Peter Arkadiev, Axel Holvoet, Björn Wiemer (Eds.)
Contemporary Approaches to Baltic Linguistics

Trends in Linguistics
Studies and Monographs

Editor
Volker Gast

Editorial Board
Walter Bisang
Jan Terje Faarlund
Hans Henrich Hock
Natalia Levshina
Heiko Narrog
Matthias Schlesewsky
Amir Zeldes
Niina Ning Zhang

Editors responsible for this volume
Volker Gast

Volume 276

Contemporary Approaches to Baltic Linguistics

Edited by
Peter Arkadiev
Axel Holvoet
Björn Wiemer

DE GRUYTER
MOUTON

ISBN 978-3-11-057854-6
e-ISBN (PDF) 978-3-11-034395-3
e-ISBN (EPUB) 978-3-11-039498-6
ISSN 1861-4302

Library of Congress Cataloging-in-Publication Data
A CIP catalog record for this book has been applied for at the Library of Congress.

Bibliographic information published by the Deutsche Nationalbibliothek
The Deutsche Nationalbibliothek lists this publication in the Deutsche Nationalbibliografie;
detailed bibliographic data are available on the Internet at http://dnb.dnb.de.

© 2015 Walter de Gruyter GmbH, Berlin/Boston
This volume is text- and page-identical with the hardback published in 2015.
Typesetting: Compuscript Ltd., Shannon, Ireland
Printing: CPI books GmbH, Leck

♾ Printed on acid-free paper
Printed in Germany

www.degruyter.com

Contents

Contributors —— vii

Peter Arkadiev, Axel Holvoet and Björn Wiemer
1 Introduction: Baltic linguistics – State of the art —— 1

Hans Henrich Hock
2 Prosody and dialectology of tonal shifts in Lithuanian and their implications —— 111

Anna Daugavet
3 The lengthening of the first component of Lithuanian diphthongs in an areal perspective —— 139

Ineta Dabašinskienė and Maria Voeikova
4 Diminutives in spoken Lithuanian and Russian: Pragmatic functions and structural properties —— 203

Daiki Horiguchi
5 Latvian attenuative *pa*-verbs in comparison with diminutives —— 235

Cori Anderson
6 Non-canonical case patterns in Lithuanian —— 263

Axel Holvoet
7 Non-canonical subjects in Latvian: An obliqueness-based approach —— 299

Ilja A. Seržant
8 Dative experiencer constructions as a Circum-Baltic isogloss —— 325

Nijolė Maskaliūnienė
9 Morphological, syntactic, and semantic types of converse verbs in Lithuanian —— 349

Eiko Sakurai
10 Past habitual tense in Lithuanian —— 383

Aurelija Usonienė
11 Non-morphological realizations of evidentiality: The case of parenthetical elements in Lithuanian —— 437

Kirill Kozhanov
12 Lithuanian indefinite pronouns in contact —— 465

Bernhard Wälchli
13 *Ištiktukai* "eventives" – The Baltic precursors of ideophones and why they remain unknown in typology —— 491

Andrii Danylenko
14 The chicken or the egg? Onomatopoeic particles and verbs in Baltic and Slavic —— 523

Index of languages —— 543

Index of subjects —— 546

Contributors

Cori Anderson
Rutgers University
Dept. of Germanic, Russian, and East European Languages and Literatures
172 College Avenue, New Brunswick, NJ 08901
anderson.cori@gmail.com

Peter Arkadiev
Institute of Slavic Studies of the Russian Academy of Sciences / Russian State University for the Humanities / Sholokhov Moscow State University for the Humanities
Leninsky prospekt 32A, Moscow, 119991, Russia
peterarkadiev@yandex.ru

Ineta Dabašinskienė
Vytautas Magnus University
Department of Linguistics
K. Donelaičio gatvė 58, Kaunas, 44248, Lithuania
i.dabasinskiene@hmf.vdu.lt

Andrii Danylenko
Pace University
Dyson College of Arts and Sciences, Modern Languages and Cultures Department
41 Park Row, New York, NY 10038, USA
adanylenko@pace.edu

Anna Daugavet
Saint-Petersburg State University
Department of General Linguistics
Universitetskaya naberezhnaya 11,
Saint-Petersburg, 199034, Russia
anna.daugavet@gmail.com

Hans Henrich Hock
University of Illinois
Department of Linguistics
707 S. Mathews, Urbana IL 61801, USA
hhhock@illinois.edu

Axel Holvoet
University of Warsaw / Vilnius University
Wydział Polonistyki
Krakowskie Przedmieście 26/28, 00-927 Warszawa, Poland
axel.holvoet@uw.edu.pl

Daiki Horiguchi
Iwate University
Faculty of Humanities and Social Sciences
3-18-8, Ueda, Morioka, Iwate, 020-8550, Japan
sirdspuksti@gmail.com

Kirill Kozhanov
Institute of Slavic Studies of the Russian Academy of Sciences
Leninsky prospekt 32A, Moscow, 119991, Russia
kozhanov.kirill@gmail.com

Nijolė Maskaliūnienė
Vilnius University
Faculty of Philology, Department of Translation Studies
Universiteto gatvė 5, Vilnius, LT-01513, Lithuania
nijole.maskaliuniene@flf.vu.lt

Eiko Sakurai
Tokyo University of Foreign Studies / Osaka University
World Language and Society Education Center
3-11-1, Asahi-cho, Fuchu-shi, Tokyo 183-8534, Japan
sakurainek2@ybb.ne.jp

Ilja A. Seržant
Johannes-Gutenberg-Universität Mainz
Institut für Slavistik
Jakob-Welder-Weg 18, Mainz, 55128, Germany
ilja.serzants@uni-mainz.de

Aurelija Usonienė
Vilnius University
Faculty of Philology, Department of English Philology
Universiteto gatvė 5, Vilnius, LT-01513, Lithuania
aurelia@usonis.lt

Maria Voeikova
Institute for Linguistic Studies of the Russian Academy of Sciences / Saint Petersburg State University, Department of Russian Language
Tuchkov pereulok 9, Saint-Petersburg, 199053, Russia
maria.voeikova@gmail.com

Bernhard Wälchli
Stockholm University
Department of Linguistics
SE-106 91 Stockholm, Sweden
bernhard@ling.su.se

Björn Wiemer
Johannes-Gutenberg-Universität Mainz
Institut für Slavistik
Jakob-Welder-Weg 18, Mainz, 55128, Germany
wiemerb@uni-mainz.de

Peter Arkadiev, Axel Holvoet and Björn Wiemer
1 Introduction: Baltic linguistics – State of the art

This introductory chapter to the volume is meant to give an overview of the state of research in the description of extant Baltic languages. Of course, we cannot supply a fully comprehensive account of all aspects of these languages. We will mainly focus on synchronic linguistics. We have not let ourselves be guided by functionalists' or formalists' prominence, although the survey to some extent reflects those domains and frameworks for which we ourselves felt competent enough. Sometimes we decided to be more explicit on noteworthy research results if these have been published in one of the Baltic languages or another language the knowledge of which cannot be assumed to be very much widespread among Western linguists. In any case, we are eager to account for the study of Baltic languages in the light of theoretically interesting issues and methods.

Before beginning our survey, we will give some basic introduction concerning the general typological "outfit" of the contemporary Baltic languages and their genealogical affiliation. This includes short explanations about the main differences between Lithuanian, Latvian, and Latgalian and the internal dialectal fragmentation of East Baltic (Section 1). Sections 2 and 3 contain the main body of our task. Section 2 is subdivided according to rather traditional levels of structural description (from phonetics to the syntax of complex sentences). Derivation is given an extra subsection (2.4). Section 3 is devoted to semantics and pragmatics and also fragmented following generally accepted linguistic disciplines. Subsequently, in Section 4, we will give some cursory information concerning aspects of areal linguistics, including dialect geography. Section 5 overviews typological studies into which Baltic data have been incorporated (Section 5.1) and highlights typologically outstanding features and rarities (Section 5.2). This subsection should show why more linguistic research into Baltic languages need not be judged just as the fancy occupation of a handful of scholars and why the Baltic languages are not to be dismissed as, on the one hand, only another tiny group of European languages (and thus not exotic enough from a global perspective), and yet, on the other hand, too obscure and hardly accessible in order to be worth labor (and thus too exotic on a European background). In the conclusion, we will sum up some outlines and add comments on paradoxes of the linguistic study of Baltic languages (Section 6) and briefly summarize the contents of the individual chapters of the volume (Section 7). The references list at the end does not pretend to be exhaustive but contains only work that has been mentioned in this introduction.

1 General outfit of Baltic languages

This section is meant to supply a rough survey of the internal subdivision of Baltic or, essentially, East Baltic, and some basic diachronic background (Section 1.1) as well as to give an overview of grammars and other general sources on Baltic languages (Section 1.2) and of electronic corpora that are currently accessible (Section 1.3).

1.1 Diachronic background, general genealogical, and dialectological issues

Originally, i.e., by more or less the mid-first millennium AD, Baltic dialects were dispersed over a large area stretching approximately from the region of today's Berlin over to eastwards of today's Moscow (Toporov 1997: 148). "Hard proof" for this extension comes from hydronymy (cf. Toporov & Trubačev 1962, Tret'jakov 1966, Vasmer 1971). The Baltic-speaking territory known from historical documents of the second millennium is usually divided into a western and an eastern branch. Old Prussian, which died out at the beginning of the eighteenth century AD, belonged to the western branch, whereas the only extant Baltic languages (Lithuanian, Latvian, Latgalian) form part of the eastern branch. On the next taxon, Lithuanian is usually divided into Aukštaitian (High Lithuanian) and Žemaitian (Samogitian or Low Lithuanian), with further subdivisions each. Latvian splits into High Latvian and Low Latvian, with the former constituted by Latgalian and Selonian dialects. Low Latvian further divides into Semigalian and Curonian. Tamian and Livonian dialects (in the north and northwest) are most affected by Finnic contact.

Figure 1 pictures the global splits that have occurred within the former Baltic dialect continuum and that are most relevant with respect to their contemporary stage (for the most recent diachronically oriented survey, cf. Petit 2010b: 3–51). Note that the two-dimensional arrangement does not reflect the real geographic location of the subdivisions of the former dialect continuum.

Both Lithuanian and Latvian have been heavily standardized, even if the process was late in comparison to other European languages (it started only at the end of the nineteenth century). Especially for non-specialists relying mostly on reference grammars and textbooks, it is crucial to remark that through standardization some features were introduced that did not exist in any dialect. As an example, we could cite the introduction of dedicated second plural imperative forms in standard Latvian, e.g., *ejiet* 'go:IMP.2PL' as against *(jūs) ejat* '(you) go:PRS.2PL'. In fact, the endings *-at* and *-iet* are used without functional difference in all Latvian dialects, and the distinction was artificially introduced in the 1920s by Endzelin, who had noted it in seventeenth-century Latvian texts and decided it should be restored in the modern language. In the case of Lithuanian,

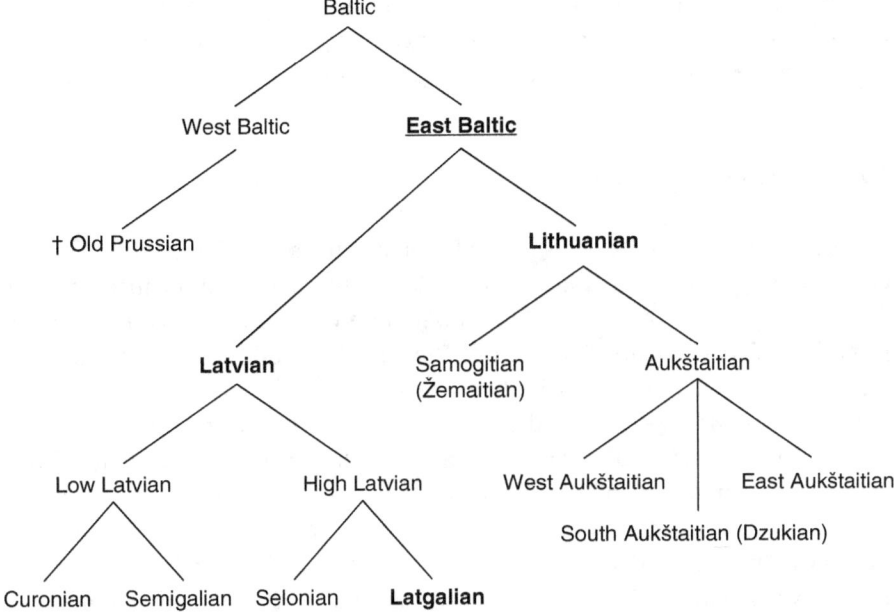

Fig. 1: Main areal and genealogical breakup relevant for contemporary Baltic.

the choice of the dialectal basis for the standard language was not definitively settled until the late nineteenth century. The West Aukštaitian dialects served as a vehicle for a tradition of Lithuanian writing in Prussian Lithuania from the sixteenth century onward, but in the Grand Duchy, it had to face competition from the Eastern Aukštaitian and (from the eighteenth century onward) Samogitian dialects. The ultimate choice in favor of West Aukštaitian was not only due to the prestige of this variety, established mainly in Prussian Lithuania, but also to the fact that this dialect is phonetically the most conservative, which seemed to make it particularly fit to serve as a metadialectal standard.

The Latvian standard language has been based, since the earliest texts (which date from the sixteenth century), on the so-called central dialect (*vidus dialekts*). This dialect area comprises the dialects of Vidzeme (former Swedish Livonia) and those of Kurzeme (Courland) and Zemgale (Semigalia). The dialects around Jelgava (German *Mitau*) are considered closest to the standard language. In addition to the central dialect, Low Latvian also comprises the so-called Livonian (*lībiskais*) dialect, whose distinguishing features are mostly connected with the influence of the Livonian (Finnic) substratum on which it developed. High Latvian (*augšzemnieku dialekts*) comprises the Latgalian dialects of former Polish Livonia as well as the Selonian dialects of what used to be called Upper Courland (the region south and north of the Daugava around Jēkabpils).

A separate writing tradition in High Latvian, associated mainly with the activities of the Roman Catholic Church, has been in existence since the eighteenth century and has become the basis of what is now often called the Latgalian language.

1.2 Sources on Baltic languages

General book-length overviews of the Baltic language family include the classical monographs of Stang (1942, 1966), Eckert, Bukevičiūtė, and Hinze (1994, in German), and Toporov (ed. 2006, in Russian); a concise overview in English is given by Holvoet (2011b). The work of Dini (1997, in Italian and translated into Lithuanian, Latvian, and Russian) contains a useful overview of the history of Baltic studies and especially of the historical-comparative tradition.

Existing grammars of Lithuanian have been largely guided by the Neogrammarian ideology of the end of the nineteenth century (e.g., Senn 1966) or by the Russian (Soviet) grammatical tradition, to which the fundamental three-volume Academy Grammar (LKG)[1] as well as the more recent and somewhat less comprehensive work DLKG (1996 edited by Ambrazas) and LG (1997 edited by Ambrazas, reprinted in 2006) are greatly indebted. The latter is to date the most comprehensive description of Lithuanian in English, having superseded the oft-cited non-academic textbook by Dambriūnas, Klimas, and Schmalstieg (1966). Among recent reference grammars written outside Lithuania, worth noting are the works of Mathiassen (1996a) in English and Chicouene and Skūpas (2003) in French.

Endzelin's (1923) German-language grammar of Latvian has remained, paradoxically, the most important source of information on Latvian available in a western language. The Latvian Academy Grammar (MLLVG 1959, 1962), heavily dependent on Soviet Russian grammar, is rich in information but is difficult to use and outdated in many respects. While preparing this introduction, a new academy grammar appeared (LVG 2013); thus, it will now become obvious whether this updated grammar is written with an account of modern linguistic approaches. Apart from that, *A Grammar of Modern Latvian* (Fennell & Gelsen 1980) is, despite its title, a textbook rather than a grammar, but it contains comprehensive and reliable grammar sections. *A Short Grammar of Latvian*, by Mathiassen (1997), is marred by numerous mistakes and should be used with caution. *Lettische Grammatik*, by Forssman (2001), is predominantly diachronic, and the synchronic sections also show a diachronic bias that often makes them misleading. *Lettische Grammatik*, by Holst (2001), is idiosyncratic and should be used with a certain caution. *Die lettische Sprache und ihre*

---

[1] A much shorter Russian version based on this grammar is GLJa (1985). Remarkably, there is no equivalent for Latvian.

Dialekte, by Gāters (1977), is not about grammar but is a general introduction to the Latvian language, with ample coverage of the dialects. Nau (1998) is a short though quite useful grammatical sketch, while Nau (2001b) is a principled investigation into problems related to part of speech distinctions (in particular of pronouns), which basically deals with Latvian.

Of the Baltic languages, Latgalian remains the most poorly described. There exist some largely outdated grammars written in Russian and Latgalian in the first half of the twentieth century (Skrinda 1908, Trasuns 1921, Strods 1922), and the only modern description is the short and far from comprehensive sketch by Nau (2011a), apart from the grammatical handbook by Bukšs and Placinskis (1973) and a comparative study by Lelis (1961).

1.3 Electronic corpora of Baltic languages

The corpora of Lithuanian include DLKT (The Corpus of Contemporary Lithuanian, compiled at the Vytautas Magnus University, Kaunas), containing more than 140 million tokens, more than a half of which come from newspapers. The corpus includes texts produced during the post-Soviet period, including fiction translations from various languages. The publicly available version of DLKT does not have any kind of morphological or part of speech annotation, and the interface is only in Lithuanian. The other available corpus of Lithuanian is CorALit (The Corpus of Academic Lithuanian, compiled at Vilnius University), containing about 9 million tokens, coming from various academic publications. The corpus does not contain morphological annotation, but the interface exists both in Lithuanian and in English. Another drawback of both corpora worth mentioning is the lack of a convenient way of exporting search results.

For Latvian, there exists LVTK (The Corpus of Contemporary Latvian, compiled at the University of Latvia in Riga), which is morphologically annotated, but the interface is only in Latvian; the current size of the corpus is ca. 4.5 million tokens. Curiously, the size of the corpus is not indicated on its website. There also exists a small Latgalian corpus (MLTK, compiled by a joint Lithuanian-Latvian research program), containing 1 million tokens, without morphological annotation, and a parallel Latvian-Lithuanian corpus (LILA, compiled by the same joint program), which contains more than 9 million tokens from texts translated from Latvian to Lithuanian, from Lithuanian to Latvian, and from English into both of them; again, there is no morphological annotation. Both the Latgalian and the parallel corpora have interface in Latvian, Lithuanian, and English. A parallel Russian-Latvian corpus, yet unannotated and containing less than 1 million tokens, has been recently launched under the auspices of the Russian National Corpus project (http://www.ruscorpora.ru/search-para-lv.html). A collection of Latgalian texts (mostly transcripts of folklore texts collected in the late nineteenth century) with Polish translations has been recently made available at the Adam Mickiewicz University in Poznań (http://inne-jezyki.amu.edu.pl/Frontend/Language/Details/1).

The only diachronic corpus of Baltic languages known to us is LVSTK (compiled at the Latvian University in Riga), comprising less than 1 million tokens. This corpus does not seem to have morphological annotation, and the interface is only in Latvian. The collection of digitalized Old Lithuanian texts compiled at the Institute of Lithuanian language in Vilnius (http://www.lki.lt/seniejirastai) cannot be considered a corpus even in the most relaxed sense of the term, since it only contains downloadable transcripts and concordances of individual texts. There also exists a searchable database of Old Prussian texts compiled at the University of Vilnius (http://www.prusistika.flf.vu.lt/zodynas/apie/).

2 Description of structural levels

2.1 Phonetics and phonology

Phonetics is among the best-studied fields of Baltic linguistics, at least in what concerns the description of the data in a predominantly Neogrammarian manner. Remarkably poorer is the state of the arts concerning phonology. Moreover, most of the modern and empirically adequate descriptive materials are published in Lithuania and Latvia in the respective languages, thus being virtually inaccessible to the broader linguistic audience. This has resulted in that discussions of Baltic phonetic and phonological data in modern theoretical and typological works are scarce, and those that exist often suffer from outdated, simplistic, and inadequate data. Thus, comprehensive book-length descriptions of the phonological systems of Lithuanian, Latvian, and Latgalian and their dialects, written from modern theoretically and typologically informed perspective and published in English, are badly needed.

One aspect that has to date received little attention in comparison to the description of phonological phenomena in individual Baltic languages and dialects or cross-dialectal surveys, is contrastive phonology of Latvian and Lithuanian. Works where phonological phenomena from both languages would be simultaneously taken into account and contrasted are not numerous (cf. e.g., Dogil 1999b, Daugavet 2010, this volume). Notably, Latvian and Lithuanian dialectologists have cooperated with each other rather insufficiently (with the notable exception of Marta Rudzīte, Zigmas Zinkevičius, and, more recently, Edmundas Trumpa). All these circumstances have seriously impeded areal research. Below we will give the basics of the phonological systems of Standard Lithuanian, Latvian, and Latgalian, together with the orthographic conventions, and briefly outline the state of the research in this domain.

2.1.1 Lithuanian

The phonological inventory of Lithuanian is given in Tables 1 (consonants) and 2 (vowels); these tables mostly follow those presented by Balode and Holvoet (2001a: 46, 48); we give the Latin-based letters corresponding to the IPA symbols in brackets < >.

Each Lithuanian consonant, except /j/, has a palatalized counterpart; palatalized consonants occur automatically before all front vowels and diphthongs, but may also freely occur before mid and back vowels, in which case, palatalization is indicated by <i>. Thus, *niūkia* Prs3 'mumble; urge' is phonologically /nʲuːkʲæ/.

The most comprehensive treatment of the Lithuanian phonological system, comprising not only segmental units but also such complex issues as vowel length, syllable structure, and the so-called syllable intonations (often somewhat misleadingly called "tones"), is contained in the works of Antanas Pakerys (Pakerys 1982, [1986] 1995) and Aleksas Girdenis (1981, [1995] 2003) (these books include summaries in Russian and in German or English; the English translation of Girdenis' book has just appeared as Girdenis 2014). On accentuation in Lithuanian from a diachronic perspective, cf. also Kazlauskas (2000a: chapter 1). There also exist numerous works written by Aleksas Girdenis and Antanas Pakerys and their collaborators and students dealing with various particular

Tab. 1: Lithuanian consonants

	Labial		Dental and alveolar		Palato-alveolar		Palatal	Velar	
Plosive	p	pʲ	t	tʲ				k	kʲ
	b	bʲ	d	dʲ				g	gʲ
Nasal	m	mʲ	n	nʲ					
Affricate			ts <c>	tsʲ	tʃ <č>	tʃʲ			
			dz <dz>	dzʲ	dʒ <dž>	dʒʲ			
Fricative	f	fʲ	s	sʲ	ʃ <š>	ʃʲ		x <ch>	xʲ
	v	vʲ	z	zʲ	ʒ <ž>	ʒʲ		ɣ <h>	ɣʲ
Approximant							j		
Lateral			l	lʲ					
Trill			r	rʲ					

Tab. 2: Lithuanian vowels and diphthongs (cf. Daugavet, this volume)

ɪ <i> iː <y,į> iːə <ie>				ʊ <u> uː <ū,ų> uːə <uo>
				ui
ɛ <e> eː <ė>			ɔ <o> oː <o>	
ɛi <ei>				
æː <e,ę>			a <a>, aː <a,ą>	
æu <iau>			ai <ai>, au <au>	

issues of phonology and phonetics of both standard language and its dialects, including both theoretical discussion and experimental research. Girdenis is also the author of the phonology chapters of the recent academic grammars of Standard Lithuanian, including the English edition LG ([1997] 2006). One of Girdenis' former students, Vytautas Kardelis, has presented an account of the differentiation of the Northeastern Aukštaitian dialect area (Kardelis 2009). This is, to our knowledge, the first truly dialect-geographic attempt at describing a dialect area of Lithuania not in terms of vaguely conceived "sound variations", but entirely based on structural phonology. The book is written in Lithuanian, but has a German and a Russian summary (see further in Section 4). Besides that, one could mention Vykypěl (2003), an original analysis of the Lithuanian phonological system based on Glossematics.

A somewhat separate trend of research concerns the description and interpretation of accentuation of standard and dialectal Lithuanian. Lithuanian has free mobile stress determined by morphological and phonological properties of morphemes and word forms (see Daugavet, this volume, for a short overview) and rules of stress placement in Lithuanian have attracted attention of both synchronic and historical-comparative linguists starting with Leskien (1876) and most prominently known from Ferdinand de Saussure (1894, 1896); cf. also Joseph (2009) and Petit (2010a) for recent studies. The most comprehensive description of accent rules of Standard Lithuanian are by Pakerys (1994, 2002), Stundžia (1995, 2009), and Mikulėnienė, Pakerys, and Stundžia (2007), written in Lithuanian but containing summaries in Russian and/or English. Notable works written outside Lithuania include those by Garde (1968: 160–165), which may be regarded as one of the sources of Lithuanian accentological theory, Young (1991), which contains standard as well as dialectal data, Halle and Vergnaud (1987: 190–203), Blevins (1993), Dogil (1999a,b), and Dogil and Möhler (1998). The works by Halle and Vergnaud and Blevins propose treatments of accentuation in metrical and autosegmental theories, unfortunately based on an inadequate view that Lithuanian has a tonal opposition (cf. also an early proposal in Kenstowicz 1972: 52–83, Dudas 1972, Dudas & O'Bryan 1972). The contributions by Dogil are important in that they take into account the works written in Lithuania and present an unbiased treatment of the phonetic representation of stress and accent in Lithuanian, comparing it to that of other languages including Latvian. Vykypěl (2004) formulates some interesting considerations arising from the relation between word-prosodic features and the shape of morphemes (and their allomorphs) in Lithuanian; his considerations are embedded into a general typological background.

Yet another major research area is the historical-comparative research into Baltic accentuation and its comparison with Slavic, represented by a huge and growing number of works, with which we cannot deal here. For a recent overview, see e.g., Olander (2009: 14–46) and Petit (2010b: 52–139).

In contrast to the rich ingenious tradition of comprehensive experimental and theoretical study of standard and dialectal phonology in Lithuania, actually not much has been done in this domain outside of the country or published in languages other than Lithuanian. In addition to works already mentioned, one may add a few experimental studies such as the work of Balšaitytė (2004) or Campos-Astorkiza (2012) dealing with acoustic features of vowels and several theoretical studies such as Daugavet (2009, 2010, this volume) on the issues of syllable structure, length, and accents. (More numerous studies dealing with morphophonological processes will be referred to in the next section.) Worth mentioning are Geyer's (2011) considerations concerning the phonological treatment of Lithuanian diphthongs as monophonemic ("gliding") or biphonemic ("combined") sound units.

Finally, sentence prosody of Lithuanian and its relation to syntax and information structure have received very little treatment (and are not covered in reference grammars). Works we know include mainly contributions by Gintautas Kundrotas written in Lithuanian and Russian, see e.g., Kundrotas (2002, 2003, 2004, 2008), inspired by the tradition of the study of sentence intonation in Russian, and Zav'jalova (2006), where interesting preliminary observations are made on the relation of word order and sentence prosody.

2.1.2 Latvian

The phonological system of Latvian, which differs from that of both its more distant relative Lithuanian and its closest kin Latgalian in many important

Tab. 3: Latvian consonants

	Labial	Dental and alveolar	Palato-alveolar	Palatal	Velar and laryngeal
Plosive	p b	t d		c <ķ> ɟ <ģ>	k g
Nasal	m	n		ɲ <ņ>	
Affricate		ts <c> dz <dz>	tʃ <č> dʒ <dž>		
Fricative	f v	s z	ʃ <š> ʒ <ž>		x <h>
Approximant				j	
Lateral		l		ʎ <ļ>	
Trill		r			

Tab. 4: Latvian vowels and diphthongs (cf. Daugavet, this volume)

i <i> iː <ī> iə <ie>				u <u> uː <ū> uːə <o>	
iu <iu, iv>					ui
	e <e> eː <ē>			ɔ <o> ɔː <o>	
	ei <ei>, eu <ev>			ɔi <oi>, ɔu <ov>	
	æ <e> æː <ē>	ɑ <a>, ɑː <ā>			
		ɑi <ai>, ɑu <au, av>			

respects, is given in Tables 3 (consonants) and 4 (vowels), with Latin letter correspondences given in < > (cf. Balode & Holvoet 2001b: 10–12).

Experimental research on Latvian phonetics started in the interwar period; it was conducted mainly by Anna Ābele (1915, 1924, 1932), and its results were published mainly in Latvian. Book-length studies of Latvian phonetics include Laua ([1969] 1997) and Grigorjevs (2008, in Latvian); the latter is an acoustic and auditive investigation of Latvian vowels, with a chapter on phonology. To our knowledge, there is no counterpart for the consonant system, except for Grigorjevs' (2012, in English) study on sonorants. A number of studies on particular problems, available in English, are mentioned below.

Prosody is the part of the Latvian sound system that has attracted most attention because of its unique features. Like Lithuanian, Latvian has a system of syllable accents, traditionally referred to as intonations; rather than being purely tonal, they involve a cluster of features including tone, length, and glottalization. The earliest experimental study is by Ābele (1915), and a book-length study is by Ekblom (1933). A characteristic and rare feature of Latvian is the existence of differences in syllable accent not only under stress (as in Lithuanian), but in unstressed position as well. Syllable accents in unstressed syllables are dealt with by Seržant (2003). The distinctive nature of the oppositions of syllable accents in both stressed and unstressed syllables is shown by Grīsle (1996/1997, 2008).

Vowel quantity is closely bound up with syllable accents. Vowels with the so-called level pitch are ultra-long, inviting comparison with the putative distinction of three degrees of length in neighboring Estonian; conversely, Estonian overlength seems to involve tonal features, so that an areal account is called for; on possible Latvian-Finnic parallels in vowel and syllable length, cf. Koptjevskaja-Tamm and Wälchli (2001: 641–645) and Daugavet (2008a,b, 2009, this volume). On vowel length and word length, cf. Bond (1991).

Consonant quantity is a very interesting but insufficiently investigated feature of Latvian phonetics and phonology. Non-distinctive variation in obstruent quantity in correlation with syllable structure (voiceless obstruents are automatically lengthened between short vowels of which the first is stressed) is undoubtedly an areal feature induced by a Finnic substratum – it is completely unknown in Lithuanian. Its Finnic origins are convincingly shown by Daugavet (2013). There are a number of phonetic studies (in Latvian) on obstruent length in different phonetic contexts and in correlation with word length, but many details remain to be established.

On syllable length in general and the interplay between vocalic and consonantal length, cf. Daugavet (2008b, 2009). On phonotactics in connection with syllable structure, cf. Bond (1994a).

Latvian has abandoned the Common Baltic mobile stress in favor of fixed initial stress, probably under Finnic influence, although this is occasionally called into question, cf. Hock (this volume). On secondary stress, cf. Daugavet (2008a).

On vowel quality in stressed and unstressed syllables, cf. Bond (1994b). A characteristically Latvian feature is the optional voiceless realization or complete loss of short unstressed vowels in word-final position, as discussed by Kariņš (1995). On sentential intonation, there is one study by Bond (1998).

The effects of Latvian-Russian and Latvian-English bilingualism on Latvian phonetics and the properties of non-native Latvian are investigated by Bond (1978), Bond, Markus, and Stockmal (2003), Stockmal, Markus, and Bond (2005), and Bond, Stockmal, and Markus (2006).

The first attempt at a phonological description of Latvian, with focus on phonotactics, was proposed by Matthews (1959). The only book-length study of Latvian phonology is Steinbergs' (1977) unpublished PhD thesis. An overall analysis of the Latvian system of syllable accents in the framework of autosegmental phonology is given in a PhD thesis by Kariņš (1996).

2.1.3 Latgalian

The phonological system of Latgalian shares certain important features both with Latvian and Lithuanian but differs substantially from both, e.g., in allowing word-final palatalized consonants (see Tables 5 and 6, based on Nau 2011a: 9–13).

Tab. 5: Latgalian consonants

	Labial	Dental and alveolar		Palato-alveolar	Palatal	Velar and laryngeal	
Plosive	p pʲ	t	tʲ			k	kʲ \<ķ\>
	b bʲ	d	dʲ			g	gʲ \<ģ\>
Nasal	m mʲ	n	nʲ \<ņ\>				
Affricate		ts \<c\>	tsʲ	tʃ \<č\>			
		dz \<dz\>	dzʲ	dʒ \<dž\>			
Fricative	f fʲ	s	sʲ	ʃ \<š\>		x \<h\>	xʲ
	v vʲ	z	zʲ	ʒ \<ž\>			
Approximant					j		
Lateral		l	lʲ \<ļ\>				
Trill				r			

Tab. 6: Latgalian vowels and diphthongs

i, iː: \<ī\>, ie, iu	ɨ \<y\>, ɨu \<yu\>		u, uː: \<ū\>, uɔ \<uo, ō\>
e		ɔ \<o\>	
æ \<e\>, æː \<ē\>		a, aː \<ā\>	
ei, æi \<ei\>		ai, au	

The major works on Latgalian phonetics and phonology remain the theses by Lelis (1961) and Breidaks ([1989] 2007), as well as a number of works by Breidaks published in his two-volume *Selected Writings* (Breidaks 2007).

2.2 Morphophonology

The rich and complex phonological processes occurring throughout Lithuanian inflection and derivation have attracted attention of various linguists both inside and outside of Lithuania (unfortunately, to our knowledge, much less attention has been paid to no less intricate and in many respects different morphophonological processes in Latvian). In addition to the descriptions of major phonological processes in grammars and special publications in Lithuanian, as well as such classic works as Leskien (1884) on ablaut, several influential works appeared during the last decades dealing with Lithuanian morphophonology from the perspective of various versions of generative phonological theory. These include Heeschen (1968) and Kenstowicz (1972), as well as a paper by Bulygina (1970); a number of contributions deal specifically with morphophonological processes occurring in verbs, e.g., Schmalstieg (1958), Clair (1973), Bulygina (1977: 238–269), Regier (1977), Arkadiev (2012a). Hoskovec (2002) examines Lithuanian morphophonology from the point of view of Prague School structuralism. On Lithuanian morphophonological issues, cf. further Akelaitienė (1987, 1996) and Karosienė (2004).

There also exist a number of theoretically oriented works devoted to specific phonological processes of Lithuanian, among recent ones, see e.g., Hume and Seo (2004) on metathesis, Flemming (2005: 294–300) on nasal deletion, Baković (2006) on *i*-insertion in verbal prefixes, Dressler, Dziubalska-Kołaczyk, and Pestal (2006: 57–61) on morphotactics and consonant clusters, Kamandulytė (2006a) on the acquisition of morphotactics. On Latvian morphophonology, cf. Kalnača (2004), and in the generative framework, Fennell (1971a) and Halle (1986).

The Latgalian morphophonological system, where nominal and verbal inflection and derivation involve an interaction of consonant and vowel adjustments between suffixes and roots, is by far the most complex and non-trivial among the Baltic languages. Although preliminarily described by Lelis (1961: 121–131) and Nau (2011a: 15–21), the full range of these alternations still begs for a comprehensive description and theoretical interpretation.

Morphophonological phenomena of Lithuanian and Latvian dialects, where various alternations absent from standard languages have arisen, e.g., due to vowel reduction, stress retraction, etc., have, to our knowledge, not received any systematic treatment so far.

2.3 Inflectional morphology

In general, academy and comprehensive grammars written in Lithuania and Latvia after World War II were skewed by structural descriptions of Russian during Soviet times (e.g., in the Russian academy grammars; see above). This holds for the division into morphological categories as well as for the treatment of stem derivational patterns.

The only contrastive study of Lithuanian and Latvian inflection (both nominal and verbal) is the unpublished dissertation by Andronov (1999); the Latvian part, however, has been published in Andronov (2002: 323–402). The morphology of Lithuanian is contrasted with that of Russian in the still useful monograph Mustejkis (1972).

In terms of morphotactic rules, morphological subparadigms in contemporary Baltic are very regular. Although the relation between past and present tense forms of verbs are often quite opaque (see Section 2.3.2), in the Baltic languages (perhaps with the exception of Latgalian), there are overall less morphophonological alternations than in the neighboring Slavic languages, and paradigms are astonishingly void of suppletive forms. There are only a few clear cases of inflectional suppletion in modern Lithuanian, first of all the paradigm of the copula and existential verb *būti* 'be' (present: 1SG *es-u*, 2SG *es-i*, 1PL *es-ame*, 2PL *es-ate* vs. 3 *yra*; all other forms are based on the stem *bū-* with a regular alternant *buv-* before vowels, cf. past 3 *buvo*, imperative 2SG *būk*); *yra* (as well as its Latvian cognate *ir*)[2] has replaced the older, non-suppletive form *esti*, which is still in use, but only as a copula and in stylistically marked contexts. In Latvian and Latgalian, there is one more suppletive verb ('go', cf. Latvian present 1SG *eju* vs. 3 *iet* vs. Past *gāja*). Besides that, there is suppletion for personal pronouns (e.g., Lithuanian 1SG.NOM *aš* vs. 1SG.ACC *mane*).

The distinction between inflection ("endings") and derivational morphology (suffixes, stem extensions) is not always straightforward, and not always have decisions on how to distinguish them in practice been realized with consequence (cf., for instance, Holvoet 2006 for a criticism concerning Lithuanian grammaticography).

On inflection in the acquisition of Latvian as a first language, cf. Rūķe-Draviņa (1973).

---

[2] Its etymology might go back to a demonstrative pronoun (cf. Mańczak 2003).

2.3.1 Nominal morphology

Baltic nominal morphology is relatively well described, at least in what concerns the standard languages. From the diachronic perspective, nominal morphology has been dealt with, among others, by Kazlauskas (2000a: chapter 2, which is a reprint of his book from 1968). Nominals in Baltic inflect for number and case as well as for gender and definiteness (adjectives and some pronouns) and degree (adjectives). The two genders (masculine and feminine) constitute an inflectional (agreement or concord-based) category for adjectives and pronouns and a classificatory (inherent) category for nouns. However, both in Lithuanian and Latvian, many nouns denoting humans, especially professions, have both a masculine and a feminine variant formally distinguished by the choice of inflectional paradigm only (not by any derivational affixes), e.g., Lith. *darbinink-as* 'worker (M)' vs. *darbinink-ė* 'worker (F)'. Thus, for these nouns, gender can arguably be considered an inflectional feature; cf. Džežulskienė (2001, 2003), Judžentis (2002a: 41f.), Vykypěl (2006: 98f.), Smetona (2005: 84) for discussion concerning Lithuanian. Stołowska's (2014) work is a recent investigation on the techniques by which conflicts between grammatical gender (masculine vs. feminine) and biological sex (male vs. female) are resolved in Latvian. Cf. also Armoškaitė (2014) on a generative treatment of gender features in Lithuanian derivation.

Baltic nominal morphology shares with Slavic and older Indo-European languages such basic principles as cumulative exponence of case and number (and gender). These parallels do not, however, pertain to animacy distinctions, which are practically inexistent in Baltic, to the extent that the common interrogative pronoun *kas* does not distinguish 'who' and 'what' (cf. Nau 1999, among others). Baltic nominal morphology is furthermore characterized by a rich system of (synchronically) unmotivated inflectional classes, some instances of inflectional homonymy (syncretisms), and, notably, non-trivial interaction between inflectional morphology and stress (in Lithuanian). However, the data from Baltic has largely remained outside of the scope of theoretical and typological studies of such issues as declension classes, syncretism, stem alternations, and other inflectional phenomena abundant in the Baltic languages (cf. however, the study of Baltic pluralia tantum in Koptjevskaja-Tamm and Wälchli 2001: 629–637).

A general, but typologically not that infrequent, feature of Baltic is the disappearance of the neuter gender. Disappearance is stepwise, both in areal and diachronic terms. One can observe it in Old Prussian (cf. Petit 2000, 2010b: 141–169), in particular, in its vocabularies. From the synchronic viewpoint, Lithuanian (more precisely, Aukštaitian) has preserved remnants of the neuter in a handful of demonstrative pronouns (*(ta)tai* 'this', *čia* 'here, this', and *viskas* 'everything'), and the marker of the neuter singular is productive in adjectives and participles (i.e., in syntactic classes that are regularly used as predicates; see Section 2.5.2). This can be interpreted as a situation in which the number of target genders (masculine, feminine, neuter) exceeds that of controller genders (in terms of Corbett 1991, 2007), for which the neuter has become extinct. However, the neuter singular of potential agreement targets remains exploited as a default in all cases of lack of agreement on clause level.[3] In participles, it has been re-interpreted for both grammatical and lexical marking of evidential functions (see Sections 2.3.2.2 and 3.3, respectively). Latvian (besides some last traits in certain dialects) has not kept any remnants of the neuter at all, and the same applies to Latgalian. As default for lack of agreement, the masculine singular is used, and this two-gender system thus reminds of French and Italian.

2.3.1.1 Lithuanian

Standard Lithuanian nouns distinguish two numbers (singular and plural); the dual is now obsolete, although it has been optionally in use in the written language up to the beginning of the twentieth century. Its relics have been preserved in some dialects (Vykypěl 2002), and dual forms of personal pronouns (which are highest on the animacy hierarchy) are still used (at least optionally) in Standard Lithuanian. For this reason, one might argue that the dual still forms part of the number system in Lithuanian (cf. Roduner & Čižik-Prokaševa 2006).

There are seven unequivocal cases (comprising the vocative, which is distinct from the nominative only in the singular). Lithuanian nouns fall into four major declension types, each further divided into several subtypes, in most cases, according to the distinction between stems ending in a non-palatalized ("hard") vs. palatalized ("soft") consonant. Most inflectional classes are at least by default associated with just one gender, although, in fact, most of them contain exceptional nouns of the opposite gender. Declension classes are cross-cut by four major stress classes usually called "accentual paradigms" (see e.g., Daugavet, this volume); in the general case, membership of a noun in a declension class is completely independent from its membership in an accentual paradigm, although

---

[3] From this perspective, one could admit, together with Sawicki (2004: 158), that "the nominals in neuter gender represent in fact not a third gender (beside masculine and feminine) but rather a negative statement about gender: 'neither masculine nor feminine'". Semėnienė (2003), by contrast, focuses on substantivized adjectives, for which the neuter forms refer to inanimate notions (e.g., *gẽra* '(the) good', *pìkta* '(the) evil', **Raudona** *yra ryški spalva* '**Red** is a bright colour') in contrast to substantivized forms of masculine or feminine gender, which always refer to persons. Because of this, one can, of course, say that Lithuanian displays a (sort of reanalyzed) system with three controller genders.

Tab. 7: Sample paradigms of Lithuanian nouns

		I hard 'man' (M) I a.p.	I soft 'horse' (M) III a.p.	II hard 'day' (F) IV a.p.	II soft 'bee' (F) II a.p.	III hard 'son' (M) III a.p.	IV soft 'night' (F) IV a.p.
SG	NOM	výras	arklỹs	dienà	bìtė	sūnùs	naktìs
	GEN	výro	árklio	dienõs	bìtės	sūnaũs	naktiẽs
	DAT	výrui	árkliui	diẽnai	bìtei	sū́nui	nãkčiai
	ACC	výrą	árklį	diẽną	bìtę	sū́nų	nãktį
	INS	výru	árkliu	dienà	bìte	sūnumì	naktimì
	LOC	výre	arklyje	dienojè	bìtėje	sūnujè	naktyjè
	VOC	výre	arklỹ	diẽna	bìte	sūnaũ	naktiẽ
PL	NOM	výrai	arkliaĩ	diẽnos	bìtės	sū́nūs	nãktys
	GEN	výrų	arklių̃	dienų̃	bičių̃	sūnų̃	naktų̃
	DAT	výrams	arkliáms	dienóms	bìtėms	sūnùms	naktìms
	ACC	výrus	árklius	dienàs	bìtes	sū́nus	naktìs
	INS	výrais	arkliaĩs	dienomìs	bìtėmis	sūnumìs	naktimìs
	LOC	výruose	arkliuosè	dienosè	bìtėse	sūnuosè	naktysè

certain statistical tendencies exist. In Table 7, we give sample paradigms representative of major declension classes and accentual paradigms (a.p.), of course, not aiming at an exhaustive representation.

Lithuanian adjectives, in addition to number and case, inflect also for gender, degree, and definiteness. The declension of indefinite adjectives in the feminine completely follows the II declension of nouns (except for the special nominative singular ending -i of the "soft" stems), while the declension of adjectives in the masculine has certain peculiarities, i.e., special inflectional suffixes not appearing in the declension of nouns as well as a non-trivial mixture of "hard" and "soft" stems in the declension of adjectives with the nominative singular masculine in -us (see Table 8, where the special forms are highlighted).

Lithuanian definite adjectives are formed by the agglutination (and partial fusion) of the inflected forms of the third-person pronoun (formerly a demonstrative) *jis* with the inflected forms of indefinite adjectives. This creates a peculiar instance of "pleonastic" inflection (cf. Stolz 2007, 2010) (see Table 9). The development of the definite declension has been a salient topic for the study of adjectives from a diachronic perspective as well (cf. Zinkevičius 1957, Kazlauskas [1972] 2000, Rosinas 1988: 163–166). In addition to that, recently, Ostrowski (2013, forthcoming) has written two studies on the development of the comparative and superlative forms of adjectives.

Tab. 8: Sample paradigms of Lithuanian indefinite adjectives

		'High' III a.p.		'Calm' IV a.p.	
		Masculine	Feminine	Masculine	Feminine
SG	NOM	áukštas	aukštà	ramùs	ramì
	GEN	áukšto	aukštõs	ramaũs	ramiõs
	DAT	aukštám	áukštai	ramiám	rãmiai
	ACC	áukštą	áukštą	rãmų	rãmią
	INS	áukštu	áukšta	ramiù	ramià
	LOC	aukštamè	aukštojè	ramiamè	ramiojè
PL	NOM	aukštì	áukštos	rãmūs	rãmios
	GEN	aukštų̃	aukštų̃	ramių̃	ramių̃
	DAT	aukštíems	aukštóms	ramíems	ramióms
	ACC	áukštus	áukštas	ramiùs	ramiàs
	INS	aukštaĩs	aukštomìs	ramiaĩs	ramiomìs
	LOC	aukštuosè	aukštosè	ramiuosè	ramiosè

Tab. 9: Sample paradigm of Lithuanian definite adjectives

		'High' III a.p.	
		Masculine	Feminine
SG	NOM	aukštàsis	aukštóji
	GEN	áukštojo	aukštõsios
	DAT	aukštájam	áukštajai
	ACC	áukštąjį	áukštąją
	INS	aukštúoju	aukštą́ja
	LOC	aukštájame	aukštõjoje
PL	NOM	aukštíeji	áukštosios
	GEN	aukštų̃jų	aukštų̃jų
	DAT	aukštíesiems	aukštósioms
	ACC	aukštúosius	aukštą́sias
	INS	aukštaĩsiais	aukštõsiomis
	LOC	aukštuõsiuose	aukštõsiose

In addition to the detailed descriptions of the declension of Lithuanian nouns, adjectives, and pronouns found in all major reference grammars, one can point out the book-length study of Marvan (1978), which addresses the Lithuanian data from an original, although admittedly highly idiosyncratic, theoretical perspective (see Carstairs 1981 for a very critical review) and the monograph on nominal categories of Paulauskienė (1989). More recently, insights of Natural Morphology have been applied to Lithuanian declension in Savickienė, Kazlauskienė, and Kamandulytė (2004); cf. also Savickienė (2005) on the frequency of cases and its relation to markedness. Note also Armoškaitė (2011), studying the interaction of syntactic categories (parts of speech specifications), derivational and inflectional morphology, and roots in Lithuanian from the perspective of Distributed Morphology.

An issue that has received quite extensive treatment in the literature concerns the origins, form, and use of the now largely obsolete "secondary" local cases in Lithuanian, going back to combinations of case markers with postpositions. Special works dedicated to this topic include, inter alia, Smoczyński (1974), Zinkevičius (1982), Rosinas (1999, 2001: 136–152), Kavaliūnaitė (2001, 2002, 2003), and Seržant (2004a,c). Cf. also Rosinas (1995: 53–76) on Baltic in general, Seržant (2004b) on East Baltic (i.e., excluding Old Prussian) and Nilsson (2002) on the illative in Old Latvian.

It is also worth noting several contributions paying attention to such poorly studied phenomena as "Suffixaufnahme" in Old Lithuanian (Parenti 1996) and in some Lithuanian peripheral and insular dialects at the border with or in Belarus (cf. Grinaveckienė 1969: 221, discussed by Wiemer 2009b: 357), "double inflection" of definite adjectives and dual pronouns (Stolz 2007, 2010), the grammatical status of numerals (Boizou 2012), and the morphology and functioning of indefinite pronouns (Haspelmath 1997: 275–276; Kozhanov 2011, this volume).

2.3.1.2 Latvian and Latgalian

Latvian declension differs from Lithuanian in many respects, including the organization of inflectional classes, presence of non-phonologically determined stem alternations, and the number of morphological cases (Latvian lacks a distinct instrumental, which has merged with the accusative in the singular and with the dative in the plural, see also below; the status of the vocative form is not unequivocal, either, see Holvoet 2012, and in the plural, case distinctions have retreated, cf. Wälchli 1998). The sample paradigms are given in Table 10.

The declension of adjectives in Latvian is much more unified than that of Lithuanian, comprising just one major declension type, completely coinciding with the noun declension I for masculine gender and with noun declension III for feminine gender. The definite declension has become largely opaque, with most of the suffixes being no longer segmentable (see Table 11).

Latvian nominal inflection has attracted attention of linguists because of various mismatches between syntax and morphology that it presents. The most well-known problem is the status of the instrumental case, which does not have

Tab. 10: Sample paradigms of Latvian nouns[4]

		I 'father' (M)	II 'brother' (M)	III 'sister' (F)	IV 'mother' (F)	V 'ice' (M)	VI 'night' (F)
SG	NOM	tēvs	brālis	māsa	māte	ledus	nakts
	GEN	tēva	brāļa	māsas	mātes	ledus	nakts
	DAT	tēvam	brālim	māsai	mātei	ledum	naktij
	ACC	tēvu	brāli	māsu	māti	ledu	nakti
	LOC	tēvā	brālī	māsā	mātē	ledū	naktī
PL	NOM	tēvi	brāļi	māsas	mātes	ledi	naktis
	GEN	tēvu	brāļu	māsu	māšu	ledu	nakšu
	DAT	tēviem	brāļiem	māsām	mātēm	lediem	naktīm
	ACC	tēvus	brāļus	māsas	mātes	ledus	naktis
	LOC	tēvos	brāļos	māsās	mātēs	ledos	naktīs

Tab. 11: Declension of adjectives in Latvian (*augsts* 'high')

		Indefinite		Definite	
		Masculine	Feminine	Masculine	Feminine
SG	NOM	augsts	augsta	augstais	augstā
	GEN	augsta	augstas	augstā	augstās
	DAT	augstam	augstai	augstajam	augstajai
	ACC	augstu		augsto	
	LOC	augstā		augstajā	
PL	NOM	augsti	augstas	augstie	augstās
	GEN	augstu		augsto	
	DAT	augstiem	augstām	augstajiem	augstajām
	ACC	augstus	augstas	augstos	augstās
	LOC	augstos	augstās	augstajos	augstajās

a dedicated exponence; this issue has been discussed by Fennell (1975), Lötzsch (1978), Holvoet (1992, 2010a), and Andronov (2001). An account of Latvian declension in terms of early Distributed Morphology is presented by Halle (1992). Another interesting issue is the defective paradigms of reflexive action nominals and participles treated in Kalnača and Lokmane (2010). From a more general

---

[4] The numbering of inflection classes in Table 11 differs from the traditional one reflected in grammars and textbooks.

Tab. 12: Sample paradigms of Latgalian nouns (based on Nau 2011b: 155, 162)[5]

		I 'end' masc. hard	II 'cock' masc. soft	III 'edge' fem. hard	IV 'mouse' fem. soft	V 'fire' masc. soft
SG	NOM	gols	gaiļs^j	mola	pele	guņs^j
	GEN	gola	gaiļa	molys	pelis^j	guņs^j
	DAT	golam	gaiļam	molai	pelei	gunei
	ACC	golu	gaili	molu	peli	guni
	LOC	golā	gailī	molā	pelē	gunī
PL	NOM	goli	gaili	molys	pelis^j	guņs^j, gunis^j
	GEN	golu	gaiļu	molu	peļu	guņu
	DAT	golim	gailim	molom	pelem	gunim
	ACC	golus	gaiļus	molys	pelis^j	guņs^j, gunis^j
	LOC	golūs	gaiļūs	moluos	pelēs^j	gunīs^j

perspective, nominal paradigms in Latvian and Latgalian were addressed by Nau (2011a: 21–42, 2011b), which, together with Lelis (1970), are actually the only works in English treating Latgalian declension. A structuralist account of nominal inflection in Latvian can be found in the study of Rosinas (2005), and a theoretical analysis from the perspective of the "No Blur Principle" can be found in Carstairs-McCarthy's (2014) work.

Latgalian nominal inflection is superficially similar to the Latvian one but differs from it in certain important, although intricate, respects, see in particular Nau (2011b), e.g., in a consistent differentiation between "hard" and "soft" stems. Sample paradigms of nouns are given in Table 12.

On Latgalian pronouns, see Stafecka (1989, 1997), based on older texts.

2.3.2 Verbal morphology

General overviews of Lithuanian and Latvian verbal morphology, both inflectional and derivational, can be found in any of the standard and academy grammars (see the introduction to this section). The hitherto unsurmounted standard reference books on Baltic verbal morphology from a diachronic perspective have remained Stang (1942, 1966: 309–482), on Lithuanian cf. also Kazlauskas (2000a: chapter 3), and more generally on Baltic diachronic morphology the collection of papers by Kazlauskas (2000b) and the useful handbook by Schmalstieg (2000).

---

[5] The superscript <j> indicates palatalization not marked in the standard orthography.

The acquisition of Lithuanian verbal morphology (both inflectional and derivational) is dealt with by Wójcik (2000).

The four most general features of Baltic verbal morphology are (a) the consistent lack of number distinctions in the third person of all finite forms, (b) the entire architecture of inflectional categories of the Baltic verb is based on stem alternations involving suffixation, infixation,[6] consonant alternations, and qualitative and/or quantitative vowel changes, cf. Arkadiev (2012a) for a recent overview of these issues in Lithuanian; (c) the inflectional endings (person-number markers) of all tenses belong to a uniform set, with slight morphophonological changes for individual subparadigms (cf. Schmid 1966 with the diachronic background, on Lithuanian cf. also Otrębski 1965, II: 307).

The system of verbal categories consistently shows an inflectional distinction of past, present, and future tenses (see Tables 15–17) plus a series of periphrastic perfect tenses, which will be considered separately (see Section 2.3.2.4). The same holds for grammatical marking of evidential functions, synchronically based on participles (see Section 2.3.2.4). The mood system is rather poor. Apart from the subjunctive and imperative in all extant languages, contemporary Latvian and Latgalian have a special debitive construction (see Section 2.3.2.2), and all three languages have analytical hortatives. The latter have ousted what is sometimes referred to as the permissive mood, i.e., a set of third-person hortative forms ending in *-ie*, *-ai* going back (as the original Baltic imperative does) to the Indo-European optative; modern Lithuanian has retained only a few fossilized instances like *te-būn-ie* 'let it be'.[7]

In a most schematic (and somewhat simplified) way, we can say that Baltic verbs formally distinguish at least three stems. For instance, in Lithuanian, the infinitive stem is always the basis for the future, the past habitual, the imperative, and the subjunctive, as well as of some non-finite forms; if the present and past tense stems differ, the infinitive stem sometimes goes with the past, sometimes with the present stem (see Table 15). If the root in the infinitive stem is extended by {y}, this suffix lacks in both past and present tenses (e.g., *sak-y-ti* 'say' ⇒ *sak-iau*

---

[6] The present tense of intransitive inchoative verbs often shows an {n/m} infix or {st} suffix (cf. Stang 1942: 132–133; Temčin 1986, Ostrowski 2006: 55).

[7] This form reflects the older Lithuanian synthetic hortative with the prefix *te-* (cf. Kazlauskas 2000a: 373–379). In modern Lithuanian, it shows up as a permissive-restrictive prefix (cf. Arkadiev 2010).

'I said', *sak-au* 'I say'). The imperative and subjunctive forms are late innovations; here the extant Baltic languages differ and show non-cognate forms.[8]

According to the composition and mutual relations between stems, Lithuanian verbs are traditionally classified into the so-called primary verbs, i.e., those where neither of the three stems contains a syllabic suffix; (ii) the suffixal verbs, which are derived from verbs or words of other parts of speech by syllabic suffixes; and (iii) the so-called mixed verbs, which have syllabic suffixes (*-o-*, *-ė-*, or *-y-*) in their infinitive stem and lack it in one or both of the remaining stems. This classification can be, *mutatis mutandis*, extended to the verbs of Latvian and Latgalian as well.

It is also worth noting that although all three Baltic languages have quite complex systems of morphophonological vowel and consonant alternations in their conjugation, their functional load is different. In Lithuanian, stem alternations are almost always subsidiary, co-occurring with, and often conditioned by overt segmental affixes serving as a primary exponence of particular morphosyntactic features. By contrast, in Latvian and especially in Latgalian, there are many cases where stem alternations become the primary means of differentiation between forms with identical (not always zero!) affixal markers (see some examples in Tables 13 and 14).

Tab. 13: Stem alternations as primary exponence in Latvian conjugation

	vest 'lead'		*pirkt* 'buy'	
	Present	**Past**	**Present**	**Past**
1SG	ved-u [væd-u]	ved-u [ved-u]	pērk-u [pæ:rku]	pirk-u
2SG	ved-ø [ved]	ved-i [ved-i]	pērc-ø [pe:rts]	pirk-i
3	ved-ø [væd]	ved-a [ved-a]	pērk-ø [pæ:rk]	pirk-a

Tab. 14: Stem alternations as primary exponence in Latgalian conjugation

	nest 'carry'		*ēst* 'eat'	
	Present	**Past**	**Present**	**Past**
1SG	nas-u	neš-u [nʲeʃu]	ād-u	iež-u
2SG	nes-ø [nʲæsʲ]	nes-i [nʲesʲi]	ēd-ø [æ:tʲ]	ied-i
3	nas-ø	nes-e [nʲæsʲæ]	ād-ø	ēd-e [æ:dʲæ]
Supine	nas-t(u)		ās-t(u)	

---

[8] For the provenance of the contemporary imperative forms, cf. Stang (1942: 245–248), Kazlauskas (2000a: 380–385), on the rise of the subjunctive inflection, cf. Stang (1942: 250–254, 1966: 428–434), Smoczyński (1988: 861; 1999), and Michelini (2004).

2.3.2.1 Lithuanian

The basic pattern of verbal stems and verbal forms in contemporary Lithuanian is given in Table 15. Unless otherwise indicated, in this and similar tables for other languages verbs are given in the third person.

Various varieties of Lithuanian demonstrate innovations in the aspect-tense domain. The Lithuanian standard variety has, based on West Aukštaitian dialects, entrenched the past habitual (sometimes misleadingly called "frequentative") (cf. Geniušienė 1989, Roszko & Roszko 2006). Holvoet and Čižik (2004: 141–142) include it as a third member in an opposition of aspect, which, in their opinion, is tightly connected to the semantics of "imperfective" verbs (Holvoet & Čižik 2004: 153–154). For an elaborate treatment of this gram in Standard Lithuanian, see Sakurai (this volume). From an areal point of view, it is remarkable that although languages with a past habitual gram are not that rare all over the world (cf. Bybee, Perkins & Pagliuca 1994: 154–155), Standard Lithuanian is the only variety in Europe marking this function with a bound morpheme (suffix). It does have functional equivalents in other Baltic varieties, namely in those to the west and north

Tab. 15: The basic relation between stems of verbal inflectional categories in Lithuanian

Infinitive	Present	Simple past	Future	Imperative	Subjunctive
I Primary verbs					
dirb-ti 'work'	dirb-a	dirb-o	dirb-s	dirb-k	dirb-tų
tap-ti 'become'	ta-m-p-a	tap-o	tap-s	tap-k	tap-tų
ding-ti 'disappear'	ding-st-a	ding-o	ding-s	din-k (<*ding-k)	ding-tų
kirs-ti 'cut'	kert-a	kirt-o	kir-s	kirs-k	kirs-tų
drėb-ti 'throw'	dreb-ia	drėb-ė	drėb-s	drėb-k	drėb-tų
kel-ti 'raise'	kel-ia	kėl-ė	kel-s	kel-k	kel-tų
gau-ti 'get'	gau-n-a	gav-o	gau-s	gau-k	gau-tų
bū-ti 'be'	1SG es-u, 3 yra	buv-o	bu-s	bū-k	bū-tų
II Mixed verbs					
kalb-ė-ti 'speak'	kalb-a	kalb-ė-jo	kalb-ė-s	kalb-ė-k	kalb-ė-tų
myl-ė-ti 'love'	myl-i	myl-ė-jo	myl-ė-s	myl-ė-k	myl-ė-tų
žin-o-ti 'know'	žin-o	žin-o-jo	žin-o-s	žin-o-k	žin-o-tų
dar-y-ti 'do'	dar-o	dar-ė	dar-y-s	dar-y-k	dar-y-tų
III Suffixal verbs					
tikr-in-ti 'check'	tikr-in-a	tikr-in-o	tikr-in-s	tikr-in-k	tikr-in-tų
dėk-o-ti 'thank'	dėk-o-ja	dėk-o-jo	dėk-o-s	dėk-o-k	dėk-o-tų
rag-au-ti 'taste'	rag-au-ja	rag-av-o	rag-au-s	rag-au-k	rag-au-tų
maž-ė-ti 'diminish'	maž-ė-ja	maž-ė-jo	maž-ė-s	maž-ė-k	maž-ė-tų

of the Aukštaitian territory: Samogitian (Lithuanian) and Latvian. However, these grams are formed analytically around verbs with an original meaning of 'like': Samogitian *liuobėti* (which still occurs as an independent verb with this meaning as well) and Latvian *mēgt* (which has come to be used only as an auxiliary) (cf. Arkad'ev 2012b: 83–85).[9] From the point of view of the inner-Baltic dialect continuum (and from a diastratic viewpoint), the Standard Lithuanian "synthetic" habitual and the analytical habituals are in complementary distribution.

Another peculiarity of Lithuanian is the productive use of inflectional prefixes (in addition to the derivational prefixes, see Sections 2.3.2.5 and 2.4.1). These include, in addition to the negative prefix *ne-*, attested in all Baltic languages, two polyfunctional prefixes, *te-* and *be-*. Both *te-* and *be-* can be used in isolation and in combination with each other and with negation. The uses of *te-* include permissive (mostly with third-person present; see (1a)) and restrictive (with any verbal forms; see (1b)) (cf. Arkadiev 2010).

(1) Lithianian
   a. *T-as,*   *kur-is*   *sukurt-as*   *rašy-ti –*
      that-NOM.SG.M   which-NOM.SG.M   created-NOM.SG.M   write-INF
      te-raš-o,   *kalbė-ti –*   **te-kalb-a...**
      PRM-write-PRS.3 speak-INF   PRM-speak-PRS.3
      'Let that who is created to write, write, and that who is created to speak, speak.' (DLKT)

   b. *...man*   *ne-atrod-o*   *natūral-u,*   *kad*   *j-is*
      I:DAT   NEG-seem-PRS.3   natural-N   that   3-NOM.SG.M
      vis-ą   *laik-ą*   *apie*   *tai*   **te-kalb-a.**
      all-ACC.SG   time-ACC.SG   about   that   RSTR-speak-PRS.3
      'It does not seem natural to me that he is always speaking only about that.' (DLKT)

The prefix *be-* is very polyfunctional, and its interpretation often depends on the type of verbal form (e.g., finite vs. non-finite) to which it attaches as well as to the broader context, see Arkadiev (2011b). The most salient uses of *be-* include the continuative and the avertive. The continuative comes in two kinds distinguished

---

[9] According to the material presented in Zinkevičius (1966: 357f.) and Eckert (1996a,b), Samogitian dialects differ among each other for both the form of *liuobėti* (= auxiliary) and the lexical verb: *liuobėti* can occur either as an inflected verb or as a particle (*liuob*); the lexical verb can occur as infinitive or in the future form. Irrespective of the formal marking, the Samogitian constructions always carry past reference and the Latvian ones (with *mēgt*) inflect and distinguish tense (Arkad'ev 2012b: 84).

by polarity: a positive one (with the additional prefix *te-* to yield *te-be-*) and a negative one (with the prefix *ne-* giving *ne-be-*), cf. (2a,b).

(2) Lithuanian
    a.   ...*miestel-yje*   **te-be-gyven-o**   *daug*   *našli-ų.*
       small.town-LOC.SG   POS-CNT-live-PST.3   many   widow-GEN.PL
       '... in the town there still lived many widows.' (DLKT)

    b. *Tada*   *j-is*   *jau*   **ne-be-gyven-o**   *su*   *žmon-a...*
       then   3-NOM.SG.M   already   NEG-CNT-live-PST.3   with   wife-INS.SG
       'Then he already no longer lived with his wife...' (DLKT)

In the avertive construction, the prefix *be-* attaches to a present active participle in combination with the inflected auxiliary *būti* in the past tense (cf. 3). On Lithuanian avertive, sometimes misleadingly called "continuative", besides Arkadiev (2011b), see also Sližienė (1961, 1995: 227–228) and Mathiassen (1996b: 8–9).

(3) Lithuanian
    Kai   *aš*   *jau*   **buv-au**   **be-iš-ein-ąs,**
    when   1SG.NOM   already   AUX-PST.1SG   CNT-out-go-PRS.PA.NOM.SG.M
    paprašė manęs stiklinės vandens.
    'When I was already going to exit, he asked me [to bring him] a glass of water.' (DLKT)

2.3.2.2 Latvian and Latgalian

Tables 16 and 17 illustrate the general patterns of verb inflection in Latvian and Latgalian, respectively. On the classification of Latvian verbs, see e.g., Fennell (1971b, 1986).

Tab. 16: The basic relation between stems of verbal inflectional categories in Latvian

Infinitive	Present	Past	Future	Subjunctive
I Primary verbs				
nes-t 'carry'	*nes*	*nes-a*	*nes-īs*	*nes-tu*
pirk-t 'buy'	*pērk*	*pirk-a*	*pirk-s*	*pirk-tu*
cel-t 'raise'	*ceļ*	*cēl-a*	*cel-s*	*cel-tu*
bār-t 'scold'	*bar*	*bār-a*	*bār-s*	*bār-tu*
bruk-t 'collapse'	*brūk*	*bruk-a*	*bruk-s*	*bruk-tu*
grim-t 'sink'	*grim-st*	*grim-a*	*grim-s*	*grim-tu*
sie-t 'tie up'	*sie-n*	*sē-ja*	*sie-s*	*sie-tu*
ie-t 'go'	1SG *eju*, 3 *iet*	*gā-ja*	*ie-s*	*ie-tu*
bū-t 'be'	1SG *esmu*, 3 *ir*	*bi-ja*	*bū-s*	*bū-tu*
II Mixed verbs				
tur-ē-t 'hold'	*tur*	*tur-ē-ja*	*tur-ē-s*	*tur-ē-tu*
zin-ā-t 'know'	*zin-a*	*zin-ā-ja*	*zin-ā-s*	*zin-ā-tu*

continued

Tab. 16: (Continued)

Infinitive	Present	Past	Future	Subjunctive
aic-in-ā-t 'bid'	aic-in-a	aic-in-ā-ja	aic-in-ā-s	aic-in-ā-tu
las-ī-t 'read'	las-a	las-ī-ja	las-ī-s	las-ī-tu
III Suffixal verbs				
run-ā-t 'speak'	run-ā	run-ā-ja	run-ā-s	run-ā-tu
mekl-ē-t 'search'	mekl-ē	mekl-ē-ja	mekl-ē-s	mekl-ē-tu
lab-o-t 'correct'	lab-o	lab-o-ja	lab-o-s	lab-o-tu

Tab. 17: The basic relation between stems of verbal inflectional categories in Latgalian (based on Nau 2011a: 42–49; Leikuma 2003: 30–37, Aleksej Andronov, p.c.)

Infinitive	Present	Past	Future	Subjunctive
I Primary verbs				
nes-t [nʲæsʲtʲ] 'carry'	nas	nes-e [nʲæsʲæ]	nes-s [nʲæsʲ:]	nas-tu
seg-t [sʲæktʲ] 'cover'	sadz	sedz-e [sʲædzʲæ]	seg-s [sʲæksʲ]	sag-tu
jim-t [jimtʲ] 'take'	jam	jēm-e [jæ:mʲæ]	jim-s [jimsʲ]	jim-tu
stum-t [stumtʲ] 'push'	stum	styum-e [stʲumʲæ]	stum-s [stumsʲ]	stum-tu
krau-t [krautʲ] 'pile'	krau-n	kruov-e [kruovʲæ]	krau-s [krausʲ]	krau-tu
snig-t [sʲnʲiktʲ] 'snow'	snīg	snyg-a	snig-s [sʲnʲiksʲ]	snyg-tu
grim-t [grimtʲ] 'sink'	grym-st	grym-a	grim-s [grimsʲ]	grym-tu
ī-t [i:tʲ] 'go'	1SG īm-u, 2SG ej [æj], 3 īt [i:t]	guoj-a	ī-s [i:sʲ]	ī-tu
byu-t [bʲutʲ] 'be'	1SG asm-u, 2SG es-i [esʲi], 3 ir	bej-a [bʲeja]	byu-s [bʲusʲ]	byu-tu
II Mixed verbs				
dar-ei-t [dareitʲ] 'do'	dor-a	dar-e-ja [darʲeja]	dar-ei-s [darʲeisʲ]	dar-ei-tu [darʲeitu]
tic-ē-t [tʲitsʲæ:tʲ] 'believe'	tic [tʲitsʲ]	tic-ē-ja [tʲitsʲæ:ja]	tic-ē-s [tʲitsʲæ:sʲ]	tyc-ā-tu
tec-ē-t [tʲætsʲæ:tʲ] 'flow'	tak	tec-ē-ja [tʲætsʲæ:ja]	tec-ē-s [tʲætsʲæ:sʲ]	tac-ā-tu
III Suffixal verbs				
mekl-ē-t [mʲækʲilʲæ:tʲ] 'search'	mekl-e-j [mʲækʲilʲæj]	mekl-ē-ja [mʲækʲilʲæ:ja]	mekl-ē-s [mʲækʲilʲæ:sʲ]	makl-ā-tu
run-uo-t [runuotʲ] 'speak'	run-o-j	run-uo-ja / run-ov-a	run-uo-s [runuosʲ]	run-uo-tu
peln-ei-t [pʲelʲnʲeitʲ] 'earn'	peln-e-j [pʲelʲnʲej]	peln-e-ja [pʲelʲnʲeja]	peln-ei-s [pʲelʲnʲeisʲ]	peln-ei-tu [pʲelʲnʲeitu]

A peculiarly Latvian innovation in the verbal system is the debitive, an inflectional form expressing necessity. It consists of a basic form with the prefix *jā-* added to the third-person present of the verb, and the verb 'be' as an auxiliary, e.g., *bija jā-strādā* 'one had to work'. Originally, the base was probably the infinitive, retained in the case of 'be': *jā-būt* 'one has to be'. The person on whom an obligation is imposed is in the dative, the original accusative object of the verb is usually in the nominative (cf. 4a). In many dialects, however, the second argument is in the accusative; in all dialects, the second argument is in the accusative if it is a first- or second-person pronoun or a reflexive pronoun (cf. Schmalstieg 1990) (see 4b).

(4) Latvian
    a. Man   jā-no.pērk   cimd-i.
        1SG.DAT   DEB-buy   glove-NOM.PL
        'I must buy gloves.'

    b. Man   jā-sa.tiek   tevi.
        1SG.DAT   DEB-meet   2SG.ACC
        'I must meet you.'

The debitive has arisen from a biclausal structure containing an infinitival relative clause: an original structure **man nav jā pirkt* 'I do not have [anything] which to buy' (≅ 'I have nothing to buy') gave rise to the modal meaning 'I need not buy' (the original meaning is attested in Old Latvian). On the grammaticalization process that led to the rise of the debitive as a modal form, cf. Holvoet (1998).

An interesting feature of the Latvian verbal system is the morphologization of evidential marking (cf. Holvoet 2001c). This marking originally consisted, like in Lithuanian (see Section 2.3.2.4), in the use of participles instead of finite verb forms, but in Latvian declinable participles have been replaced with converbs in *-ot*, and this ending has become dissociated from its original function and has become a dedicated evidential marker that can be added to many forms already marked for other categories, e.g., there is an evidential debitive, e.g., *jā-domāj-ot* 'one reportedly has to think', and some dialects have an evidential irrealis of the type *būt-ot* 'would reportedly be'. The evidential marker can also spread over the whole verbal form and be added to both auxiliary and main verb, e.g., *es-ot jā-strādāj-ot* 'one reportedly has to work'. Because of this "syntactic emancipation", Nau (1998: 27) and Holvoet (2001a: 117f., 2007: 83–89) treat the evidential suffix *-ot* as a finite (or "finitized") part of the regular verbal paradigm.

After having illustrated the general outfit of the verbal morphology of individual Baltic languages, we will now deal with several issues relevant for all of these languages, without artificially distributing information among subsections.

2.3.2.3 Participles and other deverbal nominal categories

Baltic languages betray a rich inventory of participles, which covers all tenses and fulfills a central role in different parts of the grammar (TAM system, including taxis, voice, evidentiality, all sorts of complex sentences), which we will come across at different places below. In Lithuanian, the inventory tends toward symmetry in terms of voice distinctions, while in Latvian and Latgalian, such a symmetry is lacking.

Inflected and uninflected participles have to be distinguished. The latter can for their most part be characterized as converbs, but inflected participles can also serve as adverbial ("semi-predicative") additions to the main predicate when the subjects of the participle and of the matrix verb are identical (cf. Sakurai 2008; see Section 2.5.3). From the diachronic viewpoint, the most comprehensive work on participles has been done by Ambrazas (1979, 1990); from a synchronic point of view, cf. also Gruzdeva (1958), Wiemer (2001b, 2007b: 201–206), Arkadiev (2011a, 2012c, 2013a, 2014b) on Lithuanian, Eiche (1983) on Latvian, and Nau (2011a: 57–60) on Latgalian. Uninflected participles in Lithuanian are consistently used as sort of switch reference markers in clause combining when the overt or understood subject of the participle does not coincide with the (nominative) subject of the matrix clause (cf. Wiemer 2001b: 78–80, 2009a: 183–200; Arkadiev 2012c, 2013a). By contrast, in Latvian and Latgalian, uninflected participles are productive in same-subject clauses as well, occur as components of the debitive construction, and are used as a productive marker of reportive evidentiality (see Section 2.3.2.4).

In Lithuanian, participles can be formed from any verb of any tense stem (including the past habitual). The most convenient way to subcategorize the paradigmatic organization of inflected participles is to distinguish between active and passive orientation and between participles with agreement categories (case, number, gender) and those without them, i.e., showing default agreement (active participles in *-ą, -į, -ę*, passive participles in unstressed *-a*). The latter are consistently used to mark lack of agreement with the highest-ranking (mostly the single) semantic argument, which with the passive participles can only be expressed in the genitive; in fact, these participles are predominantly derived from one-place verbs (e.g., *Čia žmoni-ų*.GEN.PL *given-ta* 'People must have lived here').

The symmetry of voice orientation is not perfect (even in Lithuanian), for two reasons: first, passive participles of future stems, although usually indicated in reference grammars, are extremely rare. Second, so-called passive participles – marked with {m} for the present stem and with {t} for the past stem – should generally better be characterized as devices of deranking the syntactic valency, irrespective of the transitivity of the verb (cf. also Sawicki 2004: 164). Both suffixes are exploited in the *ma/ta*-evidential of Lithuanian (see Section 2.3.2.4), in which one-place verbs predominate (see above). Moreover, *m*-participles are consistently used in the derivation of nouns (together with pronominal or definite inflection, see Section 2.3.1.2) to denote generic terms irrespective of any voice orientation, e.g., (*sprog-ti* 'explode' >) *sprog-st-a-m-o-ji medžiag-a* 'explosive material', (*valg-y-ti* 'eat' >) *valg-o-m-as-is kambar-ys* 'dining room', (*raš-y-ti* 'write' >) *raš-o-m-o-ji mašin-ėl-ė* 'typing machine' (cf. Wiemer 2006b: 279).

In Latvian, participles in *-am-/-ām-* have acquired a modal meaning of either possibility or necessity, as in *viņu dzīvība ir glābjama* 'their lives can/must be saved'. In its original premodal meaning, this participle is used in shortened form, as a truncated accusative in *-am/-ām-*, in complement clauses of verbs of sensory perception and a few others; here, however, their value has switched from passive to active as a result of reanalysis shown in examples (5a,b); the construction has then spread to intransitive verbs, as in example (5c).

(5) Latvian
   a. *Es   redz-ēj-u   [viņ-u ved-am   uz   iecirkn-i].*
      1SG.NOM see-PST-1SG he-ACC lead-PRS.PP to   police.station-ACC.SG
      'I saw him being led to the police station.'

→ b. *Es   redz-ēj-u   [Ø   viņ-u ved-am*
      1SG.NOM see-PST-1SG Ø   he-ACC lead-PRS.PART
      uz   iecirkn-i].
      to   police.station-ACC.SG
      'I saw how they were leading him to the police station.'

   c. *Es   dzird-u   [kād-u   dzied-am].*
      1SG.NOM hear-PRS.1SG somebody-ACC sing-PRS.PART
      'I hear somebody singing'.

2.3.2.4 Resultatives, the perfect, and grammatical evidentiality

All Baltic languages have a full-fledged system of perfect tenses (or "anterior grams" in the sense of Thieroff 2000), which is based on the nominative of the gender-number inflected past active participles occurring together with the 'be'-verb (Lithuanian *būti*, Latvian *būt*, Latgalian *byut*) as an auxiliary inflected for tense and agreement categories. This system is presented in every reference and academy grammar of the Baltic languages. For concise treatments concerning Latvian cf. Nau (2005), concerning Lithuanian cf. Wiemer (2007b: 206–210; 2009a: 168–172). It must be noted, however, that the use of the perfect tenses in Lithuanian and Latvian diverges in many respects (the Latvian perfect seems to be more grammaticalized than the Lithuanian one, which in many cases is in free or stylistic variation with the simple past tense), most of which are still to be investigated.

Close to the perfect in functional terms are resultatives; the subject-oriented resultative formally coincides with the (present) perfect, whereas the object-oriented resultative is based on participles with the {t}-suffix used also for the passive and the non-agreeing evidential (see below). A striking feature of Baltic resultatives is the perfectly complementary distribution of marking types (i.e., participial suffixes) over subject- vs. object-oriented resultatives (cf. Geniušienė & Nedjalkov 1988, Wiemer & Giger 2005: chapter 4; see further Section 4). Another fact striking only for Lithuanian (but not Latvian) is the occurrence of a weakly grammaticalized HAVE-perfect (Geniušienė & Nedjalkov 1988: 385–386; Wiemer & Giger 2005: 47ff; Arkad'ev 2012b: 105–106), which is outstanding both from an areal and a structural perspective: it is composed of the inflected transitive verb *turėti* 'have' and **active** anteriority participles agreeing in number and gender with the (nominative) subject, not the object (as was the case in initial stages of Germanic and Romance leading to the perfect, and what has been observed for centuries in all West Slavic languages). The reasons that might have led to this peculiar situation were discussed by Wiemer (2012b).

All extant Baltic languages display an evidential extension of the present perfect based on inflected participles. The reportive function clearly predominates. From a syntactic viewpoint, it is probable that a certain role in the rise of the reportive function of inflected active participles was played by syntactically embedded complement clauses[10] (as illustrated in 6a). However, this function is fulfilled by these participles also in independent (main) clauses. Insofar as the present perfect appears to have been the primary source for the spread of reportive marking in the northeastern part of the Circum-Baltic Area (CBA) (Wälchli 2000), in the Baltic languages, a second source construction proves to be no less important, namely, logophoric constructions based on a complement-taking predicate (CTP) of speech and the predicate of the complement expressed by a nominative active participle of past, present, or future tense agreeing in number and gender with the subject of the CTP (cf. Ambrazas 1979: 96–128, 1990: 124–141; Wiemer 1998, 2007b: 228–232; Arkadiev 2012b) (see 6).

---

10 On alternative assumptions, participles in reportive use might have evolved from a sort of syntactic tightening of erstwhile juxtaposed (asyndetic) coordination (finite predicate+inflected participle, with the latter re-interpreted as clausal argument of the former). This hypothesis, which is also tightly linked to the rise of logophoric constructions (as will be discussed later), does not invalidate assumptions about a development out of subordination. Rather, both assumptions may complement each other if different stages are assessed (Ambrazas 1990: 129f.; Wiemer 1998: 236–240).

(6) Lithuanian
Vaik-as   skund-ė-si
child(M)-NOM.SG   complain-PST.3-RFL
'The child complained
  a. *prarad-ęs   žaisliuk-ą.*
    lose-PST.PA.NOM.SG.M   toy-ACC.SG
    that it had lost its toy.'
  b. *nor-įs   valgy-ti.*
    want-PRS.PA.NOM.SG.M   eat-INF
    that it wanted to eat.'
  c. *šiandien ne-maty-s-iąs   draug-o.*
    today   NEG-see-FUT-PA.NOM.SG.M   friend-GEN.SG
    that it wouldn't see its friend today'.

Basically, this sort of logophoric construction is a prominent case in point to illustrate the rather widespread role of participles in the complementation of clausal arguments (see Section 2.5.3). However, this syntactically rather tight construction represents but the canonical case of a logophoric construction (Nau 2006: 64). Another, syntactically "loose" way of marking logophoricity will be discussed in Section 3.4.2.

Only Lithuanian has developed a second device of marking evidentiality, with a predominant inferential function. This "second" grammatical evidential is based on non-agreeing participles ending in *-ma* (simultaneous) and *-ta* (anterior), with the highest-ranking argument in the genitive (cf. Holvoet 2007: chapter 4, Wiemer 2006a, 2007b: 213–216, Lavine 2006, 2010). In a sense, this functional extension turns out to be an indirect consequence of the disappearance of the neuter as a control gender (see Section 2.3.1). Another remarkable observation is the almost complementary distribution of the *ma/ta*-evidential in comparison to the passive (see Section 4).[11]

Apart from this, it should be stressed that for both types of evidentials, the functional association with voice-related operations has remained weak, since particular context conditions can cancel the evidential interpretation (cf. Roszko 1993: chapter 3; Wiemer 2007b: 206–208). This annulation is not possible with the specialized morphological evidential marker *-ot* in Latvian (see Section 2.3.2.2).

2.3.2.5 The quest of aspect

Even trying to give an only brief account of this issue would go beyond the limits of this general survey, because, among other things, such an account would require

---

[11] The most recent attempt at accounting for the syntactic peculiarities of the Lithuanian *ta/ma*-impersonal (inferential evidential) from a generative perspective is by Lavine (2010). Here diachronic considerations do not play any role whatsoever.

not only "stock taking" for Baltic, but also a comparison with Slavic, whose perfective vs. imperfective opposition has often influenced (not always fortunately) the discussion of aspect in Baltic. Here we can but mention the most basic things. For more comprehensive discussions and analyses, cf. Dambriūnas (1960), Holvoet (2001a: chapter 8), Wiemer (2001a), Kardelis and Wiemer (2002, 2003: 59–64), Holvoet and Čižik (2004), Wiemer and Pakerys (2007), Arkad'ev (2008a, 2009, 2011c), Holvoet (2014), and the probably most up-to-date treatment in Arkad'ev (2012b). On more particular problems, cf. Dambriūnas (1959, 1975), Sawicki (2000, 2010), and Mikulskas (2005: 32–38). As for Latvian, cf. also Hauzenberga-Šturma (1979).

From the notional perspective, aspect is usually defined as a category of the verb by which the internal contours of a situation (event, process, state), distinctions between singular and iterated situation tokens, and speaker's representation of the eventuality as bounded or unbounded (limited or unlimited) are distinguished. However, when aspect is regarded as a *grammatical* category, one has to consider whether such distinctions are expressed regularly and predictably by means of language-particular morphosyntactic devices. From a typological point of view (cf. Dahl 1985, 2000, Bybee & Dahl 1989, Bybee, Perkins, & Pagliuca 1994), aspect is most often expressed in one of two ways: either by inflectional markers (e.g., past tenses of conservative Romance), or in an analytical way by a combination of an auxiliary with some sort of nonfinite form of the lexical verb (e.g., the English progressive or the past habitual with *used to*). Syncretisms of aspectual categories with tense functions are commonplace.

By contrast, an aspectual opposition of the Slavic type, which rests on stem derivation, is cross-linguistically much less widespread. Most briefly, it results from an evolution "whereby stems related by morphological derivation can eventually substitute each other as lexical synonyms, but with complementary grammatical functions" (Wiemer 2011: 743). By the same process, the whole stock of verb stems is being divided up into different (in the Slavic case: two) classes with specific inventories of grammatical functions (Wiemer 2001a, Lehmann 2004). In this sense, aspect based on stem derivation yields a classificatory type of morphological oppositions, which can be compared to gender systems of nouns, albeit with more restrictions caused by lexically inherent aspectual distinctions carried by the stems themselves (such as state vs. process, instantaneous vs. durative, telic vs. atelic etc.). These are partially known as Vendlerian aspectual types of predicates, but they also pertain to lexical modifications of the verbal meaning known as "Aktionsarten" in the Indoeuropeanist tradition (after Agrell 1908). Both sorts of lexicon-internal divisions have played a role in standard and academy grammars of the Baltic languages (certainly to some extent framed on the model of Soviet academy grammars in post-war Russia); thus, we occasionally encounter sections on "lexico-semantic" or "semantico-derivational" classes of verbs (cf., e.g., GLJa 1985: 250–277).¹² Influence from (Soviet) Russian grammaticography can also be explained from the fact that Baltic shares with Slavic basically the same inherited stem-derivational patterns of verbal morphology.

Let us summarize where parallels between Baltic (mainly Lithuanian) and Russian or Polish aspect indeed exist and what the crucial differences are. The most basic common feature is productive derivation of verb stems (by prefixes **and** suffixes) itself. Since inflection is of no concern, all finite and nonfinite verb forms distinguish what is considered as aspect (Lith. *veikslas*). Importantly, stem derivation includes suffixation of verbal stems to yield new verbal stems (further on this issue in Sections 2.4 and Section 4). Latvian shares the use of perfectivizing prefixation with Lithuanian, but has acquired additional means of opposing imperfective and perfective aspect: perfective verbs with spatial prefixes have exact imperfective counterparts in the form of phrasal verbs containing adverbs semantically corresponding to the prefix in combination with the simple verb, e.g., *ie-nāca istabā* 'entered the room' (perfective) vs. *nāca **iekšā** istabā* 'was entering the room' (imperfective). Although basically restricted to spatial prefixes, this pattern also comprises many of their more abstract or metaphorical uses, e.g., *iz-putēja* 'went bankrupt (perfective)' vs. *putēja ārā* 'was going bankrupt (imperfective)'. Still, there is a predominant group of verbs containing prefixes radically changing lexical meaning for which phrasal imperfectives are not available, and they are bi-aspectual, e.g., *iz-mantot* 'use, exploit' (perfective and imperfective).

The differences in comparison to Slavic aspect are of three kinds: first, despite very productive patterns of prefixation and suffixation on token level (i.e., in discourse), pairs of stems acquired by derivation do not pervade the stock of verb stems (i.e., types) with the same consequence as in, say, Russian or Polish (cf. Holvoet & Čižik 2004: 148; Arkad'ev 2009, 2012a: 60–78). Second, where pairs of lexically identical stems exist, their functional distribution over grammatically definable contexts is often not very clear-cut and unpredictable (Wiemer 2001a). Third, each verb stem regardless of its assignment to "perfective" or "imperfective" aspect (Lith. *įvykio* vs. *eigos veikslas*) can be used in any inflectional and infinite form and does not show virtually any restrictions in combination with other grammatical categories (simple and compound tenses, mood, voice, etc.). East Slavic and Polish, by contrast, show severe restrictions in both regards: neither can a Russian or Polish perfective verb be used in all tenses, nor can it derive all kinds of participles. Notice further that many Lithuanian verbs called "perfective" can occur

---

12 On discussion concerning comparisons with Russian by Lithuanian scholars, cf., Galnaitytė (1962, 1963, 1966, 1979a) and Mustejkis (1972).

in the scope of a phasal verb denoting the final stage, or with a proximative reading of a goal-directed activity or process (e.g., *baigė per-skaityti knygą* 'finished reading the book', *baigė už-migti* 'was about to fall asleep'; cf. e.g., Brauner 1961); this is generally impossible for perfective verbs in any (standard) Slavic language. Phasal verbs denoting the initial stage of (bound or unbound) processes are less well accepted by many native speakers (e.g., *pradeda nu-si-rengti* 'begins to undress'). As shown in Holvoet (2014), these differences (both with regard to Slavic languages and between ingressive and egressive phasal verbs in Lithuanian) can be explained as a distinction of two construction types: instead of simply a phasal meaning, the combination 'finish, end'+"pfv." verb by default yields a proximative reading, i.e., "refers to an imminent event viewed as the outcome of a (basically unexpressed) process that is in its final phase" at some reference interval. Note that Latvian does not show this behavior.

Another important difference between Baltic and Slavic languages in the domain of aspect lies in the existence in Baltic of a large and heterogeneous class of verbs (many of which belong to the most basic and frequent lexemes), which cannot be ascribed to any of the alleged "aspects", being able to occur both in bounded (associated to perfective) and unbounded (associated to imperfective) contexts. Cf. the following Lithuanian examples with a typical (and very frequent) "bi-aspectual" verb *patikti* 'like'.

(7) Lithuanian
    a. *J-ai   labiau **pa.tik-o**, kai   t-ie*
       3-DAT.SG.F rather like-PST.3 when DEM-NOM.PL.M
       pašnekesi-ai   vyk-o   be   j-os.
       conversation-NOM.PL occur-PST.3 without 3-GEN.SG.F
       'She rather liked [state] when such conversations happened without her.' (DLKT)

    b. *Tai,   k-ą   iš.vyd-a-u,   man   **pa.tik-o**.*
       DEM   what-ACC.SG see-PST-1SG 1SG.DAT like-PST.3
       'I liked [event of entry into a state] what I saw.' (DLKT)

    c. *J-am   **pa.tik-o**   š-is   tilt-as.*
       3-DAT.SG.M like-PST.3 DEM-NOM.SG.M bridge-NOM.SG
       'He liked [ambiguous as to state vs. event] this bridge.' (DLKT)

Of course, Slavic languages have "bi-aspectual" verbs as well; however, almost all of them are either exceptional and infrequent archaisms or recent borrowings, and by no means constitute a salient part of the core of the verbal lexicon of Slavic languages.

We conclude this discussion by saying that despite important differences between Baltic and Slavic languages in the domain of expression of aspectual distinctions, there is no difference of principle, rather a difference of degree of grammaticalization. Both Baltic and Slavic have aspectually marked lexical classes rather than inflectional aspect, and the differences between them are in (i) degree of generality and obligatoriness of choice between verb stems related to each other by derivational means and (ii) the extent of the rule-based interaction of aspectual marking with other verbal categories and morphosyntax.

2.4 Derivational morphology

Among works dealing with word formation in Baltic languages in general, the following can be mentioned: Bammesberger (1973) on abstract nouns, Rosinas (1988, 1996) on pronouns (cf. also Nau 2001b for Latvian pronouns), Kozhanov (2011, this volume) on indefinite pronouns in Lithuanian, Petit (2012) in Latvian. Forssman (2003) deals with adverb formation in Latvian, Ulvydas (2009) in Lithuanian.

Among the salient features of all Baltic languages, we find the abundant use of the reflexive marker (RM) with verbs. Cf. Geniušienė (1983, 1987) for a systematic taxonomic account on a typological background (see also in Section 3.1). Kalnača and Lokmane (2012) is an attempt at applying this taxonomy to Latvian. That reflexivization is an instance of derivational rather than inflectional morphology is usually taken for granted, obviously under the influence of Russian grammar. Holvoet (forthcoming a, cf. also Holvoet & Semėnienė 2004a) argues that reflexive morphology is actually closer to inflection than to derivation according to most criteria. The motivation for relegating reflexivity from the morphological category of voice to word formation is that anticausative reflexives such as Lith. *už-si-degti*, Latv. *iedegties* 'light up, start burning' tend to be interpreted as an instance of valency-decreasing derivation; but the existence of mediopassives in many languages militates against such a strict division between voice (as valency-preserving morphology) and valency-changing derivation. Besides, anticausatives, the main argument in favor of valency-decreasing derivation, are just one among the numerous types of middle-voice reflexives. Many reflexives do not mark a change in argument structure, cf., for instance, Latvian *es apēdu kūku* 'I.NOM ate the cake.ACC' vs. *man apēdā-s kūka* 'I.DAT inadvertently ate the cake.NOM'. For a detailed study, cf. Holvoet, Grzybowska, and Rembiałkowska (forthcoming).

Apart from that, it should be stressed that a truly reflexive passive (without any additional connotations, as in the last example from Latvian) has shown up in Baltic dialects only under extreme contact conditions with (East) Slavic; cf. Holvoet (2000e) on Latgalian and Wiemer (2004a: 501–504) on Southeast Lithuanian.

Most verbs still hold a derivational relation to existent non-RM verbs, and as just mentioned, the dominant function is that of argument demotion (on a syntactic and/or semantic level), but we also find two groups of verb pairs for which argument increase occurs, namely, causative-reflexives, as in (8), and reflexive-benefactives. Compare, for instance, Lith. *nu-si-pirkti knyg-ą* 'buy oneself a book.ACC', *ap-si-žiūrėti parod-ą* 'inspect (for one's own pleasure) an exhibition.ACC', *už-si-dėti kepurę ant galvos* 'put a cap.ACC on one's head'. In Latvian this type has become archaic ("almost non-existent in [contemporary] Latvian", Geniušienė 2007: 637), while in Latgalian, it seems to be productive, like in Lithuanian (Lidija Leikuma and Aleksej Andronov, p.c.).

(8) Lithuanian
    a. *Kirpėj-as   ap-kirp-o   Jon-ą.*
        hairdresser-NOM.SG   PRV-cut-PST.3   Jonas-ACC.SG
        'The hairdresser cut Jonas' hair' (lit. cut Jonas)
    b. *Jon-as   ap-si-kirp-o   pas   mading-ą*
        Jonas-NOM.SG   PRV-RFL-cut-PST.3   at   fashionable-ACC.SG
        kirpėj-ą.
        hairdresser-ACC.SG
        'Jonas cut his hair at the hairdresser's' (lit. cut himself at the hairdresser)

As for other derivational extensions of verb stems, one should look separately at prefixation and suffixation. Latvian has lost most of its productive derivational suffixation, the only exclusion being causative suffixes. Instead, it has developed a rich inventory of 'verbal particles', see Section 4. Here (standard) Lithuanian proves much more conservative.

2.4.1 Lithuanian

General overviews of Lithuanian derivational morphology are supplied by Otrębski (1965), Senn (1966: 316–351), DLKG (1996: 86–167, 191–238). A general theoretical background applied to Lithuanian is given by Urbutis (1978). On diachronic studies, see Section 3.2. The pervading force of analogy in derivation was illustrated by Mikelionienė (2002). She also gave a structural classification of occasional formations and tried to find criteria to differentiate between potential and occasional words. Traditional methods of classifying derivational types in Lithuanian were criticized by Smetona (2005), who proposed an alternative, more bottom-up-like method.

    Shorter grammars, as a rule, do not contain information on derivational morphology (cf. Mathiassen 1996a), nor does LG ([1997] 2006); obviously, derivation was considered as belonging rather to the lexicon, even if productive rules in verbal morphology have given rise to the assumption that Lithuanian has been developing a perfective vs. imperfective aspect opposition of the Slavic type (see Section 2.3.2.5). GLJa (1985: 250–277), however, does account for stem derivational patterns as far as they concern rather regular semantic distinctions of ±transitivity, inchoativity-causativity, or the temporal shape of situations (phasal, iteration). DLKG (1996: 282–290) and LG ([1997] 2006: 221–237) supply extensive lists of affixes used to derive verb stems and correlating them with certain semantic (aspectual, diathetical) distinctions. It would be justified to discuss at least some of them from the perspective of lexical semantics (see Section 3.1), but we treat them in this subsection for the sake of systematicity, restricting ourselves to the most salient and productive patterns.

Nominal derivational morphology of Lithuanian has been extensively treated in the classic reference works by August Leskien (1891) and Pranas Skardžius ([1943] 1996), written from a Neogrammarian historical-comparative perspective. Works in English include Klimas (1975) on word formation in general and Klimas (1994) on reflexive nouns. The only issue that has received detailed treatment in more modern work is the formation, use, and acquisition of Lithuanian diminutives, see Savickienė (1998, 2001, 2007), Savickienė, Kempe, and Brooks (2009), and Dabašinskienė and Voeikova (this volume and references therein). Besides that, several studies exist dealing with the acquisition of nominal morphology of Lithuanian, e.g., Savickienė (2002, 2003), Kamandulytė (2006b).

Lithuanian shows two productive patterns of verbal suffixation. The first one is the suffix {elė/er(ė)} used for marking semelfactives derived from unprefixed stems, sometimes combined with ablaut (e.g., *baub-ti* ⇒ *baubt-elė-ti* 'bellow, low (of a cow)', *šok-ti* ⇒ *šokt-elė-ti* 'jump', *žvelgti* 'look, watch' ⇒ *žvilgt-erė-ti* 'catch sight, have a look', *laukti* ⇒ *lukt-er(ė)-ti* 'wait') (cf. Srba 1911, Galnaitytė 1979b, Geniušienė 1997: 224f.). Often these stems bear an inherently multiplicative semantics (in the sense of Xrakovskij 1997). Interestingly, the reversed order of derivation can be observed with so-called eventives (Lithuanian *ištiktukai*), a special word class discussed by Danylenko (this volume) and Wälchli (this volume), which can signal multiple action (subsumed under 'iterativity' by Wälchli) if the eventive is reduplicated. A single eventive (e.g., *cypt* 'squeak', *takš* 'hit') can thus be treated as an equivalent of a semelfactive verb, whereas reduplicated eventives (*cypt-cypt*, *takš-takš* etc.) can be considered as equivalents of multiplicatives.

The other productive suffix is {(d)inė}; its functional range is broader. As a rule, it serves to mark iterativity, multiplicativity, and (with certain restrictions often having to do with style and dialect) durativity. Verbs with this suffix can non-redundantly be combined with the habitual past (cf. Galnaitytė 1966, Geniušienė 1987, 1997, and references therein, as well as Sakurai, this volume).

The productivity of {(d)inė} seems to be especially high in Eastern Lithuania and in Lithuanian islands in Belarus. Since Fraenkel's (1936: 76–79, 104) study on Southeast Lithuanian, this fact has repeatedly been interpreted as an indication of the development of an aspect system of the Slavic type (cf. Vidugiris 1998, among others).

Formation of morphological causative verbs in Lithuanian, especially of the so-called curative verbs based on transitive predicates, has received some attention, cf. Galnajtite (1980), Savičiūtė (1985), Toops (1989), Rackevičienė (2005), Naktinienė (2011), Žeimantienė (2011), and Arkadiev and Pakerys (forthcoming).

As for prefixes, a first systematic treatment for Lithuanian was undertaken by Paulauskas (1958). From his analysis, one can deduce five types of prefixation, if one distinguishes the semantic relation to the deriving base: (i) prefixes that preserve the lexical prototype of the base, but add some (i.a) spatial (e.g., *eiti* 'go' ⇒ ***iš**-eiti* 'go out'), (i.b) temporal (e.g., *sėdėti* 'sit' ⇒ ***pa**-sėdėti* 'sit for a while'), or (i.c) other specification (e.g., *rašyti* 'write' ⇒ ***per**-rašyti* 'write sth. over, again'); (ii) prefixes that do not change the lexical meaning of the base stem (e.g., *sakyti* 'say' ⇒ ***pa**-sakyti* 'say'); (iii) prefixes that disambiguate a lexically diffuse meaning (e.g., *braukti* 'brush, draw, rub' ⇒ ***iš**-braukti* 'strike out, erase', ***pa**-braukti* 'underline'); (iv) prefixed stems for which the deriving base has been lost (e.g., †*prasti* ⇒ ***pri**-prasti* 'become accustomed'); (v) prefixed stems with a meaning largely dissociated from the (still existent) deriving base (e.g., *nešti* 'carry' ⇒ ***pra**-nešti* 'report', *tikti* 'be suitable' ⇒ ***pa**-tikti* 'like, please', ***pa-si**-tikti* 'meet (deliberately)').

2.4.2 Latvian

Latvian (let alone Latgalian) derivational morphology has not attracted much attention, with the exception of diminutives, cf. Rūķe-Draviņa (1953, 1959) and Horiguchi (this volume). A discussion of the relationship between inflectional and derivational morphology in Latvian is offered by Nau (2001c), Soida (2009), and the academy grammars (MLLVG, I: 75–374; LVG: 190–299). Latvian morphological causatives are discussed in Holvoet (forthcoming c) and Nau (forthcoming); on agent nouns see Nau (2013). On Latgalian, some aspects of word formation have been touched in work by Breidaks ([1966] 2007).

2.5 Syntax

Syntactic phenomena of Baltic languages have received very unequal attention and treatment in the existing literature. Sections of reference grammars of Lithuanian and Latvian devoted to syntax are usually written from an outdated perspective (often, again, influenced by the traditional academy grammars of Russian) and do not cover most of the issues on the agenda of contemporary syntactic theories. Theoretically and typologically informed studies of syntactic and morphosyntactic phenomena in Baltic treat only certain selected issues, and the general picture remains largely understudied.

Work on Lithuanian syntax, in a sense, starts with Jablonskis (1922: 241–254). General reference works, in addition to the relevant sections in grammars, include Labutis (1976, 1998) and Sirtautas and Grenda (1988). Many aspects of Lithuanian syntax have been described from a more theoretically informed perspective by Holvoet and Judžentis (eds. 2003), Holvoet and Semėnienė (eds. 2004b), Holvoet and Mikulskas (eds. 2005, 2006, 2009), all published in Lithuanian. Work on Latvian syntax starts with Karl Mühlenbach (Kārlis Mülenbachs); the information on syntax in Endzelin's well-known German language grammar of Latvian (Endzelin 1923) is also due to Mühlenbach. Traditional descriptions of Latvian syntax can be found in MLLVG (by Bergmane, Grabis, Lepika, & Sokols 1962) and in the work of Ceplītis, Rozenbergs, and Valdmanis (1989). Gāters (1993) is a study of the language of the Latvian folk songs; it contains relatively little on syntax in the modern sense, concentrating mainly on the use of grammatical forms; it is rich in facts, but difficult to use because of the obsolete terminology. This is deplorable, since, in general, folk songs provide a very valuable body of primary data for Baltic linguistics.[13]

There is no good syntax based on more modern linguistic notions, but there are a number of studies on particular aspects of Latvian syntax, to be briefly overviewed below. On syntax in the acquisition of Latvian as a first language, there is a detailed study by Rūķe-Draviņa (1963).

Latgalian syntax, which in many respects differs from that of both Lithuanian and Latvian, remains largely undescribed. For a general overview and a preliminary description of many interesting patterns, see Nau (2011a); on the issue of differential object marking (i.e., the choice of accusative vs. genitive case of the object), see Nau (2014).

Some specific syntactic issues in Baltic, like constructions with nominative objects, have received attention first and foremost from the point of view of areal linguistics, see e.g., Larin (1963), Timberlake (1974), Lavine (1999), and Ambrazas (2001a) (see Section 4 for further discussion).

Complex predicates do not fit common divisions into morphology vs. syntax, but since their formation ultimately goes back to syntactic patterns (or restrictions), it

---

13 Of particular importance are the work of Ozols ([1961] 1993), a monograph on the use of folk songs, and the collection of songs by Barons ([1894–1915] 1922).

seems justified to treat them briefly here. Complex predicates traditionally coincide with analytical predicates in the TAM domain or for marked voice constructions (provided the latter are based on participles). Passives are discussed in Section 2.5.3.1 (as for the status of 'middle voice' see Section 2.4); complex predicates related to tense (perfect), aspect, and evidentiality are discussed in Sections 2.3.2.3 and 2.3.2.4. Modal auxiliaries were comprehensively described by Holvoet (2009), particular modal constructions by Holvoet (2001b, 2003b). Jasionytė (2012) described the two Lithuanian non-epistemic necessity-modals *reikėti* 'need' and *tekti* 'be gotten', Usonienė and Jasionytė's (2010) study is devoted to acquisitive modals. Wiemer, Vladyko and Kardelis (2004) is a study on the behavior of possibility modals in the dispositional domain, which seem to show convergent patterns in the Baltic-Slavic contact zone. On the Latvian and Latgalian debitive, see Section 2.5.3.2.

2.5.1 Diachronic matters

The hitherto fullest account of Lithuanian syntax from a diachronic perspective has been presented by Ambrazas (2006). The standard reference work in English is by Schmalstieg (1988), which is largely based on previous work of Ambrazas (mainly Ambrazas 1979) and other scholars. The syntax of participial constructions in Baltic is treated from a diachronic perspective in the seminal monograph of Ambrazas (1990, in Russian, with a German summary), which has served as a basis for some diachronic-typological observations of Arkadiev (2013a).

Claims concerning an alleged "ergative pre-history" of Baltic (cf., among others, Palmaitis 1977, Schmalstieg 1982, 1988, etc.) could be refuted (cf. Ambrazas 1994, 2004, Holvoet 2000d; Wiemer 2004d: 96–102 for a survey of the pros and cons). The question of 'esse'- vs. 'habere'-based predicative possession was discussed by Holvoet (2003a).

Holvoet (2004a) gave a comprehensive analysis of changes in the case marking of predicative nominals with finite and non-finite predicates in Lithuanian and Latvian.

The most systematic account of NP-internal word order patterns in Lithuanian from the sixteenth to the nineteenth century was supplied by the monograph of Vasiliauskienė (2008, written in Lithuanian with an English summary) (cf. also Say 2004). Vasiliauskienė (2001) is a more specialized study on NP-internal word order in the eighteenth-century religious writings of Lukauskas. She also paid attention to discontinuous NPs, which by that time had come to be characteristic of writings in Eastern Lithuania.

There are only some few articles on the diachronic rise of complex sentence patterns, all but one (Holvoet 2010c) in Lithuanian. Judžentis and Pajėdienė (2001, 2005) analyzed clausal coordination and clause order (2001) as well as the use of comparative constructions (2005) in Daukša's *Katekizmas*. Judžentis (2002b) looked at complement clauses in this and another of Daukša's texts. He concluded that these texts did not yet show a clear differentiation between adverbial and complement clauses, since there was no complementizer void of additional semantic shades (see further Holvoet 2010c). An account of causal clauses and pertinent conjunctions was given by Kibildaitė (2001).

2.5.2 Noun phrases

Noun phrase structure in standard Baltic languages is typologically non-trivial in that it requires that agreeing modifiers (adjectives) go before non-agreeing ones (genitive noun phrases). NP structure in Baltic languages in comparison with Finnic is discussed by Christen (2001). A separate question concerns the use of definite and indefinite adjectives, see e.g., Gāters (1959); for a useful recent survey of the situation in both Baltic languages, see Holvoet and Spraunienė (2012). On the structure of phrases including numerals, see e.g., Cerri (2010, 2013).

Noun phrase structure in Lithuanian has been studied by Vaskelaitė (2003) and Holvoet and Mikulskas (eds. 2006). It has also received some treatment in the recent generative literature, see Rutkowski (2007, 2008), Rutkowski and Progovac (2006). From a diachronic and grammaticalization perspective, NP structure in Lithuanian is addressed by Say (2004). On definite adjectives, in addition to the already mentioned work by Holvoet and Spraunienė (2012), see also Valeckienė (1957, 1986), Baldauf (1967), Levin (1979), and Spraunienė (2011). The last mentioned paper was, to a large extent, based on Holvoet and Tamulionienė (2006) and Mikulskas (2006b), who argued for a treatment of definite adjectival forms as markers on the level of noun phrases (i.e., not as an adjectival category, contrary to Lithuanian academy grammars).

2.5.3 Simple sentences

2.5.3.1 Lithuanian

Quite a lot has been written on the uses of cases in Lithuanian, starting with the classic books by Ernst Fraenkel (1928, 1929) on the syntax of Lithuanian cases and adpositions. The most comprehensive reference work concerning the use of cases (and adpositions) in Standard Lithuanian is the monograph by Šukys (1998). The diachronic development of case relations, in particular of the adverbal genitive, was elaborated on by Ambrazas (2001b). Non-trivial aspects of case morphosyntax in Lithuanian and Latvian are discussed in the already mentioned paper of Holvoet (2010a).

Theoretically and/or typologically oriented studies of Lithuanian case syntax and semantics include the works of Mo (1977), Sawicki (1992), Klaas (1996),

Ambrazas (2004), Park (2005), Roduner (2004, 2005), Franks and Lavine (2006), Kerevičienė (2008), Anderson (2011, 2013, this volume), Aleksandravičiūtė (2013), Arkadiev (2013a, 2014a), and Seržant (2013a,b). Valency patterns of the comparative and the superlative degrees of adjectives were described in Semėnienė (2002). Some specific issues of case usage have received more extensive treatment, e.g., the case marking of predicate nominals (the opposition between predicate nominal agreement and predicative instrumental), see Fraenkel (1926), Nichols (1980), Timberlake (1988, 1990), Holvoet (2004a, 2005a, 2008), and Semėnienė (2004). As for predication by "neuter" adjectives (see Section 2.3.1), cf. Tekorienė (1990), Semėnienė (2003), and Ruskan (2013).

The problem of grammatical relations and subjecthood in Lithuanian has been first discussed from a modern perspective by Christen (1995), where different subjecthood criteria were applied and the distinction between "canonical" (nominative) and "non-canonical" (non-nominative) subjects was drawn. Since then, various problems associated with "non-canonical" subjects and objects have been studied from theoretical, typological, and diachronic perspectives; see various contributions to Holvoet and Mikulskas (eds. 2009), Holvoet (2013, this volume), Seržant (2013a,b, this volume), Piccini (2008), Holvoet and Nau (eds. 2014b). Seržant (2014a,b) treats the ACC-GEN and NOM-GEN alternation of Lithuanian on the background of differential object and subject marking. On differential subject marking cf. also Semėnienė (2005).

The problem of subjecthood and grammatical relations is also closely tied to voice-oriented phenomena like the passive. Passive and impersonal constructions in Lithuanian have received quite an extensive treatment in the literature, being approached from diverse perspectives. On Lithuanian passives in general, see Geniušienė (1974, 1976, 2006), Klimas (1993), Wiemer (2004a, 2006b). On impersonal passives, and in particular on the so-called evidential passives, see Timberlake (1982), Nuñes (1994), Christen (1998), Danylenko (2005), Lavine (2006, 2010), Privitelli and Roduner (2006), Holvoet (2001a: chapters 10–11; 2001e, 2007: chapter 4), Ambrazas (2004), and Wiemer (2006b: 284–303, forthcoming: Sections 2.2.2. and 3.3.2). From a diachronic viewpoint, the passive in Baltic was dealt with by Ambrazas (2001c) and Wiemer (2004b); an attempt at sketching its developmental relation to the impersonal for Lithuanian and Latvian was given by Holvoet (2001e) and for Lithuanian, by Wiemer (2006b, forthcoming: Section 2.2). Special attention to the rise of the *genetivus auctoris* in Baltic was paid by Holvoet (1995). From a synchronic perspective cf. also Roduner (2004).

Works on word order in Lithuanian and its relations to constituency, grammatical relations, and information structure are scarce and include, e.g., Schwentner (1922), Valeika (1974), and such more recent but sporadic contributions as the already mentioned Franks and Lavine (2006), Zav'jalova (2006), and Murakami (2011).

Syntactic properties of specific constructions have been studied in the works of Mo (1978), Toops (1989, 1994), Arkadiev and Pakerys (forthcoming, see references therein) on causative constructions, Mikulskas (2007), Vaičiulytė-Semėnienė (2007), and Čižik (2003) on comparative constructions, Kalėdaitė (2002, 2008, 2012) on existential clauses, Giparaitė (2010) on small clauses, Holvoet (2003a) and Mazzitelli (2014, 2015) on predicative possession, and Kerevičienė (2004) and Holvoet (2011a) on external possession; on copular constructions from the perspective of Cognitive Grammar, cf. Mikulskas (2009, 2014a,b).

2.5.3.2 Latvian

A complex issue in Latvian syntax is that of grammatical relations, due to the frequent occurrence of sentence patterns without nominative subjects but with least-oblique datival arguments for which the status of 'oblique subjects' could be considered. This is examined, with reference to Keenan's list of subject properties, by Berg-Olsen (2001). The Latvian passive is investigated by Holvoet (1994). It is interesting in that it is only agentless (whereas Lithuanian has developed an agented passive), but occurs alongside a construction also based on passive participles but clearly distinct from the dynamic passive, serving to identify the agent; it is called 'agentive construction' by Holvoet (2001e), where the areal links to Finnic are also pointed out. When expanded with a dative, the resultative passive with the auxiliary 'be' yields a kind of possessive perfect, with parallels in neighboring Finnic and Eastern Slavic (cf. 9) (see Section 4).

(9) Latvian
Man   t-as   jau   noskaidro-t-s.
1SG.DAT   DEM-NOM.SG.M   already   sort.out-PST.PP-NOM.SG.M
'I've got this sorted out.'

A related topic is that of grammatical relations with the debitive, an affixal form expressing modality but with a specific valency pattern (see Section 2.3.2.2). The discussion starts with Fennell (1973); for a more recent view, cf. Holvoet and Grzybowska (2014).

Latvian 'impersonal' constructions, i.e., constructions with referential and non-referential implicit animate subjects (with zero realization in syntax) are dealt with, in an areal Balto-Finnic context, by Holvoet (1995, 2001e). Agreement of predicative participles reveals a difference between a third-person-plural type also known in Slavic and many other Indo-European languages, and a singular type with clear areal connections to Finnic.

The syntax of case and prepositions comprises a number of interesting issues. The demise of the genitive as a case governed by verbs is the subject of work by Berg-Olsen (1999, 2000). Case semantics, specifically those of the genitive and dative, are dealt with from a cognitive point of view by Berg-Olsen (2004). A constructional analysis of an instance of case variation in intransitive subjects is given by Berg-Olsen (2009). The loss of the opposition of stative and lative meanings in local cases is discussed in an areal context by Wälchli (1998). A problem of verbal government is dealt with by Holvoet (2001d). The peculiarities of case agreement in vocative noun phrases, apparently an instance of agreement with morphological case rather than with syntactic case, are discussed by Holvoet (2012). The place of Latvian with regard to the typology of head and dependent marking is the object of a study by Stolz and Urdze (2001). The Latvian constructions with external possessor datives, conspicuous for the lack of the constraints well known from other European languages, especially with regard to animacy, dynamicity, and affectedness, are dealt with by Holvoet (2001f; 2011a).

An interesting feature of Latvian is the widespread use of relational adverbs and relational nouns instead of prepositions, a feature perhaps influenced by a Finnic substratum. On relational adverbs, see in particular Stolz (1984, 1990), Lagzdiņa (1998); on relational nouns, cf. Holvoet (1993, 2011a). The category of relational adverbs is, in its turn, closely bound up with that of adverbs functioning as verbal particles in what, in English grammar, would be called phrasal verbs. These can also be found in neighboring Livonian and Estonian, and Wälchli (2001b) argues for parallel development of the Latvian and Baltic Finnic verbal particle systems. Such phrasal verbs are rudimentarily developed in Lithuanian (with a greater productivity and frequency in the northern dialects; cf. Mikulskas 2003, with reference to Girdenis and Kačiuškienė 1986) and absent from Finnish, which suggests a local Latvian-Finnic innovation perhaps connected with German influence.[14] Particles render the verb telic, but have perfectivising effect only in Estonian, whereas in Latvian, this function is reserved for prefixes (cf. Holvoet 2000a for details). Phrasal verbs have, at any rate, acquired an important function in the Latvian aspect system (see 2.3.2.5 and Section 4).

2.5.4 Complex sentences

Baltic languages possess quite elaborate systems of clause combining comprising both "balanced" structures employing finite sentences introduced by conjunctions or complementizers and "deranked" structures built around various nonfinite verbal forms. Although clause combining features in most contemporary reference grammars of Lithuanian and Latvian, the patterns attested in Baltic

---

[14] Recently (and probably for the first time), the development of this phenomenon in Latvian-Finnic contact has been investigated from a usage-based perspective by Karjus (2012).

languages have hardly ever been subject to a comprehensive theoretically and typologically informed treatment or contrastive comparison, and many empirical issues still remain unresolved.

2.5.4.1 Lithuanian

The only works accounting for sentential complementation in Lithuanian from a contemporary theoretical perspective are the not easily accessible overview article by Gronemeyer and Usonienė (2001) and Holvoet (2010c, forthcoming b), who has supplied a first attempt at a systematic account of complementizer choices in Lithuanian and Latvian. His criteria encompass contrasts between truth- and non-truth-valued complements, the realis/irrealis distinction as well as degrees of control and epistemic (i.e., truth-qualifying) complementizers. This study also takes account of diachronic changes in the distribution of complementizers (*jog, kad, idant*) over the named distinctions and indicative vs. subjunctive mood of the embedded predicate. Other more specific contributions to the study of functional range of complementizers are Wiemer's (2010a,b) case studies devoted to Lith. *esą*, which can function as a complementizer with speech act denoting matrix predicates (see Section 3.3).

Works dealing with the syntax of participial constructions, in addition to the already mentioned books Ambrazas (1979, 1990), include Schmalstieg (1986), Wiemer (1998, 2000, 2001b, 2007b), Greenberg and Lavine (2006), Sakurai (2008), and Arkadiev (2011a, 2012b, 2013a). The key role of participles in taxis relations was described by Wiemer (2004c, 2009a).

In general, as concerns the role of participles in contemporary Baltic, they can be used both to adjoin adverbial (adjunct) clauses and clausal arguments. This holds not only for inflected participles,[15] but also for uninflected ones. By contrast, uninflected participles in the closest Slavic languages have practically lost this ability (cf. Greenberg and Lavine 2006, Wiemer 2014: 202–205). Participial complement clauses involving both agreeing (same-subject) and non-agreeing (different-subject) participles have attracted attention primarily from the diachronic point of view (cf. e.g., Tangl 1928, Ambrazas 1979, 1990). For a recent synchronic analysis of the morphosyntax of participial complements in Lithuanian, cf. Arkadiev (2012b); for a typologically oriented account of

---

[15] For a detailed study dealing with inflected participles used as adjuncts, cf. Sakurai (2008). She demonstrated that "adjectival past participles and main verbs construct one predicate as a single entity where the combinatory possibilities are strictly constrained by the principle of semantic consistency in stativity and intransitivity" (2008: 81).

case-marking strategies in Lithuanian participial constructions in general (including a comparison with Latvian and Latgalian), cf. Arkadiev (2013a).

Infinitive constructions of different kinds are treated in the work of Ambrazas (1981, 1987), Holvoet (2000b,c, 2003b), Franks and Lavine (2006), and Arkadiev (2013a, 2014a); see also Geniušienė (1985) on varieties of phasal constructions, which involve different kinds of non-finite forms. In Lithuanian, case assignment rules turn out to be construction-based (rather than governed by lexical requirements of verbs) in at least some adjunct infinitival clauses. This obtains for the so-called dative and genitive of goal.[16] For the diachronic background of these constructions, cf., Ambrazas (1995, 2006: 313–326). The genitive-plus-supine construction has been documented for earlier stages of Lithuanian (Ambrazas 2006: 222ff, 321ff) and attested in the northeastern Aukštaitian dialects (Zinkevičius 1966: 390) and is still productive in Latgalian (Nau 2011a: 61; 2014).

Syntax and semantics of complement clauses are treated by Usonienė (2001, 2002). Pajėdienė (2004) investigated Lithuanian adverbial temporal clauses using a variety of criteria, among which we find [±finite] predicate of the subordinate clause, taxis relations (simultaneity vs. sequence), subject deletion, and types of subordinators.

2.5.4.2 Latvian and Latgalian

Apart from what is said in the grammars, there is no study of adverbial clauses in Latvian. Relative clauses are dealt with by Nau (2009). A specific type of them, viz. infinitival relative clauses (a kind of relative purpose clauses) is discussed by Holvoet (1999, 2000b), who argues that they might have arisen from the purposive *dativus cum infinitivo* construction discussed above (see Section 2.5.4.1). A subtype of infinitival relative clauses gave rise to the Latvian debitive, an inflectional form expressing necessity (see Section 2.3.2.2); this process is dealt with by Holvoet (1998). In the domain of clausal complementation, only complementizers have received some coverage (Holvoet 2010c, forthcoming b), but not complementation strategies in general.

---

[16] They were briefly mentioned by Anderson (this volume, see her examples 3 and 4), but cf. also Wiemer (2000: 287f.), Schmalstieg (2004), and Valiulytė (2001) for the genitive of goal.

3 Semantics and pragmatics

Apart from sociolinguistics and syntax, semantics and pragmatics have remained the worst investigated parts in the description of all Baltic languages.

3.1 Lexical semantics (including derivation)

There is no theoretically original work on lexical relations in Baltic languages. However, quite useful for an overview of modern theories of lexical semantics and as an introduction into their application to contemporary Standard Lithuanian are the monographs by Gudavičius (1985, 2007) and Jakaitienė (2010); for a rough analogue concerning Latvian, cf. Veidemane (1970). These books are largely semasiologically oriented and usually reflect on Lithuanian resp. Latvian material via comparison to previous research done in Slavic (mostly Russian) and Germanic languages (among some others). Nepokupnyj's (2005) work is a collection of semasiologically oriented studies on the semantic development of selected roots in Lithuanian and their remote cognates in Germanic and Slavic. Mikulskas (2002a) attempted to set up a functional model of correlated denomination systems (based on the spatial figure of the 'hook' in Lithuanian dialects). The onomasiological perspective was based on semiotic assumptions about the visual conceptualization of the natural world (cf. also Mikulskas 2002b for an abridged presentation).

Kabašinskaitė (1998) captures different types of folk etymology and gives a first account of the involved processes.

A critical analysis of the usage of motion verbs in a cognitive framework has been provided by Mikulskas (2005, 2006a). His primary interest lies in corroborating claims about cognitive foundation in the widespread use of verbs of motion (and of related changes of state) for the description of static, primarily oblong objects (e.g., *Per lygumas **bėga** vieškelis* 'Through the plain a road **runs**'; *Kelias lengvai **kilo** į kalną* 'The way smoothly **rised** upwards the hill'). Other sparse work on cognitive semantics in Lithuanian are by Šeškauskienė (2004) on spatial relations and Vaičenonienė (2000) on conduit metaphors, both with comparisons to English.

Papaurelytė (2003) analyzed the lexical field of sadness in Lithuanian, in particular the relation between an emotional state and its causes. Šileikaitė (2004) studied expressions meaning 'heart' in a comparative Lithuanian-German-Georgian analysis. For Latvian, Trumpa (2010) has recently published a monographic comparison on etymologically related Latvian and Lithuanian adjectives and their semantic differences and shifts.

Quite a few works exist dealing with the syntax-semantics interface from the perspective of lexical typology or closely to lexicalistic syntax. Thus, Lithuanian verbs of "aquamotion" were described by Arkadiev (2007). A comprehensive account of lexical converses in Lithuanian is given in Maskaliūnienė (this volume, with further references) and, more particularly, for reflexive-marked verb lexemes, by Geniušienė (1987: 118–124) and Wiemer (2006b: 291–297). Geniušienė (2007) is a concise and impressive study of the lexical groups of verbs belonging to natural reciprocals and of their polysemy with other argument-deranking functions of the RM. This article presents a more subtle account of the taxonomy of reflexives (cf. Geniušienė 1983, 1987) applied to this specific semantic group. A systematic survey and coherent analysis of different alternations in the marking of arguments typical for certain lexical groups of verbs has recently been provided by Lenartaitė in her unpublished PhD thesis (Lenartaitė 2011) (cf. also Lenartaitė 2007, 2009, Lenartaitė-Gotaučienė 2014).

In some more elaborate grammars, stem derivation of the main parts of speech is treated quite extensively, particularly in sections on verbal morphology (see Section 2.3.2). Actually, in most cases, the stem classes should be regarded as classificatory categories, since it is the stems that determine the class the whole word form belongs to (often as well as the type of inflection added to the stem). The analysis of Arkadiev (2005, 2006a,b, 2008b), following earlier work by Leskien (1884: 381ff), Stang (1942: 132–133), Arumaa (1957), Toporov (1973), Temčin (1986), Wiemer (2004d), showed that the two inflectional classes of primary verbs, which are marked with *j*- and *n/st*-stem extensions, are obviously semantically motivated by the parameters [±agentive] and [±change of state] (cf. similar observations in Metuzāle-Kangere 2000 on *st*-verbs in Latvian). Cf. also Arkadiev (2010, 2013b) on the link between valency- and event-related oppositions of Lithuanian inflectional classes.

Starting from a systematic revision of extant research, Pakerys (2004) laid the ground for a three-way classification of denominal (including deadjectival) verbs: essive, inchoative, and causative (e.g., *kvail-as* 'stupid' ⇒ *kvail-**io**-ti* 'behave like an idiot' – *kvail-ė-ti* 'become/start behaving like an idiot' – *kvail-**in**-ti* 'mock, make an idiot out of sb.'). As for Latvian, studies into the Latvian lexicon and specific lexical groups are numerous (they are increasingly inspired by cognitive semantics), but virtually nothing of this research is accessible in languages other than Latvian. A notable exception is Urdze's (2010) important work on Latvian sound verbs, which includes their phonetic, phonological, morphophonological, and morphological aspects. The richness of the Baltic languages in sound verbs and the related category of onomatopoeic 'eventives' (dealt with in contributions by Wälchli, this volume, and Danylenko, this volume) is a typologically significant feature.

3.2 Lexicography and diachronic derivational morphology

Until now, Lithuanian and Latvian lexicography lacks a coherent methodology.[17] No operative principles have been formulated of what is to count as a lexical unit, nor is there any theoretical foundation of the way lexical units interact with grammatical distinctions. There are no theoretical guidelines concerning a share between lexicon and grammar. Consequently, the vast "gray zones" between lexicon and grammar have hardly been reflected upon, let alone integrated into lexicographic work. An analogous problem concerns a differentiation between lexicographic accounts of the standard language vs. dialects (or other non-standard varieties); as concerns Lithuanian, cf. the discussion of Kardelis and Wiemer (2003: 47–54, 66–68).

Work on the largest Lithuanian dictionary (LKŽ, 20 volumes, Internet version at http://lkz.lt/; henceforth LKŽe) started before World War II, the last volume was issued in 2002.[18] The biggest problem with this dictionary is not that its first volumes had become obsolete by the time the last ones appeared, but that there have never been any clear principles of selection and description. As a consequence, one can find promiscuously various dialect data reaching back to the nineteenth century, even without any qualification. Murmulaitytė (2000) criticized LKŽ's practice of listing nominal derivatives in the entry of the deriving verbs (verb stems). The lexicographic practice does not satisfactorily distinguish between regular and more idiomatic (less predictable) items. As concerns speech act verbs, Zaikauskas (2006) reports that in LKŽe, their semantics was described incoherently.

A motivated argument concerning the lexicographic treatment of motion verbs (primary usage vs. figurative use in which they are stative) has been given by Mikulskas (2006a). In a sense, the mirror image to verbs, i.e., the lexicographic treatment of so-called verbal particles in northern and western Lithuanian dialects was analyzed by Mikulskas (2003) (see also Section 4).

The existence of the frequency dictionary of Lithuanian based on a 1 million token annotated corpus should be mentioned here as well (cf. Utka 2009, available online at http://donelaitis.vdu.lt/publikacijos/).

---

[17] For an overview of current standards in lexicography oriented toward Lithuanian, see the handbook *Leksikografija* by Jakaitienė (2005).
[18] Work, headed by Juozas Balčikonis, started in 1930. The first volume appeared in 1941, the second in 1947. Then the work on the dictionary was held up by Soviet authorities, the editorial board changed, and the third volume of the LKŽ, based on principles of officially accepted Soviet lexicography, appeared only in 1956. Later, in 1968–1969, the already published first two volumes were considered to reflect "bourgeois-nationalistic" ideology and re-edited on "new" principles.

Traditionally, lexicographers have been devoting much attention to etymology and the diachrony of word semantics as well as of the system of derivational affixes, many of which became unproductive a long time ago. As for derivational morphology, Saulius Ambrazas (1993, 2000a) presented onomasiologically oriented monographs on the diachronic formation of derivational categories of nouns with verbal or nominal origin, respectively.[19] As a partial diachronic equivalent on the side of the verb lexicon and the involved derivational suffixes of Lithuanian, one may regard Kaukienė (1994, 2002). This approach has been applied more broadly to the entire Baltic area by Kaukienė and Jakulis (2009). Ostrowski's (2006) selection of studies focuses on the diachrony of aspectually relevant suffixation and denominal verbs in Lithuanian. Larsson (2002) deals with nominal compounds from a diachronic perspective (with an Indo-European background).

Fraenkel's etymological dictionary (Fraenkel 1955–1965) is quite well known, but one has to have in mind that Fraenkel was not able to account for a great many of important lexical items, because when he was writing the dictionary only the first few volumes of the LKŽ had been issued (Sabaliauskas 1990: 5). The recent etymological dictionary by Smoczyński (2007, an expanded English version, to be published by Peter Lang, is under preparation) comprises a smaller amount of lexemes than Fraenkel's, but the selection is based on the entire LKŽ (since 2000), and the author deliberately included borrowings.

To our knowledge, apart from work on derivational morphology and Mikulskas (2002a,b) (see above), no onomasiologically oriented studies of lexical fields have been undertaken, although one occasionally finds discussions of word meanings arranged by onomasiological fields scattered over the lexicon (see, for instance, in Gudavičius 1985). Furthermore, Sabaliauskas (1990) subdivided his annotated dictionary into lexical groups that correspond to periods beginning with common Indo-European heritage and ending with layers restricted to Lithuanian. The last third of his book is dedicated to different layers of borrowed lexemes, among which Slavicisms occupy the most prominent place. Despite this fact, a coherent methodology for the lexicographic treatment of Slavicisms, in general, and for the differentiation of different Slavic languages as particular sources still waits for its master (cf. Kardelis & Wiemer 2003: 46–54). Kardelis (2003) gives a survey of the

---

19 The sections of these books are organized according to notional types (e.g., *nomina actoris, resultati, instrumenti, actionis* for deverbal nouns, collective, diminutives, etc., for denominal nouns). S. Ambrazas (2001) deals with the provenance of certain Lithuanian adjectives derived from numerals. S. Ambrazas (2000b) discusses the most striking differences in the derivation of nouns between Lithuanian and Latvian. First of all, they concern *nomina actionis*, diminutives, and collective nouns.

problems connected to establishing the concrete source language of Slavicisms and applies a principled method to the chronology and phonological integration of Slavic loans into Lithuanian.

Admittedly, the problem of identifying the specific Slavic source language is partly rooted in objective difficulties, and it is even aggravated by the fact that often one can hardly discern between borrowings from Slavic, on the one hand, and root morphemes and derivational affixes from a common Slavic-Baltic stock, on the other hand. This issue proves particularly problematic in the lexicon and morpheme layers of Lithuanian dialects whose speakers have for centuries been in intense contact with speakers of (East) Slavic (cf. Wiemer 2009b: 358–385 for a comprehensive investigation; see Section 4 for further discussion of contact phenomena).

Modern Latvian lexicography starts with the dictionary commonly referred to as 'Mühlenbach-Endzelin' 1923–1932 (with two supplement volumes: Endzelin and Hausenberg 1934–1946), a dictionary covering the nineteenth- and early twentieth-century written language, the dialects, and the language of oral folklore, started by Karl Mühlenbach and, after his death, completed and provided with brief etymological notes by Jānis Endzelīns. It is still the only dictionary of any use for historical linguists as it marks syllable accents, a tradition since abandoned in Soviet Latvian dictionaries.

The Soviet period saw the compilation of a comprehensive dictionary of the modern Latvian literary language (LLVV). Although obviously valuable as the main lexicographical source on modern written Latvian, especially the language of the post-war period, it has several drawbacks: its normative character leads to exclusion of large parts of the lexicon, such as loanwords considered undesirable, much of the colloquial vocabulary etc.; there is no phonetic or prosodic information.

Latvian historical lexicography is still in its childhood, but the compilation of a corpus of Old Latvian texts from the sixteenth and seventeenth centuries (LVSTK) is to be the foundation of an Old Latvian dictionary, work on which started in 2004.

Several dialect dictionaries have been compiled in Lithuania since Vitkauskas (1976) as well as in Latvia during and after the Soviet period. The most useful among them is probably that of the High Latvian dialect of Kalupe, compiled by Antoņina Reķēna (1998), as it gives an image of the lexical stock and also (through its illustrative material) of the morphosyntax and syntax of one of the dialects of Latgalian, for which but few descriptions are available at this moment (see Section 1.2). As long as no comprehensive Latgalian dictionary is available (see, however, Bukšs 1969, Bērzkalns 2007), Reķēna's work will remain the principal gap filler.

In addition to the etymological notes in Mühlenbach and Endzelin's dictionary, there is a separate etymological dictionary of Latvian by Konstantīns Karulis (1992). It does not quite meet modern standards, being based on the Neogrammarian paradigm of Indo-European reconstruction and offering mostly root etymologies, but it certainly is a valuable work, with lots of useful information on word history, and it offers a synthesis of earlier research as well as an overview of the relevant literature.

3.3 Function words (particles etc.)

Under the label of function words, we subsume units traditionally labeled 'syncategorematic', or similar. Extensionally, they comprise adpositions, conjunctions, complementizers, sentence and stance adverbs, and different sorts of particles and discourse markers. Intensionally, they can be united as subclasses of connective lexemes; the units they connect are of different formats (in terms of constituency), beginning from NPs (as for adpositions) via clauses (conjunctions, complementizers) up to entire sentences or utterances (particles). On higher levels, they scope over propositions or even illocutions. As an umbrella term, one might therefore call them 'connectives'. Some other function words primarily serve as attractors of the addressee's attention or carry just an expressive function (in the sense of Bühler's [1934] 'Ausdruck'). Consequently, we can roughly subdivide function words into units operating within or between constituents (adpositions, complementizers, conjunctions) or as operators scoping over propositions or illocutions, without being integrated into constituent structure (modal particles, hedges, all sorts of epistemic, evidential, or quotative modifiers). In practice, this division is sometimes difficult to maintain because many units fit into two or more subclasses, thus being heterosemic (in the sense of Lichtenberk 1991) (see further below).

To begin with adpositions, one cannot but mention the classical work by Fraenkel (1929). In more recent times, Šukys (1998) took up this issue, somewhat as an updated and joint equivalent of Fraenkel (1928, 1929) (see Section 3.5.3.1). Although this modern source is written largely from a prescriptive perspective, it is a useful reference book concerning the standard language. Lithuanian prepositions as means of structuring space were looked at from the point of view of cognitive semantics by Malesa (2003).

The most up-to-date collection of papers on particles, conjunctions, and complementizers in Baltic is by Nau and Ostrowski (eds. 2010). First, the editors themselves supplied a very valuable survey of the state of the art in reference grammars of Baltic languages, the notional distinctions made by various authors, the diachronic development of selected groups of units and a cursory typological background. The case studies account primarily for discourse markers, causal conjunctions, focus, and question particles as well as for paths leading to them (e.g., from coordinative connectors).

Some articles deal with heterosemic units. Chojnicka (2010) analyzes the functions of Latv. *it kā* ≈ 'as if' as a particle and a conjunction. Wiemer (2010a,b) does the same for Lith. *esą* used as particle and complementizer with reportive function. It derives from the paradigm of the present active participle of *būti* 'be', from which it has been isolated and petrified. Interesting is the comparison with its Latvian cognate *esot*, because their status differs markedly. Latv. *esot* is just a trivial case of the application of the suffix *-ot* deriving from a formerly inflected participle, which can be applied to any verb stem to mark reportive evidentiality (see Section 2.3.2.2; Wiemer 2010a: 286–288, 2010b: 187f). Other evidential particles (which are partially heterosemic) have been analyzed by Roszko (1993: chapter 4), Wiemer (2005, 2007c), Petit (2008), and Sinkevičienė (2014). On Lithuanian evidential adverbs and predicative adjectives, cf. Ruskan (2013). For a typologically oriented overview of non-grammatical markers of evidentiality in Lithuanian, cf. furthermore Wiemer (2007b: 217–223, 2010c).

3.4 Discourse syntax and semantics

Discourse-oriented case studies on the usage of forms from the grammatical core have been conducted by Sawicki (2004, 2010, 2012). Sawicki (2004) is a study of text functions of Lithuanian "neuter" participles (ending in unstressed *-a*; see Section 2.3.2.3) on the basis of a small newspaper corpus. Sawicki (2010) examined the distribution of unprefixed and prefixed verbal forms and found interesting correlations with the narrative background/foreground distinction. Finally, Sawicki (2012) deals with Lith. *kad* and *na*, used as turn-opening particles. Macienė (2002) investigated the textual functions of Lithuanian diminutives in contemporary belletristic and journalistic texts. Nau (2010) analyzed the discourse-pragmatic functions of the Latvian particle *neba* in internet fora.

In her case study based on Latgalian fairytales from the late nineteenth century, Nau (2008) demonstrates how participles and infinitives are exploited as means of represented speech, i.e., of "giving voice" to a character (vs. the narrator's speech). Nau stresses that for this dimension of speech the distinction between direct and indirect becomes irrelevant, and it differs from evidentiality. Similarly to Nau's study, a first attempt at a principled and corpus-based account of reported speech vs. hearsay vs. quotation in Latvian is by Chojnicka (2012a,b).

Somehow related to the differentiation of "speaking subjects" (and to quotatives) in narrative discourse is the re-interpretation of various grammatical forms (e.g., the imperative, analytical hortatives, or modal auxiliaries) as 'interpretive deontics'. This has been described, among other languages, for Lithuanian and Latvian by Holvoet (2005b) and Holvoet and Konickaja (2011).

3.4.1 Pronouns: Specific forms and uses

Kibrik (1987, 2011: 62–67) coined the notion of "referential conflict" and proposed a typology of ways how languages can solve such a conflict (Kibrik 2011: 287–333). A typical case comes up if, in a narrative setting, two human referents of equal sex are introduced one after another and, at some point, within a chain of sentences, ambiguities may arise which one of the two is being mentioned. Compare an invented, but characteristic, example (10):

(10) English
    a. *John$_i$ invited James$_k$ to meet at 6 pm.*
    b. *He$_?$ however didn't want to sit in some boring café.*

Some European languages are able to solve such ambiguities by choosing a marked pronoun; such pronouns usually derive from demonstrative pronouns and function as indicators that it is not the most topical referent (antecedent) that is "picked up" anaphorically, but its more rhematic "rival". Apart from German, where this technique is used freely, Russian and Lithuanian, in principle, allow for the same distinction.[20] See the following translational equivalents to the English text in (10):

(11) German
    a. *Hans$_i$ lud Horst$_k$ ein, sich um 18 Uhr zu treffen.*
    b. *Er$_?$ / Der$_k$ wollte aber nicht in irgendeinem langweiligen Café sitzen.*

(12) Lithuanian
    a. *Jonas$_i$ pakvietė Jurgį$_k$, kad susitiktų 18 valandų.*
    b. *Tačiau jis$_?$ / **šis**$_k$ nenorėjo sėdėti kažkokioje nuobodžioje kavinėje.*

This and similar mechanisms were surveyed on a European background for Lithuanian by Wiemer (1999). However, to date, there are no empirical studies of when referential conflicts really arise, how they are (or might be) resolved, and to what extent paradigmatic contrasts of pronouns are involved.

Apart from logophoric constructions based on clausal complementation (see Section 2.3.2.4), Latgalian (and also, but less consistently, Latvian) knows an opposition between anaphoric and logophoric pronouns, which has developed out of the inventory of former demonstrative pronouns. According to Nau (2006), in many Latgalian dialects, non-attributive pronouns of the š-series are consistently used as

---

20 For examples and discussion concerning Russian, cf. Berger and Weiss (1987: 32–52).

a means to mark co-reference between the speaker of a reported speech act and an anaphoric pronoun in an embedded clause (cf. 13) (adapted from Nau 2006: 61):

(13) Latgalian
Tagad j-is$_i$ suoka   runuot,   t-ys   bruolān-s$_j$,
now   he-NOM   start.PST.3 talk.INF DEM-NOM.SG.M   cousin(M)-NOM.SG
lai   es   precejūs   ar   j-ū$_{≠i}$ / š-ū$_j$.
COMP   1SG.NOM   marry.PST.PA.NOM.SG.F   with he=ACC   / LOG-ACC.SG.M
'Now he$_i$ started to say, this cousin$_j$, that I should marry **him** [= the uncle$_{≠i}$ / = the cousin$_j$].'

Clauses containing the logophoric pronoun are often accompanied by participial predicates, which themselves function as reportive markers as well, both in dependent and independent clauses (see Section 2.3.2.4).

3.4.2 Parentheticals and other means of taking stance

Briefly, parentheticals can be understood as discourse-driven downgrading of information "above" the propositional and illocutionary content of an utterance (cf. Kaltenböck 2007, Moroz 2010, Wiemer 2010c: 104–106). It is important to stress that parentheticals are not a separate class of words or phrases, since basically anything can be "parentheticalized". In this respect, parentheticals can be considered as non-conventionalized pieces of discursively secondary information; they cannot be focused or addressed.

Probably, Durys (1927) was the first one to have drawn attention to parentheticals (Lith. *įterpiniai*) in Lithuanian. Among his more recent followers, one should mention Balkevičius (1963, 1998) and the section on 'Parenthetical Words and Phrases' written by Zelma Dumašiūtė in LKG (1976: III, 698–719). For the first time in Lithuanian, Balkevičius (1963: 267, 275) seems to have captured parentheticals as units that serve to make prominent the speaker's subjective (emotional, cognitive) point of view. Akelaitis (2002, 2003) concentrated on parentheticals based on predicative units (verbs, adjectives).[21]

However, in Lithuanian, parentheticals have been studied primarily by Aurelija Usonienė and her collaborators, mostly in a rather strict corpus-driven approach. Usonienė claims that the most common parenthetical expressions serving the purposes of hedging and marking of epistemic stance and/or evidential functions "are synchronically traceable back to complement taking

---

[21] We are grateful to Birutė Ryvitytė for supplying us with the information conveyed in this paragraph.

predicate clauses functioning as parenthetical elements in the sentence" (Usonienė, this volume: Section 1). For similar studies taking into consideration units of different prominence, cf. Usonienė and Šolienė (2010) and Šinkūnienė (2012). Aloseviečienė (2006) provided a comparative study of hedges in Lithuanian and German political discourse, differentiating evaluative, epistemic, emphatic, and distancing as well as metalinguistic hedges.

We do not know of any similar work done on Latvian or Latgalian.

3.5 Pragmatics

Domains that are usually treated under the heading of pragmatics have hardly been studied at all. Apart from the few works on information structure mentioned in Sections 2.1.1 and 2.5.3.1, for Lithuanian, we can name only the following two articles.

Zaikauskas (2002) supplied interesting observations on how (direct and indirect) performative speech acts are realized in Lithuanian. He focuses on communicative strategies, social roles and a subclassification of notions of speaker and hearer, taking into account differences not only of illocutionary force, but also of situational settings (e.g., official vs. familiar) and other circumstances of speech. In turn, Hilbig (2008) seems to be the only methodologically well-founded study dealing with politeness. She rightly states that simply based on linguistic expressions used for purposes of politeness "no cultural community can be considered more or less polite than others", because these expressions are inherently assessed on the background of social norms and thus can have different values depending on the given semiotic system. This assumption was tested on the example of service encounters in Vilnius.

No comparable studies on Latvian or Latgalian are known to us.

4 Aspects of areality

Areally interesting properties of at least one of the Baltic languages (or some of their dialects) have already been pointed out casually at different places above. In general, from an areal viewpoint, Baltic should be considered as the eastern part of the CBA, for which a host of convergent, typologically non-trivial features (some of them discussed above) were surveyed and analyzed by Koptjevskaja-Tamm and Wälchli (2001). Furthermore, the Baltic region can be considered as a transitional zone for features regarded as typical for Standard Average European (cf. Haspelmath 2001), on the one hand, and Eurasian features, on the other.

The areal and typological significance of many features (and probably of some more yet to be discovered) remains to be established. This is not to suggest that Baltic is homogeneous. It is not; even from the perspective of larger areal clines, the southeastern part of Baltic (Aukštaitian) often patterns differently from the northwestern (Low Latvian) part, with Latgalian (High Latvian) being intermediary in many respects or even closer to East Slavic than even east and south Lithuanian dialects. A basic north(west)-south(east) layering in the dialect continuum of Baltic will become apparent below.

The purpose of this section is to pinpoint some selected morphosyntactic properties of the extant Baltic dialect continuum and its intersections with Slavic and Finnic. Although the role of language (or dialect) contact as a soil for areal convergences is obvious, no more elaborate comments on research into language contact will be made here. The same holds for Lithuanian and Latvian dialect geography, which anyway has largely remained in a stage reflecting nineteenth-century goals (frequently intermingled with issues of ethnogenesis) and/or structuralist models of dialectology. To our knowledge, no dialectological research guided by principles of modern sociolinguistics (variationist frameworks) has been conducted. Thus, it does not astonish that the first pioneering work accounting for Baltic varieties in areal terms was conducted in the domain of loanwords, as early as at the end of the nineteenth century, by Thomsen ([1890] 1931); cf. also the later studies Endzelīns ([1951] 1980), Sehwers (1953), and more recent works like Nepokupnyj (1976), Kagaine and Bušs (1985), and Wälchli (1996).

General surveys of the dialect divisions of Lithuanian and Latvian (with further references) are given in Balode and Holvoet (2001a,b), cf. also Petit (2010b: 3–51). The foundations of Latvian dialectology were laid in Bezzenberger (1885), but systematic fieldwork was initiated by Mühlenbach and Endzelin from 1901 onward; many valuable dialect descriptions were published in the *Filologu Biedrības Raksti* (*Writings of the Philological Society*) between the two world wars. A synthesis of Latvian dialectology is given in Latvian in Rudzīte (1964), but Gāters (1977) gives a useful overview in German. In Latvian dialectology, the post-war period has seen the publication of a number of dialect monographs with selections of texts. Internet sources on Latvian dialects are not (yet) available. A *Latvian Dialect Atlas* is in course of publication; it now comprises volumes on the lexicon (Laumane ed. 1999) and phonetics (Sarkanis ed. 2013).

After Jaunius' first comprehensive classification of Lithuanian dialects (cf. Javnis [Jaunius] 1908–1916), the criteria for the division of Lithuanian dialects were reconsidered by Girdenis and Zinkevičius (1966) and described feature by feature by Zinkevičius (1966). They also comprise inflectional morphology for different parts of speech (but no syntax). However, when it came to giving areal subdivisions of dialects, almost only phonetic and morphophonological features have been applied (see the maps in Zinkevičius 1966). The Lithuanian dialect atlas (LKA) comprises three published volumes dedicated to lexical items (1977), phonetics (1982), and morphology (1991); the last one takes into account also phonetic and morphological variation of some derivational affixes. Recently, Lithuanian and Latvian dialectologists started on a common Baltic dialect geographic program, based on the LKA and its Latvian equivalent (Laumane ed. 1999). According to information on http://www.tarmes.lt (accessed July 21, 2014), only some lexical items have been surveyed so far.

Kardelis (2013: Sections 6–10) concisely and critically surveys the practice of cartography for East and South Aukštaitian dialects in the most influential works on Lithuanian dialect geography since Girdenis and Zinkevičius (1966) and Zinkevičius (1966). He finds that existing maps do not allow for a clear distinction between subdivisions of Lithuanian dialects themselves and zones of overlay with heavy (east) Slavic interference or dominance. A recent critical reconsideration of the Latvian dialectological tradition can be found in the work of Trumpa (2012). A brief overview of Lithuanian island dialects and of dialects bordering with East Slavic ("peripheral dialects") is supplied in Wiemer (2009b: 350–352). Zinkevičius' (2006) renewed introduction into the division of Lithuanian dialects has remained traditional, i.e., it is predominantly based on phonetic changes and betrays a pronouncedly ethnographic bias, while Kardelis (2006) gives a short introduction into the internal division of contemporary East High Lithuanian dialects (Lith. *rytų aukštaičių vilniškių patarmės*), i.e., those dialects that, together with the southern dialects (Lith. *dzūkų patarmės*), belong to borderland dialects that have been experiencing (East) Slavic influence most intensely.

In comparison to East Slavic, contacts of Lithuanian with Polish (a West Slavic language) have been either locally highly restricted to the tiny region around the small towns Puńsk and Suwałki in northeast Poland bordering with southwest Lithuania (for recent monographs, cf. Birgiel 2002, Marcinkiewicz 2003). These contacts have been based on so-called *polszczyzna kresowa*, i.e., Polish arisen in the Lithuanian-Latgalian-East Slavic border region from a language shift from Lithuanian or Belarusian toward Polish, which, according to the most accepted theory – and apart from urban contacts lasting from approximately the fifteenth century, – took place in rural settings only during the nineteenth century and became particularly intense in the interwar period (cf. Wiemer 2003a: 218–222; 2003b: 111–114, 124–129 for summaries and further references). On a whole, the zone where Baltic and (East) Slavic dialects overlap forms part of a larger continuum stretching roughly in the southwest-northeast direction, with Podlasie and Mazowsze in the southwest and the Russian dialects of the Pskov region in the northeast. Overviews of salient features relevant for this overlap zone and its relation to embracing areas are supplied by Wiemer (2003a, 2013b), Wiemer and Erker (2011), Wiemer and Giger (2005: chapter 3–5, 12.2, 12.4), and Wiemer,

Seržant, and Erker (2014). Most important are contacts with Belarusian, which for many centuries performed the role of a transmitter in language contact, in particular in language shift from Lithuanian into Polish (see Wiemer 2003b: 109–119, 124–127 for a survey).

A good illustration of how inner-Baltic dialectal clines are "inserted" in larger areal clines is the varying preference for prefixes vs. movable particles as verb satellites marking the boundedness or modifying situations denoted by verb stems. (Low) Latvian seems to be outstanding in its rich inventory of adverbal modifiers (Wälchli 2001a). This richness appears to be due to an overlap of two larger areal clines running through Baltic territory on a north-south axis, but in opposite directions. Verb particles are quite common in Finnic to the north, whereas all Slavic languages (to the east and to the south) make abundant use of verbal prefixes, but rarely use verb particles (both on type and token level). The stepwise overlay of both clines becomes manifest if we look at its rough inner-Baltic distribution: standard (=Low) Latvian has more than 20 verb particles, northern Lithuanian dialects have some 10, while Standard Lithuanian, which is closer to dialects in the south(east), has only three more frequently used particles (*lauk* 'off, to the outside', *žemyn* 'down', *aplink(ui)* 'around'); cf. Wälchli (2001b) on Latvian-Finnic, Mikulskas (2003) for a minute analysis of verb particles in northern Lithuanian, and Wiemer (2013a) for the general picture and a comparison with Slavic minority languages under heavy contact with German. Such a broader areal perspective leads to the impression that southern East Baltic and the Slavic languages neighboring to it constitute just a relatively "particle-hostile" zone intermediate between two "particle-friendly" zones in the north(east), i.e., Latvian and Finnic, and the west, i.e., continental West Germanic.

A similar cline, more or less in north-south direction, can be observed with respect to the nominative object (see Section 2.5). Following Ambrazas (2001a), it can be assumed that this construction, with common roots in both Baltic and Slavic, spread from north to south in times prior to any written documents, and that contact with Finnic triggered this development to some considerable extent (as it did in Northwest Russian). This direction of spread would correspond to the observation that in some Northwest Russian dialects (around Pskov), the nominative object was encountered in the twentieth century not only with infinitives and other non-finite predicates, but even with finite verbs (e.g., dial. Russ. *Ja topila **pečka*** 'I.NOM heated the **stove**.NOM'). However, within Baltic, the nominative object has remained most widespread far away from this region, namely in Southeast Lithuanian dialects (whereas it seems to be absent in the immediately neighboring Slavic dialects), and there it has been retained not only with the infinitive, but also with non-agreeing participles (e.g., dial. Lith. *Kaip čia man **karvė** nusipirkus?* 'How should I now buy a **cow**.NOM?'). A plausible explanation may be found in an analogy to non-agreeing predicative constructions with neuter adjectives and *ta/ma*-participles (e.g., Lith. *Alus sveika* 'Beer.NOM.SG.M is healthy', *Laukai ariama* 'The fields.NOM.PL.M are being ploughed'); such an explanation was offered by Ambrazas (2001a: 407). These adjectives and participles do not show agreement (as remnants of the neuter as a target gender; see Section 2.3.1), and they have disappeared altogether in Latvian. Thus, together with them a possible model for the retention of the nominative with non-finite predicates vanished. On the other hand, different varieties of Slavic through various periods have known similar patterns with neuter adjectives or participles non-agreeing with a masculine, feminine, or plural nominative (cf. Wiemer 2012a). The areal distribution (and change in time) of such patterns and their impact on contact, and thus, areal convergence with Baltic still reserves many intricacies to be disclosed.

Other big parts of the complex "story" in the area of Baltic, Slavic, and Finnic associated to predication patterns concerns the relation among the perfect, grammatical evidentials, the foregrounding, and the so-called impersonal (backgrounding) passive. All of them build on participles, but the lines of development for particular constructions and subareas only cross-cut. As discussed in Section 2.3.2.4, in all Baltic languages, the perfect based on active anteriority participles (agreeing for syntactic categories with the subject) has been extended to a reportive function. This functional extension was most probably triggered by Latvian-Finnic contact in the northern part of the Baltic territory (cf. Stolz 1991, Wälchli 2000). In turn, only in Lithuanian (on the basis of Aukštaitian dialects in the south) has a second grammatical evidential, with a predominant inferential function, evolved. It is based on the same *ta/ma*-participles mentioned in the preceding paragraph, which were lost in Latvian. As surrounding Slavic nowhere shows any traits of an evidential use of neuter, non-agreeing participles, Standard Lithuanian (and the dialects on which it is based) represents a "pocket" in areal terms (for more such pockets, see below).

However, as has recently been argued by Seržant (2012), non-agreeing participles served as a starting point in the evolution of another type of perfect farther to the north, namely, in the contact region among Latvian, Finnic, and Northwest Russian dialects. Typical for this perfect is the oblique marking of the actor: in Latvian, it is marked by the dative; in Finnic, by the adessive case, and in Northwest Russian by an adessive PP (*u* 'at' + GEN); all three realizations of the actor are closely associated to the basic pattern of predicative possession typical for these three language (or dialect) groups (on the Latvian *mihi est*-pattern, see below). This connection also corresponds to the observation that Baltic (in particular Latvian), Russian (in particular its Northwestern dialects), and Finnic demonstrate non-trivial coincidences with dative experiencer constructions (cf. Seržant, this volume). On the contrary, non-agreeing, originally neuter participles at the southern end of the Baltic language continuum seem to have partially been influenced by an entirely independent development of this participle type in Polish, which rendered a passive-like impersonal with objects marked with the accusative. In Lithuanian, this pattern is attested, although only scarcely (cf. Wiemer, forthcoming: Section 2.2.2). On this background, the evolution of foregrounding passives in all areally involved Baltic and Slavic languages appears to have proceeded separately (cf. Wiemer 2004b). At least, in the whole area for which Baltic and Slavic (apart from Finnic) contact has been relevant, the evolution of the passive proper has not influenced the "new perfect" in the northern part (with Northwest Russian as the hotbed), and in the southern part (with Polish as the hotbed), the non-agreeing pattern with neuter participles ultimately went another way from the passive (not later than by the turn to the eighteenth century). For details, cf. Seržant (2012), Wiemer (forthcoming), Wiemer, Seržant, and Erker (2014: 30–36).

Furthermore, in the northern part of Baltic, the evolution of a new perfect has probably been connected to the frequent exploitation of the *mihi est*-pattern of predication (showing up also in the Latvian debitive; see Section 2.5.3.2). The Latvian possessive construction of the *mihi est* type, often mentioned in the literature as a Finnic substratum feature, is argued to be the inherited Common Baltic construction by Vykypěl (2001) and Holvoet (2003a). Its historical priority with regard to the 'have'-construction, which is now used in Lithuanian (and has never developed in Latvian and Latgalian), is shown by its providing the grammaticalization source for archaic modal 'be'-constructions in both Baltic languages and, incidentally, also in Slavic, as argued by Holvoet (2003b). Another modal construction of Latvian, based on the verbal noun in -*šana* and the existential verb 'be', is argued to be modeled on Finnic in Holvoet (2004b). The Latvian constructions with external possessor datives, which have already been mentioned above for their lack of the constraints with regard to animacy, dynamicity, and affectedness (Holvoet 2011a), find parallels in the neighboring Finnic languages (Estonian and Livonian), but the areal links of this phenomenon still await a detailed investigation. Many other details in the domain of modality still wait to be investigated thoroughly. A typical issue in this regard is the question whether convergent patterns in the use of dispositional possibility modals ('can' vs. 'be able to'), to be observed in the Baltic-Slavic contact zone (Wiemer, Vladyko, and Kardelis 2004), have resulted from contact or rather from parallel development following more universal tendencies.

The morphosyntactic realization of core arguments is another major kind of phenomena for which Baltic languages and their dialects yield an excellent example of how convergent grammatical patterns characteristic for a comparatively small region gain significance if it can be shown that these patterns are part of larger areal clines. Differential object and subject marking have been the target of quite a number of works, mostly dedicated to Lithuanian and Latgalian (see Section 2.5, 2.5.3.1), since Latvian has been reducing the use of genitival objects and subjects (see Section 2.5.3.2). Lithuanian and Latgalian inscribe very well as sort of transitory languages between

Finnic to the north and Slavic to the east, south, and west (i.e., Polish). This applies especially if we account for two gradable parameters: (a) specific reference- and clause-related rules of case alternations for subject and object; (b) restrictions to these rules by the admissible lexical input (in terms of actional classes and lexical groups). This has been shown by Koptjevskaja-Tamm and Wälchli (2001: 650–660) in an insightful comparative analysis of Polish, Russian, Lithuanian, Latvian, and different Finnic languages. Analyses of this sort have been conducted for Lithuanian (with areal comparisons) by Seržant (2014a), partially also by Lenartaitė (2011: chapter 4.3). A parallel analysis exists for Russian by Seržant (2014b), and Holvoet (1991: chapters 7–8 and 11) contributed ample succinct considerations on related facts from Polish (with comparisons to Russian, Baltic, and Finnic).

There are properties of Lithuanian that illustrate just the opposite of areal clines, insofar as they are isolated and do not (any more) occur, or have drastically been reduced, in the neighboring languages. One of these properties is the high frequency and productive formation of reflexive-benefactive verbs, which were already mentioned in Section 2.4. Latvian has reduced this type of argument-increasing derivation, it is virtually inexistent in the East Slavic neighbors and in Polish; instead, Lithuanian patterns with German, French, and Italian. Another, much more spectacular, although infrequent and lexically highly restricted, phenomenon is the Lithuanian HAVE-resultative (see Section 2.3.2.4), whose properties are probably unique even on a worldwide scale (Wiemer 2012b). On these and some other aspects of Lithuanian verbal morphology and morphosyntax that can be considered areally isolated, see Arkad'ev (2013c).

5 More from the perspective of typology

In this section, we will briefly review the representation of Baltic languages in the current typological literature and will point out some specific outstanding features of Baltic languages, that we consider of direct relevance to typological studies.

5.1 Account of Baltic in typological studies

Baltic languages have never figured prominently in work on linguistic typology. The reasons for this are manifold. First, Baltic data are not always easily accessible, and existing descriptions often do not provide sufficient empirical details and explications and are generally written from a perspective very different from that found in modern reference grammars. Second, one should have in mind the general trend of typologists to overcome the European and Indo-European bias, e.g., by means of working with balanced language samples into which Baltic languages simply have very little chance to get included. Thus, even in the strongly Indo-European-biased sample of Dahl (1985), Baltic languages do not find a place. Among well-known sample-based typological studies including data from Baltic languages, one should mention Hawkins (1983), whose 350-language sample includes Lithuanian; Stassen (1985), whose 110-language sample includes Latvian; Haspelmath (1997), whose 40-language sample includes both Lithuanian and Latvian; Stassen (1997), whose 410-language sample includes both Lithuanian and Latvian; and Wälchli (2005), whose more than 100-language sample includes both Lithuanian and Latvian.

Among typological studies not based on language samples in the strict sense of this word, the one giving prominent emphasis to Baltic languages is certainly the work of Geniušienė (1987); in general, the work by the Leningrad/Saint-Petersburg School of Linguistic Typology has systematically taken Lithuanian (but unfortunately not Latvian) into account, with chapters by Ema Geniušienė (1974, 1985, 1989, 1997, 2007, Geniušiene and Nedjalkov 1988) and recently by Björn Wiemer (2004c, 2007b, 2009a) being included into almost all collective volumes edited since the late 1990s by this research group. Also noteworthy is a current project headed by Sergej Say [Saj] in St. Petersburg dealing with alignment patterns of bivalent verbs in 16 languages, which include Latvian and Lithuanian (cf. Saj 2011, Say 2014).

Both Lithuanian and Latvian are represented in the *World Atlas of Language Structures* (Haspelmath et al. eds. 2005, online version, Haspelmath & Dryer eds. 2013, consulted in December 2013), and Latvian is included into the 200 languages core sample of WALS. In the printed version, Latvian is mentioned six times (less than, say, Lezgian), and Lithuanian, only five times. In the online database, Latvian has values for 126 WALS features out of 192, and Lithuanian is represented by just 80 features. It is worth noting that much of the Latvian data recorded in WALS are taken from the nineteenth-century grammar by Bielenstein (1863). Representation of both Baltic languages in WALS is moderately accurate. Actually, Latvian has been categorized downwardly incorrectly for at least the following WALS features[22]: (i) it is claimed to belong to languages with a moderately small consonant inventory (15–18, feature 1A compiled by Maddieson; compare with Section 2.1.2); (ii) it is classified as a language with obligatory pronouns in subject position, while Lithuanian correctly goes under languages with subject affixes on the verb, which seems to imply that subject pronouns are not obligatory (feature 101A, Dryer); (iii) Latvian is said to be zero-marking in all 3sg person forms of verbs (feature 103A, Siewierska; see Section 2.3.2); (iv) as concerns words for "tea", Latvian *tēja* is clearly derived from Min Nan Chinese *te*, and not from Sinitic *cha* (feature 138A, Dahl). In addition, it is not evident why

---

[22] Many of these shortcomings have been brought to our attention by Bernhard Wälchli.

with respect to feature 26A ("Prefixing vs. Suffixing in Inflectional Morphology", Dryer 2013) Lithuanian is treated as "strongly suffixing", while Latvian as "weakly suffixing"; if in terms of the clear definitions of the values given by Dryer (2013), the languages should be treated identically (in fact, overall, Lithuanian has more inflectional prefixing than Latvian, although this type of inflectional prefixing is not taken into account by Dryer). Finally, if one relies on WALS, one has to conclude that neither Lithuanian nor Latvian have definite affixes (in contrast to Scandinavian languages; see Section 2.3.1) and that Latvian has a "[d]emonstrative word used as definite article" and an indefinite article with the indefinite word same as 'one' (Features 37A and 38A, Dryer). First, this is wrong, and, second, Lithuanian is presented as differing from Latvian in these respects, since it is (rightly) counted among those languages (together with Polish and Czech, but also Finnish) that lack indefinite and definite articles.

Apart from such shortcomings in WALS, for many, if not most book-length wide-scale typological studies, both monographs and edited collections of articles, the norm is not to mention Baltic languages at all. Notable exceptions are constituted, first, by Boeder and Hentschel (eds. 2001) on differential case marking with Holvoet (2001g) on possessive genitive and dative, Abraham and Leisiö (eds. 2006) on passives with two papers dealing with Lithuanian (Geniušienė 2006, Wiemer 2006b), and Gast and Diessel (eds. 2012) on clause-combining (Arkadiev 2012c on participial complements), and, second, by volumes on grammaticalization co-edited by Björn Wiemer, i.e., Bisang, Himmelmann, and Wiemer (eds. 2004) (Wiemer 2004b on passives) and Wiemer, Wälchli, and Hansen (eds. 2012) (Nau 2012 on modality in Latgalian). Not much Baltic material has, to date, figured in the issues of *Linguistic Typology*, the journal of the Association of Linguistic Typology; the only article published in this journal specifically addressing Baltic data from a cross-linguistic perspective is the work of Arkadiev (2013b). The other typological journal, *Sprachtypologie und Universalienforschung*, has, however, featured a special issue on typological approaches to Latvian (Nau ed. 2001a).

If one turns to areal-typological studies, it is astonishing how little attention the Baltic languages attracted even where they could not be completely ignored, for instance, in the volumes of the EUROTYP project. The only article in the whole EUROTYP enterprise specifically devoted to Baltic languages is Dogil (1999b); if one simply browses the indices of the volumes, one finds that Latvian and Lithuanian taken together are usually mentioned on fewer pages than, say, Swedish, Portuguese, or Bulgarian. Besides EUROTYP, Baltic languages have been represented by individual chapters in such edited volumes devoted to European languages as Thieroff (ed. 1995) on tense systems (Sližienė 1995 on Lithuanian), Braunmüller and Ferraresi (eds. 2003) on multi-lingualism (Wiemer 2003b), Schroeder, Hentschel, and Boeder (eds. 2008) on secondary predicates (Holvoet 2008), Rothstein and Thieroff (eds. 2010) on mood and modality (Holvoet 2010b), Kortmann and van der Auwera (eds. 2011) on European languages in general (Holvoet 2011b); Baltic languages are amply represented in the work by Thomas Stolz and his associates, cf. Stolz, Stroh, and Urdze (2006, 2011), Stolz et al. (2008), as well as in some other recent work on the typology of European languages, e.g., Mauri (2008).

5.2 Typologically outstanding features and rarities

In the preceding sections, we have focused on both most basic features of the structure of Baltic languages and their peculiarities. Here we will briefly summarize the latter, focusing on what Baltic languages can contribute to linguistic typology.

In the domain of phonology, the following phenomena can be named as typologically outstanding: (i) the highly non-trivial and cross-linguistically by no means frequent interaction of morphologically sensitive free mobile stress and "syllable intonations" in Lithuanian, as well as "syllable intonations" in Latvian and word prosodic phenomena in Baltic dialects in general; (ii) interaction between vowel and consonant length in standard and dialectal Latvian; (iii) the so-called "diphthongal sequences" consisting of a vowel and a nasal or liquid consonant, phonologically behaving like more familiar diphthongs and, in particular, subject to "syllable intonation" contrasts; (iv) in connection with the latter, a great range of combinability and thus the occurrence of systematic mismatches between the sonority contour (vowel quality) and prominence contour (syllable peaks) in diphthongs and diphthongal sequences (otherwise called "semi-diphthongs") in Lithuanian (cf. Geyer 2011: 184–186; Daugavet, this volume); (v) various morphophonological phenomena lying on the borders of phonology and morphology, deserving a large-scale cross-dialectal study with possible non-trivial implications for both phonological and morphological typology.

In the domain of morphology, Baltic languages can offer much for the recently developing typological studies of inflectional classes, and for the understanding of the interplay of different types of inflectional exponence (affixal and non-affixal). Lithuanian can offer a fairly productive instance of inflectional infixation, otherwise absent from European languages, as well as such rarities as double inflection of definite adjectives and a "mobile" reflexive marker, while Latvian and especially Latgalian show intricate patterns of stem alternation in inflection and derivation.

Among morphological categories peculiar to Baltic, let us once again mention the Lithuanian inflectional habitual past and continuative and the Latvian debitive;

Lithuanian can also boast as being one of the very few languages of the world possessing a morphological restrictive marker with variable scope (see Arkadiev 2010 for details). Baltic systems of derivational aspect are sufficiently different from Slavic ones (and from each other) for being, in our view, indispensable for a typologically adequate characterization of this type of aspectual system (see e.g. Arkadiev 2014c). Baltic languages can offer much to students of evidentiality and modality as well. Last but not least, Latvian shows an evidently very rare pattern in the imperative: from among 547 languages accounted for in WALS, Latvian is one of but two languages (the other being Apurinã in South America) in which there exists a morphologically dedicated second plural imperative but no such second singular imperative (see feature 70a in WALS); in actual fact, however, this dedicated 2PL imperative seems to have existed in Old Latvian until the seventeenth century and was then artificially reintroduced in the twentieth century, cf. the remark in Section 1.1. Among the morphosyntactic peculiarities of Baltic languages, one can mention a wide variety of case marking patterns. Here belong phenomena such as the exclusive occurrence of the dative in the plural after all postpositions in Latvian. But, primarily, the Baltic languages demonstrate quite a few rare and typologically interesting features in the marking of core arguments, which depend on such factors as referentiality and/or partitivity, verb meaning, negation, modality, evidentiality, (non-)finiteness, and clause type. Baltic has also never shown a lexical distinction between 'who' and 'what' (the interrogative pronoun *kas* is indifferent in this respect), a feature that seems to be rare, as it has been attested only in Kayardild (Australia) (cf. Nau 1999: 134, 144–147). One should furthermore single out the Lithuanian evidential impersonal passive, which applies to all kinds of intransitive predicates, including non-agentive, copular, and even passive ones and a peculiar "participle of accompanying motion" in *-in-* (Gliwa 2003), showing, first, non-trivial restrictions on the verbs from which it may be formed, and, second, instrumental case marking of its direct object. These and many other non-trivial phenomena in the domain of argument structure found in Baltic languages can enrich the linguists' understanding of the nature of grammatical relations and case marking, see e.g., Holvoet and Nau (eds. 2014b). On the typological significance of the Lithuanian HAVE-perfect, see Sections 2.3.2.4 and 4.

In the domain of syntax, Baltic languages are classic representatives of languages with "free", i.e., information-structure determined word order of main constituents, and the interaction of constituency, information structure, sentence prosody, and word order in these languages beg for a detailed theoretically and typologically informed study. No less can Baltic languages offer to students of clause combining, complementizers, and (non-)finiteness.

6 Paradoxes and conclusions

As we hoped, the previous sections, in particular Sections 4 and 5, have made it evident that the three extant Baltic languages offer a host of phenomena to be investigated not only because many of them have remained understudied, but also because they are intriguing from the more general perspectives of typology and linguistic theory. In other words, not only would the study of Baltic languages (and their dialects) profit from a consistent application of contemporary linguistic methods, but, conversely, the empirical "check" of assumptions about the structural diversity of languages and the motives of their dynamics would gain much if typological overviews and in-depth or case studies into diverse linguistic phenomena accounted more for what linguistic variation and rare phenomena in Baltic have to offer to them. In fact, Lithuanian was one of the languages that attracted keen attention among the best linguists of the second half of the nineteenth century, not only from Neogrammarian circles. In the same period, investigations about moribund minority languages were published, for instance, Bezzenberger's (1888) and Pietsch's (1982) studies devoted to Nehrungskurisch (the latter contains a corpus with German translations). The documentation of this meanwhile extinct Baltic variety appears highly relevant for issues like the mixed-language debate. However, the aforementioned interest did not last further than by the Second World War, and many Latvian and Lithuanian linguists still do not recognize any other than Neogrammarian linguistics.

As we have shown in Section 2, quite a few phenomena attested in Baltic are peculiar not only on a European but even on a worldwide background, and already for this reason, they are interesting for general theories in phonology, morphology, or syntax. For other domains, for instance, lexical semantics or discourse-syntax and pragmatics, no reliable "prognoses" can be made about their use in cutting-edge research, since the study of such domains for Baltic has remained in its infancy (see Section 3). Moreover, as was alluded to in Section 4, insights into the rise and structure of areal clines (on different levels of granularity) can become more diversified and be posed on an empirically more solid ground if micro-variation were investigated for smaller-scale areas in which Baltic dialect continua participate.

In view of this, the first paradox consists in the fact that the more general, or even global, significance for linguistics borne by data and phenomena prominent in Baltic has almost never been brought to an audience outside the Baltic-speaking countries by "domestic" scholars specializing in Baltic studies. It was scholars educated in general linguistics who have succeeded in making Baltic languages (in the first place, Lithuanian) recognized and respectable among broader communities of linguists. As a prominent example, one may name the efforts made by linguists of the Leningrad Typology School, in particular by Ema Geniušienė (cf. Geniušienė 1987, 1997, 2006, 2007), who were among the first having highlighted outstanding features of Baltic languages and having made their structures systematically comparable to other languages and accessible for non-specialists of Baltic. As concerns merits for areal linguistics, we may name here the pioneering work by Larin (1963) and by Timberlake (1974), among some others, dedicated to syntax; cf. also Nepokupnyj (1964) as another pioneer of areal linguistic studies in the Baltic-Slavic region. As mentioned in Section 4, lexical phenomena (loanwords) attracted attention much earlier. Both domains of research have so far remained separated, but it seems desirable to integrate them for a better understanding of contact relations in past and present.

In general, although in our survey we have concentrated on the synchronic stage of Baltic languages, a more pronounced account of work dealing with diachronic issues would not have considerably shifted the general conclusion about the state of the art of the study of Baltic languages. This is so because work into diachronically interesting phenomena of these languages has largely been restricted to an Indoeuropeanist historical-comparative vantage point with a Neogrammarian or structuralist methodology. To a considerable extent, this strong bias has resulted from a belated nineteenth-century-fashioned interest in the ethnogenesis of Baltic tribes and nations. This tendency also partially explains why Baltic dialectology has either largely remained on a stage of atomistic collections of observations, or has been guided by ethnographic considerations with often linguistically rather superficial and not easily comprehensible accounts. Further serious obstacles for progress in linguistic research into dialectology and dialect geography are the lack of a sound theory of areally interesting issues and the inaccessibility of fieldwork data that have been collected and stored for about 60 years in academic institutions.[23] There do not exist any reliable and commonly accessible corpora of dialectal speech that would reflect the real structural diversity of Baltic dialects. There exist two chrestomathies of Lithuanian dialects[24] and a short, "didactic" one of Latvian dialects by Rudzīte (2005) together

---

[23] See http://www.tarmes.lt/index_meniu.php?id=1 for more detailed information on Lithuanian. It remains to be hoped whether tons of sound records and handwritten field notes can be analyzed without the participation of non-Balticist and "non-domestic" scholars in a reliable, faithful, and comprehensive enough up-to-date manner.

[24] LKT (1970) and LKTCh (2004). The latter comprises texts from a smaller amount of places than LKT (1970), but is based on Girdenis' and Zinkevičius' dialect classification (see Section 4) and also presents the texts in sound form on a CD.

with series of collections of transcripts from dialectal speech; furthermore, some appendices with transcribed dialect speech dispersed over the literature on dialects in the Baltic-Slavic contact region, and some dozen books with collections of texts from diverse Lithuanian dialects, most of them published in the last 15 years (e.g., Petrauskas & Vidugiris 1987, Mikulėnienė & Morkūnas 1997, Vidugiris & Mikulėnienė 2005, 2010, Markevičienė et al. 2009). However, the transcripts included into these book editions are highly selective; the basis of their choice often remains obscure, in particular, in view of prescriptivist thinking that sometimes intrudes also into dialect documentation. By no means do such book editions compensate for the lack of computerized corpora of non-adapted dialectal speech that would allow for independent online searches; such corpora are an indispensable prerequisite for any manageable quantificational approaches (as practiced, e.g., in variationist frameworks). The same concerns, *mutatis mutandis*, research into diachronic morphosyntax, which suffers from the lack of larger, reliably edited, and commonly accessible corpora (or of similar databases). Thus, one can at best make use of solid structuralistic descriptions (see e.g., Section 2.1.1 on the phonological system of Standard Lithuanian or Lithuanian dialects or the diachronic development and synchronic stage of Baltic pronouns by Rosinas 1988, 1995, 1996; see Section 2.4), but possibilities of falsification of claims on the basis of larger amounts of data remain severely restricted.

Finally, the richness of Baltic dialects and their significance as "witnesses" of ethnogenesis has time and again been stressed by Lithuanian and Latvian dialectologists and historical-comparative linguists. Thus, the second, and even greater, paradox lies in the surprising indifference among the same groups of scholars toward authentic, unprejudiced accounts of the observable situation that would be comprehensible for a broader audience and allow for reliable comparisons with dialects and diachronic development of language groups or areas elsewhere. After all, richness of linguistic variation (in a diatopic or diastratic dimension) can only be made visible if commonly recognizable tools of linguistic description are applied and if the observed variation is captured within coherent theoretical approaches. Otherwise, it will remain more or less a hodgepodge of accidental observations.

In sum, the paradoxes in the study of Baltic languages and dialects pointed at above arise from a self-chosen isolation of most specialists, in particular in the Baltic-speaking countries themselves. There were notable exceptions before 1989 (like Vytautas Ambrazas, Konstantins Karulis, or Jonas Kazlauskas), but even after 1989, most scholars of the generation "raised" in Soviet times have retained reluctant, if not hostile, attitudes toward modern linguistic theory. This isolation has started to slowly break down during the last decade, and we hope that the present volume is a solid contribution to this trend.

7 Structure and summary of the volume

The present volume does not, of course, aim at a comprehensive representation of current theoretically and typologically oriented approaches to Baltic languages, and – to the regret of the editors – suffers from the more general bias toward Lithuanian at the expense of Latvian and especially of Latgalian (the editors, despite their efforts, were not able to procure a contribution to the volume from the very few specialists on this language). However, we hope that the volume is able to give an impression of the diversity of current problems of Baltic linguistics and of how these problems and solutions developed by Balticists may have an impact on general linguistics.

The volume is not subdivided into thematic parts, although most of the thirteen chapters constituting the book do cluster around certain more or less broad domains such as phonology (**Hock** and **Daugavet**), diminutives (**Horiguchi, Dabašinskienė and Voeikova**), peculiarities of case syntax and grammatical relations (**Anderson, Holvoet, Seržant**, and **Maskaliūnienė**), and onomatopoetic expressions (**Wälchli** and **Danylenko**), and the order of chapters follows their thematic proximity. On the other hand, from the point of view of scope, there are areal studies with implications for contact linguistics (**Daugavet, Hock, Seržant**, and **Kozhanov**), as well as in-depth studies of particular forms or constructions in individual languages (**Horiguchi, Anderson, Sakurai, Usonienė**, and **Wälchli**), as well as contrastive or comparative studies involving Baltic and Slavic (**Dabašinskienė and Voeikova, Sakurai**, and **Danylenko**). In the following, we will briefly summarize the chapters of the volume in the order of their occurrence.

Hans Henrich Hock, in "Prosody and dialectology of tonal shifts in Lithuanian and their implications", discusses the relation between the reduction or loss of final short vowels and stress retraction occurring in many dialects of Lithuanian, with more developed stages attested to the north. Hock interprets stress retraction as the reassignment of high tone to the preceding mora or syllable when the original mora or syllable gets deleted and claims that the restriction of ictus retraction in Žemaitian to final short syllables and long syllables with the "circumflex" ("low-high") tone can be attributed to the cross-linguistically well-documented "finality effect", i.e., the tendency to avoid prosodic prominence (e.g., high tone) in the utterance-final and word-final position. This chapter presents a theoretically and typologically informed, but somewhat speculative, analysis of the quite nontrivial prosodic phenomena attested in Lithuanian dialects.

Anna Daugavet, in "The lengthening of the first component of Lithuanian diphthongs in an areal perspective", approaches the problem of the phonological interpretation of vowel length in Lithuanian in the light of comparable phenomena in Latvian and Livonian, giving a comprehensive overview of vocalic systems, syllable structure, and relevant phonological processes in these languages and their dialects. She concludes that the peculiar development that stressed diphthongs have undergone in Lithuanian is a product of two different lengthening processes found in the neighboring languages and shows how in different parts of the area these processes have led to different results. This chapter is in fact the first comprehensive account of phenomena related to syllable structure in Baltic languages and their dialects written in English, combining both solid empirical grounding and up-to-date theoretical insights.

A contrastive-linguistic perspective on diminutives is taken by **Ineta Dabašinskienė** and **Maria Voeikova** in "Diminutives in spoken Lithuanian and Russian: Pragmatic functions and structural properties". They show that despite many similarities, Lithuanian and Russian diminutives differ in such properties as morphology (Lithuanian diminutives are formally more diverse and less lexicalized than their Russian counterparts) and use (e.g., in Russian, the use of diminutives is avoided in many formal contexts, whereas Lithuanian speakers freely employ them, which suggests differences in pragmatic functions of diminutives in the two languages). From the point of view of morphology, it is shown that diminutives help the native speakers overcome the frequent irregularities and opacities of nominal paradigms and accentual patterns in both languages.

Daiki Horiguchi, in "Latvian attenuative *pa*-verbs in comparison with diminutives", takes a non-trivial perspective in comparing nominal diminutives with verbal delimitative or attenuative Aktionsart in Latvian. The chapter, based on contemporary corpus data, shows that these two morphological categories share common semantic and, notably, pragmatic features, e.g., expression of emotional attitude or familiarity. "Secondary" prefixation of the attenuative *pa*- to the already prefixed verbs is discussed in detail; this phenomenon, largely neglected by the Latvian descriptive grammars, is non-trivial for Baltic languages, which allow only one Aktionsart prefix per verb, with a couple of lexicalized exceptions. This contribution clearly shows that a proper account of word formational phenomena may require consideration of discourse pragmatic factors.

Cori Anderson, in "Non-canonical case patterns in Lithuanian", convincingly shows the relevance of Lithuanian data for the current formal approaches to case marking. She analyzes several Lithuanian constructions posing problems for the standard generative case theory, e.g., passivization promoting the non-accusative marked object of a bivalent verb to the position of the nominative subject, accusative vs. instrumental alternations with a diverse range of verbs, and substitution of the accusative case of the direct object by the genitive or dative in goal and purpose infinitival constructions. All these phenomena require a subtler conception of case than the generally assumed distinction between "structural" and "inherent" case.

Axel Holvoet in "Non-canonical subjects in Latvian: An obliqueness-based approach", deals with the problematic interpretation of grammatical relations in Latvian constructions with "dative subjects". He shows that in these constructions, it is often impossible to attribute the subject status to a particular argument and that instead we are often dealing with "diffuse grammatical relations" when behavioral properties are distributed between two arguments. To capture the peculiarities of such constructions, the obliqueness hierarchy, which involves such features as relative topicworthiness, semantic role, and morphosyntactic accessibility of arguments, is invoked instead of the notions of subject and object, which are strictly applicable only to the canonically transitive structures in relation to which they are defined.

In "Dative experiencer constructions as a Circum-Baltic isogloss", **Ilja Seržant** analyzes Baltic, Russian, and Balto-Finnic constructions with dative experiencers from an areal-typological perspective. To show that such constructions constitute a case of convergent development in all these languages, Seržant invokes the "requirement for idiosyncratic correlations", whereby an areal feature must exhibit a bundle of typologically non-trivial properties shared by non-cognate elements. In the domain of dative experiencer constructions, such idiosyncratic properties include stative morphology of pain predicates, which are often denominal, and notably, similar syntactic (behavioral) properties of arguments. From a more general perspective, Seržant supplies a case study illustrating how methods and assumptions of different disciplines dealing with linguistic variation (typology, areal linguistics, contact linguistics, and historical-comparative linguistics) should be combined to yield sound, equilibrated explanations for the rise of areally outstanding structural convergence. His study also exemplifies the necessity of looking more closely at specific alignment patterns of lexically restricted groups of predicates and the impact these patterns have for the (areally convergent) re-shaping of argument marking.

Nijolė Maskaliūnienė, in "Morphological, syntactic, and semantic types of converse verbs in Lithuanian", addresses another topic lying on the intersection of lexicon and morphosyntax, i.e., lexical and morphological converses – verbs denoting identical real-world situations with different argument structures (e.g., *buy* and *sell*). The chapter provides a detailed overview of formal and syntactic relations between members of converse pairs in Lithuanian, as well as of lexical semantic classes of predicates entering into converse relations. It also points out some phenomena that would furthermore be interesting to investigate more closely in connection with lexical typology, e.g., it calls for an explanation why certain patterns of converse pairs appear to be rarer than others.

Eiko Sakurai's chapter, "Past habitual tense in Lithuanian", is the most comprehensive description of the semantics and discourse functions of the Lithuanian past habitual tense with the suffix -*dav* to date. The author draws both on corpus and statistically analyzed experimental data to show complex correlations between the use or non-use of the past habitual and such factors as aspectual class of the predicate and presence of certain kinds of adverbials and further contrasts the Lithuanian past habitual to the Russian past imperfective, which has a much broader range of functions. The chapter yields considerable empirical feedback for aspectological theories dealing with habituals and associated functions.

Aurelija Usonienė, in "Non-morphological realizations of evidentiality: The case of parenthetical elements in Lithuanian", broadens the horizon of the studies on Lithuanian evidentiality by considering such "lexical" means of encoding evidentiality and epistemic stance as parenthetical expressions stemming from complement-taking predicates, which are actually the preferred way of expressing these meanings in modern Lithuanian. The chapter presents the results of a corpus investigation of morphosyntactic and semantic properties of Lithuanian parentheticals. It is grounded in recent corpus-driven studies dominated by investigations on English, with which the author's findings are consistently brought into relation.

Kirill Kozhanov, in "Lithuanian indefinite pronouns in contact", investigates the contact-induced changes in the Lithuanian indefinite pronouns attested in rural dialects and non-standard urban speech. These developments, mainly occurring under Slavic influence, involve both straightforward borrowing of matter and more intricate transfer of structural patterns. The author thoroughly (re-)considers Haspelmath's (1997) findings on the semantics and functional range of indefinite pronouns and thus brings to light interesting observations about the actual consequences of language contact on a general typological background.

The two last chapters of the volume are devoted to Lithuanian ideophones or onomatopoetic lexical items, which have peculiar formal and functional properties and constitute a typologically non-trivial feature for a European language. **Bernhard Wälchli**, in "*Ištiktukai* 'eventives' – The Baltic precursors of ideophones and why they remain unknown in typology", provides a general description of Lithuanian ideophones from the point of view of their morphology, morphosyntactic properties, and use in discourse and discusses them from the perspective of recent typological studies of onomatopoetic vocabulary. **Andrii Danylenko**'s chapter, "The chicken or the egg? Onomatopoeic particles and verbs in Baltic and Slavic", discusses Baltic and Slavic ideophones in the light of their derivational relation to verbs sharing the same root. Reviewing evidence from phonology, morphology, and semantics, Danylenko reaches the conclusion that ideophones are derived from verbs – even if by stripping the latter of their verb-specific morphology.

Acknowledgments

The volume stems from the conference "Contemporary Approaches to Baltic Linguistics" (organized by Peter Arkadiev at the Institute of Slavic Studies, Moscow, October 2009) and the workshop "Baltic Languages in an Areal-Typological Perspective" (organized by Peter Arkadiev and Jurgis Pakerys at the 43rd Annual Meeting of the Societas Linguistica Europaea, Vilnius University, September 2010). We thank all the participants and the audience of these events, as well as anonymous referees of the abstracts, for their enthusiasm and useful feedback. Not all of the papers presented at these conferences ended up in the current volume, and not all of the papers included into it have been presented there. We would like to express our gratitude to Bert Cornillie, Volker Gast, Östen Dahl, Andrej Malchukov, Norbert Ostrowski, and Gil Rappaport for having kindly shared with us their expertise serving as external reviewers for some of the chapters of the volume. We also thank Volker Gast and an anonymous reviewer for useful suggestions concerning the structure of the volume and content of individual chapters, as well as the De Gruyter team for their help and encouragement.

Last but not least, we also thank Aleksej Andronov, Anna Daugavet, Rolandas Mikulskas, Nicole Nau, Natalia Perkova, Bohumil Vykypěl, and Bernhard Wälchli for useful comments on the draft versions of this chapter or its parts and other help. All shortcomings remain ours.

Abbreviations

1	first person	M	masculine
2	second person	N	neuter
3	third person	NEG	negation
ACC	accusative	NOM	nominative
AUX	auxiliary	PA	active participle
CNT	continuative	PART	participle
COMP	complementizer	PL	plural
DAT	dative	POS	positive polarity
DEB	debitive	PP	passive participle
DEM	demonstrative	PRM	permissive
F	feminine	PRS	present
FUT	future	PRV	preverb
GEN	genitive	PST	past
INF	infinitive	RFL	reflexive
INS	instrumental	RSTR	restrictive
LOC	locative	SG	singular
LOG	logophoric pronoun	VOC	vocative

References

Abele [Ābele], Anna. 1915. Ob akcentuacii udarennyx prostyx glasnyx v latyšskom jazyke [On the accentuation of simple stressed vowels in Latvian]. *Izvestija Otdelenija russkogo jazyka i slovesnosti Imperatorskoj Akademii nauk,* T. 20, kn. 2, 152–196. Petrograd.
Abele [Ābele], Anna. 1924. K voprosu o sloge [On the problem of the syllable]. *Slavia.* Ročnik III, Sešit 1, 1–34. Praha.
Ābele, Anna. 1932. Par neuzsvērto zilbju intonācijām [On the intonations of unstressed syllables]. *Filologu biedrības raksti* XII. 149–163.
Abraham, Werner & Larisa Leisiö (eds.). 2006. *Passivization and typology. Form and function.* Amsterdam, Philadelphia: John Benjamins.
Agrell, Sigurd. 1908. *Aspektänderung und Aktionsartbildung beim polnischen Zeitworte: Ein Beitrag zum Studium der indogermanischen Präverbia und ihrer Bedeutungsfunktionen.* Lund: Håkan Ohlssons Buchdruckerei.
Akelaitienė, Gražina. 1987. Veiksmažodžių galūnių ir sangrąžos morfemos alternavimas [Alternations in the verbs' endings and reflexive marker]. *Kalbotyra* 38(1).
Akelaitienė, Gražina. 1996. *Morfonologinės balsių kaitos žodžių daryboje* [Morphophonological vowel alternations in word formation]. Vilnius: Vilniaus pedagoginio universiteto leidykla.
Akelaitis, Gintautas. 2002. Veiksmažodiniai pagrindinio dėmens formos įterpiniai [Parentheticals in the form of verbal heads]. *Žmogus ir žodis* 1: 3–9.
Akelaitis, Gintautas. 2003. Beasmenio pagrindinio dėmens formos įterpiniai [Parentheticals in the form of impersonal heads]. *Žmogus ir žodis* 1: 4–13.
Aleksandravičiūtė, Skaistė. 2013. The semantic effects of the Subject Genitive of Negation in Lithuanian. *Baltic Linguistics* 4: 9–38.
Aloseviečienė, Eglė. 2006. Die Rolle der Heckenausdrücke bei der Diskursstrukturierung im Deutschen und Litauischen. *Acta Linguistica Lithuanica* 54: 1–25.
Ambrazas, Saulius. 1993. *Daiktavardžių darybos raida (Lietuvių kalbos veiksmažodiniai vediniai)* [The origins of nominal word formation: Lithuanian deverbal nouns]. Vilnius: Mokslo ir enciklopedijų leidykla.
Ambrazas, Saulius. 2000a. *Daiktavardžių darybos raida II (Lietuvių kalbos vardažodiniai vediniai)* [The origins of nominal word formation: Lithuanian denominal nouns]. Vilnius: Mokslo ir enciklopedijų leidykla/Lietuvių kalbos institutas.
Ambrazas, Saulius. 2000b. Lietuvių ir latvių kalbų daiktavardžių darybos svarbiausi skirtumai [The most important differences between Lithuanian and Latvian nominal derivation]. *Acta Linguistica Lithuanica* 43: 111–127.
Ambrazas, Saulius. 2001. Dėl skaitvardinių būdvardžių su priesagomis *-(i)okas (-a)* ir *-(i)opas (-a)* kilmės [On the origins of denumeral adjectives with certain suffixes]. *Acta Linguistica Lithuanica* 45: 3–9.
Ambrazas, Vytautas. 1979. *Lietuvių kalbos dalyvių istorinė sintaksė* [The historical syntax of Lithuanian participles]. Vilnius: Mokslas.
Ambrazas, Vytautas. 1981. Zur Geschichte einer indogermanischen Konstruktion (Dativus cum infinitivo im Baltischen). *Kalbotyra* 32(3): 12–24.
Ambrazas, Vytautas. 1987. Die indogermanische Grundlage des Dativus und Nominativus cum infinitivo im Baltischen. *Indogermanische Forschungen* 92: 203–219.
Ambrazas, Vytautas. 1990. *Sravnitel'nyj sintaksis pričastij baltijskix jazykov* [Comparative syntax of participles in Baltic Languages]. Vilnius: Mokslas.
Ambrazas, Vytautas. 1994. On the interpretation of Lithuanian constructions with neuter passive participles. *Linguistica Baltica* 3: 7–11.

Ambrazas, Vytautas. 1995. Lietuvių kalbos bendraties konstrukcijų raida [The origin of Lithuanian infinitival constructions]. *Lietuvių kalbotyros klausimai* 35: 74–109.
Ambrazas, Vytautas. 2001a. On the development of the nominative object in East Baltic. In Dahl & Koptjevskaja-Tamm (eds.) 2001, 2: 391–412.
Ambrazas, Vytautas. 2001b. Lietuvių kalbos adverbalinis genityvas istorinės sintaksės požiūriu [The Lithuanian adverbial genitive from the perspective of historical syntax]. *Acta Linguistica Lithuanica* 44: 3–39.
Ambrazas, Vytautas. 2001c. Lietuvių kalbos pasyvo raidos bruožai [Characteristics of the development of the Lithuanian passive]. *Acta Linguistica Lithuanica* 45: 11–38.
Ambrazas, Vytautas. 2004. On the genitive with neuter participles and verbal nouns in Lithuanian. In Baldi & Dini (eds.) 2004: 1–6.
Ambrazas, Vytautas. 2006. *Lietuvių kalbos istorinė sintaksė* [Lithuanian historical syntax]. Vilnius: Lietuvių kalbos institutas.
Anderson, Cori. 2011. Case theory and case alternations: Evidence from Lithuanian. *Baltic Linguistics* 2: 9–35.
Anderson, Cori. 2013. *Case and event structure in Russian and Lithuanian*: Princeton University PhD dissertation.
Andronov, Aleksej V. 1999. *Sopostavitel'naja grammatika litovskogo i latyšskogo jazykov. Slovoizmenenie* [Contrastive grammar of Lithuanian and Latvian: Inflection]: Saint-Petersburg State University PhD dissertation.
Andronov, Aleksej V. 2001. A survey of the case paradigm in Latvian. *Sprachtypologie und Universalienforschung* 54(3): 197–208.
Andronov, Aleksej V. 2002. *Materialy k latyšsko-russkomu slovarju* [Materials for a Latvian-Russian dictionary]. Saint-Petersburg: SPbGU, Filologičeskij fakul'tet.
Andronovas Aleksejus [Andronov, Aleksej V.]. 2002. Dėl naujų publikacijų lietuvių kalbos teorinės fonetikos ir morfologijos klausimais [On the new publications on the issues of the Lithuanian theoretical phonetics and morphology]. *Acta Linguistica Lithuanica* 57: 117–129.
Arkadiev, Peter. 2005. On the semantic determinants of inflection class membership: Evidence from Lithuanian. In: Katrin Erk, Alissa Mellinger & Sabine Schulte im Walde (eds.), *Verb Workshop 2005. Proceedings of the Interdisciplinary Workshop on the Identification and Representation of Verb Features and Verb Classes*, 10–15. Saarbrücken: Computational Linguistics Department, Saarland University.
Arkad'ev, Petr M. [Arkadiev, Peter]. 2006a. Paradigmatičeskie klassy pervičnyx glagolov v litovskom jazyke: Formal'nye protivopostavlenija i ix semantičeskaja motivacija [Inflectional classes of primary verbs in Lithuanian: Formal distinctions and their semantic motivations]. In *Balto-slavjanskie issledovanija* [Balto-Slavic studies] *XVII*, 250–294. Moscow: Indrik.
Arkad'ev, Petr M. [Arkadiev, Peter]. 2006b. Sootnošenie meždu semantičeskimi i morfologičeskimi klassami neproizvodnyx glagolov v litovskom jazyke v tipologičeskoj perspektive [The relations between semantic and morphological classes of Lithuanian primary verbs in a typological perspective]. In: Tatiana N. Mološnaja (ed.) *Tipologija grammatičeskix sistem slavjanskogo prostranstva* [The typology of grammatical systems of the Slavic area], 128–163. Moscow: Institute of Slavic Studies of the Russian Academy of Sciences.
Arkad'ev, Petr M. [Arkadiev, Peter]. 2007. Glagoly peremeščenija v vode v litovskom jazyke [Verbs of aquamotion in Lithuanian]. In Timur A. Majsak & Ekaterina V. Raxilina (eds.) *Glagoly dviženija v vode: leksičeskaja tipologija* [Verbs of motion in water: Lexical typology], 315–334. Moscow: Indrik.

Arkad'ev, Petr M. [Arkadiev, Peter]. 2008a. Uroki litovskogo jazyka dlja slavjanskoj aspektologii [Lessons of Lithuanian for Slavic aspectology]. In Aleksandr M. Moldovan (ed.) *Slavjanskoe jazykoznanie. XIV Meždunarodnyj s"ezd slavistov (Oxrid, 10–16 sentjabrja 2008 g.). Doklady rossijskoj delegacii* [Russian contributions to the 14th International Congress of Slavicists in Oxrid], 28–43. Moscow: Indrik.

Arkadiev, Petr M. [Arkadiev, Peter]. 2008b. Lietuvių kalbos pirminių veiksmažodžių klasių semantika tipologinių duomenų kontekste [The semantics of the inflectional classes of the Lithuanian primary verbs in a typological perspective]. *Acta Linguistica Lithuanica* 49: 1–27.

Arkad'ev, Petr M. [Arkadiev, Peter]. 2009. Teorija akcional'nosti i litovskij glagol [Theory of actionality and the Lithuanian verb]. In *Balto-slavjanskie issledovanija* [Balto-Slavic studies] XVIII, 72–94. Moscow: Jazyki slavjanskix kul'tur.

Arkadiev, Peter M. 2010. Notes on the Lithuanian restrictive. *Baltic Linguistics* 1: 9–49.

Arkad'ev, Petr M. [Arkadiev, Peter]. 2011a. Problemy sintaksisa konstrukcij "accusativus cum participio" v litovskom jazyke [Problems of the syntax of accusativus cum participio constructions in Lithuanian]. *Voprosy jazykoznanija* 5: 44–75.

Arkadiev, Peter M. 2011b. On the aspectual uses of the prefix *be-* in Lithuanian. *Baltic Linguistics* 2: 37–78.

Arkadiev, Peter M. 2011c. Aspect and actionality in Lithuanian on a typological background. In Daniel Petit, Claire Le Feuvre & Henri Menantaud (eds.), *Langues baltiques, langues slaves*, 57–86. Paris: Éditions CNRS.

Arkadiev, Peter M. 2012a. Stems in Lithuanian verbal inflection (with remarks on derivation). *Word Structure* 5(1): 7–27.

Arkad'ev, Petr M. [Arkadiev, Peter]. 2012b. Aspektual'naja sistema litovskogo jazyka (s privlečeniem areal'nyx dannyx) [The aspectual system of Lithuanian (with some areal data)]. In Vladimir A. Plungjan (ed.) *Issledovanija po teorii grammatiki, vyp. 6: Tipologija aspektual'nyx sistem i kategorij* [Studies in the theory of grammar. Vol. 6. Typology of aspectual systems and categories]. *Acta Linguistica Petropolitana* 8(2): 45–121. Saint-Petersburg: Nauka.

Arkadiev, Peter M. 2012c. Participial complementation in Lithuanian. In Gast & Diessel (eds.) 2012: 285–334.

Arkadiev, Peter M. 2013a. Marking of subjects and objects in Lithuanian non-finite clauses: A typological and diachronic perspective. *Linguistic Typology* 17(3): 397–437.

Arkadiev, Peter M. 2013b. From transitivity to aspect: Causative-inchoative alternation and its extensions in Lithuanian. *Baltic Linguistics* 4: 39–78.

Arkad'ev, Petr M. [Arkadiev, Peter]. 2013c. O tipologičeskom svoeobrazii litovskoj glagol'noj sistemy [On the typological peculiarities of the Lithuanian verb]. In Arkad'ev & Ivanov (eds.) 2013: 320–361.

Arkadiev, Peter M. 2014a. Case and word order in Lithuanian revisited. In Holvoet & Nau (eds.) 2014b: 43–95.

Arkad'ev, Petr M. [Arkadiev, Peter]. 2014b. Kriterii finitnosti i morfosintaksis litovskix pričastij [Criteria of finiteness and the morphosyntax of Lithuanian participles]. *Voprosy jazykoznanija* 5: 68–96.

Arkadiev, Peter. 2014c. Towards an areal typology of prefixal perfectivization. *Scando-Slavica* 60(2): 384–405.

Arkadiev, Peter & Jurgis Pakerys. Forthcoming. Lithuanian morphological causatives: A corpus-based study. In Axel Holvoet & Nicole Nau (eds.) *Voice and argument structure in Baltic*. Amsterdam, Philadelphia: John Benjamins.

Arkad'ev, Petr M. & Vjačeslav V. Ivanov (eds.) 2013. *Issledovanija po tipologii slavjanskix, baltijskix i balkanskix jazykov* [Studies in the typology of Slavic, Baltic and Balkan languages]. Saint-Petersburg: Aletejja.
Armoškaitė, Solveiga. 2011. *The destiny of roots in Blackfoot and Lithuanian*: University of British Columbia dissertation. https://circle.ubc.ca/handle/2429/33934.
Armoškaitė, Solveiga. 2014. Derivation by gender in Lithuanian. In Ileana Paul (ed.) *Cross-linguistic investigations of nominalization patterns*, 169–187. Amsterdam, Philadelphia: John Benjamins.
Arumaa P. 1957. Von der Eigenart des Ablauts und der Diathese im Baltischen. *Zeitschrift für slavische Philologie* 26: 118–149.
Baković, Eric. 2006. Phonological opacity and counterfactual derivation. Paper presented at *GLOW Workshop: Approaches to Phonological Opacity*. http://idiom.ucsd.edu/~bakovic/work/bakovic_opacity-hdt.pdf.
Baldauf, Lucia. 1967. *Der Gebrauch der Pronominalform des Adjektivs im Litauischen*. München: Otto Sagner.
Baldi, Philip & Pietro U. Dini (eds.). 2004. *Studies in Baltic and Indo-European linguistics*. Amsterdam, Philadelphia: John Benjamins.
Balkevičius, Jonas. 1963. *Dabartinės lietuvių kalbos sintaksė* [The syntax of modern Lithuanian]. Vilnius: Valstybinė politinės ir mokslo literatūros leidykla.
Balkevičius, Jonas. 1998. *Lietuvių kalbos predikatinių konstrukcijų sintaksė* [The syntax of predicative constructions in Lithuanian]. Vilnius: Mokslo ir enciklopedijos leidybos institutas.
Balode, Laimute & Axel Holvoet. 2001a. The Lithuanian language and its dialects. In Dahl & Koptjevskaja-Tamm (eds.) 2001: 1, 41–79.
Balode, Laimute & Axel Holvoet. 2001b. The Latvian language and its dialects. In Dahl & Koptjevskaja-Tamm (eds.) 2001: 1, 3–40.
Balšaitytė, Danutė. 2004. Spektral'nye xarakteristiki glasnyx (monoftongov) sovremennogo litovskogo literaturnogo jazyka [Spectral characteristics of vowels in modern Lithuanian]. *Respectus philologicus* 5: 10. http://filologija.vukhf.lt/5-10/turinys.htm.
Bammesberger, Alfred. 1973. *Abstraktbildungen in den baltischen Sprachen*. Göttingen: Vandenhoeck & Ruprecht.
Barons, Krišjānis ([1894–1915] 1922). *Latvju dainas* [Latvian folksongs], Vols. 1–6. Rīga: Verlag F.Willmy.
Berger, Tilman & Daniel Weiss. 1987. Die Gebrauchsbedingungen des Anaphorikums 'tot' in substantivischer Verwendung. In Gerd Freidhof & Peter Kosta (eds.), *Slavistische Linguistik*, 9–93. München: Otto Sagner.
Berg-Olsen, Sturla. 1999. *A syntactic change in progress: The decline in the use of the non-prepositional genitive in Latvian, with a comparative view on Lithuanian*. Oslo University MA thesis.
Berg-Olsen, Sturla. 2000. The Latvian non-prepositional genitive – a case losing ground. *Res Balticae* 6: 95–146.
Berg-Olsen, Sturla. 2001. Subjects and valency-changing mechanisms in Latvian. *Sprachtypologie und Universalienforschung* 54(3): 209–225.
Berg-Olsen, Sturla. 2004. *The Latvian dative and genitive. A Cognitive Grammar account*: Oslo University dissertation.
Berg-Olsen, Sturla. 2009. Lacking in Latvian – Case variation from a Construction Grammar perspective. In Jóhanna Barðdal & Shobhana L. Chelliah (eds.) *The role of semantic, pragmatic, and discourse factors in the development of case*, 181–202. Amsterdam, Philadelphia: John Benjamins.

Bērzkalns, Anatolijs. 2007. *Latgaļu volūdas vōrdu krōjums* [A dictionary of Latgalian]. Rēzekne: Latgolas kulturas centra izdevnīceiba.
Bezzenberger, Adalbert. 1885. *Lettische Dialekt-Studien*. Goettingen: Vandenhoeck & Ruprecht.
Bezzenberger, Adalbert. 1888. *Über die Sprache der preussischen Letten*. Göttingen: Vandenhoeck & Ruprecht.
Bielenstein, August. 1863. *Lettische Grammatik*. Mitau: Fr. Lucas' Buchhandlung.
Birgiel, Nijole. 2002. *Procesy interferencyjne w mowie dwujęzycznej społeczności litewskiej z Puńska i okolic na Suwalszczyźnie*. [Processes of interference in the speech of the bilingual Lithuanian community in Puńsk and the region around Suwałki] Warszawa, Puńsk: Aušra.
Bisang, Walter, Nicolaus P. Himmelmann & Björn Wiemer (eds.). 2004. *What makes grammaticalization? Looks from its fringes and its components*. Berlin, New York: Mouton de Gruyter.
Blevins, Juliette. 1993. A tonal analysis of Lithuanian nominal accent. *Language* 69(2): 237–273.
Boeder, Winfried & Gerd Hentschel (eds.). 2001. *Variierende Markierung von Nominalgruppen in Sprachen unterschiedlichen Typs*. Oldenburg: Carl von Ossietzky Universität.
Boizou, Loïc. 2012. Do we need to count numerals as a part of speech in Lithuanian? In Usonienė, Nau & Dabašinskienė (eds.) 2012: 257–281.
Bond, Dzintra. 1978. Latvian long vowels and lengthened consonants: A study in phonetic interference. *Journal of Baltic Studies* 9(1): 73–79.
Bond, Dzintra. 1991. Vowel and word durations in Latvian. *Journal of Baltic Studies* 22(2): 133–144.
Bond, Dzintra. 1994a. Latvian syllable onsets and rhymes. *Linguistica Baltica* 3: 87–100.
Bond, Dzintra. 1994b. A note on the quality of Latvian vowels. *Journal of Baltic Studies* 25(1): 3–14.
Bond, Dzintra. 1998. Observations on intonational phrasing in Latvian. *Linguistica Baltica* 7: 33–50.
Bond, Dzintra, Dace Markus & Verna Stockmal. 2003. Evaluating native and non-native Latvian. *Journal of Baltic Studies* 34(2): 223–229.
Bond, Dzintra, Verna Stockmal & Dace Markus. 2006. Sixty years of bilingualism affects the pronunciation of Latvian vowels. *Language Variation and Change* 18(2): 165–177.
Brauner, S. 1961. Die Position Verbindung von 'beginnen' (bzw. 'aufhören') mit präfigierten Verben im Litauischen (Zur Frage des Verbalaspekts im Baltischen). *Zeitschrift für Slawistik* 6(2): 254–259.
Braunmüller, Kurt & Gisela Ferraresi (eds.). 2003. *Aspects of multilingualism in European language history*. Amsterdam, Philadelphia: John Benjamins.
Breidaks, Antons. [1966] 2007. *Augšzemnieku dialekta latgalisko izlokšņu dialektālā leksika un tās vēsturiskie sakari* [The dialectal lexicon of the Latgalian dialects of High Latvian and its historical connection]: University of Riga PhD dissertation. Reprinted in Breidaks, 2007: T. 1, 39–238.
Breidaks, Antons. [1989] 2007. *Fonetika latgal'skix govorov latyšskogo jazyka: diaxronija i sinxronija* [The Phonetics of the Latgalian dialects of Latvian: Diachrony and synchrony]. Habilitation, Vilnius University. Reprinted in Breidaks 2007: T. 1, 239–483.
Breidaks, Antons. 2007. *Darbu izlase* [Selected writing]], Vols. 1–2. Rīga: LU Latviešu valodas institūts.
Bühler, Karl. 1934. *Sprachtheorie: die Darstellungsfunktion der Sprache*. Jena: G. Fischer.
Bukšs, Miķelis. 1969. *Latgaļu-vōcu un vōcu-latgaļu vōrdneica: Latgalisch-deutsches und Deutsch-latgalisches Wörterbuch*. München: Latgaļu izdevnīceiba.
Bukšs, Miķelis & Jurs Placinskis. 1973. *Latgaļu volūdas gramatika un pareizraksteibas vōrdneica* [Latgalian grammar and orthographic dictionary]. München: Latgaļu izdevnīceiba.

Bulygina, Tat'jana V. 1970. Morfologičeskaja struktura slova v sovremennom litovskom jazyke (v ego pis'mennoj forme.) [Morphological structure of word in modern written Lithuanian]. In Viktor M. Žirmunskij & Nina D. Arutjunova (eds.) *Morfologičeskaja struktura slova v indoevropejskix jazykax* [Morphological structure of words in the Indo-European languages], 7–70. Moscow: Nauka.

Bulygina, Tat'jana V. 1977. *Problemy teorii morfologičeskix modelej* [Theoretical problems of morphological models]. Moscow: Nauka.

Bybee, Joan L. & Östen Dahl. 1989. The creation of tense and aspect systems in the languages of the world. *Studies in Language* 13(1): 51–103.

Bybee, Joan L., Revere D. Perkins & William Pagliuca. 1994. *The evolution of grammar. Tense, aspect, and modality in the languages of the world*. Chicago, London: The University of Chicago Press.

Campos-Astorkiza, Rebeka. 2012. Length contrast and contextual modifications of duration in the Lithuanian vowel system. *Baltic Linguistics* 3: 9–42.

Carstairs, Andrew. 1981. Review of Marvan 1978. *Linguistics* 19(5/6): 550–553.

Carstairs-McCarthy, Andrew. 2014. Affixes and stem alternants in Latvian noun inflection: A reply to Baerman. *Baltic Linguistics* 5: 59–80.

Ceplītis, Laimdots, Jānis Rozenbergs & Jānis Valdmanis. 1989. *Latviešu valodas sintakse* [Syntax of Latvian]. Rīga: Zvaigzne.

Cerri, Adriano. 2010. Morpho-syntactic behaviour of Baltic numerals in the Num-N phrase: Modern Lithuanian and Latvian. *Baltistica* 45(2): 185–204.

Cerri, Adriano. 2013. A proposito di indefinitezza nei costrutti numerali lettoni. *Res balticae* 12: 35–50.

LVSTK: *Latviešu valodas seno tekstu korpuss* [The Corpus of Early Written Latvian Texts]. http://www.korpuss.lv/senie/.

Chicouene, Michel & Laurynas-Algimantas Skūpas. 2003. *Parlons lituanien, une langue balte*. 2ème éd. Paris: L'Harmattan.

Chojnicka, Joanna. 2010. As if one were not enough: On the multiple functions of Latvian *it kā* 'as if, as though'. In Nau & Ostrowski (eds.) 2010: 39–72.

Chojnicka, Joanna. 2012a. Reportive evidentiality and reported speech: Is there a boundary? Evidence of the Latvian oblique. In Usonienė, Nau & Dabašinskienė (eds.) 2012: 170–192.

Chojnicka, Joanna. 2012b. *Linguistic markers of stance in Latvian parliamentary debates*. Saarbrücken: Lambert Academic Publishing.

Christen, Simon. 1995. *Morphologische und syntaktische Eigenschaften des Subjekts im Litauischen*: Bern University dissertation.

Christen, Simon. 1998. Unpersönliche Konstruktionen und sekundäre Personifizierung. *Linguistica Baltica* 7: 51–62.

Christen, Simon. 2001. Genitive positions in Baltic and Finnic languages. In Dahl & Koptjevskaja-Tamm (eds.) 2001: 2, 499–521.

Čižik, Veslava. 2003. Linksnių atrakcija lyginamosiose konstrukcijose [Case attraction in comparative constructions]. *Acta Linguistica Lithuanica* 48: 1–17.

Clair, Robert N. St. 1973. Lithuanian verb morphology. *Linguistics* 98: 68–87.

CorALit: The Corpus of Academic Lithuanian. http://coralit.lt/.

Corbett, Greville G. 1991. *Gender*. Cambridge: Cambridge University Press.

Corbett, Greville G. 2007. Gender and noun classes. In Timothy Shopen (ed.) *Language typology and syntactic description. Vol. III. Grammatical categories and the lexicon*, 241–279. 2nd edition. Cambridge: Cambridge University Press.

Dahl, Östen. 1985. *Tense and aspect systems*. Oxford: Blackwell.
Dahl, Östen. 2000. The tense-aspect systems of European languages in a typological perspective. In Östen Dahl (ed.) *Tense and aspect in the languages of Europe*, 3–25. Berlin, New York: Mouton de Gruyter.
Dahl, Östen & Maria Koptjevskaja-Tamm (eds.) 2001. *The Circum-Baltic languages. Typology and contact*, Vols. I–II. Amsterdam, Philadelphia: John Benjamins.
Dambriūnas, Leonardas. 1959. Verbal aspects in Lithuanian. *Lingua Posnaniensis* 7: 253–262.
Dambriūnas, Leonardas. 1960. *Lietuvių kalbos veiksmažodžių aspektai* [Verbal aspects in Lithuanian]. Boston: Lietuvių enciklopedijos leidykla.
Dambriūnas, Leonardas, Antanas Klimas & William R. Schmalstieg. 1966. *Introduction to Modern Lithuanian*. Brooklyn, New York: Franciscan Fathers.
Dambriūnas, Leonardas. 1975. Kelios pastabos dėl veikslų sampratos [Some remarks on the notion of aspect]. *Baltistica* 11(2): 171–179.
Danylenko, Andrii. 2005. Impersonal constructions with the accusative case in Lithuanian and Slavic (A reply to Axel Holvoet). *Zeitschrift für Slawistik* 50(2): 147–160.
Daugavet, Anna. 2008a. Secondary stress in Latvian compared to Lithuanian and Estonian. In Jowita Niewulis-Grablunas, Justyna Prusinowska & Ewa Stryczyńska-Hodyl (eds.) *Perspectives of Baltic Philology*, 41–48. Poznań: Rys.
Daugavet, Anna. 2008b. Slogovaja dolgota v latyšskom jazyke [Syllable length in Latvian]. *Jazyk i rečevaja dejatel'nost'* 8: 209–217.
Daugavet, Anna. 2009. *Slogovaja dolgota v baltijskix jazykax (v sopostavlenii s èstonskim i livskim)* [Syllable length in Baltic languages in comparison with Estonian and Livonian]: Saint-Petersburg State University dissertation.
Daugavet, Anna. 2010. Syllable length in Latvian and Lithuanian: Searching for the criteria. *Baltic Linguistics* 1: 83–114.
Daugavet, Anna. 2013. Geminacija soglasnyx v latyšskom jazyke: sledy pribaltijsko-finskogo vlijanija [Consonant gemination in Latvian: Traces of Fennic influence]. In Arkad'ev & Ivanov (eds.) 2013: 280–319.
Dini, Pietro U. 1997. *Le lingue baltiche*. Firenze: La Nuova Italia.
DLKG: Ambrazas, Vytautas (ed.). 1996. *Dabartinės lietuvių kalbos gramatika* [A grammar of modern Lithuanian]. Vilnius: Mokslo ir enciklopedijų leidykla.
DLKT: Dabartinės lietuvių kalbos tekstynas [The corpus of contemporary Lithuanian], http://tekstynas.vdu.lt/tekstynas/.
Dogil, Grzegorz. 1999a. The phonetic manifestation of word stress in Lithuanian, Polish, German and Spanish. In Harry van der Hulst (ed.) *Word prosodic systems in the languages of Europe*, 273–310. Berlin, New-York: Mouton de Gruyter.
Dogil, Grzegorz. 1999b. Baltic languages. In Harry van der Hulst (ed.) *Word prosodic systems in the languages of Europe*, 877–896. Berlin, New-York: Mouton de Gruyter.
Dogil, Grzegorz & Gregor Möhler. 1998. Phonetic invariance and phonological stability: Lithuanian pitch accents. In *Proceedings of the 5th International Conference on Spoken Language Processing (ICSLP)*, 75–86.
Dressler, Wolfgang U., Katarzyna Dziubalska-Kołaczyk & Lina Pestal. 2006. Change and variation in morphonotactics. *Folia Linguistica* 44(2): 51–67.
Dryer, Matthew S. 2013. Prefixing vs. suffixing in inflectional morphology. In Matthew S. Dryer & Martin Haspelmath (eds.) *The world atlas of language structures online*. Leipzig: Max Planck Institute for Evolutionary Anthropology. http://wals.info/chapter/26. Accessed on 2013-12-09.

Dudas, Karen. 1972. The accentuation of Lithuanian derived nominals. *Studies in the Linguistic Sciences* 2(2): 108–136.
Dudas, Karen & Margie O'Bryan. 1972. Lithuanian verbal accentuation. *Studies in the Linguistic Sciences* 2(2): 86–107.
Durys, Mykolas. 1927. *Lietuvių kalbos sintaksė* [Lithuanian syntax]. Kaunas: Spindulio spaustuvė.
Džežulskienė, Judita. 2001. Asmenų pavadinimai, reiškiami veiksmažodiniais mobiliaisiais daiktavardžiais (*substantiva mobilia*) [Person-denoting variable gender nouns]. *Acta Linguistica Lithuanica* 44: 55–69.
Džežulskienė, Judita. 2003. Lietuvių kalbos *substantiva mobilia* santykis su giminės kategorija [Lithuanian *substantiva mobilia* in relation to the category of gender]. In Norbert Ostrowski & Ona Vaičiulytė-Romančuk (eds.) *Prace Bałtystyczne. Język, literatura, kultura* [Baltic studies. Language, literature, culture], 11–21. Warszawa: Wydział Polonistyki UW.
Eckert, Rainer. 1996a. Zum Präteritum frequentativum im Litauischen und einer Entsprechung desselben im Lettischen. *Sborník prací Filozofické fakulty Brněnské Univerzity. Studia Minora Facultatis Philosophicae Universitatis Brunensis* A 44: 39–46.
Eckert, Rainer. 1996b. The analytic frequentative past in Samogitian and its typological correspondences. *Res Balticae* 2: 51–63.
Eckert, Rainer, Elvira-Julia Bukevičiūtė & Friedhelm Hinze. 1994. *Die baltischen Sprachen. Eine Einführung*. Leipzig: Langenscheidt.
Eiche, Aleksandra. 1983. *Latvian declinable and indeclinable participles. Their syntactic function, frequency and modality*. Stockholm: Almqvist & Wiksell.
Ekblom, Richard. 1933. *Die lettischen Akzentarten: Eine experimental-phonetische Untersuchung*. Uppsala: Almqvist & Wiksell.
Endzelīns [Endzelin], Jānis. 1923. *Lettische Grammatik*. Heidelberg: Carl Winter.
Endzelin and Hausenberg 1934–1946 = Jānis Endzelīns & Edīte Hauzenberga, *Papildinājumi un labojumi K. Mǖlenbacha Latviešu valodas vārdnīcai* [Additions and corrections to K. Mühlenbach's Latvian Dictionary]. Rīga: Kultūras Fonds, Vol. I, 1934–1938, Vol. II, 1946.
Endzelīns, Jānis. [1951] 1980. O latyšsko-finnskix jazykovyx svjazjax [On Latvian-Finnish linguistic relations]. In Boris A. Larin (ed.) *Pamjati Akademika L'va Vladimiroviča Ščerby (1880–1944)* [In memoriam academician Lev V. Ščerba], 299–305. Reprinted in: Endzelīns, Jānis. 1980. *Darbu izlase* [Selected writings] III-2, 416–422.
Fennell, Trevor G. 1971a. A phonological derivation of the forms of definite declension adjectives, reflexive nouns and reflexive verbs in Latvian. *Linguistics* 69: 24–32.
Fennell, Trevor G. 1971b. A new classification of first conjugation verbs in Latvian. *Linguistics* 72: 5–25.
Fennell, Trevor G. 1973. The subject of Latvian verbs in the debitive mood. In Arvids Ziedonis, Jaan Puhvel, Rimvydas Šilbajoris & Mardi Valgemäe (eds.) *Baltic Literature and Linguistics*, 213–221. Columbus: Association for the Advancement of Baltic Studies.
Fennell, Trevor G. 1975. Is there an instrumental case in Latvian? *Journal of Baltic Studies* 6(1): 41–48.
Fennell, Trevor G. 1986. Definitions and descriptions of first conjugation verbs in Latvian: A historical overview. *Journal of Baltic Studies* 17(2): 125–132.
Fennell, Trevor G. & Henry Gelsen. 1980. *A grammar of Modern Latvian*. 3 vols. The Hague: Mouton.
Flemming, Edward. 2005. Deriving natural classes in phonology. *Lingua* 115: 287–309.
Forssman, Berthold. 2001. *Lettische Grammatik*. Dettelbach: Röll.

Forssman, Berthold. 2003. *Das Baltische Adverb: Morphosemantik und Diachronie.* Heidelberg: Winter.
Fraenkel, Ernst. 1926. Der prädikative Instrumental im Slavischen und Baltischen und seine syntaktischen Grundlagen. *Archiv für slavische Philologie* 24: 77–117.
Fraenkel, Ernst. 1928. *Syntax der litauischen Kasus.* Kaunas: Valstybės spaustuvė.
Fraenkel, Ernst. 1929. *Syntax der litauischen Postpositionen und Präpositionen.* Heidelberg: Winter.
Fraenkel, Ernst. 1936. Der Stand der Erforschung des im Wilnagebiete gesprochenen Litauischen. *Balticoslavica* 2: 14–107.
Fraenkel, Ernst. 1955–1965. *Litauisches etymologisches Wörterbuch*, Bd. I-II (unter Mitarbeit von Annemarie Slupski, fortgeführt von Erich Hofmann und Eberhard Tangl). Heidelberg: Winter/Göttingen: Vandenhoeck & Ruprecht.
Franks, Stephen & James E. Lavine. 2006. Case and word order in Lithuanian. *Journal of Linguistics* 42(1): 239–288.
Galnaitytė, Elzė. 1962. Ginčytini lietuvių kalbos veiksmažodžių veikslo klausimai [Disputable questions of Lithuanian verbal aspect]. *Kalbotyra* 4: 119–138.
Galnajtite [Galnaitytė], Elzė. 1963. Osobennosti kategorii vida glagolov v litovskom jazyke (v sopostavlenii s russkim jazykom) [Peculiarities of the category of verbal aspect in Lithuanian in comparison with Russian]. *Kalbotyra* 7: 123–144.
Galnajtite [Galnaitytė], Elzė. 1966. K voprosu ob imperfektivacii glagolov v litovskom jazyke [On the imperfectivization of verbs in Lithuanian]. *Baltistica* 11(2): 147–158.
Galnaitytė, Elzė. 1979a. Dėl veiksmažodžių veikslų kategorijos pobūdžio [On the nature of the category of verbal aspect]. *Baltistica* 15(1): 46–51.
Galnajtite [Galnaitytė], Elzė. 1979b. K tipologii odnoaktnyx glagolov v russkom i litovskom jazykax [Towards a typology of semelfactive verbs in Russian and Lithuanian]. In *Voprosy russkoj aspektologii* IV: *Kategorija vida i ee funkcional'nye svjazi* [Problems of Russian aspectology. The category of aspect and its functional relations], 75–94. Tartu: Tartu University.
Galnajtite [Galnaitytė], Elzė. 1980. Tipologija kauzativnyx glagolov kak sposoba dejstvija (na materiale russkogo i litovskogo jazykov) [Typology of causative verbs as an Aktionsart in Russian and Lithuanian]. In *Voprosy russkoj aspektologii* V: *Aspektual'nost' i sredstva eë vyraženija* [Problems of Russian aspectology. Aspectuality and its expression], 100–114. Tartu: Tartu University.
Garde, Paul. 1968. *L'accent.* Paris: Presses universitaires de France.
Gast, Volker & Holger Diessel (eds.). 2012. *Clause linkage in cross-linguistic perspective: Data-driven approaches to cross-clausal syntax.* Berlin, New York: Mouton de Gruyter.
Gāters, Alfrēds. 1959. Das bestimmte Adjektiv im Baltischen. *Zeitschrift für die vergleichende Sprachforschung auf dem Gebiet der indogermanischen Sprachen* 76: 136–159.
Gāters, Alfrēds. 1977. *Die lettische Sprache und ihre Dialekte.* The Hague, Paris: Mouton.
Gāters, Alfrēds. 1993. *Lettische Syntax. Die Dainas.* Herausgegeben von Hildegard Radtke. Frankfurt a. M.: Peter Lang.
Geniušienė, Emma. 1974. Diatezy i zalogi v sovremennom litovskom jazyke [Diathesis and voice in modern Lithuanian]. In Alexandr A. Xolodovič (ed.) *Tipologija passivnyx konstrukcij. Diatezy i zalogi* [Typology of passive constructions. Diathesis and voice], 203–231. Leningrad: Nauka.
Geniušienė, Emma. 1976. Das Passiv des Litauischen und seine Verwendung. In Rudolf Ružička & Ronald Lötzsch (eds.), *Satzstruktur und Genus Verbi,* 139–152. Berlin: Akademie-Verlag.

Geniušienė, Emma. 1983. *Refleksivnye glagoly v baltijskix jazykax i tipologija refleksivov* [Reflexive verbs in Baltic languages and the typology of reflexives]. Vilnius: Ministerstvo Vysšego i Srednego Special'nogo Obrazovanija Litovskoj SSR.

Geniušienė, Emma. 1985. Dvupredikatnye fazovye konstrukcii v litovskom jazyke [Bipredicative phasal constructions in Lithuanian.] In Viktor S. Xrakovskij (ed.) *Tipologija konstrukcij s predikatnymi aktantami* [Typology of constructions with predicate arguments], 151–154. Leningrad: Nauka.

Geniušienė, Emma. 1987. *The typology of reflexives*. Berlin, New York: Mouton de Gruyter.

Geniušienė, Emma. 1989. Mul'tiplikativ i iterativ v litovskom jazyke [Multiplicative and iterative in Lithuanian]. In Viktor S. Xrakovskij (ed.) *Tipologija iterativnyx konstrukcij* [Typology of iterative constructions], 122–132. Leningrad: Nauka.

Geniušienė, Emma. 1997. The multiplicative and iterative in Lithuanian. In Viktor S. Xrakovskij (ed.) *Typology of iterative constructions*, 220–240. München, Newcastle: Lincom Europa.

Geniušienė, Emma. 2006. Passives in Lithuanian (in comparison with Russian). In Werner Abraham & Larisa Leisiö (eds.) *Passivization and typology. Form and function*, 29–61. Amsterdam, Philadelphia: John Benjamins.

Geniušienė, Emma. 2007. Reciprocal and reflexive constructions in Lithuanian (with references to Latvian). In Vladimir P. Nedjalkov (ed.) *Typology of reciprocal constructions*, Vol. II, 633–672. Amsterdam, Philadelphia: John Benjamins.

Geniušienė, Emma & Vladimir P. Nedjalkov. 1988. Resultative, passive, and perfect in Lithuanian. In Vladimir P. Nedjalkov (ed.) *Typology of resultative constructions*, 369–386. Amsterdam, Philadelphia: John Benjamins.

Geyer, Klaus. 2011. Diphthongology meets language documentation: The Finnish experience. In Geoffrey Haig, Nicole Nau, Stefan Schnell, & Claudia Wegener (eds.) *Documenting endangered languages (achievements and perspectives)*, 177–200. Berlin, New York: De Gruyter Mouton.

Giparaitė, Judita. 2010. *The non-verbal type of small clauses in English and Lithuanian*. Newcastle upon Tyne: Cambridge Scholars Publishing.

Girdenis, Aleksas. 1981. *Fonologija* [Phonology]. Vilnius: Mokslas.

Girdenis, Aleksas. [1995] 2003. *Teoriniai lietuvių fonologijos pagrindai* [The theoretical basis of Lithuanian phonology]. 2nd edition. Vilnius: Mokslo ir enciklopedijų leidybos insitutas.

Girdenis, Aleksas & Genovaitė Kačiuškienė. 1986. Paraleliniai reiškiniai latvių ir lietuvių veiksmažodžio sistemose [Parallel phenomena in the verbal systems of Latvian and Lithuanian]. *Kalbotyra* 37(1): 21–27.

Girdenis, Aleksas & Zigmas Zinkevičius. 1966. Dėl lietuvių tarmių klasifikacijos [On the classification of Lithuanian dialects]. *Kalbotyra* 14: 139–147.

Girdenis, Alexas (2014). *Theoretical foundations of Lithuanian phonology*. Transl. Steven Young. Vilnius: Eugrimas, 2014.

Gliwa, Bernd. 2003. Nešinas, vedinas, tekinas. *Acta Linguistica Lithuanica* 48: 19–34.

GLJa: Ambrazas, Vytautas et al. (eds.). 1985. *Grammatika litovskogo jazyka* [Grammar of Lithuanian]. Vilnius: Mokslas.

Greenberg, Gerald R. & James E. Lavine. 2006. New syntax in Russian and Lithuanian: The case of the adverbial participle. In Robert Rothstein, Ernest Scatton & Charles Townsend (eds.) *Studies in Slavic linguistics and folklore*, 143–170. Bloomington, IN: Slavica.

Grigorjevs, Juris. 2008. *Latviešu valodas patskaņu sistēmas akustisks un auditīvs raksturojums* [An acoustic and auditive characteristic of the Latvian vowel system]. Rīga: LU Latviešu valodas institūts.

Grigorjevs, Juris. 2012. Acoustic characteristics of the Latvian sonorants. *Baltistica* 47(2): 267–292.
Grinaveckienė, Elena. 1969. Lietuvių ir slavų kalbų gramatinio kontaktavimo reiškiniai pietryčių Lietuvoje [Phenomena of Lithuanian-Slavic grammatical contacts in South-Eastern Lithuania]. *Lietuvių kalbotyros klausimai* 11: 219–229.
Grīsle, Rasma. 1996/1997. The significance of Latvian syllable intonations: Heterotones. *Linguistica Baltica* 5(6): 81–88.
Grīsle, Rasma. 2008. *Heterotonu vārdnīca un heterotonijas pētījumi* [A dictionary of heterotones and studies in heterotones]. Rīga: Zinātne.
Gronemeyer, Claire & Aurelija Usonienė. 2001. Complementation in Lithuanian. In Claire Gronemeyer. *Laying the boundaries of syntax: Studies in the interfaces between syntax, semantics and lexicon*, 105–135. Lund University.
Gruzdeva, S. I. 1958. Atributivnye i predikativnye funkcii pričastija na -ęs v litovskom jazyke v sravnenii s russkimi konstrukcijami [Atributive and predicative functions of the Lithuanian participle in -ęs compared to Russian constructions]. *Učenye zapiski Leningradskogo Gosudarstvennogo Universiteta. Serija filologičeskix nauk* 38: 222–245.
Gudavičius [Gudavičjus], Aloyzas. 1985. *Sopostavitel'naja semasiologija litovskogo i russkogo jazykov* [Comparative semasiology of Lithuanian and Russian]. Vilnius: Mokslas.
Gudavičius, Aloyzas. 2007. *Gretinamoji semantika* [Contrastive semantics]. Šiauliai: Šiaulių universiteto leidykla.
Halle, Morris. 1986. The morphophonemics of Latvian declension. In Robert Channon & Linda Shockey (eds.) *In honor of Ilse Lehiste*, 375–380. Dordrecht: Foris.
Halle, Morris. 1992. Latvian declension. In Geert Booij & Jaap van der Marle (eds.) *Morphology Yearbook 1991*, 33–47. Dordrecht: Kluwer.
Halle, Morris & Jean-Roger Vergnaud. 1987. *An essay on stress*. Cambridge, MA: MIT Press.
Haspelmath, Martin. 1997. *Indefinite pronouns*. Oxford: Oxford University Press.
Haspelmath, Martin. 2001. The European linguistic area: Standard Average European. In Martin Haspelmath, Ekkehard König, Wulf Oesterreicher & Wolfgang Raible (eds.) *Language typology and language universals: An international handbook*, Vol. 2, 1492–1510. Berlin, New York: De Gruyter.
Haspelmath, Martin & Matthew Dryer (eds.) 2013. *The world atlas of language structures online*. Leipzig: Max Planck Institute for Evolutionary Anthropology. http://wals.info.
Haspelmath, Martin, Matthew Dryer, David Gil, & Bernard Comrie (eds.). 2005. *The world atlas of language structures*. Oxford: Oxford University Press.
Hawkins, John. 1983. *Word order universals*. New York, London: Academic Press.
Hauzenberga-Šturma, Edīte. 1979. Zur Frage des Verbalaspekts im Lettischen. *Zeitschrift für vergleichende Sprachforschung* 93: 279–316.
Heeschen, Claus F. E. 1968. *Einführung in die Grundprobleme der generativen Phonologie mit besonderer Berücksichtigung der litauischen Phonologie*. Bonn: Universität Bonn.
Hilbig, Inga. 2008. Mandagumas kaip reliatyvus kalbinis, socialinis ir kultūrinis reiškinys [Politeness as a relative linguistic, social and cultural phenomenon]. *Acta Linguistica Lithuanica* 58: 1–15.
Holst, Jan Henrik. 2001. *Lettische Grammatik*. Hamburg: Helmut Buske.
Holvoet, Axel. 1991. *Transitivity and clause structure in Polish (A study in case marking)*. Warszawa: Slawistyczny Ośrodek Wydawniczy.
Holvoet, Axel. 1992. Bemerkungen über die Entwicklung des lettischen Kasussystems: der Instrumental. In Wojciech Smoczyński & Axel Holvoet (eds.) *Colloquium Pruthenicum Primum*, 143–149. Warszawa: Wydawnictwa Uniwersytetu Warszawskiego.

Holvoet, Axel. 1993. On the syntax and semantics of adpositional local phrases in Latvian. *Linguistica Baltica* 2: 131–149.
Holvoet, Axel. 1994. Notes on the Latvian passive. *Linguistica Baltica* 3: 131–140.
Holvoet, Axel. 1995. Indefinite zero subjects in Latvian. *Linguistica Baltica* 4: 153–161.
Holvoet, Axel. 1998. On the rise and grammaticalisation of the Latvian debitive. *Linguistica Baltica* 7: 101–118.
Holvoet, Axel. 1999. Infinitival relative clauses in Baltic and Slavonic. *Baltistica* 34(1): 37–53.
Holvoet, Axel. 2000a. Perfectivisation in Latvian. *Linguistica Baltica* 8: 89–102.
Holvoet, Axel. 2000b. Infinitival relative clauses in Latvian: Their structure, development and tendency toward lexicalisation. *Linguistica Lettica* 7: 99–116.
Holvoet, Axel. 2000c. Lietuvių dativus cum infinitivo ir latvių infinityviniai santykiniai sakiniai [Lithuanian dative with infinitive and Latvian infinitival relative clauses]. *Acta Linguistica Lithuanica* 42: 105–113.
Holvoet, Axel. 2000d. Once more the Baltic genitive of agent. *Baltistica* 35(1): 45–58.
Holvoet, Axel. 2000e. Reflexiva typu słowiańskiego w pewnej gwarze górnołotewskiej [Reflexive verbs of the Slavic type in a High Latvian vernacular]. In Ewa Wolnicz-Pawłowska & Wanda Szulowska (eds.) *Kontakty językowe polszczyzny na pograniczu wschodnim (Prace ofiarowane Profesorowi Januszowi Riegerowi)* [Polish language contacts at the Eastern borderland region (Studies offered to Professor Janusz Rieger], 97–102. Warszawa: Semper.
Holvoet, Axel. 2001a. *Studies in the Latvian verb*. Kraków: Wydawnictwo Uniwersytetu Jagiellońskiego.
Holvoet, Axel. 2001b. Lithuanian *būti* with the infinitive as a modal expression and its Latvian counterparts. *Acta Linguistica Lithuanica* 44: 71–87.
Holvoet, Axel. 2001c. On the paradigm of the oblique mood in Lithuanian and Latvian. *Linguistica Baltica* 9: 69–81.
Holvoet, A. 2001d. Why are prepositional phrases ousted by pure case forms in Latvian? *Linguistica Baltica* 9: 87–98.
Holvoet, Axel. 2001e. Impersonals and passives in Baltic and Finnic. In Dahl & Koptjevskaja-Tamm (eds.) 2001, 2: 363–390.
Holvoet, Axel. 2001f. Zur Variation des possessiven Dativs mit dem adnominalen Genitiv im Baltischen (besonders im Lettischen). In Winfried Boeder & Gerd Hentschel (eds.), *Variierende Markierung von Nominalgruppen in Sprachen unterschiedlichen Typs*, 201–217. Oldenburg: Bibliotheks- und Informationssystem der Universität Oldenburg.
Holvoet, Axel. 2003a. Notes on possessive constructions in Baltic. In Norbert Ostrowski & Ona Vaičiulytė-Romančuk (eds.) *Prace Bałtystyczne. Język, literatura, kultura* [Baltic studies. Language, literature, culture], 36–44. Warszawa: Uniwersytet Warszawski, wydział polonistyki.
Holvoet, Axel. 2003b. Modal constructions with 'be' and the infinitive in Slavonic and Baltic. *Zeitschrift für Slawistik* 48(4): 465–480.
Holvoet, Axel. 2004a. On the marking of predicate nominals in Baltic. In Baldi & Dini (eds.) 2004: 75–90.
Holvoet, Axel. 2004b. Eine modale Konstruktion ostseefinnischer Herkunft im Lettischen. In Irma Hyvärinen, Petro Kallio & Jarmo Korhonen (eds.) *Etymologie, Entlehnungen und Entwicklungen. Festschrift für Jorma Koivulehto zum 70. Geburtstag*, 117–127. Helsinki: Société Néophilologique.

Holvoet, Axel. 2005a. Agreement strategies in infinitival clauses in Baltic. In Norbert Ostrowski & Ona Vaičiulytė-Romančuk (eds.) *Prace Bałtystyczne* [Baltic studies] 2, 31–41. Warszawa: Uniwersytet Warszawski, wydział polonistyki.
Holvoet, Axel. 2005b. Evidentialität, Modalität und interpretative Verwendung. In Björn Hansen & Petr Karlík (eds.) *Modality in Slavonic Languages (New Perspectives)*, 95–105. München: Sagner.
Holvoet, Axel. 2006. Dėl galūnių ir kamiengalių [About endings and thematic vowels]. *Acta Linguistica Lithuanica* 55: 112–116.
Holvoet, Axel. 2007. *Mood and modality in Baltic*. Kraków: Wydawnictwo Uniwersytetu Jagiellońskiego.
Holvoet, Axel. 2008. Secondary predicates in Baltic. In Christian Schroeder, Gerd Hentschel, & Winfried Boeder (eds.) *Secondary predicates in Eastern European languages and beyond*, 125–140. Oldenburg: BIS-Verlag der Carl von Ossietzky-Universität.
Holvoet, Axel. 2009. Modals in Baltic. In Björn Hansen & Ferdinand de Haan (eds.) *Modals in the languages of Europe. A reference work*, 199–228. Berlin, New York: Mouton de Gruyter.
Holvoet, Axel. 2010a. Between morphosyntax and the paradigm: Some puzzling patterns of case distribution in Baltic and their implications. *Acta Linguistica Hafniensia* 42(2): 175–198.
Holvoet, Axel. 2010b. Mood in Latvian and Lithuanian. In Björn Rothstein & Rolf Thieroff (eds.) *Mood in the languages of Europe*, 425–443. Amsterdam, Philadelphia: John Benjamins.
Holvoet, Axel. 2010c. Notes on complementisers in Baltic. In Nau & Ostrowski, eds. 2010: 73–101.
Holvoet, Axel. 2011a. Beyond external possession: Genitive and dative with locational nouns in Latvian. *Baltic Linguistics* 2: 79–107.
Holvoet, Axel. 2011b. The Baltic languages. In Bernd Kortmann & Johan van der Auwera (eds.) *The languages and linguistics of Europe. A comprehensive guide*, 3–29. Berlin, New York: Mouton de Gruyter.
Holvoet, Axel. 2012. Vocative agreement in Latvian and the principle of morphology-free syntax. *Baltic Linguistics* 3: 43–64.
Holvoet, Axel. 2013. Obliqueness, quasi-subjects and transitivity in Baltic and Slavonic. In Ilja Seržant & Leonid Kulikov (eds.) *The diachronic typology of non-prototypical subjects*, 257–282. Amsterdam, Philadelphia: John Benjamins.
Holvoet, Axel. 2014. Phasal and proximative complementation: Lithuanian *baigti*. *Baltic Linguistics* 5: 81–122.
Holvoet, Axel. Forthcoming a. Lithuanian inflection. In Matthew Baerman (ed.) *The Oxford handbook of inflection*. Oxford: Oxford University Press.
Holvoet, Axel. Forthcoming b. Semantic functions of complementizers in Baltic. In Kasper Boye & Petar Kehayov (eds.) *Semantic functions of complementizers in European languages*. Berlin, Boston: De Gruyter Mouton.
Holvoet, Axel. Forthcoming c. Extended uses of Latvian causatives. In Axel Holvoet & Nicole Nau (eds.) *Voice and argument structure in Baltic*. Amsterdam, Philadelphia: John Benjamins.
Holvoet, Axel & Veslava Čižik. 2004. Veikslo priešpriešos tipai [Types of aspectual oppositions]. In Axel Holvoet & Loreta Semėnienė (eds.) *Gramatinių kategorijų tyrimai* [Studies in grammatical categories], 141–162. Vilnius: Lietuvių kalbos institutas.
Holvoet, Axel & Marta Grzybowska. 2014. Modality and non-canonical grammatical relations: The Latvian debitive. In Holvoet & Nau (eds.) 2014b: 97–136.

Holvoet, Axel & Artūras Judžentis (eds.). 2003. *Lietuvių kalbos gramatikos darbai, 1. Sintaksinių ryšių tyrimai* [Studies in Lithiuanian grammar 1. Studies of syntactic relations]. Vilnius: Lietuvių kalbos institutas.

Holvoet, Axel & Jelena Konickaja. 2011. Interpretive deontics. A definition and a semantic map based on Slavonic and Baltic data. *Acta Linguistica Hafniensia* 43(1): 1–20.

Holvoet, Axel & Rolandas Mikulskas (eds.). 2005. *Lietuvių kalbos gramatikos darbai. 3. Gramatinių funkcijų tyrimai* [Studies in Lithuanian grammar 3. Studies in grammatical functions]. Vilnius: Lietuvių kalbos institutas.

Holvoet, Axel & Rolandas Mikulskas (eds.). 2006. *Lietuvių kalbos gramatikos darbai. 4. Daiktavardinio junginio tyrimai* [Studies in Lithuanian grammar 4. Studies in the noun phrase]. Vilnius: Lietuvių kalbos institutas.

Holvoet, Axel & Rolandas Mikulskas (eds.). 2009. *Gramatinių funkcijų prigimtis ir raiška* [Nature and expression of grammatical functions]. Vilnius: Vilnius University.

Holvoet, Axel & Nicole Nau. 2014a. Argument marking and grammatical relations in Baltic: An overview. In Holvoet & Nau (eds.) 2014b: 1–41.

Holvoet, Axel & Nicole Nau (eds.). 2014b. *Grammatical relations and their non-canonical encoding in Baltic*. Amsterdam, Philadelphia: John Benjamins.

Holvoet, Axel & Loreta Semėnienė. 2004a. Rūšies kategorija: mediumas ir pasyvas [The category of voice: Middle and passive]. In Axel Holvoet & Loreta Semėnienė (eds.) *Gramatinių kategorijų tyrimai* [Studies in grammatical categories], 35–60. Vilnius: Lietuvių kalbos institutas.

Holvoet, Axel & Loreta Semėnienė (eds). 2004b. *Gramatinių kategorijų tyrimai* [Studies in grammatical categories]. Vilnius: Lietuvių kalbos institutas.

Holvoet, Axel & Birutė Spraunienė. 2012. Towards a semantic map of definite adjectives in Baltic. *Baltic Linguistics* 3: 65–100.

Holvoet, Axel & Aurelija Tamulionienė. 2006. Apibrėžtumo kategorija [Category of definiteness]. In Holvoet & Mikulskas (eds.) 2006: 11–32.

Holvoet, Axel, Marta Grzybowska & Agnieszka Rembiałkowska. Forthcoming. Middle voice reflexives and argument structure in Baltic. In Axel Holvoet & Nicole Nau (eds.) *Voice and argument structure in Baltic*, Amsterdam-Philadelphia: John Benjamins.

Hoskovec, Tomáš. 2002. Fonologický inventář a jeho morfonologické třídení. Obecná metodologická rozvaha nad konkrétním materiálem jazyka litevského [The phonological inventory and its morphophonological alternations. General methodological considerations on the basis of Lithuanian data]. *Slavia* 71: 267–300.

Hume, Elizabeth & Misun Seo. 2004. Metathesis in Faroese and Lithuanian: From speech perception to Optimality Theory. *Nordic Journal of Linguistics* 27(1): 35–60.

Jablonskis, Jonas [Rygiškių Jonas]. [1922] 1957. *Lietuvių kalbos gramatika. Etimologija (Vidurinėms mokslo įstaigoms)* [A grammar of Lithuanian. Etymology. For middle schools]. Kaunas: Švyturys. Reprinted in: Jonas Jablonskis (1957): *Rinktiniai raštai* [Collected writings] I, 183–433. Vilnius: Valstybinės politinės ir mokslinės literatūros leidykla.

Jakaitienė, Evalda. 2005. *Leksikografija* [Lexicography]. Vilnius: Mokslo ir enciklopedijų leidybos institutas.

Jakaitienė, Evalda. 2010. *Leksikologija (Studijų knyga)* [Lexicology. A course book]. Vilnius: Vilniaus universiteto leidykla.

Jasionytė, Erika. 2012. Lithuanian impersonal modal verbs *reikėti* 'need' and *tekti* 'be gotten': A corpus-based study. In Usonienė, Nau & Dabašinskienė (eds.) 2012: 206–228.

Javnis, Kazimir (= Jaunius, Kazimieras). 1908–1916. *Grammatika litovskago jazyka* [A grammar of Lithuanian]. Petrograd: Tipografija Imperatorskoj Akademii nauk.
Joseph, John E. 2009. Why Lithuanian accentuation mattered to Saussure. *Language and History* 52(2): 182–198.
Judžentis, Artūras. 2002a. Naujas žvilgsnis į lietuvių kalbos daiktavardžių giminės kategoriją [A new look at the category of nominal gender in Lithuanian]. *Acta Linguistica Lithuanica* 46: 39–47.
Judžentis, Artūras. 2002b. Mikalojaus Daukšos *Katekizmo* (1595) sudėtiniai aiškinamieji sakiniai [Complement clauses in Mikalojus Daukša's "Catechism"]. *Acta Linguistica Lithuanica* 47: 19–29.
Judžentis, Artūras & Jūratė Pajėdienė. 2001. Mikalojaus Daukšos *Katekizmo* (1595) sudėtiniai sujungiamieji sakiniai [Coordinated clauses in Mikalojus Daukša's "Catechism"]. *Acta Linguistica Lithuanica* 45: 63–92.
Judžentis, Artūras & Jūratė Pajėdienė. 2005. M. Daukšos *Katekizmo* (1595) lyginamieji sakiniai [Comparative constructions in Mikalojus Daukša's "Catechism"]. *Acta Linguistica Lithuanica* 53: 23–31.
Kabašinskaitė, Birutė. 1998. *Lietuvių kalbos liaudies etimologija ir artimi reiškiniai* [Lithuanian folk etymology and related phenomena]. Vilnius: Mokslo ir enciklopedijų leidybos institutas.
Kagaine, Elga & Ojārs Bušs. 1985. Semantiskas paralēles (galvenokārt baltu un baltijas somu valodās) [Semantic parallels, principally between Baltic and Baltic Finnic]. *Baltistica* 21(1): 14–36.
Kalėdaitė, Violeta. 2002. *Existential sentences in English and Lithuanian. A contrastive study*. Frankfurt am Main: Peter Lang.
Kalėdaitė, Violeta. 2008. Language-specific existential sentence types: A case study of Lithuanian. *Kalbotyra* 59(3): 128–137.
Kalėdaitė, Violeta. 2012. The specifying existential sentence type in Lithuanian: A problem statement. In Usonienė, Nau & Dabašinskienė (eds.) (2012), 193–205.
Kalnača, Andra. 2004. *Morfēmika un morfonoloģija* [Morphemics and morphophonology]. Rīga: LU Akadēmiskais apgāds.
Kalnača, Andra & Ilze Lokmane. 2010. Defective paradigms of reflexive nouns and participles in Latvian. In Matthew Baerman, Greville Corbett, & Dunstan Brown (eds.) *Defective paradigms: Missing forms and what they tell us*, 53–68. Oxford: Oxford University Press.
Kalnača, Andra & Ilze Lokmane. 2012. The semantics and distribution of Latvian reflexive verbs. In Usonienė, Nau & Dabašinskienė (eds.) 2012: 229–256.
Kaltenböck, Gunther. 2007. Spoken parenthetical clauses in English. A taxonomy. In Nicole Dehé & Yordanka Kavalova (eds.) *Parentheticals*, 25–52. Amsterdam, Philadelphia: John Benjamins.
Kamandulytė, Laura. 2006a. The acquisition of morphotactics in Lithuanian. *Wiener Linguistische Gazette* 73: 88–96.
Kamandulytė, Laura. 2006b. *Acquisition of Lithuanian adjective: Lexical and morphosyntactic features*: Kaunas University dissertation summary.
Kardelis, Vytautas. 2003. *Rytų aukštaičių šnektų fonologijos bruožai* [Phonological characteristics of Eastern Aukštaitian dialects]. Vilnius: Vilniaus universitetas.
Kardelis, Vytautas. 2006. Įvadas [Introduction]. In Vytautas Kardelis, Daiva Kardelytė-Grinevičienė, Agnė Navickaitė & Inga Strungytė. *Šiaurės rytų aukštaičiai vilniškiai* [Northeastern Aukštaitian dialects of the Vilnius region], 12–44. Vilnius: Mokslo ir enciklopedijų leidybos institutas.

Kardelis, Vytautas. 2009. *Šiaurės rytų aukštaičiai vilniškiai: ribos ir diferenciacija* [Northeastern Aukštaitian dialects of the Vilnius region: Borders and differentiation]. Vilnius: Vilniaus universitetas.
Kardelis, Vytautas. 2013. Dar dėl rytų aukštaičių vilniškių patarmės ribų [More on the borders of the Northeastern Aukštaitian subdialects of the Vilnius region]. *Lietuvių kalba* 7: 1–22.
Kardelis, Vytautas & Björn Wiemer. 2002. Ausbildung von Aspektpaarigkeit in litauischen Grenz- und Inseldialekten (am Beispiel von Sprechverben). *Linguistica Baltica* 10: 51–80.
Kardelis, Vytautas & Björn Wiemer. 2003. Kritische Bemerkungen zur Praxis der Erstellung litauischer Wörterbücher, insbesondere von Mundarten – am Beispiel des slavischen Lehnguts und des 'veikslas'. In Norbert Ostrowski & Ona Vaičiulytė-Romančuk (eds.) *Prace Bałtystyczne. Język, literatura, kultura* [Baltic studies. Language, literature, culture], 45–72. Warszawa: Wydział Polonistyki, Wydawnictwo Uniwersytetu Warszawskiego.
Kariņš, A. Krišjānis. 1995. Vowel deletion in Latvian. *Language Variation and Change* 7(1): 15–34.
Kariņš, A. Krišjānis. 1996. *The Prosodic Structure of Latvian*: PhD thesis, University of Pennsylvania.
Karjus, Andres. 2012. Outdoors on the shores of the Baltic: Gradience in the grammaticalization of the exterior region. *Esuka-Jeful* 3(1), 209–225.
Karosienė, Vida. 2004. *Bendrinės lietuvių kalbos vardažodžio šaknies struktūra* [The structure of nominal roots in standard Lithuanian]. Vilnius: Vilniaus universitetas.
Karulis, Konstantīns. 1992. *Latviešu etimoloģijas vārdnīca divos sējumos* [Latvian etymological dictionary in two volumes]. Rīga: Avots.
Kaukienė, Audronė. 1994. *Lietuvių kalbos veiksmažodžio istorija* I [The history of the Lithuanian verb I]. Klaipėda: Klaipėdos universitetas.
Kaukienė, Audronė. 2002. *Lietuvių kalbos veiksmažodžio istorija* II [The history of the Lithuanian verb II]. Klaipėda: Klaipėdos universitetas.
Kaukienė, Audronė & Erdvilas Jakulis. 2009. *Bendrieji baltų kalbų veiksmažodžiai* [The common Baltic verbs]. Klaipėda: Klaipėdos universitetas.
Kavaliūnaitė, Gina. 2001. Adesyvas Chylinskio Naujojo Testamento vertime [The adessive case in Chylinski's New Testament]. *Acta Linguistica Lithuanica* 45: 93–111.
Kavaliūnaitė, Gina. 2002. Die postpositionalen Lokalkasus in Chylinskis' Übersetzung des Neuen Testaments. *Linguistica Baltica* 10: 81–97.
Kavaliūnaitė, Gina. 2003. Postpozicinių vietininkų sistema Chylinskio Naujojo Testamento vertime [The system of postpositional locative cases in Chylinskis' translation of the New Testament]. *Acta Linguistica Lithuanica* 49: 33–49.
Kazlauskas, Jonas [1972] 2000. Įvardžiuotinių būdvardžių raida baltų kalbose [The origin of pronominalized adjectives in Baltic]. *Kalbotyra* 24(1): 57–74. Reprinted in: Kazlauskas 2000b: 179–196.
Kazlauskas, Jonas. [1968] 2000a. *Rinktiniai raštai, Vol. I: Lietuvių kalbos istorinė gramatika* [Collected writings I. A historical grammar of Lithuanian]. Vilnius: Mokslo ir enciklopedijų leidybos institutas. Reprint of: Kazlauskas, Jonas. 1968. *Lietuvių kalbos istorinė gramatika*. Vilnius: Mintis.
Kazlauskas, Jonas. 2000b. *Rinktiniai raštai, II: Straipsniai. Recenzijos. Kalbos kultūra* [Collected writings II. Articles, reviews, language culture]. Vilnius: Mokslo ir enciklopedijų leidybos institutas.
Kenstowicz, Michael. 1972. Lithuanian phonology. *Studies in the Linguistic Sciences* 2(2): 1–85.
Kerevičienė, Jurgita. 2004. External possession in Lithuanian. *Acta Linguistica Lithuanica* 50: 25–33.

Kerevičienė, Jurgita. 2008. *The Lithuanian dative and its English counterparts (A case study in Cognitive grammar)*: Vilnius University PhD dissertation.
Kibildaitė, Edita. 2001. Priežasties šalutiniai sakiniai Bretkūno postilėje [Causal subordinate clauses in Bretke's Postilla]. *Acta Linguistica Lithuanica* 44: 129–144.
Kibrik, Andrej A. 1987. Mexanizmy ustranenija referencial'nogo konflikta [Mechanisms of referential conflict resolution]. In Aleksandr E. Kibrik & Aleksandr S. Narin'jani (eds.) *Modelirovanie jazykovoj dejatel'nosti v intellektual'nyx sistemax* [Modelling linguistic processing in intellectual systems], 128–145. Moscow: Nauka.
Kibrik, Andrej A. 2011. *Reference in discourse*. Oxford: Oxford University Press.
Klaas, Birute. 1996. Similarities in case marking of syntactic relations in Estonian and Lithuanian. In Mati Erelt (ed.) *Estonian: Typological Studies. I*, 37–67. Tartu: Tartu University.
Klimas, Antanas. 1975. Word-formation in Lithuanian. In Helmut Rix (ed.), *Flexion und Wortbildung*, 130–147. Wiesbaden: Reichert.
Klimas, Antanas. 1993. The two kinds of passive voice in Lithuanian. *Lituanus* 39(3).
Klimas, Antanas. 1994. Reflexive nouns in Lithuanian. *Lituanus* 40(3).
Koptjevskaja-Tamm, Maria & Bernhard Wälchli. 2001. The Circum-Baltic languages: An areal-typological approach. In Dahl & Koptjevskaja-Tamm (eds.) 2001, 2: 615–750.
Kortmann, Bernd & Johan van der Auwera (eds.). 2011. *The languages and linguistics of Europe. A comprehensive guide*. Berlin, New York: Mouton de Gruyter.
Kozhanov, Kirill. 2011. Notes on the use of Lithuanian indefinite pronouns. *Baltic Linguistics* 2: 79–110.
Kundrotas, Gintautas. 2002. Vzaimodejstvie intonacii i grammatiki v russkom i litovskom jazykax [Interaction of intonation and grammar in Russian and Lithuanian]. *Žmogus ir žodis* 3: 23–27.
Kundrotas, Gintautas. 2003. Funkcional'nye vozmožnosti intonacionnogo centra (v litovskom i russkom jazykax) [Functional load of intonation center in Lithuanian and Russian]. *Žmogus ir žodis* 3: 10–17.
Kundrotas, Gintautas. 2004. Lietuvių kalbos intonacija: teorija ir praktika [Lithuanian intonation: Theory and practice]. *Žmogus ir žodis* 1: 13–19.
Kundrotas, Gintautas. 2008. Lietuvių kalbos intonacinių kontūrų fonetiniai požymiai (eksperimentinis-fonetinis tyrimas) [Phonetic features of intonation contours in Lithuanian: An experimental study]. *Žmogus ir žodis* 1: 43–55.
Labutis, Vitas. 1976. *Žodžių junginių problemos* [Problems of phrase structure]. Vilnius: Vilnius University.
Labutis, Vitas. 1998. *Lietuvių kalbos sintaksė* [The syntax of Lithuanian]. Vilnius: Vilnius University.
Lagzdiņa, Sarmīte. 1998. Adverbien, Präpositionen oder Halbpräpositionen? *Linguistica Baltica* 7: 151–166.
Larin, Boris A. 1963. Ob odnoj slavjano-balto-finskoj izoglosse [On a Slavic-Baltic-Finnic isogloss.] *Lietuvių kalbotyros klausimai* 6: 87–107.
Larsson, Jenny Helena. 2002. Nominal compounds in the Baltic languages. *Transactions of the Philological Society* 100(2): 203–231.
Laua, Alise. [1969] 1997. *Latviešu literārās valodas fonētika* [The phonetics of standard Latvian]. 4th revised and extended edition. Rīga: Zvaigzne.
Laumane, Benita (ed.). 1999. *Latviešu valodas dialektu atlants. Leksika* [Latvian dialect atlas. Vocabulary]. Rīga: Zinātne.

Lavine, James E. 1999. Subject properties and ergativity in North Russian and Lithuanian. In Katarzyna Dziwirek, Herbert Coats & Cynthia Vakareliyska (eds.) *Formal approaches to Slavic linguistics 7*, 307–328. Ann Arbor: Michigan Slavic Publications.

Lavine, James E. 2006. Is there a passive evidential strategy in Lithuanian? *Papers from the 42nd Regional Meeting of the Chicago Linguistic Society*, 41–55.

Lavine, James E. 2010. Mood and a transitivity restriction in Lithuanian: The case of the inferential evidential. *Baltic Linguistics* 1: 115–142.

Lehmann, Volkmar. 2004. Grammaticalization via extending derivation. In Bisang, Himmelmann & Wiemer (eds.) 2004: 169–186.

Leikuma, Lideja. 2003. *Latgalīšu volūda. 1. Intensīvā mācību kursa materiāli* [Latgalian language. Intensive study course materials]. Sanktpēterburga: Sanktpēterburgas valsts universitāte.

Lelis, Joseph. 1961. *The place of Latgalian among the Baltic dialects*: PhD Thesis, Harvard University.

Lelis, Joseph. 1970. Noun declensions in the Kõrsovan subdialect of Latvian. In Thomas F. Magner & William R. Schmalstieg (eds.) *Baltic linguistics*, 103–108. University Park and London: The Pennsylvania State University Press.

Lenartaitė, Kristina. 2007. Lietuvių kalbos argumentų raiškos alternacijos ir aplikacinės gramatikos priemonės joms aiškinti [Alternations in argument expression in Lithuanian and its explanations in Applicative Grammar]. *Acta Linguistica Lithuanica* 57: 17–44.

Lenartaitė, Kristina. 2009. Diatezės alternacijos iš skirtingų teorinių modelių tyrimų perspektyvos [Diathesis alternations from different theoretical perspectives]. *Acta Linguistica Lithuanica* 61: 61–112.

Lenartaitė, Kristina. 2011. *Argumentų raiškos alternavimas lietuvių kalboje* [Alternations in argument expression in Lithuanian]: Vilnius University unpublished PhD thesis.

Lenartaitė-Gotaučienė, Kristina. 2014. Alternations in argument realisation and problematic cases of subjecthood in Lithuanian. In Holvoet & Nau (eds.) 2014: 137–180.

Leskien, August. 1876. *Die Declination im Slavisch-Litauischen und Germanischen*. Leipzig: Fürstlich Jablonowski'sche Gesellschaft.

Leskien, August. 1884. Der Ablaut in den Wurzelsilben im Litauischen. *Abhandlungen der Phil.-Hist. Klasse der Königl. Sächsischen Gesellschaft der Wissenschaften* 9(4): 263–454.

Leskien, August. 1891. Die Bildung der Nomina im Litauischen. *Abhandlungen der Phil.-Hist. Klasse der Königl. Sächsischen Gesellschaft der Wissenschaften* 12(3): 151–618.

Levin, Jules F. 1979. The Lithuanian definite adjective as syntax and as semiotic. *Journal of Baltic Studies* 10(2): 152–161.

LG: Ambrazas, Vytautas (ed.). [1997] 2006. *Lithuanian grammar*. Vilnius: Baltos lankos.

Lichtenberk, František. 1991. Semantic change and heterosemy in grammaticalization. *Language* 67(3): 475–509.

LILA: Lygiagretusis lietuvių-latvių-lietuvių tekstynas [The parallel Lithuanian-Latvian-Lithuanian corpus]. http://tekstynas.vdu.lt/page.xhtml?id=parallelLILA

LKA: Morkūnas, Kazys et al. *Lietuvių kalbos atlasas* [Atlas of Lithuanian language], t. 1: *Leksika* [Lexicon] (1977); t. 2: *Fonetika* [Phonetics] (1982); t. 3: *Morfologija* [Morphology] (1991). Vilnius: Mokslas.

LKG: Ulvydas, Kazys (ed.). 1965, 1971, 1976. *Lietuvių kalbos gramatika* [Grammar of Lithuanian]. T. I: *Fonetika ir morfologija* [Phonetics and morphology]. Vilnius: Mintis. II. *Morfologija* [Morphology]. Vilnius: Mintis. III. *Sintaksė* [Syntax]. Vilnius: Mokslas.

LKT: Grinaveckienė, Elena & Kazys Morkūnas (eds.). 1970. *Lietuvių kalbos tarmės (Chrestomatija)* [A reader in Lithuanian dialects]. Vilnius: Mintis.
LKTCh: Bacevičiūtė, Rima & Laima Grumadienė (eds.). 2004. *Lietuvių kalbos tarmių chrestomatija* [A reader in Lithuanian dialects]. Vilnius: Lietuvių kalbos leidykla.
LKŽ: *Lietuvių kalbos žodynas* [The dictionary of Lithuanian], Vols. 1–20. Vilnius: Lietuvių kalbos institutas, 1941–2002. http://lkz.lt/.
LLVV: Grabis, Rūdolfs (ed.) 1972–1996. *Latviešu literāras valodas vārdnīca* [Dictionary of standard Latvian]. T. 1–10. Rīga.
Lötzsch, Ronald. 1978. Zur Frage des sog. Instrumentals im Lettischen. *Zeitschrift für Slawistik* 23(5): 667–671.
LVG 2013: Nītiņa, Daina & Juris Grigorjevs (eds.). 2013. *Latviešu valodas gramatika* [A grammar of Latvian]. Rīga: LU Latviešu valodas institūts.
LVTK: Līdzsvarots mūsdienu latviešu valodas tekstu korpuss [The balanced corpus of contemporary Latvian]. http://www.korpuss.lv/.
Macienė, Jurgita. 2002. Deminutyvų seka ir funkcionavimas tekste [The order and functioning of diminutives in texts]. *Acta Linguistica Lithuanica* 46: 59–71.
Malesa, Krzysztof. 2003. Some preliminary remarks on spatial distinctions in Lithuanian. *Acta Linguistica Lithuanica* 48: 59–70.
Mańczak, Witold. 2003. Étymologie du lituanien *ir* 'et' et *yra* 'est'. *Acta Linguistica Lithuanica* 49: 61–62.
Marcinkiewicz, Józef. 2002. *Polsko-litewskie kontakty językowe na Suwalszczyźnie* [Polish-Lithuanian language contacts in the Suwałki region]. Poznań: Wydawnictwo Uniwersytetu Adama Mickiewicza.
Markevičienė, Žaneta, Valdimantas Markevičius & Aurimas Markevičius. 2009. *Širvintiškių tekstai* [Texts from the region of Širvintas]. Vilnius: Lietuvių kalbos institutas.
Marvan, Jiří. 1978. *Modern Lithuanian declension: A study of its infrastructure*. Ann Arbor: University of Michigan.
Mathiassen, Terje. 1996a. *A short grammar of Lithuanian*. Columbus, Ohio: Slavica.
Mathiassen, Terje. 1996b. *Tense, mood and aspect in Lithuanian and Latvian*. Meddelelser av Slavisk-baltisk avdeling, Universitetet i Oslo, No. 75.
Mathiassen, Terje. 1997. *A short grammar of Latvian*. Columbus, Ohio: Slavica.
Matthews, William. 1959. The phonematic system of literary Latvian. In Ēvalds Sokols (ed.) *Rakstu krājums. Veltījums akadēmiķim profesoram Dr. Jānim Edzelīnam viņa 85. dzīves un 65. darba gadu atcerei* [A Festschrift for Janis Endzelins], 181–200. Rīga, Latvijas PSR Zinātņu akadēmijas izdevniecība.
Mauri, Caterina. 2008. *Coordination relations in the languages of Europe and beyond*. Berlin, New York: Mouton de Gruyter.
Mazzitelli, Lidia Federica. 2014. The expression of predicative possession in Lithuanian. *Sprachtypologie und Universalienforschung* 66(4): 354–377.
Mazzitelli, Lidia Federica. 2015. *The Expression of Predicative Possession (A Comparative Study of Belarusian and Lithuanian)*. Berlin, Boston: De Gruyter Mouton.
Metuzāle-Kangere, Baiba. 2000. Derivational processes and conjugational type -*st*- verbs in Latvian. In Jochen D. Range (ed.), *Aspekte baltistischer Forschung*, 187–195. Essen: Die Blaue Eule.
Michelini, Guido. 2004. Problems in the reconstruction of certain endings of the Lithuanian optative. In Baldi & Dini (eds.): 137–141.

Mikelionienė, Jurgita. 2002. Analogija lietuvių kalbos žodžių daryboje. Potenciniai ir okaziniai dariniai [Analogy in Lithuanian word formation. Potential and occasional formations]. *Acta Linguistica Lithuanica* 46: 73–80.

Mikulėnienė, Danguolė & Kazys Morkūnas. 1997. *Dieveniškių šnektos tekstai* [Texts of the Dieveniškis dialect]. Vilnius: Lietuvių kalbos institutas.

Mikulėnienė, Danguolė, Antanas Pakerys & Bonifacas Stundžia. 2009. *Bendrinės lietuvių kalbos kirčiavimo žinynas* [Reference book of Standard Lithuanian accentuation]. Vilnius: Vilniaus Pedagoginis Universitetas.

Mikulskas, Rolandas. 2002a. *Koreliuotų nominacinių sistemų funkcionavimas lietuvių kalbos tarmėse* [The functioning of correlated denomination systems in Lithuanian dialects]: Vytautas Magnus University (Kaunas) and Institute of the Lithuanian Language (Vilnius) PhD dissertation.

Mikulskas, Rolandas. 2002b. "Kablio" figūros nominacinės sistemos raiška lietuvių kalbos tarmėse [The figure of the 'hook' in the nominational systems of the Lithuanian dialects]. *Acta Linguistica Lithuanica* 46, 81–119.

Mikulskas, Rolandas. 2003. Postverbų pateikimo problema *Lietuvių kalbos žodyne* [The problem of the representation of postverbs in the Dictionary of Lithuanian]. *Acta Linguistica Lithuanica* 48: 71–96.

Mikulskas, Rolandas. 2005. Išilginių objektų predikacijos pobūdis. Subjektyvaus judėjimo sąvoka [Types of predication for oblong objects. The notion of abstract motion]. *Acta Linguistica Lithuanica* 52: 23–39.

Mikulskas, Rolandas. 2006a. Judėjimo reikšmės kelio predikatai. Leksikografinis aspektas [Path predicates with the meaning of motion. Lexicographic aspects]. In Danutė Liutkevičienė, Rolandas Mikulskas, Daiva Murmulaitytė & Ritutė Petrokienė (eds.) *Aiškinamųjų bendrinės kalbos žodynų aktualijos* [Current problems of explanatory dictionaries of the standard language], 138–148. Vilnius: Lietuvių kalbos institutas.

Mikulskas, Rolandas. 2006b. Apibrėžiamųjų būdvardžių aprašo perspektyva [Prospects for research into definite adjectives]. In Holvoet & Mikulskas (eds.) 2006: 33–65.

Mikulskas, Rolandas. 2007. Dėl daiktavardinės *kaip* konstrukcijomis reiškiamos antrinės predikacijos pobūdžio [On the characteristics of the secondary predication adjectival constructions with *kaip*]. *Acta Linguistica Lithuanica* 57: 123–155.

Mikulskas, Rolandas. 2009. Jungties konstrukcijos ir jų gramatinis kontekstas [Copular constructions and their grammatical context]. *Acta Linguistica Lithuanica* 61, 113–156.

Mikulskas, Rolandas. 2014a. Specifinė jungties konstrukcija [A specific copular construction]. *Prace Bałtystyczne* [Baltic studies] 5, 9–82.

Mikulskas, Rolandas. 2014b. Subjecthood in specificational copular constructions in Lithuanian. In Holvoet & Nau (eds.) 2014: 181–206.

MLLVG: Bergmane, Anna, Rūdolfs Grabis, M. Lepika & Evalds Sokols (eds.). 1959, 1962. *Mūsdienu latviešu literārās valodas gramatika* [A grammar of contemporary standard Latvian]. I. *Fonētika un morfoloģija* [Phonetics and morphology]. II. *Sintakse* [Syntax]. Rīga: Latvijas PSR Zinātņu akadēmijas izdevniecība.

MLTK: Mūsdienu latgaliešu tekstu korpuss [The corpus of contemporary Latgalian], http://hipilatlit.ru.lv/eng/.

Mo, Chien-Ching. 1977. *A case grammar of spoken Lithuanian*: University of Rochester, NY, PhD thesis.

Mo, Chien-Ching. 1978. Causative construction in Lithuanian. *Lituanus* 24(3).

Moroz, Andrzej. 2010. *Parenteza ze składnikiem czasownikowym we współczesnym języku polskim* [Parentheses with a verbal component in contemporary Polish]. Toruń: Wydawnictwo Naukowe UMK.
Mühlenbach & Endzelin 1923–1932 = Mǖlenbachs, Kārlis. *Latviešu valodas vārdnīca. Lettisch-deutsches Wörterbuch*. Redigiert, ergänzt und fortgesetzt von J[ānis] Endzelīns. Rīga: Lettisches Bildungsministerium.
Murakami, Madoka. 2011. Verb movement: The contrast between English and Lithuanian. *RANDOM* (Tokyo) 33(3): 23–45.
Murmulaitytė, Daiva. 2000. Vedinių pateikimas "Dabartinės lietuvių kalbos žodyno" pamatinių žodžių straipsniuose [The listing of derivatives in the head entries of the Dictionary of Contemporary Lithuanian]. *Acta Linguistica Lithuanica* 42: 141–159.
Musteikis [Mustejkis], Kazimieras. 1972. *Sopostavitel'naja morfologija russkogo i litovskogo jazykov* [Contrastive morphology of Russian and Lithuanian]. Vilnius: Mintis.
Naktinienė, Gertrūda. 2011. Parūpinamieji veiksmažodžiai *Bendrinės lietuvių kalbos žodyne* [Curative verbs in the Dictionary of Contemporary Lithuanian]. *Kalbos kultūra* 84: 150–164.
Nau, Nicole. 1998. *Latvian*. München: Lincom Europa.
Nau, Nicole. 1999. Was schlägt der Kasus? Zu Paradigmen und Formengebrauch von Interrogativpronomina. *Sprachtypologie und Universalienforschung* 52(2): 130–150.
Nau, Nicole (ed.). 2001a. *Typological Approaches to Latvian*. Special issue of *Sprachtypologie und Universalienforschung* 54(3).
Nau, Nicole. 2001b. *Wortarten und Pronomina. Studien zur lettischen Grammatik:* Kiel University habilitation.
Nau, Nicole. 2001c. Inflection vs. derivation: How split is Latvian morphology? *Sprachtypologie und Universalienforschung* 54(3): 253–278.
Nau, Nicole. 2005. Perfekts un saliktā tagadne latviešu valodā [Perfect and compound present in Latvian]. *Baltu filoloģija* 14(2): 137–154.
Nau, Nicole. 2006. Out of Africa: Logophoric pronouns and reported discourse in Finnish and High Latvian dialects. *Acta Linguistica Lithuanica* 55: 55–87.
Nau, Nicole. 2008. Non-finite predication as a voicing device in Stefania Ulanowska's Latgalian fairytales. In Jowita Niewulis-Grablunas, Justyna Prusinowska & Ewa Stryczyńska-Hodyl (eds.) *Perspectives of Baltic Philology*, 101–127. Poznań: Rys.
Nau, Nicole. 2009. Towards a comprehensive description of Latvian relative clauses. In Sturla Berg-Olsen (ed.) *The Baltic languages and the Nordic countries*, 93–116. Vilnius: Lietuvių kalbos institutas.
Nau, Nicole. 2010. Contradiction, contrast, and cause: On the functions of the Latvian particle *neba* in Internet discussions. In Nau & Ostrowski (eds.) 2010: 103–133.
Nau, Nicole. 2011a. *A short grammar of Latgalian*. München, Newcastle: LINCOM Europa.
Nau, Nicole. 2011b. Declension classes in Latvian and Latgalian: Morphomics vs. morphophonology. *Baltic Linguistics* 2: 141–177.
Nau, Nicole. 2012. Modality in an areal context: The case of a Latgalian dialect. In Wiemer, Wälchli & Hansen (eds.) 2012: 465–508.
Nau, Nicole. 2013. Latvian agent nouns: Their meaning, grammar, and use. *Baltic Linguistics* 4: 79–131.
Nau, Nicole. 2014. Differential object marking in Latgalian. In Holvoet & Nau (eds.) 2014: 207–255.
Nau, Nicole. Forthcoming. Morphological causatives in contemporary Latvian. In Axel Holvoet & Nicole Nau (eds.) *Voice and argument structure in Baltic*. Amsterdam, Philadelphia: John Benjamins.

Nau, Nicole & Norbert Ostrowski. 2010. Background and perspectives for the study of particles and connectives in Baltic languages. In Nau & Ostrowski (eds.) 2010: 1–37.
Nau, Nicole & Norbert Ostrowski (eds.). 2010. *Particles and connectives in Baltic*. Vilnius: Vilniaus Universitetas.
Nepokupnyj, Anatolij P. 1964. *Areal'nye aspekty balto-slavjanskix jazykovyx otnošenij* [Areal aspects of Balto-Slavic linguistic relations]. Kiev: Naukova dumka.
Nepokupnyj, Anatolij P. 1976. *Balto-severnoslavjanskie jazykovye svjazi* [Baltic-North Slavic linguistic relations]. Kiev: Naukova dumka.
Nepokupnyj, Anatolij P. 2005. *Očerki po sravnitel'noj semasiologii germanskix, baltijskix i slavjanskix jazykov* [Studies in comparative semasiology of Germanic, Baltic and Slavic languages]. Kiev: Dovira.
Nichols, Johanna. 1980. Predicate instrumental and agreement in Lithuanian: A contrastive analysis. *International Review of Slavic Linguistics* 5: 1–21.
Nilsson, Torbjörn K. 2002. The illative in Old Latvian: Analysis of its functions and its relations to the Baltic-Finnic illative. *Linguistica Baltica* 10: 123–140.
Nuñes, Jairo. 1994. Another look at Lithuanian impersonal passives. *Studies in the Linguistic Sciences* 24(1/2): 347–360.
Olander, Thomas. 2009. *Balto-Slavic accentual mobility*. Berlin, New York: Mouton de Gruyter.
Ostrowski, Norbert. 2006. *Studia z historii czasownika litewskiego (Iteratiwa. Denominatiwa)* [Investigations on the history of the Lithuanian verb (Iteratives. Denominatives]. Poznań: Wydawnictwo Naukowe Uniwersytetu Adama Mickiewicza.
Ostrowski, Norbert. 2013. Rozwój kategorii stopnia w języku litewskim (studium historyczno-typologiczne) [The evolution of degrees of comparison in Lithuanian (a historical-typological investigation)]. In Stanisław Puppel & Teresa Tomaszkiewicz (eds.) *Res Novae, scripta manent*, 291–300. Poznań: Wydawnictwo Naukowe Uniwersytetu Adama Mickiewicza.
Ostrowski, Norbert. Forthcoming. From focus marker to comparative suffix – The original character of the Lithuanian comparative *-iau*. *Historische Sprachforschung*.
Otrębski, Jan. 1956–1965. *Gramatyka języka litewskiego* – t. I (1958): *Wiadomości wstępne. Nauka o głoskach*; t. II (1965): *Nauka o budowie wyrazów*; t. III (1956): *Nauka o formach* [Lithuanian grammar, vol. I (1958): Introductory information. About the sounds; vol. II (1965): About the architecture of words; vol. III (1956): About forms (morphology)]. Warszawa: Państwowe Wydawnictwo Naukowe.
Ozols, Arturs [1961] 1993. *Latviešu tautasdziesmu valoda* [The language of Latvian folksongs]. Rīga: Latviešu Valsts Izdevniecība.
Pajėdienė, Jūratė. 2004. Dabartinės lietuvių kalbos prijungiamieji laiko sakiniai [Temporal clauses in modern Lithuanian]. *Acta Linguistica Lithuanica* 50: 35–53.
Pakerys, Antanas. 1982. *Lietuvių bendrinės kalbos prozodija* [The prosody of Standard Lithuanian]. Vilnius: Mokslas.
Pakerys, Antanas. [1986] 1995. *Lietuvių bendrinės kalbos fonetika* [The phonetics of Standard Lithuanian]. Vilnius: Mokslas.
Pakerys, Antanas. 1994. *Akcentologija. I. Daiktavardis ir būdvardis* [Accentology. I. Nouns and adjectives]. Kaunas: Šviesa.
Pakerys, Antanas. 2002. *Akcentologija. II. Skaitvardis, įvardis, veiksmažodis, prieveiksmis, dalelytė, prielinksnis, jungtukas, jaustukas, ištiktukas* [Accentology. II. Numerals, pronouns, verbs, adverbs and other parts of speech]. Vilnius: Mokslo ir enciklopedijų leidybos institutas.

Pakerys, Jurgis. 2004. Dėl lietuvių kalbos priesaginių denominatyvinių veiksmažodžių semantikos [On the semantics of denominal suffixal verbs in Lithuanian]. *Acta Linguistica Lithuanica* 50: 55–77.
Palmaitis, M. Letas. 1977. Dėl baltų kalbų nenominatyvinės praeities [On the non-nominative past of Baltic languages]. *Baltistica* II, *Priedas:* 114–123.
Papaurelytė, Silvija. 2003. Kai kurios liūdesio koncepto raiškos ypatybės lietuvių kalboje [On some peculiarities of the expression of the concept of sadness in Lithuanian]. *Acta Linguistica Lithuanica* 48: 105–118.
Parenti, Alessandro. 1996. Suffixaufnahme-like constructions in Lithuanian. *Res Balticae* 2: 65–76.
Park, Yeong-Woon. 2005. Instrumental case in Korean and Lithuanian: A contrastive analysis. *Language and Linguistics* 36: 21–46.
Paulauskas, Jonas. 1958. Veiksmažodžių priešdėlių funkcijos dabartinėje lietuvių literatūrinėje kalboje [Functions of verbal prefixes in contemporary standard Lithuanian]. In *Literatūra ir kalba* 3: 303–453.
Paulauskienė, Aldona. 1989. *Gramatinės lietuvių kalbos vardažodžių kategorijos* [Grammatical categories of Lithuanian nominals]. Vilnius: Mokslas.
Petit, Daniel. 2000. Quelques observations sur les substantifs de genre neutre en vieux prussien. *Baltistica* 35(1): 29–43.
Petit, Daniel. 2004. *Apophonie et catégories grammaticales dans les langues baltiques*. Leuven, Paris: Peeters.
Petit, Daniel. 2008. Zum Ausdruck der Evidentialität im Baltischen: die litauische Partikel *neva*. *Acta Linguistica Lithuanica* 59: 57–80.
Petit, Daniel. 2010a. New insights on Lithuanian accentuation from the unpublished manuscripts of Ferdinand de Saussure (1857–1913). *Baltic Linguistics* 1: 143–166.
Petit, Daniel. 2010b. *Untersuchungen zu den baltischen Sprachen*. Leiden: Brill.
Petit, Daniel. 2012. On the Latvian indefinite pronoun *kaût kas*. *Baltic Linguistics* 3: 101–150.
Petrauskas, Jonas & Aloyzas Vidugiris. 1987. *Lazūnų tarmės tekstai* [Texts from the Lazūnai dialect]. Vilnius: Mokslas.
Piccini, Silvia. 2008. Traces of non-nominative alignment in Lithuanian: The impersonal constructions in Indo-European perspective. *Baltistica* 43(3): 437–461.
Pietsch, Richard [1982] 2004. *Fischerleben auf der Kurischen Nehrung: dargestellt in kurischer und deutscher Sprache*. (Mit einer Einleitung von Prof. Dr. Friedrich Scholz und mit 24 Zeichnungen des Verfassers / Bearbeitet von Heinz Ischreyt). Berlin: Camen. Reprinted in 2004.
Privitelli, Tobias & Markus Roduner. 2006. Der Genitiv des Agens/Experiencers in litauischen und russischen Dialekten. *Acta Baltico-Slavica* 30: 403–425.
Rackevičienė, Sigita. 2005. Typology of morphological causatives in Lithuanian, Finnish and Norwegian. *Norsk Lingvistisk Tidsskrift* 23(1): 55–74.
Regier, Philip J. 1977. Lithuanian conjugation. A closer examination. *Linguistics* 190: 47–77.
Reķēna, Antoņina. 1998. *Kalupes izloksnes vārdnīca* [Dictionary of the Kalupe dialect]. 2 vols. Ed. by Alberts Sarkanis. Rīga: Latviešu valodas institūts.
Roduner, Markus. 2004. Partizip und Genitiv im Litauischen. In Robert Hodel (ed.), *Zentrum und Peripherie in den slavischen und baltischen Sprachen und Literaturen*, 299–310. Bern: Peter Lang.
Roduner, Markus. 2005. Der Nominativ in Zeitadverbien im Litauischen. *Acta Linguistica Lituanica* 52: 41–59.

Roduner, Markus & Veslava Čižik-Prokaševa. 2006. Skaičiaus kategorija [The category of number]. In Holvoet & Mikulskas (eds.) 2006: 67–100.
Rosinas, Albertas. 1988. *Baltų kalbų įvardžiai* [Pronouns of the Baltic languages]. Vilnius.
Rosinas, Albertas. 1995. *Baltų kalbų įvardžiai: morfologijos raida* [Pronouns in the Baltic languages: The origins of morphology]. Vilnius.
Rosinas, Albertas. 1996. *Lietuvių bendrinės kalbos įvardžiai (funkcijos ir semantika)* [Pronouns in standard Lithuanian (functions and semantics)]. Vilnius: Mokslo ir enciklopedijų leidykla.
Rosinas, Albertas. 1999. Inesyvo ir adesyvo formų kilmės ir raidos klausimu [On the problem of the genesis of inessive and adessive]. *Baltistica* 34(2): 173–183.
Rosinas, Albertas. 2001. *Mikalojaus Daukšos tekstų įvardžių semantinė ir morfologinė struktūra* [Semantic and morphological structure of pronouns in the texts of Mikalojus Daukša]. Vilnius: Mokslo ir enciklopedijų leidybos institutas.
Rosinas, Albertas. 2005. *Latvių kalbos daiktavardžio linksniavimo sistema. Sinchronija ir diachronija* [The system of Latvian nominal declension. Synchrony and diachrony]. Vilnius: Mokslo ir enciklopedijų leidybos institutas.
Roszko, Roman. 1993. *Wykładniki modalności imperceptywnej w języku polskim i litewskim* [Markers of imperceptive modality in Polish and Lithuanian]. Warszawa: Slawistyczny Ośrodek Wydawniczy.
Roszko, Danuta & Roman Roszko. 2006. Lithuanian frequentativum. *Études cognitives* 7: 163–172.
Rothstein, Björn & Rolf Thieroff (eds.). 2010. *Mood in the languages of Europe*. Amsterdam, Philadelphia: John Benjamins.
Rudzīte, Marta. 1964. *Latviešu dialektoloģija* [Latvian dialectology]. Rīga: Latvijas valsts izdevniecība.
Rudzīte, Marta. 2005. *Latviešu izlokšņu teksti* [Latvian dialectal texts]. Rīga: LU Akadēmiskais apgāds.
Rūķe-Draviņa, Velta. 1953. Adjectival diminutives in Latvian. *The Slavonic and East European Review* 31(77): 452–465.
Rūķe-Draviņa, Velta. 1959. *Diminutive im Lettischen*. Lund: Håkan Ohlsson.
Rūķe-Draviņa, Velta. 1963. *Zur Sprachentwicklung bei Kleinkindern. 1. Syntax. Beitrag auf der Grundlage lettischen Sprachmaterials*. Lund: Håkan Ohlsson.
Rūķe-Draviņa, Velta. 1973. On the emergence of inflection in child language: A contribution based on Latvian speech data. In Charles A. Ferguson & Dan I. Slobin (eds.) *Studies of child language development*, 252–267. New York: Rinehart & Winston.
Ruskan, Anna. 2013. *Nemorfologinio evidencialumo raiška ir turinys lietuvių kalboje: bevardės giminės būdvardžiai ir prieveiksmiai* [Non-morphological expressions of evidentiality in Lithuanian: Neuter adjectives and adverbs]: Vilnius University PhD dissertation.
Rutkowski, Paweł. 2007. Some remarks on the syntax of genitival phrases in Lithuanian. In Nicole Carter et al. (eds.) *Simon Fraser University working papers in linguistics* 1, 221–231. Burnaby: Simon Fraser University.
Rutkowski, Paweł. 2008. From apposition to classification: Polish vs. Lithuanian. In Anastasia Smirnova & Matthew Curtis (eds.) *Issues in Slavic syntax and semantics*, 1–13. Newcastle upon Tyne: Cambridge Scholars Publishing.
Rutkowski, Paweł & Ljiljana Progovac. 2006. Classifying adjectives and noun movement in Lithuanian. In Changguk Yim (ed.) *Minimalist views on language design*, 265–277. Seoul: Hankook.
Sabaliauskas, Algirdas. 1990. *Lietuvių kalbos leksika* [Lithuanian lexics]. Vilnius: Mokslas.

Saj [Say], Sergej S. 2011. Nekanoničeskoe markirovanie aktantov mnogomestnyx predikatov: opyt kvantitativno-tipologičeskogo issledovanija [Non-canonical marking of arguments of polyvalent predicates: A quantitative-typological study]. *Acta Linguistica Petropolitana* 7(3): 424–430.
Sakurai, Eiko. 2008. Combination of past participles functioning as adverbials with main verbs in Lithuanian: Aspect and transitivity. *Acta Linguistica Lithuanica* 59: 81–108.
Sarkanis, Alberts (ed.). 2013. *Latviešu valodas dialektu atlants. Fonētika. Apraksts, kartes un to komentāri* [Latvian dialect atlas. Phonetics. Description, maps, commentaries]. Rīga: LU Latviešu valodas institūts.
Saussure, Ferdinand de. 1894. À propos de l'accentuation lituanienne (intonations et accent proprement dit). *Mémoires de la Société de linguistique de Paris* 8: 425–446.
Saussure, Ferdinand de. 1896. Accentuation lituanienne. *Indogermanische Forschungen, Anzeiger* 6: 157–166.
Savičiūtė, Gertrūda. 1985. Parūpinamųjų veiksmažodžių semantika [Semantics of curative verbs]. *Lietuvių kalbotyros klausimai* 24: 236–251.
Savickienė, Ineta. 1998. The acquisition of diminutives in Lithuanian. In Steven Gillis (ed.) *Studies in the acquisition of number and diminutive marking. Antwerp Papers in Linguistics* 95: 115–135.
Savickienė, Ineta. 2001. The role of diminutives in Lithuanian child language acquisition. *Linguistica Baltica* 9: 109–118.
Savickienė, Ineta. 2002. The acquisition of gender. *Kalbotyra* 51(3): 133–143.
Savickienė, Ineta. 2003. *The acquisition of Lithuanian noun morphology*. Wien: Verlag der Österreichischen Akademie der Wissenschaften.
Savickienė, Ineta. 2005. Linksnių vartojimo dažnumas ir daiktavardžio reikšmė [The frequency of case usage and the meaning of the noun]. *Acta Linguistica Lithuanica* 52: 59–65.
Savickienė, Ineta. 2007. Form and meaning of diminutives in Lithuanian child language. In Ineta Savickienė & Wolfgang U. Dressler (eds.) *The acquisition of diminutives: A cross-linguistic perspective*, 13–41. Amsterdam, Philadelphia: John Benjamins.
Savickienė, Ineta, Asta Kazlauskienė & Laura Kamandulytė. 2004. Naujas požiūris į lietuvių kalbos linksniavimo tipus pagal natūraliosios morfologijos teoriją [New approach to Lithuanian inflectional classes according to the theory of Natural Morphology]. *Acta Linguistica Lithuanica* 50: 1–20.
Savickienė, Ineta, Vera Kempe & Patricia J. Brooks. 2009. Acquisition of gender agreement in Lithuanian: Exploring the effect of diminutive usage in an elicited production task. *Journal of Child Language* 36: 477–494.
Sawicki, Lea. 1992. Genitive and dative in goal and purpose expressions in contemporary Lithuanian. *Linguistica Baltica* 1: 93–101.
Sawicki, Lea. 2000. Remarks on the category of aspect in Lithuanian. *Linguistica Baltica* 8: 133–142.
Sawicki, Lea. 2004. Neuter passive participles in modern Lithuanian. In Baldi & Dini (eds.) 2004: 157–164.
Sawicki, Lea. 2010. Preverbation and narrativity in Lithuanian (The distribution of finite simplex and compound verbs in narrative main clauses). *Baltic Linguistics* 1: 167–192.
Sawicki, Lea. 2012. Responsive discourse particles in Lithuanian dialog. *Baltic Linguistics* 3: 151–175.
Say [Saj], Sergey. 2004. Grammaticalization of word order: Evidence from Lithuanian. In Olga Fischer, Muriel Norde & Harry Perridon (eds.) *Up and down the cline: The nature of grammaticalization*, 363–384. Amsterdam, Philadelphia: John Benjamins.
Say [Saj], Sergej. 2014. Bivalent verb classes in the languages of Europe. *Language Dynamics and Change* 4(1): 116–166.

Schmalstieg, William R. 1958. A descriptive study of the Lithuanian verbal system. *General Linguistics* 3(3): 85–105.
Schmalstieg, William R. 1982. The shift of intransitive to transitive passive in the Lithuanian and Indo-European verb. *Baltistica* 17(2): 119–134.
Schmalstieg, William R. 1986. Lithuanian participles in the nominative case as the modifier of the phrase subject. *Lituanus* 32(2).
Schmalstieg, William R. 1988. *A Lithuanian historical syntax*. Columbus, Ohio: Slavica.
Schmalstieg, William R. 1990. A comment on the Latvian debitive. In Baiba Metuzāle-Kangere, (ed.) *Symposium Balticum: A Festschrift to honour Professor Velta Rūķe-Draviņa*, 427–432. Hamburg: Buske.
Schmalstieg, William R. 2000. *The historical morphology of the Baltic verb*. Washington, DC: Institute for the Study of Man.
Schmalstieg, William R. 2004. The Balto-Slavic dative complement with the verb 'to be'. *Acta Linguistica Lithuanica* 51: 45–48.
Schmid, Wolfgang. P. 1966. Baltische Beiträge IV: Zur Bildung des litauischen Präteritums. *Indogermanische Forschungen* 71: 286–296.
Schroeder, Christian, Gerd Hentschel & Winfried Boeder (eds.). 2008. *Secondary predicates in Eastern European languages and beyond*. Oldenburg: BIS-Verlag der Carl von Ossietzky-Universität.
Schwentner, Ernst. 1922. *Die Wortfolge im Litauischen*. Heidelberg: Winter.
Sehwers, Johannes. 1953. *Sprachlich-kulturhistorische Untersuchungen vornehmlich über den deutschen Einfluss im Lettischen*. Berlin: Osteuropa-Institut an der Freien Universität Berlin.
Semėnienė, Loreta. 2002. Aukštesniojo ir aukščiausiojo laipsnio būdvardžių valentingumas [Valency of comparative and superlative adjectives]. *Acta Linguistica Lithuanica* 46: 131–144.
Semėnienė, Loreta. 2003. Būdvardžio derinimas ir būdvardžio bevardės giminės problema [Adjectival concord and the problem of neuter gender]. *Acta Linguistica Lithuanica* 48: 119–136.
Semėnienė, Loreta. 2004. Die prädikative Verwendung von Substantiven im Litauischen: Nominativ vs. Instrumental. *Acta Linguistica Lithuanica* 50: 99–125.
Semėnienė, Loreta. 2005. Intranzityvinio subjekto žymėjimas vardininku ir/arba kilmininku [The expression of intransitive subject by nominative and/or genitive]. *Acta Linguistica Lithuanica* 52: 67–82.
Senn, Alfred. 1966. *Handbuch der litauischen Sprache*, Bd. I: *Grammatik*. Heidelberg: Winter.
Seržant, Ilja. 2003. Die Intonationen der suffixalen und Endsilben im Lettischen. Synchronie und Diachronie. *Baltu filoloģija* 12(1): 83–122.
Seržant, Ilja. 2004a. Einige Bemerkungen zur Geschichte des Illativs. *Baltu Filoloģija* 13(1): 113–120.
Seržant, Ilja. 2004b. K voprosu ob obrazovanii adessiva [On the problem of the genesis of the adessive]. *Acta Linguistica Lithuanica* 51: 49–57.
Seržant, Ilja. 2004c. Zur Vorgeschichte des Inessivs im Urostbaltischen. *Acta Linguistica Lithuanica.* 51: 59–67.
Seržant, Ilja. 2012. The so-called possessive perfect in North Russian and the Circum-Baltic area. A diachronic and areal approach. *Lingua* 122(4): 356–385.

Seržant, Ilja. 2013a. Acquisition of canonical subjecthood. In Ilja Seržant & Leonid Kulikov (eds.) *The diachronic typology of non-prototypical subjects*, 283–310. Amsterdam, Philadelphia: John Benjamins.
Seržant, Ilja. 2013b. Acquisition of canonical objecthood by the Lithuanian verbs of pain. *Baltic Linguistics* 4: 187–211.
Seržant, Ilja. 2014a. The independent partitive genitive in Lithuanian. In Holvoet & Nau (eds.) 2014: 257–299.
Seržant, Ilja A. (2014b). The independent partitive genitive in North Russian. In Ilja A. Seržant & Björn Wiemer (eds.) *Contemporary approaches to dialectology: The area of North, Northwest Russian and Belarusian vernaculars* (Slavica Bergensia 13), 270–329. Bergen: John Grieg AS.
Sinkevičienė, Jurgita. 2014. Lietuvių *neva* – daugiafunkcinis diskurso markeris [Lithuanian *neva* – A polyfunctional discourse marker]. *Prace Bałtystyczne* [Baltic studies] 5. Warszawa, 83–100.
Sirtautas, Vytautas & Česys Grenda. 1988. *Lietuvių kalbos sintaksė* [Lithuanian syntax]. Vilnius: Mokslas.
Skardžius, Pranas. [1943] 1996. *Lietuvių kalbos žodžių daryba* [Lithuanian word formation]. (Rinktiniai raštai, 1.) Vilnius: Mokslo ir enciklopedijų leidybos institutas 1st edition. Vilnius: Lietuvių kalbos institutas.
Skrinda, Ontons. 1908. *Latyšskaja grammatika letgal'skago narečija* [A Latvian grammar of the Letgalian dialect]. Saint-Petersburg.
Sližienė, Nijole. 1961. Apie sudurtines pradėtines veiksmažodžių formas [On the compound inceptive verbal forms]. *Lietuvių kalbotyros klausimai* 4: 67–72.
Sližienė, Nijole. 1995. The tense system of Lithuanian. In Rolf Thieroff (ed.) *The tense systems in European languages*, Vol. II, 215–232. Tübingen: Niemeyer.
Smetona, Antanas. 2005. Pagrindinių darybos būdų skyrimo klausimu [On the classification of basic derivational types]. *Acta Linguistica Lithuanica* 52, 83–89.
Smoczyński, Wojciech. 1974. Przypadki lokalne języków bałtyckich [Local cases of Baltic languages]. *Sprawozdania Oddziału Krakowskiego PAN za rok 1974* 18(1): 36–38.
Smoczyński, Wojciech. 1988. Języki bałtyckie [Baltic languages]. In Leszek Bednarczuk (ed.) *Języki indoeuropejskie*, t. II [Indo-European languages, vol. II], 817–905. Warszawa: Państwowe Wydawnictwo Naukowe.
Smoczyński, Wojciech. 1999. Geneza starolitewskiego conditonalis na *-biau, -bei, -bi-* [The rise of the Old Lithuanian conditionalis in *-biau, -bei, -bi-*]. *Acta Baltico-Slavica* 24: 13–18.
Smoczyński, Wojciech. 2007. *Słownik etymologiczny języka litewskiego* [Etymological dictionary of Lithuanian]. Vilnius: Vilniaus Universitetas.
Soida, Emīlija. 2009. *Vārddarināšana* [Word formation]. Rīga: Latvijas Universitāte.
Spraunienė, Birutė. 2008. Paprastųjų ir įvardžiuotinių būdvardžių opozicija lietuvių kalboje kaip apibrėžtumo sistema [The opposition of simple and pronominalized adjectives in Lithuanian as a system of definiteness]. *Acta Linguistica Lithuanica* 59: 109–139.
Spraunienė, Birutė. 2011. *The marking of definiteness in Lithuanian. Against the background of Danish and other article languages*: Vilnius University summary of doctoral dissertation. http://vddb.library.lt/obj/LT-eLABa-0001:E.02~2011~D_20110519_082052-38010.
Srba, Adalbert. 1911. Über die Momentativ-Verba im Litauischen (Ein Beitrag zur litauischen Syntax). *Lietuvių tauta* 2(1): 51–71.

Stafecka, Anna. 1989. Sistema mestoimenij v pamjatnikax latgaľskoj pis'mennosti (1753–1871) [Pronominal system in Latgalian written monuments]. In *Verxnelatyšskij dialekt. Sbornik naučnyx trudov* [The High Latvian dialect], 100–142. Rīga: Latvijskij gosudarstvennyj universitet im. P. Stučki.

Stafecka, Anna. 1997. Vietniekvārds senākajos latgaliešu rakstos un mūsdienu Latgales izloksnēs [The pronoun in the oldest Latgalian texts and in the modern Latgalian dialects]. In *Savai valodai (Latvija Zinātņu Akadēmijas goda loceklim Rūdolfam Grabim veltīts piemiņas krājums)* [For the Native Language. A collection of articles in remembrance of academician Rūdolfs Grabis], 272–281. Rīga: LZA Vēstis.

Stang, Christian S. 1942. *Das slavische und baltische Verbum*. Skrifter utgitt av det Norske Videnskaps-Akademi i Oslo 1942. II. Historisk-Filosofisk Klasse, No.1. Oslo.

Stang, Christian S. 1966. *Vergleichende Grammatik der Baltischen Sprachen*. Oslo, Bergen, Tromsö: Universitetsforlaget.

Stassen, Leon. 1985. *Comparison and universal grammar*. Oxford: Blackwell.

Stassen, Leon. 1997. *Intransitive predication*. Oxford: Oxford University Press.

Steinbergs, Aleksandra. 1977. *The phonology of Latvian*: University of Illinois PhD dissertation.

Stockmal, Verna, Dace Markus & Dzintra Bond. 2005. Measures of native and non-native rhythm in a quantity language. *Language and Speech* 48(1): 5–63.

Stolz, Thomas. 1984. Para-Präpositionen, Präpositionen, Adverbien und (Pseudo-)Postpositionen im Lettischen. *Indogermanische Forschungen* 89: 241–269.

Stolz, Thomas. 1990. Natural morphosyntax, grammaticalization, and Balto-Finnic vs. Baltic case-marking strategies: A study of the nature of periphrases. *Papiere zur Linguistik* 42(1): 9–29.

Stolz, Thomas. 1991. *Sprachbund im Baltikum? Estnisch und Lettisch im Zentrum einer sprachlichen Konvergenzlandschaft*. Bochum: Brockmeyer.

Stolz, Thomas. 2007. Word-internal agreement. *Sprachtypologie und Universalienforschung* 60(3): 219–251.

Stolz, Thomas. 2010. Pleonastic morphology dies hard: Change and variation in definiteness inflection in Lithuanian. In Franz Rainer, Wolfgang U. Dressler, Dieter Kastovsky & Hans Christian Luschützky (eds.) *Variation and change in morphology*, 217–245. Amsterdam, Philadelphia: John Benjamins.

Stolz, Thomas & Aina M. Urdze. 2001. Head-marking and dependent-marking in modern Latvian. *Sprachtypologie und Universalienforschung* 54(3): 279–297.

Stolz, Thomas, Cornelia Stroh & Aina Urdze. 2006. *On comitatives and related categories: A typological study with special reference to the languages of Europe*. Berlin, New York: Mouton de Gruyter.

Stolz, Thomas, Cornelia Stroh & Aina Urdze. 2011. *Total reduplication. The areal linguistics of a potential universal*. Berlin: Akademie-Verlag.

Stolz, Thomas, Sonja Kettler, Cornelia Stroh & Aina Urdze. 2008. *Split possession. An areal-linguistic study of the alienability correlation and related phenomena in the languages of Europe*. Amsterdam, Philadelphia: John Benjamins.

Stołowska, Ewa. 2014. Uwagi o żywotności i wyznaczaniu rodzaju we współczesnym języku łotewskim [Remarks on animacy and gender marking in contemporary Latvian]. *Prace Bałtystyczne* [Baltic studies] 5. Warszawa, 101–110.

Strods, Pīters. 1922. *Latwìšu wolùdas gramatika latgališim*. [A Latvian grammar for Latgalians.] Rēzekne.

Stundžia, Bonifacas. 1995. *Lietuvių bendrinės kalbos kirčiavimo sistema* [The accentuation system of standard Lithuanian], Vilnius: Vilniaus universitetas.

Stundžia, Bonifacas. 2009. *Bendrinės lietuvių kalbos akcentologija* [The accentology of standard Lithuanian]. Vilnius: Vilniaus universitetas.
Šeškauskienė, Inesa. 2004. The extension of meaning: Spatial relations in English and Lithuanian. In Barbara Lewandowska-Tomaszczyk & Alina Kwiatkowska (eds.) *Imagery in language: Festschrift in honour of Professor Ronald W. Langacker*, 373–384. Bern: Peter Lang.
Šileikaitė, Diana. 2004. Der Somatismus 'Herz' als phraseologisches Weltbildelement im Deutschen, Litauischen und Georgischen. *Kalbotyra* 54(3): 84–93.
Šinkūnienė, Jolanta. 2012. Adverbials as hedging devices in Lithuanian academic discourse: A cross-disciplinary study. In Usonienė, Nau & Dabašinskienė (eds.) 2012: 137–167.
Šukys, Jonas. 1998. *Lietuvių kalbos linksniai ir prielinksniai: vartosena ir normos* [Cases and prepositions of Lithuanian: Usage and norm.] Kaunas: Šviesa.
Tangl, Eberhard. 1928. *Der Accusativus und Nominativus cum Participio im Altlitauischen*: Doctoral Dissertation, Berlin.
Tekorienė, Dalija. 1990. *Bevardės giminės būdvardžiai* [Neuter adjectives]. Vilnius: Mokslas.
Temčin, Sergej. 1986. Semantika *-n-* i *-sta-* glagol'nyx osnov litovskogo jazyka [The semantics of *-n-* and *-sta-* verbal stems in Lithuanian]. *Kalbotyra* 37(1): 87–98.
Thieroff, Rolf. 2000. On the areal distribution of tense-aspect categories in Europe. In Östen Dahl (ed.) *Tense and aspect systems in the languages of Europe*, 265–303. Berlin, New York: Mouton de Gruyter.
Thieroff, Rolf (ed.). 1995. *The tense systems in European languages*, Vol. II. Tübingen: Niemeyer.
Thomsen, Vilhelm. [1890] 1931. *Berührungen zwischen den finnischen und den baltischen (litauischlettischen) Sprachen*. Copenhagen: Fjerde Bind.
Timberlake, Alan. 1974. *The nominative object in Slavic, Baltic and West Finnic*. München: Sagner.
Timberlake, Alan. 1982. The impersonal passive in Lithuanian. *Proceedings of the 8th Annual Meeting of the Berkeley Linguistics Society*, 508–524.
Timberlake, Alan. 1988. Case agreement in Lithuanian. In Michael Barlow & Charles A. Ferguson (eds.) *Agreement in natural language: Approaches, theories, descriptions*, 181–199. Stanford, CA: CSLI Publications.
Timberlake, Alan. 1990. The aspectual case of predicative nouns in Lithuanian texts. In Nils B. Thelin (ed.) *Verbal aspect in discourse. Contributions to the semantics of time and temporal perspective in Slavic and Non-Slavic languages*, 325–347. Amsterdam, Philadelphia: John Benjamins.
Toops, Gary H. 1989. The syntax and semantics of Lithuanian curative constructions. In Howard Aronson (ed.) *The Non-Slavic languages of the USSR*, Vol. 5, 249–282. Chicago: Chicago Linguistics Society.
Toops, Gary H. 1994. Notes on reflexivity and causativity in Lithuanian. *Journal of Baltic Studies* 25(1): 53–62.
Toporov, Vladimir N. 1973. Neskol'ko zamečanij o baltijskix glagolax na *-sta* v svjazi s proisxoždeniem ètogo formanta (indoevropejskaja perspektiva). [Some remarks on the Baltic *-sta* verbs with respect to the genesis of this formant (an Indo-European perspective)]. *Baltų kalbų veiksmažodžio tyrinėjimai* [Studies in the Baltic verb], 151–168. Vilnius.
Toporov, Vladimir N. 1997. Baltijskie jazyki [The Baltic languages]. In Valentina N. Jarceva et al. (eds.) *Jazyki Rossijskoj Federacii i sosednix gosudarstv. Ènciklopedija* [The Languages of The Russian Federation and the neighbouring countries. An encyclopaedia], Vol. I: *A-I*, 143–154. Moscow: Nauka.

Toporov, Vladimir N. (ed.). 2006. *Jazyki mira. Baltijskie jazyki* [Languages of the world. The Baltic languages]. Moscow: Akademia.
Toporov, Vladimir N. & Oleg N. Trubačev. 1962. *Lingvističeskij analiz gidronimov Verxnego Podneprov'ja* [A linguistic analysis of the hydronymy of the Upper Dnepr]. Moscow: Izdatel'stvo Akademii nauk SSSR.
Trasuns, Francis. 1921. *Łatwišu vołudas gramatika del łatgališim* (A Latvian grammar for the Latgalians). Riga: Valters un Rapa.
Tret'jakov, Petr N. 1966. *Finno-ugry, balty i slavjane na Dnepre i Volge* [Finno-Ugrians, Balts and Slavs on the banks of Dnepr and Volga]. Moscow, Leningrad: Nauka.
Trumpa, Anta. 2010. *Adjektīvu semantiskā diferenciācija latviešu un lietuviešu valodā* [Semantic differentiation of adjectives in Latvian and Lithuanian]. Rīga: LU Latviešu valodas institūts.
Trumpa, Edmunds. 2012. *Latviešu ģeolingvistikas etīdes* [Latvian geolinguistic studies]. Rīga: Zinātne.
Ulvydas, Kazys. 2009. *Lietuvių kalbos prieveiksmiai* [Lithuanian adverbs]. Vilnius: Mokslo ir enciklopedijų leidybos institutas.
Urbutis, Vincas. 1978. *Žodžių darybos teorija* [A theory of word formation]. Vilnius: Mokslas.
Urdze, Aina M. 2010. *Ideophone in Europa. Die Grammatik der lettischen Geräuschverben.* Bochum: Brockmeyer.
Usonienė, Aurelia. 2001. On direct/indirect perception with verbs of seeing and seeming in English and Lithuanian. *Working Papers, Lund University, Dept. of Linguistics* 48: 163–182.
Usonienė, Aurelia. 2002. Types of epistemic qualification with verbs of perception. *Kalbotyra* 52(3): 147–154.
Usonienė, Aurelija & Erika Jasionytė. 2010. Towards grammaticalization: Lithuanian acquisitive verbs *gauti* ('get') and *tekti* ('be gotten'). *Acta Linguistica Hafniensia* 42(2): 199–220.
Usonienė, Aurelija Nicole Nau & Ineta Dabašinskienė (eds.). 2012. *Multiple perspectives in linguistic research on Baltic languages.* Newcastle upon Tyne: Cambridge Scholars Publishing.
Usonienė, Aurelija & Audronė Šolienė. 2010. Choice of strategies in realizations of epistemic possibility in English and Lithuanian. *International Journal of Corpus Linguistics* 15(2): 291–316.
Utka, Anrdius. 2009. *Dažninis rašytinės lietuvių kalbos žodynas 1 milijono žodžių morfologiškai anotuoto tekstyno pagrindu* [A frequency dictionary of written Lithuanian based on a 1 million token morphologically annotated corpus]. Kaunas: Vytauto Didžiojo Universitetas. http://donelaitis.vdu.lt/publikacijos/Dazninis_zodynas.pdf.
Vaičenonienė, Jūratė. 2000. The conduit metaphor in English and Lithuanian. *Darbai ir dienos* 24: 143–167.
Vaičiulytė-Semėnienė, Loreta. 2007. Daiktavardinės *kaip* konstrukcijos kaip analitinis predikatyvų žymėjimo rodiklis [Adjectival *kaip*-constructions as a n analytical marker of predicates]. *Acta Linguistica Lithuanica* 56: 73–101.
Valeckienė, Adelė. 1957. Dabartinės lietuvių kalbos įvardžiuotinių būdvardžių vartojimas [The use of pronominalized adjectives in modern Lithuanian]. *Literatūra ir kalba* 2: 159–355.
Valeckienė, Adelė. 1986. Apibrėžtumo/neapibrėžtumo kategorija ir pirminė įvardžiuotinių būdvardžių reikšmė [The category of definiteness/indefiniteness and the primary meaning of pronominalized adjectives]. *Lietuvių kalbotyros klausimai* 25: 168–189.
Valeika, Laimutis. 1974. *Word-order in Lithuanian and English in functional sentence perspective.* Vilnius: Vilnius State University.

Valiulytė, Elena. 2001. Lietuvių kalbos tikslo konstrukcijos su slinkties veiksmažodžiais [Goal constructions with motion verbs in Lithuanian]. *Acta Linguistica Lithuanica* 44: 201–225.
Vasiliauskienė, Virginija. 2001. Atributinė frazė su derinamuoju komponentu Kiprijono Lukausko *Pamoksluose* [Attributive phrases with agreeing components in Cyprian Lukauskas' Sermons]. *Acta Linguistica Lithuanica* 45: 151–178.
Vasiliauskienė, Virginija. 2008. *Lietuvių kalbos žodžių tvarka XVI-XIX a. (atributinės frazės)* [Word order in attributive phrases in 16th–19th century Lithuanian]. Vilnius: Lietuvių kalbos institutas.
Vaskelaitė, Ramunė. 2003. Lietuvių kalbos daiktavardiniai junginiai sintaksinių ryšių požiūriu [Lithuanian noun phrases from the point of view of syntactic relations]. *Acta Linguistica Lithuanica* 48: 143–158.
Vasmer, Max. 1971. *Schriften zur slavischen Altertumskunde*, Bd. I. Wiesbaden: Harrassowitz.
Veidemane, Ruta. 1970. *Latviešu valodas leksiskā sinonīmija* [Lexical synonymy in Latvian]. Rīga: Zinātne.
Vidugiris, Aloyzas. 1998. Dėl daugkartinio veiksmo raiškos pietrytinėse lietuvių kalbos tarmėse [On the expression of iterative events in Southeastern Lithuanian dialects]. *Lietuvių kalbotyros klausimai* 39: 183–191.
Vidugiris, Aloyzas & Danguolė Mikulėnienė. 2005, 2010. *Zietelos šnektos tekstai* [Texts of the Zietela dialect], I dalis + II dalis. Vilnius: Lietuvių kalbos institutas.
Vitkauskas, Vytautas. 1976. *Šiaurės rytų dūnininkų šnektų žodynas* [Glossary of the south-eastern *dūnininkai* dialects]. Vilnius: Mokslas.
Vykypěl, Bohumil. 2001. Zwei lettonistische Bemerkungen. In Ondřej Šefčík & Bohumil Vykypěl (eds.) *Grammaticus. Studia linguistica Adolfo Erharto quinque et septuagenario oblata*, 211–223. Brno: Masarykova univerzita.
Vykypěl, Bohumil. 2002. Zum Schicksal der Dualformen (ein tschechisch-lettisch-litauisch-sorbischer Vergleich mit einigen allgemeinen Bemerkungen). *Acta Linguistica Lithuanica* 47: 103–107.
Vykypěl, Bohumil. 2003. Das phonologische Inventar und seine morphonologische Klassifizierung (einige Bemerkungen). *Acta Linguistica Lithuanica* 48: 159–175.
Vykypěl, Bohumil. 2004. Zur Prosodie in der Typologie. *Acta Linguistica Lithuanica* 50: 127–134.
Vykypěl, Bohumil. 2006. Eine Bemerkung zum Genus. *Acta Linguistica Lithuanica* 54, 95–100.
Wälchli, Bernhard. 1996. *Letto-livisches und Livo-lettisches. Eine Studie zur Bedeutungskonvergenz im nordosteuropäischen Kontaktraum*. Lizenziatsarbeit, Universität Bern.
Wälchli, Bernhard. 1998. Der Synkretismus der Lokalkasus im Lettischen und Livischen. *Linguistica Baltica* 7: 207–228.
Wälchli, Bernhard. 2000. Infinite predication as a marker of evidentiality and modality in the languages of the Baltic region. *Sprachtypologie und Universalienforschung* 53(2): 186–210.
Wälchli, Bernhard. 2001a. A typology of displacement (with special reference to Latvian). *Sprachtypologie und Universalienforschung* 54(3): 298–323.
Wälchli, Bernhard. 2001b. Lexical evidence for the parallel development of the Latvian and Livonian verb particles. In Dahl & Koptjevskaja-Tamm 2001, 1: 413–441.
Wälchli, Bernhard. 2005. *Co-compounds and natural coordination*. Oxford: Oxford University Press.
Wiemer, Björn. 1998. Pragmatical inferences at the threshold to grammaticalization. The case of Lithuanian predicative participles and their functions. *Linguistica Baltica* 7: 229–243.
Wiemer, Björn. 1999. K tipologii anaforičeskoj topikalizacii v jazykax Evropy (s osobym učetom roli substantivnyx mestoimenij) [Towards a typology of anaphoric topicalization in the European languages, with special reference to substantive pronouns]. In Violeta Koseska-Toszewa & Zbigniew Greń (eds.) *Semantyka a konfrontacja językowa 2*, 231–249. Warszawa: Slawistyczny Ośrodek Wydawniczy.

Wiemer, Björn. 2000. Diffusität und Synkretismus in der diachronen Syntax. Ein Klärungsversuch anhand von Kasussystemen, insbesondere der Objektmarkierung im Nordslavischen und Litauischen. In Walter Breu (ed.) *Slavistische Linguistik XXV. (Referate des XXV. Konstanzer Slavistischen Arbeitstreffens, Konstanz 7.-10.9.1999)*, 277–313. München: Sagner.

Wiemer, Björn. 2001a. Aspektual'nye paradigmy i leksičeskoe značenie russkix i litovskix glagolov (Opyt sopostavlenija s točki zrenija leksikalizacii i grammatikalizacii) [Aspectual paradigms and lexical meaning of Russian and Lithuanian verbs (A comparison from the perspective of grammaticalization and lexicalization)]. *Voprosy jazykoznanija* 2: 26–58.

Wiemer, Björn. 2001b. Partizipien zwischen Syntax, Semantik und Pragmatik: Ein Überblick zu aspektuellen, diathesebezogenen und diskursrelevanten Eigenschaften im modernen Litauischen. In Bernhard Wälchli & Fernando Zúñiga (eds.), *Sprachbeschreibung und Typologie*, 65–81. Bern: Universität Bern.

Wiemer, Björn. 2003a. Zur Verbindung dialektologischer, soziolinguistischer und typologischer Methoden in der Sprachkontaktforschung (am Beispiel slavischer und litauischer Varietäten in Nordostpolen, Litauen und Weißrußland). *Zeitschrift für Slawistik* 48(2): 212–229.

Wiemer, Björn. 2003b. Dialect and language contacts on the territory of the Grand Duchy of Lithuania from the 15th century until 1939. In Kurt Braunmüller & Gisela Ferraresi (eds.) *Aspects of multilingualism in European language history*, 105–143. Amsterdam, Philadelphia: John Benjamins.

Wiemer, Björn. 2004a. Population linguistics on a micro-scale. Lessons to be learnt from Baltic and Slavic dialects in contact. In Bernd Kortmann (ed.) *Dialectology meets typology (dialect grammar from a cross-linguistic perspective)*, 497–526. Berlin, New York: Mouton de Gruyter.

Wiemer, Björn. 2004b. The evolution of passives as grammatical constructions in Northern Slavic and Baltic languages. In Walter Bisang, Nikolaus P. Himmelmann & Björn Wiemer (eds.) *What makes grammaticalization? A look from its fringes and its components*, 271–331. Berlin, New York: Walter de Gruyter.

Wiemer, Björn. 2004c. Taksis i koincidencija v zavisimyx predikacijax: litovskie pričastija na *-damas* [Taxis and coincidence in subordinate predications: Lithuanian participles in *-damas*]. In Viktor S. Xrakovskij, Andrej L. Mal'čukov & Sergej Ju. Dmitrenko (eds.) *40 let Sankt-Peterburgskoj tipologičeskoj škole* [40 years of the Saint-Petersburg School of typology], 53–73. Moscow: Znak.

Wiemer, Björn. 2004d. Grammatische Kernbereiche, deren Rekonstruktion und deren Relevanz für historisch belegte Sprachstufen des Baltischen und Slavischen. *Acta Linguistica Lithuanica* 51: 81–112.

Wiemer, Björn. 2005. Conceptual affinities and diachronic relationships between epistemic, inferential and quotative functions (preliminary observations on lexical markers in Russian, Polish and Lithuanian). In Björn Hansen & Petr Karlík (eds.) *Modality in Slavonic languages. New perspectives*, 107–131. München: Sagner.

Wiemer, Björn. 2006a. Grammatical evidentiality in Lithuanian (a typological assessment). *Baltistica* 41(1): 33–49.

Wiemer, Björn. 2006b. Relations between Actor-demoting devices in Lithuanian. In Werner Abraham & Larisa Leisiö (eds.) *Passivization and typology. Form and function*, 274–309. Amsterdam, Philadelphia: John Benjamins.

Wiemer, Björn. 2007a. Sud'by balto-slavjanskix gipotez i segodnjašnjaja kontaktnaja lingvistika [The fate of Balto-Slavic hypotheses and contemporary contact linguistics]. In Vjačeslav Vs. Ivanov & Petr M. Arkad'ev (eds.) *Areal'noe i genetičeskoe v strukture slavjanskix jazykov* [Areal and genetic in the structure of Slavic languages], 17–30. Moscow: Probel-2000.

Wiemer, Björn. 2007b. Kosvennaja zasvidetel'stvovannost' v litovskom jazyke [Indirect evidentiality in Lithuanian]. In Viktor S. Xrakovskij (ed.) *Èvidencial'nost' v jazykax Evropy i Azii* [Evidentiality in the languages of Europe and Asia], 197–240. Saint-Petersburg: Nauka.

Wiemer, Björn. 2007c. Lexical markers of evidentiality in Lithuanian. In Mario Squartini (ed.) *Evidentiality between lexicon and grammar. Rivista di Linguistica* special issue 19(1): 173–208.

Wiemer, Björn. 2009a. Taksisnye konstrukcii v litovskom jazyke [Taxis constructions in Lithuanian]. In Viktor S. Xrakovskij (ed.) *Tipologija taksisnyx konstrukcij* [Typology of taxis constructions], 161–216. Moscow: Znak.

Wiemer, Björn. 2009b. Zu entlehnten Präfixen und anderen morphosyntaktischen Slavismen in litauischen Insel- und Grenzmundarten. In Lenka Scholze & Björn Wiemer (eds.) *Von Zuständen, Dynamik und Veränderung bei Pygmäen und Giganten (Festschrift für Walter Breu zu seinem 60. Geburtstag)*, 347–390. Bochum: Brockmeyer.

Wiemer, Björn. 2010a. Lithuanian *esą* – a heterosemic reportive marker in its contemporary stage. *Baltic Linguistics* 1: 245–308.

Wiemer, Björn. 2010b. On the lexicographic treatment of Lith. *esą* (on the background of other particles in Lithuanian and elsewhere). In Nau & Ostrowski (eds.) 2010: 171–212.

Wiemer, Björn. 2010c. Hearsay in European languages: Toward an integrative account of grammatical and lexical marking. In Gabriele Diewald & Elena Smirnova (eds.) *Linguistic realization of evidentiality in European languages*, 59–129. Berlin, New York: Mouton de Gruyter.

Wiemer, Björn. 2011. Grammaticalization in Slavic languages. In Bernd Heine & Heiko Narrog (eds.) *The Oxford handbook of grammaticalization*, 740–753. Oxford: Oxford University Press.

Wiemer, Björn. 2012a. Zum wechselnden Status nicht-kongruierender Prädikationstypen im nördlichen Slavischen und Litauischen. In Andrii Danylenko & Serhii Vakulenko (eds.), *Studien zur Sprache, Literatur und Kultur bei den Slaven (Gedenkschrift für George Y. Shevelov aus Anlass seines 100. Geburtstages und 10. Todestages)*, 31–57. München: Sagner.

Wiemer, Björn. 2012b. The Lithuanian HAVE-resultative – A typological curiosum? In *Lingua Posnansiensis* 54(2): 69–81.

Wiemer, Björn. 2013a. Značimost' sposobov modifikacii glagol'nyx osnov dlja ocenki areal'noj differenciacii baltijskix jazykov (po sravneniju s rjadom slavjanskix mikrojazykov) [The relevance of the means of modification of verbal stems for the assessment of areal differentiation of Baltic languages (in comparison with a number of Slavic micro-languages)]. In Arkad'ev & Ivanov (eds.) 2013: 220–246.

Wiemer, Björn. 2013b. Zur arealen Stufung im baltisch-slavischen Kontaktgebiet (und dabei auftretenden methodischen Desideraten). In Norbert Franz, Miranda Jakiš, Sebastian Kempgen & Monika Wingender (eds.) *Deutsche Beiträge zum 15. Internationalen Slavistenkongress, Minsk 2013*, 313–324. München: Sagner.

Wiemer, Björn. 2014. Sprachwandeltypen im litauisch-slavischen Kontakt: ein Überblick. In Tat'jana V. Civ'jan, Marija, V. Zav'jalova & Artūras Judžentis (eds.) *Baltai ir slavai: dvasinių kultūrų sankirtos* [Balts and Slavs: Intersections of spiritual cultures], 196–217. Vilnius: Versmė.

Wiemer, Björn. Forthcoming. On the rise, establishment and continued development of subject impersonals in Polish, East Slavic and Baltic. In Seppo Kittilä & Leonid Kulikov (eds.) *Diachronic typology of voice and valency-changing categories*. Amsterdam, Philadelphia: John Benjamins.

Wiemer, Björn & Aksana Erker. 2011. Manifestations of areal convergence in rural Belarusian spoken in the Baltic-Slavic contact zone. *Journal of Language Contact* 4: 184–216.

Wiemer, Björn & Markus Giger. 2005. *Resultativa in den nordslavischen und baltischen Sprachen (Bestandsaufnahme unter arealen und grammatikalisierungstheoretischen Gesichtspunkten)*. München, Newcastle: LINCOM Europa.

Wiemer, Björn & Jurgis Pakerys. 2007. Building a partial aspect system in East Aukštaitian Vilnius dialects of Lithuanian (Correlations between telic and activity verbs). *Acta Linguistica Lithuanica* 57: 45–97.

Wiemer, Björn, Ilja Seržant & Aksana Erker. 2014. Convergence in the Baltic-Slavic contact zone. Triangulation approach. In Juliana Besters-Dilger, Cynthia Dermarkar, Stefan Pfänder & Achim Rabus (eds.) *Family effects in language contact (Modeling congruence as a factor in contact induced change)*, 15–42. Berlin, Boston: De Gruyter Mouton.

Wiemer, Björn, Irina Vladyko & Vytautas Kardelis. 2004. *Moč'* i *umet'* – funkcional'nye peresečenija dvux modal'nyx glagolov v govorax litovsko-slavjanskogo pogranič'ja [Functional intersections of two modal verbs in the vernaculars of the Lithuanian-Slavic border area]. *Balto-slavjanskie issledovanija* [Balto-Slavic studies] *XVI*, 142–167. Moskva: Indrik.

Wiemer, Björn, Bernhard Wälchli & Björn Hansen (eds.). 2012. *Grammatical replication and borrowability in language contact*. Berlin, Boston: Mouton de Gruyter.

Wójcik, Paweł. 2000. *The acquisition of Lithuanian verb morphology (A case study)*. Cracow: Universitas.

Xrakovskij, Viktor S. 1997. Semantic types of the plurality of situations and their natural classification. In Viktor S. Xrakovskij (ed.) *Typology of iterative constructions*, 3–64. München, Newcastle: Lincom Europa.

Young, Steven. 1991. *The prosodic structure of Lithuanian*. New York: University Press of America.

Zaikauskas, Egidijus. 2002. Šnekos akto dalyvių strategija, socialiniai vaidmenys ir tipai lietuvių kalboje [Strategies of speech act participants, social roles and types in Lithuanian]. *Acta Linguistica Lithuanica* 46: 145–172.

Zaikauskas, Egidijus. 2006. Ilokucinių veiksmažodžių reikšmės aiškinimas bendrinės kalbos žodyne [The explanation of illocutionary meanings of verbs in the dictionary of the standard language]. In Danutė Liutkevičienė, Rolandas Mikulskas, Daiva Murmulaitytė & Ritutė Petrokienė (eds.) *Aiškinamųjų bendrinės kalbos žodynų aktualijos* [Current problems of explanatory dictionaries of the standard language], 149–169. Vilnius: Lietuvių kalbos institutas.

Zav'jalova, Marija. 2006. Nekotorye zamečanija po povodu porjadka slov v litovskom jazyke v sravnenii s russkim [Some observations on word order in Lithuanian in comparison with Russian]. In Tatiana N. Mološnaja (ed.) *Tipologija grammatičeskix sistem slavjanskogo prostranstva* [Typology of grammatical systems of the Slavic area], 164–174. Moscow: Institute of Slavic Studies of the Russian Academy of Sciences.

Zinkevičius, Zigmas. 1957. *Lietuvių kalbos įvardžiuotinių būdvardžių istorijos bruožai* [Characteristics of the history of the Lithuanian pronominalized adjectives]. Vilnius: Valstybinės politinės ir mokslinės literatūros leidykla.

Zinkevičius, Zigmas. 1966. *Lietuvių dialektologija: Lyginamoji tarmių fonetika ir morfologija* [Lithuanian dialectology: Comparative phonetics and morphology of the dialects]. Vilnius: Mintis.

Zinkevičius, Zigmas. 1982. Lietuvių kalbos postpoziciniai vietininkai [Lithuanian postposition-based locative cases]. *Baltistica* 18(1): 21–38.

Zinkevičius, Zigmas. 2006. *Lietuvių tarmių kilmė* [The genesis of Lithuanian dialects]. Vilnius: Lietuvių kalbos institutas.

Žeimantienė, Vaiva. 2011. Zur Verwendung und Bedeutung ausgewählter litauischer kurativer Verben mit Ausblick auf das Deutsche. *Moderne Sprachen* 55(2): 123–133.

Hans Henrich Hock
2 Prosody and dialectology of tonal shifts in Lithuanian and their implications

1 Introduction

Standard Lithuanian final vowels and their prosodies are fairly stable. Colloquial varieties of southern Aukštaitian, as well as more northern dialects of Aukštaitian and especially the Žemaitian dialect area, exhibit a variety of changes. I focus on two developments – the loss of final short vowels and reassignment of their pitch properties to preceding syllables and ictus[1] retraction from the final syllable to the penult and beyond, culminating in initial ictus in northwest varieties of Žemaitian. My aim is to provide comprehensive, theoretically and cross-linguistically grounded explanations of these developments.

I draw on a broad range of sources of information on the phenomena under consideration in Lithuanian and its dialects, especially Stang (1966), Senn (1966), Girdenis (1982),[2] Young (1991),[3] Atkočaitytė (1999/2000), Balode and Holvoet (2001b), and Petit (2010). None of these provide a complete or detailed overview of Lithuanian dialectology, tending instead to focus on certain "privileged" dialects. A fuller test of my account – as well as those of others – against the entire range of relevant Lithuanian dialects remains a desideratum.

The chapter is organized as follows. Section 2 provides brief theoretical and typological background information. Section 3 focuses on the issue of traditional, somewhat idiosyncratic terminology regarding Lithuanian prosody and how to interpret the terminology in more up-to-date linguistic terms. Section 4 is devoted to the phenomenon of apocope and pitch retraction. Section 5 contains a summary of evidence regarding the more complex problem of ictus retraction not dependent on apocope, a process with more far-reaching effects. Section 6 presents my interpretation of the evidence. Alternative accounts are discussed in Section 7. Finally, Section 8 discusses the implications of my findings, including the issue of Latvian word-initial ictus, its relation or non-relation to the Lithuanian developments, and the question of a Balto-Finnic substratum.

---

[1] See Section 3 regarding the term "ictus" and why, in Lithuanian linguistics, it is preferable to the more usual term "accent".
[2] The article by Girdenis became available to me in February 2012. I have benefited from a translation by Tatyana Luchkina.
[3] I am grateful to Peter Arkadiev for making this monograph available to me.

2 Theoretical and typological background

As is well known, there is a cross-linguistic tendency for various segmental reductions and losses in word-final position (see e.g., Hock [1986] 1991: 88, 92–93, 95–96). What is not so well known is that there is a similar tendency for prosodic, suprasegmental changes in the same context. A detailed discussion is found in Hock (1999). In the following, I summarize the major issues and arguments, with primary focus on prosodic developments.

A variety of changes can be attributed to the conflict between the prosodic prominence of accent or high pitch and the low pitch and reduced prominence that is characteristic of unmarked falling intonation in utterance-final position – the Utterance Finality Effect (see Figure 1). Developments of this type include accent or pitch retraction to the penult, generalized retraction toward word-initial position, or even loss of accent or pitch.

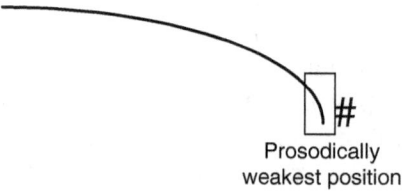

Fig. 1: Falling intonation and utterance-final prosodic weakness.

As early as 1917, Bloomfield noted that in Tagalog, "an accent on the last syllable of a sentence often entirely loses its pitch-rise." Cheng and Kisseberth (1979: 34–35) posit a rule of "phrase-final lowering" for Makua and justify it is "an expected accentual phenomenon – lowering of pitch at the end of an utterance." More far-reaching developments are found in the Mesoamerican language Huichol and in Vedic Sanskrit, with a near-parallel in Modern Persian.

In Huichol, underlying tonal contrasts are neutralized in utterance- (and phrase-) final position, in favor of the intonational pitch properties associated with that position; see (1) and (2), where (a) illustrates the neutralization and (b) the underlying tonal properties (accent marks or their absence indicate tonal distinctions; numerals, different final pitch contours) (see Grimes 1959).[4]

---

[4] The glosses are approximate.

Huichol (Uto-Aztecan, Mexico)

(1) a. yaawi+   kámʌ́+   **maa³na¹#**
        coyote   look   there
        'Look! There's a coyote'

   b. **mána** +   ʔukaitʌ +   náayaa³¹ ni³
        there   living   he took-up
        'He took up living there.'

(2) a. **yaa⁴wi¹**
        coyote
        'A coyote!' (uttered with surprise)

   b. **yaawi**+   kámʌ́+   maa³na¹#
        coyote   look   there
        'Look! There's a coyote'

In Vedic Sanskrit, finite verbs lose their pitch accent in main clauses[5] (MCs) but not in dependent clauses (DCs) (see 3a). The MC accent loss is plausibly explained as originally conditioned by utterance-final position and then extended to non-canonical, non-final positions, including MC-DC configurations (see Klein 1992, Hock 2014, and the summary in 3b). As Hock (1999) notes, the development has a near-parallel in Modern Persian, with accent retraction on verbs in MCs and complement clauses – which are prototypically utterance-final, but not in preposed, non-utterance-final DCs (see e.g., 4a,b vs. 4c).

(3) Vedic (Indo-European>Indo-Aryan)
    a. [tásmai   víśaḥ   svayám   evā́   **namante**]$_{MC}$
        CP.DAT.SG.M   people.NOM.PL self   PCLE   bow.PRS.3PL
        [yásmin   brahmā́   pū́rva   **éti**]$_{DC}$
        RP.LOC.SG.M   brahmin.NOM.SG first.NOM.SG.M go.PRS.3SG
        'Even the common people bow to him for whom the brahmin goes first.' (Rigveda 4.50.8)

---

5 Unless the verb is initial in the clause or the poetic prosodic phrase.

b. i.   Original canonical word order: s   o   v#
    ii. Original canonical clause order: DC   MC
    iii. Hence: [s   o   v]$_{DC}$ [s   o   v]$_{MC}$ ##
    iv. Finality-conditioned accent loss: [s   o   v]$_{DC}$ [s   o   v]$_{MC}$ ##
                                                                                  [– accent]
    v.   Polarization: MC   :   DC
                                                  [verb: – accent]   [verb: + accent]

Persian (Indo-European>Iranian)
(4) a. **kā̂r**   mi-kon-am
        work   do-PRS-1SG
        'I do the work/I work.'

    b. [hàqqas   **ín**   ast]$_{MC}$ [ke   **púl**   nà-dār-am]$_{DC}$
        truth   it.OBL   be.PRS.3SG   COMP   money   NEG-have-1SG
        'The truth of it is that I do not have money.'

    c. [àgar   be-rav-**ád**]$_{DC}$ [kàsi   digàr   níst]$_{MC}$
        if   OPT-go-3SG   nobody   left   NEG.be.PRS.3SG
        'If he goes, nobody will be left.'

Most relevant for present purposes is the work by Becker (1977, 1979), who uses dialectological data to argue that the well-known Serbian-Croatian accent retraction originated in utterance-final position. The most peripheral, also otherwise conservative varieties (dialects of Čakavian) show no accent shift at all (5a); neighboring Čakavian dialects exhibit the change only utterance-finally, as a shift of high pitch from the final to the penultimate MORA (5b); in the standard (Štokavian) language, by contrast, we find generalized accent retraction (5c–e).

(5) Serbian-Croatian accent retraction (Becker 1977, 1979)
    a. Čakavian 1   krãl^y =   [kraál^y]   'king'
    b. Čakavian 2   krãl^y =   [kráal^y]   / ___ ##
        vs.   krãl^y =   [kraál^y]   elsewhere
    c. Štokavian   krãl^y =   [kráal^y]   everywhere
    d. Štokavian   lopàta   >   lòpata   'shovel'
    e. Štokavian   vodá   >   vòda   'water' (NOM.SG)
        vs.   vódu   >   vòdu   'water' (ACC.SG)

Significant for the further discussion are the following observations:
i. As shown by the change from (5b) to (5c), originally utterance-final changes can be extended to ALL word-final contexts.
ii. Accent retraction can be further extended to affect non-final syllables, leading to a generalized process of retraction (5d).

iii. Accent retraction may lead to new tonal phenomena on syllables that receive the accent (5e).

Since both segmental weakening and suprasegmental prominence shifts can be triggered by utterance-finality, the two phenomena can potentially interact. One such case is reported by Canger (1990): Nahuatl final short vowels become super-short, and final long vowels have a falling or low tone (vs. rising or high tone elsewhere) and their duration is more similar to the (short) vowels of Spanish (see 6). Thus, in the domain of final long vowels, reduction is accompanied by left dislocation of prominence.

(6) Nahuatl (Uto-Aztecan) according to Canger (1990) (where *a* represents any vowel)
    a. -*a*   >   -^{a} / ___ #
    b. -*aá* >   -*à* / ___ #

Utterance-finality then can be a powerful trigger for both segmental and suprasegmental changes, or even a combination of these. In many cases, however, it remains an explanation in principle. As Serbian-Croatian shows, utterance-final developments can easily be extended to word-final position, and in many cases, we may not get a glimpse of the original utterance-final change, but only its word-final extension. Note further that originally utterance- or word-final prosodic retractions can be extended to become generalized phenomena, as in Serbian-Croatian.

3 Traditional terminology in Lithuanian prosody and its interpretation

Traditional[6] Standard Lithuanian has a distinction between falling and rising pitch on accented long vowels and diphthongs, where "diphthong" includes sequences of vowel+tautosyllabic non-vocalic sonorant (as in *gérti* 'drink', *ber̃ti* 'strew').[7] A convenient cover term for both types of syllables is "LONG". Accented short vowels do not exhibit this distinction. Traditionally, the term ACUTE

---

6 In much of contemporary Lithuanian, the system here described is breaking down or has already done so (see Young 1991 for a recent discussion). The changes discussed in this chapter operate in the traditional system.
7 Recent publications based on contemporary evidence, such as Dogil (1999) (see also Daugavet, this volume), question the phonetic characterization of these distinctions. Unfortunately, they do not necessarily agree with each other in the alternative characterizations that they propose. Moreover, the question must arise whether these recent characterizations may be the result of linguistic changes from an earlier stage at which the pitch-accent characterizations of late nineteenth- and early twentieth-century descriptions were appropriate.

is employed for accented long syllables with falling pitch (such as *výras* [víiras] 'man'); CIRCUMFLEX for accented long syllables with rising pitch (e.g., *gẽras* [gɛɛ́ras] 'good'); GRAVE for accented short vowel (e.g., *manè* [manɛ́] 'me'), and these different accent patterns are referred to as INTONATIONS or "accents".

Although not felicitous from the general linguistic perspective, the terms are so deeply ingrained in discussions of Lithuanian prosody that replacing them with more transparent terminology would be counterproductive. The one exception is the term "accent", not only because it is confusing (all the Standard Lithuanian intonations are accented after all), but also because it creates even greater confusion when referring to unaccented pitch (contour) distinctions in other dialects (see further below).

To avoid terminological confusion, INTONATION will be used in the remainder of this chapter, and following Stang (1966), the term ICTUS designates (main) accent or stress.

In contrast to Standard Lithuanian, many Žemaitian dialects as well as Latvian do not have a one-to-one correspondence between ictus and (contour) pitch – even syllables not carrying the ictus may bear pitch, such as the non-initial syllables in Žemaitian *àtvìrà* 'open (NOM.SG.F)' (Standard *atvirà*) or *dár,bẹ̀nĩnks*[8] 'worker' (Standard *darbiniñkas*). Lithuanian linguists tend to refer to the non-ictus-bearing syllables as having a secondary "accent", but given general principles of "stress-clash" avoidance (see Section 7), it is highly unlikely that structures of this sort contain three accented or stressed syllables in a row. For this reason, the so-called secondary accents are analyzed as pitch phenomena in syllables not bearing the ictus.

In the same dialects, the circumflex symbol is used to refer to weak rising-falling (or level) rather than rising pitch (as in *dár,bẹ̀nĩnks*), and several additional "intonations" are recognized, the most important of which is the "broken tone" (Germ. Brechton) – generally, a falling pitch contour whose most salient feature is a glottal stop or constriction – as in the final syllable of *šà,kâ* 'branch (DAT.SG.F)' (Standard *šãkai*). These facts will be important in the discussion of Žemaitian ictus retraction.

Finally, it is important for the subsequent discussion that Lithuanian distinguishes between "FIXED" and "MOBILE accent" paradigms. In mobile paradigms, ictus placement varies between stem and ending under purely morphological conditions; in fixed paradigms, the ictus is on the stem (with shift to certain endings only under morphophonological conditions). The majority of MOBILE nouns

---

8 The publications consulted for dialectal data employ a variety of symbols such as the comma in *dár,bẹ̀nĩnks* without explaining what they stand for.

and adjectives show variation between the initial syllable and the ending (e.g., Standard *ãtvirą* (ACC.SG.F): *atvirà* (NOM.SG.F 'open'), but some have non-initial stem ictus (e.g., Standard *nedraũgas* (N sg.m.): *nedrauguosè* (LOC.PL.M) 'enemy').

4 Aukštaitian apocope and pitch retraction

In much of Aukštaitian, short vowels in final syllables tend to undergo apocope, whether accented or not (see 7).[9] According to the handbook accounts, if the lost vowel bears the ictus (and grave intonation), a long preceding syllable receives circumflex intonation, i.e., rising pitch (LH) (see 7a). If it does not, a long preceding syllable receives the acute, i.e., falling pitch (HL) (cf. 7b) (see e.g., Stang 1966: 167–168). What is not included in this account is the fate of preceding short syllables. As shown by (7c), from Senn (1966: 190), in such cases, an unaccented preceding syllable receives the so-called grave, i.e., simple, non-contour high pitch (H). (Note that Lithuanian <o>=[ō] and <y>=[ī].)

(7)   Standard   dialect
  a.   *manè*   *mañ*   'me (ACC)'
       tomìs   *tõms*   'they (INS.PL)'

  b.   *gēras*   *gérs*   'good (NOM.SG.M)'
       výras   *výrs*   'man (NOM.SG)'

  c.   *tavè*   *tàv*   'you (ACC.SG)'

While descriptively adequate, this account does not amount to an explanation; moreover, it presupposes a more detailed knowledge of Lithuanian phonology than can be expected for general linguistic audiences.

Let me begin with the latter issue. What needs to be explained is the intonational difference between *mañ* and *tõms* in (7a), as well as the yet different situation in (7c). These differences follow from the fact that only short vowel + glide, liquid, or nasal can form a diphthong, whose second mora can bear high pitch. So, *man* contains a legitimate diphthong and hence can bear high pitch on the nasal (*mañ*), but *toms* contains a long *o* [o:], which cannot combine with the following nasal into a diphthong and hence the high pitch cannot be expressed on the nasal but must be expressed on the second mora of *o* (hence *tõms*). As for *tàv* in (7c), the combination *a* + *v* is not a legitimate diphthong and hence no

---

[9] There is a fair amount of variation, both geographically and socially. For instance, the process takes place more commonly in the colloquial than in the standard language.

bimoraic sequence exists to carry a rising pitch; therefore, only a simple high pitch can be expressed.[10]

What is more important is the lack of explanation for the differences between (7a,c) on the one hand and (7b) on the other.

A first approximation might follow Hock (1999) by considering the developments in (7a,c) to involve segmental loss with compensatory pitch displacement, along the lines of (8). That is, apocope leaves behind a floating high pitch, which then attaches to the next preceding mora or pitch-bearing element, whether that is the second element of a diphthong or of a long vowel (7a) or simply a short vowel (7c). In bimoraic configurations (7a), the result is a rising pitch, marked by circumflex; in monomoraic configurations (7c), the high pitch attaches to the short vowel and is marked by grave.

(8) Written representation   *manè*   *toomìs*   *tavè*

H	H	H
|	|	|
man e	toom is	tav e

Apocope

H	H	H
|	|	|
man Ø	toom Øs	tav Ø

Pitch reattachment

H	H	H
|	|	|
man	tooms	tav

Written representation   *mañ*   *tõms*   *tàv*

However, this account fails for (7b), since here the final syllable does not have high pitch. To account for both (7a,c) and (7b), a more comprehensive approach is needed, which pays attention not just to high pitch, but to the MELODY of high pitch ± following low pitch, see (9), where *tomìs* represents all of (7a,c), and *gẽras* stands for (7b).[11] For *tomìs/tõms*, the effect is the same as in the previous analysis, since no low pitch follows the suffixal H. But now, we can also account for *gẽras/gérs*. Reattachment of the HL melody to the syllable that remains after apocope

---

10 Some varieties have *taũ* instead, with sonorant [u̯], rather than non-sonorant [v].
11 The acute on *výrs* reflects vacuous application.

produces a falling intonation and thus changes the intonation of that syllable from circumflex (rising) to acute (falling).

(9)

	H	H L
	|	| |
	toomis	geer as

Apocope	H	H L
	|	| |
	toomØs	geer Øs

Melody reattachment	H	H L
	|	| |
	toomØs	g e r Øs
	tõms	gérs

The Aukštaitian developments covered in this section have been discussed in terms of pitch or HL melody reassignments, but because in this variety the location of pitch and ictus coincides, it would have been possible, with appropriate changes, to treat the developments in terms of ictus.[12] This coincidence of pitch and ictus is not shared by the more northern dialects, and retraction phenomena in these dialects are therefore more complex.

5 Ictus retraction in Žemaitian: General observations

While the Žemaitian dialects of Lithuanian may also exhibit apocope, the major process that differentiates these dialects from Aukštaitian consists in the retraction of the ictus from final syllables to the penult, and even further to the left. Significantly, ictus retraction takes place no matter whether there is apocope or not

---

[12] In Lithuanian grammatical descriptions, it is customary to recognize a special type of apocope with pitch readjustment, which takes place with greater regularity than the cases examined above. This is apocope in longer inflectional endings, such as *nedrauguosè* (Loc. pl. m.) 'enemy'>*nedrauguõs*. The purpose is often said to be making these endings conform to the pattern of the more common shorter endings (see e.g., Senn 1966: 97). While this may be a valid synchronic account, historically, the process may simply reflect the fact that apocope often is sensitive to syllable structure, with, e.g., trisyllabic words undergoing the process in preference to disyllabic ones. According to another perspective, discussed in Young (1991: 75–76), with reference to Kazlauskas (1968: 87), the starting point is ictus retraction, which columnarizes the ictus on the post-stem syllable of the suffix. While this explanation may hold for varieties that retain the final vowel, it does not address the case of dialects with apocope.

(see e.g., 10). (Here as elsewhere, underlining in Žemaitian forms indicates ictus.) The process becomes more advanced the further north or northwest the dialect is located, ultimately culminating in initial ictus.

(10) a. Without apocope
Southern pl*ĩ*·ta 'brick' (Standard plytà)
More northern mètèl'ùs 'coat' (Standard meteliùs)

b. With apocope
Southern p*ĩ*ˢeštǫks 'pencil' (Standard pieštùkas)

Shift of the ictus to long syllables tends to introduce new intonations, indicated by special symbols such as the raised ˢ of p*ĩ*ˢeštǫks, which indicates "intermediate" intonation (see Derksen 1991 for a good summary).

The following sections present an overview of the major phenomena and developments.

5.1 Retraction in the southern dialects

Ictus retraction is least regular and most restricted in the southern dialects of Žemaitian. As Atkočaitytė (1999/2000) observes, ictus retraction in the dialect of Raseinai is still a change in progress, with a high degree of variation.[13] In its phonologically most restricted form, ictus retraction takes place from short final-syllable vowel to long but not short penult (see 11 and compare Petit 2010: 72).

(11) pl*ĩ*·ta 'brick' (Standard plytà)
vs. šakà, Gen.Sg šakūos 'branch' (Standard šakà, šakõs)

In more advanced dialects, retraction also takes place from final syllables with circumflex and/or to short penults (in addition to long ones) (see 12). What complicates matters is that there is also a common phenomenon of "secondary accent", i.e., some retention of the original pitch property on the final syllable, as in (12a,b). Stang (1966: 169–170) notes that this phenomenon is found in dialects that do not lengthen the vowel of the new ictus syllable, while it is absent in dialects that do lengthen it.

(12) a. šàkà 'branch' (vs. more southern Žemaitian and Standard šakà)
atvìrà 'open (NOM.SG.F)' (vs. southern Žemaitian and Standard atvirà)
b. gèrã· 'well' (vs. southern Žemaitian and Standard geraĩ)

---

[13] See also Girdenis (1982), who, however, does not specifically identify the geographical location.

Retraction may also take place from original penult syllables that have become final through apocope, as in (13) (see Young 1991: 26).

(13) *pieštọ̀kas (Standard pieštùkas) > *pieštọ̀ks > pi̯eštọ̀ks 'pencil'

Especially important for present purposes is the fact that ictus retraction does not take place from syllables with acute intonation, as in *laukáms* 'field (DAT. PL.M)', where second-syllable ictus remains unchanged (but see Section 5.3 for extreme northern dialects).

5.2 Retraction farther north

In an intermediate dialect area, farther to the north, ictus retraction tends to be extended, largely along morphological lines: In MOBILE paradigms, the ictus tends to be shifted further left, from the penult to the syllable that bears the ictus in the corresponding stem-accented variant (STEM ICTUS for short), as in (14a,b). Grinaveckis (1973: 152), however, observes that some varieties retract the ictus to initial position even in forms that do not have initial stem ictus, as in (14c) from Váiguva, or fail to retract to the initial stem ictus, as in (14d) from Kelmė.

(14) a. *atvirà>atvìrà>a̰tvìrà* 'open (NOM.SG.F)' (compare stem ictus *ãtvirą*, ACC.SG.F)
  b. *negyvà>negỹvà* 'dead (NOM.SG.F)' (compare stem ictus *negývą*, ACC.SG.F)
  c. *mẹ̀tėl'ùs*: Standard *meteliùs* 'coat' (compare *metēliai* NOM.PL, with non-initial stem ictus)
  d. *vargṵ̄·sè*: *vargusè* 'in miseries' (compare Standard *var̃gą* ACC.SG.M, with initial stem ictus)

Significantly, forms such as those in (15a) show that ictus retraction – and "secondary accent", i.e., trace of original pitch properties – normally skips syllables between the penult and the stem ictus syllable, but there seem to be exceptions with pitch even on the antepenult, such as those in (15b) from Kelmė and (15c) from Junkilai, cited by Grinaveckis (1973: 152, 153). These examples suggest that ictus retraction took place syllable-by-syllable in these dialects, rather than directly from penult to the stem ictus syllable. In addition, some dialects exhibit only initial ictus, without penult ictus, as in (15d) from Šaukėnai (see Girdenis 1982: 185).

(15) a. nè̠supîntè̠: Standard *nesupintì* 'unbraided (NOM.PL.M)
 b. pà̠beˢnktùvės: Standard *pabengtùvės* 'harvest festival'
 c. bè̠sieˢduñ.tì: Standard *besėdantì* 'sitting'
 d. pà̠žastìs: Standard *pažastìs* 'armpit'

Note further that in forms with original stem ictus, synchronically long syllables in post-ictus position ("POST-ICTUS" syllables) receive a "SECONDARY DISPLACED" broken tone irrespective of their original intonation (as in 16) (see Young 1991: 27).

(16) a. *darbûdavûomûos* 'we used to work': Standard *darbúodavomės*
 b. *kãlvâ·* 'hill': Standard *kaĩvai*

5.3 The extreme northwest

The extreme northwestern varieties of Žemaitian exhibit a further, phonological extension of ictus retraction to the first syllable, overriding the morphological conditions for retraction in the intermediate area (see e.g., 17 and compare Girdenis 1982).

(17) *latàk(a)s* 'tray, gutter'>*là̠tàks*[14]

Some extreme northern dialects exhibit further peculiarities. For instance, some dialects show a difference between original acute and circumflex where the intermediate dialects only have the "secondary displaced" "broken tone" (Grinaveckis 1964: 6, cited by Young 1991, note 5, p. 90). This system is more similar to the one found in Latvian.

Further, in contrast to the rest of the Žemaitian dialects, some northern dialects exhibit (not completely regular) ictus retraction even from original acute, as in *laukáms*>*la̠ˢukâms*/*la̠ũkams* 'field (DAT.PL.M) (Grinaveckis 1964: 16, cited by Young 1991, note 3, p. 89). Again, this is something that brings these dialects closer to Latvian.

---

14 The original stem ictus is on the second syllable, compare genitive singular *lataˢ.ka*.

5.4 The realization of the circumflex

As noted in Section 3, Žemaitian differs from Aukštaitian in the realization of the circumflex. The Aukštaitian circumflex is characterized by rising pitch (LH); that of Žemaitian has been variously characterized as weak rising-falling (Stang 1966: 125), simple falling (Stang 1966: 139, Petit 2010: 73), and falling, varying with level pitch (Balode & Holvoet 2001b: 73). Young (1991: 5) suggests that the "weak rising-falling" realization is a feature of western dialects. What is shared by all of these realizations is a retraction of (pitch or ictus) prominence to the left. The retraction, however, does not lead to merger with the old acute, which becomes broken tone and according to Young is realized as "rising-falling ... interrupted at its peak by a glottal stop". Put differently, circumflex and acute→broken tone seem to differ not only by the glottal stop or constriction of the latter, but also by the degree of initial rise – weak in the circumflex, strong in the broken tone.

5.5 The type Standard Lithuanian *mataū*/Žemaitian *matâu*

The Standard Lithuanian type *mataū* 'I see', and its Žemaitian counterpart *matâu*, presents difficulties from the historical/comparative perspective. As noted, e.g., by Young (1991: 27), the ictus on the ending suggests an original acute intonation, contrary to the synchronic circumflex. Many scholars have therefore suggested that the original ending must have been of the type *-ā-ō*, with simple long *ā*, which would attract the ictus from the root to the ending by Saussure's Law, yielding an intermediate stage *-ā́-ō* with acute.[15] Scholars like Stang (1966: 116) find support for this stage in Žemaitian *matâu*, whose broken tone is the normal reflex of an original acute. The problem with this account is the (Standard) third-person form *mãto*, with root accent rather than shift to the ending, suggesting that the suffix of this verb class had circumflex rather than acute intonation. Petit (2010: 246–247) tries to account for the intonational properties of the type *mãto* as analogical, based on the first and second plural persons, but given the centrality of the third person (which serves to mark singular, dual, and plural), this account is problematic.

---

[15] Saussure's Law refers to a prehistoric shift of ictus form an original circumflex or "grave" syllable to a following acute syllable (Saussure 1894, 1896). Its effect may be obscured by subsequent shortening of final acute syllables by Leskien's Law (Leskien 1881). Compare *nẽšúo>*nešúo̯>nešù̯.

Significantly, any account operating with a long, acute suffix vowel *-ā́- is difficult to reconcile with up-to-date Indo-European reconstructions, which would have to operate with structures of the type *-eh_2-oh_2 (sg. 1) and *-eh_2-e/o (third singular→general third person), which, with loss of intervocalic laryngeal and other changes would yield structures like *-a-ō and *-a-e/a>ā̃ respectively, neither of which have the long, acute *-ā́- postulated by scholars like Stang. In fact, in his review of Petit, Villanueva Svensson (2010) makes precisely this point, comparing Rau's (2009) derivation of the "athematic" Greek contract verb inflection from the Old Hittite factitive type newaḫḫ- 'make new', with an original inflection *neu̯ah_2-h_2e(i), *neu̯ah_2-th$_2$e(i), *neu̯ah_2-e(i).

Under the circumstances, it appears that the standard intonation mataũ (with circumflex) is original and the broken tone of Žemaitian matâu innovated. The ictus on the ending then can be explained as analogical to the Saussure's Law ictus variation in the thematic verbs (see 18).

(18) 3rd person   nẽš-a   mãt-o
      sg. 1   neš-ù   X=mat-aũ

6 A prosodically grounded account of Žemaitian ictus retraction

Let us now put together the different strands of evidence assembled in Section 5 and try to develop an explanatory hypothesis. What is important is that this explanation accounts both for the fact that short and circumflex final syllables – including secondarily final ones as in (13) – trigger ictus retraction and acute final syllables do not (except in some extreme northwestern dialects; see Section 5.3).

Just as other scholars (e.g., Young 1991: 25, Petit 2010: 71), this account assumes that accent retraction is a process that spreads from a northern core area and loses momentum on the southern periphery, which like conservative Čakavian dialects in the case of Serbian-Croatian, preserve earlier stages of the development.

6.1 First approximation

The phonologically most restricted form of ictus retraction is from final short syllable to long penult (see 11). It is also the process that appears to exhibit the greatest variability, partly in terms of morphological conditions, suggesting a change in progress (Atkočaitytė 1999/2000). These facts suggest that this form of the change constitutes the first step of ictus retraction.

Given the parallels cited in Section 2, especially the Serbian-Croatian one, the change can be attributed to the Finality Effect, the avoidance of final prosodic prominence, originally in utterance-final position and then extended to word-final. Support for the hypothesis that the change originated in utterance-final position may be seen in Atkočaitytė's (1999/2000) observation that one of the factors favoring ictus retraction in southern Žemaitian is phrase- or utterance-final position. The phonological restriction that the ictus only shifts to long penult can be explained by the well-known tendency for ictus ("accent", "stress") to be associated with "weight" and vice versa (see Hock 1999, with references).

The more northern extension of retraction to short penults and/or to shift from final circumflex can be explained along the same lines as the extension of pitch (and ictus) retraction in Serbian-Croatian. In this context, it is important to note that the original realization of circumflex is rising, i.e., LH.[16]

What is shared by these two triggers – final short and circumflex syllables – is that they have prominence on the final (or only) mora. This fact distinguishes them from final acute syllables, which have HL, i.e., prominence on the initial mora, and which do not trigger ictus retraction (except in some extreme northwestern dialects).

These facts permit the generalization that ictus retraction originates in structures with prosodic prominence (H) on the final mora (see 19a, items i and ii). By contrast, there is no retraction from an original acute syllable (HL) in which the H is not final (see 19a, item iii). At this point, the change has to be formulated as ictus retraction from the syllable containing final H (see Section 6.2). (The difference between extreme southern dialects that limit retraction to short triggers and long penult targets and the slightly more northern ones that remove these limitations can, provisionally, be attributed to some kind of "parameterization", including the restriction of "shift to weight".)

In the "intermediate", more northern dialects retraction is evidently extended beyond the penult, a change again comparable to the Serbian-Croatian shift. However, in contrast to Serbian-Croatian, the extension normally is sensitive to morphology, with the target of retraction being the stem ictus syllable (see Section 5.2 and example 14a,b). Moreover, the retraction generally skips directly from the

---

16 Convincing arguments against an opposing view going back to Endzelin (1899), which holds that circumflex originally was falling (HL), are found in Stang (1966: 125) (see also Poljakov 1997).

penult to the stem ictus syllable, rather than in syllable-by-syllable fashion (15a). What may have helped in this process is the fact that in monosyllabic stems such as *lángas* 'window', the stem ictus syllable is also the penult for most of the forms of the paradigm; only forms with disyllabic endings such as the locative plural (e.g., *languosè*) are an exception.

There are, however, some cases where the retraction does not go to the stem ictus syllable (14c,d), as well as some instances that suggest syllable-by-syllable retraction with even the antepenult showing a trace of ictus retraction (15b,c), or retraction to the stem ictus syllable skipping the penult (15d). Examples like these suggest the need for a great deal of more detailed research into the way in which retraction plays out in these dialects.

There is, thus, considerable variation in the "intermediate" dialects, as well as a fair amount of non-phonological, morphological conditioning, facts that suggest that the change is still in progress, even though further progressed than in the extreme south. The general tendency, however, is clear and can be formulated, as in (19b).

The extreme northern (and northwestern) dialects exhibit the most far-reaching extension, with retraction to the initial syllable, i.e., in terms of purely phonological conditions (see Section 5.3 and example 17). (Further developments, in some extreme northern dialects, are dealt with in Section 8.) This final step in the development can be formulated as in (19c). Like the preceding extension, this step, too, can be explained in terms of a reanalysis of monosyllabic stems, in so far as the stem ictus syllable is also the initial syllable. In addition, as noted in Section 3, the majority of mobiles, whether monosyllabic or polysyllabic, have initial stem ictus.

(19) a. Variable syllabic ictus from final syllable in H, with various restrictions

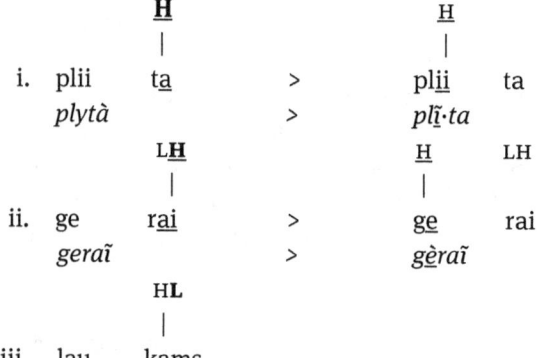

b. Variable extended ictus retraction, generally morphologically conditioned

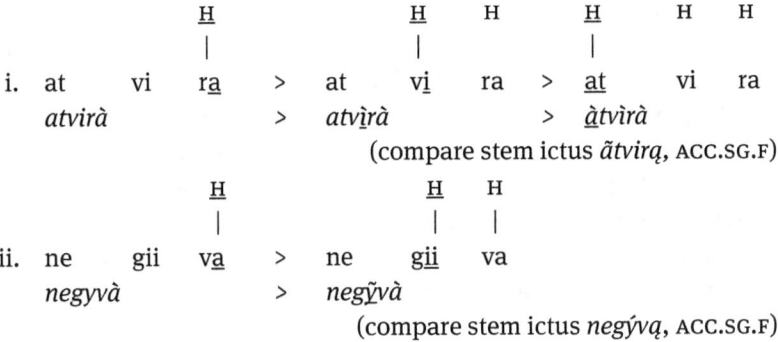

```
                H                      H   H              H    H   H
                |                      |                  |
   i.   at   vi   ra    >    at   vi   ra    >    at   vi   ra
        atvirà             >    atvìrà            >    àtvìrà
                                   (compare stem ictus ātvirą, ACC.SG.F)

                        H                    H   H
                        |                    |   |
   ii.  ne   gii   va   >    ne   gii   va
        negyvà              >    negỹvà
                                   (compare stem ictus negývą, ACC.SG.F)
```

c. Phonological ictus retraction to initial syllable

```
                     H                   H                H    H
                     |                   |                |    |
   i.   la   ta   kas    >    la   taks    >    la   taks
        latakàs              >    latàks         >    làtàks
                                   (vs. stem ictus lataˢ.ka, GEN.SG)
```

6.2 Second attempt: The Žemaitian change in circumflex realization and beyond

The hypothesis just outlined operates with the interpretation of circumflex as having rising (LH) pitch. This is, of course, the correct characterization for Aukštaitian, as well as for earlier Baltic in general (see note 10). As observed in Section 5.4, however, the Žemaitian circumflex has a weak rising-falling contour, i.e., something like $_L$HL (or $_L$H$_L$?). Similarly, while the characterization HL is correct for the acute of Aukštaitian and earlier Baltic in general, the intonation has changed to broken tone in Žemaitian, i.e., something like H$^?$L. These different realizations of the original circumflex and acute offer both a challenge and an opportunity.

The challenge is that the Žemaitian circumflex no longer ends in H, and as a consequence, the explanation of ictus retraction in terms of avoidance of final prominence (H) may appear problematic. This problem, however, is not insurmountable. All we need to do is assume that ictus retraction began before the change from LH to $_L$HL or $_L$H$_L$ or at an early intermediate phase of the change (something like LH$_L$).

The opportunity focuses on the fact that the Žemaitian change of the circumflex intonation involves a pitch or ictus RETRACTION within the circumflex syllable. While the fact of the change is well established (even if there may be differences regarding the precise nature of the new pitch contour; see Section 5.4), to my knowledge, no attempts have been made to link this retraction with the general phenomenon of Žemaitian ictus retraction – the similarities between the two phenomena are not accounted for.

A unified account becomes possible if the following change (20) is added to or before change in example (19a, item i). In both cases, final H is avoided through retraction, the difference being attributable to difference in structure – short final vowel in (19a, item i), final diphthong in (20). Perhaps significantly, the change in (20) is remarkably similar to the first step in Becker's account of Serbian-Croatian retraction, except that at an early stage, H is not shifted to the first mora of the final syllable, but merely farther to the left. (The retraction evidently was then extended from final position to all positions within the word.)

(20) Retraction of H/ictus within the circumflex intonation

```
             LH                    ₗHL
             ||                     V\
   ii.   ge    rai      >      ge    ra i
         geraĩ                      geraĩ
```

6.3 A speculative account for the type *matâu*

As shown in Section 5.5, the broken tone of the Žemaitian type *matâu* must be an innovation. A speculative explanation for this innovation is possible along the following lines.

A growing body of evidence suggests that in SOV languages, the Finality Effect discussed in Section 2 has special consequences for FINITE VERBS (which are utterance-final in unmarked utterances). In addition to the Vedic Sanskrit and Persian accent retractions summarized in Section 2, I have shown elsewhere that in a number of early Indo-European languages – Italic, Insular Celtic, and Baltic-Slavic – a process of *i*-apocope preferentially targets finite verbs (Hock 2006, 2007, 2012).[17] (see e.g., the Baltic-Slavic developments summarized in 21). As can be seen, *i*-apocope affects nouns only if the original penult has a long vowel (21a vs. 21b), but this restriction does not hold in verbs (21c). (The Slavic

---

[17] The Finality Effect is not limited to Indo-European SOV languages (see e.g., Harms 1990 for Finnish).

variation *bere:beretŭ* reflects an earlier **beret*, with loss of *-t* or anaptyxis of *-ŭ* due to the Slavic Open Syllable Conspiracy. Lithuanian has thematic vowel *-a-* throughout the paradigm.)

(21) a. **sūnumi*   > OCS   *synŭmĭ* 'son (INS.SG.M)'
                                    Lith *sūnumì*

      b. **ronkāmi* → **ronkayāmi* > OCS *rǫkajǫ* 'hand (INS.SG.F)' (via *-ām*)

      c. **bhereti*   > (o)cs *bere(tŭ)* 'gather (3SG)'
          **wegheti*   > Lith. *vě̃ža* 'convey (3rd person)'

Now, unlike most other European members of Indo-European, Lithuanian preserved SOV order (varying with V2) until fairly late; even Schleicher's grammar of 1856 contains a large number of verb-final utterances. Further, the putative change of *mataũ* to the **matáu* underlying Žemaitian *matâu* appears to be restricted to finite verb forms (the first and second singular of *o-* and *ė-*verbs).

Under the circumstances, it is possible to speculate that the change from *mataũ* to **matáu* arose as an utterance-final ictus/pitch retraction in finite verbs when SOV was the predominant word order (see the summary in 22). Note that if this account is correct, the change to **matáu* must have taken place early enough that the resulting acute (>broken tone) blocked the Žemaitian ictus retraction from final non-acute.

(22) a. Original canonical word order: s   o   v#
      b. Utterance-final ictus/pitch retraction: mataũ [mataú]>matáu / __ ##
      c. Extension to other contexts: mataũ [mataú]>matáu
      d. Change of acute to broken tone: matáu>matâu

7 Alternative accounts

This section addresses two alternative accounts of Žemaitian ictus retraction. One goes back to Jaunius in 1891–1900, and the other is Girdenis' more recent attempt in 1982.

7.1 Ictus retraction starting as stress-clash avoidance

According to Jaunius (1891–1900) (see Petit 2010: 72), retraction originates in a sandhi process that avoids clash between stressed final syllables and following stressed initial syllables, through retraction of word-final ictus to the preceding syllable (see 23).

(23) a. *vienà rópė* > *vienà rópė* 'one turnip'
  b. *šešiàs dẽšimtis* > *šẽšias dẽšimtis* '60 (ACC.F)'

As noted by Senn (1966: 76), the stress clash avoidance in (23) is limited to cases where the ending of the first word contains a short vowel. While the more general Žemaitian ictus retraction from final short and circumflex could be considered an extension of the process, the restriction that acute endings do not trigger retraction would remain unexplained.

This hypothesis therefore does not provide a likely explanation of the origin of Žemaitian ictus retraction.

7.2 Girdenis' account of 1982

A more comprehensive account has been proposed by Girdenis (1982). In his view, several factors contributed to Žemaitian ictus retraction – weakening or loss of vowels in final syllables, Jaunius' stress-clash avoidance, and a cross-linguistic tendency toward penult, rather than final accentuation.[18] In addition, the extension of retraction was favored by the morphological factor of what in Section 5.2 is called stem ictus in mobile paradigms, as well as an emphatic initial accent.

Two of these factors are similar to the ones considered relevant in this chapter's account – the preference for penult over final ictus and the morphological condition for the extension of ictus retraction.[19] Perhaps emphatic initial accentuation played a role too, but the account in Section 5.3 is a viable alternative.

Some of Girdenis' factors, however, are problematic. As shown in the preceding section, Jaunius' stress-clash avoidance is an unlikely starting point for Žemaitian ictus retraction. Further, Žemaitian ictus retraction does not depend on weakening or loss of vowels in final syllables (see again 10a along with 10b).

---

18 For the latter, Girdenis refers to Hyman (1975).
19 In fact, this part of my explanation is greatly indebted to Girdenis's account. At the same time, as noted in Sections 5.2 and 5.3 as well as in Section 6.1, in some, cases retraction does not go to the stem ictus syllable and some instances suggest syllable-by-syllable retraction. There clearly is a need for further research.

(10) a. Without apocope
Southern *plį̇́·ta* 'brick' (Standard *plytà*)
More northern *mẹ̇tėl'ùs* 'coat' (Standard *meteliùs)*

b. With apocope
Southern *pi̭eštǫks* 'pencil' (Standard *piẽštùkas*)

Most problematic, however, is Girdenis' attempt to account for why acute does not trigger ictus retraction. His argument is opaque at points, but the general thrust seems to be the claim that, in contrast to retraction from final circumflex, retraction from final acute would have led to loss of distinctiveness, as in Girdenis' examples *kr̂ǫšâ·* 'you (SG) dug out': *kr̂ǫšâ·*'hail (DAT.SG)'.

Prima facie, the claim that potential loss of distinctiveness can block sound change is questionable. As noted in a similar context by Hock ([1986] 1991: section 8.2), Middle Indo-Aryan had extensive consonant assimilations as well as sibilant merger, even though these led to massive loss of distinctions (see e.g., 24).

(24) Sanskrit   Middle Indo-Aryan
      sapta ⎫   'seven'
      śapta ⎪   'cursed'
      satta ⎬   satta   'sat'
      sakta ⎪   'attached'
      śakta ⎭   'able'

More specifically, the identity of the endings in *kr̂ǫšâ·*:*kr̂ǫšâ·* is not old. The second-singular ending of *kr̂ǫšâ·* reflects earlier Žemaitian acute *-ái*. The dative-singular ending of *kr̂ǫšâ·* by contrast represents a "secondary displaced" broken tone (Section 5.2). Significantly, this intonation appears on post-ictus syllables, irrespective of their original intonation. In fact, the original intonation of the dative ending is circumflex, not acute (>broken tone),[20] so the broken tone of *-â* in *kr̂ǫšâ·* cannot reflect an original acute. Further, as Grinaveckis (1964: 6) notes, the preservation of post-ictus intonational differences in extreme northern Žemaitian as well as Latvian suggests that the "secondary displaced" broken tone of the more southern dialects reflects NEUTRALIZATION of the contrast circumflex: acute (>broken tone).

Given these problems, the explanation in Section 6 is preferable.

---

[20] Consider the lack of Saussure's law shift in forms like *rañkaĩ>rañkai* 'hand (DAT.SG) vs. shift in *rañką́>rañką́>>ranką̀* (NOM.SG), with original acute ending.

8 Conclusions and implications

Lithuanian thus adds to the cross-linguistic evidence for finality effects, in terms both of segmental changes (apocope) and suprasegmental ones (ictus retraction). The latter development can be motivated as starting out with avoidance of utterance-final high pitch and thus is remarkably similar to the motivation of the Serbian-Croatian shift. In addition, Lithuanian adds to the examples of interaction between segmental and suprasegmental finality effects, in so far as apocope entails reassignment of stranded pitch melodies.

Beyond their cross-linguistic significance, the Lithuanian developments are relevant for East Baltic linguistics and the question of a Finnic substratum in Latvian.

First, the Žemaitian ictus retraction, culminating in initial accent in the northern dialects, is remarkably similar to the well-known fact that Latvian, too, has undergone ictus retraction to the first syllable – with one important difference: Unlike Žemaitian, Latvian does not have a non-acute limitation on ictus retraction. That this similarity is not accidental is suggested by Grinaveckis' observation that some extreme northern Žemaitian dialects, too, have (somewhat irregular) ictus retraction to the first syllable without the usual Žemaitian acute restriction. The boundary between Latvian and (Žemaitian) Lithuanian, thus, appears to be porous.

What is especially interesting in this regard is that, based on Endzelin (1922), Stang argues for a two-stage process of Latvian ictus retraction, first to the penult and then to the initial syllable, as in *galvāsę̄>*galvā̇sę̄>galvās(ę̄) / ga̍l̂vâs 'head (LOC. PL), with the broken tone on the first syllable and the penult resulting from retraction (1966: 142–143). This two-stage development is of course highly reminiscent of the fact that Žemaitian ictus retraction (outside the south) also unfolds in two stages – retraction to the penult, followed by retraction to the stem ictus syllable and beyond.

Under the circumstances, it is possible to argue for a larger scenario of ictus retraction embracing both Žemaitian and Latvian, which with some simplifications can be summarized as in (25). In its early phases, the process is a highly variable phenomenon; along the way, it becomes more regular, but still generally sensitive to morphological factors; a further stage is the phonological retraction to the first syllable; finally, the restriction that retraction takes place only from non-acute endings is lifted and the change is completely regularized. In northern Žemaitian dialects that have this retraction, the change is not completely regular, while in Latvian it is.[21]

---

[21] A reviewer notes that modern Latvian has exceptions to initial ictus. But these exceptions either are recent borrowings such as *ragū̱* 'ragout' or are words such as *neka̱s* 'nobody', which, as the reviewer notes, can be explained as having emphatic stress. (For a similar phenomenon in German, note forms like *u̱nmöglich* vs. emphatic *unmö̱glich* 'impossible', where non-initial ictus is hardly an archaism.)

(25) a. Variable retraction to penult (limited to non-acute) — Southern Žemaitian
b. Variable retraction to stem ictus syllable (limited to non-acute) — Intermediate area
c. Generalized retraction (limited to non-acute) — Northern Žemaitian
d. Generalized retraction (even from acute; not fully regular) — Extreme Northern Žemaitian
e. Generalized retraction (even from acute; fully regular) — Latvian

The most likely hypothesis regarding the historical geographical spread of ictus retraction is that it started in the north (somewhere within the Latvian dialect continuum) and spread south petering out in the extreme south of Žemaitian.[22] Not only does this hypothesis conform to the general dialectological spread pattern of innovations, it is also supported by the fact that retraction has been complete in Latvian since at least the nineteenth century but is still a highly variable change in progress in the south.

As an anonymous reviewer points out, Girdenis and Rosinas (1974) have criticized the view that Latvian and Žemaitian ictus retraction are related. Petit (2010: 74–75) argues that there are considerable differences between Latvian and Žemaitian – in his view, the Latvian broken tone "obviously" developed in originally unaccented syllables, while the (Kretinga) Žemaitian counterpart developed in originally accented syllables.[23] Moreover, while Latvian preserves intonational contrasts in originally post-ictus syllables, Žemaitian normally has only broken tone. Further, as noted by Stang (1966: 125), Latvian distinguishes between three intonations – circumflex (falling), "Dehnton" (weakly rising or level), and broken tone (with glottal stop or constriction), while some of Žemaitian has four – circumflex (rising-falling), broken tone (with glottal stop or constriction), Dehnton (level), and "geschnittener Dehnton" (not clearly characterized).

Such differences in detail, however, are to be expected, especially if the four-way distinction of some of the northern Žemaitian dialects might be original (Žinkevičius 1966: 40, referred to by Young 1991: 90, note 3). Non-standard, regional varieties of Latvian show that rich intonational systems of this sort tend to be simplified through various mergers/neutralizations. As noted earlier, this is no doubt true in the case of post-ictus intonations – the general Žemaitian "secondary displaced" broken tone appears to be an innovation compared to the preservation of original intonational distinctions of Latvian and some of extreme

---

22 See also Young (1991: 25); Petit (2010: 71) makes a similar claim, but limited to Žemaitian.
23 At the same time, Petit does raise the question whether the typologically unusual stød-like broken tone in two close neighbors can be accidental.

northern Žemaitian. Further, note that the "secondary displaced" broken tone of Žemaitian appears in originally unaccented syllables – contrary to Petit's claim that Žemaitian broken tone is limited to originally accented syllables.

Most important, trying to completely separate the Latvian and Žemaitian ictus retractions is tantamount to saying that the remarkable similarities between these varieties of East Baltic are accidental. More than that, it fails to account for the existence of extreme northern Žemaitian dialects that share the Latvian intonational distinctions in post-ictus syllables and, like Latvian, relax the restriction against acute triggers. Moreover, the fact that this relaxation is not completely regular in the Žemaitian dialects, but regular in Latvian shows that the Žemaitian dialects in question form a transition area between Latvian and Žemaitian – within a larger, Latvian-Žemaitian dialect continuum.

Finally, there are implications for the widespread claim that the Latvian generalized ictus retraction or initial accent results from contact with Uralic/Finnic (see e.g., Bojtár 1999: 219, Balode and Holvoet 2001a: 9, Thomason and Kaufman 1988: 241). That claim is difficult to reconcile with the fact that ictus retraction is not limited to Latvian but constitutes a change that spread into neighboring Žemaitian dialects and that, moreover, the change can be explained as an internal development, resulting from a series of extensions. In fact, the first stage of the change – ictus retraction to avoid final prominence – cannot conceivably be attributed to the initial accent of Finnic. It is therefore not surprising that scholars such as Stang (1966: passim) or Koptjevskaja-Tamm and Wälchli (2001: 639) question the Finnic-influence hypothesis (although their approach differs from the one of this chapter). Perhaps Koptjevskaja-Tamm and Wälchli are right in suggesting that the Finnic "influence could still have played an important role in strengthening the tendency to repeat the process of stress retraction, which might have arisen due to language-internal mechanisms". But I do not see any way of testing this compromise proposal.

Acknowledgments

This is a revised and updated version of a paper read at the workshop "Baltic Languages in an Areal-Typological Perspective" at the 2010 Annual Meeting of the Societas Linguistica Europaea in Vilnius, Lithuania. An earlier, much less detailed version is contained in Hock (1999). I have benefited from comments received at the meeting, as well as feedback by two anonymous reviewers. The responsibility for the views in this chapter remains with me.

Abbreviations

1	first person	MC	main clause
3	third person	NEG	negation
ACC	accusative	NOM	nominative
COMP	complementizer	O	object
CP	correlative pronoun	OBL	oblique
DAT	dative	OPT	optative
DC	dependent clause	PCLE	particle
F	feminine	PL	plural
H	high pitch	PRS	present
INS	instrumental	RP	relative pronoun
L	low pitch	S	subject
LOC	locative	SG	singular
M	masculine	V	verb

References

Atkočaitytė, Daiva. 1999/2000. Kirčio atitraukimas pietų žemaičių raseiniškių tarmėje [Shift of stress from endings in the South Žemaitian dialect of Raseinai]. *Baltistica* 34(2): 151–172 (English summary, p. 171).

Balode, Laimute & Axel Holvoet. 2001a. The Latvian language and its dialects. In Östen Dahl & Maria Koptjevskaja-Tamm (eds.) *Circum-Baltic languages. Vol. 1: Past and present*, 3–40. Amsterdam, Philadelphia: John Benjamins.

Balode, Laimute & Axel Holvoet. 2001b. The Lithuanian language and its dialects. In Östen Dahl & Maria Koptjevskaja-Tamm (eds.) *Circum-Baltic languages. Vol. 1: Past and present*, 41–79. Amsterdam, Philadelphia: John Benjamins.

Becker, Lee A. 1977. *Leftward movement of high tone*. Paper at the 1977 Annual Meeting of the Linguistic Society of America.

Becker, Lee A. 1979. A contribution to an explanation of the Neo-Stokavian accent retraction. *Zbornik za filologiju i lingvistiku* 22(1). 87–94.

Bloomfield, Leonard. 1917. Tagalog texts with grammatical analysis. *University of Illinois Studies in Language and Literature* 3(2–4).

Bojtár, Endre. 1999. *Foreword to the past: A cultural history of the Baltic people*. Budapest, New York: Central European University Press.

Canger, Una. 1990. Philology in America: Nahuatl. In Jacek Fisiak (ed.) *Historical linguistics and philology*, 107–118. Berlin, New York: Mouton de Gruyter.

Cheng, Chin-Chuan & Charles W. Kisseberth. 1979. Ikorovere Makua tonology (part 1). *Studies in the Linguistic Sciences* 9(1). 31–63.

Derksen, Rick. 1991. An introduction to the history of Lithuanian accentuation. In A. A. Barentsen, B. M. Groen, & R. Sprenger (eds.) *Studies in West Slavic and Baltic linguistics*, 45–84. Amsterdam: Rodopi.

Dogil, Gregorz. 1999. Baltic languages. In Harry van der Hulst (ed.) *Word prosodic systems in the languages of Europe*, 877–896. Berlin, New York: de Gruyter.

Endzelin, Janis. 1899. Über den lettischen Silbenakzent. *Beiträge zur Kunde der indogermanischen Sprachen* 25: 259–274.

Endzelin, Janis. 1922. *Lettische Grammatik*. Riga: Gulbis. (Also published in 1923, Heidelberg: Winter.)

Girdenis, Aleksas. 1982. Opyt morfologičeskoj interpretacii severožemajtskoj attrakcii udarenija. [On the morphological interpretation of North Žemaitian accent retraction.] *Baltistica* 18(2): 179–188.

Girdenis, Aleksas & Albertas Rosinas. 1974. Review of V. Grinaveckis *Žemaičių tarmės istorija (Fonetika)*, 1973. *Baltistica* 10(2): 187–207.

Grimes, J. E. 1959. Huichol tone and intonation. *International Journal of American Linguistics* 25: 221–232.

Grinaveckis, Vladas. 1964. Istoričeskoe razvitie udarenija i intonacii žemajtskix govorov litovskogo jazyka (v sravnenii s latyšskim). [Historical development of stress and intonation in the Žemaitian dialects of Lithuanian, in comparison with Latvian]. In V. D. Koroljuk (ed.) *Slavjanskaja i baltijskaja akcentologija* [Slavic and Baltic accentology], 1–17. Moscow: Nauka. (Cited in Young 1991.)

Grinaveckis, Vladas. 1973. Kirčiavimo sistemos reikšmė kirčio atitraukimui [On the role of accentual system in accent retraction]. *Baltistica* 9(2): 151–160. (Cited in Young 1991.)

Harms, Robert T. 1990. Synchronic rules and diachronic "laws": The Saussurean dichotomy reaffirmed. In Edgar C. Polomé (ed.) *Research guide on language change*, 313–323. Berlin, New York: Mouton de Gruyter.

Hock, Hans Henrich. [1986] 1991. *Principles of historical linguistics*. 1st and 2nd editions. Berlin, New York: Mouton de Gruyter.

Hock, Hans Henrich. 1999. Finality, prosody, and change. In Osamu Fujimura, Brian D. Joseph, & Bohumil Palek (eds.) *Proceedings of LP'98*, 15–30. Prague: The Karolinum Press.

Hock, Hans Henrich. 2006. The Insular Celtic absolute : conjunct distinction once again: A prosodic proposal. In Karlene Jones-Bley, Martin E. Huld, Angela Della Volpe, & Miriam Robbins Dexter (eds.) *Proceedings of the Sixteenth UCLA Indo-European Conference. Los Angeles, Nov. 5–6, 2005, Journal of Indo-European Studies Monograph* 50: 153–172. Washington: Institute for the Study of Man.

Hock, Hans Henrich. 2007. Morphology and *i*-apocope in Slavic and Baltic. In Karlene Jones-Bley, Martin E. Huld, Angela Della Volpe, & Miriam Robbins Dexter (eds.) *Proceedings of the Eighteenth UCLA Indo-European Conference. Los Angeles, Nov. 3–4, 2006, Journal of Indo-European Studies Monograph* 53: 65–76. Washington: Institute for the Study of Man.

Hock, Hans Henrich. 2012. Phrasal prosody and the Indo-European verb. In H. Craig Melchert (ed.) *The Indo-European verb: Proceedings of the Conference of the Society for Indo-European Studies, Los Angeles, 13–15 September 2010*, 115–126. Wiesbaden: Reichert.

Hock, Hans Henrich. 2014. Vedic verb accent revisited. In Jared Klein & Elizabeth Tucker (eds.) *Vedic and Sanskrit historical linguistics: Papers from the 13th World Sanskrit Conference, 153–178*. Delhi: Motilal Banarsidass.

Hyman, Larry M. 1975. *Phonology: Theory and analysis*. New York: Holt, Rinehart & Winston.
Jaunius, Kazimieras. 1891–1900. *Dialektologiniai darbai* [Dialectological works]. Kaunas. (Cited in Petit 2010.)
Kazlauskas, Jonas. 1968. *Lietuvių kalbos istorinė gramatika* [Historical grammar of Lithuanian]. Vilnius: Mintis. (Cited in Young 1991.)
Klein, Jared S. 1992. *On verbal accentuation in the Rigveda*. (American Oriental Society Essay Number 11.) New Haven, CT: American Oriental Society.
Koptjevskaja-Tamm, Maria & Bernhard Wälchli. 2001. The Circum-Baltic languages: An areal-typological approach. In Östen Dahl & Maria Koptjevskaja-Tamm (eds.) *Circum-Baltic languages. Vol. 2: Grammar and typology*, 615–750. Amsterdam, Philadelphia: John Benjamins.
Leskien, August. 1881. Die Quantitätsverhältnisse im Ablaut des Litauischen. *Archiv für slavische Philologie* 5: 188–190.
Petit, Daniel. 2010. *Untersuchungen zu den baltischen Sprachen*. Leiden, Boston: Brill.
Poljakov, Oleg. 1997. Über Herkunft und Entwicklung der Silbenakzente im Lettischen. *Baltistica* 32(1): 57–69.
Rau, Jeremy. 2009. Myc. *te-re-ja* and the athematic inflection of the Greek contract verbs. In Kazuhiko Yoshida & Brent Vine (eds.) *East and west: Papers in Indo-European studies*, 181–188. Bremen: Hempen.
Saussure, Ferdinand de. 1894. A propos de l'accentuation lituanienne. *Mémoires de la Société de Linguistique de Paris* 8: 435–446.
Saussure, Ferdinand de. 1896. Accentuation lituanienne. *Indogermanische Forschungen* 6 (Anzeiger): 157–166.
Schleicher, August Wilhelm. 1856. *Handbuch der litauischen Sprache*. Prag: Calve.
Senn, Alfred. 1966. *Handbuch der litauischen Sprache*. Heidelberg: Winter.
Stang, Christian S. 1966. *Vergleichende Grammatik der [b]altischen Sprachen*. Oslo, Bergen, Tromsö: Universitetsforlaget.
Thomason, Sarah Grey & Terrence Kaufman. 1988. *Language contact, creolization, and genetic linguistics*. Berkeley, Los Angeles: University of California Press.
Villanueva Svensson, Miguel. 2010. Review of Petit 2010. *Baltistica* 45: 364–369.
Young, Stephen R. 1991. *The prosodic structure of Lithuanian*. Lanham, New York, London: University Press of America.
Žinkevičius, Zigmas. 1966. *Lietuvių dialektologija* [Lithuanian dialectology]. Vilnius: Mintis. (Cited in Young 1991.)

Anna Daugavet
3 The lengthening of the first component of Lithuanian diphthongs in an areal perspective

1 Introduction

The main impetus for the chapter lies in the controversy surrounding the so-called tonal contrast in Lithuanian. A closer acquaintance with its facts shows that at some level of simplification, this contrast turns out to be no more than a peculiar pronunciation of some diphthongs that has little to do with pitch. Compare the realization of the contrasting tones in the examples below.[1] (I will further refer to the tonal contrast as that between the accents traditionally called "acute" and "circumflex". In the orthography, the acute accent is marked as <´> on the first component of diphthongs and the circumflex accent as <˜> on the second component of diphthongs.)

(1) a. acute
    áukštas [ˈɑˑʊk.ʃtas] 'high'
    táiką [ˈtɑˑɪ.kaː] 'aim; apply' (PRS.PRTC.NOM.PL)

   b. circumflex
    aũkštas [ˈʊuˑk.ʃtas] 'storey of a building'
    taĩką [ˈtəiˑ.kaː] 'peace' (ACC.SG)

Under the acute accent, the first component of diphthongs is lengthened (it is marked as half-long [ˑ] in the transcription) and the second component is short (1a). The circumflex accent is distinguished from the acute by the reduction of the first component and the lengthening of the second component (also marked as half-long) (1b). The realization of the circumflex is especially striking in so-called diphthongal sequences, i.e., diphthongs having sonorants *n, m, l, r* as their second components (2b).[2] The less sonorous second element sounds as

---

[1] All examples are rendered in the IPA transcription, which facilitates the comparison but may lead to some inaccuracies, as the symbols that I use to substitute the national transcription are not always based on phonetic studies. Grammatical information in the examples is only supplied if it is different from the nominative singular (masculine) for nouns and adjectives, but it may be present if relevant for the context.
[2] In Lithuanian and Latvian, diphthongs may be viewed as diphthongal sequences with [j], [v] acting as their second components (Girdenis 2003: 100–101; cf. Pakerys 1995: 166–167). In fact, the same may be also true for Livonian (see the discussion in Viitso 2008: 168 and Livonian examples in Section 3.4).

if it were syllabic, whereas the more sonorous preceding vowel is perceived as non-syllabic.

(2) a. acute
 káltas [ˈkɑˑl.tas] 'chisel'

 b. circumflex
 kaĩtas [ˈkəlˑ.tas] 'guilty'

The accents on diphthongs and diphthongal sequences are much better distinguished than on long monophthongs where the contrast tends to be lost in dialects and the colloquial standard language.

The chapter concentrates on changes that brought about the current situation in Lithuanian. I view it as a result of two lengthening processes. The first process is the lengthening of the first components of diphthongs and diphthongal sequences, as in Lithuanian examples under the acute in (1a) and (2a). Similar processes are found in the neighboring languages Latvian and Livonian. In all the three languages, I analyze the process as the reassignment of the second mora, linked to the less sonorous second component, to the more sonorous first component. (The lengthened first component in Latvian (3a) and Livonian (3b) is identified as a long vowel.)

(3) a. Latvian
 *varna>vārna [ˈvɑːrnɑ] 'crow'[3]

 b. Livonian
 *aiga>āiga [ˈɑːigɑ(ː)] 'time'
 *jalga>jālga [ˈjɑːlgɑ(ː)] 'leg; foot'

The second process is the lengthening of vowels and consonants in stressed syllables in order to make the stressed syllable heavy. The process is only found in Latvian and Lithuanian. In Latvian, an intervocalic consonant following a stressed vowel is geminated, thus supplying the closure for the stressed syllable (4a). In Lithuanian, the stressed syllable is made heavy by simply lengthening the stressed vowel (4b). (This type of lengthening is not reflected in either Latvian or Lithuanian orthography due to the regularity of the process. In the examples below, the lengthened stressed vowel is marked as long.) I analyze this change as the addition of a second mora, which is further attributed to the intervocalic consonant in Latvian and to the stressed vowel in Lithuanian. The link

---

[3] Reconstructed forms in the chapter may be unaccurate with regard to changes other than those under discussion.

between stress and vowel length in Lithuanian is reinforced by the shortening of unstressed long vowels.

(4) a. Latvian
rati>['ratti] 'wheels; cart'

b. Lithuanian
ratai>['raːtai] 'wheels; cart'

I believe the two lengthening processes, which were initially independent, to come into interaction with each other in Lithuanian, where they use the same phonetic material. Besides, they often apply to different forms of the same morphemes so that in one form the vowel is lengthened as the first component of a diphthongal sequence, and in another form as a single vowel under stress (see 5). In my opinion, the lengthened first component of diphthongs and diphthongal sequences under the acute was reinterpreted as the stressed element. The second component was consequently perceived as unstressed.

(5) diphthongal sequence   monophthong
     kálti>['kaˑlʲ.tʲɪ] (INF)   *kãla*>['kaː.la] (PRS.3)   'hammer; forge'

According to my hypothesis, the identification of the bimoraic first component of diphthongs and diphthongal sequences as the stressed element led to the reinterpretation of circumflex diphthongs and diphthongal sequences. As distinct from acute syllables, they retained short vowels in the position of the first component. Latvian (6a) and Livonian (6b) show that it is common for diphthongs and diphthongal sequences that have a short vowel as their first component to lengthen the moraic second component. (It is marked as half-long or long depending on various factors.) This is different from the pronunciation of circumflex diphthongs and diphthongal sequences in modern Lithuanian as neither Latvian nor Livonian has the reduction of the first component.

(6) a. Latvian
maina ['maiːna] 'change' (PRS.3)
maisis ['maiˑsis] 'bag'
balts [balːts] 'white'
balsis ['balˑsis] 'voice' (NOM.PL)

b. Livonian
aigõ ['aiˑgə] 'time' (PART.SG)
jalgõ ['jalˑgə] 'leg; foot' (PART.SG)

Initially, the pronunciation of circumflex syllables in Lithuanian must have been roughly the same as in the above examples from Latvian and Livonian.

The first component was short but unreduced; the second component was lengthened, which is easy to explain by its moraic status.

My idea is that the lengthened second component of circumflex diphthongs and diphthongal sequences was reinterpreted, on the grounds of its length, as the only stressed element in the syllable. A mora that was initially connected to the short first component was assigned to it. The reduction of the first component, which is the most remarkable feature of circumflex diphthongs and diphthongal sequences in modern Lithuanian, is thus a consequence of the vowel's becoming non-moraic.

The chapter deals with the material of the Baltic languages Lithuanian and Latvian, and the Finnic language Livonian. The latter is a now almost extinct minority language in the north of Kurzeme (Courland), Latvia, its speakers having been assimilated by Latvians in the course of several centuries. In the chapter, I will discuss phonetic and phonological features, some of which are shared, to a different extent, by all three languages and may thus be viewed as an areal phenomenon, and some which are only found in Lithuanian.

The three languages have in common the differentiation between short and long monophthongs and the existence of diphthongs. They also distinguish between light and heavy syllables so that syllables containing a long monophthong or a diphthong are grouped together with syllables containing a short monophthong followed by a (sonorant) consonant. The grouping is based on the ability of heavy syllables to serve as the domain for a suprasegmental opposition that otherwise takes rather different forms in each of the three languages, that is, the acute and circumflex accents in Lithuanian, the three Latvian tones, and the Livonian *stød*.

The extent to which the lengthening processes under discussion apply to the three languages is different. While the lengthening of the first component of diphthongs is found in Lithuanian, Latvian, and Livonian, the lengthening of stressed syllables is only present in the Baltic languages.

The chapter is the first attempt to juxtapose the sound systems of the three languages instead of analyzing in isolation phenomena such as polytonicity, initial stress, and overlength (see Koptjevskaja-Tamm & Wälchli 2001: 637–646 and the literature therein). Nevertheless, my task is not to give a full-scale comparison but to illuminate the presented facts under a specific angle provided by the focus on lengthening processes.

The following three sections are dedicated to the three languages discussed. I start with Latvian because, as different from the other languages, it only lengthens the first component of diphthongal sequences with *r*. Livonian is more similar to Lithuanian in that the lengthening of the first components is found in all types of diphthongs and diphthongal sequences. Lithuanian comes last, since it combines the lengthening in diphthongs and diphthongal sequences with the lengthening of stressed vowels, which is a complication absent from the other languages.

The description of each of the languages includes information about vocalism, syllable weight, stress, the above-mentioned suprasegmental opposition, and the conditions under which the components of diphthongs and diphthongal sequences are lengthened. Since the conditions of the lengthening are subject to considerable dialectal variation in Latvian and Lithuanian, the information about dialects is added to the corresponding sections.

2 Latvian

I will begin with the redistribution of moras to the more sonorous first component of diphthongs and diphthongal sequences as it is found in Latvian and Livonian. In Latvian, this change is confined to diphthongal sequences where the second component is *r*, but dialects show variation with regard to the exact conditions for the lengthening.

2.1 Phonemic inventory and syllable weight

The Latvian vowel inventory is given in Table 1, which mainly follows the discussion by Grigorjevs (2008: 194–213), but in accordance with Girdenis (2003: 103) *ie* [iə] and *o* [uə] are placed together with long monophthongs.[4]

The symbols for vowels used in the Latvian orthography (written in italics) do not reflect some of the contrasts, such as the one between the open [æː], [æ] and close [eː], [e]. The orthographic *o* stands for [uə] in most cases including borrowings, although many borrowings are pronounced with either [ɔː] or [ɔ], which sometimes may be realized as long and sometimes as short in the same word. Standard Latvian does not have [ɔː], [ɔ] in native words.

Tab. 1: Latvian monophthongs

Long		Short	
ī [iː]	*ū* [uː]	*i* [i]	*u* [u]
ie [iə]	*o* [uə]		
ē [eː]	*o* [ɔː]	*e* [e]	*o* [ɔ]
ē [æː]	*ā* [ɑː]	*e* [æ]	*a* [ɑ]

---

4 The traditional transcription in both Latvian and Lithuanian is [ie], [uo], but only Lithuanian consequently uses both symbols in orthography; cf. Lithuanian *pienas*, Latvian *piens* 'milk', and Lithuanain *uodas*, Latvian *ods* 'gnat'.

Diphthongs include combinations of any short vowel except [æ] with the subsequent *i* or *u*, although *oi* and *ou* are only possible in borrowings. Diphthongal sequences also include combinations of short vowels with palatal *ņ* [ɲ] and *ļ* [ʎ].

Consonants in Latvian contribute to syllable weight in more than one way (see also Kariņš (1996: 43–46)).

First, diphthongal sequences are equivalent to diphthongs and long monophthongs because they all form heavy syllables, distinguished from light syllables by their ability to serve as the domain for the tonal opposition (see Section 2.2).

Second, as distinct from Lithuanian, but similar to the Finnic languages, Latvian allows gemination of consonants. Any consonants may form geminates on morpheme boundaries, but inside morphemes, only long sonorants and voiceless obstruents are found (Laua 1997: 62–66, 83). While sonorants contrast for length (7a), voiceless obstruents appear automatically between two short vowels, if the first of the short vowels bears stress (7b). Voiceless geminates are not reflected in the orthography.

(7) a. sonorant geminates
galli ['gɑl.li] 'Gaul' (NOM.PL), cf. *gali* ['gɑ.li] 'end' (NOM.PL)

b. voiceless obstruent geminates
saki ['sɑk.ki] 'say' (2SG.PRS)

The main purpose of the automatic gemination of voiceless obstruents seems to be to turn underlyingly light stressed syllables into heavy (8a), as it does not affect syllables that are underlyingly heavy, that is, syllables with long monophthongs, diphthongs, and diphthongal sequences (8b) (see Daugavet 2013 for more details).

(8) a. after short vowels
saka ['sɑk.kɑ] 'say' (PRS.3)

b. after long vowels, diphthongs, and diphthongal sequences
sāka ['sɑː.kɑ] 'begin' (PST.3)
sveika ['svei.kɑ] 'healthy' (NOM.SG.F)
sarka ['sɑr.kɑ] 'turn red' (PST.3)

Thus, gemination of intervocalic obstruents adds the second mora to the stressed syllable, which is a process playing a crucial part in the other Baltic language Lithuanian where it interacts with the process of redistribution of moras to the more sonorous component of diphthongs and diphthongal sequences. In Latvian, these processes are kept apart from each other.

2.2 Tones

Latvian distinguishes three tones, traditionally called "level", "falling", and "broken". (See the examples in Table 2, where they are indicated according to the tradition. I deviate from the tradition in that I combine the diacritics for tone with the macron from the orthography.) In everyday orthography, tones are not marked. The importance of tones for the present discussion is that in Latvian the tonal contrast creates one of the conditions for the lengthening of the first components of diphthongal sequences with *r*.

For the phonological analysis of the Latvian tones, see Kariņš (1996) and Daugavet (2012). The phonetic manifestation of the Latvian tones involves pitch, intensity, and duration. The names of the level and the falling tones roughly reflect their pitch characteristics, although the level tone may also have a slightly rising pitch contour (Ekblom 1933: 34, Ceplītis et al. 1995: 24–25, Kariņš 1996: 131–132, Laua 1997: 104–105). Intensity is reported as falling for both level and falling tones (Ekblom 1933: 48, Laua 1997: 104–105), but some authors claim that the level tone has the same pattern for both pitch and intensity (Ceplītis et al. 1995: 24).

The level tone lengthens the syllable nucleus (Ekblom 1933: 10–11; cf. Kariņš 1996: 126). It is noteworthy that in Markus and Auziņa (2008: 55–58), long monophthongs under the level tone are transcribed as overlong (9a), whereas under the falling tone, they are represented as having the normal length (9b).

(9) a. level tone
 mãsa ['mɑːːsɑ] 'sister'

 b. falling tone
 lȃse ['lɑːse] 'drop (of liquid)'

Under the level tone, the second components of diphthongs and diphthongal sequences are long (10a) (see the transcription of diphthongs by Markus and

Tab. 2: Latvian tones

	Level	Falling	Broken
Long monophthong	*mīt* 'change' (INF)	*mìt* 'exist' (PRS.3)	*mȋt* 'tread' (INF)
Diphthong	*aũksts* 'cold'	*ràuks* 'pucker' (FUT.3)	*aȗgsts* [ksts] 'high'
			raȗgs [ks] 'yeast'
Diphthongal sequence	*vaĩgs* [ks] 'tether' *kaĩšana* 'forging'	*kàlšana* 'drying up'	*vaȋgs* [ks] 'humid'

Auziņa 2008: 55–58; for diphthongal sequences, see Laua 1997: 64). Under the two other tones, the second components are marked as short by Markus and Auziņa, but Laua claims that the second components of diphthongal sequences are half-long under the falling and broken tones, and my impression is that is also true for diphthongs (10b,c).

(10) a. under level tone
laĩks [ˈlaiːks] 'time'
aũksts [ˈauːksts] 'cold'
mañta [ˈmanːta] 'belongings'

b. under falling tone
màisis [ˈmaiˑsis] 'bag'
bàlsis [ˈbalˑsis] 'voice' (NOM.PL)

c. under broken tone
jaûns [jauˑns] 'young; new'
jum̂ti [ˈjumˑti] 'roof' (NOM.PL)

The broken tone stands aside from the other Latvian tones as its main phonetic feature is glottal stop or creaky voice. In Markus and Auziņa (2008: 55–58), it is transcribed accordingly as in (11). From the standpoint of pitch and intensity, the broken tone has the falling-rising pattern (Kariņš 1996: 132; cf. Laua 1997: 105).

(11) jûgs [juːʔks] 'yoke'
jaûns [jauʔns] 'young; new'

In this chapter, I will transcribe the Latvian tones according to the convention proposed by Markus and Auziņa (2008).[5] In orthography and in reconstructed forms, I will retain the traditional diacritics and combine them with the macron on long vowels.

A few words must be said about the relationship between tones and stress. Latvian normally has initial stress, but tones are claimed to be found in both stressed and unstressed syllables (Ābele 1932; Ceplītis et al. 1995: 25; cf. Laua

---

[5] The rendering of the level tone with the help of an additional length mark is actually problematic because it may be interpreted as an indication that a syllable with the level tone has more than two moras, which is not my intention. One and the same word in this chapter may be transcribed as having a long or "overlong" vowel (e.g., vārna [vaːrna] or vãrna [vaːːrna]) depending on whether I include information about tones in its transcription and orthographic representation.

1997: 107). The example of the tonal contrast in an unstressed position is given in (12). More information on the tonal contrast in unstressed position can be found in Endzelīns (1951: 35) and Ābele (1932).

(12) êdin*ā̃t* [ˈeːˀ.di.nɑˀːt] (INF)   êdin*ā̃t* [ˈeːˀ.di.nɑːːt] (2PL.PRS)   'feed'

It may be due to the presence of contrastive tones in unstressed syllables that in Latvian the lengthening of vowels before a tautosyllabic *r* is equally found in stressed and unstressed position, although an alternative explanation is also possible (see the next section).

2.3 Lengthening of vowels before *r*

At some point in the history of Latvian, vowels acting as the first components of diphthongal sequences were lengthened if the second component was *r* (Endzelīns 1951: 147–152, Rudzīte 1993: 251–258). In the dialects on which the standard language is based, this change only affected non-high vowels [ɑ], [æ], [e] in syllables with either the level or the falling tone (13). In syllables under the broken tone (14a), and with high vowels [u], [i] under any tone (14b), no lengthening is found.

(13) a. non-high vowels under the level tone
varna>vãrna [ˈvɑːːrnɑ] 'crow'
berzi>bẽrzi [ˈbæːːrzi] 'birch' (NOM.PL)
bert>bẽrt [beːːrt] 'pour' (INF)

b. non-high vowels under the falling tone
dàrzi>dàrzi [ˈdɑːrzi] 'garden' (NOM.PL)
bèrni>bẽrni [ˈbæːrni] 'children'
vèrst>vẽrst [veːrst] 'turn' (INF)

(14) a. non-high vowels under the broken tone
dar̂bi [ˈdɑrˀbi] 'labor' (NOM.PL)
ver̂gi [ˈværˀgi] 'slave' (NOM.PL)
dzer̂t [ʥerˀt] 'drink' (INF)

b. high vowels under any tone
kur̃pe [ˈkurːpe] 'shoe'
bir̃ze [ˈbirːze] 'grove'
ùrba [ˈurbɑ] 'drill' (PST.3)
pìrkt [pirkt] 'buy' (INF)
pur̂ns [purˀns] 'snout'
zir̂gi [ˈzirˀgi] 'horse' (NOM.PL)

Although the lengthening might have been connected with the phonetic manifestation of the tones at the time of the change, it cannot be treated as such at present. Short vowels are possible, even under the level or the falling tone, before the tautosyllabic *r* in borrowings (15) and words where *r* historically belonged to the next syllable[6] (16). There is also no lengthening of [ɔ] in [ɔr], as the vowel is only found in borrowings. The examples in (15) are taken from Ceplītis et al. (1995); the IPA transcription is mine.

(15) a. borrowings with the level tone
  ar̃mija [ˈɑrːmijɑ] 'army'
  ver̃sija [ˈverːsijɑ] 'version'
  ver̃bs [værːps] 'verb'
  or̃bīta [ˈɔrːbiːːtɑ] 'orbit'

  b. borrowings with the falling tone
  àrtẽrija [ˈɑrteːːrijɑ] 'artery'
  bèrbèrs [ˈberbers] 'Berber'
  hèrcõgs [ˈhærtsɔːːks] 'duke'
  òrķestris [ˈɔrcestris] 'orchestra'

(16) *garas>*gàrs* [gɑrs] 'spirit'
  *keras>*cèrs* [tsærs] 'shrub'

It is not entirely clear if the lengthening of the first components in diphthongal sequences with *r* was only conditioned by tone or by both tone and stress. In the previous section, I link the lengthening in unstressed position with the fact that in Latvian the tonal contrast is relatively independent of stress (see 17). But it is possible that the lengthening initially took place in stressed syllables, but later, the lengthened vowel became associated with certain morphemes, so that now it appears every time when one of such morphemes is used even if the corresponding syllables turns out to be in unstressed position. In that case, the presence of lengthened vowels in unstressed syllables may serve as additional evidence that the lengthening process is no longer operative.

(17) *uzvãrdi* [ˈuzvɑːrdi] 'surname' (NOM.PL)
  aizbẽrt [aizbeːːrt] 'fill up' (INF)

---

[6] In some Latvian dialects, the vowel before *r* is also lengthened in words with resyllabification like [gɑːrs] 'long' (Endzelīns 1951: 147).

2.4 Latvian dialects

The main division of Latvian dialects is between Low Latvian and High Latvian. Low Latvian is further divided into Central Latvian, which is the base of the standard language, and the so-called Livonianized dialect (Rudzīte 1964: 28–34) (also see Balode & Holvoet 2001a: 4, 16–39). For the term "Livonianized", see Strelēvica-Ošiņa (2009). See the full classification in (18).

(18) Classification of Latvian dialects
    1. Low Latvian
       a. the Livonianized dialect
          i. Kurzeme
          ii. Vidzeme
       b. Central Latvian
          i. Vidzeme
          ii. Zemgale (Semigalian)
          iii. Kurzeme (Curonian)
    2. High Latvian
       a. Selonian
       b. non-Selonian (Latgalian)

High Latvian has only two tones: falling and broken, with the falling tone corresponding to both the level and the falling tone of Standard Latvian. In a part of High Latvian known as Selonian, the broken tone is replaced with the rising tone, which is a unique Selonian feature. The part of High Latvian that preserves the broken tone is simply called non-Selonian or (less precisely) Latgalian.[7]

The three tones of Standard Latvian are found only in a relatively small area of Low Latvian in Vidzeme, belonging to Central Latvian. In the rest of Low Latvian, the distinction between the falling and the broken tone has disappeared (see Table 3). The result of the merger is traditionally transcribed with the symbol of the broken tone, although the phonetic manifestation may include either the falling contour or the laryngealization. This type of the two-way contrast is also commonly found among Standard Latvian speakers. For more details on the development of tones in dialects of Latvian, see Rudzīte (1993: 108–110) and Andronov (1996).

---

[7] Latgalian proper, which is sometimes viewed as a separate Baltic language, includes only part of the non-Selonian subdialect of High Latvian.

Tab. 3: Tones in Latvian dialects

	Low Latvian		High Latvian
The rest of low Latvian	Standard Latvian Central Latvian in Vidzeme		
Level	Level		Falling
Falling/broken	Falling		
	Broken		Broken/rising

Tab. 4: Distinctions between Latvian dialects

	Low Latvian	High Latvian	Translation
The Livonianized dialect	Central Latvian (Standard Latvian)		
['lɑːbs]	['lɑbus]	['lobus]	'good' (ACC.PL.M)
['mɑːs]	['mɑːsɑs]	['muəsis]	'sister' (GEN.SG)

Apart from the merger of the level and the falling tones, High Latvian differs from Low Latvian due to vowel changes, first of all, labialization of [ɑ]>[o] and [ɑː]>[oː]>[uə]. The difference between Central Latvian and the Livonianized dialect lies in the loss of vowels in final syllables that has taken place in the latter (see Table 4).

2.5 Diphthongal sequences with *r* in Latvian dialects

The lengthening of vowels before the tautosyllabic *r* may take different forms depending on the dialect. This feature is even used as one of the criteria in the classification of dialects. The traditional division of Central Latvian into three parts (those in Vidzeme, Zemgale, and Kurzeme) follows the different development of diphthongal sequences with *r*. In fact, the same criterion may be used with respect to the whole Latvian area because the results of the lengthening in the central part of Vidzeme belonging to Central Latvian are the same as in the western part, included in the Livonianized dialect, and it is also true for the two dialects in Kurzeme. As for High Latvian, it is characterized by its own type of vowel lengthening before *r*, which nevertheless continues the trend seen in Vidzeme. The following characterization is based on Rudzīte (1964, 1993), Endzelīns (1951), and partly on Rūķe (1939, 1940).

The situation in Standard Latvian coincides with that in Vidzeme and part of Zemgale. Non-high vowels are lengthened before the tautosyllabic *r* under the level and the falling tones. Non-high vowels under the broken tone are not lengthened, and high vowels remain short independently of the tone (see 13 and 14, here partly repeated as 19 and 20; for the sake of space, I only give examples with back vowels).

(19) Lengthened non-high vowels under the level and the falling tones (Vidzeme, Zemgale)
vaȓna>['vaːːrnɑ] 'crow'
dàrzi>['daːrzi] 'garden' (NOM.PL)

(20) a. short non-high vowels under the broken tone (Vidzeme, Zemgale)
['dɑrˀbi] 'labor' (NOM.PL)

b. short high vowels (Vidzeme, Zemgale)
['kurːpe] 'shoe'
['urba] 'drill' (PST.3)
['purˀns] 'snout'

In areas where the falling and the broken tones have merged together, the vowels are long in syllables with the historical falling tone (21a) and short under the historical broken tone (21b).

(21) a. historical falling tone (Vidzeme, Zemgale)
dàrzi>['daːrzi]>['daːˀrzi] 'garden' (NOM.PL)

b. historical broken tone (Vidzeme, Zemgale)
['dɑrˀbi] 'labor' (NOM.PL)

High Latvian is similar to the Vidzeme area in that it also confines the lengthening to syllables with the falling tone (22a), which corresponds to both the falling and the level tones in the Vidzeme subdialect of Central Latvian. Under the broken tone (the rising tone in Selonian), no lengthening occurs (22b).[8] But, as distinct from Vidzeme, the lengthening in High Latvian affects high vowels.

(22) a. lengthened vowels under the falling tone (High Latvian)
dàrzi>['duərzʲi] 'garden' (NOM.PL)
kùrpe>['kuːrpʲæ] 'shoe'

b. short vowels under the broken tone (High Latvian)
['dorˀbi] 'labor' (NOM.PL)
[purˀns] 'snout'

---

8 The lengthening of the first components of all diphthongal sequences, rather than only those with r, is found under the broken/rising tone in some High Latvian areas, but this is a much later change as can be easily seen from the vocalism; cf. ['dɑrzi] 'garden' (NOM.PL)>['daːrzi]>['duərzi] and [kɑlˀns] 'hill'>[koːˀlns].

In the Kurzeme area of Central Latvian (traditionally called the Curonian sub-dialect) and the northern part of Kurzeme belonging to the Livonianized dialect, the vowel lengthening before *r* involves both non-high and high vowels and occurs independently of the tone (23). The lengthening of [i], [u] may yield not only long [iː], [uː] but also [iə], [uə].

(23) Lengthened vowels in all contexts (Kurzeme)
['vaːːrnɑ] 'crow'
['dɑːrzi] 'garden' (NOM.PL)
['dɑːˀrbi] 'labor' (NOM.PL)
['kuːːrpe] or ['kuəːrpe] 'shoe'
['uːˀrbɑ] or ['uəˀrbɑ] 'drill' (PST.3)
[puːˀrns] or [puəˀrns] 'snout'

Still, in several smaller areas in the northern part of Kurzeme tone-related restrictions are applied to high vowels in a way not dissimilar to Vidzeme and High Latvian. Here, high vowels are only lengthened if the diphthongal sequences bear the level tone (24a), whereas under the merged broken-falling tone no lengthening takes place (24b).

(24) a. lengthened high vowels under the level tone (northern Kurzeme)
mir̃t>[miːːrt] or [miəːrt] 'die'
dur̃t>[duːːrt] or [duəːrt] 'stab'

b. short high vowels under the merged broken-falling tone (northern Kurzeme)
['zirˀgɑm] 'horse' (DAT.SG)
[purˀns] 'snout'

At least one of these smaller areas, namely, Dundaga, is reported to actually have no tone on those diphthongal sequences with *r* that bear the merged broken-falling tone in other places in Kurzeme (see 25) (Adamovičs 1923: 103). The tautosyllabic *r* is described as being shorter in comparison to other sonorants in "normal" diphthongal sequences under either of the tones (cf. Section 2.2). I will return to this anomaly in Section 2.6.

(25) Short high vowels under the merged broken-falling tone (Dundaga in northern Kurzeme)
['zirˀgɑm]>['zirgɑm] 'horse' (DAT.SG)
[purˀns]>[purns] 'snout'

The part of the Zemgale area of Central Latvian that does not follow the Vidzeme pattern has a special place in the classification, because instead of lengthening the vowel before *r*, here, a short anaptyctic vowel is inserted after *r* (and *l*). The insertion is found under the same conditions as the lengthening in Kurzeme, that is, after any vowel and under any of the tones (see 26).

(26) Anaptyctic vowel in Zemgale
 vařna>[ˈvarana] 'crow'
 daȓbi>[ˈdarabi] 'labor' (NOM.PL.)
 kuȓpe>[ˈkurape] 'shoe'

The reflexes of diphthongal sequences with *r* in different Latvian dialects are summed up in Table 5. It is not hard to notice that the Latvian language area splits up into two major parts with respect to the conditions of this change. In Vidzeme, the adjacent part of Zemgale, and the whole High Latvian territory, the change does not happen if the syllable has the broken, or the corresponding rising, tone. This will be further referred to as East Latvian. In Kurzeme, as well as the rest of Zemgale (with anaptyxis), the change has no restrictions on either tone or vowel quality. I will refer to these dialects as West Latvian. The uniformity of the conditions in West Latvian is especially striking because the processes themselves are different in Kurzeme and Zemgale.

To complete the picture of the changes affecting diphthongal sequences with *r* in Latvian dialects, one more development must be mentioned, namely, the deletion of *r* after the lengthened vowel, which sporadically takes place in Central Latvian (see 27).

(27) *vařna*>[ˈvaːːrna]>[ˈvaːːna] 'crow'
 svàrki>[ˈsvaːrki]>[ˈsvaːki] 'coat'

I will comment on the deletion of *r* in Section 2.7.

Tab. 5: Lengthening of vowels before tautosyllabic *r* in Latvian dialects

Standard Latvian Vidzeme and Zemgale (without anaptyxis)	High Latvian	Kurzeme	Zemgale (with anaptyxis)
Non-high vowels	Any vowel		Any vowel
Not under broken tone	Not under broken/ rising tone		Any tone
	East Latvian		West Latvian

2.6 Analysis

The following largely repeats Daugavet (2010: 96–100). I believe that the key to the phenomenon of vowel lengthening before *r* is provided by the treatment of the diphthongal sequences with high vowels in Dundaga (see 25, here repeated as 28). The syllable loses its tone if the vowel before *r* is not lengthened.

(28)   Short high vowels under the merged broken-falling tone (Dundaga in northern Kurzeme) [ˈzirˀgam]>[ˈzirgam] 'horse' (DAT.SG) [purˀns]>[purns] 'snout'

In toneless syllables, *r* is shorter than the sonorants occupying the same position in syllables that retain their tones. Additionally, the further development of such *r* is completely parallel to the development of obstruents (Adamovičs 1923: 103, 1925: 138). For instance, in case of apocope, which is regular in this area of Kurzeme, compensatory lengthening affects different segments in apocopated forms depending on the syllable structure (see Table 6). In diphthongs and diphthongal sequences, apocope leads to the lengthening of the second component, not dissimilar to the lengthening that normally takes place under the level tone. But if a short vowel is followed by an obstruent or *r*, it is the vowel itself that has to be lengthened in order to compensate for the loss of the next syllable. My suggestion is that the similar behavior of *r* and obstruents reflects the non-moraic status of *r*.[9]

In my view, the loss of the tone in Dundaga is the consequence of not lengthening the vowel when the following *r* becomes non-moraic. Evidently, the necessity of lengthening the vowel before *r* in other dialects comes from the fact that *r* is no longer able to act as a constituent of a heavy syllable on which tones can

Tab. 6: Apocope in Dundaga

Conditions	No apocope (DAT.SG)	Apocope (GEN.SG)	Translation
Obstruent and *r*, no tonal contrast, lengthening of the preceding vowel	[ˈgadam] [ˈtirgam]	*gada*>[gaːd] *tirga*>[tiːrg]	'year' 'market'
Sonorants, tonal contrast, lengthening of the sonorant	[ˈgalˀdam]	*gaîda*>[galˀːd]	'table'

---

9 The lengthening of different components of the syllable due to apocope must not be confused with the lengthening of components of diphthongal sequences that takes place in absence of apocope and is the main subject of the present chapter.

be distinguished. The lengthening of the vowel was, in its nature, compensatory, as it resulted from reassigning the stranded mora to the preceding vowel (29a). The case of Dundaga shows us what would have occurred to the other dialects of Latvian if they had not lengthened the vowels before *r*.

(29) a. Reassignment of the stranded mora in most Latvian dialects

   μμ   μμ   μμ
   | | > | ⸸ > \/
   vɑrːnɑ   vɑrnɑ   vɑːrnɑ

 b. Reassignment of the stranded mora in Zemgale

   μμ   μμ   μ μ
   | | > | ⸸ > | |
   vɑrːnɑ   vɑrnɑ   vɑrɑnɑ

The anaptyctic vowel in Zemgale serves the same purpose as the lengthening of vowels in the rest of Latvian area, although here, instead of lengthening the vowel **before** *r*, a new short vowel was created **after** *r* in order to support the weakened sonorant so that it would be able to remain moraic (29b). But this does not seem as successful as lengthening the preceding vowel, since the resulting sequence of two light syllables does not allow to maintain the tonal contrast – a task that is easily accomplished by the long vowel.

2.7 Conclusion on Latvian

The fact that vowels were only lengthened before *r* (the anaptyxis is also found after *l*) suggests that in Latvian the change sprang from some inherent properties of rhotic sounds, probably responsible for similar changes in other languages as well (see Ladefoged & Maddieson 1996: 216). One may also suppose that, eventually, the lengthening came to be perceived as unmotivated reassignment of moras and further spread to dialects where *r* was not weakened.

The question remains as to what gives us the different types of vowel lengthening shown in Section 2.5. I do not assign much importance to the lengthening being sensitive to vowel height in Central Latvian, as this can be easily seen as the initial stage of the development. In the rest of East Latvian where the change has gone further, it affects all vowels irrespectively of their height. However, the sensitivity to the tonal contrast, which characterizes East Latvian, needs more attention. One may doubt the unrestricted loss of moraicity on *r* in dialects where *r* is still capable of acting as the second part of a diphthongal sequence under the broken/rising tone, even if it is not found under any other tone.

The lack of lengthening under one of the tones may also be explained as an attempt to maintain the tonal contrast by means of different vowel duration when the second component, after losing its moraic status, is no longer able to participate in the manifestation of the contrast. On the contrary, those dialects that lengthen the vowel under all of the tones clearly choose the other solution, i.e., to transfer the tonal contrast to the preceding long vowel.

The deletion of *r* after the lengthened vowel in (27) can have two opposite interpretations. First, it may be seen as the final stage of the weakening of *r*. Second, it may result from *r* retaining its moraic status and thus creating a hypercharacterized syllable after the lengthening of the preceding vowel. In this case, *r* is deleted in order to simplify the syllable structure. Which of the answers is correct can only be found out after thoroughly investigating the dialect areas where the deletion occurs.

3 Livonian

The Finnic language Livonian shares more than one feature with the neighboring Baltic languages. Among other things, Livonian lengthens the first components of diphthongs and diphthongal sequences, which is most important for the current chapter.

As distinct from Latvian, the lengthening of the first component in Livonian is found in all types of diphthongs and diphthongal sequences as Livonian puts no constraints on the quality of either the first or the second components with respect to this change. However, the lengthening does not apply to all instances of the same diphthong or diphthongal sequence, so that the lengthened variants alternate with those without lengthening in inflection and derivation.

3.1 Phonemic inventory

The vocalism in Table 7 is largely based on Vijtso (1993: 77–78), except for the IPA symbols which I add at my own risk, as their choice is not verified by experimental research (cf. Lehiste et al. 2008: 84–91).

Livonian is different from the Baltic languages in that it has central vowels, among them [ɑ(ː)]. All monophthongs can be long or short, with the exception of ǭ [ɔː] < *ā; the latter is sometimes not differentiated from [oː] in the orthography.

In having *ie* [iːə], *uo* [uːə], Livonian is more similar to the Baltic languages. The main deviation from Viitso and all other authors writing about Livonian is

Tab. 7: Livonian monophthongs

Long			Short		
ī [iː]	ȭ [ɯː]	ū [uː]	i [i]	õ [ɯ][11]	u [u]
īe [iːə]		ūo [uːə]	ie [iə]		uo [uə]
ē [eː]	ȱ [ɜː]	ō [oː]	e [e]	ȯ [ɜ]	o [o]
ǟ [æː]	ā [ɑː]	ǭ [ɔː]	ä [æ]	a [ɑ]	

Tab. 8: Livonian geminates

	NOM.PL	PART.SG	Translation
Voiced obstruents	single consonants	geminates	
	sugūd [suguːd]	suggõ [suˀggə]	'relative'
Voiceless obstruents	short geminates	long geminates	
	sukād [sukkɑːd]	sukkõ [suk·kə]	'sock'

that I include *īe* [iːə], *ūo* [uːə], and their short counterparts *ie* [iə], *uo* [uə] among monophthongs rather than diphthongs, which is a solution directly inspired by Girdenis' analysis of Lithuanian.[10] In fact, the existence of the short counterparts makes it even easier to interpret these sounds as equivalent to monophthongs in Livonian than in the Baltic languages (see Girdenis 2003: 103). On the quality of the second part of [i(ː)ə], *ūo* [u(ː)ə], see Pajupuu and Viitso (1986).

All short vowels combine with *i* [i], *u* [u] to form diphthongs with minor exceptions. It is important that the short [ie], [uo] combine with *i* [i], *u* [u] to form diphthongs [ieu] and [uoi] like "normal" short monophthongs (cf. Viitso 2008 and other authors who call [ieu] and [uoi] triphthongs).

As in Latvian, the division into sonorants and obstruents correlates with the ability to contribute to syllable weight in Livonian, although the resemblance is only partial.

Even though orthography gives an impression that, intervocalically, both voiceless and voiced consonants occur as either single or geminates in a parallel way, voiceless obstruents are always geminated between vowels, and what is represented as a single voiceless consonant in orthography is, in fact, a geminate with a short first component (Table 8) (see Viitso 2008: 297 n. 14 for a short summary of different views on the subject).

---

10 On Lithuanian, see also Buch (1968) and the literature she shows.
11 In unstressed syllables, the letter <õ> in Livonian orthography stands for [ə].

When acting as syllable closure after a short vowel, voiced obstruents are always accompanied by a glottal stop [ʔ] – a suprasegmental feature that is often called *stød* by analogy with a similar feature in Danish. This will be discussed in the next subsection.

3.2 Livonian *stød*

Livonian has a suprasegmental contrast manifested in the presence or absence of glottal stop or laryngealization, which is often referred to as the "Livonian *stød*" (see minimal pairs in Table 9). The phonetic manifestation of *stød* involves glottal stop or laryngealization and pitch (Lehiste et al. 2008: 67–84). The latter is reflected in the use of the alternative terms "broken tone" and "rising tone" by Kettunen (1938) and Penttilä and Posti (1941). For more details on these and other phonetic parameters of the Livonian *stød*, see Tuisk and Teras (2009). The phonological analysis of the Livonian *stød* is found in Kiparsky (1995–2006).

3.3 Syllable weight

I suggest two different criteria of syllable weight in Livonian that yield different results for sonorants and obstruents. The first criterion is the ability of a syllable to serve as the domain for the suprasegmental opposition between *stød* and its absence (see Table 9). Short vowels followed by tautosyllabic sonorants form combinations that are equivalent to long monophthongs and diphthongs. No special term for such combinations is used in works on Livonian, but nothing prevents us from calling them "diphthongal sequences", as in the Baltic languages.

Tab. 9: Minimal pairs for the Livonian *stød*

	stød	no *stød*
Long monophthong	*ūdō* [ˈuːˀdə] 'strain' (INF)	*ūdō* [ˈuːdə] 'fry' (INF)
Diphthong	*jovd* [joˀud] 'flour' (PART.SG)	*joud* [jouˑd] 'strength'
Short vowel plus sonorant	*kallō* [ˈkaˀllə] 'fish' (PART.SG)	*kallō* [ˈkalˑlə] 'island' (PART.SG)
Short vowel plus voiced obstruent	*sugḑi* [ˈsuˀgdʲi] 'relative' (PART.PL)	–
Short vowel plus voiceless obstruent	–	*sukṭi* [ˈsukˑtʲi] 'sock' (PART.PL)

While in Latvian diphthongal sequences are easily differentiated from combinations with obstruents because in the Baltic languages, the latter are never identified with one of the tones or accents, in Livonian the division is blurred, as *stød* is actually present in what must be seen as a type of light syllables. In combinations with obstruents *stød* is possible, but it is not contrastive, since in such syllables, the absence or presence of *stød* is conditioned by voicing. Voiced obstruents are always accompanied by *stød*, but voiceless obstruents may only be realized without it.

The second criterion involves lengthening of post-stressed vowels (see Lehiste et al. 2007: 30–42, 2008: 41–67, Tuisk & Teras 2009: 241–248, Tuisk 2012). After a light stressed syllable, the vowel in the post-stressed syllable is long, and after a heavy stressed syllable, the vowel in the post-stressed syllable can be either short or long. (In some cases, the lengthening is reflected in the orthographic representation, as in *mõtsā* 'forest', but in others, it is not, as in *lēba* 'bread'.) See examples in Table 10.

With regard to post-stressed vowel lengthening all closed syllables including those with the obstruents must be considered heavy, together with syllables containing diphthongs and long monophthongs. Light syllables must only encompass open syllables containing short monophthongs.

There is a controversy as to what structural types of stressed heavy syllables are expected to be followed by a lengthened post-stressed vowel. For instance, both *āigal* 'at the time' and *aigõ* (PART.SG) 'time' are given a short post-stressed vowel in Lehiste et al. (2008: 47), whereas in Tuisk and Teras (2009: 243–244), the structurally identical pairs *rānda* (NOM.SG) and *randõ* (PART.SG) 'shore', *jālga* (NOM.SG), and *jalgõ* (PART.SG) 'leg; foot' are characterized as differentiated by post-stressed vowel lengthening in *rānda* [rɑːndɑː], *jālga* [jɑːlgɑː].

Tab. 10: Post-stressed lengthening in Livonian

	Post-stressed lengthening	No post-stressed lengthening
Light syllables	*kadāg* [kɑdɑːg] 'juniper' (NOM.SG)	–
	jemā [jemɑː] 'mother' (NOM.SG)	
Heavy syllables	*võrōz* [vɯːrəːz] 'stranger' (NOM.SG)	*võrõd* [vɯːrəd] 'stranger' (NOM.PL)
	pūdōz [puːˀdəːz] 'clean' (NOM.SG)	*vīmõ* [viːˀmə] 'rain' (PART.SG)
	aigā [ɑigɑː] 'shore' (NOM.SG)	*leibõ* [leiˑbə] 'bread' (PART.SG)
	jālga [jɑːlgɑː] 'foot' (NOM.SG)	*jalgõ* [jɑlˑgə] 'foot' (PART.SG)
	mõtsā [mɯtsɑː] 'forest' (NOM.SG)	*mõtsõ* [mɯtˑsə] 'forest' (PART.SG)
	sukād [sukkɑːd] 'sock' (NOM.PL)	*sukkõ* [sukˑkə] 'sock' (PART.SG)
		jemmõ [jeˀmmə] 'mother' (PART.SG)
		suggõ [suˀggə] 'relative' (PART.SG)

3.4 Gradation

In Livonian, gradation comprises two types of alternation. One gradation type is illustrated in the alternation of intervocalic consonants shown in Table 8. Together with other examples of this type, it is repeated in Table 11. Forms with voiceless obstruents actually belongs to a separate type in Viitso (2008: 297–298), but the difference between them is not important for the purposes of this chapter.

On the whole, the type of gradation in Table 11 involves an intervocalic consonant and the following post-stressed vowel. The intervocalic consonant is shorter in the weak grade and longer in the strong grade, while the duration of the post-stressed vowel is exactly opposite to the duration of the consonant. The post-stressed vowel is lengthened in the weak grade, and in the strong grade, it is short (very often õ [ə]). This type of gradation is found with all consonants, but there is difference between sonorants and voiced obstruents, on the one hand, and voiceless obstruents, on the other. While the former appear as single consonants in the weak grade and geminates in the strong grade, the latter are in both cases represented by geminates and consonant clusters, their duration being shorter in the weak grade and longer in the strong grade. As a result, words with voiceless obstruents have heavy syllables in both the strong and the weak grade so that the grades are differentiated due to the coda obstruent being short in the weak grade and half-long in the strong grade. (Some authors claim coda obstruents to be long in the strong grade, instead of half-long.) Words with sonorants and voiced obstruents have light syllables in the weak grade and heavy syllables in the strong grade. Geminated sonorants and voiced obstruents are additionally accompanied by *stød* in the strong grade, which is absent with voiceless obstruents.

Another type of gradation, illustrated in Table 12, entails lengthening of a short vowel that forms the first part of a diphthong or a diphthongal sequence. Consequently, it is only possible before sonorants and *i*, *u*. Lengthened vowels are marked as long in the Livonian orthography, and I will transcribe them as such (cf. Viitso 2008: 167).

Tab. 11: Gemination of intervocalic consonants in Livonian

	Weak grade (NOM.PL)	Strong grade (PART.SG)	
Voiced obstruents and sonorants	sugūd [ˈsuguːd]	suggō [ˈsuˀggə]	'relative'
	suodād [ˈsuədaːd]	suoddō [ˈsuəˀddə]	'war'
	piņīd [ˈpinʲiːd]	piņņō [ˈpiˀnʲnʲə]	'dog'
	kalād [ˈkalaːd]	kallō [ˈkaˀllə]	'fish'
Voiceless obstruents	siepād [ˈsiəppaːd]	sukkō [ˈsiəpˑpə]	'smith'
	mõtsād [ˈmɯtsaːd]	mõtsō [ˈmɯtˑsə]	'forest'

The lengthened first component appears in the weak grade, but it remains short in the strong grade where the second part of diphthongs and diphthongal sequences is half-long (long by some authors); one can compare it to the half-long coda obstruents in the weak grade of the first type of gradation in Table 11. In the weak grade, the second component is short and may even be deleted, as in Table 13. This type of gradation is characterized by heavy syllables in both the strong and the weak grade. *Stød* is not typical for words participating in this type of gradation. Sometimes, the lengthening of the first component is accompanied by resyllabification (Table 14); in that case, the strong grade has a geminate sonorant in case of diphthongal sequences or a combination of *ij*, respectively, *uv* in case of diphthongs, where *i*, respectively, *u* is the second component of the diphthong.

It is not entirely clear when the type of gradation illustrated in Tables 12–14 has a lengthened post-stressed vowel in weak-grade forms, which is regular for the type of gradation shown in Table 11. Compare the weak-grade forms *rānda* [raːndaː], *jālga* [jaːlgaː] in Tuisk and Teras (2009: 243–244) with the weak-grade

Tab. 12: Lengthening of the first components of diphthongs and diphthongal sequences

Weak grade (NOM.PL)	Strong grade (PART.SG)	Translation
āigad [ˈɑːigɑ(ː)d]	aigō [ˈɑiˑgə]	'time'
jālgad [ˈjaːlgɑ(ː)d]	jalgō [ˈjalˑgə]	'leg; foot'
kūondad [ˈkuːəndɑ(ː)d]	kuondō [ˈkŭonˑdə]	'heel'

Tab. 13: Deletion of the second components of diphthongs and diphthongal sequences

Weak grade (NOM.PL)	Strong grade (PART.SG)	Translation
lēbad [ˈleːbɑ(ː)d]	leibō [ˈleiˑbə]	'bread'
lōdōd [ˈloːdə(ː)d]	loulō [ˈlauˑdə]	'bird'
pūogad [ˈpuːəgɑ(ː)d]	pȯigō [ˈpɔiˑgə]	'son'

Tab. 14: Resyllabification

Weak grade (NOM.PL)	Strong grade (PART.SG)	Translation
nǭļad [ˈnɔːlʲɑ(ː)d]	naļļō [ˈnalʲˑlʲə]	'joke'
kīelad [ˈkiːələ(ː)d]	kiellō [ˈkiəlˑlə]	'clock'
kōvōd [ˈkoːvə(ː)d]	kouvō [ˈkouˑvə]	'water-well'
lǭjad [ˈlɔːjɑ(ː)d]	laijō [ˈlaiˑjə]	'boat'

Tab. 15: No post-stressed lengthening after voiceless obstruents

Weak grade (NOM.PL)	Strong grade (PART.SG)	Translation
āitad ['ɑːitɑd]	aitõ ['ɑi·tə]	'threshing-barn'
kõnkad ['kɯːŋkɑd]	kõnkõ ['kɯŋ·kə]	'dune'

form āigal 'at the time' in Lehiste et al. (2008: 47) (see Section 3.3). (Could it be that the lengthening does not apply after diphthongs?) But the authors seem to be in agreement that before the voiceless consonant, the lengthening of the first component takes place without a simultaneous lengthening of the post-stressed vowel (Table 15). It is remarkable that the post-stressed lengthening in Livonian is not even connected to the word being in the weak grade, since it is found with forms like võrõz [vɯːrəːz] 'stranger' in (30) (Lehiste et al. 2008: 64–67, Tuisk & Teras 2009: 243), which do not participate in gradation. It must be concluded that in Livonian, the post-stressed lengthening and the lengthening in the rhyme of stressed syllables are relatively independent from each other.

(30) võrõz ['vɯːrəːz] (NOM.SG) võrõd ['vɯːrəd] (NOM.PL) 'stranger'

3.5 Alternation pattern of heavy syllables

In this section, I consider the durational characteristics of heavy stressed syllables in the weak and strong grades of both types of gradation. I put aside those words in the first type of gradation (Table 11) that show light syllables in the weak grade (those with sonorants and voiced obstruents) and concentrate on words that have heavy syllables in both weak-grade and strong grade forms (those with voiceless obstruents in Table 11 and all examples in Tables 12–15).

Apart from the post-stressed lengthening in the weak grade, the lengthening of the first components of diphthongs and diphthongal sequences is the only feature that distinguishes the gradation types. The latter seems to be a recent development (Kettunen 1938: XXII; Viitso 2008: 306), and one can easily reconstruct the stage when diphthongs and diphthongal sequences only distinguished the strong and the weak grade by the duration of the second component. At this stage, the alternation pattern for syllables with diphthongs and diphthongal sequences must have been the same as the one for syllables where a short vowel is followed by a voiceless obstruent (Table 16).

Tab. 16: Alternation pattern of heavy syllables

Weak grade (NOM.SG)			Strong grade (PART.SG)		Translation
siepā ['siəppɑ:]		< *seppa	sieppõ ['siəp·pə]	< *sep·pa	'smith'
mõtsā ['mʉtsɑ:]		< *metsa	mõtsõ ['mʉt·sə]	< *met·sa	'forest'
āiga ['ɑ:igɑ(:)]		< *aiga	aigõ ['ɑi·gə]	< *ai·ga	'time'
āita ['ɑ:itɑ]		< *aita	aitõ ['ɑi·tə]	< *ai·ta	'threshing-barn'
rānda ['rɑ:ndɑ(:)]		< *randa	randõ ['rɑn·də]	< *ran·da	'shore'
lēba ['le:bɑ(:)]	< *lēiba	< *leiba	leibõ ['lei·bə]	< *lei·ba	'bread'
lǭda ['lɔ:dɑ(:)]	< *lāuda	< *lauda	laudõ ['lɑu·də]	< *lau·da	'table'
pūoga ['pu:əgɑ(:)]	< *pōiga	< *poiga	põigõ ['pɘi·gə]	< *poi·ga	'son'
kīela ['ki:əlɑ(:)]	< *kēlla	< *kella	kiellõ ['kiəl·lə]	< *kel·la	'clock'
lǭja ['lɔ:jɑ(:)]	< *lājja	< *lajja	laijõ ['lɑi·jə]	< *laj·ja	'boat'

Tab. 17: Gradation of related words in Estonian

Weak grade (GEN.SG)	Strong grade (PART.SG)	Translation
´sepa ['seppɑ]	`seppa ['sep·pä]	'smith'
´metsa ['metsɑ]	`metsa ['met·sä]	'forest'
´ranna ['rɑnnɑ]	`randa ['rɑn·dä]	'shore'
´leiva ['leivɑ]	`leiba ['lei·bä]	'bread'
´laua ['lɑuwɑ]	`lauda ['lɑu·dä]	'table'
´kella ['kellɑ]	`kella ['kel·lä]	'clock'

At the stage reconstructed in Table 16, the gradation of heavy syllables in Livonian must have looked very similar to the alternation in related words in Estonian[12] (Table 17) where (apart from the alternation of consonants) strong-grade forms differ from weak-grade forms in what is called Estonian overlength.[13] "Normal" (long) diphthongs have a short second component, whereas in overlong diphthongs, the second component is half-long. Intervocalic consonant clusters and geminates have a short first part is they are "simply" long and a half-long first part if they are overlong.

---

[12] One must bear in mind that forms showing the weak and strong grades in Livonian and Estonian may be different.
[13] In Estonian, there is no straightforward relationship between overlength and the strong grade. For instance, a form in the strong grade may have a short syllable, and a form in the weak grade an overlong syllable, as in ´lagi ['lɑgi·] (NOM.SG, strong grade) and `lae [lɑe·] (GEN.SG, weak grade).

As distinct from shortness and the "normal" length, overlength is a property of syllables or feet where it contrasts with the absence of overlength. The interaction between segmental and suprasegmental length creates the three degrees of length in the surface. The contrast for overlength is sometimes described in terms of accents, so that syllables with overlength have the heavy accent and syllables without overlength the light accent (see the overview of the analyses in Hint 1997: 285–287).[14] Short vowels and consonants are identified with the light accent. When necessary, in orthography, the heavy accent is marked with the grave <`> before the syllable and the light accent with the acute <´>.

When represented as a result of interaction between segmental and suprasegmental length, Estonian overlength is reminiscent of the suprasegmental oppositions in the other languages of the region, including the Latvian tones.[15] The two Estonian accents only contrast in heavy syllables that comprise syllables with long monophthongs or diphthongs and syllables where short monophthongs are followed by any consonant in the coda (see Table 18). Unlike the other languages, in Estonian, the accents are differentiated not only on "diphthongal sequences" with sonorants, but also on combinations of vowels with obstruents, normally, the strong ones.[16] (After short vowels, weak obstruents only occur in coda position of unstressed syllables, where the accents are absent.) Light syllables are automatically given the light accent.

---

14 I do not like the terminology in Viitso (2003: 11), where he differentiates between short and long syllables, on the one hand, and light and heavy syllables, on the other, because "long" and "heavy", respectively, "short" and "light" usually mean the same things when applied to syllables.

15 Estonian is different from the other languages in that it uses duration as the main phonetic parameter of the suprasegmental contrast, which presents a challenge for those trying to represent the difference between overlength and the "normal" length in terms of moras (see Bye 1997). Another phonetic parameter of the Estonian accents is pitch. Overlength is associated with a falling contour, probably inherited from the disyllabic sequence that was substituted with the overlong syllable after syncope and apocope took place (Lehiste 2003: 55).

16 The manifestation of the accents on diphthongs and vowel-plus-consonant combinations in Estonian is comparable to the durational difference between the second components of diphthongs and diphthongal sequences under different tones in Latvian (see Section 2.2.), except that in Latvian the second component is claimed to be long under the level tone and half-long under the two other tones. The shortness of the second component, which is associated with the light accent in Estonian, in Latvian, leads to the loss of the tonal contrast, as I have shown by the development of *r* in Section 2.6.

Tab. 18: Syllables weight and accents in Estonian

	Light accent		Heavy accent
Q1	Q2		Q3
Light syllables (V)	Heavy syllables (V:, VV, VC)		

Tab. 19: Reconstructed accents in Livonian

Weak grade Light accent (NOM.SG.)	Strong grade Heavy accent (PART.SG.)	Translation
*seppa	*sep·pa	'smith'
*metsa	*met·sa	'forest'
*aiga	*ai·ga	'time'
*aita	*ai·ta	'threshing-barn'
*randa	*ran·da	'shore'
*leiba	*lei·ba	'bread'
*lauda	*lau·da	'table'
*poiga	*poi·ga	'son'
*kella	*kel·la	'clock'
lajja	*lai·ja	'boat'

The comparison between Tables 16 and 17 shows that the Estonian-like contrast between the heavy and the light accents can be also postulated for the previous stage of Livonian where the strong grade of heavy syllables must have had the heavy accent and the weak grade the light accent, as shown in Table 19.[17] The forms with intervocalic obstruents must have looked very similar to what they look now. The main difference from the Estonian accents is that the realization of post-stressed vowels as short or extra-short in Estonian automatically follows from the length of the preceding syllable, whereas in Livonian, there is no strict correlation between the reconstructed light accent and the post-stressed lengthening. In other words, the difference in the duration of the second component, connected to the accents, was not regularly accompanied by the post-stressed lengthening.

---

[17] See also Viitso (1974) and Kuleshov (2012), where accents are proposed for modern Livonian.

I propose that it is the lack of support from the post-stressed lengthening in weak-grade forms that initiated the lengthening of the first components of diphthongs and diphthongal sequences in order to further differentiate the contrast between the syllables bearing the different accents. After the change, the Estonian-like contrast between the accents was replaced by the alternation of long and short vowels acting as the first component, the short vowel being automatically followed by a half-long second component in the strong grade. But with respect to the main issue of the chapter, it is important that the first components of diphthongs and diphthongal sequences were lengthened under one of the contrasting accents.

3.7 Comparison between Livonian and Latvian

The Livonian development *aiga>āiga [ɑːigɑ(ː)] 'time', *jalga>jālga [jɑːlgɑ(ː)] 'leg; foot' is analogous with the Latvian change *varna>vārna [vɑːrnɑ], as in both languages, it involves lengthening of a short vowel, which acts as the first component of a diphthongal sequence or diphthong. Since we assume that the Livonian gradation is historically based on an alternation of accents, the retaining of the short first component in the strong grade in Livonian is comparable to the lack of lengthening under the broken/rising tone in East Latvian. Even the further deletion of r, which occurs in some Latvian dialects, is mirrored in the Livonian deletion of the second component after the lengthened vowel. Compare (31a) vs. (31b).

(31) a. Latvian
   vãrna [ˈvɑːːrnɑ]>*vãna* [ˈvɑːːnɑ] 'crow'
   daȓbi [ˈdɑrˀbi] 'labor' (NOM.PL.)

   b. Livonian
   leiba>lēba [ˈleːbɑ(ː)] 'bread' (NOM.SG.)
   leibõ [ˈleiˑbə] 'bread' (PART.SG.)

I suggest that the lengthening of the first component of diphthongs and diphthongal sequences in Livonian may be represented in the same terms as the lengthening before r in Latvian, that is, as reassignment of the second mora, previously linked to the second component, to the preceding vowel (see 32). One may also view the process as the result of a synchronic rule that is applied to the underlying form. But I do not think that one may speak about some sudden loss of moraicity in Livonian as the reason for the change. Rather, Livonian must have been on the verge of losing moraicity of the second components at the stage when they were made maximally short in weak-grade forms in order to distinguish them from the longer second components in strong-grade forms. Then, the first components were lengthened so that the contrast could be realized in another way, with the second component giving over its mora in the process.

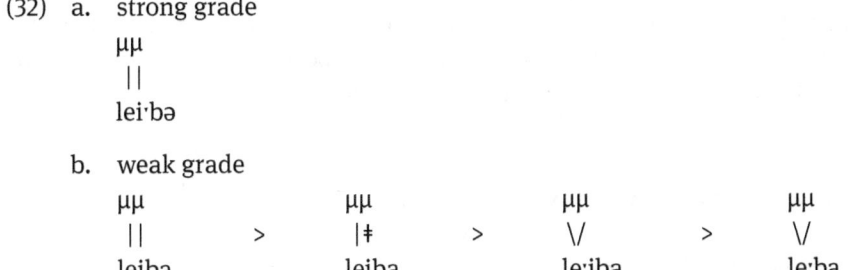

While the deletion of *r* in Latvian may be given two alternative explanations, that is, as either the further weakening of the non-moraic sound or the simplification of the hypercharacterized syllable, the major cause behind the similar change in Livonian seems to be the pressure to further increase the difference between the strong and the weak grade. But the fact that, as opposed to the lengthening itself, the deletion of the second component is only found in diphthongs, where it is more sonorous than in diphthongal sequences, testifies to the simplification of the hypercharacterized syllable.

3.8 Conclusion on Livonian

Comparison with Estonian allows us to reconstruct a stage in Livonian when the latter had a contrast on heavy syllables analogous to the contrast between the heavy and the light accents in Estonian. This contrast in Livonian was destroyed by the lengthening of the first components of diphthongs and diphthongal sequences, which has no parallels in Estonian and, in some cases, the consequent drop of the second component.

This change is similar to the lengthening of vowels in the diphthongal sequences with *r* in Latvian in that in both languages it is easily interpreted as redistribution of moras to the more sonorous of the two components of the diphthongal sequence. But the similarity with Latvian is not complete, as in Latvian, the change is largely determined by the individual properties of *r*, which is confirmed to behave in a unique way in some other languages of the world. In Livonian, the change is triggered by the need to intensify the distinction between the forms with the different accents, even though the contrast itself is eliminated in the change. This factor is also present in Latvian where it plays a subordinate role.

4 Lithuanian

The coexistence of the lengthening of the first components of diphthongs and diphthongal sequences with the lengthening of stressed syllables is not a unique Lithuanian feature because both processes are also present in Latvian. However, it is only in Lithuanian that the two lengthening processes come into interaction with each other resulting in rather unusual changes.

4.1 Phonemic inventory and syllable weight

The vocalism in Table 20 essentially repeats the Lithuanian vowel system as presented in Girdenis (1997a: 24, 28) (see also Garšva & Girdenis 1997: 21, 23). The transcription is supplemented with the letters used in Lithuanian orthography. The rendering of *ie, uo* as [iːə], [uːə] reflects the phonetic study by Girdenis (2009: 237).[18]

In general, the Lithuanian vowel inventory is similar to the one in Latvian in the number of vowels they contain and the position of vowels in the articulatory space. As distinct from Latvian, short vowels differ in quality from their long counterparts.[19] The different origin of the same vowels is reflected in the use of different letters, for instance, *y* and *į* for [iː], as well as *ą* and *a* for [ɑː]. The so-called nasal letters *į, ų, ą, ę* stand for long monophthongs that developed from diphthongal sequences with nasals[20] and still alternate with them in many morphemes (33).

Tab. 20: Lithuanian monophthongs

Long		Short	
y, į [iː]	*ū, ų* [uː]	*i* [ɪ]	*u* [ʊ]
ie [iːə]	*uo* [uːə]		
ė [eː]	*o* [oː]	*e* [e]	*o* [ɔ]
ę, e [æː]	*ą, a* [ɑː]	*e* [ɛ]	*a* [a]

---

[18] Girdenis (1997a: 25) transcribes *ie* and *uo* as [ⁱɛ_a] and [ᵘɔ_a] and refers to them as "polyphthongs" that "have no distinct components".
[19] Contrary to what may seem from Table 20, long *ė* [eː] and *o* [oː] do not really have short counterparts, since both [e] and [ɔ] are only present in borrowings, and many speakers of Standard Lithuanian do not differentiate between the short [e] and [ɛ].
[20] This convention is not always strictly followed, cf. *šyla* [ʃiːla]<*ʃinla 'warm' (PRS.3).

(33) *kansti>kąsti [ˈkɑːsʲtʲɪ] (INF)   kanda [ˈkɑˑnda] (PRS.3)   'bite'

Initially, monophthongs designated by the "nasal" letters were indeed nasalized but eventually lost nasalization and merged with ordinary vowels. The high non-nasalized vowels were historically long, often corresponding to the long *ū*, *ī* in other Indo-European languages. The low non-nasalized vowels, on the contrary, were historically short and only later lengthened under stress (34). Consequently, they are automatically replaced with short vowels in an unstressed position; in orthography, such lengthened vowels are given the same letters as short monophthongs of the same quality.

(34) *ratas* [ˈrɑːtas] (NOM.SG)   *ratu* [raˈtʊ] (INS.SG)   'wheel'

The class of diphthongs includes combinations of almost any short vowel with the subsequent *u* [ʊ] or *i* [ɪ], but some of the possible combinations are only found in borrowings. Although both the initial and final components of diphthongs are here identified with short monophthongs, it must be borne in mind that their duration and quality depend on the accent (see examples in 35).

Every consonant with the exception of *j* can be palatalized. Since the issue is not of much interest for the present chapter, I will not discuss the palatalization and its impact on vowel quality.

Although both sonorants and obstruents may act as a syllable closure in Lithuanian, only sonorants count as weight-bearing units forming diphthongal sequences with the preceding vowel. Together with long vowels and diphthongs, diphthongal sequences belong to the group of sounds that make up heavy syllables. Heavy syllables serve as a domain for what is known as the contrast between the acute and the circumflex accents (see the next subsection).

As opposed to the other languages, Lithuanian does not have consonant geminates. In fact, it does not even tolerate sequences of identical consonants on morpheme and word boundaries, where potential geminates are always simplified to a single sound (Pakerys 1995: 233–234). Due to this, it is only vowels that can be lengthened in Lithuanian in order to make the stressed syllable bimoraic.

4.2 Accents

Lithuanian distinguishes between acute and circumflex, which are usually called "accents" or "tones". The accents are only found in heavy stressed syllables. Minimal pairs are given in Table 21.

Tab. 21: Lithuanian accents

	Acute	Circumflex
Long monophthong	rúgti ['ruːkʲtʲi] 'sour' (INF)[21]	rū̃kti ['ruːkʲtʲi] 'smoke' (INF)
Diphthong	áukštas ['ɑˑukʃtas] 'high'	aũkštas ['ɒukʃtas] 'floor, level'
Diphthongal sequence	káltas ['kɑˑltas] 'chisel'	kal̃tas ['kəlˑtas] 'guilty'

Tab. 22: Accents as phonological categories and diacritic marks

	Heavy syllables		Light syllables
	Acute	Circumflex	No accent
Grave <`>	ùiti, pìlkas, òrdinas		àkti, pìktas
Acute <´>	rúgti		
	áukštas, káltas		
	dúona, píenas		
Circumflex <˜>		rū̃kti	
		aũkštas, kal̃tas	
		uõlos, pliẽnas	
		muĩlas, pil̃vas	

Sometimes, three accents are claimed for Lithuanian, with the "grave" beside the acute and circumflex (Blevins 1993: 242 f7, Dogil 1999a: 278). Grave is then reported as the accent of light syllables. However, the Lithuanian school of phonology draws a clear difference between accents as phonological/phonetic entities and accents as diacritic marks that serve to convey the information about the former (Girdenis 2003: 275; see also Girdenis 1997a: 55). Grave entirely belongs to diacritic marks, its function being to designate the presence of stress on a light syllable (Table 22). Light syllables themselves, however, are left outside the domain of accents as phonological/phonetic entities. Although both heavy and light syllables can be stressed, only heavy syllables can contrast for the accents (Girdenis 2003: 274). This chapter follows the view that grave is a diacritic mark rather than a phonological category. It is necessary to add that the grave mark may also appear on heavy syllables due to the convention that the acute accent is signaled by the grave mark if the heavy syllable contains a diphthong or diphthongal sequence with a high vowel as the first component, for example, ùiti [ʊɪ] 'hound' (INF.), pìlkas [ɪl] 'gray'.[22] The notable exception is ie, uo on which the acute accent is always marked by the acute mark, for example, píenas 'milk', dúona 'bread'. Contrary to what may seem, these three diacritical marks are not part of the usual Lithuanian orthography and only used in dictionaries and textbooks.

---

[21] The IPA transcription here does not reflect the difference between the Lithuanian accents in syllables with long monophthongs.

[22] In borrowings, the grave mark is also used with [ɔ] and [e], as in òrdinas 'medal', koncèrtas 'concert'.

The difference between the acute and the circumflex is often assumed to be one in pitch,[23] especially in works published outside Lithuania (see e.g., Hock, this volume). This view is based on the classic works by Kurschat (1876: 57–63) and Javnis (1908–1916: 34, 44–5), propagated by Senn (1966). These authors define the acute as falling, and the circumflex as rising. Another classic view also expressed by Javnis (1908–1916) is that the contrast is created by stressing different moras inside a heavy syllable. The acute is then understood as "strong in the beginning" and the circumflex as "strong in the end" (Lithuanian *tvirtapradė* and *tvirtagalė*). This approach clearly associates the contrast with intensity.

Nevertheless, the exact phonetic manifestation of the accents is a matter of controversy (see Blevins 1993: 241–242, Dogil 1999a: 278–279, and the literature they mention). Based on the study by Pakerys (1982: 182–189), the view now prevailing among Lithuanian phonologists is that the phonetic correlates of the accents include not only fundamental frequency and intensity but also duration and spectral structure. According to this view, the importance of different correlates depends on the syllable type. For a survey on phonetic studies of the Lithuanian accents, see also Kudirka (2005: 1–4) and Bacevičiūtė (2009).

The main difference lies between syllables with long monophthongs and those with diphthongs and diphthongal sequences. On long monophthongs, including *ie* [iːə], *uo* [uːə], accents are indeed mostly differentiated by pitch, other parameters being less important. But rather than concentrating on the shape of the tonal contour, more recent studies pay attention to the difference in the average pitch level, the time and value of the peak, and the distance between the highest and the lowest pitches in the contour. It is typical for the acute to have a lower pitch level and an earlier time of the peak in comparison to the circumflex. The distance between the highest and the lowest pitches is greater for the acute than for the circumflex; in acute syllables, the value of the pitch (and intensity) also changes more rapidly.

On diphthongs and diphthongal sequences, accents are differentiated by the different duration and quality of the components, although it is only true for diphthongs and diphthongal sequences that have low vowels as their first components. In acute syllables, the first component is lengthened if it is a low vowel (35a). High vowels remain short in this position, as does *o* [ɔ] in borrowings (35b). In circumflex syllables, the second component is lengthened in all cases, whereas the low vowel acting as the first component is reduced (35c). The lengthened first components are usually identified as half-long or long, the lengthened second components as half-long (Girdenis 1997a: 56; see also Garšva & Girdenis 1997: 39).

---

[23] Cf. Garšva (2003: 12), who actually calls pitch "the least probable of all possible phonetic correlates" of the Lithuanian accents.

The accent mark is traditionally placed on the component that undergoes lengthening, so that the acute diacritic appears on the first component and the circumflex diacritic on the second. The use of the grave mark in the Lithuanian phonological tradition instead of the acute symbol in diphthongs and diphthongal sequences with high vowels is motivated by the fact that high vowels are not lengthened under the acute.

(35) a. acute (low vowels)
 šáuk [ʃɑˑʊk] or [ʃɑːʊk] 'shoot' (2SG.IMP)
 káilis [ˈkɑˑɪlʲɪs] or [ˈkɑːɪlʲɪs] 'hide, fur'
 káltas [ˈkɑˑltas] or [ˈkɑːltas] 'chisel'
 pavérgti [paˈvʲæˑrʲkʲtʲi] or [paˈvʲæːrʲkʲtʲi] 'subdue, enslave' (INF)

b. acute (high and mid vowels)
 gìnti [ˈgʲɪnʲtʲi] 'defend' (INF)
 kùrpė [ˈkʊrʲpʲeː] 'shoe'
 spòrtas [ˈspɔrtas] 'sport'

c. circumflex (all vowels)
 šaũk [ʃʊʊˑk] 'call' (2SG.IMP)
 gaĩla [ˈgəiˑla] 'regrettably'
 kaĩtas [ˈkəlˑtas] 'guilty'
 veȓkti [ˈvʲerʲˑkʲtʲi] 'weep' (INF)
 kuȓpė [ˈkʊrʲˑpʲeː] 'do smth clumsily or badly' (PST.3)

Since high (and mid) vowels are not lengthened under acute, pitch still plays a significant part in producing the contrast in diphthongs and diphthongal sequences having high vowels as their first components (Pakerys 1982: 186–187).

In a framework that views the Lithuanian accents as differentiated mainly by pitch, heavy syllables are given two moras as distinct from light syllables that have only one, and either the first or the second mora of the heavy syllable is assigned a H(igh tone). This H tone may be assigned to the mora directly (Blevins 1993), or the mora may be identified as stressed and then given the H (Halle & Vergnaud 1987: 190–203). The only mora of the light syllable is also associated with the H (directly or through the connection with stress), but, for obvious reason, no contrast arises. The assignment of the H to one of the two moras is clearly connected with the classic description of the acute as falling and the circumflex as rising. The idea of the different stress locations inside the heavy syllable, corresponding to the two moras, reflects another traditional view on the acute as "strong in the beginning" and the circumflex as "strong in the end".

Since the importance of such phonetic parameters as pitch, intensity, duration, and spectral structure has been shown to depend on the type of the syllable

(Pakerys 1982), none of the above-mentioned characteristics of the accents is taken to be the primary parameter by Lithuanian phonologists, and the complex nature of the accents is put forward instead. Girdenis (2003: 273–274) even insists on terms that do not name any phonetic properties, considering the designations *intonation rude* and *intonation douce* by Saussure (1922: 491) to be a close ideal. He prefers to call the acute *staiginė priegaidė* (from Lithuanian *staigus* 'sudden') and the circumflex *tęstinė priegaidė* (from *tęsti* 'extend, spread'). In Girdenis (1997a: 55), the acute is defined in English as "sharp falling" and the circumflex as "smooth rising".

As Dogil's (1999a,b) analysis is based on the same study by Pakerys (1982), it shares the spirit of Girdenis' proposal. Dogil assigns the acute and the circumflex different underlying prosodic representations so that the moraic structure is underlyingly specified only in acute morphemes. The circumflex morphemes have syllabic representations, and the accent is realized on the whole syllable (Dogil 1999b: 887; see also Kačiuškienė & Girdenis 1997: 33–34).

I intend to show that none of the interpretations is fully compatible with what is found in modern Lithuanian, although Dogil's approach can be seen as the most accurate.

4.3 Stress

Lithuanian is the only language under discussion that has free and mobile stress, and it is also the only language that lengthens stressed vowels. The peculiarities of the Lithuanian accentuation system concern us only as far as they are determined by the acute and circumflex. For more details on Lithuanian accentuation, see Young (1991: 13–24), Stundžia (1995), and Dogil (1999b: 878–883).

There are two types of stress mobility in Lithuanian. The first type is dictated by the lexically specified properties of morphemes, labeled "strong" and "weak" or, alternatively, "accented" and "unaccented". Stress is assigned to the first strong morpheme; if all morphemes in a word are weak, stress is assigned to the first of them. The strong morphemes in Table 23 are in capital letters. As can be surmised from the examples, the accent plays no part in this type of stress mobility.

Tab. 23: Strong and weak morphemes

NOM.SG	NOM.PL	Translation
KĒL-IS	KĒL-IAI	'knee'
kēl-ias	kel-IAĨ	'road'

The second type of stress mobility depends on the properties of syllables and also partly on the properties of morphemes, although of another kind. Heavy syllables with the circumflex and also short syllables yield the stress to certain endings and derivational suffixes known as "attractive", whereas long acute syllables retain the stress. In Table 24, the attractive morphemes are set in bold.

The second type of mobility initially was phonetically motivated, as attractive morphemes had long acute syllables later shortened as the result of the so-called Leskien's Law (Zinkevičius 1980: 105–107, Collinge 1985: 115–116). The shift of stress from non-acute syllables onto the following acute syllables is known as Saussure's Law; sometimes, the synchronic rule behind the second type of stress mobility is also called Saussure's Law (see Zinkevičius 1980: 49–52, Collinge 1985: 149–152).

Stress causes lengthening of short low monophthongs *a* [a] and *e* [ɛ] (Girdenis 1997b: 62–63; see also Garšva & Girdenis 1997: 41–42). The accent of lengthened vowels is traditionally identified with the circumflex in Standard Lithuanian. Compare different forms of the same words in stressed and unstressed position in Table 25.

In unstressed syllables *a* [a] and *e* [ɛ] remain short, which sets them apart from the historically long *ą* [aː] and *ę* [æː] that are long in both stressed and unstressed position (Table 26).

The lengthening does not apply in several phonological and morphological contexts. The former include monosyllables and final syllables of polysyllabic words (36), whereas the latter encompass certain pronouns (37a), the comparative suffix (37b), verbal prefixes (37c), certain forms of verbs that do not contain

Tab. 24: Attractive morphemes

	NOM.SG	ACC.PL	Translation
long circumflex syllable	vilk-as	vilk-**ùs**	'wolf'
short syllable	pikt-as	pikt-**ùs**	'evil; angry'
long acute syllable	pilk-as	pilk-**us**	'gray'

Tab. 25: Stress-based alternation of low vowels

Stressed	Unstressed	Translation
nãmas [ˈnɑːmas] (NOM.SG)	namaĩ [naˈmaiˑ] (INS.SG)	'house'
rãktas [ˈrɑːktas] (NOM.SG)	raktù [raˈktʊ] (INS.SG)	'key'
lẽdas [ˈlʲæːdas] (NOM.SG)	ledù [lʲɛˈdʊ] (INS.SG)	'ice'
nẽša [ˈnʲæːʃa] (PRS.3)	nešù [nʲɛˈʃʊ] (1SG.PRS)	'carry'

Tab. 26: Historically long low vowels in stressed and unstressed syllables

Stressed	Unstressed	Translation
šą́la [ˈʃɑːla] (PRS.3)	šąlù [ʃɑːˈlʊ] (PRS.1SG)	'freeze'
rą́stas [ˈrɑːstas] (NOM.PL)	rąstùs [rɑːˈstʊs] (ACC.PL)	'log'
grę́žė [ˈgʲrʲæːʒʲeː] (PST.3)	gręžiaũ [gʲrʲæːˈʒʲeuˑ] (PST.1SG)	'spin'
tę́sė [ˈtʲæːsʲeː] (PST.3)	tęsiaũ [tʲæːˈsʲeuˑ] (PST.1SG)	'continue'

syllabic suffixes (37d), and a few other cases. See the full list in Girdenis (1997b: 62–63) and Garšva and Girdenis (1997: 41–42). For a recent discussion of verbal stems in Lithuanian, including their accentuation, see Arkadiev (2012).

(36) a. final syllables of polysyllabic words
  valandà 'hour' (NOM.SG)
  rankàs 'arm; hand' (ACC.PL)
  galvojè 'head' (LOC.SG)
  upès 'river' (ACC.PL)

  b. monosyllables
  àš 'I'
  kàs 'who, what'
  bèt 'but' (cf. *mḗs* 'we'[24])

(37) a. pronouns
  màno 'my'
  tàvo 'your'

  b. comparative suffixes
  jaunèsnis (NOM.SG.M), *jaunèsnė* (NOM.SG.F) 'younger'

  c. verbal prefixes
  àtneša 'bring' (PRS.3)
  tebèneša 'still carry' (PRS.3)

  d. "primary" verbs
  kàsti (INF), *kàsdavo* (HAB.3), *kàsiu* (1SG.FUT), *kàstume* (1PL.SBJV) 'dig'
  dègti (INF), *dègdavo* (HAB.3), *dègsiu* (1SG.FUT), *dègtume* (1PL.SBJV) 'burn'

---

[24] The lengthened vowel in *mḗs* 'we' is explained by analogy with the historically long vowel in the 2PL pronoun *jū̃s*.

As can be seen from comparison with (35a), the lengthening of underlyingly short monophthongs and that of the first components of diphthongs and diphthongal sequences has in common that in both cases it affects low vowels. It must be specified that lengthening of components in diphthongs and diphthongal sequences only occurs under stress, since the acute and the circumflex are normally found in stressed syllables (sometimes also under secondary stress). The similarity is even closer if we remember that some phonological interpretations of the Lithuanian accents identify the first components of acute diphthongs and diphthongal sequences with the stressed mora. Nevertheless, it will be shown below that the relationship between the two types of lengthening is not so simple as it may seem from the first glance.

4.4 Lithuanian dialects

Accents and stress in Lithuanian are connected with their respective lengthening processes: accents with the lengthening of the first components of diphthongs and diphthongal sequences, and stress with the lengthening of the stressed vowels. Both accents and stress are subject to dialectal variation.

Standard Lithuanian is archaic in comparison with dialects, so that the lengthening (and shortening) processes seen in the standard language only reach their full potential in dialects. Nevertheless, many facts about dialects may be relevant for the colloquial variety of Standard Lithuanian as well. In this section, I provide a brief outline of the main distinctions among Lithuanian dialects, based on Zinkevičius (1966, 1994) (see also Balode & Holvoet 2001b: 42, 51–78).

The two major dialects are Aukštaitian and Žemaitian, Standard Lithuanian being basically Aukštaitian. Aukštaitian are further divided into Western, Southern, and Eastern Aukštaitian. Žemaitian, correspondingly, consists of Southern, Northern, and Western Žemaitian. Four of the above-mentioned six dialects are made up of smaller areas, named after the nearest urban center; for example, the dialect that is closest to Standard Lithuanian is called the Western Aukštaitian dialect of Kaunas. The classification in (38) is repeated, with some omissions, from Zinkevičius (1994: 124).

(38) Classification of Lithuanian dialects
    1. Aukštaitian
        a. Western
            i. Kaunas
            ii. Šiauliai
        b. Southern

    c. Eastern
        i. Vilnius
        ii. Utena
        iii. Anykščiai
        iv. Kupiškis
        v. Širvintos
        vi. Panevėžys
2. Žemaitian
    a. Southern
        i. Raseiniai
        ii. Varniai
    b. Northern
        i. Telšiai
        ii. Kretinga
    c. Western

The classification is based on the following features. Žemaitian does not have *ie* [iːə], *uo* [uːə] where Aukštaitian (and Standard Lithuanian) has them. Instead, Southern Žemaitian has [iː], [uː], Northern Žemaitian [ei], [ou], and Western Žemaitian [eː], [oː] (see Table 27 for illustrations).

The division of Aukštaitian is associated with another feature, namely, the reflexes of the once-nasalized low long vowels *ą*, *ę* (39a) and combinations of a short low vowel with a tautosyllabic nasal stop *an*, *am*, *en*, *em* (in morphemes where such combinations were not turned into nasal long vowels) (39b). The low vowels may be either retained or raised to high vowels.

(39)   a. *kąsnis* [ˈkɑːsʲnʲis] or [ˈkuːsʲnʲis] 'bite' (NOM.SG)
        b. *kanda* [ˈkɑˑnda] or [ˈkuˑnda] 'bite' (PRS.3)

Long low vowels are only retained in Western Aukštaitian. In Southern and Eastern Aukštaitian, high vowels are found in their stead. Historical, short low vowels before nasal stops are retained in both Western and Southern Aukštaitian, and only Eastern Aukštaitian replaces them with high vowels (Table 28). The

Tab. 27: Correspondences of *ie*, *uo* in Žemaitian

Standard Lithuanian and Aukštaitian	Žemaitian		
	Southern	Northern	Western
ie [iːə], *uo* [uːə]	[iː], [uː]	[eɪ], [oʊ]	[eː], [oː]
pienas 'milk'	[pʲiːns]	[peɪns]	[peːns]
duona 'bread'	[duːna]	[doʊna]	[doːna]

Tab. 28: The development of *ą*, *an* in Lithuanian dialects

Standard Lithuanian and Western Aukštaitian	[ˈkaːsʲnʲɪs]	[ˈkaˑnda]
Southern Aukštaitian	[ˈkuːsʲnʲɪs]	[ˈkaˑnda]
Eastern Aukštaitian	[ˈkuːsʲnʲɪs]	[ˈkuˑnda]

situation in Western Aukštaitian coincides with Standard Lithuanian. (Note that, even though the first component of the diphthongal sequence in *kanda* is now pronounced as long under the acute, its fate in Southern Aukštaitian is different from that of the long vowel.)

The classification does not represent the whole Lithuanian area as it ignores the territories of what used to be East Prussia called *Lithuania Minor* (at present, Kaliningrad Oblast of Russia). Although not part of the Lithuanian-speaking area anymore, it played a crucial part in the development of the Lithuanian language and provided material for the first researchers of Lithuanian including Saussure and Kurschat. *Lithuania Minor* encompassed two sub-areas identified with the Žemaitian and Aukštaitian dialects, the Aukštaitian part being close to the current Western Aukštaitian dialect of Kaunas and the standard language.

4.5 Lengthening of the first component in Lithuanian dialects

Girdenis (2003: 276–277) states that the contrast between the acute and the circumflex is shared by all dialects of Lithuanian, even though the phonetic correlates may differ from Standard Lithuanian (see also Kudirka 2005: 3, Bacevičiūtė 2011: 14–15) for surveys on phonetic studies of the accents in Lithuanian dialects. The phonetic variation of each of the accents still fits within the bounds of the impressionistic designations by Girdenis, that is, the variants of the acute are still "sharper" and more "sudden" than the circumflex in a given dialect, and the circumflex is "smoother" and more "spread out" than the acute. The major distinctions in the dialect realization of the accents are the following.

First, the acute in most part of the Žemaitian dialect (including Northern Žemaitian, Western Žemaitian, and the adjoining part of Southern Žemaitian) may be pronounced with glottal stop (Zinkevičius 1966: 34) (see map 106 in Grinaveckienė et al. 1982). This type of acute is marked with the diacritic <^>[25] in the transcription used by Lithuanian dialectologists, but I will mark it with the

---

[25] The symbol <^> is not normally called "circumflex" in the Baltic linguistics.

symbol [ʔ] also used in Latvian in Section 2.2 (Table 29). Nevertheless, since the variant of the acute without glottal stop is also common, Lithuanian dialectologists do not view the glottal stop as the main phonetic property of the Žemaitian acute. Instead, the latter is described as being shorter and having a more rapidly falling pitch in comparison with the circumflex. For more details on the phonetic correlates of the Žemaitian acute and circumflex, see Girdenis (1967, 1974, 1996, 1998), Mažiulienė (1996), Atkočaitytė (2002), Murinienė (2007), and other authors.

Second, in Žemaitian and the neighboring part of the Western Aukštaitian, phonetic correlates of the accents are less dependent on the type of the syllable, in that pitch is as important for the contrast in diphthongs and diphthongal sequences as for long monophthongs (Pakerys 1982: 154, 183–184) (see also Kačiuškienė & Girdenis 1997). This is closely connected with the third parameter of dialectal variation, namely, the duration of the components, as well as the reduction of the first component under the circumflex.

In most part of the Aukštaitian dialect, both low and high vowels acting as the first components of diphthongs and diphthongal sequences are lengthened under the acute. The situation as in Standard Lithuanian, when only low vowels are lengthened in this position, is solely found in a part of Western Aukštaitian (Zinkevičius 1966: 108) (see map 20 in Grinaveckienė et al. 1982; compare examples in Table 30).

Thus, the lengthening of the first component under the acute and the second component under the circumflex knows no exception in most Aukštaitian dialects. In order to maintain the contrast between the accents, these dialects rely on differences in duration and spectral structure even to a greater extent than Standard

Tab. 29: Acute in Northern Žemaitian compared to Standard Lithuanian

Standard Lithuanian	Northern Žemaitian	Translation
pūti [ˈpuːtʲɪ]	[ˈpuːʔte]	'rot' (INF)
káulas [ˈkaˑʊlas] or [ˈkaːʊlas]	[ˈkaˑʔʊls] or [ˈkaːʔʊls]	'bone'
kálnas [ˈkaˑlnas] or [ˈkaːlnas]	[ˈkaˑʔlns] or [ˈkaːʔlns]	'hill, mountain'

Tab. 30: Lengthening of high vowels in Aukštaitian

Standard Lithuanian	Most Aukštaitian dialects	Translation
pìrmas [ˈpʲɪrmas]	[ˈpʲiˑrmas] or [ˈpʲiːrmas]	'first'
kùrmis [ˈkʊrmɪs]	[ˈkuˑrmis] or [ˈkuːrmis]	'mole'

Lithuanian does. In addition, these differences are more pronounced than in Standard Lithuanian. At least in Eastern Aukštaitian, the lengthened components of diphthongs and diphthongal sequences are longer in both acute and circumflex syllables, and the initial vowels, reduced under the circumflex, are more closed (Kačiuškienė & Girdenis 1997: 31–32). The transcription in Table 31, based on the examples of Kačiuškienė and Girdenis (1997), shows the different quality of the first components of the circumflex diphthongs in Standard Lithuanian and Eastern Aukštaitian.

In most part of the Žemaitian dialect – corresponding to the area where the acute is realized with glottal stop (see map 106 in Grinaveckienė et al. 1982) – the first component of diphthongs and diphthongal sequences is lengthened under both the acute and the circumflex, and the second component under both accents is short (Zinkevičius 1966: 109) (see examples in Tables 32 and 33). Consequently, there is no reduction of the first components under the circumflex. As opposed to Aukštaitian and Standard Lithuanian, the main phonetic correlates of the acute and the circumflex in diphthongs and diphthongal sequences in Žemaitian are pitch and intensity (Kačiuškienė & Girdenis 1997: 33–34).

In two adjoining areas of Southern Žemaitian and Western Aukštaitian, forming, perhaps, a transition zone, the circumflex induces lengthening of both the first and the second components of diphthongs and diphthongal sequences (Zinkevičius 1966: 109) (see map 106 in Grinaveckienė et al. 1982).

Tab. 31: Circumflex diphthongs in Eastern Aukshayt

Standard Lithuanian	[ʊuˑ], [əiˑ]
Eastern Aukštaitian	[ɔuˑ], [ɨiˑ]

Tab. 32: Acute diphthongs and diphthongal sequences in Žemaitian

Standard Lithuanian	Žemaitian	Translation
káulas [ˈkaˑʊlas] or [ˈkaːʊlas]	[ˈkaˑʔʊls] or [ˈkaːʔʊls]	'bone'
kálnas [ˈkaˑlnas] or [ˈkaːlnas]	[ˈkaˑʔlns] or [ˈkaːʔlns]	'hill, mountain'

Tab. 33: Circumflex diphthongs and diphthongal sequences in Žemaitian and other dialects

Standard Lithuanian	Southern Žemaitian and part of Western Aukštaitian	Žemaitian	Translation
laūkas [ˈlɔuˑkas]	[laˑuˑks]	[laˑʊks] or [laːʊks]	'field'
kaȓtas [ˈkərˑtas]	[kaˑrˑts]	[kaˑrts] or [kaːrts]	'time; occasion'

Lithuanian dialectologists transcribe such diphthongs and diphthongal sequences with the circumflex diacritics on both components, although this is actually meant to be a typographic substitute for the longer circumflex symbol that should cover the letters for both components (Zinkevičius 1994: 32) (see examples in Table 33).

The lengthening of the first component may be accompanied by the drop of the short second component. This process is found in the western part of the Lithuanian area including both Žemaitian and Aukštaitian varieties. In Žemaitian, the second components of the diphthongs *ai*, *ei* are deleted under both accents (Zinkevičius 1966: 90–91). The result of the monophthongization is a long vowel, identical to the lengthened first component of the former diphthong (40).

(40) Žemaitian (acute and circumflex)
vaĩkas>[vɑːks] 'child'[26]
sveĩkas>[sʲvʲæːks] 'healthy'
mergáitė>[mʲɛrˈgɑːtʲɪ] 'girl'
par̃šai>[ˈpɑːrʃɑː] 'pig' (NOM.PL)

The second component is only regularly deleted in endings, while in stems, the deletion is subject to areal variation, the exception being some words that only exist with monophthongs in the stem. The monophthongization takes place in both acute and circumflex syllables, which is easily connected to the fact that both accents involve lengthening the first component in Žemaitian.

Although not found in the Aukštaitian dialect of the modern Lithuanian, a similar process is known to have affected the Aukštaitian area of *Lithuania Minor* in East Prussia (Zinkevičius 1966: 91, 1994: 34). Examples from East Prussia in (41a) also include the diphthong *au*, which does not undergo the change in Žemaitian.

(41) Aukštaitian in East Prussia
   a. acute
      dáiktas>[dɑːkts] 'thing'
      pavéikslai>[paˈvʲæːkslaɪ] 'picture' (NOM.PL)
      šáukštai>[ˈʃɑːkʃtaɪ] 'spoon' (NOM.PL)

   b. circumflex
      žemaĩtis [ʒʲɛˈmarˑtʲɪs] 'Žemaitian person'

In Prussian Aukštaitian, the second component is retained under the circumflex, where the first component is short, thus confirming the idea that the

---

[26] The more archaic Standard Lithuanian forms are conventionally shown as the input for the change. Post-stressed syllables in Žemaitian may have accents as well as stressed ones.

deletion of the second component simply accompanies the lengthening of the preceding vowel (41b). (In Prussian Aukštaitian, the monophthongization is also absent from unstressed position.)

4.6 Comparison with Latvian and Livonian

Evidently, the conditions that determine the lengthening of the first component resemble the restrictions on the lengthening of vowels before the tautosyllabic *r* in Latvian dialects. In both languages, they include suprasegmental features and vowel height. High vowels are not lengthened in the standard languages and the areas on which they are based (Western Aukštaitian, Central Latvian). This may be connected with the fact that, accidentally, both standard languages are based on more archaic dialects where the change only affects low vowels. Another matter is the lack of lengthening under one of the tones/accents as it shows similar geographic distribution. The first component is short under the broken (or the corresponding rising) tone in East Latvian (42a) and under the circumflex accent in the eastern and southern parts of the Aukštaitian dialect in Lithuanian (42b). In the western parts of both Latvia (Kurzeme) and Lithuania (in Žemaitian), the first component is lengthened under any of the contrastive tones/accents (43).

(42) a. East (Central and High) Latvian
 *vaȓna>[ˈvaːːrnɑ] 'crow'
 *dàrzi>[ˈdɑːrzi] 'garden' (NOM.PL)
 *daȓbi>[ˈdɑrˀbi] 'labor' (NOM.PL) – no lengthening

 b. Aukštaitian
 *káulas>[ˈkɑːʊlɑs] 'bone'
 *laũkas>[ˈlɒuˑkɑs] 'field' – no lengthening

(43) a. West (Curonian) Latvian
 *vaȓna>[ˈvaːːrnɑ] 'crow'
 *dàrzi>[ˈdɑːrzi] 'garden' (NOM.PL)
 *daȓbi>[ˈdɑːˀrbi] 'labor' (NOM.PL)

 b. Žemaitian
 *káulas>[kɑˑˀʊls] or [kɑːˀʊls] 'bone'
 *laũkas>[lɑˑʊks] or [lɑːʊks] 'field'

Lithuanian and Latvian dialectologists have paid surprisingly little attention to these similarities between the two Baltic languages, with the exception of the development of high vowels into [i(ː)ə], [u(ː)ə], which may accompany their lengthening (see Grinaveckis 1973: 245) (44).

(44) a. Sourthern Žemaitian (Viduklė-Nemakščiai)
   pìrmas>[ˈpʲiːərms] 'first'
   pùlti>[ˈpuːəlʲtʲɪ] 'attack' (INF)

   b. Curonian Latvian
   kur̃pe>[ˈkuəːrpe] 'shoe'
   zir̂gs>[ziə˺rks] 'horse'

One of the reasons for the neglect may be the different status that the results of the lengthening receive in Latvian and Lithuanian. In Latvian, vowels that are lengthened before *r* are identified with historically long vowels both in duration and as part of the vowel inventory. It is also important that in Latvian, the lengthening of the first component is independent of stress (see Section 2.2). In Lithuanian, the lengthened first components of diphthongs and diphthongal sequences waver between long and half-long, and their lengthening is traditionally seen as the enhancement of the acute-circumflex contrast, which only appears under stress. The difference in the treatment of the lengthened component is even reflected in the orthography (45).

(45) a. Standard Latvian
   vàrdi [ˈvaːrdi] 'word; name' (NOM.PL), cf. *uzvàrdi* [ˈuzvaːrdi] 'surname' (NOM.PL)

   b. Standard Lithuanian
   dárbas [ˈdɑˑrbas] or [ˈdɑːrbas] 'labor', cf. *ùždarbis* [ˈuʒdarʲbʲɪs] 'wage'

It is less surprising that specialists on Lithuanian do not compare it with the unrelated language Livonian, separated from the Lithuanian area by Latvian. Nevertheless, with respect to the lengthening of the first component, Livonian shows similarity to Aukštaitian Lithuanian. Livonian places no restriction on the quality of vowels that are subject to lengthening, but this feature is less important, as it probably only reflects the less advanced stage of the development in Lithuanian. The main similarity with Lithuanian is that, in accordance with my understanding of the process outlined in Section 3.8, Livonian only induces lengthening under one of the reconstructed accents (the one comparable to the light accent/"normal" length in Estonian). In this regard, Livonian groups together with East Latvian and Aukštaitian Lithuanian as opposed to West Latvian and Žemaitian where lengthening is universal. But Livonian and Lithuanian, either Žemaitian or Aukštaitian, crucially differ from Latvian, in that in Latvian, the lengthening was triggered by some individual properties of *r* that prevented this sound from being moraic. This is obviously not the case in Lithuanian (46a) and Livonian (46b) where lengthening involved diphthongs and diphthongal sequences as whole classes.

(46) a. Livonian
   *aiga>āiga [ˈɑːigɑ(ː)] 'time'
   *lauda>*lāuda>lǭda [ˈlɔːdɑ(ː)] 'table'
   *jalga>jālga [ˈjɑːlgɑ(ː)] 'leg; foot'
   *randa>rānda [ˈrɑːndɑ(ː)] 'shore'

   b. Lithuanian
   káilis [ˈkɑˑɪlʲɪs] or [ˈkɑːɪlʲɪs] 'hide; fur'
   áukštas [ˈɑˑʊkʃtas] or [ˈɑːʊkʃtas] 'high'
   káltas [ˈkɑˑltas] or [ˈkɑːltas] 'chisel'
   kánda [ˈkɑˑnda] or [ˈkɑːnda] 'bit' (PRS.3)

The similarity between Lithuanian and Livonian is made more striking by the fact that the alternation between the acute and the circumflex (known as metatony), which often accompanies Lithuanian word formation, clearly resembles one of the types of the Livonian gradation (Table 34).

As I already said in Section 3.7, I do not consider the lengthening of the first components in Livonian as resulting from the loss of moraicity on the second components, and the same pertains to Lithuanian. (Although the second components must have indeed lost the moraic status, it happened as a consequence of the change rather as its cause.) While the properties of *r* made it difficult to maintain the tonal contrast, as well as syllable weight, on the relevant diphthongal sequences in Latvian, it was the problems with the suprasegmental contrast itself that forced the change in Livonian and Lithuanian.

I mentioned in connection with the Latvian change (see Section 2.7) that I view the two types of lengthening (both the one which is sensitive to the suprasegmental

Tab. 34: Alternation in Lithuanian and Livonian

Lithuanian	ADJ	INF
	sveĩkas [ˈsʲvʲɛiˑkas] 'well; whole'	svéikinti [ˈsʲvʲæˑikʲinʲtʲi] 'greet'
	kaĩtas [ˈkəlˑtas] 'guilty'	káltinti [ˈkɑˑlʲtʲinʲtʲi] 'blame'
Livonian	PART.SG	NOM.SG
	aigō [ˈɑiˑgə] 'time'	āiga [ˈɑːigɑ(ː)] 'time'
	jalgō [ˈjɑlˑgə] 'leg; foot'	jālga [ˈjɑːlgɑ(ː)] 'leg; foot'

contrast and the one which is not) as two ways of intensifying the contrast between the tones on diphthongs and diphthongal sequences. One solution is to substitute the diphthong or diphthongal sequence with a long vowel, created by lengthening the first component and transferring the tonal contrast to the long vowel, which, in some cases, may be better suited for expressing the contrast. This is what has happened in Žemaitian Lithuanian and West Latvian (Kurzeme) where the first components of diphthongs and diphthongal sequences were lengthened under all accents/tones. Another solution is to replace the suprasegmental contrast with contrasting sequences of different phonemes. In this case, the first component is only lengthened under one of the tones/accents in order to distinguish it from the contrasting tone/accent. This scenario is found in Aukštaitian Lithuanian, East Latvian, and Livonian.

It is not always easy to explain why the former or the latter course is chosen, even though one may refer to differences in either phonological status or phonetic parameters of the contrast. In case of Aukštaitian Lithuanian, however, the direction of the choice is obviously linked to the fact that the acute-circumflex contrast on long monophthongs tends to disappear in the major part of this dialect, which is also reflected in colloquial style of the standard language.

4.7 Loss of accents on long monophthongs

The eastern part of the Lithuanian language area, including not only Eastern, but also Southern Aukštaitian and part of Western Aukštaitian has a tendency to lose the acute-circumflex contrast in syllables with long monophthongs and [iːə], [uːə] (Zinkevičius 1966: 33; see also Young 1991: 6).[27] Diphthongs and diphthongal sequences preserve the contrast due to the lengthening of the different components under the different accents, which helps to identify the accent. In the western part of Western Aukštaitian and in Žemaitian, the acute-circumflex contrast in long monophthongs is preserved.

Although the rules of the Standard Lithuanian language require that the accents must be distinguished in all types of heavy syllables, the colloquial language used

---

27 Later, this opinion was revised by Girdenis (1971: 206) and Zinkevičius (1974) (cf. Pakerys 1982: 154); nevertheless, the contrast in syllables with long monophthongs and [iːə], [uːə] is still considered to be less salient and treated as possible, but not necessary (Girdenis 2003: 276, f50). Other authors find it difficult to deny that the accents in long monophthongs and [iːə], [uːə] are indeed susceptible to neutralization – see Leskauskaitė (2004: 191–192) for Southern Aukštaitian and Bacevičiūtė (2011: 15) for the eastern part of Western Aukštaitian.

by educated people actually resembles the eastern dialects in that the contrast between the accents is only maintained in diphthongs and diphthongal sequences (Pakerys 1982: 151–154, Garšva 2003: 13, Kudirka 2005: 20).

In addition to long monophthongs, in the standard language, neutralization also affects diphthongs and diphthongal sequences with high vowels as the first components because high vowels are not lengthened under the acute in this position. According to Pakerys (1982: 152–153), the acute syllable in (47a) can be perceived as the circumflex one (47b) due to the shortness of the first component.

(47) Standard Lithuanian
    a.   *vìrto* [ˈvɪrtoː] 'boiled' (GEN.SG.M)

    b.   *vir̃to* [ˈvɪrˑtoː] 'collapse; change' (PST.3)

Pakerys explains the confusion between the acute and the circumflex in such cases as (47) by the fact that pronouncing an acute diphthong or diphthongal sequence with a short initial vowel poses difficulties for many speakers of the standard language with either Aukštaitian or Žemaitian background. As a result, the initial high vowel may be lengthened, as in dialects, or the acute may be replaced with the circumflex (see also Pupkis 1980: 94).

4.8 Reduction of the first component under the circumflex

Aukštaitian Lithuanian resembles Livonian in that diphthongs and diphthongal sequences have a lengthened second component if the first component remains short. The longer second component is found in circumflex syllables in Aukštaitian Lithuanian and in strong-grade forms in Livonian (48a). In East Latvian, too, *r* is known to be half-long under the broken tone (Laua 1997: 65), which blocks the lengthening of the first component (48b). But Aukštaitian Lithuanian still stands apart from the other languages in the region in that it has the lengthened second component accompanied by reduction of the first component (48c).

(48)   a.   Livonian
             aigõ [ˈaiˑgə] 'time' (PART.SG.)
             jalgõ [ˈjalˑgə] 'leg; foot' (PART.SG.)

       b.   East Latvian
             dar̂bi [ˈdarˀbi] 'labor' (NOM.PL)

       c.   Aukštaitian Lithuanian
             gaĩla [ˈgəiˑla] 'regrettably'
             kaĩtas [ˈkəlˑtas] 'guilty'

The first component is reduced if it is a low vowel. In the standard language, [a] is turned into [ɒ] before [u] and into [ə] before all other sounds acting as the second components. In Eastern Aukštaitian, the reduction is even more pronounced as the circumflex *au* becomes [ɔuˑ] and *ai* [ɨiˑ][28] (see Sections 4.2 and 4.5).

There is a controversy among Lithuanian scholars as to which sounds belong to the nucleus of a syllable containing a circumflex diphthong or diphthongal sequence (Pakerys 1970). It is assumed traditionally that a syllable with a diphthong (or diphthongal sequence) is considered heavy because it has two elements while a light syllable only has one. It must be logical therefore to treat both the first and the second components of diphthongs and diphthongal sequences as belonging to the nucleus. In other terms (usually not used by Lithuanian phonologists), both sounds must be treated as moraic (see van der Hulst 1999: 13). But this approach fails to account for a considerable reduction of the first component of a diphthong (or diphthongal sequence) that occurs under the circumflex.

The reduction of the first component looks very unusual in that it affects what otherwise is expected to be the most sonorous sound in the syllable while the inherently less sonorous sound, the high vowel in diphthongs or the sonorant in diphthongal sequences, is given the maximum duration. (Under the acute accent, the lesser duration of the second component does not seem "unnatural", as it correlates with the lesser sonority of the corresponding sounds.) Based on the actual properties of the components of diphthongs and diphthongal sequences, rather than theoretical assumptions, the second component of the circumflex diphthongs and diphthongal sequences must be acknowledged as the only sound in the syllable nucleus, and the only moraic sound – see Abele (1924: 30–31) where she discusses, without mentioning Lithuanian, the possibility of a less sonorous sound being syllabic instead of the more sonorous sound in the same syllable.

The solution offered by Pakerys (1970) is to give different labels to different groups of elements. The components of diphthongs and diphthongal sequences, whose presence is crucial for the weight of the syllable, are named "syllable constituent sounds" (*skiemens sudaromieji garsai* in Lithuanian), whereas the components that receive additional lengthening under either acute or circumflex are identified as "syllabic" (*skiemeniniai garsai*). Evidently, giving labels only highlights the controversy instead of solving it. I believe the conflict in terminology to

---

28 It is interesting to note that the first components of circumflex diphthongs and diphthongal sequences sometimes develop in the way characteristic for unstressed vowels. In a part of Panevėžys subdialect of Eastern Aukštaitian, the original sequences *an, en* are only turned into *un, in* under the acute. Under the circumflex and in unstressed position, *on, en* are found instead (Zinkevičius 1966: 99).

reflect the real conflict in the language, originating from language change. In my opinion, both diphthongs and diphthongal sequences, taken as whole units, and their components are candidates for the same role, but at different stages in the history of Lithuanian. The functioning of diphthongs and diphthongal sequences as nuclei of heavy syllables is being replaced by single long sounds in the syllable nucleus, either vowels or sonorants. The acute-circumflex contrast is consequently being reinterpreted as the one between different strings of segments.

4.9 Stressed-vowel lengthening in dialects

The discussion on stress in Lithuanian dialects usually involves the issues of stress retraction and vowel lengthening under stress. I discuss the lengthening of stressed vowels, which is more important for this study. In dialects, the lengthening of vowels under stress is paralleled by their shortening in unstressed syllables, thus strengthening the connection between stress and vowel length. Since no vowel lengthening is found under the retracted stress, I will not go into discussion of stress retraction.

Historically, short monophthongs are lengthened under stress in dialects as well as in Standard Lithuanian. Lengthened vowels in the standard language are traditionally viewed as being identical to historically long vowels under the circumflex. But in most dialects, lengthened vowels are reported to be shorter in comparison with historically long vowels, although occasionally, they may occur with the full length (see Bacevičiūtė 2004: 31–33 and the literature there). In dialectal texts, lengthened vowels are usually transcribed with the "middle accent" (Lithuanian *vidurinė priegaidė*), which is considered a shorter, and more abrupt, variety of the circumflex, even though before voiceless obstruents, they actually resemble the acute (Girdenis 2002: 211). (The middle accent has a special symbol [ˢ], which I do not reproduce in the examples below.) It is interesting that lengthened vowels are also believed to be half-long in the part of Western Aukštaitian, which is known as the base for the standard language (Table 35).

In Standard Lithuanian as well as Western and Southern Aukštaitian, it is only low vowels that are lengthened under stress, whereas high vowels remain

Tab. 35: Lengthening of low vowels in Lithuanian dialects

Standard Lithuanian	Western Aukštaitian	Translation
lēdas [ˈlʲæːdas]	[ˈlʲæˑdas]	'ice'
rātas [ˈrɑːtas]	[ˈrɑˑtas]	'wheel'

Tab. 36: Lengthening of high vowels in Eastern Aukštaitian

	Standard Lithuanian	Eastern Aukštaitian	Translation
Historically short vowels	bùvo [ˈbʊvoː]	[ˈbuˑva]	'be' (PST.3)
	mìškas [ˈmʲiʃkas]	[ˈmʲiˑʃkas]	'forest'
Historically long vowels	dū̃ko [ˈduːkoː]	[ˈduːka]	'rampage' (PST.3)
	nȳko [ˈniːkoː]	[ˈniːka]	'vanish' (PST.3)

short. But in other dialects, lengthening affects all historically short vowels irrespectively of height (Zinkevičius 1966: 103–108; see map 19 in Grinaveckienė et al. 1982). Lengthened high monophthongs are never identified with historically long high vowels, but one has to add that they still become tenser, approaching the articulation of historically long vowels (Table 36).

Despite the fact that the lengthened vowels may have a lesser duration in comparison with historically long vowels, I will nevertheless analyze them as bimoraic, since I believe that they were lengthened in order to make the stressed syllable heavy. Since in Lithuanian (as opposed to Latvian, see Section 2.1), lengthening only affects vowels, the initial correlation between stress and syllable length may have been replaced with that between stress and vowel length.

4.10 Parallelism between lengthening processes

The stressed vowel lengthening seems to be parallel with the lengthening of the first component of diphthongs and diphthongal sequences in that both changes go through the same two stages corresponding to different vowel height. In the Western Aukštaitian subdialect of Kaunas, which is the base of the standard language, both lengthening processes only affect low vowels (49). This variety of Lithuanian is known as the most archaic one.

(49) Western Aukštaitian of Kaunas
   a. low vowels as components of diphthongs and diphthongal sequences
      šáuk [ˈʃɑˑʊk] or [ˈʃɑːʊk] 'shoot' (IMP.2SG)
      méilė [ˈmʲæˑɪlʲeː] or [ˈmʲæːɪlʲeː] 'love'
      káltas [ˈkɑˑltas] or [ˈkɑːltas] 'chisel'
      pavérgti [paˈvæˑrʲkʲtʲi] or [paˈvæːrʲkʲtʲi] 'subdue, enslave' (INF)

   b. low short monophthongs
      rãtas [ˈrɑˑtas] or [ˈrɑːtas] 'wheel'
      lẽdas [ˈlʲæˑdas] or [ˈlʲæːdas] 'ice'

In other dialects, both types of lengthening spread to high vowels. The examples in (50) are from Eastern Aukštaitian.

(50) Eastern Aukštaitian
a. high vowels as components of diphthongs and diphthongal sequences
['pʲiˑrmas] or ['pʲiːrmas] 'first'
['kuˑrmis] or ['kuːrmis] 'mole'

b. high short monophthongs
['mʲiˑʃkas] or ['mʲiːʃkas] 'forest'
['buˑva] or ['buːva] 'be' (PST.3)

Both lengthening processes are not simply parallel – there may seem to be an inner connection between them. One can easily imagine the lengthening in diphthongs and diphthongal sequences as secondary to the lengthening of stressed monophthongs. This hypothesis sounds especially promising if we recall that the acute and the circumflex may be viewed as differentiated by the placement of the stress on the first mora in acute syllables and the second mora in circumflex syllables. This would mean that the lengthening takes place on any low vowel linked to a stressed mora.

This hypothesis, however, is not supported by dialect data, which shows that the first components of acute diphthongs and diphthongal sequences may be lengthened without lengthening of monophthongs. In Southern Aukštaitian and the adjacent part of Western Aukštaitian, high monophthongs remain short under stress (51b), as in Standard Lithuanian, whereas the same vowels acting as the first components of diphthongs and diphthongal sequences in acute syllables are lengthened (51a) (compare maps 19 and 20 in Grinaveckienė et al. 1982). As a consequence, the lengthening in acute syllables cannot be interpreted as induced by stress on the first mora because, otherwise, we would also expect the lengthening of the only stressed mora in monophthongs.

(51) Southern Aukštaitian
a. high vowels as first components of diphthongal sequences
['kuˑrmis] or ['kuːrmis] 'mole'
['piˑrmas] or ['piːrmas] 'first'

b. high vowels as short monophthongs under stress
['bʊvoː] 'be' (PST.3)
['mɪʃkas] 'forest'

Historically, the lengthening of short monophthongs must have occurred later than the lengthening in diphthongs and diphthongal sequences, at least for Southern Aukštaitian. The two changes must be unconnected with each other because, while it is easy to think of diphthong components as being influenced by the change in short monophthongs, the opposite seems not to be true. Nevertheless, this does not exclude the results of both processes from being re-identified in the minds of speakers as coming from the same source.

4.11 Interaction between two types of lengthening

Although the conditions for the lengthening of the first component of diphthongs and diphthongal sequences are not strictly parallel to those for the stressed-vowel lengthening, I still maintain that in the history of Lithuanian and its dialects both processes were, at least partly, equated. This led to the re-analysis of the acute-circumflex distinction in diphthongs and diphthongal sequences, which phonetically manifested itself in the reduction of the first component under the circumflex.

The analysis that I propose for (Aukštaitian) Lithuanian essentially repeats the view on Eastern Aukštaitian advanced by Kazlauskas (1968: 5) in that contrastive length in Lithuanian is lost as length becomes associated with stress. On long monophthongs, the contrast between the accents disappears, whereas on diphthongs and diphthongal sequences, it is replaced by the contrastive placement of stress. The former acute diphthongs have the stress on the vowel, and the former circumflex diphthongs on the sonorant. But, unlike Kazlauskas, I admit that this was only a general trend that never came to fruition as the link between stress and length was severed in all dialects, albeit at different stages. As a consequence, Lithuanian retains the contrastive length on vowels, at least in stressed syllables.

I believe the reduction of the first components of circumflex diphthongs and diphthongal sequences to be the evidence for the interaction between the lengthening of components in heavy syllables and the lengthening of stressed vowels. First, the reduction of the more sonorous elements, accompanied by the lengthening of less sonorous elements, is peculiar in itself and must have arisen due to some special circumstances. Second, nothing like the reduction of the first component is found in the other languages of the region, even though the lengthening of either the first or the second component has strong parallels in Latvian, Estonian, and, especially, Livonian.

The reduction of the first component only makes sense if the latter was reinterpreted as unstressed, which could have only happened if the second component started to be perceived as the only bearer of stress in the syllable. The conditions for such shift in perception were created by stressed vowel lengthening, which established the link between stress and vowel length. The analogy between lengthening of vowels and sonorants may seem far-fetched, but I think that, initially, the re-analysis may have only applied to the first components lengthened under the acute, as they are exclusively vowels. After the lengthened first components of acute diphthongs and diphthongal sequences were reinterpreted as the stressed elements and the second components as unstressed, it was not unnatural to identify the lengthened second components of circumflex diphthongs and diphthongal sequences as the bearer of stress as well, even if in diphthongal sequences the second components are represented by sonorant consonants. The acute-circumflex contrast was thus replaced with the contrastive placement of stress within the syllable.

Different varieties of Aukštaitian, including Standard Lithuanian, reflect different stages of the process. The most advanced stage is found in Eastern Aukštaitian where all stressed vowels (both high and low) are lengthened in historically short syllables as well as in diphthongs and diphthongal sequences. The least developed stage is that in Standard Lithuanian and its base, the Kaunas subdialect of Western Aukštaitian, where stressed high vowels are unaffected by lengthening in either of the two positions. Since Western Aukštaitian and Standard Lithuanian are also believed to preserve the acute-circumflex contrast on long monophthongs, they must have a mixed system where the new features are combined with the more archaic ones. While the acute-circumflex contrast may be preserved in its more traditional shape in diphthongs and diphthongal sequences with high vowels, it seems to be replaced by stressing either the first or the second component of diphthongs and diphthongal sequences with low vowels. The identification of the lengthened component of a diphthong or diphthongal sequence with a lengthened stressed monophthong may be hindered by the fact that lengthening under stress is no longer automatic. In a number of positions, short vowels remain short even when stressed. One may ask then how it may be that the lengthening of components in diphthongs and diphthongal sequences is universal while it is not so with short vowels? Actually, these positions are indeed exceptions because it is normal for a short vowel to be lengthened under stress rather than not, and it is also much easier to list the positions where the lengthening does not apply than define the context where it does.

4.12 Differences from the traditional moraic analysis

At first glance, my approach may seem identical to the well-known analyses of Lithuanian that explain the acute-circumflex contrast as the different placement of stress on one of the two moras. But these analyses also presume the same treatment of the accents on long vowels so that both long monophthongs and diphthongs (diphthongal sequences) are seen as having stress on one of the two moras. I claim, on the contrary, that modern Lithuanian does not have the contrast between stressed and unstressed moras in stressed syllables. Instead, the lengthened elements in diphthongs and diphthongal sequences must be treated as corresponding to two moras, as well as long vowels (either lengthened or historically long).

Under the acute accent, the considerable lengthening of the first component, which made it comparable, if not equal, to long monophthongs, could only mean that the second component was banished to the periphery of the syllable, which is confirmed by the drop of the second component in some Lithuanian dialects. The stranded mora was given to the first component (52a). This part of the change is shared by Livonian and, to some extent, Latvian. But the main argument against the unstressed moras is the first component of circumflex diphthongs and diphthongal sequences, which, after the reduction, has clearly become non-moraic. Its mora must have been transferred to the second component (53). Lengthening the stressed elements meant making them bimoraic, and the second component of circumflex diphthongs and diphthongal sequences was re-analyzed as lengthened under stress. Although ascribing two moras to less sonorous element of the syllable, when the more sonorous element has none, may seem very unusual, it is justified by the unusualness of the situation it is meant to capture.

(52) a. Lithuanian *káltas* ['kaˑltas] or ['kaːltas] 'chisel'

$$\begin{array}{ccccc} \mu\mu & & \mu\mu & & \mu\mu \\ || & > & |\ddag & > & \backslash/ \\ \text{kaltas} & & \text{kaltas} & & \text{kaːltas} \end{array}$$

b. Livonian **leiba>lēba* ['leːba(ː)] 'bread'

$$\begin{array}{ccccccc} \mu\mu & & \mu\mu & & \mu\mu & & \mu\mu \\ || & > & |\ddag & > & \backslash/ & > & \backslash/ \\ \text{leiba} & & \text{leiba} & & \text{leːiba} & & \text{leːba} \end{array}$$

c. Latvian **var̂na>vãrna* [vaːːrna] 'crow'

$$\begin{array}{ccccc} \mu\mu & & \mu\mu & & \mu\mu \\ || & > & |\ddag & > & \backslash/ \\ \text{varːna} & & \text{varna} & & \text{vaːːrna} \end{array}$$

(53) Lithuanian *kaĩtas* ['kəlˑtas] 'guilty'

$$\begin{array}{ccc} \mu\mu & & \mu\mu \\ || & > & \backslash/ \\ \text{kalˑtas} & & \text{kəlˑtas} \end{array}$$

My approach is similar to that of Dogil (1999b: 887), who explains the contrast between acute and circumflex syllables as determined by their different prosodic structures. In my analysis, the structure is essentially the same, but the way it is linked to the segments of the former acute syllable is different from that of the former circumflex syllable.

5 Conclusion

The difference in the realization of Lithuanian diphthongs and diphthongal sequences, such as in *aũkštas* ['ɒuˑkʃtas], *taĩką* ['təiˑkaː] vs. *áukštas* ['aˑʊkʃtas], *táiką* ['taˑɪkaː], goes beyond the phonetic manifestation of the tonal contrast. The traditional analysis of the distinction as the one between the accents, acute and circumflex, is only true in a historical sense, as the modern pronunciation has indeed developed from the tonal contrast. At present, diphthongs and diphthongal sequences differ in the way how the two moras of the heavy stressed syllables correspond to the components of the diphthong or diphthongal sequence. In former acute diphthongs and diphthongal sequences, the two moras are linked to the first component, whereas in former circumflex diphthongs and diphthongal sequences, the two moras are connected to the second component. The reduction of the first component under the former circumflex is explained by its being nonmoraic.

The unusual development of former circumflex diphthongs and diphthongal sequences, where the more sonorous element is reduced while the less sonorous element is lengthened, was made possible under special circumstances. It is the product of two independent lengthening processes that are also found in the neighboring languages, both related and unrelated. One is the lengthening of the more sonorous component of diphthongs and diphthongal sequences and the other is the lengthening of stressed syllables. The latter established the connection between stress and vowel length in Lithuanian, and both changes were identified as resulting in bimoraic vowels under stress.

The lengthening of the first component was created by the reassignment of the second mora, which initially corresponded to the second component. The change was mainly brought about by the need to intensify the suprasegmental contrast on diphthongs and diphthongal sequences, and this was achieved in two different ways in different dialects and languages. Aukštaitian Lithuanian, East Latvian, and Livonian preferred to replace contrasting accents (tones) with different syllable structures. In this case, the lengthening of the first component, which led to the substitution of a diphthong or diphthongal sequence with a long monophthong, only applied under one of the contrasting accents (tones).

Žemaitian and West Latvian chose to completely transfer the accentual (tonal) contrast from diphthongs and diphthongal sequences to long monophthongs, which resulted in the lengthening of the first component and the consequent change of syllable structure independently of the accent (tone).

The choice between the two opportunities may have been conditioned by the ability of long monophthongs to maintain the suprasegmental contrast, at least in Lithuanian. The fact that the lengthening of the first component in Aukštaitian only occurs under one of the accents seems to be related to the progressing loss of the contrast on long monophthongs. In Latvian, the change was specifically aimed at preserving not only the tonal contrast, but also the syllable weight in diphthongal sequences with *r*. Notwithstanding the special nature of the change in Latvian, it is interesting that the adjoining areas of Latvian and Lithuanian dialects show the same preference for the lengthening of the first component with respect to the suprasegmental contrast. But Livonian, which is more similar to Lithuanian in that it lengthens the first component in all diphthongs and diphthongal sequences, only has the lengthening under one of the contrasting accents, although the surrounding Latvian dialects, for the most part, are indifferent to the tone of the syllable in which the lengthening is found.

Although the lengthening of stressed vowels applied in the whole Lithuanian area (with a minor exception), its interaction with the lengthening of the first component was different for Aukštaitian and Žemaitian. In Aukštaitian, where the first component was only given the second mora under the acute, the second component of circumflex diphthongs and diphthongal sequences retained its mora, which was phonetically manifested as the lengthening of the second component. But due to the newly developed connection between length and stress, the second component was re-analyzed as corresponding to two moras, the additional mora being taken over from the first component. Consequently, the non-moraic first component was reduced.

It is possible that the area comprising Southern Žemaitian and the northern part of the Kaunas subdialect of Western Aukštaitian, where the first component of the circumflex diphthongs and diphthongal sequences is not reduced, corresponds to the more archaic stage in the development of Aukštaitian, but the lack of reduction (actually reported as the lengthening on both the first and the second component) may as well be a product of the Žemaitian influence. In Northern Žemaitian, where the lengthening of the first component took place under both acute and circumflex, the identification of the two types of lengthening did not have much impact on the further development of diphthongs and diphthongal sequences.

What is very important for the understanding of the changes I postulate for Lithuanian is that they are not completed, and some of them will probably never be completed. The vowels resulting from both lengthening processes are only partly identified with historically long vowels, since they may be realized as only half-long, which impedes their analysis as bimoraic. In some varieties of Lithuanian, including the standard language, the lengthening processes only apply to low vowels. The loss of the acute-circumflex contrast on long monophthongs in Aukštaitian is an ongoing process that is not complete even in Eastern Aukštaitian. The connection between stress and length has not been fully established, since the lengthening of stressed vowels is not automatic and vowels contrast for length at least in stressed syllables. In many dialects and in the standard language, the length contrast is also preserved in unstressed syllables. This means that the analysis that I propose for Lithuanian can only be viewed as a tendency that may be stronger or weaker depending of the dialect. Still I maintain that if this tendency is not recognized, Lithuanian phonology cannot be fully understood.

Acknowledgments

I would like to thank Peter Arkadiev and an anonymous reviewer for highly useful comments and suggestions on the earlier version of my chapter. All errors are my own.

Abbreviations

ACC	accusative		M	masculine
DAT	dative		NOM	nominative
F	feminine		PART	partitive
FUT	future		PL	plural
GEN	genitive		PST	past
HAB	habitual		PRS	present
IMP	imperative		PRTC	participle
INF	infinitive		SBJV	subjunctive
INS	instrumental		SG	singular
LOC	locative			

References

Abele [Ābele], Anna. 1924. K voprosu o sloge [On the issue of syllable]. *Slavia* 3: 1–34.
Ābele, Anna. 1932. Par neuzsvērto zilbju intonācijām [On the intonations of unstressed syllables]. *Filologu biedrības raksti* 12: 148–163.

Adamovičs, Fricis. 1923. Dundagas izloksne [The dialect of Dundaga]. *Filologu biedrības raksti* 3: 94–106.
Adamovičs, Fricis. 1925. Dundagas izloksne (turpinājums) [The dialect of Dundaga (continuation)]. *Filologu biedrības raksti* 5: 125–142.
Andronov, Aleksej. 1996. Nekotoryje zamečanija o prosodičeskix javlenijax v dialektax latysškogo jazyka i ix predstavlenii na karte [Some remarks about prosodic phenomena in dialects of Latvian and their representation on the map]. *Baltistica* 31(2): 201–212.
Arkadiev, Peter. 2012. Stems in Lithuanian verbal inflection (with remarks on derivation). *Word Structure* 5(1): 7–27.
Atkočaitytė, Daiva. 2002. *Pietų žemaičių raseiniškių prozodija ir vokalizmas* [The prosody and vocalism of the Southern Žemaitian dialect of Raseiniai]. Vilnius: Lietuvių kalbos instituto leidykla.
Bacevičiūtė, Rima. 2004. *Šakių šnektos prozodija ir vokalizmas* [The prosody and vocalism of the Šakiai dialect]. Vilnius: Lietuvių kalbos instituto leidykla.
Bacevičiūtė, Rima. 2009. Dėl baltų kalbų priegaidžių eksperimentinių tyrimų [On the experimental research of accents in the Baltic languages]. *Baltu filoloģija* 18(1/2): 17–30.
Bacevičiūtė, Rima. 2011. Vakarų aukštaičių kauniškių monoftongų priegaidžių fonetiniai požymiai [The phonetic features of syllable accents on monophthongs in the Western Aukštaitian dialect of Kaunas]. *Baltistica, VII Priedas*: 13–26.
Balode, Laimute & Axel Holvoet. 2001a. The Latvian language and its dialects. In Östen Dahl & Maria Koptjevskaja-Tamm (eds.) *Circum-Baltic languages. Vol. 2: Past and present*, 3–40. Amsterdam, Philadelphia: John Benjamins.
Balode, Laimute & Axel Holvoet. 2001b. The Lithuanian language and its dialects. In Östen Dahl & Maria Koptjevskaja-Tamm (eds.) *Circum-Baltic languages. Vol. 2: Past and present*, 41–79. Amsterdam, Philadelphia: John Benjamins.
Blevins, Juliette. 1993. A tonal analysis of Lithuanian nominal accent. *Language* 69(2): 237–273.
Buch, Tamara. 1968. Zur phonologischen Wertung von lit. *ie, uo* und lit. *ę, e*. *Lingua Posnaniensis* 12/13: 77–80.
Bye, Patrik. 1997. A generative perspective on 'overlength' in Estonian and Saami. In Ilse Lehiste & Jaan Ross (eds.) *Estonian prosody: Papers from a symposium*, 36–70. Tallinn: Institute of Estonian Language.
Ceplītis, Laimdots, Aina Miķelsone, Tamāra Porīte, & Silvija Raģe. 1995. *Latviešu valodas pareizrakstības un pareizrunas vārdnīca* [The orthographic and orthoepic dictionary of Latvian]. Rīga: Avots.
Collinge, Neville. 1985. *The laws of Indo-European*. Amsterdam, Philadelphia: John Benjamins.
Daugavet, Anna. 2010. Syllable length in Latvian and Lithuanian: Searching for the criteria. *Baltic Linguistics* 1: 83–114.
Daugavet, Anna. 2012. Register and contour in the analysis of Latvian and Lithuanian tones. Paper presented at the 45th Annual Meeting of the Societas Linguistica Europaea, Stockholm.
Daugavet, Anna. 2013. Geminacija soglasnyx v latysškom jazyke: sledy pribaltijsko-finskogo vlijanija [Consonant gemination in Latvian: traces of Finnic influence]. In Petr M. Arkad'jev & Vjacheslav V. Ivanov (eds.) *Issledovanija po tipologii slavjanskix, baltijskix i balkanskix jazykov* [Studies in the typology of Slavic, Baltic and Balkan languages], 280–319. Saint Petersburg: Aletheia.
Dogil, Grzegorz. 1999a. The phonetic manifestation of word stress in Lithuanian, Polish, German and Spanish. In Harry van der Hulst (ed.) *Word prosodic systems in the languages of Europe*, 273–310. Berlin, New York: Mouton de Gruyter.

Dogil, Grzegorz. 1999b. Baltic languages. In Harry van der Hulst (ed.) *Word prosodic systems in the languages of Europe*, 877–896. Berlin, New York: Mouton de Gruyter.
Ekblom, Richard. 1933. *Die lettischen Akzentarten*. Uppsala: Almquist and Wiksells Boktryckerei.
Endzelīns, Jānis. 1951. *Latviešu valodas gramatika* [The grammar of Latvian]. Rīga: Latvijas valsts izdevniecība.
Garšva, Kazimieras. 2003. Lietuvių kalbos priegaidės [Lithuanian syllable accents]. *Kalbų studijos* 4: 12–16.
Garšva, Kazimieras & Aleksas Girdenis. 1997. Fonologija [Phonology]. In Vytautas Ambrazas (ed.) *Dabartinės lietuvių kalbos gramatika* [Grammar of contemporary Lithuanian]. Vilnius: Mokslo ir enciklopedijų leidybos institutas.
Girdenis, Aleksas. 1967. Mažeikių tarmės priegaidžių fonetinės ypatybės [The phonetic properties of syllable accents in the dialect of Mažeikiai]. *Kalbotyra* 15: 31–41.
Girdenis, Aleksas. 1971. Review of: Lietuvių kalbos tarmės (Chrestomatija), Leidykla „Mintis", Vilnius, 1970. *Baltistica* 7(2): 201–209.
Girdenis, Aleksas. 1974. Prozodinės priegaidžių ypatybės šiaurės žemaičių tarmėje [The prosodic properties of syllable accents in Northern Žemaitian]. In Antanas Pakerys (ed.) *Eksperimentinė ir praktinė fonetika* [Experimental and practical phonetics], 160–198. Vilnius: Vilniaus pedagoginis institutas.
Girdenis, Aleksas. 1996. Energetinė šiaurės žemaičių tarmės priegaidžių fonetinės prigimties interpretacija [The energetic interpretation of the phonetic manifestation of syllable accents in Northern Žemaitian]. *Baltistica* 31(1): 71–84.
Girdenis, Aleksas. 1997a. Phonology. In Vytautas Ambrazas (ed.) *Lithuanian grammar*, 13–58. Vilnius: Baltos lankos.
Girdenis, Aleksas. 1997b. Morphonology. In Vytautas Ambrazas (ed.) *Lithuanian grammar*, 61–84. Vilnius: Baltos lankos.
Girdenis, Aleksas. 1998. Šiaurės žemaičių priegaidžių skiriamieji požymiai [The differentiating features of syllable accents in Northern Žemaitian]. In Kazys Morkūnas (ed.) *Lietuvių kalba: tyrėjai ir tyrimai: Kazimiero Jauniaus 150-osioms gimimo ir 90-osioms mirties metinėms paminėti: konferencijos pranešimų tezės, 1998 m. spalio 22–23 d.* [Lithuanian language: Scholars and studies: Abstracts from the conference dedicated to Kazimieras Jaunis], 37–38. Vilnius: Lietuvių kalbos institutas.
Girdenis, Aleksas. 2002. Dėl kirčiuotų pusilgių balsių prozodijos [On the prosody of stressed half-long vowels]. *Baltistica* 37(2): 211–213.
Girdenis, Aleksas. 2003. *Teoriniai lietuvių fonologijos pagrindai* [The theoretical grounds of Lithuanian phonology]. Vilnius: Moklso ir enciklopedijų leidybos insitutas.
Girdenis, Aleksas. 2009. Vadinamųjų sutaptinių dvibalsių [ie uo] garsinė ir fonologinė sudėtis [The phonetical and phonological structure of the so-called gliding diphthongs]. *Baltistica* 44: 213–242.
Grigorjevs, Juris. 2008. *Latviešu valodas patskaņu sistēmas akustisks un auditīvs raksturojums* [The acoustic and auditory analysis of the Latvian vowel system]. Rīga: LU Latviešu valodas institūts.
Grinaveckienė, Elena, Aldona Jonaitytė, Jonina Lipskienė, Kazys Morkūnas, Birutė Vanagienė & Aloyzas Vidugiris. 1982. *Lietuvių kalbos atlasas II. Fonetika* [The atlas of the Lithuanian language II. Phonetics.]. Vilnius: Mokslas.
Grinaveckis, Vladas. 1973. *Žemaičių tarmių istorija (Fonetika)* [The history of the Žemaitian dialects (phonetics)]. Vilnius: Mintis.
Halle, Morris & Jean-Roger Vergnaud. 1987. *An essay on stress*. Cambridge, MA: MIT Press.

Hint, Mati. 1997. Two issues in Estonian phonology. In Mati Hint, *Eesti keele astmevahelduse ja prosoodiasüsteemi tüpoloogilised probleemid* [Typological problems of the system of gradation and prosody in Estonian]. Tallinn, Helsinki: Eesti Keele Sihtasutus.
Hulst, Harry van der (ed.): 1999. *Word prosodic systems in the languages of Europe*. Berlin, New York: de Gruyter.
Javnis, Kazimir [Kazimieras Jaunis]. 1908–1916. *Grammatika litovskogo jazyka. Litovskij original i russkij perevod* [The grammar of Lithuanian. Lithuanian original and Russian translation]. Petrograd: Imperatorskaja Akademija Nauk.
Kačiuškienė, Genovaitė & Aleksas Girdenis. 1997. Rytų aukštaičių ir šiaurės žemaičių priegaidės: Bendrybės ir skirtumai [Syllable accents in Eastern Aukštaitian and Northern Žemaitian: Similarities and differences]. *Kalbotyra* 46(1): 31–36.
Kariņš, Krišjānis. 1996. *The prosodic structure of Latvian*. Institute for Research in Cognitive Science, University of Pennsylvania PhD dissertation.
Kazlauskas, Jonas. 1968. *Lietuvių kalbos istorinė gramatika (kirčiavimas, daiktavardis, veiksmažodis)* [The historical grammar of Lithuanian (accentuation, substantive, verb)]. Vilnius: Mintis.
Kettunen, Lauri. 1938. *Livisches Wörterbuch mit grammatischer Einleitung*. (Lexicae Societatis Fenno-Ugricae V.) Helsinki: Suomalais-ugrilainen Seura.
Kiparsky, Paul. 1995–2006. Livonian stød. http://www.stanford.edu/~kiparsky/. Accessed 28 July 2012.
Koptjevskaja-Tamm, Maria & Bernhard Wälchli. 2001. The Circum-Baltic languages: An areal-typological approach. In Östen Dahl & Maria Koptjevskaja-Tamm (eds.) *Circum-Baltic languages. Vol. 2: Grammar and typology*, 615–750. Amsterdam, Philadelphia: John Benjamins.
Kudirka, Robertas. 2005. Lietuvių bendrinės kalbos monoftongų priegaidžių akustiniai požymiai [The acoustic features of syllable accents on monophthongs in Standard Lithuanian]. *Acta Linguistica Lithuanica* 52: 1–21.
Kuleshov, Vyacheslav. 2012. Livonian word accent system. In Natalya V. Kuznetsova (ed.) *Fenno-Lapponica Petropolitana*, 104–131. (*Acta Linguistica Petropolitana*. Volume VIII, part 1). Sankt-Peterburg: Nauka.
Kurschat, Fridrich. 1876. *Grammatik der litauischen Sprache*. Halle: Verlag der Buchhandlung des Waisenhauses.
Ladefoged, Peter & Jan Maddieson. 1996. *The sounds of the world's languages*. Oxford: Blackwell.
Laua, Alise. 1997. *Latviešu literārās valodas fonētika* [The phonetics of Standard Latvian]. Rīga: Zvaigzne ABC.
Lehiste, Ilse. 2003. Prosodic change in progress. In Paula Fikkert and Haike Jacobs (eds.) *Development in prosodic systems*, 47–65. Berlin, New York: Mouton de Gruyter.
Lehiste, Ilse, Pire Teras, Valts Ernštreits, Pärtel Lippus, Karl Pajusalu, Tuuli Tuisk, & Tiit-Rein Viitso. 2008. *Livonian prosody*. Helsinki: Suomalais-ugrilainen seura.
Lehiste, Ilse, Pire Teras, Karl Pajusalu & Tuuli Tuisk. 2007. Quantity in Livonian: Preliminary results. *Linguistica Uralica* 48(1): 29–44.
Leskauskaitė, Asta. 2004. *Pietų aukštaičių vokalizmo ir prozodijos bruožai* [The characteristics of vocalism and prosody of Southern Aukštaitian]. Vilnius: Lietuvių kalbos institutas.
Markus, Dace & Ilze Auziņa. 2008. Fonētika un fonoloģija [Phonetics and phonology]. In Inga Jansone (ed.) *Latviešu valodas gramatika: koncepcija, prospekts, atsevišķu nodaļu pirmvarianti, diskusijas materiāli* [Latvian grammar: Conception, prospect, initial descriptions, discussions], 52–58. Rīga: LU Latviešu valodas institūts.

Mažiulienė, Irena. 1996. Centrinės šiaurės žemaičių tarmės prozodija: Instrumentinis ir sociolingvistinis tyrimas [The prosody of central Northern Žemaitian: An instrumental and sociolinguistic study]. *Kalbotyra* 44(1): 5–115.
Murinienė, Lina. 2007. *Rytinių šiaurės žemaičių fonologija: vokalizmas ir prozodija* [The Phonology of East Northern Žemaitian: Vocalism and prosody]. Vilnius: Lietuvių kalbos institutas, Vilniaus pedagoginis universitetas.
Pajupuu, Hille & Tiit-Rein Viitso. 1986. Livonian polyphthongs. In *Estonian Papers in Phonetics 1984–1985*, 96–131. Tallinn: Academy of Sciences of the E.S.S.R. Institute of Language and Literature.
Pakerys, Antanas. 1970. Skiemenų sudaromieji ir skiemeniniai garsai [Syllable constituent sounds and syllabic sounds]. *Tarybinė mokykla* 10: 29–30.
Pakerys, Antanas. 1982. *Lietuvių bendrinės kalbos prozodija* [The prosody of Standard Lithuanian]. Vilnius: Mokslas.
Pakerys, Antanas. 1995. *Lietuvių bendrinės kalbos fonetika* [The phonetics of Standard Lithuanian]. Vilnius: Žara.
Penttilä, Aarni & Lauri Posti. 1941. Uber die steigende und sog. Stossintonation im Livischen. *Finnisch-Ugrische Forschungen* 27: 235–272.
Pupkis, Aldonas. 1980. *Kalbos kultūros pagrindai* [The grounds of speech culture]. Vilnius: Mokslas.
Rudzīte, Marta. 1964. *Latviešu dialektoloģija* [Latvian dialectology]. Rīga: Latvijas valsts izdevniecība.
Rudzīte, Marta. 1993. *Latviešu valodas vēsturiskā fonētika* [A historical phonology of Latvian]. Rīga: Zvaigzne.
Rūķe, Velta. 1939. Latgales izloksņu grupējums [The grouping of dialects in Latgale]. *Filologu biedrības raksti* 19: 133–188.
Rūķe, Velta. 1940. Kurzemes un Vidzemes lībiskais apgabals [The Livonian region in Kurzeme and Vidzeme]. *Filologu biedrības raksti* 20: 75–128.
Saussure, Ferdinand de. 1922. *Recueil des publications scientifiques*. Heidelberg: Winter.
Senn, Alfred. 1966. *Handbuch der litauischen Sprache*. Heidelberg: Carl Winter.
Strelēvica-Ošiņa, Dace. 2009. Latviešu valodas lībiskais dialekts un tā lietotāju identitāte: pārdomas pēc pētījuma [The Livonianized dialect of Latvian and the identity of its speakers: Thoughts after research]. *Acta Universitatis Latviensis 746. Linguistics. Latvian Studies and Finno-Ugristics*, 94–112.
Stundžia, Bonifacas. 1995. *Lietuvių bendrinės kalbos kirčiavimo sistema* [The accentuation system of Standard Lithuanian]. Vilnius: Petro ofsetas.
Tuisk, Tuuli & Pire Teras. 2009. The role of duration ratios and fundamental frequency in spontaneous Livonian. *Lingustica Uralica* 45(4): 241–252.
Tuisk, Tuuli. 2012. Tonal and temporal characteristics of disyllabic words in spontaneous Livonian. *Linguistica Uralica* 48(1): 1–11.
Viitso, Tiit-Rein. 1974. On the phonological role of stress, quantity, and stød in Livonian. *Sovetskoe finno-ugrovedenie* 20(3): 159–169.
Viitso, Tiit-Rein. 2003. Structure of the Estonian language: Phonology, morphology and word formation. In Mati Erelt (ed.) *Estonian language* (Linguistica Uralica. Supplementary Series 1), 9–92. Tallinn: Estonian Academy Publishers.
Viitso, Tiit-Rein. 2008. *Liivi keel ja läänemeresoome keelemaastikud* [The Livonian language and Finnic linguistic landscapes]. Tartu, Tallinn: Eesti Keele Sihtasutus.

Vijtso, Tiit-Rein. 1993. Livskij jazyk [Livonian language]. In Jurij Eliseev & Klara E. Maitinskaja (eds.) *Jazyki mira. Ural'skie jazyki* [The languages of the world. The Uralic languages], 76–90. Moskva: Nauka.

Young, Steven R. 1991. *The prosodic structure of Lithuanian*. Lanham, New York, London: University Press of America.

Zinkevičius, Zigmas. 1966. *Lietuvių dialektologija: lyginamoji tarmių fonetika ir morfologija* [Lithuanian dialectology: Comparative phonology and morphology of dialects]. Vilnius: Mintis.

Zinkevičius, Zigmas. 1974. Dėl akūto ir cirkumflekso skyrimo rytų Lietuvos tarmėse [On distinguishing between acute and circumflex in dialects of East Lithuania]. *Baltistica* 11(1): 85–86.

Zinkevičius, Zigmas. 1980. *Lietuvių kalbos istorinė gramatika. T. I: Įvadas; Istorinė fonetika; Daiktavardžių linksniavimas* [A historical grammar of Lithuanian. Volume 1: Introduction; Historical phonology; Declination of substantives]. Vilnius: Mokslas.

Zinkevičius, Zigmas. 1994. *Lietuvių kalbos dialektologija* [Dialectology of Lithuanian]. Vilnius: Mokslo ir enciklopedijų leidykla.

Ineta Dabašinskienė and Maria Voeikova
4 Diminutives in spoken Lithuanian and Russian: Pragmatic functions and structural properties

1 Introduction

Usually, the diminutive is understood as "1. A derivational affix which may be added to a word to express a notion of small size, often additionally (or even instead) a notion of warmth and affection: Spanish -*it*-, -*ill*-; 2. A word formed by the use of such an affix: Spanish *gatito* 'kitten' (*gato* 'cat'), *pallilo* 'toothpick' (*palo* 'stick'), *hijito* 'son' (affectionate) (*hijo* 'son', unmarked)..." (Trask 1995: 82). This definition is based on two different functions of diminutives, namely the semantic function of expressing smallness and the pragmatic function of indicating endearment, sympathy, empathy, pleasure, or irony. Some researchers consider smallness to be the basic meaning of diminutives, whereas connotations associated with emotions and assessment are dealt with in the field of pragmatics (Jurafsky 1996). Other investigations show that pragmatic functions may play a leading role (cf. Sifianou 1992, Dressler 1994, Dressler & Merlini Barbaresi 1994, Gillis 1997, Stephany 1997, Savickienė & Dressler 2007).

Furthermore, diminutives function as markers of certain speech registers, such as child- or pet-centered speech; they are also found in the intimate language of lovers and serve as a mitigation device in face-threatening speech acts and "downgrading of the request" (Dressler & Merlini Barbaresi 1994: 17, 242). However, neither the semantic nor pragmatic functions can sufficiently explain the cross-linguistic differences in the type and token frequency of diminutives.

Research has provided sufficient evidence to assume that some languages are more diminutive-prone than others, with Slavic and Mediterranean languages (more than other European languages) belonging to this group, as well as Hungarian and Austrian German (cf. Dressler & Merlini Barbaresi 1994: 409ff). A cross-linguistic study of diminutives in child (CS) and child-directed speech (CDS) of eleven morphologically rich languages[1] (Savickienė & Dressler 2007) has shown a clear hierarchy of languages in the usage of these derivatives. These languages

---

[1] The notion of *morphologically rich* and *poor* languages is used here in the sense of quantitative typology and is based on specific calculations of several measures elaborated in the framework of natural morphology, such as the mean size of paradigm, level of transparency, etc. (see details in Dressler 2005, Xanthos et al. 2011).

formed the following continuum according to the frequency of diminutives (starting from the highest frequency and ending with the lowest frequency) in the CDS and CS corpora: Lithuanian, Russian, Croatian, Italian, Greek, Spanish, Hungarian, German, Finnish, and Turkish. The scarcity of Turkish diminutives in CS as well as in CDS can be attributed to the complex nature of the Turkish diminutive system (see Ketrez & Aksu-Koç 2007: 284). An interesting phenomenon was observed in Dutch, which showed the highest frequency of diminutives in adult-directed speech (ADS) among all the investigated languages, whereas in CDS and CS, it was Lithuanian that appeared to have the highest frequency (Savickienė & Dressler 2007: 243).

These differences in the use of diminutives could be associated with pragmatic functions in various speech situations. Another possible area in which to look for explanations may be the structural properties of the languages.

In this chapter, we are going to examine the data from two spoken language corpora – the corpus of Lithuanian spoken language[2] and the oral subcorpus of the Russian national corpus.[3] Our aim is to find out what the differences in the use of diminutives in these two morphologically rich and genetically related languages are. We will present the main features of diminutives in both languages, describe their pragmatic functions in different speech situations, discuss their grammatical structures, and finally discuss the conclusions.

2 Diminutives in Lithuanian

Lithuanian noun diminutives provide the largest group of suffixed noun derivatives. The diminutive suffixes are claimed to perform a very distinct modifying function. To quote Urbutis (1978: 168, our translation), "the notion expressed by the derivative noun always falls within the limits of the initial concept; however, the diminutivized form differs in its quantificational (small size or big size) or qualitative (showing affection or attenuation) connotations, or both".

Lithuanian is characterized by an extensive formation of diminutives from almost any noun by adding to it one or several suffixes. The most frequent and productive suffixes of diminutive formation are the masculine forms *-elis/-ėlis*, *-(i)ukas*, *-utis*, *-ytis*, *-aitis*, and their feminine counterparts in *-ė*: *-elė/-ėlė*, *-(i)ukė*,

---

[2] The corpus of Lithuanian spoken language can be found at http://donelaitis.vdu.lt/sakytines-kalbos-tekstynas. Different from the Russian oral subcorpus, the Lithuanian corpus is much smaller in size.
[3] The Russian national corpus can be found at http://www.ruscorpora.ru.

-utė, -ytė, -aitė. Other diminutive suffixes are less productive and usually occur in various dialects; examples of these are -ulis (-ė), -užis (-ė), -(i)ūkštis (-ė), -okšnis (-ė), -ušis (-ė), -ikė, -(i)okas (-ė), etc. (cf. LKG 1 1965: 256–288, Ambrazas 1997: 88–94).

Academic Lithuanian grammars (Ambrazas 1997: 90) claim that simplex disyllabic nouns tend to be diminutivized more often than polysyllabic ones (this point is also supported by empirical studies, see Savickienė 2003, 2007), e.g., stal-as 'table'– stal-el-is, stal-iu-kas, saul-ė 'sun'– saul-yt-ė, saul-ul-ė, saul-el-ė. However, diminutives can also be formed from three- or four-syllable nouns, e.g., sausain-is 'biscuit'– sausain-iuk-as, sausain-ėl-is, bezdžion-ė 'monkey'– bezdžion-ėl-ė, bezdžion-yt-ė, krokodil-as 'crocodile' – krokodil-iuk-as.

The most prominent structural feature of Lithuanian diminutives is that at least three or four different suffixes can be attached interchangeably to the same stem, e.g., kepur-ė 'cap'→ kepur-yt-ė, kepur-ait-ė, kepur-ėl-ė, kepur-iuk-ė. Moreover, there also exists the possibility of adding more than one suffix simultaneously; thus, for example, the simplex noun bern-as 'boy' can be diminutivized as bern-už-is, bern-el-is, bern-už-ėl-is, bern-ait-is, bern-iok-as, bern-iok-ėl-is, bern-iūkšt-is, bern-iūkšt-ėl-is, bern-ykšt-is, bern-ykšt-ėl-is, bern-ėk-as, bern-iokšl-is, etc. Here, the simplex noun yields many different forms with a wide range of meanings, ranging from that of endearment to the pejorative meaning. Pejorative diminutive suffixes (most frequent one is (i)ūkštis, but also -ykštis, -ėzas), encompass a double meaning, i.e., the semantic meaning of smallness is coded together with the pejorative sense, as in nam-iūkšt-is 'house-DIM:PEJ' (from nam-as 'house'), vaik-iūkšt-is 'child-DIM:PEJ' (from vaik-as 'child').

A variety of suffixes are employed to form diminutives from nouns belonging to different lexico-semantic groups. Semantically, these groups include the names of animals, food, and drinks; objects found in everyday life, body parts, etc. Moreover, diminutives can be formed not only from the names of physical entities, but also from nouns denoting more abstract entities by adding the most productive suffix, -elis/-elė (-ėlis/-ėlė), e.g., nuotaik-a 'mood'– nuotaik-ėl-ė 'mood-DIM', sveikat-a 'health'– sveikat-ėl-ė 'health-DIM', or-as 'weather'– or-el-is 'weather-DIM', darb-as 'work'– darb-el-is 'work-DIM'. The diminutivization of abstract nouns is not a frequent phenomenon in other languages (including Russian), and therefore, this language-specific feature may explain the higher token frequency of diminutives in Lithuanian as compared to other languages on the "diminutive continuum" mentioned above.

In modern Lithuanian, there are "double-diminutives" (i.e., those with two subsequent suffixes), as in žmog-el-iuk-as 'man-DIM-DIM', saul-ut-ėl-ė 'sun-DIM-DIM' where double suffixation reinforces the pragmatic effectiveness or the meaning of smallness of the diminutive. Moreover, the number of subsequent diminutive suffixes in one word may amount to six, as in occasional derivatives, as *puod-el-ait-uk-ėl-yt-ėl-is* 'cup-DIM(6)'.⁴ Such words are extremely rare in everyday usage.

The formation of noun diminutives is very productive, while the diminutivization of adjectives (*ger-as* – *ger-ut-is* 'good'), ordinal numerals (*penkt-as* – *penkt-uk-as* 'the fifth', with a class shift to nouns), adverbs (*truput-į* – *truput-ėl-į* 'a little bit'), and verbs (*šok-ti* 'jump' – *šok-telė-ti* 'to jump up a little bit') is less frequent. Greetings (such as *lab-as* 'hello'– *lab-uk-as*, *lab-ut-is* 'hello-DIM'; *labanakt-is* 'goodnight' – *labanakt-uk-as* 'goodnight-DIM'; *ačiū* 'thanks' – *ač-iuk-as* 'thanks-DIM', *iki* 'see you' – *iki-uk-as* 'see you-DIM'), and wishes (e.g., *ger-os dien-os* 'good day' – *ger-os dien-yt-ės/dien-el-ės* 'good day-DIM', *sėkm-ės* '(good) luck' – *sėkm-yt-ės* '(good) luck-DIM') are often used as diminutives in the colloquial speech of adults, especially young adults.

Hypocoristics (informal variants of personal or pet names),⁵ e.g., *Aušr-a* – *Aušr-el-ė*, *Aušr-yt-ė*, *Rok-as* – *Rok-ut-is*, *Rok-el-is*), and special names in CDS, such as *mam-a* 'mother' – *mam-yt-ė*, *mam-ut-ė* 'mother-DIM', *tėv-as* 'father'– *tėv-el-is*, *tėv-uk-as* 'father-DIM', are very common and are used very frequently. Hypocoristics, as well as common nouns, are more often formed from two-syllable nouns than from trisyllabic ones.

3 Diminutives in Russian

According to the Academic Russian grammar (Švedova 1980: 208), diminutives express personal, evaluative, caressing, hypocoristic, and pejorative semantic values. The meaning of smallness in their semantic structure is usually accompanied by the pragmatic nuance of endearment. In many cases, the expressive meaning is their only pragmatic function.

Diminutives are productively formed from Russian nouns by adding suffixes and combinations of suffixes to a stem, e.g., *syn-ok*, *syn-oč-ek*, *syn-ulj-a* 'son-DIM' from the simplex *syn* 'son' or *mam-očk-a*, *mam-ulj-a* 'mommy-DIM' from *mama* 'mommy'. Some of diminutive suffixes have special semantics, e.g., *-onok/-ënok* serves to name baby animals, as in *slon-ënok* 'baby elephant' from *slon*. The most frequent diminutives are formed from monosyllabic and disyllabic masculine and feminine nouns, thus lengthening them with one extra syllable. The benefits of diminutivization are stable stress and homogeneous stem finals. Therefore, longer

---

[4] This diminutive was invented by a philologist Kristupas Jurkšaitis, as claimed by Rūta Kazlauskaitė (2012: 27).
[5] See definition in http://oxforddictionaries.com/definition/american_english/hypocoristic.

words may also get diminutive suffixes; compare *begemot-ik* 'hippopotamus-DIM' from *begemot* 'hippopotamus' or *velosiped-ik* 'bicycle-DIM' from *velosiped* 'bicycle'. Thus, the users of diminutives may not be simply striving for a certain optimal word length or shape: It is certain that there are other structural reasons for using diminutives of longer stems alongside with their pragmatic function to signal the informal and friendly manner of conversation. Some simplex nouns are seen as an obstacle for diminutive formation. For example, abstract feminine nouns ending in *-ost'* like *večn-ost'* 'eternity' or *beskonečn-ost'* 'infinity' are never given diminutive suffixes. This happens not only because of their semantics but also due to morphopragmatic reasons: Diminutive suffixes seem not to be able to follow other derivational suffixes except those historically ending in *-k*. Thus, the form *načal'nič-ek* 'boss-DIM' from *načal'nik* 'boss' accompanied by the palatalization of the suffix *-nik* occurs in the Internet 79,200 times, whereas the form *pisatel'-čik* 'writer-DIM' from the noun *pisatel'* 'writer' has a clear sarcastic meaning and occurs only 507 times. At the same time, abstract semantics is not an obstacle for the diminutivization of non-derivatives or diminutive-like derivatives, e.g., *vrem-ečk-o* 'time-DIM' from *vremja* 'time' or *pogod-k-a* 'weather-DIM' from *pogoda* 'weather'. Thus, in most cases, the reason to use or to avoid diminutives is both semantic/pragmatic and morphonological.

Unlike Lithuanian, in Russian, the existence of several diminutive variants from one and the same noun is an exception typical only for the most frequent words (like *kniž-k-a, kniž-eč-k-a, kniž-onk-a, kniž-onoč-k-a, kniž-ul'-k-a kniž-ul-eč-k-a* 'book-DIM' from *knig-a* 'book'). Most of these variants have slight semantic differences, mostly evaluative ones, e.g., using the variant *kniž-eč-k-a*, speakers express their endearment, whereas with *kniž-onk-a*, they show their negligence of the object. The usage of double diminutives as well as several diminutives from one and the same stem is restricted to some familiar objects, hypocoristics, animals, and kinship terms.[6]

Diminutives may also be formed from parametric and perceptual adjectives and adverbs, but these are not as frequent as noun diminutives. They may denote the same features as the corresponding simplex with the additional meaning of smallness or endearment, e.g., *bel-en'k-ij* 'white-DIM' means 'white and small' or 'white and pretty (dear, attractive)'. It is not by accident that diminutive adjectives usually refer to diminutive nouns (the form *bel-en'-kij* also demands to pick out the noun *dom-ik* 'house-DIM' or *zajč-ik* 'hare-DIM' instead of their simplex forms). Vinogradov (1947: 113) regarded this tendency as an "emotional agreement", saying that "evaluative terms are infectious". Indeed, the use of noun diminutive triggers

---

[6] In other cases, diminutive formation is restricted to one or two lexicalized forms. These observations show that in Russian diminutivization is a less productive process than in Lithuanian.

adjective or adverb diminutives in the same utterance (Rusakova & Rusakov 2002, Rusakova 2004, 2009: 526–535; 2013: 354–371). Consider example (1):

(1) Russian
Ėto by-l daže skoree ne čelovek, a
this be-PST(SG.M) even rather not man(NOM.SG) but
čeloveč-ek. **Krugl-en'k-ij,** **tolst-en'k-ij.**
man-DIM (NOM.SG) round-DIM-NOM.SG.M fat-DIM-NOM.SG.M
'It was rather not a man, but a little man. Roundy, fatty' (*Live Journal* 2004).

It may be due to the emotional component that other parts of speech may also be used in a quasi-diminutive form without any semantic indication to smallness. Several verbs in CDS may obtain diminutive suffixes. A good example is the verb *kuš-en'k-at'* 'eat-DIM' from *kuš-at'* 'eat'; *kuš-en'k-a-em, kuš-en'k-a-et* in 1Pl and 3Sg, etc.[7] Other verb-like diminutives lose their verb markers and may not be conjugated (cf. *spat-en'ki* 'sleep-DIM', *rost-en'ki* – 'grow up-DIM') where the diminutive suffix *-en'k-* follows the infinitive marker. They are used in certain games and everyday rituals instead of the corresponding simplex infinitives. Even if not many examples were found in the corpus, this type of language play may still be used in a family-dependent way (see Protasova 2001).

Uninflected words, such as particles, pronouns, interjections, and adverbs, are also subject to diminutivization, e.g., *net-uški* 'no-DIM:PL' from *net* 'no', *tut-očki* 'here-DIM:PL' from the adverb *tut* 'here', and *aj-uški* 'aj-DIM', *xoroš-en-eč-ko* 'accurately-DIM-DIM' from the adverb *xorošo* 'well'. Typical of these forms is the final *-i* comparable to the "false plural" *-i* in exclamations such as *mamoč-k-i* 'lit. mommy-DIM-PL' from *mama* 'mommy'. Thus, prototypical diminutives are nouns, and even if other parts of speech are diminutivized, it happens due to the features of the objects under description and to the emotional attitude of the speaker to these objects.

Unlike Lithuanian, Russian also has augmentative suffixes. These are not as productive as the diminutive ones. Augmentatives are formed from nouns and adjectives by attaching suffixes such as *-ušč-/-jušč-, -išč-* to the stem (cf. *bol'š-ušč-aja sobač-išč-a* 'big-AUG-SG.FEM dog-AUG from *bol'š-aja sobak-a* 'big dog'). The suffix *-išč-* (with the corresponding consonant alternations) is accompanied by the inflectional ending *-e* for masculine and neuter and *-a* for feminine nouns, while the suffix *-in-* has the ending *-a* for all genders (cf. *kozl-išč-e* and *kozl-in-a*

---

[7] The simplex verb *kušat'* is already pragmatically loaded: it is used only in the second and third person and is not recommended for use in the first person singular when referring to an adult speaker.

'goat-AUG' formed from the root *kozël* 'goat').⁸ Thus, the choice of the augmentative suffixes and/or prefixes expressing different degrees of quality or pejorative meaning depends on the individual characteristics of the speaker.

4 Pragmatic functions of diminutives

Our speech is determined by continuous lexical choice. Consciously or unconsciously, we consider what to say and how to say it, which words, intonation, gestures, body language, and other signals to choose. In this complicated process, some semantic and pragmatic nuances are chosen not for every single word form or utterance but rather for the whole speech act. The pure semantic use of diminutives is based on the small size of the object described. However, the choice of diminutives may also depend on the social roles of the interlocutors, their level of familiarity, the attitude toward the object described, and on the illocutionary force of the utterance.

Diminutives are usually used in familiar, informal, intimate interactions involving people who are close to each other. Speech situations of this kind are characterized by a high degree of cooperativeness and a low degree of psychological distance. Meanwhile, formality signals an increased psychological distance, which disfavors the use of diminutives. The distance between the interlocutors, as suggested by Koch and Österreicher (1994: 588–589), is measured by a system of indicators that include, among others, openness, emotionality, trust, and role changing. Other important issues concerning distance and politeness are discussed by Brown and Levinson (1987: 101–135) and Levinson (2000: 274). The scholars distinguish between negative and positive politeness on the basis of different expectations and draw attention to the emergence of a certain "interactional pessimism", which imposes different means of mitigation of requests.

4.1 Diminutives in informal interactions

In some languages, Lithuanian and Russian included, diminutives play a crucial role in CDS (cf. Savickienė & Dressler 2007). The direct influence of CDS is seen

---

8 It is also important for acquisition that there are other possibilities to express the intensification of the quality, e.g., the augmentative prefix in the adjectives *pre-sladkij* 'AUG-sweet' from *sladkij* 'sweet'. Such augmentatives are usually used in the reduplicative form with their simplicia, e.g., *bol'šaja-prebol'šaja* 'big-AUG-big' or simply *bol'šoj-bol'šoj* 'very big', lit. 'big-big'.

in diminutive suffixes occurring among the first emerging morphemes in CS. However, diminutives have been studied very little in adult interactions.

The use of diminutives may depend on the speech situation: Adults overuse diminutives not only talking to their children but also addressing their good friends, parents or grandparents, loved ones, and pets. It is obvious that the situations just mentioned are related to friendly or intimate exchanges, and Dressler and Merlini Barbaresi (1994: 218) refer to them as "non-serious" situations. In all these cases the use of diminutives is a manifestation of emotions. Love and kindness are demonstrated in particular when the addressee is a dear person, especially a small child.

4.1.1 Pragmatic functions of diminutives in CDS and CS

The use of diminutive suffixes in child-centered situations is mainly determined by pragmatics. As pointed out by Dressler and Merlini Barbaresi (1994: 224), diminutive suffixes are "firstly attributed to the nouns which describe the child, the parts of his body, or other objects which belong to that child".

Lithuanian and Russian mothers usually use a high number of diminutives. However, it should be noticed that the frequencies of diminutive usage may vary greatly. Under- or over-usage of emotional words depends on the communicative styles/strategies of families (see Dabašinskienė 2012 for Lithuanian; Protassova & Voeikova 2007 and Kempe et al. 2007 for Russian). In Russia, some mothers and also fathers (especially young and educated ones) assume that children must not be condemned to the artificial, "bad taste" input. On the contrary, elder caregivers, especially grandmothers, are normally fond of using diminutives. However, in the only case when we could make calculations for the input from a Russian mother and a grandmother of the same child, the percentage of diminutives in their speech was comparably low in both cases, especially in the speech of the grandmother (grandmother, 34.9% of diminutive types vs. 27.8% of diminutive tokens; mother, 40.9% of diminutive types vs. 35.5% of diminutive tokens). In other cases, their percentage may reach 50% in Russian CDS (Kempe et al. 2007), whereas in Russian CS, this percentage varies from 20% to 35% (Protassova & Voeikova 2007). Lithuanian data also show differences in input as well as in output: from 35% to 50% in CDS and from 25% to 72% in CS (Savickienė 2003, Dabašinskienė 2012) at the earliest periods of language acquisition (up to 3 years).

Diminutives in child language situations often occur in orders, requests, prohibitions, and questions: The use of diminutives mitigates the strictness of the speech act. Lithuanian mothers and children often use diminutives in orders or requests, as in (2) and (3):

(2) Lithuanian
    Atneš-k   **mam-yt-ei**   *t-ą*   **žaisl-iuk-ą.**
    bring-IMP(2SG)   mother-DIM-DAT.SG   that-ACC.SG   toy-DIM-ACC.SG
    'Bring that toy to mother' (in CDS);

(3) Lithuanian
    Mama,   *staty-k,*   *staty-k,*   **mam-yt-e.**
    mother:VOC   build-IMP(2SG)   build-IMP(2SG)   mother-DIM-VOC
    'Mother, build up, build up, mother' (in CS).

Quite often orders can be expressed indirectly, using the first-person plural verb form instead of imperative, as in *tuoj eisime* **miegučio** '(we) will go get some sleep:DIM soon'.

In our Russian data, diminutives were used quite frequently in orders and requests as well, see (4) for CS and (5) for CDS:

(4) Russian
    Postroj   **dom-ik,**   *net, postroj*   **dom-ik.**
    build:IMP(2SG)   house-DIM(ACC.SG)   no   build-IMP(2SG)   house-DIM(ACC.SG)
    'Build a little house, no, build a little house'.

(5) Russian
    Vanja,   *nu*   *podar-i*   *mne*   *kakuju-nibud'*   **mašin-k-u,**
    Vanja,   now   give-IMP(2SG)   me.DAT   some   car-DIM-ACC.SG
    a to   *u*   *menja*   *netu.*
    since   at   me:GEN   no.
    'Vanja, give me any of the cars as a present because I have none'.

Since diminutive suffixes may be added to any noun in the sentence, we may attribute such uses to a feeling of special affection for the addressee. Our data suggest that such a style is more typical of girls than of boys.

Hypocoristics are chiefly used to express warm feelings, love, and kindness. Nevertheless, the basic forms of names in our data are not rare at all. Actually, the names used by the mothers in the base form have acquired a different pragmatic value, compare the use of basic forms of personal names in (6) and (7) to their diminutive forms in (8) and (9).

(6) Lithuanian
    Ne-kramty-k   *čiulptuk-o,*   **Elvij-au.**
    NEG-chew-IMP(2SG)   dummy-GEN.SG   Elvijus-VOC
    'Don't chew a dummy, Elvijus'.

(7) Lithuanian
Monik-a, *padė-k* *į* *viet-ą.*
Monika:VOC put-IMP(2SG) in place-ACC.SG
'Monika, put (this) back to where it belongs'.

In the situations referred to above, the mothers used the basic form of the name in order to discipline their children, whereas in other situations, the mothers use the diminutives mostly to emphasize their love and tender feelings, as in (8) and (9):

(8) Lithuanian
Taip *ne-laksty-k,* **Elvij-uk-ai!**
like.this NEG-run-IMP(2SG) Elvijus-DIM-VOC
'Don't run like this, Elvijus'.

(9) Lithuanian
Atei-k *čia,* **Monik-ut-e.**
come-IMP(2SG) here Monika-DIM-VOC
'Come here, Monika'.

Thus, the basic form of the name used in such situations acquires an entirely different, i.e., negative, pragmatic meaning (Savickienė & Dressler 2007). In Russian, the usage of basic forms is also unusual – hypocoristics are used in all everyday situations. This trend has morphophonological reasons: Masculine full names end with a consonant, thus violating the tendency for using open syllables. Disyllabic hypocoristics are usually shorter than simplex, compare *Lisa* from *Elizaveta*, *Varja* from *Varvara*, or *Nastja* from *Anastasia* and are close to the ideal shape of the Slavic word form containing a stem and an inflectional ending.[9] Thus, in the whole high-density corpus of the boy Vanja, the full name of the child was never used. In Filipp's corpus, different hypocoristics and diminutives of the boy's name were used twice as frequently as his full name, compare (10) and (11) with hypocoristics and (12) with the simplex:

(10) Russian
Filip-uš-en'k-a, *a* *chto* *ty* *interesnogo*
Filipp-DIM-DIM-NOM.SG and what you(SG).NOM interesting-GEN.SG
segodnja *vide-l?*
today see-PST(SG.M)
'Filipp, my little, have you seen something interesting today?'

---

9 The term *inflectional ending* is used here to distinguish the morphological markers from the final phonological part of the word that does not necessarily correspond to any inflectional suffix.

(11) Russian
Filip-uš-a, na odejal-e chto èt-o tak-oe?
Filipp-DIM-NOM.SG on blanket-LOC.SG what this-NOM.SG.N such-NOM.SG.N
'Filipp, my little, what is it here, on the blanket?'

(12) Russian
Filipp, ne nado.
Filipp not need
'Filipp, don't do it!'

As in Lithuanian, the base form of the name is rather used to discipline the child, whereas the usual form of addressing is hypocoristic or diminutive.

In Lithuanian, children also use hypocoristics quite frequently while addressing their mothers. Some utterances are actually demands directed to the mother to perform something expressed by an imperative verb form. In addition to the demand, a new nuance of discontent emerges indicated by the simplex form of the address. In the first utterance, the diminutive **Mamyte**, *statom!* 'Mother-DIM, let's build' appears as the first item, but the simplex *Mama!* follows immediately. Moreover, the simplex is used with a specific intonation conveying impatience, irritation, and discontent; obviously, all these emotions express negative connotations. Such difference in pragmatic meaning is evident only when used with the children's names and *mama* 'mother'.

In Russian, gender-specific preferences are also observed. The boys do not form many diminutives from the word *mama* 'mother', whereas all the girls under observation use diminutive forms in 50% of cases. Varja has many different forms like *mamaka, mamat'ka, mamuset'ka* for addressing her mother, and similar diminutives and hypocoristics were used by Lisa. Lithuanian and Russian data show that hypocoristics usually appear as unmarked items, whereas simplex forms are marked in terms of the pragmatic meanings they express, such as seriousness, reprimand, or anger.

Another aspect of the pragmatic use of diminutives is related to situations that are unpleasant for the child. Mothers use diminutive forms and hypocoristics when they want to alleviate an unpleasant situation, as in (13) and (14).

(13) Lithuanian
Ei-si-m kirp-ti **nag-uč-ius.**
go-FUT-1PL cut-INF nail-DIM-ACC.PL
'(We) will go to cut nails'.

(14) Lithuanian
*Reikia   ger-ti   **vaist-uk-us***
necessary drink-INF medicine-DIM-ACC.PL
'It is necessary to take medicine'.

Compare similar use of diminutives in Russian (15 and 16):

(15) Russian
*Sejčas   **tablet-očk-u**   prim-i!*
now   pill-DIM-ACC.SG   take-IMP(2SG)
'Now take the little pill'.

(16) Russian
***Volos-ik-i**   pričeš-em   i   bud-et   Filj-a*
hair-DIM-ACC.PL   comb-FUT.1PL and be-FUT.3SG Filja-NOM.SG
krasiv-yj.
beautiful-NOM.SG.M
'Now we shall comb the little hair and Filja will be beautiful'.

Making children familiar with unpleasant but necessary procedures is manifested in a similar way in both languages.

4.1.2 Pragmatic functions of diminutives in ADS

Lithuanian and Russian diminutives, however, are not restricted only to interaction with children. They might have originated in such contexts and then their use has been expanded to other contexts related to ADS. The use of diminutives often depends on the speech situation: Their highest frequency of occurrence is in CDS followed by lover- and pet-directed speech. Adults also use diminutives when they talk to good friends, and this is especially true for women talking to their female friends (Tannen 1986). The calculation of diminutives compared to all noun forms in spontaneous conversations in Lithuanian and Russian shows similar results. Depending on the speech situation, their frequency in the spoken variety of Russian fluctuates between 4% and 9% of all noun tokens, and the Lithuanian data show an average of 5% of ADS usage of diminutives. In Russian, ADS diminutives seem to be slightly more frequent than in Lithuanian. This percentage depends on the individual style of the speaker and on the pragmatic situation.

CDS situations can be metaphorically transferred into the language of love, which can be explained as realizing the pragmatic feature "non-serious" or "non-important" (Dressler & Merlini Barbaresi 1994). When used in speech acts involving lovers, diminutives usually convey an emotional aspect. An emotional component is brought out when diminutives are used to express tenderness, compassion, pleasantness, and even soft irony. The language of love could be seen as CDS only in some contexts. Diminutives in such situations have a meaning of tenderness and intimacy; they sometimes convey specific erotic connotations. The main difference is the participants' responsibility for defining the speech situation. Usually, only two people (a speaker and a listener) participate in a conversation and create intimate exchanges. Another person or a wider audience would disturb the nature of a lover-directed speech situation and the naturalness of the emotions.

In lover-directed speech, the most frequently used diminutivized forms are vocatives, i.e., the noun forms by which lovers call each other. Some of the examples for Lithuanian are *Rasele, Mildute, Linute* (female names); beloved women are often called by the names of various animals, e.g., *zuikeli* 'rabbit-DIM', *paukšteli* 'bird-DIM', *meškiuk* 'bear-DIM'. In Russian, lovers also use special suffixes of diminutives and hypocoristics, which may be similar for men and women, e.g., *Olečka, Borečka, Lenočka, Petečka*. In addition to vocatives, body parts, food, and objects of belonging are frequently diminutivized. The use of several diminutives in one utterance is common for such situations in Lithuanian, e.g., (17) and (18):

(17) Lithuanian
Maž-ul-e,   lukter-k   dar   **minut-ėl-ę,**
little-DIM-VOC wait.a.bit-IMP(2SG)   more   minute-DIM-ACC.SG
tuoj   bu-s   **kav-yt-ė.**
soon   be-FUT:3   coffee-DIM-NOM.SG
'Little one, wait a minute, coffee will be soon'.

(18) Lithuanian
Tuoj   baig-si-u   **darb-el-ius**   ir   grįši-u
soon   finish-FUT-1SG work-DIM-ACC.PL   and   return:FUT-1SG
nam-uč-ių.
home-DIM-GEN.PL
'I will finish my work and will be back home soon'.

The same tendency may be found in Russian, compare (19) from modern colloquial speech to (20) taken from the nineteenth-century novel:

(19) Russian
*Značit,   ja   sebe   sši-l-a   **plat'-ic-e***
so   I:NOM   self:DAT   sew-PST-SG.F   dress-DIM-ACC.SG
*tak-oe,   sitcev-oe,   letn-ee   i   **kusoč-k-i***
such-ACC.SG.N   chintz(ADJ)-ACC.SG.N   summer(ADJ)-ACC.SG.N   and   piece-DIM-
                                                                            NOM.PL
*osta-l-i-s',   tak-aja   **beret-oč-k-a**   u   menja.*
remain-PST-PL-REFL   such-NOM.SG.F   beret-DIM-DIM-NOM.SG   at   I:GEN
'So I had sewn for myself such a dress, a chintz dress for summer, and some little pieces remained, and now I have such a little beret'.

It has been observed that fiction or biographies, including letters to loved ones, represent lover-directed speech situations as well. This feature is often manifested in Russian classical literature. Note example (20) from the speech of the noble countryman Manilov in Gogol's *Dead Souls*:

(20) Russian
*Otkroj   svoj   **rot-ik,**   **dušen'-k-a,***
open:IMP(2SG)   your(ACC.SG.M)   mouth-DIM(ACC.SG)   soul-DIM-NOM.SG
*ja   polož-u   tuda   ėt-u   **konfet-k-u.***
I:NOM   put-FUT.1SG   there   this-ACC.SG.F   candy-DIM-ACC.SG
'Open your little mouth, my little soul, I shall put there this little candy'.

Nevertheless, such intimate utterances can be seen as being in "bad taste" if the partners use this register outside of their close intimate circle. Playfulness is a characteristic feature of the language of love; as regards the linguistic creativity of lovers, the phenomenon of a "childish behavior of lovers" is often observed. Therefore, some special words and names are created for specific purposes when memories and experiences of two people are shared (Dabašinskienė 2009b).

In both languages, one of the favorite speech games in lover-directed speech and CDS is a kind of gender shift, e.g., *moj **malen'kij Len-ok*** 'my-M little-M Lena-DIM:M' when speaking to a girl or *moja **milaja Lenjav-očk-a*** 'my-F dear-F Leonid-DIM:F' when speaking to a boy, as described by Gavrilova (2002: 54) discussing CDS in Russian. The Lithuanian data also demonstrate gender shift, especially in addressing female speakers, e.g., *mano **Linukas*** 'my Lina-DIM:M', *mano **nabagėlis žvirblelis*** 'my poor-DIM:M sparrow-DIM:M'. Compare also the non-standard feminine gender agreement for the Russian masculine word *zajka moja* 'hare-DIM my-F' in a popular song. The feminine gender sounds very natural in this context, as this is a usual form of addressing a woman. Some linguists (e.g., Nesset 2001: 202) believe that masculine hypocoristics in Russian are formed intentionally to refer to children or women; it is treated as a manifestation of a certain sexist ideology in grammar.

It is interesting to note that in lover-directed speech, men use more diminutives than women. This could be explained by the inequality of their status. Women are usually treated as weaker and smaller, therefore, metaphorically they are compared to children – both of them belong to a weaker group and thus the stronger side always has the right to use diminutives (Dabašinskienė 2009b).

4.1.3 Diminutives in pet-directed speech

In pet-directed speech, small/young dogs and cats are usually treated like children; thus, they can also be addressed accordingly. Interestingly, diminutives are used not only in the vocative form; other nouns, mostly referring to body parts and food, are diminutivized as well. Diminutives are used in different speech acts, such as greetings, orders, and questions in Lithuanian pet-directed speech (see 21–23).

(21) Lithuanian
 Sveikas, ***maž-yl-i,*** *ko* ***snuk-el-is*** *nelinksm-as?*
 hello little-DIM-VOC why muzzle-DIM-NOM.SG unhappy-NOM.SG.M
 'Hello, little-one, why is your face so unhappy?'

(22) Lithuanian
 Im-k, *palak* ***pien-el-io.***
 take-IMP(2SG) lap:IMP(2SG) milk-DIM-GEN.SG
 'Take, have some milk'.

(23) Lithuanian
 K-o *nor-i* ***šun-el-is?***
 what-GEN want-PRS(3) dog-DIM-NOM.SG
 'What does the dog want?'

In Russian, pets are usually addressed in the form of the third person exactly as children are (see 24–26):

(24) Russian
 Vot *on* *id-ët,* ***malyš-eč-k-a!***
 here he:NOM.SG.M go-PRS.3SG baby-DIM-DIM-NOM.SG
 'Here he comes, the dear little'.

(25) Russian

A	*u*	*k-ogo*	*èto*	*tak-ie*	**uš-k-i?**
and	at	who-GEN	there	such-NOM.PL	ear-DIM-NOM.PL

'And who has such little ears?'

Note that such sentence has nothing to do with the real size of the animal; all these diminutives have a pure pragmatic function expressing affection (compare also 26).

(26) Russian

Sejčas	**lap-k-i**	*pomo-et*	*naš-a*
now	paw-DIM-ACC.PL	wash-FUT.3SG	our-NOM.SG.F

sobač-k-a.
dog-DIM-NOM.SG
'Now our doggy will wash her little paws'.

These examples demonstrate the pragmatic meaning of friendliness, closeness, and tenderness. Diminutives are used in requests and orders to mitigate the strictness of the speech act. Adults use diminutives not only in pet-directed speech, but also in conversations about their pets (as well as about their children). For example, in Lithuanian: *kaip mano* **šuniukas** *mėgsta* **varškytę** 'My dog-DIM loves curd-DIM a lot'; *jo mėgstamiausias* **žaisliukas** – **kamuoliukas** 'his favorite toy-DIM is a ball-DIM.' This does not always work the same way in Russian – it may be true if both speech partners are caregivers of the same cat or dog or, at least, both of them have animals. In this case, a special kind of familiarity exists pretending that the pet is always present in the speech situation. Pet-owners speak about their pets with other people without diminutive suffixes. Thus, they only demonstrate their affection being sure that their speech partner will understand and appreciate it. As our data show, the use of diminutives mostly depends on the relations between the participants, namely, on the solidarity, familiarity, and friendliness existing between them.

4.2 Diminutives in formal interactions

As discussed in the previous sections, diminutives are most frequently used in situations between close participants and in familiar settings, as a rule, at home. Therefore, we expect diminutives to be used in familiar, informal, and intimate interactions involving people who are close to each other. Formality, meanwhile, is present in a speech situation marked by an increased psychological distance and thus disfavors the use of diminutives. Let us consider other situations where diminutives in ADS occur quite often, even when people do not know each other. These situations usually include speech acts of offers, questions, suggestions, requests, etc. (Dressler & Merlini Barbaresi 1994). Interactions that occur between strangers in formal institutional contexts, for example, in banks, hospitals, and supermarkets, could also be marked by the use of diminutives. The pragmatic meaning of "non-serious" is the main condition for such speech situations. The diminutives most often used here are signs of reduced psychological distance and signal the playful character of the exchange. Service providers, while speaking to their clients, pretend to establish a certain kind of intimacy and friendship via the use of diminutives, which are more likely to accompany positive rather than negative emotions. Examples of emotions that seem to disfavor the use of diminutives are fear, pain, and anger. Thus, if diminutives are used in connection with these emotions, then they are used for the purpose of mitigation. Sympathy is another area that elicits the use of diminutives. According to Dressler and Merlini Barbaresi (1994: 206), "sympathy is a direct, dyadic relation between speaker and referent, it represents the speaker's affinity to, and positive attitude towards, persons or things".

Examples where sympathy is expressed in the contexts of fear and pain may also influence the professional speech of medical personnel in Lithuania; therefore, diminutives are used by nurses and doctors (see 27–30).

(27) Lithuanian
Ar dar **galv-yt-ę** *šiandien skaud-a?*
Q still head-DIM-ACC.SG today hurt-PRS(3)
'Do you still have a headache today?'

(28) Lithuanian
Neš-ki-te ten t-ą **šlapim-ėl-į**
bring-IMP-2PL there that-ACC.SG urine-DIM-ACC.SG
'Bring that urine there'.

(29) Lithuanian
Spaudim-ėl-į *pamatuo-si-me.*
blood.pressure-DIM-ACC.SG measure-FUT-1PL
'(We) will measure your blood-pressure'.

(30) Lithuanian
Dabar išger-si-m **vaist-uk-us**.
now drink-FUT-1PL medicine-DIM-ACC.PL
'Now (we) will take medicines'.

Nowadays, this sphere, which was traditionally overloaded with diminutives, has become very official in Russia: We found only twelve instances of diminutives, and in only one example was it used by a medical assistant (see 31).

(31) Russian
U vas nebol'š-aja **dyr-oč-k-a** *v*
at you(PL):GEN little-NOM.SG.F hole-DIM-DIM-NOM.SG in
nižn-em zub-e, tak čto bud-em plombirova-t'.
lower-LOC.SG.M tooth-LOC.SG so be-FUT.1PL fill-INF
'You have a small hole in the lower tooth, so we shall fill it'.

In (31), the diminutive may express smallness, so it may not be interpreted as a pure pragmatic use. The other eleven instances were used by patients in their conversations.

Similar situations occur in banks when a client may need help or feel fear or confusion. The speech acts of requests and questions involve the use of diminutives in Lithuanian (32–34).

(32) Lithuanian
Pin **kod-uk-ą** *saugo-ki-te.*
pin code-DIM-ACC.SG guard-IMP-2PL
'Keep safe the pin-code'.

(33) Lithuanian
T-ą **sąskait-ėl-ę** *gal-i-te tvarky-ti ir*
that-ACC.SG account-DIM-ACC.SG can-PRS-2PL manage-INF and
elektroniniu būdu, per Internet-ą.
electronically thorugh Internet-ACC.SG
'You can manage this account electronically, via the Internet'.

(34) Lithuanian
Kiek perves-ti **pinig-ėl-ių?**
how.much transfer-INF money-DIM-GEN.PL
'How much money do you need to transfer?'

In Russian, the use of diminutives in this sphere is very unusual. All financial negotiations require seriousness, and the use of diminutives may be interpreted as a lack of professionalism and thus produces a negative impression. However, restrictions of diminutive use do not concern the business relations of equal partners – that state of affairs, on the contrary, triggers their frequent use (e.g., 35).

(35) Russian
Sejčas **dogovor-čik** *podpiš-em* *i* *svobodn-y.*
now agreement-DIM:NOM.SG sign-FUT.1PL and free-PL
'Now we shall sign the little agreement and we are free.'

The extensive use of diminutives related to the expression of politeness might be observed in the interactions of customer and service provider, mainly in the speech acts of offers and questions (this applies to both Lithuanian and Russian). People use diminutives in requests and/or orders in offices, shops, and restaurants when they buy food and drinks, tickets, choose clothes, etc. (see the following Lithuanian examples 36–40).

(36) Lithuanian
Duo-ki-te, *pakabin-si-u* **palt-uk-ą.**
give-IMP-2PL hang-FUT-1SG coat-DIM-ACC.SG
'Give it to me, I will hang your coat'.

(37) Lithuanian
Gal *norė-si-te* **kav-yt-ės,** **desert-uk-o?**
maybe want-FUT-2PL coffee-DIM-GEN.SG dessert-DIM-GEN.SG
'Maybe you want some coffee or dessert?'

(38) Lithuanian
Ar **sąskait-ėl-ę** *jau* *išrašy-ti?*
Q bill-DIM-ACC.SG already write-INF
'Should I already write the bill [for you]?' (in a restaurant/cafe).

(39) Lithuanian
Prie **kas-yt-ės** *ei-ki-te*
at cashier-DIM-GEN.SG go-IMP-2PL
'Go to the cashier' (in a supermarket).

(40) Lithuanian
Gal **lašiš-ėl-ės** *karšt-o* **rūkym-ėl-io?**
maybe salmon-DIM-GEN.SG hot-GEN.SG.M smoking-DIM-GEN.SG
'Maybe some salmon of hot smoking' (in a market).

In Russian, negotiations are also triggered by diminutives (see 41 and 42).

(41) Russian
Podskaza-t' *vam* *čto-nibud'?* **Bibliotec-k-u?**
prompt-INF you(PL):DAT something(ACC) library-DIM-ACC.SG
'Should I recommend you something? A little library?'

(42) Russian
*I   odin   **škaf-čik**   peredviga-et-sja   po   ix*
and one   bookshelf-DIM:NOM.SG   move-PRS.3SG-REFL   along   their
osnovanij-u.
basis-DAT.SG
'And one bookshelf moves along their basis' (in a furniture shop).

Being polite is largely a matter of the minimization of impositions while using proper mitigation devices. Such special devices have to be used especially in the speech acts of requests, as in Lithuanian examples (43) and (44).

(43) Lithuanian
*Ar   galė-čiau   gau-ti   **kav-yt-ės?***
Q   can-SBJV:1SG   get-INF   coffee-DIM-GEN.SG
'Could I have (some) coffee?'

(44) Lithuanian
*Bū-ki-te   malon-i,   perduo-ki-te   **biliet-ėl-į.***
be-IMP-2PL   nice-NOM.PL.M   pass-IMP-2PL   ticket-DIM-ACC.SG
'Would you be so nice as to pass the ticket?'

All these spheres are qualified as strictly personal and unofficial, as can also be seen from Russian examples (45)–(47).

(45) Russian
*Davaj-te   vyp'j-em   **kofej-k-u.***
let:IMP-2PL   drink-FUT.1PL   coffee-DIM-PART.SG
'Let's have some coffee'.

(46) Russian
*Daj-te,   požaluista,   **upakovoč-k-u**   molok-a.*
give:IMP-2PL   please   packet-DIM-ACC.SG   milk-GEN.SG
'Give me, please, a packet of milk'.

(47) Russian
*Tri,   navernoe,   vot   tak-ix   **kružeč-k-i.***
three   probably   here   such-GEN.PL   mug-DIM-ADNUM
'(Give me), probably, three of those little mugs'.

The examples of diminutives in requests encompass the pragmatic feature "non-serious" that has the primary function of the mitigation of the request, of making the request more acceptable by decreasing the obligation of the addressee. By uttering a request, the speaker may obtain the satisfaction of his/her needs, but may also sound arrogant or obtrusive. By mitigating the request via a diminutive, the speaker may minimize the negative effect and get what he/she needs. According to Sifianou (1992: 161), the everyday function of diminutives is not mainly to soften impositions but to express the speaker's wish to maintain or establish common ground and solidarity with the addressee.

Different speech situations in formal institutions (e.g., hospitals, banks) show that diminutives in Lithuanian seem to be more appropriate than in Russian, where they are not felicitous in contexts requiring a serious professional attitude or if they may perform a different pragmatic function. With these differences in mind, it seems that the use of Lithuanian diminutives has extended into areas where they satisfy a wide variety of politeness needs. Such derivates usually express politeness by showing solidarity toward the addressee. In other words, the use of diminutives marks the interaction as positively polite (Sifianou 1992: 159).

5 The grammar of diminutives

In the early research on CDS, it has already been stated that diminutives or hypocoristics are not only more frequently used in CDS as compared to ADS, but also play a role in the development of a child's grammar (Berko 1958, Rūķe-Draviņa 1959). Recent research into a number of languages has also demonstrated that diminutives are especially frequent when talking to children, and thus, they may facilitate the acquisition of noun morphology (Olmsted 1994, Kempe et al. 2003, Savickienė & Dressler 2007, Savickienė et al. 2009), conversational interaction, and the acquisition of discourse strategies (King & Melzi 2004). Therefore, the formal features of languages make children prefer diminutives to simplex forms. The length of the diminutivized word does not seem to cause difficulties for children and adults, as both groups use them for different purposes: Adults prefer to employ them for pragmatic reasons, while children, especially during first years of language development, use them for the facilitation of the acquisition process.

Despite the fact that adults can use diminutives in various speech situations for different pragmatic purposes, the analysis of our data allows us to suggest that the base form of the noun may predict its potential to be diminutivized. As was briefly mentioned in the description of Lithuanian and Russian (see Sections 1 and 2), the most frequent diminutives are formed from disyllabic nouns. In the Lithuanian data, 70% of disyllabic and 30% of trisyllabic simplex nouns were used for diminutive formation. In the Russian data, up to 48% of all diminutivized masculine nouns were disyllabic and thus formed from monosyllabic nouns (compare also the description of such diminutives by Polivanova 2008). Feminine diminutives are, in general, longer: In our examples, 42% of all feminine diminutives are trisyllabic, as *polos-k-a* 'stripe-DIM-NOM.SG' from *polosa* 'stripe'. Such preferences for a certain form of the word may be explained in terms of the subtheory of typological adequacy of natural morphology (Kilani-Schoch & Dressler 2005).[10] Viewed from this perspective, it may be claimed that in Russian, word length may serve as an extra bootstrapping mechanism of gender distinction: Longer words are more likely to belong to the feminine gender, whereas shorter ones will belong to the masculine gender.

Diminutive formation from shorter stems is supported by the principles of language economy (Bybee & Hopper 2001, Vicentini 2003): Shorter words are always preferred by the speaker not only for reasons of articulation, but also for the sake of a higher speech tempo. The following examples clearly demonstrate the preference for less-syllabic nouns to be diminutivized (note that their pragmatic functions and the speech situation are the same in both languages): ***Kav-yt-ė*** *ir arbat-a* 'coffee-DIM and tea' (Lituanian) and *Kofe i **čaj-ok*** 'coffee and tea-DIM' (Russian). In Lithuanian, *kava* 'coffee' is a two-syllable noun; therefore, it appeared in a diminutive form, while in Russian, it is the word *čaj* 'tea' that is a monosyllabic noun and therefore was diminutivized.[11]

In both languages, diminutive formation triggers the shift of a word to a more productive declensional class. However, in Russian and Lithuanian, the formal features of diminutives differ.

In some languages, both the gender and word class of the base are maintained in the diminutive form, while in others, one of them or even both may change. Thus, in German, diminutives are easy to identify because they are always nouns and always neuters (Korecky-Kröll & Dressler 2007).

In Lithuanian, the change of inflectional class[12] and gender is also possible, but this is not the case in Russian, where there is no gender shift. Masculine

---

[10] "La répartition typologiques des mots selon leur taille peut être esquissée comme suit: ... Les langues flexionnells et introflexionnelles préfèrent des mots à un pied binaire ou ternaire ..." (Kilani-Schoch & Dressler 2005: 80).

[11] Some cultural habits must also be taken into consideration: in Lithuania, coffee is preferred to tea, whereas in Russia, it is vice versa. In both languages, the shorter noun and the name of the preferable drink tend to be diminutivized. As we already observed in several other cases, the combination of pragmatic and morphonological features is the strongest reason for using diminutives.

[12] In this chapter, we use the term "inflectional class" (see Savickienė 2003, Savickienė, Kazlauskienė, & Kamandulytė 2004), although traditional grammars use the term "declensions" (cf. Ambrazas 1997).

diminutives ending with -*o* (like *nos-išk-o* 'nose-DIM:M') agree with neuter adjectives in colloquial speech, but such agreement is treated as erroneous (see Table 1, row 1). Diminutives belong to productive inflectional classes, therefore, when diminutivized, nouns switch from unproductive classes to classes with productive inflections (Table 1, row 2). Thus, the Lithuanian inflection class of the simple noun *dantis* 'tooth' is unproductive, whereas the derived diminutive *dantukas* belongs to a productive class. In Russian, the class shift from unproductive to productive is observed in feminine nouns, but does not work for masculine nouns; a derived diminutive form becomes opaque[13] due to the historical consonant change of the stem, compare *sok* 'juice' with *soč-ok* 'juice-DIM'. In Lithuanian, differently from Russian, diminutive forms may be more transparent (for example, they do not demonstrate stem alternation) than those of their simple bases (Table 1, row 3). Thus, the derivation of diminutives often leads to inflectional simplification or inflection class shift (Savickienė 2003, 2007, Dabašinskienė 2009a). In Russian, masculine diminutive suffixes may even make the stems more opaque as compared to the simplex. However, the prevocalic -*k* of diminutive suffixes makes inflectional endings in Russian more salient; these derivates are prosodically uniform having final trochees and salient case and number marking. Compare the nominative-genitive opposition of simplex forms and the corresponding diminutives: *dver'/dver-i* 'door-Nom/Gen' vs. *dver-k-a/dver-k-i* 'door-DIM-NOM/GEN', *ulic-a/ulic-y* 'street-NOM/GEN' vs. *uloč-k-a/uloč-k-i* 'street-DIM-NOM/GEN', and *stol/stol-a* 'table-NOM/GEN' vs. *stol-ik/stol-ik-a* 'table-DIM-NOM/GEN' (Table 1, row 4). Diminutive forms have homogeneous contrasting final parts whereas all simplex forms sound differently. In Lithuanian, for example, a base form may be stressed on the final syllable, as in *knyg-à* 'book', whereas in diminutives, nearly all case forms are accented on the penultimate syllable.

---

[13] Morphosemantic parameter of transparency/opacity shows whether the derived word form may be easily recognized as a composition of morphological elements.

Tab. 1: Diminutives in the target adult languages: Lithuanian and Russian

	Lithuanian	Russian
1. Word class shift/ category shift	Class shift to nouns from numerals; gender shift	No class or gender shift. However, some Dim/Pejor:M tend to erroneously be treated as neuter: e.g., *nos-išk-o, dom-išk-o, volč-išk-o* (nose-DIM, house-DIM, wolf-DIM) get the neuter inflectional ending that is rare in Masc.
2. Inflectional class shift: unprod.→prod.	fem. in *-is*: *žuvis→žuv-ytė* 'fish' masc. in *-is*: *dantis→dant-ukas* 'tooth' masc. in *-uo*: *vanduo→vand-en-ukas* 'water'	fem. in consonant *dver'→dver-k-a* 'door-DIM-NOM.SG', *myš'→myš-k-a* 'mouse-DIM-NOM.SG' Masc do not change class and even become opaque because of historical changes: *zamok→zamoč-ek* 'lock-DIM', *drug→druž-ok* 'friend-DIM' Neuter do not change class.
3. Transparency	In base form the noun *dviratis* 'bike' possess the sterm alternation, but diminutive is transparent, *dviratis* (NOM.SG), *dviračio* (GEN.SG), *dviratį* (ACC.SG), *dviračiui* (DAT.SG)→*dviratukas* (NOM.SG), *dviratuko* (GEN.SG), *dviratuką* (ACC.SG), *dviratukui* (DAT.SG) 'bike:DIM', etc.	Masculine become opaque, all Dims gain in the similarity of final syllables.
4. Stress shift	*knygà→knygėlė* 'book' (always final trochees, except INS.SG, LOC. SG, ACC.PL)	Stress shift is not a rule but is characteristic of some suffixes, e.g., *knížka→kníž-eč-ka, kniž-ónoč-k-a* 'book-DIM-DIM-NOM.SG, especially pejoratives.

The use of diminutives in Russian also helps to get rid of the unproductive feminine declension class ending in consonants (see the last column in Table 2). However, as shown in Table 1, diminutive formation may also have formal disadvantages, such as opaque gender, greater word length, and vowel syncope in the suffix. All these disadvantages are characteristic of masculine diminutives.

Tab. 2: Impact of diminutivization on the word forms of different declension classes for Russian

No change	No change	Disadvantage (opaque gender)	Advantage (non-productive → productive)
Fem Cl. 1→Fem Cl. 1(+P)	Masc Cl. 2 →Masc Cl. 2	Masc Cl. 2 → Masc Cl.1	Fem Cl. 3→Fem Cl. 1
sobaka→sobač-k-a 'dog-DIM-NOM.SG'	mjač→mjač-ik 'ball-DIM' zajac→zajč-ik 'hare-DIM'	zajac→zaj-k-a 'hare-DIM-NOM.SG' drug→druž-k-a 'friend of the fiance-DIM-NOM.SG'	myš'→myš-k-a 'mouse-DIM-NOM.SG' dver'→dver-k-a 'door-DIM-NOM.SG'

However, the clear advantage of masculine diminutives is their stable accentual scheme (see Polivanova 2008: 9). Noun declension in Russian may be accompanied by stress shift; thus, note the contrast between the nominative and the genitive for some simplexes, as in *topór* 'axe(NOM.SG)' – *topor-á* 'axe-GEN.SG'. Diminutives, meanwhile, always have a permanent stress, as in *topór-ik* 'axe-DIM:NOM.SG' – *topór-ik-a* 'axe-DIM-GEN.SG'. The stress may only move from the suffix to the inflectional ending when the suffix displays vowel syncope, e.g., *petuš-ók* 'cock-DIM(NOM.SG)' – *petuš-k-á* 'cock-DIM-GEN.SG'. In brief, even masculine diminutives, which seem to be opaque, have clear formal advantages compared to their simplex forms.

In general, Table 2 shows the strengthening of the second declension class as a result of diminutive use, as well as similar derivational patterns in the informal spoken language, as in the colloquial diminutives of indeclinable nouns such as *metro-šk-a* (DIM-FEM) from *metro* (NEUT) 'metro'. Such diminutives are used in informal settings and mostly occur in the slang of children and teenagers. It has to be emphasized that this type of diminutive formation is expanding and illegal feminine diminutives like *apel'sin-k-a* 'orange-DIM-FEM*', *pomidor-k-a* 'tomato-DIM-FEM*', *morož-k-a* 'ice cream-DIM-FEM*', *souvenir-k-a* 'souvenir-DIM-FEM*' frequently occur instead of standard masculine and neuter variants *apel'sin-čik, pomidor-čik, morožen-c-e, souvenir-čik*.[14]

---

[14] In parallel, colloquial derivates from NPs have the same structure: *vstrečnaja polosa → vstrečka* 'opposite side of the road'. The dominance of the feminine second declension is strengthened by the non-accentuated endings of the neuter, which are understood as *-a*.

As we have shown, diminutives in Lithuanian and Russian exhibit many similarities in their frequency, distribution across word classes, and form preferences. However, Russian diminutives are more lexicalized and rather stored in the mental lexicon than spontaneously derived; in the contrary, Lithuanian diminutive formation is highly productive and show almost unlimited derivational possibilities: Their suffixes may function in a free variation, and numerous derivates from one and the same stem may be simultaneously used in the same function. Unlike this, in Russian diminutives, suffixes must be kept in memory; using the wrong suffix is considered to be an error both by parents and by speech pathologists.

6 Conclusions

Diminutives in spoken Russian and Lithuanian are extremely frequent for several reasons: They are used to perform the pragmatic functions of showing politeness and the mitigation of requests or other necessary actions. They also mark a close and friendly "little world" as opposed to the hostile world of "other people". Such pragmatic functions seem very important for modern conversational strategies. The use of diminutives enables us to change the pragmatic values usually attributed to asking questions, giving orders, making requests, and offers. In both languages, the use of diminutives is strongly favored due to their formal characteristics. They all belong to the most productive inflectional classes, and their use helps to avoid the use of unproductive word forms. They have salient inflectional endings and thus are easier for processing and acquisition. They are characterized by stable accent schemes and in our languages represent an ideal word structure, i.e., disyllabic or trisyllabic nouns, belonging to productive inflectional classes with no or little stress shift throughout the whole paradigm (see also Kempe et al. 2005). We assume that these features are important not only for young children, but also for adults in their everyday conversations.

However, there are differences in the functioning of diminutives in the two languages. In Lithuanian, diminutives may be formed with different suffixes from the same bases and such alternative variants co-exist in free variation for almost all the nouns. In Russian, diminutive formations are more lexicalized, so that several different forms from one simplex exist only for some frequently occurring items. Taken that diminutive formation is a process having both inflectional and derivational properties, we may assume that Russian diminutive building is lexicalized and thus closer to derivation, whereas in Lithuanian, it is closer to inflection (Dressler 1994). Russian diminutives are stored in the mental lexicon as a whole, whereas Lithuanian ones are produced online during the conversation.

This assumption is preliminary and needs further investigation. Russian diminutive adjectives were examined from this point of view by Marina V. Roussakova (Rusakova 2013: 360 ff.). Her investigation shows that only 7% of diminutive adjectives used in the National Russian Corpus were not cited in the grammatical dictionary of modern Russian. For nouns, this percentage might be lower; however, we also expect that Russian native-speakers keep in mind the etalon diminutive form of most frequent nouns.

Pragmatic rules are not always similar in the two languages either. In Russian, diminutives are rather used by customers and avoided by staff, whereas in Lithuanian, these derivatives are often used while serving people in restaurants, banks, shops, or hospitals. In Russian, there are contexts that disfavor their use, such as the financial or medical sphere. Diminutives are not welcomed in medical communication since they manifest in informal, non-serious and thus non-competent conversation. In Lithuanian, the use of diminutives in such situations ensures a different pragmatic function, which is not related to non-competence, but emphasizes the sympathy and/or friendly relations between the parties. In both languages, they remain very frequent in all spheres of service related to consuming (like eating and buying clothes or cosmetic procedures).

Conversational strategies and formal devices may show the level of speakers' involvement. While using diminutives in formal or familiar and intimate situations, we try to reduce psychological distance, eliminate hierarchies, and become equal, despite our social status, age, or gender. However, even when an advantageous position or a superior status of one of the speakers is established, very close and intimate exchanges can still occur. Socio-economic changes also influence the structure of communication, favoring the use of informal markers in public discourse. A good command of using diminutive suffixes manifests itself in language mastery. Nevertheless, native speakers repeatedly report that diminutives are overly expressively loaded and therefore in certain circumstances may seem irrelevant, false, or signal socio-communicative incompetence.

Acknowledgments

We are grateful to the editors and reviewers for their extremely helpful and informative comments to the earlier versions of the paper. Different parts of this investigation were supported for the second author in 2013 by the Foundation of the President of Russian Federation SS-3135.2014.6 "Saint Petersburg School of Functional Grammar", the corpus investigation was granted by the Program of Fundamental Studies of Russian Academy of Sciences, project "Development of the Syntactic Component for the Russian National Corpus", and in 2014, by the

Russian National Foundation, grant 14-18-03668 "Mechanisms of the Acquisition of Russian and the Acquisition of the Communicative Competence at the Early Stages of Child's Development".

Abbreviations

ACC	accusative	N(EUT)	neuter
ADJ	adjective	NEG	negation
ADNUM	adnumerative	NOM	nominative
AUG	augmentative	PART	partitive
DAT	dative	PEJ	pejorative
DIM	diminutive	PL	plural
F(EM)	feminine	PRS	present tense
FUT	future tense	PST	past tense
GEN	genitive	Q	question particle
IMP	imperative	REFL	reflexive
INF	infinitive	SBJV	subjunctive
INS	instrumental	SG	singular
LOC	locative	VOC	vocative
M(ASC)	masculine		

References

Ambrazas, Vytautas (ed.). 1997. *Lithuanian grammar*. Vilnius: Baltos lankos.
Berko, Jean. 1958. The child's learning English morphology. *Word* 14: 150–177.
Brown, Penny & Stephen Levinson. 1987. Universals in language use: Politeness phenomena. In Esther N. Goody (ed.) *Questions and politeness: Strategies in social interaction*, 56–311. Cambridge: Cambridge University Press.
Bybee, Joan & Paul J. Hopper (eds.). 2001. *Frequency and the emergence of linguistic structure*. Amsterdam, Philadelphia: John Benjamins.
Dabašinskienė, Ineta. 2009a. Easy way to language acquisition: Diminutives in Lithuanian child language. *Ad verba liberorum: Linguistics and Pedagogy and Psychology* 1: 11–22.
Dabašinskienė, Ineta. 2009b. Intimacy, familiarity and formality: Diminutives in modern Lithuanian. *Lituanus* 55(1): 65–79.
Dabašinskienė, Ineta. 2012. Gender differences in language acquisition: Case study of Lithuanian diminutives. *Journal of Baltic Studies* 43(2): 177–196.
Dressler, Wolfgang U. 1994. On prototypical differences between inflection and derivation. *Zeitschrift für Sprachwissenschaft und Kommunikationsforschung* 42: 3–10.
Dressler, Wolfgang U. 2005. Morphological typology and first language acquisition: Some mutual challenges. In Geert Booij, Emiliano Guevara, Angela Ralli, Salvatore Sgroi, & Sergio Scalise (eds.) *Morphology and linguistic typology*. On-line proceedings of the

fourth Mediterranean Morphology Meeting (MMM4). Catania 21-23.9.2003, University of Bologna, 2005. http://morbo.lingue.unibo.it/mmm/.
Dressler, Wolfgang U. & Lavinia Merlini Barbaresi. 1994. *Morphopragmatics. Diminutives and intensifiers in Italian, German, and other languages.* Berlin: Mouton de Gruyter.
Gavrilova, Tatjana O. 2002. *Registr obščenija s det'mi: strukturnyj i sociolingvističeskij aspekty* [Register of communication with children: Structural and sociolinguistic aspects.] Unpublished dissertation of the candidate of philological sciences. Saint Petersburg: European University.
Gillis, Steven. 1997. The acquisition of diminutives in Dutch. In Wolfgang U. Dressler (ed.). *Studies in Pre- and Protomorphology*, 165–179. Vienna: Österreichische Akademie der Wissenschaften.
Jurafsky, Daniel. 1996. Universal tendencies in the semantics of the diminutive. *Language* 72: 533–578.
Kazlauskaitė, Rūta. 2012. Pragmatics of occational diminutives. *Language studies for the 21st century: From sound to text* (conference abstracts). Vilnius, 27 September 2012.
Kempe, Vera, Patricia J. Brooks, Natalia Mironova, & Olga Fedorova. 2003. Diminutivization supports gender acquisition in Russian children. *Journal of Child Language* 30: 471–485.
Kempe, Vera, Patricia J. Brooks, & Steven Gillis. 2005. Diminutives in child-directed speech supplement metric with distributional word segmentation cues. *Psychonomic Bulletin and Review* 12: 145–151.
Kempe, Vera, Patricia J. Brooks, & Steven Gillis. 2007. Diminutives provide multiple benefits for language acquisition. In Ineta Savickienė & Wolfgang U. Dressler (eds.) *The acquisition of diminutives: A cross-linguistic perspective*, 319–342. Amsterdam, Philadelphia: John Benjamins.
Ketrez, Nihan F. & Ayhan Aksu-Koç. 2007. The (scarcity of) diminutives in Turkish child language. In Ineta Savickienė & Wolfgang U. Dressler (eds.) *The acquisition of diminutives: A cross-linguistic perspective*, 279–295. Amsterdam, Philadelphia: John Benjamins.
Kilani-Schoch, Marianne & Wolfgang U. Dressler. 2005. *Morphologie naturelle et flexion du verbe français*. Tübingen: Narr.
King, Kimbell & Giuliana Melzi. 2004. Intimacy, imitation and language learning: Spanish diminutives in mother-child conversation. *First Language* 24(2): 241–261.
Koch, Peter & Wulf Österreicher. 1994. Schriftlichkeit und Sprache [writing and language]. In Hugo Steger & Herbert Ernst Wiegand (hgs.), *Schrift und Schriftlichkeit. Ein interdisziplinäres Handbuch internationaler Forschung* [Writing and its use. An interdisciplinary handbook of international research], Bd. 10.1, 587–604. Berlin, New York: Walter de Gruyter.
Korecky-Kröll, Katharina & Wolfgang U. Dressler. 2007. Diminutives and hypocoristics in Austrian German (AG). In Ineta Savickienė & Wolfgang U. Dressler (eds.) *The acquisition of diminutives: A cross-linguistic perspective*, 207–230. Amsterdam, Philadelphia: John Benjamins.
Levinson, Stephen. 2000. *Pragmatics*. Cambridge: Cambridge University Press.
LKG 1. 1965. *Lietuvių kalbos gramatika: Fonetika ir morfologija* [Lithuanian grammar: Phonetics and morphology], Vol. 1. Vilnius: Mintis.
Nesset, Tore. 2001. How pervasive are sexist ideologies in grammar? In René Dirven, Bruce Hawkins, & Esra Sandikcioglu (eds.) *Language and ideologies. Volume 1: Theoretical cognitive approaches*, 197–227. Amsterdam, Philadelphia: John Benjamins.

Olmsted, Hugh. 1994. Diminutive morphology of Russian children: A simplified subset of nominal declension in language acquisition. In *Alexander Lipson: In memoriam*, 165–207. Columbus, OH: Slavica Publishers.

Polivanova, Anna K. 2008. Obrazovanie umen'šitel'nyx suščestvitel'nyx mužskogo roda [Formation of masculine diminutive nouns]. In Anna K. Polivanova, *Obščee i russkoe jazykoznanie* [*General and Russian Linguistics*], 8–23. Moscow: Russian State Humanitarian University.

Protasova, Ekaterina. 2001. Rol' diminutivov v sovremennom russkom jazyke [The role of diminutives in modern Russian language]. In Irina P. Külmoja (ed.) *Russkij jazyk: sistema i funkcionirovanie* [*Russian language: System and functioning*], 72–88. Tartu: Tartu ülikool.

Protassova, Ekaterina & Maria D. Voeikova. 2007. Diminutives in Russian at the early stages of acquisition. In Ineta Savickienė & Wolfgang U. Dressler (eds.) *The acquisition of diminutives: A cross-linguistic perspective*, 43–73. Amsterdam, Philadelphia: John Benjamins.

Rusakova, Marina V. 2004. Ob okkazional'nom soglasovanii v razgovornom russkom jazyke [On the occasional agreement in spoken Russian]. In *Russkij jazyk: istoričeskie sud'by I sovremennost'. II Meždunarodnyj congress issledovatelej russkogo jazyka. Trudy i materialy* [*Russian language: Historic development and modern state. II International Congress of the Researchers of Russian Language. Proceedings and materials*], 322–323. Moscow: Izdatel'stvo MGU.

Rusakova, Marina V. 2009. *Realizacija grammatičeskix javlenij russkogo jazyka v reči i v rečevoj dejatel'nosti* [*Realisation of grammatical phenomena of Russian in the speech production*]. Unpublished habilitation. Saint Petersburg: Saint Petersburg State University.

Rusakova, Marina V. 2013. *Èlementy antropocentričeskoj grammatiki russkogo jazyka* [*Elements of anthropocentric grammar of Russian*]. Moscow: Jazyki slavjanskix kul'tur.

Rusakova, Marina V. & Aleksandr Ju. Rusakov. 2002. Russkie diminutivy: sočetaemost', funkcionirovanie, semantika: k postanovke problemy [Russian diminutives: Their co-occurrence, functions, and semantics: Formulation of the problem]. In *Materialy konferencii, posvjaščennoj 90-letiju so dnja roždenija A.V. Desnickoj* [Proceedings of the conference dedicated to the 90th anniversary of A.V. Desnickaja], 267–275. Saint Petersburg.

Rūķe-Draviņa, Velta. 1959. *Diminutive im Lettischen*. Lund: Håkan Ohlsoons Boktryckeri.

Savickienė, Ineta. 2003. *The acquisition of Lithuanian noun morphology*. Wien: Verlag der Österreichischen Akademie der Wissenschaften.

Savickienė, Ineta. 2005. Morfopragmatika: deminutyvų vartojimas dabartinėje lietuvių kalboje [Morphopragmatics: The use of diminutives in modern Lithuanian]. *Kalbotyra* 54(1): 91–100.

Savickienė, Ineta. 2007. Form and meaning of diminutives in Lithuanian child language. In Ineta Savickienė & Wolfgang U. Dressler (eds.) *The acquisition of diminutives: A cross-linguistic perspective*, 13–41. Amsterdam, Philadelphia: John Benjamins.

Savickienė, Ineta & Violeta Kalėdaitė. 2007. The role of child's gender in language acquisition. *Estonian Papers in Applied Linguistics* 3: 285–299.

Savickienė, Ineta & Wolfgang Dressler (eds.). 2007. *The acquisition of diminutives. A cross-linguistic perspective*. Amsterdam, Philadelphia: John Benjamins.

Savickienė, Ineta, Asta Kazlauskienė, & Laura Kamandulytė. 2004. Naujas požiūris į lietuvių kalbos linksniavimo tipus pagal natūraliosios morfologijos teoriją [New approach to Lithuanian inflectional classes according to the theory of Natural Morphology]. *Acta Linguistica Lituanica* 50: 79–98.

Savickienė, Ineta, Kempe Vera & Patricia J. Brooks. 2009. Acquisition of Gender Agreement in Lithuanian: Exploring the Effect of Diminutive Usage in an Elicited Production Task. *Journal of Child Language* 36: 477–494.

Sifianou, Maria. 1992. The use of diminutives in expressing politeness: Modern Greek versus English. *Journal of Pragmatics* 17: 155–173.

Stephany, Ursula. 1997. Diminutives in early Greek. In Wolfgang U. Dressler (ed.). *Studies in Pre- and Protomorphology*, 145–156. Vienna: Österreichische Akademie der Wissenschaften.

Švedova, Natalia Ju. (ed.). 1980. *Russkaja grammatika* [Russian Grammar], V.1. Moscow: Nauka.

Tannen, Deborah. 1986. *That's not what I meant!* New York: Ballantines Books.

Trask, Robert Lawrence. 1995. *A dictionary of grammatical terms in linguistics*. London, New York: Routledge.

Urbutis, Vincas. 1978. *Žodžių darybos teorija* [The theory of word formation]. Vilnius: Mokslas.

Verschueren, Jef. 1987. *Pragmatics as a theory of linguistic adaptation*. IPrA Working Document, 1. Antwerp: International Pragmatics Association.

Vicentini, Alessandra. 2003. The economy principle in language. *Mots, Palabras, Words* 3: 37–57. http://www.ledonline.it/mpw/allegati/mpw0303vicentini.pdf.

Vinogradov, Victor V. 1947. *Russkij jazyk. Grammatičeskoe učenie o slove* [Russian language. The grammatical study of the word]. Moscow, Leningrad: Učpedgiz.

Xanthos, Aris, Sabine Laaha, Steven Gillis, Ursula Stephany, Ayhan Aksu-Koç, Anastasia Christofidou, Natalia Gagarina, Gordana Hrzica, Nihan Ketrez, Marianne Kilani-Schoch, Katharina Korecky-Kröll, Melita Kovačević, Klaus Laalo, Marian Palmović, Barbara Pfeiler, Maria D. Voeikova, & Wolfgang U. Dressler. 2011. On the role of morphological richness in the early development of noun and verb inflection. *First Language* 31: 461–479. http://fla.sagepub.com/email?gca=spfla;31/4/461&current-view-path=/content/31/4/461.full.pdf+html.

Daiki Horiguchi
5 Latvian attenuative *pa*-verbs in comparison with diminutives

1 Introduction

Referring to denotative and evaluative aspects (*denotativnyj i modusnyj aspekty*) of certain Russian *po*-verbs with attenuative meaning, Karavanov (2006: 107) makes a brief and slight allusion to a possibility of comparing them with the corresponding two aspects of diminutive nominals. Analyzing the choice of attenuative *po*-verbs from the point of view of the communication act, Mustajoki and Pussinen (2008: 265–266, 273) observe an expansion of Russian *po*-verbs and regard the *po*-verbs as "functional and propositional passwords (*slovoparoli*)", which reflect the speaker's attitude to action and ensure the act of communication more effectively.

Despite the fact that Russian and Latvian are two different languages with different systems of verbal aspect,[1] they have similar prefixes – *po*- and *pa*-, respectively – both regarded as aspectual formants mostly expressing delimitative and attenuative *Aktionsarten*. Both languages possess also diminutive forms in the nominal domain.

In this chapter, I further examine the possibility of comparing Latvian attenuative *pa*-verbs like **palasīt** 'to read a little' with diminutives and to shed light on a subjective side of attenuative *pa*-verbs, that is, the speaker's subjective attitude to the action.

The structure of this chapter is as follows. In Section 2, I will give an overview of the diminutives in Latvian and their objective and subjective meanings. Then, in Section 3, I will look at the Latvian verbal aspect in general and in particular at aspectual meanings of "smallness of action" – delimitative and attenuative – expressed by the prefix *pa*-. Based on a parallel between diminutives and

---

[1] In this chapter, by "verbal aspect", I broadly understand all aspectually relevant meanings including perfective and imperfective, which, especially in Slavic linguistics, are often regarded as grammatical aspect, and other meanings such as iterative, inchoative, attenuative, and so forth, usually characterized as lexical aspect (*Aktionsarten*) in respect to grammatical aspect. A strict distinction of grammatical and lexical aspect in Latvian is problematic, as it is true for the distinction of grammatical and lexical categories in general (Dahl 1985: 26–27), and it is not the aim of this research (see Sections 2.1 and 2.2 of this chapter).

attenuative *pa*-verbs drawn in the previous sections, Section 4 is dedicated to the analysis of attenuative *pa*-verbs.

As the corpus for my analysis, I used the *Laikrakstu bibliotēka* 'Newspaper Library' provided by Lursoft (http://news.lv), Google (http://www.google.lv), and other periodicals and radio programs. As to the *Newspaper Library*, although it is not a linguistic corpus per se, it can be used as a tool for analyzing the language of mass media with a word searching system. It provides articles from more than 60 Latvian newspapers and journals dating from the last 15–20 years. For this chapter, I intentionally use examples where base verbs and *pa*-verbs are used in the same text or utterance to elucidate the semantic relation of *pa*-verbs with their base verbs, and thus I show how a speaker intentionally or unintentionally uses *pa*-verbs in contrast to base verbs.

2 The combination of objectivity and subjectivity in diminutives

2.1 Diminutives in Latvian

It has been recognized throughout a wide range of languages that the semantics of diminutives has two complicatedly related objective and subjective sides. Diminutives designate the smallness of an object, evaluated more or less objectively and denotatively. They also designate the speaker's subjective attitude toward an object. Their semantic and pragmatic elements are as complicated as human emotions, ranging from endearment, affection, intimacy to irony, or disdain. Thus diminutives, along with their counterparts, i.e., augmentatives, have been studied in the framework of morphopragmatics and evaluative morphology (Wierzbicka 1980: 53–60, Scalise 1984: 131, Stump 1993: 18, Tovena 2011: 49–51, see also Dabašinskienė & Voeikova, this volume). Studies of language acquisition have also focused on diminutive morphology, because, diminutives in many languages, due to their pragmatic functions, are the first word-formation models to emerge (Savickienė & Dressler 2007b: 343).

The grammar of contemporary standard Latvian (Bergmane et al. 1959: 112–121) refers to meanings both of real diminution (*reāls pamazinājums*) and emotionally subjective evaluation (*emocionāli subjektīvs vērtējums*) for diminutive endings like *-iņ-š*, *-iņ-a*, and so on. The denotative meaning of diminutives can be objectively defined if we investigate them only from a denotative point of view, that is, related to the real size of objects. Here is an example from the magazine *Mans Mazais* [My Little One]. Baby clothes are objectively of a small size, to be expressed in diminutive forms.

(1) (...) uzadīju   vairāk-us   kombinezon-iņ-us,
       knit:PST.1SG   several-ACC.PL   romper.suits-DIM-ACC.PL
    jac-iņ-as,   biks-īt-es,   cepur-īt-es,   zābac-iņ-us (...).
    jacket-DIM-ACC.PL trousers-DIM-ACC.PL hat-DIM-ACC.PL   boots-DIM-ACC.PL
    'I knitted several romper suits, jackets, trousers, hats, boots.' (MM: Jun/2010)

However, it is also widely known that objective and subjective sides can be combined in a single diminutive. This is true for Latvian (Bergmane et al. 1959: 113, Rūķe-Draviņa 1959). The subjective side of diminutives can be hardly established when they are investigated only from a denotative point of view. In example (1), besides the objective meaning of the real size of the clothes, one can find a certain endearment for the child, because the fact that diminutives are often used in speech addressed to or related to children is difficult to dispute (Nieuwenhuis 1985: 80, Jurafsky 1996: 563, Savickienė & Dressler 2007a: 1, see also Dabašinskienė & Voeikova, this volume).

Here are two examples where base-nouns and diminutives are used in the same utterance. In example (2), the writer uses the word *bizness* 'business', but then adds, in his own considerations, the diminutive form *biznesiņš*. The scale of a just-opened restaurant is far from gigantic and the writer refashions the word in diminutive form. Meanwhile, the business is developing and promising, and the writer manifests his positive evaluation, objectively clarifying the scale of business at the same time. This subjective evaluation is motivated with the positive adjectives that follow. In example (3), there is a diminutive of the base-word *projekts* 'project'. It designates the scale of this project, but according to the context as a whole, the speaker, diminutivizing the word, undervalues the importance of his project, although this undervaluing function is linked to the denotative meaning of scale.

(2) Tas   tad   arī   ir   Mārtiņ-a,   pēc   izglītīb-as
    that:NOM.SG then   too   be:PRS.3   Mārtiņš-GEN   by   education-GEN.SG
    žurnālist-a,   jaun-ais   biznes-s.   Nu,   vai
    journalist-GEN.SG new-NOM.SG.DEF   business-NOM.SG   well   or
    biznes-iņ-š.   Gard-s,   sātīg-s,   un
    business-DIM-NOM.SG tasty-NOM.SG   satisfying-NOM.SG   and
    galven-ais,   savēj-ais.
    main.thing-NOM.SG.DEF   own-NOM.SG.DEF
    'That then is Mārtiņš', a qualified journalist's, new business. Well, or little business. Tasty, satisfying, and, most importantly, his own.' (K: Jul/2010)

(3) "Strādāju   vien-u   labdarīb-as   projekt-u.   (...)
    work:PST.1SG one-ACC.SG charity-GEN.SG project-ACC.SG
    Projekt-iņ-š   ir   projekt-iņ-š,   bet   gribēju   es
    project-DIM-NOM.SG be:PRS.3 project-DIM-NOM.SG but want:PST.1SG I:NOM
    kaut k-o   tād-u,   kas   ir   vis-u   mūž-u."
    something-ACC such-ACC.SG that be:PRS.3 all-ACC.SG lifetime-ACC.SG
    'I worked on a charity project. A little project is a little project, but I wanted something that would be for life.' (LR: 22.10.2009)

2.2 Diminutives in relation to not-diminutivized words

It is often said that it is in relation to the diminutivized object that the objective evaluation of real size and/or emotional subjective attitude is expressed, as in the examples above (*biznesiņš, projektiņš*). In example (1), the subjective attitude is oriented not only to small clothes, but rather to the possessor of the clothes (*kombinezoniņi*). Example (4) shows that the diminutive does not represent the real size of the object, nor the speaker's attitude to the phenomenon named by the diminutivized word. The diminutive form of the base-word *e-pasta adrese* 'e-mail address' is replaceable with the base-noun, and the use of the diminutive is optional.

(4) "Atkal   tur   vajadzīg-a   tikai   e-past-a
    again   there   needed-NOM.SG.F   only   e-mail-GEN.SG
    adres-īt-e   apstiprināšan-ai."
    address-DIM-NOM.SG   confirmation-DAT.SG
    'There again, just an e-mail address is needed for confirmation.'
    (LR:09.02.2010)

Contextually, the speaker is advertising an Internet site and invites listeners to register on it. Does the speaker show any attitude to the e-mail address? It is clear that he is not talking about the smallness or shortness of the e-mail address, not to mention sympathy or disdain for it. Here, the e-mail address is a tool for an action that the speaker wants listeners to perform, that is, to register on the site. Troublesomeness of this procedure is expressed by the adverb *atkal* 'again', but it is neutralized by the diminutive together with the adverb *tikai* 'only'.

Regarding Russian diminutive suffixes as an emotive device, Volek (1987: 149–150) argues that "a specific feature of the diminutive suffix is its ability to express the emotive attitude of the addressor both toward the phenomenon named in the base of the diminutive derivative and toward phenomena not named in it", and in some cases, "the base of the diminutive plays only the role of a mediator of the expression of the emotive attitude toward a certain phenomenon of extralinguistic reality". Her study shows that uses of diminutives are highly dependent on the speaker's attitude to his/her addressee and his/her intention to achieve successful communication. This means that the evaluative meaning of diminutives does not remain encapsulated in the phenomenon named in the diminutives themselves, but can spread over a whole utterance, as in example (4).

This ability of single diminutives to affect the whole utterance complicates linguistic inquiries, and it has led to the necessity for more global and pragmatic studies on and around diminutives. For example, Nieuwenhuis, in his doctoral thesis about typological studies of diminutives in languages around the world, outlines the universal areas of meanings linked with diminutives as follows: hypocoristic, immature, origin or offspring, relatedness, likeness/similarity, collective, female/feminine, reverential (respect) (Nieuwenhuis 1985: 39). Jurafsky (1996: 535–536) similarly summarizes the major senses of the diminutives. He proposes to treat the semantics of diminutives as a radial category, which "consists of a central sense of proptotype [sic] together with conceptual extensions" (Jurafsky 1996: 542). These statements show us how difficult it is to deal with diminutives as such just from a morphological or word-formational point of view, and how important it is to study them from a pragmatic perspective, because the semantics of diminutives depends to a great extent on the context.

2.3 Emotivity and expressivity

Linguistic inquiries of diminutives are also complicated by the fact that they represent emotivity, which is part of the subjective side of language. Linguists have been wondering whether and to what extent emotivity can be investigated in linguistics (Bally 1952, Šaxovskij 2009, 2010). Because if we regard grammar as a system of rules – more or less systematic, central, absolute, objective, denotative, logical, unambiguous, tangible, obligatory, constant – we would have to characterize emotivity as a phenomenon that is more or less unsystematic, marginal, relative, subjective, connotative, illogical, ambiguous, elusive, optional, and momentary.

However, categorizing emotivity in language and emphasizing the importance of emotivity in linguistics, Šaxovskij (2010: 21) states that "emotions represent variants of human passions which penetrate all spheres of human life and reflect themselves on all the levels of language" (my translation), ranging from lexica and morphology to syntax, not to mention phonetics. Many researchers have shown that the studies on diminutives would be impossible without reference to emotivity (Galkina-Fedoruk 1958, Nieuwenhuis 1985, Volek 1987). According to Šaxovskij (2009: 24), emotivity as a linguistic term represents "a semantic property that is eminently characteristic of language to express by the system of its means emotionality as a fact of mentality, social and individual emotions reflected in semantics of linguistic units" (my translation).

Meanwhile, morphemes carrying emotivity have an expressive function, manifesting the speaker's personal, individual, subjective attitude by special linguistic means. As to expressivity of diminutives, Galkina-Fedoruk (1958: 111) states that "expressivity of speech manifests itself most of all in special suffixes – augmentative-diminutive, caressing-pejorative". Therefore, diminutives can be adequately regarded as more or less emotionally non-neutral ("emotivated") linguistic units and their use gives expressivity to utterances and texts.

Before going on to the next section, we should take a look at verbal aspect in relation to emotivity and expressivity. In literature, this relationship has not been directly examined. There seems to exist a certain difficulty on the scientific level to talk about emotivity or expressivity, or respectively, emotive or expressive markedness/unmarkedness in connection with verbal aspect. Especially in Russian, where verbal aspect is a grammatical category, the interests of linguists are related to phenomena that are reduced to the opposition of two features – perfective and imperfective, even if the research is conducted from a pragmatic perspective. Meanwhile, if we shift our scope oriented for emotivity and expressivity to the semantic and derivational category of *Aktionsarten*, we find a lot of morphologically emotivated and thus expressive verbs. The reason for this is that word formation, which has often been a framework of studies on *Aktionsarten*, is a creative process where the speaker employs linguistic means in order to reflect verbally a phenomenon that describes his/her attitude. Further, we see a necessity to examine the comparable objects – diminutives and *pa*-verbs – in relation to emotivity and expressivity as well.

3 Delimitativity and attenuativity as aspectual features

3.1 From diminutivity toward verbal aspect

Speaking about two different categories across two different parts of speech – nouns and verbs – diminutivity and aspect in Latvian represent not grammatical, but rather lexical-semantic categories. This seemingly abrupt transition from diminutive toward aspect and the comparison between the two is based on the fact that diminutives typologically concern not only nouns, but a full range of parts of speech: adjectives, adverbs, numerals, personal pronouns, demonstratives, interrogatives, interjections, and verbs (Nieuwenhuis 1985: 64–73, for Russian, see Ximik 2010: 380).

As to diminutive verbs, besides the diminutive verbs mostly used to address children and lovers, Nieuwenhuis mentions verbs expressing "repetition of an action or repeated interruption" and verbs referring to "a smaller amount than usual or an action which is somehow less important or which involves 'smallness' in its widest sense" (Nieuwenhuis 1985: 70–73). It is indisputable that these two semantic features represent, respectively, *iterativity* (or *multiplicity*) and *attenuativity* often mentioned in aspectological literature.

Rūķe-Draviņa (1959: 27) in her monograph on Latvian diminutives names verbs used in child-directed speech like *stāviņāt* 'to stand' or *nāciņ!* 'come! (imperative)' in contrast to *stāvēt* and *nāc!*

As to iterativity and diminutivity in Latvian verbs, we find iterative verbs with the suffixes *-aļā-*, *-alē-*, *-elē-*, *-uļo-* like *skraidelēt* (from the base verb *skraidīt* 'run around-iter.') or *raudulot* (from the base verb *raudāt* 'cry'), which carry a nuance of pejorative meaning (Soida 2009: 196). Pejorativity is, by the way, one of the meanings often manifested by diminutives. However, in this chapter, I do not focus on iterativity because these suffixes are not as productive as prefixes.

Bergmane et al. (1959) mentions *Aktionsarten* only cursorily as lexical aspect in contrast to grammatical aspect constituted by an aspectual opposition *perfective* vs. *imperfective* like in Slavic languages. In a small description of *Aktionsarten* by Bergmane et al. (1959), we find the term *deminutīvie verbi* 'diminutive verbs' referring only to verbs like **pajokoties** 'to have a little joke' or 'to joke around' (from the base verb *jokot* 'joke') and **pielabot** 'to make small repairs' (from the base verb *labot* 'repair') (Bergmane et al. 1959: 565).

3.2 Verbal aspect in Latvian

Aspectual categories are differently expressed across languages. But it is widely known that "aspects are different ways of viewing the internal temporal constituency of a situation" (Comrie 1976: 3) and, in a slightly different formulation, "aspectual meanings reflect the speaker's 'evaluation' and characteristics of an action named by the verb from the point of view of the action's course and its distribution in time, but without respect to the moment of speech" (Maslov 1978: 8, my translation). The "course of verbal action" is characterized by different aspectual features such as temporal duration, quantity, intensity, iterativity, and so on. The most abstract is the opposition between the perfective and the imperfective, which gives us a sense of situational completeness and situational progression, respectively (Bache 1997: 260). Referring to verbal aspect, even in

Russian, where it is a grammatical category, linguists have characterized it as belonging to "subjective-objective" (Maslov 1978: 6) and "mainly interpretational" (Bondarko 1976: 47–50) categories.

Without committing ourselves as to whether aspectual category in Latvian is a grammatical category, lexical category, "lexico-grammatical category" (Staltmane 1958: 19) or a "typical functional semantic category" (Kalnača 2004: 32), we can state that prefixation plays an important role in the formation of so-called aspectual pairs or just in expressing perfectivity of the action without forming an aspectual pair. In Latvian, prefixes modify the base verb, broadly speaking, spatially, aspectually, and by other lexical meanings. The spatial meaning is the historically original and synchronically basic meaning of the prefixes and it specifies the spatial extent of the situation denoted by the verb. Meanwhile, aspectual meanings can be divided into two subtypes: (i) the "formal" meaning of the prefix perfectivizing a base verb when the spatial meaning of the prefix corresponds to the spatiality most associable with the semantics of the base verb (*rakstīt* – **uz***rakstīt* 'to write', the prefix *uz-* 'on', *lasīt* – **iz***lasīt* 'to read', the prefix *iz-* 'through') and (ii) the quantitative-temporal meaning that forms the *Aktionsarten* category and expresses a quantity and intensity of the action (***pa***runāt* 'to speak for a short while', ***no***runāt* 'to speak for a certain time', ***ie***runāties* 'to start to speak', ***iz***runāties* 'to speak out to one's content', and so on).

An aspectual pair whose components do not differ in lexical meaning is established according to morphological and semantic oppositions. The morphological opposition is defined by the presence of the prefixes. As to the semantic oppositions, the main aspectual feature is process/non-process, or "simultaneity/non-simultaneity" (Holvoet 2001: 150). Contextually, aspectual pairs also serve to generalize/concretize an action and, to a broader extent, realia designated in the sentence (Horiguchi 2010: 142).

In Latvian aspectology, the notion *perfectivity* has not yet been well elaborated because what is generally meant by "perfective verbs" is almost all verbs with aspectualizing prefixes, without considering the necessity of classifying prefixed perfective verbs that have imperfective counterparts. For example, from a point of view of word formation, the aspectual opposition of perfective and imperfective verbs should not be discussed on the same grammatical, semantic, or syntactic level for at least three types of aspectual opposition – the opposition created by so-called *préverbes vides*, i.e., semantically empty preverbs, whose original spatial meaning is still somehow receptible (**uz***rakstīt*/*rakstīt* 'to write', the prefix *uz-* 'on', **sa***vākt*/*vākt* 'to collect', the prefix *sa-* 'together'), the opposition created by the most neutral and productive *préverbe vide no-* (**no***publicēt*/*publicēt* 'to publish'), and finally the opposition created by prefixes with fully fledged spatial meanings (*ieiet*/*iet iekšā* 'to enter') (about the problem of aspectual pairing see Horiguchi 2014: 23).

Broadly speaking, diminutivity and perfectivity share the feature of the speaker's evaluation of a given object or action designated, respectively, by nouns and verbs. If we try to discover similarities between diminutive and aspectual features, our attention is naturally directed to the attenuative and delimitative *Aktionsarten*. In the next subsections, I will review the general characteristics of delimitativity and attenuativity.

3.3 Delimitative and attenuative *Aktionsarten*

Among various aspectual features, we find delimitative and attenuative *Aktionsarten*. Verbs with these aspectual meanings generally do not have imperfective counterparts. By delimitative verbs, we understand verbs denoting durative situations that occur in a short temporal interval. Delimitative verbs are often contrasted with perdurative verbs referring to action in a non-short term. In Latvian, delimitatives have the prefix *pa-*, and perduratives are prefixed mostly by the prefix *no-*, cf. ***pa**sēdēt stundu* 'to sit for an hour' vs. ***no**sēdēt visu dienu* 'to sit for a whole day'. Base verbs of delimitatives and perduratives are usually verbs of activity (*strādāt* 'to work', *runāt* 'to speak' etc.), co-occurring with temporal accusative or temporal adverbs, but not admitting an accusative object. Delimitatives with their semantic counterparts – perduratives – are regarded as perfective verbs according to the morphological criterion (aspectual prefixes) and their semantics (non-simultaneity).

Attenuative verbs denote actions completed to a weak degree or with a weak intensity. Unlike delimitatives accompanied by obvious and objective temporal adverbs, attenuativity is a less concrete notion.

If we try to distinguish these two notions, we might state that while delimitative indicates a certain quantity of action, attenuative rather indicates a certain quality of action. However, the border between these two *Aktionsarten* is conventional: a single *pa*-verb can be regarded as both delimitative and attenuative at the same time. For instance, in example (5), the *pa*-verb is accompanied by a temporal adverb 'for a while', which allows us to regard it as delimitative. But without such an adverb, the same verb can be taken for attenuative too, and the sense of the utterance would not change, because the *pa*-verb already carries information about both short duration and weak intensity of the situation.

(5) – *Ne-baidies   no   novecošan-os?*
      NEG-be.afraid:PRS.2SG of   aging-GEN.SG
      – *Īs-u   brī-tiņ-u   **pa**-baidījos.*
      short-ACC.SG   moment-DIM-ACC.SG *pa*-be.afraid:PST.1SG

'– You're not afraid of aging?
– I was a bit afraid for a little while.' (L: Feb/2010)

From the lexicographic perspective, *pa*-verbs are often defined as a base verb with adverbs *neilgu laiku* 'for a short time', *mazliet* 'a little'. *Neilgu laiku* corresponds to the delimitative, but *mazliet* – to the attenuative meaning. *Mazliet* is a broader and more ambiguous notion than *neilgu laiku* because it may refer both to low intensity and to short duration of the action at the same time.

This shows that an attenuative action may also have a short duration, which is the feature of delimitatives and that attenuativity covers a wider and more complex semantic area than delimitativity. Attenuative verbs, potentially including delimitative verbs, are to be examined for their objective and subjective sides, as we have seen with diminutives.

3.4 The prefix *pa*- and *pa*-verbs

In her treatment of Latvian word formation, Soida (2009: 249) describes the blocks of verbs naming a partly completed action and mentions eight prefixes, the most productive of which is *pa*-. According to *Latviešu literārās valodas vārdnīca* (LLVV), the prefix *pa*- has spatial explications *zem/apakšā* 'under, at the bottom, underneath' and *gar* 'along' and also an aspectual explication "short and non-resultative action of weakened intensity", and after this explication, "action of short duration and also short-term completed action" (LLVV 6/1). Meanwhile, *pa*- can denote fully completed actions, often with a connotation 'to one's content' in such ingestive verbs like **paēst** 'to eat', **padzert** 'to drink', and their causative counterparts **paēdināt** 'to feed', **padzirdināt** 'to water'. Soida includes these *pa*-verbs into a class of verbs naming fully completed actions (Soida 2009: 252).

A high degree of desemantization of spatial meaning allows this prefix to be added to verbs with a vast variety of lexical meanings, including both transitive and intransitive verbs, verbs of state and activity, as well as verbs denoting physical actions. It is only with verbs of motion that the prefix *pa*- shows its spatial meaning. The degree of desemantization of *pa*- and *no*- is particularly apparent when we compare them to other prefixes, which, according to the description of Soida, express a partitive action as well: *aiz*-, *ap*-, *at*-, *ie*-, *pie*-, *uz*- (Soida 2009: 246–250). Generally speaking, all these prefixes often maintain their spatial meanings. Productivity of these prefixes is proven by their ability to combine with borrowed verbs (see Horiguči 2011 for the perfectivizing prefix *no*-).

The delimitative or attenuative prefix *pa*- is prefixed to verbs with a full range of lexical meanings, except verbs of directed motion: verbs of state (**pasēdēt** 'to sit'), verbs of intellectual activity (*padomāt* 'to think', *palasīt grāmatu* 'to read a book'), verbs of physical activity (*paskriet* 'to run (as activity)', *pastrādāt* 'to work'). The prefixation of *pa-* is very productive for verbs of speech – *pajautāt* 'to ask', *pasacīt* 'to say', *padot ziņu* 'to give a message', including verbs with foreign base verbs like *pacitēt* 'to cite', *pakomentēt* 'to comment'. These verbs may function as perfective counterparts of the base verbs as well because it is hard to distinguish formal and delimitative/attenuative meanings (Staltmane 1958: 80). That would especially be true for verbs of speech.

Pa- as a *préverbe vide* is not so productive: *parādīt* 'to show', *paklupt* 'to stumble', *pamosties* 'to wake'. In these verbs, delimitativity and attenuativity are hardly perceptible, and being perfective, the *pa*-verbs denote a concrete and semelfactive action.

An obstacle for the productivity of *pa-* is the fact that, being a highly active word-formation process, Latvian prefixation does not allow a prefix to be added to an already prefixed verb. This restriction is particularly evident in comparison with Russian, where we observe even triple prefixes in a single verb like *po-na-vy-dumat'* 'to invent (accumulative)'. The only exceptions are the cases where the prefix is lexicalized and the base verb is not usually used without a prefix. For example, aspectually neutral prefixed verbs like *palīdzēt* 'to help', *pazīt* 'to know, to recognize', *patikt* 'to please' allow secondary prefixation supposedly to more clearly distinguish perfective and imperfective aspects like *piepalīdzēt* 'to help', *atpazīt* 'to recognize'. By some conservative and normatively oriented native speakers double prefixes have been regarded as "ponderous" (Kuškis 2009: 188, 228).

4 Attenuative *pa*-verbs

4.1 Investigations in the subjectivity of attenuative *pa*-verbs

Before examining the objective and subjective sides of *pa*-verbs, we should remind ourselves of the general aspectual features of *pa*-verbs as perfective verbs. As other perfective verbs, *pa*-verbs cannot designate an action in its continuity or simultaneity to another action. More importantly, although *pa*-verbs usually do not form an aspectual opposition in the strict sense of the term, they specify the action named by the base verb as a short-term or one-time action. In diminutives, the real size of the object sometimes has no importance, and diminutives mainly manifest the subjective attitude of a speaker to the object or, more broadly, to the realia named in the sentence around and through this object. Here questions arise – what is then the subjective side of *pa*-verbs and how does it manifest itself?

The answer is to be sought in the attenuativity of *pa*-verbs. The subjective side of *pa*-verbs is just the same as that of diminutives – a subjective attitude of the speaker toward the action of itself and the realia designated in the sentence. When real short duration of the action becomes less important because of the unmeasurability of the action, this subjective side comes to the foreground, based on an aspectual characterization.

Returning back to Latvian *pa*-verbs, the greater importance of the subjective side of *pa*-verbs is supported by a short comment by Freimane (1993: 158) referring to the prefixes *pa-* and *pie-* which name "an incomplete and short-term action" and "give to a verb a nuance of non-serious attitude", with such examples as **pa**rakstu*rot stāvokli* 'to characterize situation', **pa**turpināt sarunu 'to continue the conversation', **pie**palīdzēt darbā 'to help in work'. Freimane's comment reminds us not only of the constraint against double-prefixed verbs, but also of certain negative features of the subjective evaluation conveyed by diminutives. Most of the following examples show that both objective and subjective sides are combined in a single *pa*-verb.

The "non-serious" attitude manifests itself in the context. Here is a very compact example from an advertisement for help. The *pa*-verb in example (6) can denote working for a while, but what is really implied here is rather a non-serious attitude to work that can be interpreted further as unreadiness for serious work or the feeling of a trial. This subjective attitude is motivated by contrastive base verb and another prefixed verb.

(6) Nevēlam-ās   īpašīb-as: Vēlm-e   nevis   strādāt,   bet
    undesirable-NOM.PL feature-NOM.PL wish-NOM.SG   not   work:INF   but
    pa-strādāt   /piestrādāt.
    -pa-work:INF   earn:INF
    'Undesirable features: the wish not to work, but to work unseriously/ make a bit of money on the side.' (http://www.vakance.lv/rus/open.php?id=21766&SID=wbnugldm – accessed on April 10 2013).

In example (7), the objective side of the action named by the *pa*-verb is indeed an attenuative – 'a little'. And thanks to the adverb *dažreiz* 'sometimes', we see that this action is repeated regularly. It is important to note that the interviewer uses the imperfective base verb *lasīt* 'to read' in order to ask whether the interviewee generally reads negative comments about himself on the Internet, but the latter, not repeating in his response the base verb, uses the *pa*-verb, expressing his own subjective attitude to comments that are not at all pleasant for him.

(7) – Vai   tu   tos   lasi?
        Q   you   they:ACC   read:PRS.2SG

– *Dažreiz* **pa**-*lasu,* *bet* *pats* *nekad* *nek-o*
sometimes pa-read:PRS.1SG but oneself never nothing-ACC
ne-esmu *komentējis.*
NEG-be:PRS.1SG comment:PST.PA.NOM.SG.M
'– Do you read them (negative comments on the Internet)?
– Sometimes I have a bit of a read, but I have never commented anything myself.' (K: Sep/2009)

Next, we have examples from an interview with a married couple. In example (8), the wife is asked about her mutual relation with her husband, while in example (9), the husband is asked about the education of their children. Here we see both base verb *lutināt* 'to spoil' and its *pa*-verb. As there is no temporal accusative, these *pa*-verbs can be interpreted as attenuative. The objective side is to be aspectually formulated as follows – *pa*-verbs as perfective verbs here specify the action as contrasted with the action named by base verb. **Palutinu** in example (8) is a form of the first person and is contrasted to the form of the base verb *lutina*. **Palutina** in example (9) realizes a coordination with another attenuative *pa*-verb – **pažēlo** 'pity'. Emotionally, attenuativity may come from conjugal affection and parental affection toward children.

(8) – *Kur-š* *kur-u* *vairāk* *lutina?*
    who-NOM.SG.M who-ACC.SG more spoil:PRS.3
    – *Liene: Ir* *reiz-es,* *kad* *viņ-š* *mani* *vairāk* **lutina**,
    Liene be:PRS.3 time-NOM.PL when he-NOM I:ACC more spoil:PRS.3
    un *ir* *reiz-es,* *kad* *es* *viņ-u* **pa**-*lutinu.*
    and be:PRS.3 time-NOM.PL when I.NOM he-ACC pa-spoil:PRS.1SG
    '– Which of you spoils the other more?
    – Liene: At times he spoils me more, and there are times when I spoil him.' (NRA: 17.02.2007)

(9) – *(...) vien-s* *sav-as* *atvas-es* *vairāk*
    one-NOM.SG.M own-ACC.PL offspring-ACC.PL more
    audzina, *norādot,* *ko* *drīkst,* *ko*
    bring.up:PRS.3 indicate:IDP what:ACC be.allowed:PRS.3 what:ACC
    ne-drīkst, *bet* *otr-s* *vairāk* **pa**-*žēlo*
    NEG-be.allowed:3 but the.other-NOM.SG.M more pa-pity:PRS.3
    un **pa**-*lutina.* *Kā* *ir* *jūsu* *ģimen-ē?*
    and pa-spoil:PRS.3 how be:PRS.3 your family-LOC.SG
    – *Normunds: Es* *ne-gribē-tu* *teikt,* *ka* *vien-s*
    Normunds I.NOM NEG-want-SBJV say:INF that one-NOM.SG.M

lutina	*vairāk,*	*otr-s*		*mazāk.*	*Bet (...)*	*es*
spoil:PRS.3	more	the.other-NOM.SG.M		less	but	I.NOM
vairāk	***pa**-lutinu.*					
more	*pa*-spoil:PRS.1SG					

'– One brings up his offspring, indicating what is allowed and what is not allowed, but the other pities and spoils more. How is it in your family?
– Normunds: I wouldn't say that one spoils more and the other less. But I spoil more.' (NRA: 17.02.2007)

Prefixation of verbs of foreign origin reflects the word-formation system of verbs with stems of Latvian origin. Here are some examples with base verbs of foreign origin and their *pa*-verbs. In example (10), we can regard the base verb *trenējos* 'I trained' as an imperfective and the *pa*-verb *patrenējos* 'I (*pa*-)trained' as a delimitative accompanied by temporal accusative *trīs dienas* 'three days'. The analysis of the objective side is to be given as follows: These two actions of the same quantity are represented in different aspects and the speaker locates himself in and outside of the process of action. The base verb is coordinated with an aspectually neutral prefixed verb *atpūtos* 'I took a rest', while the perfective *pa*-verb is coordinated with the non-prefixed, but here semantically telic verb *braucu uz turnīru* 'I went to the tournament', and a sequence of two actions is thus represented. In contrast with the same quantity of training expressed by both verbs, the *pa*-verb here shows a difference in quality of training and the speaker's non-serious or casual attitude to his conclusive training before matches. This is an example of the delimitative *pa*-verb combined with attenuativity.

(10) *Man-am treniņdarb-am ne-bija īst-as sistēm-as.*
 my-DAT.SG.M training-DAT.SG NEG-be:PST.3 real-GEN.SG system-GEN.SG
 Trīs dien-as trenējos un tad div-as
 three:ACC.PL day-ACC.PL train:PST.1SG and then two-ACC.PL.F
 dien-as atpūtos ar draug-iem. Tad vēl
 day-ACC.PL take.a.rest:PST.1SG with friend-DAT.PL then more
 *trīs dien-as **pa-trenējos** un braucu*
 three:ACC.PL day-ACC.PL *pa*-train:PST.1SG and go:PST.1SG
 uz turnīr-u. (...) Pēdēj-ās trīs
 to tournament-ACC.SG last-LOC.PL.F three:LOC.PL
 dien-ās es nopietni trenējos un, lūk, rezultāt-s.
 day-LOC.PL I.NOM seriously train:PST.1SG and see result-NOM.SG
 'There was no real system to my training. I trained three days, then I took a rest for two days with my friends. Then I trained three days more and went to the tournament. For the last three days I trained very seriously, and see, there's the result.' (D:28.04.2010)

In examples (11) and (12), the difference between verbs **pa**ironizēt 'to (pa-)ironize' and ironizēt 'to ironize' is not motivated by the real duration of the speech act, but just by the speaker's tone. A subjective attitude to the utterance is intensified by the colloquial word superduper. This example is a case where attenuativity sometimes renders pa-verbs synonymous with their base verbs, differentiated only in the expression of a subjective attitude (saki!/**pa**saki! 'say!', došu/**pa**došu ziņu 'I will let you know' (literally: 'I will give you news'), grūti teikt/**pa**teikt 'it is difficult to say', godīgi teikšu/**pa**teikšu 'I will say honestly').

(11) "Es   ne-izmantoju   kaut kād-as   superduper   lak-as",
     I   NEG-use:PRS.1SG   any.kinds-ACC.PL   superduper   lacquer-ACC.PL
     pa-ironizē   Ann-a.
     pa-ironize:PRS.3   Anna-NOM
     '"I don't use any superduper lacquers", ironizes Anna.'(D.02.02.2009)

(12) "Mēs   esam   tie   kas   taisa
     we.NOM   be:PRS.1PL   those:NOM   who:NOM   make:PRS.3
     skaist-as   bild-es",   **ironizē**   Ann-a.
     beautiful-ACC.PL   picture-ACC.PL   ironize:PRS.3   Anna-NOM
     '"We're the ones who make beautiful pictures", ironizes Anna.'
     (D.02.02.2009)

In example (13), the semantics of arestēt 'to arrest' seems to be not connected with attenuativity even in the presence of the adverb drusciņ 'a bit'. Here the author expresses his subjective attitude to the event, using the pa-verb together with diminutives like lietiņas 'things' and procesiņš 'trial' and an unusual verbal form iešūpāt with the suffix -ā- occasionally derived from iešūpot 'to set in motion'.

(13) (...) prokuror-iem   un   KNABist-iem   derē-tu
           prosecutor-DAT.PL   and   people.in.KNAB-DAT.PL   be.useful-SBJV
     pieķert   arī   daž-as   cit-as   liet-iņ-as
     catch:INF   also   some-ACC.PL   other-ACC.PL   thing-DIM-ACC.PL
     – kaut vai   bijuš-o   kolēģ-i   Šabansk-u
       if only   former-ACC.SG.DEF   colleague-ACC.SG   Šabanska-ACC.SG
     tā   drusc-iņ   **pa-arestēt.**   Un   par   laikrakst-a
     just   a.little.bit-DIM   pa-arrest:INF   and   about   newspaper-GEN.SG
     "Diena"   privatizācij-as   liet-ām   proces-iņ-u
      Diena   privatization-GEN.SG   matter-DAT.PL   trial-DIM-ACC.SG
     iešūpāt.
      set.in.motion:INF
     'Public prosecutors and people in the Corruption Prevention and
     Combating Bureau should catch also some other things – at least to arrest

a little bit former colleague Šabanska. And to set in motion a trial about the privatization of the newspaper "Diena".' (VZŽ: 23.03.2007)

As we know, double prefixation is a rare phenomenon, and as far as we have seen in the *Newspaper Library*, uses of double-prefixed *pa*-verbs are rather occasional and far from frequent: for verbs with the lexicalized prefixes like **pa-pie**-*dalīties* 'to participate' (two articles), **pa-iz**-*mantot* 'to make use of') (two articles), **pa-iz**-*meklēt* 'to investigate' (one article), **pa-iz**-*klaidēties* 'to enjoy oneself' (one article), **pa-no**-*darboties* 'to be engaged' (one article), **pa-aiz**-*mirsties* 'to forget oneself' (one article), **pa-aiz**-*vainoties* 'to take offence (one article), and perfective verbs like **pa-uz**-*būvēt* 'to build' (one article), **pa-no**-*demonstrēt* 'to demonstrate' (one article), **pa-no**-*lemt* 'to decide'(one article), and so on. It is notable that in most of cases, the texts are satirical, often addressed to politicians. *Pa*-verbs are accompanied by other stylistically expressive words, including diminutives.

In example (14), with **pa**piedalīties and **pa**izklaidēties, base verbs have a prefix already lexicalized and the meaning of the verb without the prefix differs (cf. *dalīties* 'to share'). As to *izklaidēties*, its presumable unprefixed base *klaidēties is not used in practice. Short duration of actions is to be found for both *pa*-verbs – participation in meetings between times can be interpreted as short term and there is little time left to enjoy his presidential status before the end of his term. In contrast to the neutral base verb *piedalīties* for serious presidents, the *pa*-verb **pa**piedalīties is addressed to a president who does not execute his duties. It is worth noting that the critical tone of the text is actualized not only by colloquial words such as *funktierēt* 'to think' and *dembelis* 'demob', but also by the relative mood. The relative mood indicates that the information is received by another person and show the speaker's distance to what he has heard.

(14) (...) *nopietn-i   prezident-i   (lūdzu   par   kompliment-u!)*
           serious-NOM.PL president-NOM.PL please   for   compliment-ACC.SG
     *mēdz   **piedalīties**   nopietn-os   pašākum-os,   bet   mūsu*
     tend:PRS.3 participate:INF   serious-LOC.PL   event-LOC.PL   but   our
     gadījum-ā... (...) Prezident-a   aparāt-s   funktierējot,
     case-LOC.SG   president-GEN.SG apparatus-NOM.SG   think:EVID
     ka   Ulmanis   hokejskatīšan-ās   starplaikos   varē-tu
     that   Ulmanis   watching.hockey-GEN.SG   betweentimes   can-SBJV
     arīdzan   kād-ās   valstiski   svarīg-ās   tikšan-ās
     also   some-LOC.PL   nationally   important-LOC.PL   meeting-LOC.PL
     pa-piedalīties. (...) *Lai   **pa-izklaidējas**   pirms   dembeļ-a.*
     pa-participate:INF   let   *pa*-enjoy.oneself:PRS.3 before   demob-GEN.SG

'Serious presidents (please take it for a compliment!) tend to participate in serious events, but in our case... It is said that the presidential administration thinks that in between times watching hockey Ulmanis could also participate in some nationally important meetings. Let him enjoy himself before his demob.' (JA: 13.04.1999)

In example (15), where the author ironizes about the corruption of deputies, we see a contrast between the neutral base verb *izmantot* 'to make use, exploit', included in a paragraph of the Ethics Code for Deputies, and the *pa*-verb **paizmantot** 'to (pa-)make use', used in the description of the deputies who continue to make use of their status. In example (16), the author criticizes a politician for his vocabulary abusing journalists, and he uses a *pa*-verb **papielietot** 'to (*pa*-)use' together with the diminutive of *vārds* 'word'. In example (17), the *pa*-verb intensifies the author's negative attitude toward bureaucrats designated by *puiši* 'boys'.

(15) *Beidzot   oficiāli   tika   atļau-t-a   korumpošan-ās,   un*
      finally   officially   AUX   permit-PST.PP-NOM.SG.F   corruption-NOM.SG   and
      vien-s   no   punkt-iem   skanēja   šādi: «Par
      one-NOM.SG.M   of   paragraph-DAT.PL   sound:PST.3   like.this   As
      pašcieņ-as   trūkum-u   atzīsta-m-a   deputāt-u
      self.respect-GEN.SG   lack-ACC.SG   consider-PRS.PP-NOM.SG.F   deputy-GEN.PL
      pērkamīb-a   un   ļaušan-ās   sevi   izmantot
      corruptibility-NOM.SG   and   allowing-NOM.SG   oneself:ACC   make.use:ITF
      kād-u   savtīg-u   interes-u   nolūk-os.»
      some-ACC.SG   selfish-ACC.SG   interest-GEN.PL   purpose-LOC.PL
      Deputāt-i   strīp-ām   vien   devās   uz   Ētik-as
      deputy-NOM.PL   line-DAT.PL   just   go:PST.3   to   ethics-GEN.SG
      komisij-u,   kur   atzinās,   ka   sirgst   no
      Commission-ACC.SG   where   confess:PST.3 that   ail:PRS.3   from
      pašcieņ-as   trūkum-a,   ļāva   sevi   vēl
      self.respect-GEN.SG   lack-GEN.SG   allow:PST.3   oneself:ACC   more
      *mazliet   **pa-izmantot (...).***
      a.little   *pa*-make.use:INF

'Finally corruption was officially permitted, and one of the paragraphs read as follows: "The corruptibility of deputies and their allowing themselves to be used for the furtherance of selfish interests is to be considered as a lack of self-respect." Lines of deputies went to the Ethics Commission, where they confessed that they are ailing from a lack of self-respect, and allowed themselves to be a little further exploited.' (NRA: 13.10.2003)

(16) *Un   kād-us   tik   Vārd-iņ-us   bijuš-ais*
     and   which-ACC.PL   just   word-DIM-ACC.PL   former-NOM.SG.DEF
     *ķīmiķ-is   **pa-pielietoja!** Brangi!*
     chemist-NOM.SG   *pa*-use:PST.3   jolly.good
     'And oh what kinds of words the former chemist used! Jolly good!'
     (JA: 06.09.1999)

(17) *Un   vēl   atceras,   kad   tie   puiš-i*
     and   still remember:PRS.3   when   that:NOM.PL.M   boy-NOM.PL
     iedomājas   par   taut-as   sīkaj-iem   graš-iem
     fancy:PRS.3   for   people-GEN.SG   small-DAT.PL.M   groat-DAT.PL
     *gaism-as   pil-i   **pa-uzbūvēt**.*
     light-GEN.SG   castle-ACC.SG   *pa*-build:INF
     'And still one remembers when those boys get into their heads the idea of building a Castle of Light with the nation's small coins?' (JA: 24.03.2000)

Thus, formally, by attenuating verbs with the prefix *pa-*, the speaker reflects his/her subjective attitude to the action or a phenomenon related with it. For examples (6)–(13), it is rather the context that actualizes the subjective side of attenuativity, which can remain covert behind the more objective aspectual interpretation. For *pa*-verbs in examples (14)–(17), the subjective attitude is more evident, because *pa*-verbs are highlighted not only by their structure (double prefixation) or semantic oddity (for **paarestēt** lit. 'to arrest a little'), but also other pejorative words used in the text. Even using the intensifier of attenuativity like *mazliet* 'a little', the speaker seems not to attenuate the action, but just to manifest his/her subjective attitude and enhance irony.

In example (18), we see a double-prefixed verb used by a journalist, while example (19) cites the same utterance of the same journalist criticizing politicians in the article quoted in example (18), but here, the prefix *pa-* is omitted (see Horiguči 2011 for similar examples of the 'disappearance' of the perfectivizing prefix *no-*). The subjective side of attenuativity would not change the propositional content of the sentence. This is especially true for double-prefixed verbs with *pa-*, where the prefix can be omitted because of the structural oddity and the subtlety of subjective attitude.

(18) *Jo   reizi   četr-os   gad-os   **pa-apčakarēt**   cilvēk-us*
     because   once   four-LOC.PL   year-LOC.PL   *pa*-fool:INF   man-ACC.PL
     ar   dažād-u   stendzeniek-u   un   Co.
     with   different-GEN.PL   man.like.Stendzenieks-GEN.PL   and   companies

	palīdzīb-u	*viņ-i*	*ir*	*iemanījušies*
	help-ACC.SG	they-NOM	be:PRS.3	contrive:PST.PA.NOM.PL.M
	gluži	*labi.*		
	quite	well		

'Because once every four years with the help of various Stendzenieks-like people and companies they have got the knack of fooling people quite well.' (AP: 01.08.2008)

(19)
	Jo	*reizi*	*četr-os*	*gad-os*	**apčakarēt**	*cilvēk-us*
	because	once	four-LOC.PL	year-LOC.PL	fool:INF	man-ACC.PL
	ar	*dažād-u*	*stendzeniek-u*		*un*	*Co.*
	with	different-GEN.PL	man.like.Stendzenieks-GEN.PL	and		companies
	palīdzīb-u	*viņ-i*	*ir*	*iemanījušies*		
	help-ACC.SG	they-NOM	be:PRS.3	contrive:PST.PA.NOM.PL.M		
	gluži	*labi.*				
	quite	well				

'Because once every four years with the help of various Stendzenieks-like people and companies they have got the knack of fooling people quite well.' (NRA: 02.08.2008)

4.2 Pragmatic uses of *pa*-verbs

As we see, diminutives have been studied with an emphasis on pragmatic and communicative points of view. It is thus worthwhile to investigate the pragmatic uses of *pa*-verbs, too. This communicative feature may be actualized in imperative forms of *pa*-verbs because the use of the imperative itself has highly pragmatic and communicative aspects. Among imperatives, we encounter many more *pa*-verbs than base verbs, if they are aspectual pairs. True, Bergmane et al. (1959) notes only imperatives of base verbs with spatial adverbs, referring to the relation between verbal aspect and imperative, but explains that these imperfective imperatives have "an expressive and categorical connotation and oversee an immediate execution of the action" (Bergmane et al. 1959: 581; my translation).

In the radio program *Kā labāk dzīvot* 'How to Live Better' on *Latvijas Radio* 'Radio of Latvia', we less frequently hear the imperative *stāstiet!* 'please tell' than **pastāstiet** 'please (*pa*-)tell', or **iz**stāstiet 'please give an account', when a presenter asks his/her guest to talk about something. Imperfective imperatives usually request to perform the action denoted by the verb regularly, as in *"Zvaniet un rakstiet mums e-pastu!"*

'Call and write us an e-mail!' But during the talk show itself, the imperative of the base verb serves to urge the speaker to talk. This is backed up by several seconds of pause before the utterance, which a presenter expects his/her guest to produce in example (20). In example (21), the guest started to talk about something that the presenter did not expect. Then the latter corrected the course of their dialog with *nē, nē* 'no, no', before requesting to restart the account immediately.

(20) "... ***stāstiet***,   *jā!*"
    tell:IMP.2PL   yes
    "'(pause) Tell us, come on!'" (LR: 10.12.2008)

(21) "*Nē,   nē,   nu*   ***stāstiet***,   *nu*   *gal-u*   *gal-ā*
    no   no   well tell:IMP.2PL   well   end-GEN.PL   end-LOC.SG
    kaut kād-a   *pieredz-e*,   *nu*   *redziet*,   *nu*
    some-NOM.SG.F   experience-NOM.SG   well   see:IMP.2PL   well
    pa-rakņājiet   *vēl*   *kaut kur*   *papildus.*"
    pa-dig:IMP.2PL   more   somewhere   additionally
    "'No, no, tell us, well, after all some kind of experience, you see, dig around a little bit more.'" (LR: 23.03.2010)

In example (21), the speaker, after urging his guest to talk about the subject of the conversation with *stāstiet*, modifies the tone of his speech with imperative *pa*-verb *parakņājiet*. In contrast to imperfective imperatives, which can sound categorical, the imperative of *pa*-verbs, expressing a single definite action – and that is no doubt the aspectual feature of *pa*-verbs – softens the request. In those cases, *pa*-verbs do not in fact denote a delimitative or attenuative action the requesting person wants the addressee to perform.

Karavanov (2006: 111) points out that in Russian attenuative verbs are sometimes accompanied with intensifying adverbs like *osnovatel'no* 'thoroughly' or *sil'no* 'hard'. The Latvian data show a similar situation.

(22) – *Ko*   *šād-ā*   *situācij-ā*   *darīt*   *sociāl-ajam*
    What   such-LOC.SG   situation-LOC.SG   do:INF   social-DAT.SG.DEF
    dienest-am?
    services-DAT.SG
    – ***Ļoti***,   ***ļoti***   ***pa-domāt***,   *pirms*   *šād-os*   *piedāvājum-os*
    very   very   pa-think:INF   before   such-LOC.PL   offer-LOC.PL
    iesaistīties.
    join:INF
    '– What should the social services do in such a situation?
    – Think very, very hard, before getting involved with these offers.'
    (LV: 27.10.2009)

(23) Šogad   ir   vislabāk – varēšu   **daudz   pa-strādāt**
     this.year be:PRS.3   the.best   can:FUT.1SG a.lot   pa-work:INF
     un   sapelnīt   direktor-am   daudz   naud-as.
     and   earn.a.lot:INF director-DAT.SG   much   money-GEN.SG
     'This year it's the best of all – I'll be able to work a lot and make a lot of money for the director.' (D: 02.09.2000)

In examples (22) and (23), the attenuative semantics of *pa*-verbs seems to be incompatible with the adverbs *ļoti* 'very' and *daudz* 'a lot, much'. In addition, in example (23), the speaker needs to earn a lot and the augmentative semantics is also expressed by a verb with the prefix *sa-*. We actually find lots of examples of *pa*-verbs combined with *pamatīgi* 'thoroughly' or *stipri* 'hard, very'. Let us once more look at the seemingly contradictory example (23) with *daudz*. On the one hand, the *pa*-verb as a perfective verb denotes a single concrete action and, accompanied by *daudz*, the action can be regarded as frequentative. On the other hand, if used in the infinitive form like in both examples (22) and 23, perfective verbs show that the action has not yet started, nor is it in process. In these cases, the *pa*-verb is used to express a pre-initial stage of action. These two interpretations are based on aspectual considerations, that is, concreteness and semelfactivity of perfective verbs. In addition, one could establish a certain subjective attitude that is based on attenuativity and combined with higher degree of intensity, as we will examine emotivity and expressivity in connection with *pa*-verbs.

4.3 Expressivity of the repeated use of *pa*-verbs

Expressivity in language manifests itself at different linguistic levels. Here we will examine this problem from the point of view of *pa*-verbs. What is interesting is the repeated use of *pa*-verbs. Repeated use of prefixed verbs with the same base verb or of prefixed verbs with the same prefix is an issue often discussed in Russian word-formation studies as an expressive means (Blinova 2010: 133, Zemskaja 2009: 167–169, 177–179). Referring to the repeated use of words belonging to the same word-formation type, Zemskaja (2009: 167) states that, "it is used as a means of cohesion and emphasis mainly for the purpose of artistic expressivity" (my translation). Such repetitive use of verbs with the same prefix places verbs on the same semantic level and emphasizes the semantics of the prefix in the sentence. The following examples show that this observation is definitely true for Latvian, too.

Repeated use of two or more *pa*-verbs is encountered quite frequently. In example (24), objectively listening to critics and experiencing bitterness take place in a short period of time. The use of two aspectually perfective *pa*-verbs in a sequence contextually juxtaposes two actions or just connects the aspect of coordinated parts of the sentence. Simultaneously, the speaker, who is an actress, shows the unimportance of accepting criticism by attenuating these actions.

(24) Nu,   ja   ir   kād-s   aizvainojum-s,   rūgtum-s,
     well   if   be:PRS.3   some-NOM.SG.M   offence-NOM.SG   bitterness-NOM.SG
     es   **pa-klausos,**   **pa-raudu**   kaut kur   kakt-iņ-ā,
     I.NOM pa-listen:PRS.1SG   pa-cry:PRS.1SG   somewhere   corner-DIM-LOC.SG
     un –   vis-i   ejam   tālāk.   Tas   man
     and   all-NOM.PL.M   go:PRS.1PL   further   that:NOM.SG.M   me:DAT
     ir   sāpīgi,   bet   laikam   šajā
     be:PRS.1PL   painful   but   probably   this:LOC.SG
     amat-ā   normāli.
     profession-LOC.SG   normal
     'Well, if there is some offence or bitterness, I have a listen, have a cry somewhere in a corner, and – we all move on. It's painful for me, but probably normal in this profession.' (D: 14.08.2010)

Example (25), with three actions named by *pa*-verbs, is from an utterance by a mother about her leisure time with her children. Interestingly, in example (26), we see diminutives of 'books' *grāmatiņas*, which are envisaged to read, glue, and paint together (all are attenuative *pa*-verbs), and the augmentative verb *savest* 'bring in a great quantity' that can be regarded as an intensifier of the expressivity of the utterance.

(25) Ar   maz-ajiem   kopā   **pa-dziedu,**
     with   little.one-DAT.PL.M.DEF   together   pa-sing:PRS.1SG
     pa-dejoju,   **pa-spēlējos.**
     pa-dance:PRS.1SG   pa-play:PRS.1SG
     'I sing, dance, play together with my little ones.' (MM: June/2010)

(26) Kad   atbrauc   pilsēt-as   om-e,   viņ-a
     when   come:PRS.3   city-GEN.SG   granny-NOM.SG   she-NOM
     saved   visād-as   interesant-as   grāmat-iņ-as,
     bring:PRS.3   all.kinds.of-ACC.PL   interesting-ACC.PL   books-DIM-ACC:PL
     k-o   kopā   **pa-lasīt,**   **pa-līmēt,**   **pa-krāsot.**
     which-ACC   together   pa-read:INF   pa-glue:INF   pa-paint:INF
     'When city granny comes over, she brings all kinds of interesting books to read, glue and paint together.' (MM: June/2010)

Example (27) contains five imperatives of *pa*-verbs. The speaker, changing his tone of speech, ironically imitates a person longing for others' attention. Aspectually, the speaker requests to execute a concrete and single action, but the imperatives of *pa*-verbs make the utterance softened so as to attract others' attention and, most importantly, so that the imitated and ironized person gains their sympathy.

(27) *"Psiholoģij-ā   tur   droši vien   dēvē-tu   par uzmanīb-as*
    psychology-LOC.SG   there   supposedly   call:SBJV   as   attention-GEN.SG
    deficīt-a   sindrom-u.   Nu   redziet,   tajā
    deficit-GEN.SG   syndrome-ACC.SG well   see:IMP:2PL   that-LOC.SG
    brīdī,   kad   tu   šitā   izspēlējies,   jā,
    moment-LOC.SG   when   you(SG).NOM   like.this   act.out:PRS.2SG   yes
    tu   patiesībā   ko   saki?
    you(SG).NOM   fact:LOC.SG   what:ACC   say:PRS.2SG
    *«Nu   **pa-žēlo**   mani,   nu   **pa-skaties**,   cik*
    well   pa-pity:IMP.2SG   I:ACC   well   pa-look:IMP.2SG   how
    man   ir   slikti,   atnāc   pa-runāt   ar   mani,
    me:DAT   be:PRS.3   bad   come:IMP.2SG   pa-talk:INF   with   I:ACC
    pa-turi   *man-u   rok-u,   **pa-žēlo**   mani,*
    pa-hold:IMP.2SG   my-ACC.SG hand-ACC.SG   pa-pity:IMP.2SG   I:ACC
    pa-lasi   *man   pasac-iņ-u   priekšā!» Tas*
    pa-read:IMP.2SG   I:DAT   tale-DIM-ACC.SG   ahead   it:NOM.SG.M
    ir   tas,   ka   nu   «Pievērsiet   taču
    be:PRS.3   it:NOM.SG.M   that   well   pay:IMP.2PL   yet
    mums   uzmanīb-u!.
    we:DAT   attention-ACC.SG

'"In psychology it would probably be called attention deficit syndrome. You see, at that moment when you behave like this, what in fact are you saying? «Well comfort me, look how bad it is for me, come here to talk to me, hold my hand, comfort me, read a story to me!» It's like «Pay attention to us, will you!»."' (LR: 29.04.2010)

The expressivity of the repeated use of *pa*-verbs can be studied textually. In example (28), from a local newspaper, we find the feature *"Burts aiz burta"* 'Letter by letter', where all the words start with the same letter. The text titled *"Pirtiņa"* 'Sauna (diminutive)' contains altogether 342 words starting with the letter *p*, including 118 verb forms. Of these 118 verb forms we count 74 forms of *pa*-verbs. Excluding lexicalized *pa*-verbs like *palīdzēt* 'to help', *patikt* 'to please', *pamest* 'to leave', *pateikties* 'to thank', we identify at least 48 attenuative *pa*-verbs. A text with such a feature is already expressive enough, but *pa*-verbs play an important role in creating a global expressivity of the text, and most importantly, attenuative *pa*-verbs account for more than half of all *pa*-verbs. Here is a fragment of the text where in two sentences we count nine *pa*-verbs, which are all identifiable as attenuative.

Repeated use of *pa*-verbs, which are perfective, represents attenuated actions as performed in a sequence. All verbs refer to physical actions and are thus physically attenuated.

(28) **Pa-slaucīja,** **pa-mazgāja,** **pa-berza** pirt-iņ-u,
pa-wipe:PST.3 *pa*-wash:PST.3 *pa*-scrub:PST.3 sauna-DIM-ACC.SG
pa-lasīja pustukš-ā pašbrūvēt-ā
pa-gather:PST.3 half-empty-GEN.SG.DEF home.brewed-GEN.SG.DEF
punš-a plastmas-as pudel-es, **pa-nesa** paklāj-u
toddy-GEN.SG plastic-GEN.SG bottle-ACC.PL *pa*-bring:PST.3 mat-ACC.SG
pirt-iņ-as priekšā, **pa-purināja,** **pa-karināja**
sauna-DIM-GEN.SG front *pa*-shake:PST.3 *pa*-hang:PST.3
pa-žāvēties. Pamatīgi **pa-strādāja.**
pa-dry:INF thoroughly *pa*-work:PST.3
'They wiped, washed, scrubbed the sauna, gathered half-empty plastic-bottles of home-brewed toddy, brought the mat to the front of the sauna, shook it, hung it out to dry. They worked quite hard.' (V: July/2008, http://www.valdgale.lv/docs/773/av ize.7.2008.pdf)

As in example (1), where we see a sequence of diminutives, in examples (24)–(28) attenuativity radiates globally across the whole text and the repeated use of *pa*-verbs make the text especially expressive.

5 Conclusion

Although the parts of speech that the two derivations apply to differ, diminutive nominals and attenuative *pa*-verbs have a common subjective side, and the diminutive suffixes and the attenuative prefix are both regarded as markers of a subjective attitude on the part of the speaker. It should not be so surprising because the aspects themselves, including individual aspectual meanings (*Aktionsarten*), represent the speaker's evaluation of events in their internal structure.

This common feature of "evaluation" unites these two different categories covering two different parts of speech, but it somehow shades the subjective side of this feature in the aspectual domain. While diminutives sometimes show only their subjective side, most attenuative *pa*-verbs keep in some way their objective side backed up by aspectual interpretations, and a few of them are definitely subjective, where the evaluative overtone prevails over the aspectual meaning. Thanks to this subjective side, both diminutives and *pa*-verbs serve as emotive and expressive means in communication.

Naturally, an object is evaluated on the basis of not only its "smallness", but also "largeness". Despite the absence of augmentative nouns in Latvian, a parallel would be similarly drawn between augmentative nouns and aspect. It would broaden the studies on the connection between the verbal aspect and the speaker's subjective evaluation.

Acknowledgments

I am grateful to the editors and reviewers for their valuable comments to the earlier versions of this chapter.

Abbreviations

ACC	accusative	NEG	negation
DAT	dative	NOM	nominative
DEF	definite	PA	active participle
DIM	diminutive	PL	plural
EVID	evidential	PP	passive participle
FUT	future	PRS	present
GEN	genitive	PST	past
IDP	indeclinable participle	Q	question particle
IMP	imperative	SBJV	subjunctive
INF	infinitive	SG	singular
LOC	locative		

Data sources

AP:	Apollo portāls (website)
D:	Diena (newspaper)
JA:	Jaunā Avīze (newspaper)
K:	Klubs (magazine)
LA:	Latvijas Avīze (newspaper)
LR:	Latvijas Radio, daily program Kā labāk dzīvot?
LV:	Latvijas Vēstnesis (newspaper)
L:	Lilita (magazine)
MM:	Mans Mazais (magazine)
NRA:	Neatkarīgā Rīta Avīze (newspaper)

V: Talsu rajona Valdgales pagasta padomes informatīvais izdevums (newspaper)
VZŽ: Vakara Ziņu Žurnāls (magazine)

References

Bache, Carl. 1997. *The study of aspect, tense, and action: Towards a theory of the semantics of grammatical categories.* 2nd revised edition. Frankfurt am Main: Peter Lang.
Bally, Charles. 1952. *Le langage et la vie.* 3rd edition. Genève: Droz.
Bergmane, Anna, Rūdolfs Grabis, Milda Lepika, & Evalds Sokols (eds.). 1959. *Mūsdienu latviešu literārās valodas gramatika I. – fonētika un morfoloģija* [Grammar of contemporary standard Latvian I. – Phonetics and morphology]. Rīga: Latvijas PSR Zinātņu akadēmija.
Blinova, Olga. 2010. *Motivologija i ee aspekty* [Motivology and its aspects]. 3rd edition. Moskva: KRASAND.
Bondarko, Aleksandr. 1976. *Teorija morfologičeskix kategorij* [Theory of morphological categories]. Leningrad: Nauka.
Comrie, Bernard. 1976. *Aspect.* Cambridge: Cambridge University Press.
Dahl, Östen. 1985. *Tense and aspect systems.* Oxford, New York: Basil Blackwell.
Freimane, Inta. 1993. *Valodas kultūra teorētiskā skatījumā* [Culture of language in a theoretical view]. Rīga: Zvaigzne.
Galkina-Fedoruk, Evdokija. 1958. Ob ékspressivnosti i émocional'nosti v jazyke [About expressivity and emotionality in language]. In *Sbornik statej po jazykoznaniju. Prof. Moskovskogo universiteta akademiku V.V. Vinogradovu v den' ego 60-letija* [A collection of linguistic papers presented to Prof. Viktor Vinogradov on the occasion of his 60th birthday], 103–124. Moscow: Moskovskij universitet.
Holvoet, Axel. 2001. *Studies in the Latvian verb.* Kraków: Uniwersytet jagielloński.
Horiguchi, Daiki 2010. Aspectual opposition and facultativity of its expression in Latvian. *Journal of the Institute of Language Research* 15: 131–150. Tokyo: Tokyo University of Foreign Studies. (In Japanese).
Horiguči [=Horiguchi], Daiki. 2011. Perfektīvie citvalodu izcelsmes *no*-verbi plašsaziņas līdzekļos [Perfective *no*-verbs of foreign origin in mass media]. *Vārds un tā pētīšanas aspekti* 15(1), 100–108. Liepāja: Liepājas universitāte.
Horiguchi, Daiki. 2014. Some remarks on Latvian aspect. In Andra Kalnača & Ilze Lokmane (eds.) *Valoda: nozīme un forma* 4 [Language: Meaning and form 4], 22–32. Rīga: Latvijas Universitāte.
Jurafsky, Daniel. 1996. Universal tendencies in the semantics of the diminutive. *Language* 72: 533–578.
Kalnača, Andra. 2004. Darbības vārda veida kategorijas realizācija latviešu valodā [Realization of verbal aspect category in Latvian]. *Linguistica Lettica* 13: 5–34.
Karavanov, Aleksej. 2006. Denotativnyj i modusnyj aspekty semantiki attenuativnosti [Denotative and modal aspects of semantics of attenuativity]. *Vestnik moskovskogo universiteta. Serija 9. Filologija* 4: 104–111.
Kušķis, Jānis. 2009. *Mūsu valoda* II [Our language II]. Rīga: Latvietis.
Maslov, Jurij. 1978. K osnovanijam sopostavitel'noj aspektologii [Prolegomena to comparative ascpectology]. In Jurij Maslov (ed.) *Voprosy sopostavitel'noj aspektologii* [Problems of Comparative Aspectology], 4–43. Leningrad: Leningradskij universitet.

Mustajoki, Arto & Olga Pussinen. 2008. Ob èkspansii glagol'noj pristavki PO v sovremennom russkom jazyke [About the expansion of the verbal prefix PO in contemporary Russian]. *Slavica Helsingiensia* 34: 247–275.
Nieuwenhuis, Paul. 1985. *Diminutives*. University of Edinburgh PhD dissertation.
Rūķe-Draviņa, Velta. 1959. *Diminutive im Lettischen*. Lund: Håker Ohlssons Boktryckeri.
Savickienė, Ineta & Wolfgang Dressler. 2007a. Introduction. In Ineta Savickienė & Wolfgang Dressler (eds.) *The acquisition of diminutives. A cross-linguistic perspective*, 1–12. Amsterdam, Philadelphia: John Benjamins.
Savickienė, Ineta & Wolfgang Dressler. 2007b. Conclusions. In Ineta Savickienė & Wolfgang Dressler (eds.) *The acquisition of diminutives. A cross-linguistic perspective*, 343–349. Amsterdam, Philadelphia: John Benjamins.
Scalise, Sergio. 1984. *Generative morphology*. Dordrecht: Foris.
Soida, Emīlija. 2009. *Vārddarināšana* [Word-formation]. Rīga: Latvijas universitāte.
Staltmane, Velta. 1958. *Verbu veidi mūsdienu latviešu literārajā valodā* [Verbal aspects in contemporary standard Latvian]. Latvijas PSR Zinātņu akadēmijas Valodas un literatūras institūts PhD dissertation.
Stump, Gregory. 1993. How peculiar is evaluative morphology? *Journal of Linguistics* 29(1): 1–36.
Šaxovskij, Viktor. 2009. *Kategorizacija èmocij v leksiko-semantičeskoj sisteme jazyka*. [Categorization of emotions in the lexico-semantic system of language]. 3rd edition. Moskva: LIBROKOM.
Šaxovskij, Viktor. 2010. *Èmocii: dolingvistika, lingvistika, lingvokul'turologija* [Emotions: Prelinguistics, linguistics, linguaculturology]. Moskva: LIBROKOM.
Tovena, Lucia M. 2011 When small is many in the event domain. In Lívia Körtvélyessy & Pavol Stekauer (eds.) *Lexis. 6. Diminutives and augmentatives in the languages of the world*, 41–58. http://lexis.univ-lyon3.fr/IMG/pdf/Lexis_6_-_Tovena.pdf.
Volek, Bronislava. 1987. *Emotive signs in language and semantic functioning of derived nouns in Russian*. Amsterdam, Philadelphia: John Benjamins.
Wierzbicka, Anna. 1980. *Lingua mentalis: The semantics of natural language*. Sydney: Academic Press.
Ximik, Vasilij. 2000. Èkspressivno-ocenočnyj potencial russkogo modifikacionnogo slovoobrazovanija. [Expressive evaluative potencial of Russian modificational word-formation]. In *Novye javlenija v slavjanskom slovoobrazovanii: sistema i funkcionirovanie* [New phenomena in Slavic word-formation: System and function], 376–389. Moscow: Moskovskij universitet.
Zemskaja, Elena. 2009. *Slovoobrazovanie kak dejatel'nost'* [Word-formation as activity]. 4th edition. Moskva: LIBROKOM.

Cori Anderson
6 Non-canonical case patterns in Lithuanian

1 Introduction

In this chapter, I propose that the standard version of case theory in generative/Minimalist syntax (Chomsky 1986, 1995) does not adequately capture the range of case licensing phenomena. Such a view has been advanced by Babby (1986, 1994), as well as more recently by Woolford (2006), Richardson (2008), and Matushansky (2008, 2010). The major shortcoming of the standard theory, which Babby and Woolford in particular address, is that there are only two kinds of case: structural case, which is dependent on the structural position of the noun phrase when case is licensed in the derivation, and inherent case, which is not. Inherent case, I will argue, includes idiosyncratic lexical case, which is dependent on a lexical item, and semantic case, which is linked to a particular theta role and contributes to the semantic interpretation of the sentence.

In Lithuanian, there is evidence for a finer distinction between types of case than just structural and nonstructural, based on instances of internal arguments marked with a morphological case other than accusative. I consider these to be non-canonical case markings, since accusative is the expected morphological case for the object. First, I consider oblique passivization: verbs that use an oblique (genitive, dative, or instrumental) case to mark the object and yet undergo passivization (contra Freidin 1992), resulting in a nominative subject in passive, as in (1). Not all oblique case-marking verbs passivize, but this is evidence that passivization is not a true test for structural or non-structural case. Further evidence comes from passives with subjects apparently derived from adjuncts, as in (2).

(1) a. *Advokat-as   atstovav-o   **darbinink-ui**/*darbinink-ą.*
       lawyer-NOM.SG represent-PST.3 worker-DAT.SG/*ACC.SG
       'The lawyer represented the worker.'

   b. ***Darbinink-as** buvo   advokat-o   atstovau-t-as.*
       worker-NOM.SG AUX.PST.3 lawyer-GEN.SG represented-PST.PP-NOM.SG.M
       'The worker was represented by the lawyer.'

(2) a. *Žvėr-ys   gyven-a   **urv-uose**.*
       animal-NOM.PL inhabit-PRS.3 cave-LOC.PL
       'Animals live in caves.'

b. **Urv-ai** yra žvėri-ų gyven-am-i.
   cave-NOM.PL AUX.PRS.3 animal-GEN.PL inhabit-PRS.PP-NOM.PL.M
   'Caves are lived in by animals.' (Ambrazas 2006: 322)

Next, I turn to object case in purpose infinitival clauses, in which the accusative usually seen with the verb is replaced by dative or genitive, as in (3) and (4). If the main clause verb is a verb of motion, genitive case is licensed on the internal argument of the lower clause. Otherwise, dative case is licensed. In this construction, it is the semantics of the clause that determine the morphological case, rather than structural position or a lexical item.

(3) Padovano-jau vyr-ui patog-ų krėsl-ą
    give-PST.1.SG husband-DAT.SG comfortable-ACC.SG.M chair-ACC.SG
    knyg-ams skaity-ti.
    books-DAT.PL read-INF
    'I gave my husband a comfortable chair to read books in.'

(4) Berniuk-as nuėjo į parduotuv-ę **knyg-os** nupirk-ti.
    boy-NOM.SG go:PST.3 to store-ACC.SG book-GEN.SG buy-INF
    'The boy went to the store to buy a book.'

Finally, I examine case alternations: Certain verbs in Lithuanian allow either accusative or instrumental case on the internal argument. I will argue that this is not only an alternation in morphological case, but in argument structure as well. The difference in case correlates to a difference in interpretation. I will show that accusative is not only a structural case, but associated with prototypical patients, in the sense of Dowty (1991), and that instrumental case is not a lexical requirement of the verb, but contributes to the overall meaning of the phrase. Examples of verbs that participate in this case alternation are shown in (5).

(5) a. Berniuk-ai mėt-ė **akmen-imis/akmen-isį** lang-ą.
       boy-NOM.PL throw-PST.3 stone-INS.PL/ACC.PL in window-ACC.SG
       'The boys threw stones at the window.'

    b. Šuo vizgin-o **uodeg-a/uodeg-ą**.
       dog:NOM.SG wag-PST.3 tail-INS.SG/ACC.SG
       'The dog wagged its tail.'

    c. Apsaugininh-as žvangin-o **rakt-us/rakt-ais**.
       guard-NOM.SG jingle-PST.3 key-ACC.PL/INS.PL
       'The guard jingled the keys.'

d. *Mergait-ė   apsireng-ė   **džins-us/džins-ais**.*
   girl-NOM.SG   dress-PST.3   jeans-ACC.PL/INS.PL
   'The girl put on jeans.'

The examples in (1)–(5) pose a problem for traditional case theory, which has focused more on the licensing of noun phrases than on accounting for the morphological case in which they appear. A similar point is made by Matushansky (2008, 2010) and McFadden (2004) regarding licensing non-structural case. However, in this chapter, I do not address issues of licensing, but rather discuss the relationship between case and event structure. There is a growing body of literature connecting case to aspect (Tenny 1994, Kiparsky 1998 broadly, although see Armoškaitė 2006 for evidence against such an analysis for Lithuanian), suggesting that structural position is not the only relevant factor for case licensing. Additionally, there is an increasing amount of research on the relationship between syntax and event structure (Borer 2005, Ramchand 2008), so examining morphological case marking is proving to be insightful to approaches to argument realization. The purpose of the current article is to show that Lithuanian alone presents several problems for the standard view of case theory.

The organization of the chapter is as follows: In Section 2, I will present a background on case theory, both the standard view as well as alternatives that propose additional types of case, as mentioned above. Next, in Section 3, I will discuss the oblique passive and show that not only structural case positions are available for promotion under passivization, contra Freidin (1992) and Woolford (2006). I will also distinguish between inherent and lexical case on the basis of the distribution of oblique passivization. In Section 4, I will discuss the dative and genitive case in purpose clauses as evidence for semantic case, a type of non-structural case that is predictable from the theta role, yet unlike inherent case, makes a contribution to the interpretation of the sentence. In Section 5, the instrumental/accusative case alternations are presented in detail, with further evidence for semantic case, and showing that event structure influences the morphological case marking of an argument. I conclude with a revised case theory, which follows the spirit of Babby (1986, 1994), in proposing the distinction between three types of non-structural case: lexical, inherent, and semantic case.

2 Case theory

Case theory originated as a means of explaining why certain non-finite clauses allowed overt subjects and others did not (Chomsky 1981: 49, building on ideas from Rouveret & Vergnaud 1980). The first discussions of case[1] in the generative literature were to account for the licensing of NPs, in particular, syntactic structures, which have little to do with morphological case. Early case theory did initially distinguish inherent case from structural case, on the basis of differences in morphological case in languages like German, and "quirky" case subjects in Icelandic. In earlier generative syntax, when deep (D) and surface (S) structures were distinguished, inherent case was licensed at the D structure, by association with a particular theta role or lexical item, and structural case was licensed at the S structure by virtue of the final position of the noun phrase in the syntactic structure. The current Minimalist approach (Chomsky 1995) does not distinguish between the D and the S structures, yet there is still a division between structural and non-structural case, although relatively little attention is paid to how inherent case is licensed.

There is growing evidence that this two-way division misses some of the facts, notably that not all instances of non-structural case are entirely idiosyncratic or are they all linked to a theta role. Three distinct varieties have been identified in the literature (cf. Babby 1986, 1994, Richardson 2008): purely lexical case, inherent case, and semantic case. The first is the unpredictable, "quirky" variety, which must be stipulated in the lexical entry of the word that requires this case. There is little debate whether this type of case is necessary: Many languages with rich morphological case systems do have verbs or prepositions that require a certain case for no apparent semantic or syntactic reason. Whether and how to further categorize the non-structural case seen in natural language is still under debate, but the goal of this chapter is to show that not all non-structural case is a pure lexical requirement of the verb.

In addition to the distinction between structural and non-structural case, case theory attempts to account for the licensing of a particular case, which may have different morphological reflexes cross-linguistically. Assuming that morphological case is related to abstract case features that may appear in the syntax, examining languages like Lithuanian with rich morphological case systems can provide unique insight. While this chapter is primarily descriptive, presenting three puzzles for case theory, I will focus on the distinction between structural and non-structural case and the distinction among semantic (meaningful) case, inherent (theta-related) case, and (purely) lexical case.

---

[1] Aside from Fillmore's (1968) "Case Grammar" which was more related to the interpretation of noun phrases, but still divorced from actual morphological case.

2.1 Structural case

Structural, or grammatical (cf. Holvoet & Semėnienė 2004), case has two primary features: It is licensed by virtue of the structural position of the noun phrase, and it is regular and predictable. Subjects, regardless of their particular theta role, are generally marked nominative, and objects are generally marked with accusative case. This is because these grammatical functions occupy the same syntactic structure in the clause. Subjects are licensed in the specifier of T, and objects in the specifier of *v*, and the case is licensed in these positions.

Other instances of structural case have been suggested in addition to the subject of the clause and object of the verb. Deverbal nouns often occur with genitive case on the object of the verb. In English, this appears as a prepositional phrase with *of* or as the possessive in *'s*.

(6) a. *The Romans destroyed the village.*
 b. *The destruction of the village.*
 c. *The village's destruction.*

The structural relationship between the nominalized verb and the object allows for case to be licensed, but the structure is different than in a verb phrase, and accusative is not licensed. Instead, the preposition *of* is inserted in English, but other languages, such as Russian or Lithuanian, may use a different morphological case for the same structural relationship.

2.2 Non-structural case

Inherent case, unlike structural case, is determined by a particular lexical item or a theta role, rather than a structural position (Chomsky 1986: 193, 1995: 114). For instance, verbs that license a case other than accusative on their direct object are said to license inherent case, such as dative case on the argument of *padėti* 'to help' in Lithuanian. Prepositions can also have an inherent case requirement; assuming that all prepositions have the same structure, this would be the only way to account for the fact that different prepositions require different cases.

While Babby (1986, 1994) was the first to note the flaw in ascribing both the lexical and theta requirements of inherent case to a single type of case, there are also recent proposals for splitting this category of case into two groups. Woolford (2006) argues that there is one type of non-structural case that is unpredictable (in terms of the morphological case that is licensed) and dependent on the particular lexical item and another type that is predictable and associated with a theta role rather than a structural position. Thus, the truly idiosyncratic, unpredictable lexical case, which is seen on dative subjects of Icelandic verbs and non-accusative objects in languages like Russian or Lithuanian, is set apart from the inherent case seen on indirect (goal) objects, which are overwhelmingly (and, Woolford argues, predictably) dative. She concludes that lexical and inherent cases are in complementary distribution, based on theta positions: Lexical case can only occur on internal arguments or themes, and inherent case only on external arguments and (shifted) DP goals.

However, there are some case patterns that still are not captured by inherent or lexical case. Babby (1986) argued for "semantic case", given that these usages of case contribute to the overall meaning of the sentence. There are two types of semantic case that Babby identifies: semantic case that can alternate with a structural case, and adverbial case, found on bare noun phrase adverbials. The first group includes such alternations as partitive genitive, where the partitive meaning comes exclusively from the use of genitive in place of the accusative, as in (7).

(7) a. *J-is   upirk-o   **duon-os**.*
       he-NOM.SG buy-PST.3   bread-GEN.SG
       'He bought some bread.'

   b. *J-is   nupirk-o   **duon-ą**.*
       he-NOM.SG buy-PST.3   bread-ACC.SG
       'He bought (the) bread.'

Both cases are licensed in the same structural position,[2] and presumably receive the same theta role, but the choice of accusative or genitive changes the interpretation of the sentence. Other languages have case alternations based on a semantic feature of a noun, such as animacy or definiteness. This is also known as differential object marking (see Aissen 2003 for an overview of this phenomenon).

The second type of semantic case I call "adverbial" because it is commonly seen in bare-NP adverbials, as in the following examples.

Russian
(8) *Cel-ymi   dnj-ami   my   exa-l-i   **les-om**.*
    whole-INS.PL   day-INS.PL   we:NOM travel-PST-PL forest-INS.SG
    'For entire days we travelled through the forest.' (Babby 1994:647)

Lithuanian
(9) a. *Nupirk-au   biliet-us   **pirmadien-į**.*
       buy-PST.1SG   tickets-ACC.PL Monday-ACC.SG
       'I bought tickets on Monday.'

---

2 An alternative analysis of the partitive genitive in Russian, and presumably also in Lithuanian, is that there is a null quantifier in the structure that gives both the genitive case and the quantificational interpretation.

b. *Nupirk-au biliet-us   kreditin-e   kortel-e.*
   buy-PST.1SG tickets-ACC.PL credit(ADJ)-INS.SG.F card-INS.SG
   'I bought tickets with a credit card.'

In (8) and (9), there is a strong connection between the morphological case and the interpretation of the adjunct noun phrase. Unlike lexical case, this meaning is predictable, and like inherent case, there is an association with a theta role. But the association cannot be one to one: Instrumental case, for example, can be associated with many different meanings (Wierzbicka 1980 identifies seventeen in Russian), and while there may be some overlap, there is unlikely one theta role that can cover all of these meanings. I take semantic case to be distinct from inherent in its contribution to the overall semantic interpretation of the sentence.

A final, compelling reason for distinguishing between non-structural cases comes from the correlation between case and event structure. Finnish provides the clearest example. Accusative is licensed only on direct objects in bounded events, when the object is a measurer of the event (Tenny 1994). However, partitive case is licensed in unbounded events. Thus, a difference in event structure shows up only on the noun phrase, rather than on the verb, as shown in (10).

Finnish
(10) a. *Ammu-i-n   karhu-a   / kah-ta   karhu-a   / karhu-j-a.*
        shoot-PST-1SG bear-PART / two-PART bear-PART / bear-PL-PART
        'I shot at the (a) bear / at (the) two bears / at (the) bears.'

   b. *Ammu-i-n   karhu-n   / kaksi   karhu-a   / karhu-t.*
      shoot-PST-1SG bear-ACC / two-ACC bear-PART / bear-PL.ACC
      'I shot the (a) bear / two bears / the bears.' (Kiparsky 1998:267)

Richardson (2008) shows that structural case is connected to telicity in the Slavic languages. However, Armoškaitė (2006) shows that case and telicity are separate in Lithuanian. This type of case licensing, which depends on a difference in event structure, should be considered semantic, since it does contribute to the meaning of the sentence, even if it is licensed based on its structural position.

In the rest of this chapter, I will present evidence against the traditional two-way distinction between structural and non-structural case on the basis of data from Lithuanian. With more types of case than in the standard view of the theory, the non-canonical case patterns we see in Lithuanian will seem less exceptional and fall out from the revisions proposed to case theory. I will show that in many instances, the morphological case contributes to the meaning of the sentence, and affects various aspects of the verb: the ability to passivize, the word order, and the event structure.

3 Oblique passivization[3]

There are two[4] primary passive participles in Lithuanian: present passive and past passive. An example of a typical passive, with a verb that licenses accusative on the direct object, is shown in (11), in both the present and past passive. Both of these participles are compatible with the past tense auxiliary. The *by*-phrase in Lithuanian is represented by a genitive noun phrase, which can occur before or after the participle. Geniušienė (2006) gives a thorough overview of the Lithuanian passive.

(11) a. *Jon-as   stat-ė   **nam-ą**.*
       John-NOM.SG build-PST.3 house-ACC.SG
       'John was building/built the house.'

   b. ***Nam-as**   buvo   Jon-o   stat-om-as.*
      house-NOM.SG AUX.PST.3 John-GEN.SG build-PRS.PP-NOM.SG.M
      'The house was being built by John.'

   c. ***Nam-as**   buvo   Jon-o   staty-t-as.*
      house-NOM.SG AUX.PST.3 John-GEN.SG build-PST.PP-NOM.SG.M
      'The house was built by John.'

There are several verbs in Lithuanian that take genitive and dative internal arguments that can passivize like accusative-licensing verbs (Ambrazas 2006: 278–279, contra Freidin 1992, Woolford 2006) in (12) and (13). Although the object is marked with an "oblique" case (i.e., dative, genitive) in the active (a) sentences, the passive sentences show nominative case subjects, like the passive of accusative-case verbs. I refer to this phenomenon as oblique passivization. However, this is more felicitous with the present passive participle, shown in the (b) sentences, than with the past passive participle, the (c) sentences.

(12) a. *Jon-as   atstovav-o/vadovav-o   **komand-ai**.*
       John-NOM.SG represent-PST.3/manage-PST.3 team-DAT.SG
       'John represented/managed the team.'

---

[3] Thanks to Kristina Lenartaitė for very helpful data and grammaticality judgments in this section. Unless otherwise indicated, the data and judgments are from her.
[4] Reference grammars include a future passive participle, but this form is "exceedingly rare" (Björn Wiemer, p.c.).

b. **Komand-a** buvo Jon-o atstovau-jam-a/vadovau-jam-a.
team-NOM.SG AUX.PST.3 John-GEN.SG represent/manage-PRS.
PP-NOM.SG.F
'The team was (being) represented/managed by John.'

c. ?**Komand-a** buvo Jon-o atstovau-t-a/vadovau-t-a.
team-NOM.SG AUX.PST.3 John-GEN.SG represent/manage-PST.
PP-NOM.SG.F
'The team was repesented by John.'

(13) a. *Policij-a ieško-jo* **nusikaltėli-ų/vaik-ų**.
police-NOM.SG search-PST.3 criminal-GEN.PL/child-GEN.PL
'The police looked for the criminals/children.'

b. **Nusikaltėli-ai/vaik-ai** buvo ieško-m-i
criminals-NOM.PL/child-NOM.PL AUX.PST.3 search-PRS.PP-NOM.PL.M
policij-os.
police-GEN.SG
'Criminals/children were looked for by the police.'

c. ??**Nusikaltėli-ai/vaik-ai** buvo ieško-t-i
criminal-NOM.PL/child-NOM.PL AUX.PST.3 search-PST.PP-NOM.PL.M
policij-os.
police-GEN.SG
'Criminals/children were looked for by police.'

The fact that the present passive is more acceptable than the past passive could have to do with the fact that these verbs are atelic.[5] It is also important to note the distinction between true verbal passives and adjectival passives. Emonds (2006) distinguishes between true verbal passives, with an activity sense, and adjectival passives, indicating a resultant state. Similarly, Geniušienė (1974) discusses the types of passive in Lithuanian: actional, or 'real' passive, with the present passive participle and statal or resultative passive, which occurs with the past passive participle. Thus, the oblique passives in (12) and (13) are not entirely equivalent to the canonical passive, found in verbs that license accusative case, as shown in (11). This could be related to a difference in tense or aspect, the latter of which has been shown to play a role in case licensing (cf. conative alternations in Finnish by Kiparsky 1998; also discussed in Richardson 2008 for Russian).

---

[5] In Lithuanian, aspect is a semantic property of the verb, rather than a grammatical category, as in Slavic.

While it is not uncommon outside of Lithuanian for verbs that do not license accusative case to passivize, it is often the case that the promoted NP remains marked with the same case, as in the Icelandic example in the following.

Icelandic

(14) a. *Skipstjórinn sökkti **skipinu**.*
captain:DEF.NOM.SG sank.PST.3.SG ship:DEF.DAT.SG
'The captain sank the ship.'

b. ***Skipinu** var sökkt af skipstjóranum.*
ship:DEF.DAT.SG be.PST.3SG sunk.PP by captain:DEF.DAT.SG
'The ship was sunk by the captain.' (Zaenen & Maling 1990, quoted after Svenonius 2006)

The phenomenon of oblique passivization in Lithuanian is surprising, given the claims that passivization is a test for structural case. It is claimed (Freidin 1994, Woolford 2006) that only verbs that license structural accusative case should be able to form the passive with an agreeing nominative subject. However, the data above from Lithuanian and similar data from Russian (Fowler 1996) contradict these claims.

A key part of understanding the case-theory implications of oblique passivization comes from the fact that not all oblique-case verbs in Lithuanian (or Russian) do passivize. I propose that passivization can still be used as a diagnostic for distinguishing between types of case, but not for diagnosing structural vs. non-structural case. I will discuss better diagnostics for structural case, followed by a discussion of the differences between the passivizing and the non-passivizing oblique-case verbs.[6]

3.1 Testing for structural case: Genitive of negation and deverbal nouns

In Lithuanian, accusative case on internal arguments is replaced with genitive case when the verb is negated, as in (15). This is referred to as the genitive of negation and is obligatory in Lithuanian. The genitive of negation does not hold for non-accusative licensing verbs, as in (16).

---

[6] In this chapter, I will not discuss non-agreeing passives, which can be formed from almost any verb, including zero- and one-place predicates, but with a different semantic function, namely evidential mood. For more on these, see Wiemer (2006), Lavine (2006), inter alia.

(15) a. J-is   mėgsta   **al-ų**.
       he-NOM.SG   like:PRS.3   beer-ACC.SG
       'He likes beer.'

  b. J-is   ne-mėgsta   **al-aus**/*al-ų.
     he-NOM.SG NEG-like:PRS.3   beer-GEN.SG/*ACC.SG
     'He doesn't like beer.'

(16) a. J-is   atstovau-ja   **darbinink-ams**.
       he-NOM.SG   represent-PRS.3 worker-DAT.PL
       'He represented the workers.'

  b. J-is   ne-atstovau-ja   **darbinink-ams**/*darbinink-ų.
     he-NOM.SG NEG-represent-PRS.3   workers-DAT.PL/*GEN.PL
     'He didn't represent the workers.'

A strict distinction between structural accusative and other cases licensed by the verb can be established on the basis of genitive of negation. The only possible exception is with genitive case licensed by the verb: It is impossible to test if the case marking is due to the negation or the verb, but this does not affect my analysis greatly.

It should also be noted that the genitive of negation can also, but need not, apply to accusative adverbs of time, as discussed by Holvoet and Judžentis (2004).

(17) a. J-is   musų   firm-oje   išdirb-o   **vien-us**   **met-us**.
       he-NOM.SG our   firm-LOC.SG   worked-PST.3 one-ACC.PL.M   year-ACC.PL
       'He worked a year in our firm.'

  b. J-is   musų   firm-oje   ne-išdirb-o   **vien-ų**
     he-NOM.SG our   firm-LOC.SG   NEG-worked-PST.3   one-GEN.PL
     met-ų   /?vien-us   met-us.
     year-GEN.PL   /?one-ACC.PL.M   year-ACC.PL
     'He didn't work a year in our firm.' (Holvoet & Judžentis 2004: 71)

Certain accusative adverbials seem to function like accusative direct objects, highlighting the complex situation of transitivity in Lithuanian. Similarly, certain unaccusative verbs also allow genitive case marking on the subject.

(18) Pas mus   atvažiav-o   **sveči-ų**.
     at   we:ACC arrive-PST.3 guests-GEN.PL
     'Some guests arrived at our place.' (Holvoet & Judžentis 2004: 64)

A second instance of structural case behaving consistently differently from non-structural case is the case preservation of internal arguments with deverbal nouns. For verbs that license accusative case, the object is expressed in the genitive case under nominalization of the verb. The genitive case-marked noun precedes the noun it is associated with, as in other instances in Lithuanian (e.g., genitive of possession, quality), as in (19).

(19) *laišk-ą/**laišk-o**   rašymas
     *letter-ACC.SG/GEN.SG   writing
     'the writing of letters.'

This instance of genitive case, like the genitive of negation, appears to be structural: It is not associated with any semantic relationship, but is due to the structural relation between the noun and the nominalized verb.

In nominalizations from verbs that license genitive case, it is unclear if the object occurs in genitive due to the verb or the nominalization. The word order is the same as for accusative verbs, perhaps indicating that the case is structural as for accusative verbs.

(20) a. **tams-os**   baimė
        dark-GEN.SG   fear
        'fear of the dark'

   b. *baimė   tams-os
       fear   dark-GEN.SG

Nominalizations from verbs that license an oblique case (other than genitive) differ in two ways from their accusative counterparts. First, they retain the morphological case on the object, and second, the word order is reversed: The object follows the nominalized verb, as in (19).

(21) a. vadovavimas   **darbinink-ams**/*darbininkų
        representing   worker-DAT.PL/*GEN.PL
        'the representing of the workers'

   b. tikėjimas   **ateit-imi**
      belief   future-INS.SG
      'belief in the future'

Babby (1994) identifies instances in which two possible cases being licensed as "case conflicts". According to him, lexical case can override structural case in such conflicts but not vice versa, accounting for the difference in case for numerical expressions in Russian. This account can be extended to the Lithuanian genitive of negation: While it may be an obligatory structural case, licensed by the negation, it cannot override a non-structural case. Similarly, the genitive under nominalization only applies to structural case objects. The word order difference creates a problem, however, because it does not appear that the accusative objects and oblique objects are in the same structural position relative to the deverbal noun they are associated with. One possibility is that all objects are initially in the same position, but the genitive case marking activates movement to the specifier position of the noun phrase, yielding the object-verb word order. Another analysis, suggested by Peter Arkadiev (p.c.) is that the deverbal noun does not contain the *v* head that would normally license Accusative case, triggering the movement to SpecNP for genitive case assignment.

The facts of genitive under negation and under nominalization show that there is a difference in syntactic behavior between verbs that license accusative objects and those that license an oblique case. Because it is genitive case in such constructions that is the defining feature of a structural-case licensing verb, it is unclear how to categorize verbs that license genitive case.

One piece of evidence that genitive on internal arguments is strutural case comes from the fact that this case can be overridden with the distributive preposition *po* (Axel Holvoet, p.c.).

(22) a. *suvalg-ė* **obuol-į**.
   eat-PST.3 apple-ACC.SG
   '(S)he/They ate an apple.'

   b. *suvalg-ė* **po** **obuol-į**.
   eat-PST.3 PREP apple-ACC.SG
   'They ate an apple each.'

(23) a. *Ar* *nor-ite* **obuoli-o?**
   Q want-PRS.2.PL apple-GEN.SG
   'Do you want an apple?'

   b. *Ar* *nor-ite* **po** **obuol-į?**
   Q want-PRS.2.PL PREP apple-GEN.SG
   'Do you want an apple each?'

(24) a. *Atstovav-o* **darbinink-ui**.
   represent-PST.3 worker-DAT.SG
   '(S)he/they represented the worker.'

   b. **Atstovav-o* **po** **darbinink-ą**.
   represent-PST.3 PREP worker-DAT.SG
   'They represented a worker each.'

The examples in (22) and (23) show that accusative and genitive internal arguments have the same behavior when in the scope of *po* 'each', while (24) shows that the lexical dative case cannot be overridden (cf. Babby 1994: 643 for similar data in Russian). Thus, it is unclear if the passivization of verbs that require genitive case marked internal arguments should be considered oblique passivization or not.

3.2 Passivization as a test for objecthood and transitivity

Not all verbs that license non-structural case can equally passivize with a promoted, agreeing subject. The examples in (25)–(28) show oblique passivization of verbs that license dative and instrumental on the internal argument. For some verbs, only the present passive is possible, as in (26b), while for others, neither is acceptable, as shown in (27). Finally, (28) shows that both forms of the participle are acceptable.

(25) a. *Jon-as   pirmininkav-o   **posėdži-ui**.*
       John-NOM.SG   chair-PST.3   meeting-DAT.SG
       'John chaired the meeting.'

   b. ***Posėd-is**   buvo   Jon-o   pirmininkau-jam-as.*
       meeting-NOM.SG   AUX.PST.3   John-GEN.SG   chair-PRS.PP-NOM.SG.M
       'The meeting was (being) chaired by John.'

   c. *??**Posėd-is**   buvo   Jon-o   pirmininkau-t-as.*
       meeting-NOM.SG   AUX.PST.3   John-GEN.SG   chair-PST.PP-NOM.SG.M
       'The meeting was chaired by John.'

(26) a. *Vaik-as   padė-jo   **motin-ai**.*
       child-NOM.SG   help-PST.3   mother-DAT.SG
       'The child helped the mother.'

   b. ***Motin-a**   būdavo/buvo   vaik-o   paded-am-a.*
       mother-NOM.SG   AUX.HAB.3/AUX.PST.3   child-GEN.SG   help-PRS.
                                                               PP-NOM.SG.F
       'The mother usually was/was being helped by the child.'

   c. ***Motin-a**   buvo   vaik-o   padė-t-a.*
       *mother-NOM.SG   AUX.PST.3   child-GEN.SG   help-PST.PP-NOM.SG.F
       Intended: 'The mother was helped by the child.'

(27) a. *Lietuv-a   prekiau-ja   **gintar-u**.*
       Lithuania-NOM.SG   trade-PRS.3   amber-INS.SG
       'Lithuania trades (in) amber.'

b. ***Gintar-as**   *Lietuv-os*   *prekiau-jam-as.*
   amber-NOM.SG Lithuania-GEN.SG trade-PRS.PP-NOM.SG.M
   'Amber is traded by Lithuania.'

(28) a. *Alkohol-is*   *(pa)-kenk-ė*   **kepen-ims.**
   alcohol-NOM.SG (PRF)-harm-PST.3 liver-DAT.PL
   'Alcohol harmed liver.'

b. **Kepen-ys**   *yra/buvo*   *pa-kenk-t-os/kenki-am-os*
   liver-NOM.PL AUX.PRS.3/PST.3 PRF-harm-PST.PP-NOM.PL.F/harm-
                                                               PRS.PP-NOM.PL.F
   alkoholi-o.
   alcohol-GEN.SG
   'The liver was harmed by alcohol.'

Additionally, the animacy of the argument can affect ability of a verb to passivize (Kristina Lenartaitė, p.c.). Note the unacceptability of the passive for the animate argument in (29), as compared with the inanimate argument in (28).

(29) a. *Alkohol-is*   *(pa)-kenk-ė*   **Jon-ui.**
   alcohol-NOM.SG (PRF)-harm-PST.3 John-DAT.SG
   'Alcohol harmed (the) liver.'

b. ***Jon-as**   *yra/buvo*   *pa-kenk-t-as/kenki-am-as*
   Jonas-NOM.SG AUX.PRS.3/PST.3 PRF-harm-PST.PP-NOM.SG.M/harm-
                                                                PRS.PP-NOM.M.SG
   alkoholi-o.
   alcohol-GEN.SG
   Intended: 'John was harmed by alcohol.'

A further issue for oblique passivization is that not only direct internal arguments (which i hear take to include patients and themes) can become subjects under passivization, as discussed by Lenartaitė (2009: 74–75). Noun phrases marked with other theta roles can be appear as agreeing nominative subjects of passive participles, including locations, shown in (2), repeated hear as (30); instruments, shown in (31); and means, shown in (32). These noun phrases, while not direct internal arguments of the verbs, may not be adjuncts. Details of such a distinction are beyond the scope of this chapter.

(30) a. *Žvėr-ys*   *gyven-a*   **urv-uose.**
   animal-NOM.PL live-PRS.3 cave-LOC.PL
   'Animals inhabit caves.'

b. **Urv-ai** yra žvėri-ų gyven-am-i.
cave-NOM.PL AUX.PRS.3 animal-GEN.PL live-PRS.PP-NOM.PL.M
'Caves are inhabited by animals.' (From Ambrazas 2006: 322)

(31) a. Tu valg-ai **šit-uo** **šaukšt-u**.
you(SG):NOM eat:PRS.2SG this-INS.SG.M spoon-INS.SG
'You are eating with this spoon.'

b. **Š-is** **šaukšt-as** tavo valg-om-as.
this-NOM.SG.M spoon-NOM.SG your(SG) eat-PRS.PP-NOM.SG.M
Literally: 'This spoon is being eaten by you.' (Jablonskis [1922] 1997: 132, in Lenartaitė 2009: 75)

(32) a. Žmon-ės **šit-uo** **keli-u** dabar ne-be-važiuo-ja.
people-NOM.PL this-INS.M.SG road-INS.SG now NEG-CNT-drive-PRS.3
'People don't drive this way anymore.'

b. **Šit-as** **keli-as** dabar (žmoni-ų)
this-NOM.SG.M road-NOM.SG now (people-GEN.PL)
ne-be-važiuo-jam-as.
NEG-CNT-drive-PRS.PP-NOM.SG.M
'The road isn't driven by people anymore.' (Jablonskis [1922] 1997: 132, in Lenartaitė 2009: 75)

In addition to the locative and instrumental noun phrases shown above, even an internal argument inside a prepositional phrases can become nominative subjects of passives, as in (33), somewhat like the English pseudo-passive *This bed has been slept in*.

(33) a. J-is atsak-ė **į** **klausim-ą**.
he-NOM.SG answer-PST.3 in question-ACC.SG
'He answered the question.'

b. **Klausim-as** j-o yra/buvo
question-NOM.SG he-GEN.SG AUX.PRS.3/AUX.PST.3
atsaky-t-as.
answer-PST.PP-NOM.SG.M
'The question was answered by him.'

All of these examples of non-canonical passives show that passivization is not a useful test for either structural vs. lexical case, or (internal) argumenthood. This could have to do with the fact that passivization involves two changes to the syntactic structure: The external argument is demoted, and (generally), the internal argument (or some NP, in the case of, e.g., English pseudo-passives) is promoted. For Lithuanian, it appears that the first change is key, while the second is less important. This is evidenced by the existence of (non-agreeing) passive participles from one-place predicates, such as *miegoti* 'to sleep' (see Wiemer 2006 for more on such impersonal passives). Thus, the fact that many different types of non-external arguments/participants can become the agreeing subject of a passive is not entirely unjustifiable. However, there are differences in acceptability between verbs and between the present and the past passive.

At the very least, this is evidence that the traditional distinction between structural and inherent case is not adequate enough to capture the different (morphological) case patterns and voice alternations in Lithuanian. In the next subsection, I will attempt to show how a finer distinction of non-structural case can be useful in interpreting the above data, relying on previous analyses in which arguments marked with different cases can occupy different structural positions.

3.3 Passivization and case theory

In light of new data brought to my attention by Kristina Lenartaitė (p.c.), it appears that there is no clear semantic distinction between the verbs that allow oblique passivization, either present or past, such as *atstovauti* 'to represent', *ieškoti* 'to search for', *kenkti* 'to harm', and those that do not allow oblique passivization, such as *prekiauti* 'to trade in', contra Anderson (2009). However, there is a subtle difference in the acceptability of the past passive. In (26), the past passive participle *padėtas* 'helped:PST.PASS' is completely ungrammatical, while the past passive participles for other verbs are not. In Anderson (2009), I argued that the difference could be based on the fact that some verbs have a semantic motivation for the particular case that is used, while others have a purely lexical case. Dative case is highly associated with recipients and bene/malefactives in Lithuanian, and other languages (cf. Cuervo 2003 for datives in Spanish). Instrumental is associated with the means of performing an action (e.g., *write with a pen*). Thus, the infelicity of the (past) passive with the verbs *padėti* 'to help' and *prekauti* 'to trade in' could be due to the fact that these verbs have inherent case, predictable from the theta role, on the internal argument, rather than either structural or lexical case. Recall that Woolford (2006) proposes a distinction between inherent and lexical on the basis of passivization. While her claim that lexical case-governing verbs cannot undergo passivization is refuted by the data above, there still may be something to her distinction between two types of non-structural case.

Additionally, I claim that the examples with non-internal arguments, as shown in (31)–(33), have semantic case, given the fact that the morphological case in these examples contributes to the overall meaning of the sentence. Note that these are also shown with the present, rather than past, passive participles.

I suggest in Anderson (2013a,b) that the past passive, being more resultative in nature than the present passive, only allows affected arguments to be promoted, and that only lexical case can occur on noun phrases in the internal argument position. This position is in the scope of the past passive participle. Noun phrases that receive inherent or semantic case (both of which involve theta roles), however, occur in a different position, where the present passive participle can have scope. As shown above, the present passive participle is acceptable for more verbs, and the past passive participle is not entirely grammatical for the verbs that seem to lack this semantic connection with the case licensed on the internal argument, e.g., the judgment on (26c).

Thus, the arguments whose case marking is related to their theta role cannot become subjects of past passives as easily as they can in present passives. This would require the non-accusative internal arguments that can be promoted in the past passive to be considered patients. Thus, my earlier claims may still hold true: Verbs that license a case on the internal argument (or adjunct) that is based on the theta role the verb assigns are not patients. However, not all patients are marked with structural case; accusative may be overridden by a strong lexical requirement of the verb.

We can see how this plays out with two verbs that license instrumental on the internal argument, but do not both allow the past passive participle: *prekauti* 'to trade in' and *tikėti* 'to believe in'. The item that is traded can be construed as the means of performing the action of trading, while the thing or person that is believed in is not the means of believing. I conclude that the instrumental case that occurs on the argument with *prekauti* is an instance of semantic case, while *tikėti* has a strong lexical requirement for instrumental case, which is not based on the meaning of instrumental in other contexts. However, the lexical semantics of this verb may preclude it from having the right structure for forming the past passive participle, as not all accusative-assigning verbs form this participle either. The type of event described by the verb, i.e., the state described by *tikėti*, also plays a role in determining the ability of a verb to passivize. This conclusion is still tentative, as there must be established a clear diagnostic for distinguishing between the "statal" and the "actional" passive for Lithuanian, as well as a better understanding of the lexical semantics of more verbs that appear to license purely lexical case.

4 Case in purpose clauses

Another instance of non-canonical case marking is found in the behavior of internal arguments in infinitival purpose clauses, discussed in great detail by

Franks and Lavine (2006) and Arkadiev (2014). Unlike these works, which present analyses for the case and word order, I will focus on the facts relevant to case typology. In these purpose clauses, the structural accusative case that is usually licensed by the verb is apparently overridden by dative or genitive in these non-finite subordinate clauses. Additionally, there is a strong preference for object-verb word order with dative and a weak preference for the same word order with genitive (rather than the default[7] verb-object word order). Genitive case occurs when the main-clause verb is a motion verb; dative occurs elsewhere, as shown in (34)–(35).

(34) **Genitive** (from Ambrazas 2006: 557)
    a. *Išsiunt-ė*   *sūn-ų*   ***daktar-o***   *pakvies-ti.*
       send-PST.3   son-ACC.SG   doctor-GEN.SG   invite-INF
       'He sent his son to get the doctor.'

    b. *Išvažiav-o*   ***keli-o***   *taisy-ti.*
       arrive-PST.3   road-GEN.SG   fix-INF
       'They came to fix the road.'

(35) **Dative** (from Ambrazas 2006: 557)
    a. *Iššov-ė*   ***žmon-ėms***   *pagąsdin-ti.*
       fire-PST.3   people-DAT.PL   scare-INF
       'He fired to scare people.'

    b. *Pastat-ė*   *daržin-ę*   ***šien-ui***   *sukrau-ti.*
       build-PST.3   hayloft-ACC.SG   hay-DAT.SG   keep-INF
       'They built a hayloft to keep hay.'

The genitive and dative case in such purpose clauses is related to the overall interpretation of the sentence, like semantic case found on nominal adverbial expressions. Additionally, it generally occurs with infinitives of verbs that license accusative on their direct objects. The examples below show the ungrammaticality of the dative and genitive in a purpose clause with the verb *rūpintis* 'to take care of', which requires an instrumental argument. The dative or genitive is not possible; as seen elsewhere with "case conflicts" (cf. Babby 1994), lexical case cannot be "overridden". The word order is also important here: OV is possible under certain discourse conditions, such as shift in functional sentence perspective.

---

[7] Lithuanian, as other languages with rich morphological case marking, has relatively free word order, which is largely determined by information structure. The constituents of a sentence occur in the order subject, verb, object in neutral circumstances. Scrambling is permitted for expressing differences in functional sentence perspective (Ambrazas 2006: 691–692).

(36) a. Mes pastat-ėme ligonin-ę [rūpintis **vaik-ais**].
we:NOM build-PST.1.PL hospital-ACC.SG take.care:INF child-INS.PL
'We built a hospital to take care of children.'

b. Mes pastatėme ligoninę [#**vaik-ais** rūpintis].
children-INS.PL take.care:INF

c. Mes pastatėme ligoninę [***vaik-ams** rūpintis].
children-DAT.PL take.care:INF
(Franks & Lavine 2006: 250)

(37) a. Atėj-o [rūpintis **draug-u**].
arrive-PST.3 take.care:INF friend-INS.SG
'He came to take care of his friend.'

b. Atėjo [#**draug-u** rūpintis].
friend-INS.SG take.care:INF

c. Atėjo [***draug-o** rūpintis].
friend-GEN.SG take.care:INF (Franks & Lavine 2006: 255)

As noted in Section 3.1, genitive internal arguments seem to be somewhere between structural and non-structural. Both lexically required and quantificational genitive can be overridden by dative in purpose infinitivals, as demonstrated by Arkadiev (2014).

(38) a. Jie nor-i [išveng-ti **kar-o**].
they:NOM.PL want-PRS.3 avoid-INF war-GEN.SG
'They want to avoid war.'

b. %Jie dė-jo pastang-as [**kar-ui** išveng-ti].
they:NOM.PL put-PST.3 efforts-ACC.PL war-DAT.SG avoid-INF

c. %Jie dė-jo pastang-as [išveng-ti **kar-ui**].
they:NOM.PL put:PST.3 efforts:ACC.PL avoid:INF war:DAT.SG
'They made efforts to avoid war.' (Arkadiev 2014: 61–62)

Dative can also occur on the subject[8] of the infinitival clause if it is interpreted as benefitting from the action described by the main verb (Ambrazas 2006: 557–558).

---

[8] Infinitives may have the subject expressed as a dative argument under other circumstances as well, such as non-finite modal sentences, so I will focus on the object case in these constructions.

(39) a. *Pastūm-ė   kėd-ę   **sveči-ui**   atsisės-ti.*
       move-PST.3 chair-ACC.SG guest-DAT.SG sit.down-INF
       'He moved the chair for the guest to sit down.'

   b. *Iškas-ė   griov-į   **vandeni-ui**   nutekė-ti.*
       dig-PST.3 ditch-ACC.SG water-DAT.SG   flow-INF
       'They dug a ditch for the water to flow away.'

The genitive and dative of purpose are not limited to subordinate clauses but can also occur without an infinitive in the lower clause.

(40) *Išsiunt-ė   sūn-ų   **daktar-o**   (pakvies-ti).*
     sent-PST.3   son-ACC.SG doctor-GEN.SG   invite-INF
     '(He) sent his son {for the doctor / to get the doctor}.' (Ambrazas 2006: 557)

(41) *Parvež-ėm   lent-ų   **nam-ui**   (apmuš-ti).*
     bring-PST.1.PL board-GEN.PL house-DAT.SG   cover-INF
     'We brought some boards {for the house/to cover the house}.' (Ambrazas 2006: 557)

However, the infinitive is not always optional.[9] Compare (35a) with (42).

(42) *Iššov-ė   **žmon-ėms**   *(pagąsdin-ti).*
     fire-PST.3 people-DAT.PL   frighten-INF
     'He fired for people.' (Franks & Lavine 2006: 271)

The dative without the infinitive, as in (41) and (42), is only possible if the action in the main clause is done for the benefit of the people. This seems to indicate the there is a strong association with the dative and the meaning of "for X purpose". Dative case-marked noun phrase can be added in many contexts to indicate a purpose or goal.

(43) *Nusipirk-au   kiaušini-ų   **pyrag-ui**.*
     buy-PST.1.SG   egg-GEN.PL   pie-DAT.SG
     'I bought some eggs for the pie'

(44) *Įvyk-o   vakar-as,   skirt-as   rašytoj-ui.*
     take.place-PST.3 evening-NOM.SG dedicated-NOM.SG.M writer-DAT.SG
     'There was an evening dedicated to the writer'

---

9 The order of the asterisk and parenthesis indicates that the exclusion of the infinitive is ungrammatical.

There is a semantic correlation between a benefactive or recipient theta role and dative case in Lithuanian. For dative noun phrases like those in (43), it appears that the dative noun phrase is an adjunct modifying the first noun: The eggs are for the pie. In (44), the dative is an argument of the adjective *skirtas* 'meant for, dedicated to'. The actual status of such datives as adjuncts or an optional argument is unclear, but does not affect my claims. Likewise, the genitive has a similar meaning: The noun phrase is always interpreted as the goal of the motion in the main clause, even without an infinitive in the lower clause. The default interpretation is "to get". Examples of the genitive without an infinitive are shown in (45) and (46), which were overheard outside a cornerstore in Vilnius.

(45) a. *Išėj-o*   **pien-o.**
        go.out-PST.3   milk-GEN.SG
        'He went out for milk.'

    b. *Išsiunt-ė*   *sūn-ų*   **daktar-o.**
        sent-PST.3   son-ACC.SG   doctor-GEN.SG
        'He sent his son for the doctor.' (Ambrazas 2006: 557)

(46) – *Kur*   *eini?*   – *Al-aus.*
         where   go:PRS.2.SG   beer-GEN.SG
         'Where are you going?' 'For beer.'

The goal of the present work is not to account for the assignment or licensing of case; Franks and Lavine (2006) and Arkadiev (2014) offer two potential analyses. Rather, my goal here is to highlight the problem presented by the case patterns in such constructions in Lithuanian. The main issue for the dative and genitive case in purpose clauses is that the semantics of such clauses allow a case other than (the expected) accusative to be licensed on the direct object. Further evidence that these should be considered semantic case, rather than structural, or inherent, is that the morphological case can affect the semantic interpretation of the sentence. This is also supported by the fact that the case marking is possible without the verb present, particularly with dative. While there are many interesting facts regarding the distribution, summarized in Arkadiev (2014), issues of analysis are beyond the scope of the current work.

The evidence presented by Arkadiev (2014) regarding "case conflicts" in these constructions, e.g., the (in)ability of the dative to override another case, also shows that semantic case "takes precedence" (Richardson 2008: 44) over structural case. While this particular semantic case pattern may be on its way out (Arkadiev 2014 claims that accusative is acceptable, or required for some speakers), the next section features a different semantic case that has various applications in Lithuanian: instrumental, alternating with accusative in a variety of verb classes.

5 Instrumental alternations

The final non-canonical case pattern is the alternation of accusative and instrumental with certain verbs. There are four semantic classes of verbs that license either accusative or instrumental on the internal argument (Ambrazas 2006: 512–513): verbs of throwing, verbs of moving a body part, verbs of making sound, and verbs of dressing/wearing clothing, shown in (47a–d), respectively.

(47) a. *Berniuk-ai mėt-ė* **akmen-is/akmen-imis** *į lang-ą.*
 boy-NOM.PL throw-PST.3 stone-ACC.PL/INS.PL in window-ACC.SG
 'The boys threw stones at the window.'

 b. *On-a trauk-ė* **peči-us/peči-ais.**
 Ona-NOM.SG shrug-PST.3 shoulder-ACC.PL/INS.PL
 'Ona shrugged her shoulders.'

 c. *Apsauginink-as žvang-in-o* **rakt-us/rakt-ais.**
 guard-NOM.SG jingle-CAUS-PST.3 key-ACC.PL/INS.PL
 'The guard jingled the keys.'

 d. *Moter-is avėsi/avėjo* **bat-us/bat-ais.**
 woman-NOM.SG put.on:PST.3/wear:PST.3 shoe-ACC.PL/INS.PL
 'The woman put on/wore shoes.'

For each of the verbal classes, there is a slight difference in meaning associated with the difference in case. Generally, this difference is related to whether the internal argument is interpreted as an (affected) patient or a means of performing the action (Šukys 2006, Anderson 2011, 2013b, c). As argued by Anderson (2011), the accusative is used with these verbs when the internal argument has more features of a prototypical patient in the sense of Dowty (1991). When the internal argument is not a proto-patient, instrumental is licensed. This also corresponds with the claims of Lenartaitė (2010: 204–205) that verbs of throwing and verbs of dressing not only involve a case alternation, but a diathetic (argument structure) alternation: Only the accusative internal object is an argument of the verb, while the instrumental is more of an adjunct.

Because of these differences in meaning and argument structure, based on the morphological case assigned to the internal argument, I propose that the instrumental is an instance of semantic case, rather than lexical case. Furthermore, the accusative case also plays a role in the interpretation of these sentences, accounting for why this structural case is not always replaced by the semantic case, as is the case with infinitival purpose clauses, discussed in Section 4. First, I will review the facts for each of the verbal classes (Sections 5.1–5.4) and then further discuss the implications of this alternation for case theory (Section 5.5).

5.1 Verbs of throwing

Perhaps the smallest class of verbs that allow this alternation are those that refer to throwing an object. The Lithuanian grammar (Ambrazas 2006: 227) claims that accusative occurs with non-reflexive verbs, and instrumental with reflexive ones, as in (48).

(48) a. *mėtyti/svaidyti* **akmen-is**
throw/toss stones-ACC.PL

b. *mėtyti-s/svaidyti-s* **akmen-imis**
throw-REFL/toss-REFL stone-INS.PL

Similar examples are discussed by Geniušienė (1987: 94–97). She describes the difference between (48a) and (48b) as one of prominence: The reflexive verb has a less-prominent internal argument, while the action described by the predicate is promoted in prominence.

However, examples of non-reflexive verbs with instrumental can be found in the Lithuanian online corpus (LKT)[10] and elsewhere on the Internet, with examples in (49). No examples of a reflexive verb with an accusative internal argument could be found.

(49) ...*visi žmonės ėmė mėtyti į mane kas* **kuo** *galėjo:*
...all people took throw in me who what:INS could
purv-u, akmen-imis, smėli-u, šluot-omis.
mud-INS.SG stones-INS.PL sand-INS.SG brooms-INS.PL
'...all the people started throwing at me whatever they could: mud, rocks, sand, brooms.' (Dainius Juozėnas, Faustina Ir Jėzus [Faustina and Jesus], published in "Šiaurės Atėnai" [Northern Athens] 2005-11-19, http://www.culture.lt/satenai/?leid_id=773&kas=straipsnis&st_id=4468)

For some speakers, the difference in meaning is connected with a difference in entailment. For non-reflexive verbs, accusative case is used when the target is

---

[10] Corpus of Lithuanian Language (LKT; http://tekstynas.vdu.lt/).

not hit, or is not likely to be hit. The instrumental case, meanwhile, indicates the target is affected. This fits with Geniušienė's description of the reflexive alternations in (48) (see also Holvoet 1991 for a discussion of similar alternations).

A similar case alternation with verbs of throwing in Russian is discussed by Demjjanow and Strigin (2000). They claim that the difference is due to a "change in perspective", as seen with *spray/load* alternations, in which either of the two internal arguments is eligible for being the proto-patient. However, verbs of throwing have only one internal argument, which can either be the direct or indirect object. The choice of whether the sole argument is direct or indirect depends on the focus of the speaker: The direct internal argument is more prominent and seen as undergoing the action, whereas the indirect internal argument is peripheral.

Based on this difference in meaning for sentences with a target, we can conclude that instrumental case on the internal argument indicates the thrown object is less affected, and the focus is on the target. Accusative case indicates the object is more affected than the target. This difference in meaning is related to the lack of accusative licensing with reflexive verbs of throwing, as in (48b).

While the reflexive verbs do not allow accusative, it is not surprising that instrumental is licensed in such semantic contexts: The internal argument is not affected, nor the focus of the speaker (e.g., the sentence is not about what happens to the object thrown). Meanwhile, there is the semantic context for the accusative, albeit the default one in which the agent is acting upon an entity. While accusative case on internal arguments is generally considered to be licensed solely based on the structural position, in these alternations it is also a marker of patienthood. In Anderson (2011), I put forth an analysis in which the accusative and instrumental are indeed in different structural positions, based on their different status in the argument and event structure. For the present work, the largest issue is how to classify the instrumental case in such verb alternations. As will be demonstrated more fully for the other classes of verbs that have this alternation, the instrumental is an instance of semantic rather than lexical case: The use of instrumental rather than any other "oblique" case is motivated by the general meaning and function of instrumental in Lithuanian, which is to encode an argument as a means for performing an action (cf. Šukys 2005).

5.2 Verbs of moving a body part

Many verbs that describe the movement of a body part can mark the internal argument with either accusative or instrumental case, as shown above in (47b).

As with the verbs of throwing, there is a subtle difference in meaning for the two morphological cases. Accusative case indicates that something is happening to the body part, whereas instrumental case is used to indicate a movement was performed by means of the body part. This can be shown by creating a context in which only one meaning is possible, as in (50).

(50) *Trauky-k* *peči-us/*peči-ais* *iki* *aus-ų.*
 shrug-IMP.2SG shoulder.ACC.PL/*INS.PL to ears-GEN.PL
 'Shrug your shoulders to your ears.'

The addition of a directional resultative prepositional phrase requires accusative case, as the body part is distinctly changing position. This lines up with the claim of Anderson (2011) that accusative case is used with proto-patients; change of state or position is a feature of prototypical patients. This also explains why certain verbs that involve movement of a body part never allow instrumental. The verb *sukryžiuoti* 'to cross' entails a change of position, thus only accusative is permissible on the internal argument.

(51) *On-a* *sukryžiav-o* *koj-as/*koj-omis.*
 Ona-NOM.SG cross-PST.3 leg-ACC.PL/*INS.PL
 'Ona crossed her legs.'

Instrumental case, meanwhile, is possible when the body part is a "true" instrument, e.g., a means of performing the action. Letučij (2007) analyzes similar case alternations in Russian, arguing that with the instrumental case, the body part is construed as an extension of the agent, and thus cannot be interpreted as a proto-patient. This can account for the fact that many of the verbs that bar accusative denote gestures or autonomous physical responses: The agent cannot exert control over the chattering of teeth and the gesture is performed using a body part (or some other object, e.g., *waving with a handkerchief*).

(52) *gūžčio-ti* *peči-ais/*peči-us*
 shrug-INF shoulder-INS.PL/*ACC.PL
 'to shrug one's shoulders'

The verb *gūžčioti* 'to shrug' in (52) can only refer to the movement made to express uncertainty. Meanwhile, *traukyti pečius/pečiais* 'to shrug shoulders:ACC/INS' can refer to this movement, as well as the movement of the shoulders up to the ears, as in some sort of exercises. Thus, it is possible to add to the latter, but not the former, the phrase *iki ausų* 'to one's ears' (as in 51), indicating that the shoulders have changed position without returning to their original state. However, this is only possible with the accusative licensed because the shoulders are interpreted as an affected patient of the action, rather than the means, when marked with accusative case. As I claimed above for verbs of throwing, accusative has a semantic function.

Thus, the event structure of the verb, e.g., the presence of a resultative to indicate a change of state or position, can affect which case appears. Additionally, the choice of instrumental is further motivated for its correlation with the meaning of instrument or means. Unsurprisingly, this is also seen in the next class of verbs: verbs of making sound.

5.3 Verbs of making sound

The third class of verbs that allows the internal argument to either appear with accusative or instrumental case is those describing making a sound. In addition to a case alternation, there is also an argument structure alternation, shown in (53).

(53) a. *Baršk-a*   **ind-ai.**
 rattle-PRS.3   dish-NOM.PL
 'The dishes are rattling.'

     b. *Moter-is*   *baršk-a*   ***ind-ais/*ind-us.***
         woman-NOM.SG   rattle-PRS.3   dish-INS.PL/*ACC.PL
         'The woman rattles the dishes.'

     c. *Moter-is*   *baršk-in-a*   ***ind-us/ind-ais.***
         woman-NOM.SG   rattle-CAUS-PRS.3   dish-ACC.PL/INS.PL
         'The woman rattles the dishes.'

     d. ****Ind-ai***   *baršk-in-a.*
         dish-NOM.PL   rattle-CAUS-PRS.3
         Intended: 'The dishes are rattling.'

There are two verbs with the same root: the unsuffixed, in (53a,b) and the causative, (53c,d). For the unsuffixed verb, the verb can have a sole (nominative) argument representing the source of the sound, as in (53a), or two arguments, with the source of the sound exclusively an instrumental internal argument. The causative verb always has two arguments, and the internal argument (the source of the sound) can be either instrumental or accusative. The focus of this section is the alternation in (53c) (for a more detailed discussion of the argument structure alternation, see Anderson 2013c). As shown in the following, examples of the causative verb with either accusative, as in (54a), or instrumental, as in (54b), can be found.

(54) a. *Poet-as,   barškin-dam-as   **rašomąja mašinėl-e**,   atsak-ė:*
       poet-NOM.SG   rattle-CNV-SG.M   typewriter-INS.SG   answer-PST.3
       - Palauk   minut-ėl-ę.
       wait:IMP.2SG   minute-DIM-ACC.SG
       'The poet, rattling at the typewriter, replied "Wait a minute".' (LKT)

   b. *Mortūnien-ė   liaujasi   barškin-us-i   **ind-us***
       Mortuniene-NOM.SG   stop.PRS.3   rattle-PST.PA-NOM.SG.F   dishes-ACC.PL
       ir   į   lėkšt-es   krov-us-i   kaln-us   mės-os.
       and   to   plates-ACC.PL   load-PST. PA-NOM.SG.F   hill-ACC.PL   meat-GEN.SG
       'Mortuniene stops rattling the dishes and loading mounds of meat onto the plates.' (LKT)

The case alternation with verbs of making sound reflects a similar difference in meaning for each case to that for the verbs of moving a body part: If the internal argument can be conceived of as an affected undergoer of some action, it will be marked accusative, and interpreted as more like a proto-patient. If it can only represent an unaffected source of the sound, only the instrumental is possible, and it will be interpreted as the means for producing the sound.

5.4 Verbs of dressing

The final category of case-alternating verbs is the most complicated, as it has the least semantic difference between the two possible morphological cases. These verbs allow the item of clothing to be expressed either in accusative or instrumental case, as in (5d), repeated here as (55a). A verb of wearing clothing is shown in (55b).

(55) a. *Mergait-ė   apsireng-ė   **džins-us/džins-ais.***
       girl-NOM.SG   dress-PST.3   jeans-ACC.PL/INS.PL
       'The girl put on jeans.'

   b. *Mergait-ė   devė-jo   **džins-us/džins-ais.***
       girl-NOM.SG   wear-PST.3   jeans-ACC.PL/INS.PL
       'The girl wore jeans.'

It may be the case that there is also a diathetic change, with the instrumental noun phrase demoted from being an internal argument, suggested by Kristina Lenartaitė (p.c.). First, I will address the types of verbs that allow for this alternation.

As Table 1 shows, there are two kinds of verbs related to clothing in Lithuanian: Those that denote an act of putting clothes onto the body and those that

Tab. 1: Verbs of dressing

Dressing	Wearing	Translation	Items of clothing
rengtis	devėti	'get dressed/wear'	all clothes
autis	avėti	'put on/wear shoes'	shoes, boots, footwear
gaubtis	gobėti	'wrap on/wear'	wraps, shawls
juostis	juosėti	'girdle/wear a belt'	belts
mautis	mūvėti	'slide on/wear'	gloves, pants, rings
ryštis	ryšėti	'tie on/wear'	scarves, ties
segtis	segėti	'fasten, button/wear'	skirts, broches, buttons
vilktis	vilkėti	'cover, put on/wear'	outerwear, suits, uniforms
–	nešioti	'wear'	all clothes, accessories

denote having clothes on the body. A different verb stem is used for various types of clothing, roughly varying with the type of action required to put it on.

The verbs of dressing are reflexive, shown with the -s reflexive marker on the infinitives in Table 1, but they have non-reflexive counterparts for dressing someone else, shown in (56).

(56) a. *Ras-a   (ap)reng-ė   vaik-ą*
   Rasa-NOM.SG (PRF-)dress-PST.3 child-ACC.SG
   (marškini-ais/*marškini-us).
   shirt-INS.PL/*ACC.PL
   'Rasa dressed the child (in a shirt).'

   b. *Ras-a   (ap)reng-ė   **marškini-us/*marškini-ais***
   Rasa-NOM.SG (PRF-)dress-PST.3 shirt-ACC.PL/*INS.PL
   vaik-ui.
   child-DAT.SG
   'Rasa put the shirt on the child.'

The non-reflexive verbs also allow an alternation, as seen in (56). The item of clothing can be instrumental if the argument denoting the person being dressed is in accusative, as in (56a), or the item of clothing can be accusative if the other argument is dative. The reflexive verbs of dressing appear to allow a similar alternation, given that the reflexive affix in Lithuanian can be interpreted as either accusative or dative; that is, accusative overt arguments are not incompatible with reflexive verbs (see Geniušienė 1987 for a much more detailed discussion of reflexive verbs in Lithuanian).

Argument structure alternations, rather than just case alternations, can occur with the addition of certain prefixes. In some instances the number of arguments a verb can take is augmented when a prefix is added. The reflexive marker in (57) and (58) is benefactive (Geniušienė 1987).

(57) ap-(si-)riš-ti galv-ą **skarel-e/*skarel-ę**
 PRF-(REFL-)tie-INF head-ACC.SG kerchief-INS.SG/*ACC.SG
 'to tie a kerchief around one's head'

(58) su-si-juos-ti keln-es **dirž-u/*dirž-ą**
 PRF-REFL-girdle-INF trousers-ACC.PL belt-INS.SG/*ACC.SG
 'to girdle one's trousers with a belt'

The examples in (57) and (58) show that if a direct object is introduced by the prefix, the accusative is no longer possible on the item of clothing. Only instrumental can be licensed on the item of clothing. If the prefix introduces a prepositional phrase indicating the location, only accusative is licensed on the clothing argument, not instrumental:

(59) už-si-riš-ti ant galv-os **skarel-ę /*skarel-e**
 PRF-REFL-tie:INF on head-GEN.SG kerchief-ACC.SG/*INS.SG
 'to tie a kerchief on one's head'

(60) su-si-juos-ti **juost-ą/*juost-a** ant marškini-ų
 PRF-REFL-put.on-INF belt-ACC.SG/*INS.SG on shirt-GEN.PL
 'to tie a belt on one's shirt'

(61) (į)seg-ti **sag-ę** į suknel-ę
 (PRF-)fasten-INF brooch-ACC.SG in dress-ACC.SG
 'to fasten a brooch to one's dress'

The differences in case for these prefixed verbs are reminiscent of spray/load alternations, in which the two internal arguments can switch positions. One must be the direct object, marked with accusative, and the other is an indirect object, usually occurring in a prepositional phrase or an oblique case, depending on the language. However, this alternation occurs without the presence of a second argument for the unaugmented verbs in Table 1.

Based on the other classes of case-alternating verbs in Lithuanian, it appears that the same trend is followed: Instrumental case, particularly when not obligatory, indicates that the argument is peripheral to the event, and crucially, not as highly affected by the action. Accusative case, meanwhile, indicates that the argument is more central or affected by the event in some way. While the differences are subtle with only one internal argument, it seems that the alternation for verbs of dressing is like a spray/load alternation, but rather than switching prominence relations with another argument, the sole argument can occupy either position, depending on the relation. For the prefixed verbs with two internal arguments, the prominence relations are fixed. For each of the examples in (57)–(61), the accusative argument changes position, or is affected, and the other argument is the new location (when a prepositional phrase), or the instrument by which the action is performed. By analogy, the verbs in this class with only one internal argument undergo a similar argument structure alternation, but only one of the possible arguments is expressed: If the item of clothing is marked with accusative case, it is interpreted as changing position, but if it is marked with instrumental case, it is the means for performing the action.

Thus, all of the accusative-instrumental case alternations have a similar interpretation. Accusative case is marked on an argument that is a prototypical patient, and instrumental case is marked on an instrument, or the means of performing the action. The case alternation is a morphological representation of the difference in event structure and argument structure. In the next section, I outline what implications such case alternations have for case theory.

5.5 Alternations and case theory

Semantic case, as I have discussed above, is associated with the semantic interpretation of a noun phrase or sentence based on the morphological case. The instrumental case that can be licensed by the verbs described in this section is an instance of semantic case: The difference in case results in a difference in interpretation of the sentence based on the relationship between the noun phrase and the rest of the clause. Furthermore, instrumental case is associated with a few specific meanings when it is used as a semantic case (e.g., in adverbial noun phrases, such as *valgyti šaukstu* 'to eat with a spoon:INS'). The interpretation of the instrumental arguments in the examples above is that of a true instrument or a means of performing the action. The choice of case is not based on a particular lexical item (as is true with lexical case), but based on meaning, so it must be a semantic case.

Finally, there is the question as to why not all verbs participate in this alternation. One possible solution is that these verbs are unique in the theta role that they assign to their internal arguments. Parsons (1990) suggests that certain arguments can have two theta roles, such as instrument-theme or agent-theme (p. 81). This, however, means that the case licensing is not solely related to either the theta role or the semantic relationship between the verb and the object, but relies on both. Thus, the case alternation is limited to the specific classes of verbs where both the multiple theta-role assignment occurs, and the difference in prominence is possible.

These accusative-instrumental case alternations reflect the event structure and argument structure: The morphological case is a reflection of the argument's role in the clause and in determining the type of event. As seen with the verbs of moving a body part, for instance, the addition of a directional resultative prepositional phrase eliminates the possibility of an alternation. Similarly, Levin and Rappaport Hovav (1997) discuss resultatives as a test for ergativity and unaccusativity and determining event type. Therefore, the accusative-instrumental alternation may be limited to verbs whose event structure is flexible enough to accommodate these differences in interpretation.

Finally, these case alternations show that a difference in case can reflect a difference in event structure. Here, the morphological case is not necessarily connected to a particular lexical item, although the theta role assigned by the verb may still play an important role. Case is also an important indicator of argument structure alternations, as seen with verbs of dressing in particular.

6 Conclusion

There are many instances of non-canonical morphological case in Lithuanian that appear to violate the tenets of case theory that hold that case must either be based on the structural position or is tied to a particular lexical item or theta role in some way. In this chapter, I explored three constructions with internal arguments marked with a case other than accusative: instrumental-accusative alternations on internal arguments, dative and genitive objects in purpose clauses, as well as the passivization of oblique case-licensing verbs with agreeing passive participles and nominative subjects.

These constructions are exceptional because each instance has elements of structural case and semantic case licensing. I have argued that there are multiple types of non-structural case and that the traditional view of inherent case is too narrow to account for the variety of case licensing found in Lithuanian. Rather, there are three kinds of case in addition to structural: lexical, inherent, and semantic. Lexical case is a strong requirement on a particular verb or preposition and can be overridden in passivization in Lithuanian. Inherent case is, as with the traditional definition, associated with a particular theta role. Following Woolford (2006), dative recipients and goals are examples of inherent case. Semantic case is found when the morphological case contributes significantly to the overall interpretation of the sentence. This sometimes corresponds with a particular theta role that may be assigned instead of the usual patient role for direct objects. By examining a language with rich morphological case like Lithuanian, we can gain a better understanding of how case can interact with other elements in the clause, as well as how case can reflect the argument structure and event structure of a verb.

Acknowledgments

Thanks to Leonard Babby, James Lavine, and Edwin Williams for their useful comments and to the participants of the Contemporary Approaches to Baltic Linguistics conference and the audience at FASL 20 and the Syntax Supper at the CUNY Graduate Center. Thanks also go to the reviewers of a previous version of this article and the editors of this volume for their useful comments. I am also very grateful to the native speakers who helped with the Lithuanian data: Artūras Judžentis, Kristina Lenartaitė, Rolandas Mikulskas, Žydrūnė Mladineo, Elvyra Petrašiūnienė, Giedrius Subačius, Martynas Vasiliauskas, and Virginija Vasiliauskienė.

Abbreviations

1	first person	NEG	negation
2	second person	NOM	nominative
3	third person	PA	active participle
ACC	accusative	PART	partitive
AUX	auxiliary	PP	passive participle
CNT	continuative	PL	plural
CNV	converb	PREP	preposition
DAT	dative	PRS	present
DEF	definite	PRF	(verbal) prefix
F	feminine	PRT	particle
GEN	genitive	PST	past
IMP	imperative	Q	yes-no question marker
INS	instrumental	REFL	reflexive
M	masculine	SG	singular

References

Aissen, Judith. 2003. Differential Object Marking: Iconicity vs. Economy. Natural Language and Linguistic Theory 21(3): 435–483.
Ambrazas, Vytautas (ed.). 2006. *Lithuanian grammar*. Vilnius: Baltos lankos.

Anderson, Cori. 2009. Oblique passivization: Evidence from Lithuanian and Slavic. In *Issledovanija po Slavjanskim Jazykam* [Studies in Slavic Languages] 14: 137–154.
Anderson, Cori. 2011. Case theory and case alternations: Evidence from Lithuanian. *Baltic Linguistics* 2: 9–35.
Anderson, Cori. 2013a. Passivization and argument structure in Russian and Lithuanian. Presentation at the annual meeting of American Association of Teachers of Slavic and Eastern European Languages, Boston, MA.
Anderson, Cori. 2013b. *Case and event structure in Russian and Lithuanian.* Princeton University doctoral dissertation.
Anderson, Cori. 2013c. Case alternation and event structure: Evidence from Lithuanian and Russian. In *Formal Approaches to Slavic Linguistics 20*, 1–16. Ann Arbor, MI: Michigan Slavic Publications.
Arkadiev, Peter. 2014. Case and word order in Lithuanian revisited. In Axel Holvoet & Nicole Nau (eds.) *Grammatical relations and their non-canonical encoding in Baltic*, 43–95. Amsterdam, Philadelphia: John Benjamins.
Armoškaitė, Solveiga. 2006. Accomplishment VPs: Construction of telicity. A case study of Lithuanian. In Claire Gurski & Milica Radisic (eds.) *Proceedings of the 2006 annual conference of the Canadian Linguistic Association.* http://westernlinguistics.ca/Publications/CLA2006/Armoskaite.pdf.
Babby, Leonard H. 1986. The locus of case assignment and the direction of percolation: Case theory and Russian. In Richard Brecht & James Levine (eds.) *Case in Slavic*, 170–219. Columbus, OH: Slavica.
Babby, Leonard H. 1994. Case theory. In Carlos P. Otero (ed.) *Noam Chomsky: Critical assessments (Vol I: Linguistics: Tome II)*, 630-652. London, New York: Routledge.
Borer, Hagit. 2005. *Structuring Sense. Vol. II: The normal course of events.* Oxford: Oxford University Press.
Chomsky, Noam. 1981. Lectures on Government and Binding: The Pisa Lectures. Holland: Foris Publications.
Chomsky, Noam. 1986. *Knowledge of language: Its nature, origin, and use.* New York: Praeger.
Chomsky, Noam. 1995. *The minimalist program.* Cambridge, MA: MIT Press.
Cuervo, Maria Cristina. 2003. Datives at large. Doctoral dissertation, MIT.
Demjjanow, Assinya & Anatoli Strigin. 2000. Case assignment to conceptual structures: The Russian instrumental. In Markus Kracht & Anatoli Strigin (eds.) *Papers on the Interpretation of Case*, 75–107. University of Potsdam.
Dowty, David. 1991. Thematic proto-roles and argument selection. *Language* 67(3): 547–619.
Emonds, Joseph. 2006. Adjectival passives. In Martin Everaert & Henk C. van Riemsdijk (eds.) *The Blackwell Companion to Syntax, Vol 1*, 16–60. Oxford: Blackwell.
Fillmore, Charles. 1968. The case for case. In Emmon Bach & Robert Harms (eds.) *Universals in linguistic theory*, 1–88. New York: Holt, Rinehart, and Winston.
Fowler, George. 1996. Oblique passivization in Russian. *Slavic and East European Journal* 40(3): 519–545.
Freidin, Robert. 1992. *Foundations of generative syntax.* Cambridge, MA: MIT Press.
Franks, Steven & James E. Lavine. 2006. Case and word order in Lithuanian. *Journal of Linguistics* 42(2): 239–288.
Geniušienė, Emma. 1987. *The typology of reflexives.* Berlin, Mouton de Gruyter.

Geniušienė, Emma. 2006. Passives in Lithuanian (with comparison to Russian). In Werner Abraham & Larisa Leisiö (eds.) *Passivization and typology: Form and function*, 29–61. Amsterdam, Philadelphia: John Benjamins.
Holvoet, Axel. 1991. *Transitivity and clause structure in Polish (a study in case marking)*. Warsaw: Slawistyczny Ośrodek Wydawniczy.
Holvoet, Axel & Loreta Semėnienė. 2004. Linksnio teorijos pagrindai [Basics of case theory]. In Axel Holvoet & Loreta Semėnienė (red.) *Gramatinių kategorijų tyrimai* [Research on grammatical categories], 11–33. Vilnius: Lithuanian Language Institute.
Holvoet, A. & A. Judžentis, 2004: Tranzityvumo samprata [Notion of Transitivity]. In: Holvoet & Semėnienė, eds., Gramatinių kategorijų tyrimai [Research on Grammatical Categories], Lietuvių kalbos institutas, 61–76.
Jablonskis, Jonas. [1922] 1997. *Lietuvių kalbos gramatika* [Grammar of the Lithuanian language]. Vilnius: Mokslo ir enciklopedijų leidykla.
Kiparsky, Paul. 1998. Partitive case and aspect. In Miriam Butt & Wilhelm Geuder (eds.) *The projection of arguments*, 265–308. Stanford: CSLI.
Lavine, James. 2006. "Is There a Passive Evidential Strategy in Lithuanian?" In Papers from the 42nd Meeting of the Chicago Linguistic Society, eds. Jacqueline Bunting et al., 41–55.
Lenartaitė, Kristina. 2009. Tiesioginiai objektai ir ditranzityvinių konstrukcijų klausimas lietuvių kalboje [Direct objects and questions of ditransitive constructions in Lithuanian]. In Axel Holvoet & Rolandas Mikulskas (red.) *Gramatinių funkcijų prigimtis ir raiška* [The nature and expression of grammatical functions], 69–98. Vilnius: Vilniaus universitetas & Asociacija „Academia Salensis".
Lenartaitė, Kristina. 2010. *Argumentų raiškos alternavimas lietuvių kalboje* [Alternations of argument expression in Lithuanian]. Vilnius University doctoral dissertation.
Letučij, Aleksandr. 2007. Tvoritel"nyj padež pri russkix perexodnyx glagolax: konstrukcii s ob"ektami-částiami tela [Instrumental case with Russian transitive verbs: Constructions with body parts as objects]. In *Russkaja Filologija 18. Sbornik naučnyx rabot molodyx filologov* [Russian Philology 18. Collection of works by young philologists], 50–55. Tartu University Press.
Levin, Beth & Malka Rappaport Hovav. 1997. Lexical semantics and syntactic structure. In Shalom Lappin (ed.) *The handbook of contemporary semantic theory*, 487–507. Oxford: Blackwell.
Matushansky, Ora. 2008. A case study of predication. In Frank Marušič and Rok Žaucer (eds.) *Studies in formal Slavic linguistics. Contributions from formal description of Slavic Languages 6.5*, 213–239. Frankfurt am Main: Peter Lang.
Matushansky, Ora. 2010. Russian predicate case, encore. In Gerhild Zybatow, Philip Dudchuk, Serge Minor, & Ekaterina Pshehotskaya (eds.) *Formal studies in Slavic linguistics, Proceedings of FDSL 7.5*, 117–135. Frankfurt am Main: Peter Lang.
McFadden, Thomas. 2004. *The position of morphological case in the derivation: A study on the syntax-morphology interface*. University of Pennsylvania doctoral dissertation.
Parsons, Terence. 1990. Events in the Semantics of English. Cambridge: MA: MIT Press.
Ramchand, Gillian. 2008. A first-phase syntax. Cambridge: Cambridge University Press.
Richardson, Kylie. 2008. *Case and aspect in Slavic*. Oxford: Oxford University Press.
Rouveret, Alain & Jean Roger Vergnaud. 1980. Specifying reference to the subject: French causatives and conditions on representations. *Linguistic Inquiry* 11: 97–202.
Šukys, Jonas. 2005. Veiksmo atlikimo priemonės raiška [Expressing means of performing an action]. *Kalbos kultūra* 78: 133–143.

Svenonius, Peter. 2006. Case alternations and the Icelandic passive and middle. Ms., lingBuzz/000124 ([v2 in 2005]).
Tenny, Carol. 1994. *Aspectual roles and the syntax-semantics interface*. Dordrecht: Kluwer.
Wiemer, Björn. 2006. Relations between actor-demoting devices in Lithuanian. In Werner Abraham & Larisa Leisiö (eds.) *Passivization and typology. Form and function*, 274–309. Amsterdam, Philadelphia: John Benjamins.
Wierzbicka, Anna. 1980. *The case for surface case*. Ann Arbor, MI: Karoma Publishers.
Woolford, Ellen. 2006. Lexical case, inherent case, and argument structure. *Linguistic Inquiry* 37(1): 111–130.
Zaenen, Annie & Joan Maling. 1990. Unaccusative, passive, and quirky case. In Joan Maling & Annie Zaenen (eds.) *Modern Icelandic syntax*, 137–152. New York: Academic Press.

Axel Holvoet
7 Non-canonical subjects in Latvian: An obliqueness-based approach

1 The problem stated

The article deals with the interpretation of grammatical relations in Latvian constructions like the ones shown in examples (1)–(3).

(1) Man   patīk   šī   grāmat-a.
    1SG.DAT   please.PRS.3   this.NOM.SG.F   book-NOM.SG
    'I like this book.'

(2) Man   vajag   tav-u   palīdzīb-u.
    1SG.DAT   be.needed.PRS.3 1SG.POSS-ACC.SG   help-ACC.SG
    'I need your help.'

(3) Man   jā-lasa   šī   grāmat-a.
    1SG.DAT   DEB-read   this.NOM.SG.F   book-NOM.SG
    'I have to read this book.'

These three constructions have one thing in common: They contain dative NPs that normally occur clause-initially, constitute the unmarked topic of the sentence, and might be regarded as being semantically, in some sense, the subject of the clause. In this sense, and perhaps also in other respects, they could raise claims to the status of "non-canonically marked subjects". Other things differ: (1) has a nominative marked NP that might raise rival claims to subjecthood; (2) contains no nominative and would traditionally be described as impersonal, whereas (3) is superficially similar to (1) but for the fact that the debitive *jālasa* 'one must read' is an inflectional form of the verb *lasīt* 'read' and one could be tempted to derive evidence from this fact, say, to the effect that *grāmata* 'book. NOM' must be the object of *jālasa* just as *grāmatu* 'book.ACC' is an object in *lasu grāmatu* 'I am reading a book' – a type of evidence that is not available, e.g., for (1), where the interpretation of *grāmata* as clause subject is at least an option. But if one accepts the interpretation of *grāmata* in (3) as an object, one could extend this interpretation to *grāmata* in (1). One could even adduce evidence in support of this parallel interpretation. The datives with *patikt* 'please' and with the debitive may both control reflexivization, which would plead in favor of their interpretation as subjects.[1]

(4) **Tev**   patīk   **sav-i**   klasesbiedr-i?
    2SG.DAT please.PRS.3   **REFL.POSS-NOM.PL.M**   classmate-NOM.PL
    'Do you like your classmates?'
    http://www.formspring.me/r/tev-pat-k-savi-klasesbiedri/253602291771249079 (accessed July 2012)

(5) Tik-uš-i   rīko-t-i   internacionāl-ie
    AUX-PPA-NOM.PL.M   organize-PPP-NOM.PL.M   international-NOM.PL.M.DEF
    vakar-i,   kad   **katr-am**   bij-is   jā-atnes
    evening-NOM.PL   when   **each-DAT.SG.M** be-PPA-NOM.SG.M   DEB-bring
    sav-s   nacionāl-ais   ēdien-s
    REFL.POSS-NOM.SG.M   national-NOM.SG.M.DEF   dish-NOM.SG
    http://www.icelo.lv/lat/stasti-un-galerijas/ttstasti/32795/ (accessed July 2012)
    '(It is told that) international evenings were held at which everybody had to bring their national dish with him.'

The reflexivization criterion is not a strong one, because it is not clear what exactly enables control of reflexive pronouns in general. The conditions that have been invoked in the literature on reflexives include: c-command (the standard view in generative grammar), a thematic hierarchy (as proposed by Jackendoff 1972), the obliqueness hierarchy as proposed in HPSG (Pollard & Sag 1994: 238–280), etc. Examples discussed in this article point to topichood as an important condition. But, as we will see below, for many putative "non-canonically marked subjects", control of reflexivization is the only syntactic subjecthood test that works well, and I will therefore use it as a *pis aller*: At least if there are two candidates to quasi-subjecthood, the one that can control reflexivization is probably a better candidate than the one that cannot, although control of reflexivization is not by itself a sufficient criterion of subjecthood.

---

[1] Here and in what follows, I will be using reflexivization tests involving the reflexive possessive pronoun *savs* 'one's (own)' rather than the reflexive pronoun proper, the reason for this being that constructions with the reflexive possessive pronoun are of wider application. The reflexive pronoun *sevis* lacks a nominative, so that with a verb like *patikt* (which occurs with dative and nominative NPs), the ability of the dative NP to control reflexivity can only be revealed by tests involving the reflexive possessive pronoun, which can occur in nominative NPs. The use of tests involving reflexive possessive pronouns is not quite unproblematic: for Russian, Rappaport (1986) claims that the reflexive possessive may have arbitary antecedents. These cases, however, seem to involve emphatic ("of one's own") rather than properly reflexive uses, and the antecedents are always generic. No uses of this type occur in the material dealt with here. Where tests with reflexives proper and reflexive possessives yield different results, this will be noted.

In the case of (1), the reflexivization criterion leads to difficulties: It is also possible to find examples where the stimulus argument with *patikt* controls reflexivization, although only when certain additional conditions, to be discussed below, are satisfied:

(6) *Pirmdzimtais var būt krietns lielais brālis vai laba lielā māsa.*
    Tād-s   *viņ-š*   *patīk*   ***sav-iem***
    such-NOM.SG.M 3-NOM.SG.M   please.PRS.3   **REFL.POSS-DAT.PL**
    vecāk-iem.
    parent-DAT.PL
    'The firstborn can be a decent elder brother or a good elder sister. That's how his parents like him.'
    http://wow7.blogs.lv/2010/11/10/cela-cirtejs-diplomats-vai-dumpinieks-1/ (accessed July 2012)

We will obviously need some criteria to establish which of the noun phrases in (1) should be interpreted as subject. These criteria should apply to all three types of constructions illustrated here, and they should, of course, be consistent with criteria that could be formulated for other languages with "non-canonical subjects". The aim of the article will be, then, to test explanations that have been formulated elsewhere on Latvian, and to characterize the evidence Latvian can contribute to a satisfactory account of dativi quasi-subjects.

The structure of the article is as follows. First, I will clarify the basic notions I will be invoking, especially that of obliqueness as understood in the article. Next, I will discuss grammatical relations in the three clause types illustrated by examples (1)–(3). I will show that they display no clear subject properties in any argument, that they are also intransitive, and that they can be described in terms of a demoted intransitive subject occurring alongside a less-oblique dativ quasi-subject. A comparison of the three types discussed in the article is given in the final part, and some generalizations are attempted.

2 The framework

The account I will propose for a number of Latvian constructions without nominative subjects relies heavily on the notion of **obliqueness**. Obliqueness is a hierarchy of noun phrases in a clause that, but for the fear of causing confusion with levels of structure in phrasal syntax, we could formulate as based on "relative depth of syntactic embedding". Rather than to putative levels of phrase structure, obliqueness refers to the empirically verifiable differences in "accessibility" (Keenan & Comrie 1977): Less oblique NPs are more easily accessible to various syntactic and morphosyntactic operations than more oblique ones. Obliqueness is a composite notion comprising at least the following elements: (i) relative position in the topic-comment structure, this structure being conceived not as dichotomous but as a hierarchy of primary and secondary topics (for a recent study highlighting the importance of secondary topics, cf. Dalrymple & Nikolaeva 2011); (ii) semantic role (theta role), a level of semantics whose hierarchical structure is widely recognized; (iii) inherent categorial features related to animacy and individuation; (iv) empathy (in the case of symmetrical predicates like *John met Mary*, where the hierarchy reduces to differences of perspective or vantage point).

The obliqueness hierarchy has been invoked to explain not only accessibility differences, but also universal regularities of word order (Pullum 1977) and binding (Pollard & Sag 2004). The notion may therefore be considered to be well-established in the literature. In what follows, however, I will slightly modify it.

The obliqueness hierarchy is usually formulated as a hierarchy of grammatical relations (actually Keenan and Comrie's accessibility hierarchy is formulated in this way), but I suggest there is only a default correspondence between grammatical relations and positions in the obliqueness hierarchy. By default, the least oblique NP becomes clause subject, but it is possible for the relation of subject not to be conferred at all (or, to be more precise, whether and to what extent it must be conferred will be a matter of cross-linguistic variation). Therefore, we will say that the obliqueness hierarchy constitutes the foundation of the hierarchy of grammatical relations and grammatical relations are its principal manifestation, but the two should not be completely identified. Alongside least-oblique arguments that are subjects, we will also have least-oblique arguments that are subject-like but lack one or more features of fully fledged subjecthood (especially coding properties), thereby justifying terms like "quasi-subject".

I assume that the obliqueness hierarchy is valid cross-linguistically, independently of language-specific morphosyntactic marking. For example, the same obliqueness pattern is realized morphosyntactically in the English construction *I like this book* and underlies linguists' intuition that the datival argument in Latvian example (1) is also some kind of subject – an intuition without which the whole discussion on non-canonically marked subjects would probably never have started.

As will be clear from what was said above, I do not regard obliqueness as a primitive notion: It can certainly be decomposed into more elementary principles. The default correspondences between the different hierarchies may be overridden, e.g., an NP that would be least oblique in virtue of being animate and an agent or experiencer may be outranked in topicality when a shift in topic-comment structure occurs in a specific type of communicative situation (we will see examples of this further on); still, it is the default assignment of topichood, not that associated with a particular utterance, that will be grammaticalized.

I agree with Primus (1999), who develops the "generalized hierarchy principle", that the hierarchical ordering characteristic of different levels of clause structure extends to morphosyntax. The counterpart of the obliqueness hierarchy in morphosyntax is the case hierarchy (Blake 2001: 89–90). Although there inevitably is a certain extent of cross-linguistic variation, the upper end of this hierarchy tends to take the shape NOM>ACC>DAT>OTHER. By default, the case that ranks highest in the case hierarchy is assigned to the least-oblique NP and so on. The grammatical relation of subject could thus be defined as the pairing of the status of least-oblique NP with the nominative.[2] There are, however, in certain languages at least, situations where the nominative is not assigned. When this occurs, we will still be able, in most instances, to single out a least-oblique NP, which we will then be tempted to characterize as a quasi-subject, a non-canonically marked subject etc. Without rejecting these formulations (least-oblique NPs may have many interesting syntactic properties of subjects), I want to suggest that such least-oblique NPs are only approximations to subjecthood, a canonical subject having, among other properties, that of being marked with the nominative.

Non-canonical subjects have received a lot of attention in the literature lately, cf. Aikhenvald, Dixon, and Onishi (2001), Bhaskararao and Subbarao (2004), and most recently, Seržant and Kulikov (2013), as well as numerous sundry articles. With reference to Latvian, Stolz (1987) should also be noted. These discussions focus on sentences like (1)–(3). Note that these constructions could also be interpreted as "extended intransitive constructions", with the dative as an obligatory "extension to core", marked with the symbol E in Onishi (2001: 2). This is the interpretation favored by Haspelmath (2001: 68) at least for European languages. At least one of the reasons why many investigators pose the question whether this E argument is not really a subject, and whether the S argument is not actually an object, seems to be that the extended intransitive configuration marked S-E in Onishi (2001: 2) actually looks more like E-S, that is, the E argument is clearly less oblique (in terms of unmarked topichood, semantic role, and animacy) than the S argument, which makes it look more subject-like. The impression is strengthened by non-nominative marking on the second argument in structures like (2).

---

2 This amounts, in fact, to a return to Keenan's (1976) notion of a prototypical subject defined by a cluster of properties including case features and other coding properties. Although Onishi (2001: 4–8) refers to Keenan's coding properties, the notion of "non-canonical marking of subjects and objects" (conspicuous in the title of Aikhenvald et al. 2001) actually sets coding apart from the rest and suggests that one can somehow establish subjecthood syntactically and then go on to see whether it is canonically marked or not. Although the shift may appear to be a subtle one, it is nonetheless important.

The Icelandic constructions with "quirky subjects" have been widely discussed in the literature and constitute a kind of benchmark for non-canonical subjects as they pass a series of syntactic (behavioral) subjecthood tests formulated by Zaenen, Maling, and Thráinsson (1985) on the basis of the subject properties listed by Keenan (1976). They include control of reflexivization, control of PRO in sentential complementation, coreferential deletion in coordination (pivot-controller properties), etc. Attempts at identifying non-canonical subjects in other languages, e.g., German, on the basis of these criteria have proven unsuccessful (cf. Andrews 2001, Sigurðsson 2004). Sigurðsson (2004) speaks of an "Icelandic-German dichotomy", although Barðdal and Eythórsson (2006) relativize this and suggest there are different degrees of acceptability rather than a sharp dichotomy. The situation in Baltic and Slavonic is not better than in German, although the assumption of datival subjects in Slavonic is widespread among authors representing formal approaches (cf. the brief overview by Moore & Perlmutter 2000): We find a considerable number of least-oblique NPs passing but very few subjecthood tests (most of them pass only the control-of-reflexivization test). What is more, even in Icelandic alongside the putative oblique subjects nominative-marked NPs are found, which, when occurring in clause-initial topical position, behave as fully fledged subjects (cf. Barðdal 2001). In view of all this, I propose in Holvoet (2013) that it is preferable to operate with the notion of **diffuse subjecthood**, i.e., subject properties that are spread over several NPs. Alongside a least-oblique, subject-like argument A (the so-called quasi-subject), we find a second-ranking argument B that can raise at least certain claims to subjecthood. This is most pronounced in structures where B is marked with the nominative; in this case B displays what I call **recoverable subjecthood**, i.e., it shows all or many subject properties when topicalized and occurring clause-initially. If B has oblique marking there is no recoverable subjecthood, but B shows no object properties either, even when the accusative is introduced for its marking. The construction is therefore intransitive, and the B argument can be characterized as a demoted intransitive subject occurring alongside a less-oblique datival argument (in a configuration comparable to that of demoted direct objects alongside datival recipient/experiencer NPs in ditransitive structures). Demoted intransitive subjects are characterized by nominative/accusative alternations across languages, dialects, and diachronic stages, peculiar to a configuration with less-oblique datival NPs. This account is argued in more detail by Holvoet (2013). In this article, I will discuss its applicability to the Latvian facts.

3 Constructions with nominative marked B arguments

Apart from *patikt* 'please' this group comprises *riebties* and *dergties* 'disgust'. Constructions with these verbs are the most bewildering ones because of possible rival claims to subjecthood: One argument seems to be subject semantically, another gets the coding properties. As far as the latter are concerned, they are not restricted to case marking: When a compound verb form occurs, the participle contained in it agrees with this nominative NP:

(7) *Maz-ajām*   *meiten-ēm*   *visvairāk*   *bija*
little-DAT.PL.F.DEF   girl-DAT.PL   most   be.PST.3
patik-usi   *indieš-u*   ***princes-e.***
please-PPA.NOM.SG.F   Indian-GEN.PL   **princess-NOM.SG**
'The little girls had liked the Indian princess most of all.'
http://www.jrt.lv/nijaramas-pasakas?page=1 (accessed July 2012)

Syntactically, however, things are less clear: Not only the nominative NP, but also (and, perhaps, more frequently), the dative NP is able to control reflexivization. The dative usually occurs clause-initially and is the unmarked topic. The pattern of topic-comment structure can, however, be reversed in specific circumstances, which yields a structure like (6). In such instances, the nominative NP can be recognized as a fully fledged subject. As we have seen above, it always has the coding properties. But in this case, it also has syntactic subject properties: Most importantly, it can function as pivot-controller in coordination:

(8) *Bet nu tā pa lielam jau, protams, galvenais,*
ka   **vārd-s**   *piestāv*   *un*   Ø   *patīk*   *vecāk-iem.*
that   **name-NOM.SG**   fit.PRS.3   and   Ø   please.PRS.3   parent-DAT.PL
'But, broadly speaking, the most important thing is that the name fits, and that the parents like it.'
http://www.calis.lv/forums/tema/18110672-meitenu-vardi/72/ (accessed July 2012)

By contrast, the dative NP cannot function as a pivot/controller:

(9) ***Bērn-iem***   *patīk*   *un*   ****(viņ-i)***   *prasa*   *labāk*
child-DAT.PL   please.PRS.3   and   **3-NOM.PL.M**   demand.PRS.3   rather
tās   *pasak-as,*   *nekā*   *grāmat-u.*
DEM.ACC.PL.F   fairy.tales-ACC.PL   than   book-ACC.SG
'The children like them and call for these fairy tales rather than for a book.'
http://www.apollo.lv/komentari/zinas/507005/1 (accessed July 2012)

Tab. 1: Subject properties in constructions with *patikt*

	A	B
Case marking	DAT	NOM
Control of agreement	No	Yes
Control of reflexivization	Yes	Yes*
Pivot/controller in coordination	No	Yes*

We can conclude that constructions of the *patikt* type show a certain diffuseness of subject properties, but there is a fairly strong concentration of subject properties in the nominative marked B argument, whose subjecthood is fully recoverable when the unmarked pattern of topic-comment structure is reversed. To facilitate comparison with other constructions to be discussed further on, I represent the relevant features in Table 1; those subject features recovered only if the B argument is topicalized and occurs clause-initially are marked with an asterisk.

4 Constructions with oblique B arguments

The second type of constructions to be considered here has a datival quasi-subject but argument B is marked with an oblique case. It is illustrated from modern Latvian in (2), which shows an accusative encoding the B argument. In Old Latvian, the case encoding B is still the genitive (10), a type of marking still retained in modern Lithuanian (11).

(10) Old Latvian
*Tad   eeschehlojahs   tam   Kungam   **tha***
then   be.sorry.PST.3   DEF.DAT.SG.M   lord.DAT.SG   **DEF.GEN.SG.M**
Kalpa   *un   palaide   to   un   to*
servant.GEN.SG   and   loose.PST.3   3.ACC.SG   and   DEF.ACC.SG
Parradu   atlaide   wiņśch   tam   arri.
debt.ACC.SG   forgive.PST.3 3.NOM.SG.M   3.DAT.SG.M   also
'Then the lord of that servant was moved with compassion, and loosed him, and forgave him the debt.' (*Glück's New Testament*, 1685, Mt 18.27; cf. Luther: *Da hatte der Herr Erbarmen mit diesem Knecht und ließ ihn frei und die Schuld erließ er ihm auch*)

(11) Lithuanian
Pon-ui pagailo **tarn-o.**
Lord-DAT.SG be.sorry.PST.3 **servant-GEN.SG**
'The lord felt sorry for the servant.'

Already in Old Latvian, the verb *iežēloties* could also be used as a personal verb with a nominative experiencer subject. It then takes a prepositional phrase with *par*:

(12) Old Latvian
Bet ja tu warri tad palihdsi mums
but if 2SG.NOM be.able.PRS.2SG then help.IMP.2SG 1PL.DAT
eeschehloj-ees pahr mums.
take.pity-PPA.NOM.SG.M over 1PL.DAT
'But if thou canst do any thing, have compassion on us, and help us.'
(Glück's New Testament, 1685, Mk 9.22; cf. Luther: *Wenn du aber etwas kannst, so erbarme dich unser und hilf uns!*)

This second construction is the only one to have survived into modern Latvian. We will not further consider it here. A synonymous construction with dative and genitive does exist in modern Latvian, but is composed of the predicator *žēl* (a borrowing from Old Russian *žalь*) and the auxiliary *būt* 'be' or the aspectually marked quasi-copular *kļūt* and *palikt* 'become, get, grow' (this type of construction is also dealt with, from an areal perspective, by Seržant, this volume). The following example shows the same pattern of case marking as the Old Latvian construction with *iežēloties* in (10):

(13) *Un man kļuva žēl gan tā* **puiš-a,**
and 1SG.DAT become.PST.3 sorry PTCL that.GEN.SG.M **boy-GEN.SG**
gan viņ-a **ģimen-es,** *gan mašīn-as* **šoferīt-es,**
PCLE 3-GEN.SG.M **family-GEN.SG** PTCL car-GEN.SG **driver-GEN.SG.F**
kur-ai ar to jā-sadzīvo vis-u dzīv-i pat
REL-DAT.SG.F with it DEB-live.with all-ACC.SG life-ACC.SG even
tad, ja ne-bija vainīg-a.
then if NEG-be.PST.3 guilty-NOM.SG.F
'And I felt sorry for the boy, and for his family, and for the car driver who has to cope with it for all her further life even though she was not guilty.'
http://www.zz.lv/portals/vietejas/raksts.html?offset=1&xml_id=38058&order=desc (accessed July 2012)

In the modern language, however, this genitive is being ousted by the accusative. This reflects a general tendency: As a case governed by verbs, the genitive has largely fallen into disuse in Latvian, a process dealt with in detail by Berg-Olsen (1999). The following example shows this accusative:

(14) Ir   jā-būt   reālist-am,   las-ot   šo
     be.PRS.3   DEB-be   realist-DAT.SG   read-CVB   this.ACC.SG
     rakst-u   man   kļuva   žēl   **māt-i**   un
     article-ACC.SG   1SG.DAT   become.PST.3   sorry   **mother-ACC.SG**   and
     viņ-as 5   **bērn-us**,   jo   ne   īr-iem   ne
     3-GEN.SG.F   **child-ACC.PL**   for   neither   Irishman-DAT.PL   nor
     latvieš-iem   viņ-i   nav   vajadzīg-i.
     Latvian-DAT.PL   3-NOM.PL.M   be.PRS.3.NEG   necessary-NOM.PL.M
     'Let's be realistic: while reading the article I felt sorry for that mother and her five children, because neither the Irish nor the Latvians need them.'
     http://www.apollo.lv/portal/news/articles/268859?comm_page=1 (accessed July 2012)

The genitive, however, has not yet been ousted completely. It is often found not only in literary texts but even in Internet texts written in an informal style. What is also interesting is that one finds it alongside the accusative within the same clause; the examples I have found suggest that animacy might be a factor, the accusative spreading more consistently in the case of animates:

(15) Tā   ir   tā   laim-e,
     that.NOM.SG.F   be.PRS.3   that. DEM.NOM.SG.F   happiness-NOM.SG
     dzīvo-t   tā,   lai   ne-bū-tu   žēl   **sevi**   un
     live-INF   so   so.as   NEG-be-COND   sorry   **REFL.ACC**   and
     sav-as   **dzīv-es**.
     REFL.POSS-GEN.SG   **life-GEN.SG**
     'That is happiness – to live so as not be sorry for oneself and one's life.'
     http://www.sievietespasaule.lv/slejas/ka_paspet_visu/ (accessed July 2012)

The same is suggested by the contrast between the following examples, both of which contain demonstrative pronouns, one with animate (16) and one with inanimate (17) reference:

(16) Visvairāk   žēl   **sevi**   un   **tos**   kas
     most   sorry   **REFL.ACC**   and   those.**ACC.PL.M**   REL.NOM
     sev   gribēja   iegādāties   dzīvokl-i!
     REFL.DAT   want.PST.3   acquire.INF   flat-ACC.SG
     'Most of all I feel sorry for myself and those who wished to acquire flats.'
     http://www.zz.lv/forum/reply.html?fid=24&tid=383&pid=27 (accessed July 2012)

(17) Ir   žēl   **sevi**   un   tā   kas
    be.PRS.3   sorry   **REFL.ACC**   and   that.GEN.SG.M   REL.NOM
    ir   bij-is.
    be.PRS.3   be-PPA.NOM.SG.M
    'I feel sorry for myself and that what has been,'
    http://sjuuzii.blogspot.com/2011/02/beres.html (accessed 2012)

To account for this difference, we would probably have to examine the material more closely. One thing is certain, however. The genitive is still relatively frequent and is not an archaism or a feature of literary style. This treatment is clearly different from that of direct objects of transitive verbs, where the genitive is now completely obsolete.

At a first glance, this process looks like one of transitivization, canonical object marking being introduced for argument B. This expectation would in itself be perfectly justified. The well-known case of English *like* shows the development from an Old and Middle English construction with a datival least-oblique argument (18) to a canonical transitive construction (19) of Modern English:

(18) Old English
    Ac   god-e   ne   licode   na   heora   geleafleast.
    but   God-DAT   NEG   please.PST.3SG   NEG   their   faithlessness.NOM

(19) Modern English
    But God did not like their faithlessness. (Example from Allen 1986, 390)

One could, in principle, imagine this process starting from the end, i.e., canonical object marking being introduced for B without concomitant introduction of canonical subject marking for A. But there is little evidence for transitivization at the stage of development illustrated by the Latvian structures we are dealing with here. First, as we have seen, the case marking is not what we would expect if a transitive structure were involved – the genitive is relatively well preserved whereas it has been defunct for several decades as an object case. Second, syntactic evidence for transitivity is lacking. Passivization is impossible even in the case of a verb like *vajadzēt* 'be needed', which (being non-reflexive) would formally allow it:

(20) *Tiek   vajadzē-t-a   tav-a   palīdzīb-a.
     AUX.PRS.3   need-PPP-NOM.SG.F   2SG. POSS.NOM.SG.F   help-NOM.SG
     Intended meaning: 'Your help is needed.'

Thus, without denying that the introduction of accusative marking for B can be one of the steps leading to the rise of a transitive structure as illustrated by English *like*, I would venture that the structure actually remains intransitive as long as the other indispensable step, the introduction of nominative marking for A, has not been accomplished. After all, it takes a nominative and an accusative to make a canonical transitive structure in a language with nominative alignment. The configuration "dative-accusative" is far from being canonically transitive, and it is, in many respects, close to the configuration "dative-nominative". Instances where these two cases alternate for the marking of B in constructions with datival quasi-subjects are cited from Scandinavian (Icelandic vs. Faroese) and Baltic (Lithuanian vs. Latvian with verbs of pain) by Holvoet (2013). Radically different explanations are proposed for the Baltic constructions with verbs of pain by Seržant (2013).

Between these two configurations, there is no very sharp line of division in Latvian, and some verbs seem to oscillate between the two. With *iekāroties* 'feel a craving for' three cases are attested: accusative (21), genitive (22), and nominative (23):

(21) Es   pazīstu   vien-u, kur-š   var
     1SG.NOM   know.PRS.1SG   one-ACC.SG REL-NOM.SG.M be.able.PRS.3
     nakt-ī   skrie-t   uz   veikal-u,   ja   viņ-am   iekārojas
     night-LOC.SG run-INF   to   shop-ACC.SG   if   3-DAT.SG.M   crave.PRS.3
     vafeļu   **tortīt-i.**
     wafer-GEN.PL   **cake-ACC.SG**
     http://meeting.oho.lv/meeting.php?cmd=intereses&grupaid=
     14subgrupaid=784&temaid=1384343 (accessed July 2012)
     'I know one who is capable of running to the shop at night if he feels a sudden craving for a wafer cake.'

(22) Gadās,   ka   kād-am   tūrist-am   iekārojas
     happen.PRS.3   that   some-DAT.SG.M   tourist-DAT.SG crave.PRS.3
     auglīš-a,   bet,   tavu neražu, uz   sarkan-ā   bumbuļ-a
     fruit-GEN.SG but   bad.luck   on   red-GEN.SG.M.DEF   bulb-GEN.SG
     ir   tūkstoš-iem   neredzam-u   adatiņ-u.
     be.PRS.3   thousand-DAT.PL   invisible-GEN.PL   needle-GEN.PL
     'It happens that some tourist feels a craving for a piece of fruit, but, imagine the bad luck, the red bulb is abristle with thousands of invisible needles.'
     http://www.tvnet.lv/izklaide/notikumi/52232-rietosas_saules_burviba_
     saharas_tuksnesi (accessed July 2012)

(23) Bet,   ja   iekārojas   **kād-s**   **našķ-is** [...]
     but   when   crave.PRS.3   **some-NOM.SG**   **titbit-NOM.SG**
     tad Arvīda kungs „ierūcina" mocīti un dodas uz pagasta vai novada centru.
     'When Mr. Arvīds feels a craving for some titbit, he throws his motorbike into gear and drives to the municipality or district centre.'
     http://www.novadpetnieciba.lv/re%C4%A3ioni/r%C4%ABgas-
     re%C4%A3ions/siguldas-novads/alla%C5%BEu-pagasts/7-devi%
     C5%86desmit-gadi-harmonij%C4%81-ar-dabu.html (accessed July 2012)

Tab. 2: Subject properties with *vajadzēt*

	A	B
Case marking	DAT	ACC (GEN)
Control of agreement	No	No
Control of reflexivization	Yes	No
Pivot/controller in coordination	No	No

I conclude, therefore, that the introduction of the accusative is not associated with transitivity. Just as not every nominative must reflect a subject, not every accusative must reflect a direct object. The best way of describing the constructions under discussion is to view the argument B as a demoted intransitive subject. Its encoding with the accusative rather than with the nominative results from **obliqueness adjustment**: The encoding of the more oblique NP with a nominative alongside a dative-marked least-oblique NP leads to an **obliqueness mismatch**, as the case hierarchy should normally replicate the syntactic obliqueness hierarchy. The effect of the introduction of the accusative instead of the nominative is to lessen the obliqueness mismatch.

Subject properties with *vajadzēt* are shown in Table 2.

5 Constructions with the debitive

As mentioned above, constructions with the debitive differ from the two preceding ones in that the debitive is an inflectional form of the verb characterized by a particular pattern of case marking, whereas in the other cases the valency pattern is associated with particular lexemes. We should therefore first discuss the nature of the debitive and the possible ways of explaining its morphosyntactic peculiarities.

5.1 The status of the debitive

Traditionally, the debitive is treated as a mood, which is problematic in that the debitive can itself be conjugated for mood (cf. *ir jālasa* '(one) has to read' vs. *būtu jālasa* '(one) would have to read'). It seems therefore preferable to treat the debitive marker *jā-* as a modal affix (De Haan 2006: 36–37).

Nau (1998: 39–40) suggests the debitive should be treated as a voice, alongside the passive. This proposal is not completely new, as Bielenstein (1854: 211) had treated the debitive as the only true Latvian passive (the other passive forms being periphrastic and in that sense less "true"), recognizing that this passive always has modal overtones. Nau's proposal seems to be motivated by the fact that one of the effects of the debitive is to change the valency pattern of the verb, as the passive does. But is this enough? What the passive does is to change the assignment of grammatical relations while retaining the same configuration of semantic roles (Mel'čuk 1993). With the debitive case, assignment certainly changes, but whether this reflects a change in grammatical relations is not quite clear. Maybe the same grammatical relations are just coded by different cases?

It is probably not controversial to say that deviations from canonical valency patterns can originate in several ways, of which voice is only one. Lexemes may have their idiosyncratic valency patterns, e.g., Latvian *vajadzēt* 'be needed', which covers about the same modal meanings as the debitive, requires an experiencer in the dative rather than in the nominative.

(24) Man   vajag   tav-u   palīdzīb-u.
      1SG.DAT   be.needed.PRS.3   your-ACC.SG   help-ACC.SG
      'I need your help.'

We will not say that the use of *vajadzēt* is associated with a special voice because voice is marked inflectionally on the verb (if it is marked in morphology at all), whereas the valency pattern used with *vajadzēt* is an idiosyncratic feature specified in the lexicon. Cases of suppletion, such as that of Latin *fieri*, said to be the passive of *facere*, do not alter this fundamental distinction. There is little doubt that the debitive is inflectional as well, and this is obviously the reason why Nau decides it must be an instance of voice.

We would be ill-advised, however, to use this criterion too mechanically. Splits in case marking associated with grammatical categories clearly distinct from voice are well documented. The best-known example is probably that of nominative/ergative splits associated with tense and aspect; for a recent discussion of these, cf. Malchukov, and de Hoop (2011). Still more relevant is this context is the occurrence of non-canonical case marking associated with event modality, discussed by Narrog (2010).

It is clear that the modal affix *jā*- has roughly the same valency as the modal verb *vajadzēt*. The debitive requires the second-ranking NP (the object of the semantically embedded predication) to be in the nominative in most cases, whereas with *vajadzēt*, it is usually in the accusative (although the nominative is attested in the dialects, cf. Endzelīns 1951: 554), but these are differences of detail.

Another question is whether the reassignment of case forms reflects a difference in the assignment of grammatical relations. This is an empirical issue: One would probably expect the assignment of grammatical relations associated with a verb in the lexicon to be stable throughout the tense and mood system, but this has to be examined in every specific case. The situation with the debitive is, however, clearly different. The debitive represents a higher modal predicate, which, as a result of the accretion of the modal morpheme to the verb, superimposes its own argument structure on that of the embedded verb. Compare:

(25) Es   lasu   grāmat-u.
     1SG.NOM read.PRS.1SG book-ACC.SG
     'I am reading a book.'

(26) Man   jā-lasa   grāmat-a.
     1SG.DAT DEB-read   book-NOM.SG
     'I have to read a book.'

Whereas *es* in (25) codes an agent, *man* in (26) codes not only an agent, but also an experiencer-like argument of the modal predicate expressed by the bound morpheme *jā-*. The argument structures of the modal predicate and its complement having been collapsed into one, there is a priori no reason to assume that the debitive should preserve the assignment of grammatical relations associated with the verb in the lexicon. In this sense, there is no exact parallelism between the situation with the debitive and other splits such as tense-driven nominative/ergative alternations. Tense does not introduce a superordinate predicate with its own argument structure, and one is tempted to look for stable subject and object assignments across tense distinctions, whereas there is no reason to expect these when the verb's valency pattern is fused into one with that of a modal predicate, no matter whether expressed by a free or bound morpheme.

How exactly the pattern of grammatical relations in constructions with the debitive could be characterized is a question I will deal with in the next section.

5.2 Grammatical relations in the debitive construction

Let us start from an exposition of the facts. The Latvian debitive has an A argument (the experiencer argument of the model predicate and agent of the embedded predicate) in the dative. The B argument is supposed to be in the nominative if it is a noun or a third-person pronoun. It is in the accusative if it is a first- or second-person pronoun or a reflexive pronoun (Endzelīns 1951: 972). Compare (27) with (3):

(27) Pirms   tu   ko   sak-i,   man   ir
     before   2SG.NOM   anything.ACC   say-PRS.2SG   1SG.DAT   be.PRS.3
     tevi   jā-brīdina, ka   vis-s,   ko   tu
     2SG.ACC DEB-warn   that   all-NOM.SG.M   what.ACC   2SG.NOM
     teik-si,   var   tikt   lieto-t-s   pret   tevi.
     say-FUT.2SG may.PRS.3   become.INF   use-PPP-NOM.SG.M   against   2SG.ACC

'Before you say anything I must warn you that anything you say can be used against you.'
http://zagarins.net/jg/jg182/JG182_Bekmans.htm (accessed July 2012)

That the use of the accusative for first- and second-person pronouns is an effect of the animacy hierarchy (the accusative being reserved for NPs at the upper end of the hierarchy) was already recognized by Timberlake (1974). Timberlake compares the Latvian debitive construction to the Fennic nominative object construction, which shows a similar animacy constraint, as shown in (28) and (29):

(28) Finnish
Sinu-n   täytyy   luke-a   tämä   kirja.
2SG-GEN   be.necessary.PRS.3SG   read-INF   DEM   book.NOM
'You must read this book.'

(29) Finnish
Sinu-n   täytyy   kutsu-a   minu-t.
2SG-GEN   be.necessary.PRS.3SG   invite-INF   1SG-ACC
'You must invite me.'

Although the parallel is valid in principle, it is only to a certain extent: In the Fennic construction, there is a separate embedded infinitival clause with grammatical relations largely intact apart from the use of a phonologically empty PRO subject. The complement of the infinitive is therefore clearly an object. This cannot be said of the Latvian debitive construction, which does not contain a syntactically distinguishable embedded clause. That the B-argument of a debitive construction is an object may therefore not be taken for granted.

In the dialects, the situation is different from what was stated for Standard Latvian: In many Latvian dialects, the object of a verb in the debitive is always in the accusative (Endzelīns 1951: 971). This situation is also spreading in colloquial Standard Latvian, although this tendency is opposed by prescriptive grammarians.

Historically speaking, the nominative is the original case, as the debitive construction has arisen from an existential construction or its expanded form, a possessive construction of the type *mihi est*, in which the subject was modified by an infinitival relative purpose clause (cf. Holvoet 1998 for a historical outline). In Old Latvian, the original meaning was retained:

(30) Old Latvian
Man   ir   Barriba   jaehd,
1SG.DAT   be.PRS3   food.NOM.SG   DEB.eat
ko   juhs   ne   sinnat
that.ACC   2PL.NOM   NEG   know.PRS.2PL

'I have meat to eat that ye know not of.' (*Glück's New Testament*, John 4.32)
(*Ich habe eine Speise zu essen, von der ihr nicht wisset*)

The modern meaning would be "I have to eat food". The original subject has undoubtedly lost part of the properties associated with subjecthood, the question is, however, to establish exactly how many.

Let us first look at coding properties. The alternation of nominative and accusative as cases encoding the second-ranking argument points to the obvious conclusion that we are not dealing with a canonical subject here. This impression is reinforced by the facts concerning agreement. The debitive comprises a form of the auxiliary *būt* 'be'. In the compound tenses of this auxiliary, the participle should show agreement with the nominative if it is a subject. This can be illustrated by the copular construction:

(31) Sien-as   kādreiz   ir   **bij-uš-as**   balt-as.
     wall-NOM.PL   once   be.PRS.3   **be-PPA-NOM.PL.F**   white-NOM.PL.F
     'The walls have once been white.'

In the debitive construction, however, this agreement is usually absent, and the participle is in the default agreement form, the masculine singular:

(32) Šaj-os   gad-os   ir   **bij-is**
     those-LOC.PL   year-LOC.PL   be.PRS.3   **be-PPA.NOM.SG.M**
     jā-lasa   dažād-as   ziņ-as,
     DEB-read   various-NOM.PL.F   news.item-NOM.PL
     tai skaitā arī šokējošas, kad pašai diktorei trīcējušas kājas no uztraukuma.
     http://www.diena.lv/sabiedriba/pasi-mazakie-648149 (accessed July 2012)
     'In those years one has had to read various news items, among them shocking ones, which made the newsreader's legs shake with excitement.'

But constructions with agreeing auxiliaries also occur. The Academy Grammar (Bergmane et al. 1959: 618) cites an example with agreement alongside an analogous construction without agreement. Both examples are in the so-called oblique mood, an evidential construction based on the use of a participle instead of a finite form. This participle is capable, in principle, of agreeing with the nominative NP in number and gender. In (33), there is no agreement, while (34) displays agreement with a nominative plural NP:

(33) Jau   lemeš-u   uzasināšan-ai   ogl-es
     PCLE   ploughshare-GEN.PL   sharpening-DAT.SG   coals-NOM.PL
     bij-is   jā-aizņemas   no   kalēj-a.
     be-PPA.NOM.SG.M   DEB-borrow   from   blacksmith-GEN.SG
     'The coals needed for the sharpening of the ploughshares had [reportedly] to be borrowed from the blacksmith.' (E. Birznieks-Upītis)

(34) *Lin-i*   **bij-uš-i**   *jā-kaltē,*   *un*   *vec-ais*
flax-NOM.PL   **be-PPA-NOM.PL.M**   DEB-dry   and   old-NOM.SG.M.DEF
tēv-s   *tos*   *labi*   *prat-is*   *izraudzīt.*
father-NOM.SG   3.ACC.PL.M   well   know.how-PPA.NOM.SG.M   select.INF
'The flax [reportedly] had to be dried, and the old father knew very well how to select it.' (J. Akuraters)

The *Grammar* notes, however, that this agreement is rare (Bergmane et al. 1959: 617). We may probably rely on the authors of the *Academy Grammar* when they state that constructions with agreement are less frequent, but they can certainly be found even in the present-day language. Word order probably has a certain influence on the presence of absence of agreement, cf. the following example with preverbal B argument:

(35) *Es*   *gan*   *spriežu*   *no malas,*   *jo*   *man*
1SG.NOM   PTCL   judge.PRS.1SG   from aside   because   1SG.DAT
par laimi   *šād-a*   **izvēl-e**   *nav*
fortunately   such-NOM.SG.F   **choice-NOM.SG**   be.PRS.3.NEG
bij-usi   *jā-izdara.*
be-PPA.NOM.SG.F   DEB-make
'True, I can judge only from aside, as I have never been compelled to make such a choice.'
http://www.calis.lv/forums/tema/18191705-piespiedu-karta/ (accessed July 2012)

Behavior properties yield no decisive evidence. The dative NP is capable of controlling reflexivization and does so regularly.[3]

(36) Latvian
Tā   *ir*   *pasaul-es*   *lielāk-ā*
DEM-NOM.SG.F   be.PRS.3   world-GEN.SG   greatest-NOM.SG.F.DEF
nelaime,   *ka*   **vecāk-iem**   *jā-redz*   *sav-i*
misfortune-NOM.SG   that   parent-DAT.PL   DEB-see   POSS.REFL-NOM.PL.M
bērn-i   *aizej-am.*
child-NOM.PL   go.away-CVB
http://www.calis.lv/forums/tema/15206129-engelisu-maminas/51/ (accessed July 2012)

---

3 In the construction with the debitive, reflexive pronouns proper can be controlled only by the dative NP.

The nominative NP seems to be unable to control reflexivization if the datival A argument precedes the B argument:

(37) Bet   siev-ām   **vīr-i**   aizvien   jā-redz
     but   wife-DAT.PL   **husband-NOM.PL**   always   DEB-see
     ar   vis-iem   **viņ-u**   veikal-iem
     with   all-DAT.PL   **3-GEN.PL**   business-DAT.PL (Pāvils Rozītis)
     'But wives should always view their husbands in the context of their
     (i.e., their husbands') business occupations.'

As in the case of *patikt*, however, topicalization and fronting render the nominative B argument capable of controlling reflexivization:

(38) Atgriežoties pie biskvīta, kad tas izcepies,
     tas   jā-ņem   ārā,   jā-atbrīvo   no   **sav-a**
     it.NOM.SG.M   DEB-take   out   DEB-loosen   from   **POSS.REFL-GEN.SG.M**
     follij-a   žodziņ-a   un   cepam-ā   papīr-a,
     foil-GEN   enclosure-GEN and   baking-GEN.SG.M.DEF   paper-GEN
     lai   atdziest.
     so.that   get.cold.PRS.3
     'To get back to the sponge cake, when it's ready, it should be taken out,
     loosened from its foil enclosure and from the baking paper to let it get cold.'
     http://spoki.tvnet.lv/receptes/Aromatiska-zemenu-kuka/544597
     (accessed July 2012)

When topicalized and occurring sentence-initially, such a nominative NP is also treated as a pivot/controller in coordination, as in example (39). This shows, together with pairs of contrasting sentences like (4) and (6), how important topichood is for control of reflexivization:

(39) Vid-es,   sociāl-ie   un   ekonomisk-ie
     environment-GEN   social-NOM.PL.M.DEF   and   economic-NOM.PL.M.DEF
     jautājum-i   ir   savstarpēji   cieši   saistīt-i
     issue-NOM.PL   be.PRS.3   mutually   closely   connected-NOM.PL.M
     un   Ø   ir   jā-risina   vienoti.
     and   be.PRS.3   DEB-solve   conjointly
     'Environmental, social and economic issues are closely interrelated and
     must be dealt with conjointly.' (http://archive.politika.lv/temas/vide_un_
     ilgtspeja/17419/) (accessed July 2012)

This points to the conclusion that the debitive, just as the construction with *patikt*, provides us with an example of recoverable subjecthood. This recovery of subjecthood, however, is not complete, as the nominative may not control reflexivization even when topicalized and sentence-initial, as shown by (33).

The apparently recoverable subject properties of the B argument explain the specific properties of the debitive with regard to voice. Although the debitive, as mentioned above, has been called a kind of passive, the full debitive construction, comprising both A and B argument, is more similar to the active one in that the nominative-marked NP (the original object) is normally the second-ranking argument, the dative NP (the original subject) being least oblique and normally assuming the position of unmarked topic:

(40) *Mums   ar   Kuzm-u   jā-padarin-ot   četr-i*
      1PL.DAT   with   Kuzma-ACC   DEB-make-OBL   four-NOM.M
      baļķ-u   vārt-i   un   jā-uzstat-ot   tie
      beam-GEN.PL   gate-NOM.PL   and   DEB-set.up-OBL   3.NOM.PL.M
      straum-es   vid-ū.
      stream-GEN.SG   mid-LOC.SG
      'Kuzma and I [he said] would have to make four beam gates and to set them up amidst the stream.' (Valentīns Jakobsons)

This example could be transformed into a non-debitive active construction without the slightest change in word order:

(41) *Mēs   ar   Kuzm-u   padarinājām   četr-us*
      1PL.NOM   with   Kuzma-ACC   make.PST.1PL   four-ACC.M
      baļķ-u   vārt-us   un   uzstatījām   tos
      beam-GEN.PL   gate-ACC.PL   and   set.up.PST.1PL   3.ACC.PL.M
      straum-es   vid-ū.
      stream-GEN.SG   mid-LOC.SG
      'Kuzma and I made four beam gates and set them up amidst the stream.'

But the agent/modal experiencer may be backgrounded or generalized and, as a result, may not be represented in syntactic structure. In many languages, Latvian not excluded, a typical device enabling the suppression of the agent is the passive. Passive debitives, however, do not occur.[4] For a structure like

---

4 Or rather, a debitive actional (dynamic) passive does not occur. What is possible is a debitive derived from a resultative passive (with the auxiliary *būt* rather than the regular passive auxiliary *tikt*), as in *adresei jābūt apzīmētai* (address.DAT.SG DEB-be indicate.PPP.DAT.SG.F) 'the address must be indicated' (German *die Adresse muss angegeben sein*). The corresponding actional passive **adresei jātiek apzīmētai* (German *die Adresse muss angegeben werden*) is not used; instead, we have simply *adrese jāapzīmē* (address.NOM.SG DEB-indicate).

(42) Lin-i   ir   jā-kaltē.
    flax-NOM.PL be.PRS.3   DEB-dry
    'The flax must be dried.'

the natural English translation will be in the passive. In the Latvian construction with the debitive, however, the effect otherwise achieved by passivization is achieved merely by moving the nominative NP to clause-initial, topical position – the dative NP can be deleted without further morphosyntactic changes. The nominative can be compared to the nominative subject in the corresponding passive construction:

(43) Lin-i   tiek   kaltē-t-i.
    flax-NOM.PL become.PRS.3   dry-PPP-NOM.PL.M
    'The flax is being dried.'

The resemblance is, of course, only partial, because even when occurring in the typical subject position, the nominative in the debitive construction does not always control auxiliary agreement. Still, between the active-like debitive construction and that with recovery of subject properties by the B argument there is probably a difference in the assignment of grammatical relations. Does this mean that in the active-like debitive construction, it is actually the same as in the active non-debitive construction? Could the nominative NP in debitive constructions like (3) be characterized as a nominative object that, to an increasing degree, is adjusting its case marking to its real syntactic function – that of direct object? I think not, despite appearances. It is true that the nominative NP represents the object of the "embedded" verb, but in view of the fact that in the debitive construction the argument structures of higher (modal) and embedded predicates are collapsed, we should not a priori assume identical grammatical relations for the object of the embedded verb and the second-ranking NP with the debitive. The debitive construction should be compared to other constructions with datival quasi-subjects, such as those with *vajag*, *žēl*, etc. These constructions are, as I have argued above, basically intransitive and their second-ranking (more oblique) argument is not a direct object but a demoted intransitive subject. That this interpretation applies to the debitive construction is suggested by the partial recoverability of subjecthood by the nominative NP. The behavioral properties of NPs with the debitive are shown in Table 3.

Tab. 3: Subject properties with the debitive

	A	B
Case marking	DAT	NOM/ACC
Control of agreement	No	Yes*
Control of reflexivization	Yes	Yes*
Pivot/controller in coordination	No	Yes*

6 Conclusion

When we look at the list of subject properties shown in Tables 1–3, certain regularities stand out clearly. In the left column, we find only control of reflexivization, a feature of that we cannot be sure whether it is really a subject property. In the right column, subject properties correlate in an interesting way with case marking. Nominative marked B arguments show themselves capable of recovering subject properties when they are topicalized, even though they do not fundamentally differ from oblique marked B arguments when non-topicalized; as soon as nominative marking is replaced with oblique marking, this recoverability of subject properties is lost. This shows that there is really no stable concentration of subject properties in any argument as long as we have a nominative marked argument; when there is no nominative marked argument, the distribution of subject properties (which I have described as "diffuse" in this chapter) is more stable, i.e., independent from topicalization and word order, but this does not go hand in hand with a stronger concentration of subject properties in A. The best way of accounting for the types discussed here is thus through the notion of diffuse subjecthood.

From a diachronic perspective, at least two of the three constructions discussed here had, at the outset, argument B as their subject. As we see most clearly in the case of the debitive, historical shifts lead to a loss of subject properties in B, but without a clear increase in subject properties in A. Claiming that the oblique (accusative) marking on B is a kind of object marking is pointless because an object presupposes a transitive subject. That is why I prefer to refer to the B arguments as demoted intransitive subjects. The three types discussed in this article are once more compared in Table 4, arranged in an order different from that in which they are discussed above: It shows that those subject properties of B conditional on topicalization and clause-initial position are absent when B is encoded by an oblique case, but this does not go hand in hand with an increase of subject properties in A, and the overall picture is, in all cases, that of a construction with diffuse grammatical relations.

Tab. 4: Subject properties – overview table

	Patikt	Debitive	Vajadzēt
A controls agreement	No	No	No
B controls agreement	Yes	Yes*	No
A controls reflexivization	Yes	Yes	Yes
B controls reflexivization	Yes*	Yes*	No
A is pivot/controller	No	No	No
B is pivot/controller	Yes*	Yes*	No

The three types of constructions discussed in this article present a fundamental unity: They display a least-oblique dative NP alongside an argument oscillating in its marking between nominative and accusative (and genitive, a case that can encode both intransitive subjects and direct objects). These cases compete as means of encoding what is here characterized as a demoted intransitive subject in a specific configuration with a datival quasi-subject. This configuration is diachronically quite stable, but shows minor changes in case marking characterized here as "obliqueness adjustment", i.e., a replacement of the pattern DAT-NOM with DAT-ACC not motivated by transitivity but rather by the tendency to bring the pattern of case marking in accordance with that of syntactic obliqueness.

Acknowledgments

My thanks are due to the co-editors of this volume, to an anonymous reviewer, and to Ilja Seržant, Nicole Nau, and Wayles E. Browne, for useful criticism and comments on earlier versions of this article. For its shortcomings, I remain solely responsible.

Abbreviations

ACC	accusative	OBL	oblique mood
AUX	auxiliary	PL	plural
COND	conditional	POSS	possessive pronoun
CVB	converb	PPA	past active participle
DAT	dative	PPP	past passive participle
DEB	debitive	PRS	present
DEF	definite	PST	past
DEM	demonstrative	PTCL	particle
F	feminine	REFL	reflexive pronoun
FUT	future	REL	relative pronoun
GEN	genitive	SG	singular
IMP	imperative		
INF	infinitive		
LOC	locative		
M	masculine		
NEG	negation		
NOM	nominative		

References

Aikhenvald, Alexandra Y., Robert M. W. Dixon & Masayuki Onishi (eds.) *Non-canonical marking of subjects and objects*. Amsterdam, Philadelphia: John Benjamins.
Allen, Cynthia. 1986. Reconsidering the history of *like*. *Journal of Linguistics* 22: 375–409.
Andrews, Avery D. 2001. Non-canonical A/S marking in Icelandic. In Alexandra Y. Aikhenvald, Robert M. W. Dixon, & Masayuki Onishi (eds.) *Non-canonical marking of subjects and objects*, 85–111. Amsterdam, Philadelphia: John Benjamins.
Barðdal, Jóhanna. 2001. The perplexity of Dat-Nom verbs in Icelandic. *Nordic Journal of Linguistics* 24: 47–70.
Barðdal, Jóhanna & Thórhallur Eythórsson. 2006. Control infinitives and case in Germanic: 'Performance error' or marginally acceptable constructions? In Leonid Kulikov, Andrej Malchukov, & Peter de Swart (eds.) *Case, valency and transitivity*, 147–177. Amsterdam, Philadelphia: John Benjamins.
Berg-Olsen, Sturla. 1999. A syntactic change in progress: The decline in the use of the non-prepositional genitive in Latvian, with a comparative view on Lithuanian. MA thesis, Oslo University.
Bergmane, Anna, Rūdolfs Grabis, M. Lepika & Evalds Sokols (eds.) 1959. *Mūsdienu latviešu literārās valodas gramatika 1. Fonētika un morfoloģija* [*Grammar of Modern Standard Latvian 1. Phonetics and morphology*]. Rīga: Latvijas PSR Zinātņu akadēmijas izdevniecība.
Bhaskararao, Peri & Karumuri V. Subbarao (eds.). 2004. *Non-nominative subjects*, Vols. 1–2. Amsterdam, Philadelphia: John Benjamins.
Bielenstein, August. 1863/1864. *Die lettische Sprache nach ihren Lauten und Formen erklärend und vergleichend dargestellt*, Bd. I–II. Berlin: Ferdinand Dümmler.
Blake, Barry J. 2001. *Case*. 2nd edition. Cambridge: Cambridge University Press.
Dalrymple, Mary & Irina Nikolaeva. 2011. *Objects and information structure*. Cambridge: Cambridge University Press.
De Haan, Ferdinand. 2006. Typological approaches to modality. In William Frawley (ed.) *The expression of modality*, 27–69. Berlin, New York: Mouton de Gruyter.
Endzelīns, Jānis. 1951. *Latviešu valodas gramatika* [*Grammar of Latvian*]. Rīga: Latvijas valsts izdevniecība.
Haspelmath, Martin. 2001. Non-canonical marking of core arguments in European languages. In Alexandra Y. Aikhenvald, Robert M. W. Dixon & Masayuki Onishi (eds.) *Non-canonical marking of subjects and objects*, 53–83. Amsterdam, Philadelphia: John Benjamins.
Holvoet, Axel. 1998. Notes on the rise and grammaticalization of the Latvian debitive. *Linguistica Baltica* 7: 101–118.
Holvoet, Axel. 2013. Obliqueness, quasi-subjects and transitivity in Baltic and Slavonic. In Ilja Seržant & Leonid Kulikov (eds.). 2013. *The diachronic typology of non-prototypical subjects*, 257–282. Amsterdam, Philadelphia: John Benjamins.
Jackendoff, Ray. 1972. *Semantic interpretation in generative grammar*. Cambridge MA: MIT Press.
Keenan, Edward L. 1976. Towards a universal definition of 'subject'. In Charles N. Li (ed.) *Subject and topic*, 303–333. New York: Academic Press.
Keenan, Edward L. & Bernard Comrie. 1977. Noun phrase accessibility and Universal Grammar. *Linguistic Inquiry* 8(1): 63–91.
Malchukov, Andrej L. & Helen de Hoop. 2011. Tense, aspect, and mood based differential case marking. *Lingua* 121: 35–47.

Mel'čuk, Igor. 1993. The inflectional category of voice: Towards a more rigorous definition. In Bernard Comrie & Maria Polinsky (eds.) *Causatives and transitivity*, 1–46. Amsterdam, Philadelphia: John Benjamins.

Moore, John & David M. Perlmutter. 2000. What does it take to be a dative subject? *Natural Language and Linguistic Theory* 18(2): 373–416.

Narrog, Heiko. 2010. Voice and non-canonical case marking in the expression of event-oriented modality. *Linguistic Typology* 14(1): 71–126.

Nau, Nicole. 1998. *Latvian*. München, Newcastle: LINCOM Europa.

Onishi, Masayuki. 2001. Introduction. In Alexandra Y. Aikhenvald, Robert M. W. Dixon & Masayuki Onishi (eds.) *Non-canonical marking of subjects and objects*, 1–51. Amsterdam, Philadelphia: John Benjamins.

Pollard, Carl J. & Ivan A. Sag. 1994. *Head driven phrase structure grammar*. Chicago, London: University of Chicago Press.

Primus, Beatrice. 1999. *Cases and thematic roles. Ergative, accusative and active*. Tübingen: Niemeyer.

Pullum, Geoffrey K. 1977. Word order universals and grammatical relations. In Peter Cole & Jerrold M. Sadock (eds.) *Syntax and semantics 8. Grammatical relations*, 249–277. New York: Academic Press.

Rappaport, Gilbert C. 1986. On anaphor binding in Russian. *Natural Language and Linguistic Theory* 4(1): 97–120.

Seržant, Ilja. 2013. The acquisition of canonical subjecthood. In Ilja Seržant & Leonid Kulikov (eds.). 2013. *The diachronic typology of non-prototypical subjects*, 283–310. Amsterdam, Philadelphia: John Benjamins.

Seržant, Ilja & Leonid Kulikov (eds.). 2013. *The diachronic typology of non-prototypical subjects*. Amsterdam, Philadelphia: John Benjamins.

Sigurðsson, Halldór Á. 2004. Icelandic non-nominative subjects: Facts and implications. In Bhaskararao, Peri & Karumuri V. Subbarao (eds.). 2004. *Non-nominative subjects*, Vol. 2: 137–159. Amsterdam, Philadelphia: John Benjamins.

Stolz, Thomas. 1987. Das Dativsubjekt – ein Beitrag zur lettischen Kasuslehre. *Indogermanische Forschungen* 92: 220–242.

Timberlake, Alan. 1974. *The nominative object in Slavic, Baltic, and West Finnic*. München: Verlag Otto Sagner.

Zaenen, Annie, Joan Maling & Höskuldur Thráinsson. 1985. Case and grammatical functions: The Icelandic passive. *Natural Language and Linguistic Theory* 3(4): 441–483.

Ilja A. Seržant
8 Dative experiencer constructions as a Circum-Baltic isogloss

1 Introduction

The present chapter is devoted to dative experiencer constructions in the Circum-Baltic area (established in a number of works, cf., inter alia, Stolz 1991, Koptjevskaja-Tamm & Wälchli 2001). I will primarily focus on Russian, West Finnic, and Baltic.

More specifically, I will argue that the languages of the Eastern part of the Circum-Baltic area (i.e., Latvian, Lithuanian, Estonian, Finnish, and Russian) share the same set of properties with certain predicates encoding psychological states. In these languages, there is a productive pattern according to which the experiencer is encoded with the dative case (or with another case that functions as an equivalent of the dative case in the given language[1]) and the object of the experience (stimulus) is encoded with the nominative case, cf.:

(1) Latvian
 Man patīk šī grāmata.
 I:DAT like:3.PRS this:NOM.SG book:NOM.SG
 'I like this book'

An important step toward the claim to be made here has been made primarily by Bossong (1998) and, subsequently, Haspelmath (2001) who show that the dative-like marked experiencers are very productive specifically in the northeastern part of Europe as opposed to the western part of Europe.

Furthermore, the area of dative-like marked experiencers in a subject-like position might potentially be extended to Scandinavia as well. As I will argue below, a low degree of subjecthood is also found in Baltic, Slavic, and Finnic with these predicates. Data from other languages of the area such as (Low) German, Polish, or Belarusian can be adduced.

---

[1] Thus, Finnic languages lack an exact counterpart to Russian or Latvian dative case. In these languages, such local cases as allative or adessive cover the dative domain. The adessive case fulfils the functions of the dative in the possessive *mihi est* construction in Estonian and Finnish. The recipient is usually marked with the allative case in both languages, cf. (Finnish) *Tarjoamme vieraille illallisen* (offer.1PL guest.ALL.PL dinner.ACC=GEN.SG) 'We offer the guests a dinner'.

I will claim that the dative-like marked experiencers can be regarded as a feature that originally pertained at least to the Eastern part of the Circum-Baltic linguistic area. I will concentrate on rather "idiosyncratic" parameters and properties of the constructions in order to provide evidence for the claim that there is much more than a simple typologically frequent constructional pattern found in the area. I will conclude that the presence of dative experiencer constructions across the East of the Circum-Baltic area is a contact-induced or at least contact-facilitated phenomenon, and as a whole, not a result of independent developments or genetic inheritance.

To do so, I will proceed as follows. I will first introduce the semantically oriented notion of DAT (Section 2) that will enable cross-linguistic comparison. Then, I will discuss the question about how typologically frequently recurrent patterns may be shown to be subject of language contact (Section 3). Section 4 contains the main body of the chapter presenting the data and analysis thereof. Here I will discuss two predicate types, namely, a verbal predicate *'to ache'* (Section 4.1) and adverb-like predicatives (Section 4.2), both taking dative experiencers. In these subsections, I will argue that these predicates exhibit correlations across the languages under investigation along all grammatical levels, i.e., in the morphological makeup of the predicates, in their morphosyntactic interface and in the syntactic properties of the DAT case-marked experiencers. In Section 5, I will summarize the main arguments for the claim that there are significant correlations that the pattern exhibits in the Eastern part of the Circum-Baltic area. Finally, Section 6 summarizes the main conclusions.

2 Dative domain (DAT)

In the following, I will use the term dative domain to refer to case markers that are typically used to encode dative semantics in the languages under investigation such as recipient, beneficiary, experiencer, or (external) possessor. The DAT domain is a semantic-functional domain not tied to morphological datives only. Thus, the East Slavic prepositional phrase *u*+gen. 'at sbd.', apart from its purely locative semantics, also has dative functions: It can encode experiencer, beneficiary, and external possessor. In addition, Russian has the old dative case that is in the process of losing grounds in favor of the adessive PP but is still frequently used.

Finnic languages do not have a dedicated dative case except for Livonian. Instead, they use genitive (Finnish only), adessive, or allative cases (Finnish, Estonian, Votic, amd Karelian) to express such semantic roles as recipient, experiencer, or beneficiary (Ariste 1968: 19, Sands & Campbell 2001: 275–276, 288) pertaining to the dative domain (Metuzāle-Kangare & Boiko 2001: 491). Livonian, in turn, has a dative case in -*n* in its Curonian dialect (historically stemming from the genitive and essive) and a second dative in -*l* in the Salis dialect representing a merger of the former adessive and allative case (Sjögren 1861: XLI–XLII, 75–77, 105). Morphologically different cases that are inherently linked to the semantic domain of dative case will be referred to in this chapter as DAT in order to highlight the structural correspondences across these languages and leave aside the morphological discrepancies.

Thus, in Russian and Finnic, there are several strategies that – only if taken together – cover the dative domain, while the Baltic languages have only one strategy, namely, the morphological dative case, that is responsible for this grammatical domain. As a consequence, when comparing the experiencer constructions across these languages, one will unavoidably end up with different correspondence sets because the dative case in Baltic may correspond to several cases in Finnic and to either the adessive PP or the dative case in Russian. The speakers of Estonian, e.g., do not have the same choice of cases if they would switch to Latvian, and subsequently, they would have to stick to the dative case for their adessive and allative because the directionality is not featured in Latvian (Metuzāle-Kangare & Boiko 2001: 491). Exactly as the speakers of some other Finnic languages (such as Votic or Karelian) have to stick with either the dative case or the adessive PP in Russian, whereby the latter two strategies do not have the same distribution of meanings as the adessive/allative vs. genitive case in Finnic.

These discrepancies should not leave astray in making the impression of no correspondence. It is natural that genetically unrelated languages (such as Finnic and Baltic/Slavic) do not have a clear-cut set of correspondences when they come into contact. Such a set may be created as a result of a long contact. Indeed, we observe developments toward such a set: Russian creates another "dative case", the adessive PP, that is not only functionally parallel to the adessive case in Finnic but also employs the same locational metaphor. Finnic and Russian are also parallel in another respect, both gradually replace the older experiencer and external-possessor case, the genitive case in Finnic, and the dative case in Russian with the innovative adessive case/adessive PP. Thus, one finds in older texts the genitive case-marked predicative possessor in Finnish (*minun on* I:GEN is 'I have', cf. Kettunen 1938: XLI) beside the regular adessive case-marked predicative possessor in present day Finnish (*minulla on* I:ADESS is 'I have'). At the same time, only the adessive case-marking is found in Estonian (*mul/minul on* I:ADESS is 'I have'), while the genitive is no longer grammatical in the latter. The same holds for the subject-like experiencers. Finnish allows for both *minun on kylmä* (I:GEN is cold 'I am cold') and *minulla on kylmä* (I:ADESS is cold 'I am cold'). Notably, the former is a conservative option. Estonian again does not have the older, genitive case-marking option, allowing only for adessive here. Now, Russian has undergone a very similar development in replacing the older dative with the – originally only locative – adessive-like PP formed by the preposition *u* 'at' (Veenker 1967: 117–119, Koptjevskaja-Tamm & Wälchli 2001: 676). While the earliest Old Russian still attests the original, inherited option of encoding the predicative possessor with the dative, one finds already in the Middle Russian and regular in Modern Russian the adessive PP encoding the predicative possessor (*u menja jest'* lit. 'at me is', i.e., 'I have'). Seržant and Bjarnadóttir (2014) argue that the Russian verb *bolet'* 'to ache' to be discussed in detail below originally did have the option to encode the experiencer with the dative case while Modern Russian allows the adessive PP only.

Meanwhile, Baltic languages, as has already been mentioned, attest only the original, inherited dative case with no tendency to replace it with some locative expression.[2] The situation found in Livonian is telling in this context. Its northeastern, Salis dialect does not have traces of the dative-like use of the genitive and unifies both adessive and allative into a new dative case, while its southwestern, Curonian dialect loses the non-locative readings of the adessive and allative case and introduces a new dative case (partly) stemming morphologically from the older genitive (Sjörgren 1861: 75–77 and 105). It seems that, with Livonian, one faces here a transitional zone mediating between the two patterns: the new, originally locative adessive in the east and the north as opposed to the old dative (in Livonian *genitivus pro dativo*) in the south (summarized in Table 1).

Tab. 1: Diachronic changes in the encoding of the DAT domain

	Old DAT strategy	New DAT strategy (based on a locative expression)
Russian	Dative	Adessive PP
Finnish	Genitive	Adessive and allative
Estonian	–	Adessive and allative
Livonian/northeastern, Salis dialect	–	Dative<adessive and allative
Livonian/southwestern, Curonian dialect	Dative<genitive	–
Latvian	Dative	–
Lithuanian	Dative	–

---

[2] However, both the allative and the adessive cases have existed in Old Lithuanian and Latvian, cf., inter alia, Seržant (2004a,b) and still exist lexicalized in some eastern Lithuanian subdialects. These cases had only purely locative semantics in these languages.

As can be observed, there is a common development based on the same locative metaphor, namely, '**at** the landmark', to encode meanings from the dative domain showing non-trivial correlations across the languages under investigation already at this point.

3 Areal, inherited, or independent parallelism? Some preliminary considerations

While dative experiencer pattern is not typologically infrequent (Gupta & Tuladhar 1980, Bossong 1998, Haspelmath 2001, Verhoeven 2010, inter alia), it still appears striking that the languages under investigation exhibit correspondences over a whole array of parameters and properties, e.g., the employment of the same conceptualization of the experience events, correspondences in derivational verb morphology (Sections 4.1.1 and 4.2.1), common tendencies in the renewal of the dative encoding (Section 2), correspondences in syntactic behavior (Sections 4.1.2 and 4.2.2), and a higher type frequency of this pattern than in other Standard Average European (SAE) languages, even closely related ones (Bossong 1998). That is, while, in the SAE languages, there is rather a tendency to generalize the transitive nominative (experiencer) – accusative (stimulus) alignment of the experience predicates (Haspelmath 2001), the type frequency of the dative experiencer is twice as high in Russian than in other Slavic languages (not belonging to the Eastern part of the Circum-Baltic Area) such as Bulgarian, Serbian or Czech (Bossong 1998: 285–286). Analogically, it is, furthermore, ca. four times higher in Finnic than in the related Hungarian (Bossong 1998: 282–284).

Different properties of the dative experiencer constructions can be found cross-linguistically. Vice versa, many of the properties found with the dative experiencer construction of the languages under investigation can also be found in comparable constructions of some other languages of the world. However, what matters here is that one finds merely the same set of the correlating properties across the languages under investigation. A specific composition of properties recurrent in the languages at issue makes this pattern more idiosyncratic or exclusive and less typologically general.

To give an example: On the one hand, it is typologically quite probable that a psychological predicate would subcategorize for a less canonical case pattern, construing the experiencer as goal or recipient (cf., inter alia, Bickel 2004) or as a possessor (cf., inter alia, Bossong 1998, König & Haspelmath 1998, Næss 2007: 199). On the other hand, it is less typologically motivated that the very experiencer marking, at the same time, would undergo parallel developments in the languages under investigation (as discussed in Section 2). Recall that it has the tendency to be replaced with a new case in this pattern in both Russian and Finnic, whereby the new Case is based on the same local, *at*-landmark periphrasis. There is no general or typological motivation for specifically this periphrasis and, not, say, for an *in*-landmark pattern replacing the older case marking. Such complex correlations found with the dative experiencer predicates in the East of the Circum-Baltic area make the assumption of an areal influence (at minimum, in terms of an accommodation) strongly suggested (cf. Heine 2009: 39, Seržant 2010: 194–195).[3] In other words, there is much more in common between the dative experiencer constructions in the languages of the Eastern Baltic than with other languages of the world attesting superficially the same pattern: DAT-Verb(-Nom).

One of the major problems of the areal linguistics in general and the research on the Circum-Baltic area in particular is that typologically frequently recurrent patterns are left out from the descriptions of the areas because, in these cases, diffusion cannot sufficiently be argued for against the "null hypothesis" of an independent development (Wälchli 2012, Koptjevskaja-Tamm & Wälchli 2001). The aim of the chapter is to fill this gap. The main idea here is the same as with the "quirky" areal features: For a feature to be shown to be areal, it must be individualized in contrast to its typological background. While quirky features are typologically individuated already at their superficial level by virtue of their typological idiosyncrasy, the individualization of the frequently recurrent features must be sought in a deeper level of analysis, e.g., in an idiosyncratic composition of semantic, syntactic or morphological properties. Thus, Klaiman (1980) suggests that the semantic properties of the dative-subject constructions may also be used to define an areal pattern. The selection of a complex set of implicationally unrelated properties as the main criterion for establishing language contact has been suggested already in Koptjevskaja-Tamm and Wälchli (2001: 732). Notably, these properties do not have to be necessarily central to the function of the pattern. Thus, the makeup of the predicates – e.g., whether they contain a predicative noun with a light verb or whether they are formed by full-fledged verbs – is less relevant for their very function but, at the same time, may be helpful for the typological individualization:

Requirement for idiosyncratic correlations (RIC):
The feature must exhibit correlations along some (typologically) idiosyncratic properties in the languages of the area and/or the very composition of properties in the area of concern must be typologically idiosyncratic.

---

[3] The *paired structural similarity* in Heine (2009: 39) is an important diagnostic for a contact-induced pattern; cf. also the *principle of complex correlation* in Seržant (2010), which assumes that a correlation of a feature's properties in more than one domain in two neighboring languages may be used as evidence for its areal nature.

Furthermore, it is notoriously difficult to decide whether a certain pattern is inherited or contact-induced (Heine 2009), in which case the RIC alone will not warrant areal diffusion, since the typologically idiosyncratic composition of properties or particular typologically idiosyncratic properties may potentially be due to genetic inheritance. In this case, the following requirement has to be satisfied (following Thomason 2007: 94). Note that the conservative effect of language contact is excluded here.

Requirement for the correlation in innovations (RCI):
Correlations satisfying the RIC must contain innovations.

The RCI has to be tested first of all with closely related languages such as Lithuanian and Latvian for the simple reason that in languages of a more distant relation such as, e.g., between English and Irish (both Indo-European), there will assumedly be no instances satisfying RIC that could be explained by the common inheritance. It should be emphasized that the application of RCI is not biconditional. Thus, if RCI is not satisfied, i.e., the feature is inherited in the alleged source and target language, this does not imply that language contact has not played a role here, since theoretically language contact may also be made responsible for the preservation of inherited items.

Since both inheritance and language contact may potentially interplay, I will not concentrate in this chapter on whether or not there were certain inherited prerequisites for the pattern under investigation at earlier layers of the languages involved. Instead, I will argue that regardless of what the historical basis is for this pattern, the issue that solely matters is whether, from the synchronic point of view, it correlates sufficiently across the languages along its "idiosyncratic" properties, satisfying both RIC and RCI. I will regard the evidence as satisfying the RIC and RCI if, in turn, at least one of the three following requirements is met:

i. Two synonymous non-cognate predicates in some two neighboring languages exhibit striking correlations in their derivational morphology (cf. "ähnliche innermorphologische Struktur"[4] in Holvoet 2004: 120).
ii. The predicate in one of the languages is a lexical borrowing (sensu stricto, or MAT(erial) borrowing in Matras and Sakel 2007, Sakel 2007) from another.
iii. Two predicates in two different languages entail the same syntactic status for their core arguments in terms of syntactic (behavioral) properties.

---

4 Similar intra-morphological structure.

i. The languages under discussion have different strategies at disposal to encode low transitivity on the verb. Hence, if two or more predicates from different languages, having the same meaning, but not being etymological cognates, exhibit the same derivational pattern, then this correlation of semantic and morphological properties can hardly be considered accidental. While it is typologically not unusual to mark low transitivity by special verbal morphology, the exact choice of a morphological marker is much more a matter of a particular language and a particular cognitive model involved, especially if the given language has more than one competing means to do so, as do Baltic and Russian.[5] Moreover, typical for a derivational means, the presence *vs.* absence of a particular low-transitivity marker is furthermore matter of lexicon organization in a particular language. Finally, to satisfy RCI, it must be shown that the predicates do not represent archaisms in at least one of the languages.

ii. If two neighboring languages employ the same construction for the same meaning, this in itself is not a sufficient argument in favor of the assumption that this pattern is contact-induced. However, if there are lexical predicates that assign this pattern and that simultaneously are borrowings in one language from the other then the probability of a contact-induced pattern is much higher and can indeed be assumed. The phonetic string of a lexical predicate represents an idiosyncratic feature. The correspondence in idiosyncratic features of a pattern is an indication for a non-independent development.

iii. Experiencer predicates are low on the transitivity scale and none of their arguments exhibits prototypical subjecthood or objecthood in terms of syntactic properties. I consider that a particular subset of syntactic subjecthood tests that the dative-like argument passes or fails to pass as typologically less motivated, since this is exactly the point at which languages having dative experiencers crucially distinguish themselves. Thus, Icelandic dative subjects score highest being compatible with nearly all subjecthood tests in that language, while, on the opposite end of the scale, the dative-like experiencer *to me* in English *it seems to me that* ... can hardly be argued to have any subject properties at all.

In the next section, I will present the application of these principles and the data.

---

[5] Thus, Baltic and Slavic can mark an experience event with a primarily stative marker *-ē- (cf. Lith. *skaud-ė-ti* 'ache', Latvian *sāp-ē-t* 'idem', Russ. *bol-e-t'* 'idem'), with a middle-like infix -n- in present (cf. Lith. *pati-n-ka* 'likes'), with a reflexive periphrasis, cf. Lith. *džiaugti-s* 'to joy'.

4 Analysis

4.1 Verbal predicate 'to ache'

Lithuanian *skaudėti*, Latvian *sāpēt*, and Russian *bolet'* are exact translations of each other, all meaning 'to ache' and all having the same structure: DAT_{EXP}-verb-nom_{STIM}:

(2) Lithuanian
    Man   *skauda*   *galva/galvą.*
    I:DAT   ache:PRS.3   head:NOM.SG/head:ACC.SG

    Latvian
    Man   *sāp*   *galva.*
    I:DAT   ache:PRS.3   head:NOM.SG

    Russian
    U   *menja*   *bolit*   *golova.*
    at   me.GEN   ache:PRS.3SG   head:NOM.SG

    Livonian
    Mi'n   *va'lləbəd*   *ambəd*
    I:DAT   ache:PRS.3PL   tooth:NOM.PL
    'I have a tooth pain.'[6]

    Estonian
    Mul   *valutab*   *pea.*
    I:ADESS   ache:PRS.3SG   head:NOM.SG
    'I have a headache'

    Finnish
    Minulla   *särkee*   *pää/päätä*
    I:ADESS   ache:PRS.3SG   head.NOM.SG/head.PART.SG
    'I have a headache'

It is only Standard Lithuanian and Finnish that also allow for the direct-object marking: accusative in Lithuanian and partitive in Finnish. The DAT-Verb-Acc structure replaces the older DAT-Verb-Nom in Lithuanian (discussed in detail by Seržant 2013). Otherwise, the structures are identical across these languages. It is important that there is more than just a superficial correspondence in case frames.

---

[6] Adopted from Kettunen (1938: 468) in a simplified spelling.

4.1.1 Morphological correlations

If we first limit ourselves just to the Indo-European languages of the East Circum-Baltic Area (i.e., Lithuanian, Latvian, and Russian), we see that despite not being etymological cognates in any pair of the languages, these verbs exhibit a number of morphological correspondences, which therefore can hardly be accidental:

i. In all three languages, *ache*-verbs show the same derivational morphology, namely, the traditionally stative or functionally rather deagentivizing (Seržant 2011) suffix (historically) *-ē-: Lith. *skaud-ė-ti*, Latv. *sāp-ē-t*, Russ. *bol'-e-t'*.

ii. Furthermore, this deagentivizing suffix, if added to a verbal base, required historically zero grade of the root (LIV²: 25, Seržant 2011). Thus, one would expect to find something like Lith. *skudėti, Latv. *s(a)pēt/*s(i)pēt, Russ. *blet'. Instead, one finds the unexpected *o*-grade (yielding -*a*- in the Baltic languages) in all three cases: Lith. *sk-a-udėti*, Latv. *s-ā-pēt*, Russ. *b-o-l'et'*.[7] The combination of the root *o*-grade and the deagentivizing suffix *-ē- points out that these verbs are rather denominal in their origin because the *o*-grades have been typically employed to derive nouns in Proto-Indo-European (see Seržant & Bjarnadóttir 2014 for a comprehensive historical account).[8]

iii. Not only do Russian, Lithuanian, and Latvian exhibit striking correspondences in the morphological makeup of the verb, but Estonian and Livonian also show considerable similarity as well. The Estonian and Livonian verbs both are also denominal in origin containing the noun *valu* 'pain, ache'. The Estonian verb *valu-ta-* 'ache' employs the causative/factitive suffix *-ta-*. The same is true for its Livonian cognate. Interestingly, while it is also denominal in the origin it is a causative formation, the latter being seemingly in contradiction to the deagentivizing suffix *-ē- in Baltic and Slavic. However, this issue is more complicated than appears at first glance, and there are parallels even here. In Latvian – a language that has the most intensive contacts with Estonian (Stolz 1991) – an etymologically different suffix originating from the old causative paradigm became phonetically identical to the deagentivizing suffix -*ē*- due to a series of morphological and phonetic changes (for the most comprehensive historical account, see Ostrowski 2006), cf. *aug-t* 'to grow' vs. (caus.) *audz-ē-t* 'to cultivate'. In other words, Latvian -*ē*- may have both functions: (i) derivation of less agentive denominal verbs and (ii) derivation of causatives. By this, it

---

[7] Note that this verb had the meaning of "to be sick" (with a nominative experiencer and no slot for a stimulus) in Old Russian and Old Church Slavonic.
[8] The *o*-grade has mainly been used to derive different kinds of nominal formations as well as forms of the reduplicated perfect in Proto-Indo-European.

patterns with both Lithuanian in respect to the original function and with Estonian along its secondary function. Notably, Latvia is also geographically situated between Estonian and Lithuanian. In turn, it is only Finnish that employs a lexical verb that elsewhere has the meaning 'to break' (summarized in Table 2).

Tab. 2: Distribution of the causativizing and the detransitivizing morphological strategies with the denominal verbs of pain

	Deagentivizing suffix	Causativizing suffix
Finnish	–	–
Estonian		+
Livonian		+
Latvian	+	
Russian	+	
Lithuanian	+	

4.1.2 Syntactic correlations

Additionally, there are syntactic correspondences among Baltic, Russian, and Finnic. The syntactic structure these verbs assign is also exactly the same. In all three languages, the DAT argument shows the same degree of subjecthood: It can control reflexivization (cf. 3) and it occupies the first position in an unmarked word order:

(3) Lithuanian
 Man   skauda   širdį   dėl   savo   vaiko.
 I:DAT ache:PRS.3 heart:ACC.SG for   REFL.GEN   child:GEN.SG

 Latvian
 Man   sāp   sirds   par   savu   bērnu.
 I:DAT   ache:PRS.3 heart:NOM.SG about   REFL.ADJ   child:ACC.SG

 Russian
 U   men'a   bolit   serdce   za   svoego   rebenka.
 at   me:GEN   ache:PRS.3SG   heart:NOM.SG for   REFL.ADJ   child:GEN.SG

 Estonian
 Mul   valutab   süda   oma   lapse   pärast.
 I:ADESS   ache:PRS.3SG heart:NOM.SG REFL.GEN   child:GEN.SG   for
 'I am worrying about my child.' (lit. 'I have heartache for my child')

I skip here the data from Finnish because this language lacks a possessive reflexive pronoun.

At the same time, the DAT argument lacks other subject behavioral properties, (cf. Keenan 1976, Onishi 2001), such as, the subject control in infinitival subclauses, in which the logical subject of the complement subclause is omitted on identity with the subject of the main predicate (cf. 4).

(4) Lithuanian
*Ne-noriu   skaudėti   galva/galvą.
NEG-want:PRS.1SG ache:INF   head:NOM.SG/head:ACC.SG

Latvian
*Ne-gribu   sāpēt   galva.
NEG-want:PRS.1SG ache:INF   head:NOM.SG

Russian
*Ne   xoču   bolet'   golova
NEG   want:PRS.1SG   ache:INF   head:NOM.SG

Estonian
*Ma   ei   taha   valutada   pead.
I   NEG   want   ache:INF   head:PART.SG

Finnish
*Minä   en   halua   särkeä   päätä
I:NOM   NEG.1SG   want   ache:INF   head:PART.SG
Intended meaning: 'I don't want to have headache'

I turn to the conjunction reduction test. This test is less informative in our context, because the languages under investigation allow for *pro*-drop in the first and second person and, partly, in the third person (under different conditions, however). Generally, utterances as in (5) are acceptable rather in those contexts where the DAT argument's referent is the active discourse topic anyway. The omission of the subject pronoun is rather due to the *pro*-drop effect. The referential identity between the dropped nominative argument and the DAT argument is rather due to pragmatics, and provided the right context, the co-referential interpretation might be cancelled. To conclude, the DAT argument is not good at controlling the subject left unexpressed in conjoined clauses[9]:

(5) Lithuanian
?Jam   skauda   galvą   ir   Ø
he:DAT   ache:PRS.3   head:ACC.SG   and

---

[9] Thus, the subject left unexpressed need not be co-referential with the DAT argument given the appropriate context.

ne-gali	*užmigti.*			
NEG-can:PRS.3	fall.asleep:INF			

Latvian
?Viņam	*sāp*	*galva*	*un* Ø
he:DAT	ache:PRS.3	head:NOM.SG	and
ne-var	*aizmigt.*		
NEG-can:PRS.3	fall.asleep:INF		

Russian
?U	*nego*	*bolit*	*golova*	*i* Ø
at	him	ache:PRS.3SG	head:NOM.SG	and
ne	*možet*	*zasnut'*		
NEG	can:PRS.3SG	fall.asleep:INF		

Estonian
?Tal	*valutab*	*pea*	*ja*	Ø
s/he:ADESS	ache:PRS.3.SG	head:NOM.SG	and	
ei	*saa*	*magada.*		
NEG	CAN	SLEEP:INF		

Finnish
?Hänellä	*särkee*	*pää/päätä*	*eikä*	Ø
s/he:ADESS	ache:PRS.3.SG	head:NOM.SG/PART.SG	NEG.3SG-and	
saa	*nukuttua*			
GET.PRS.3	sleep:PTC.PART			

Intended meaning: 'He has headache and cannot fall asleep'

While the first position in unmarked word order and reflexivization control both reveal a subject-like behavior of the DAT argument in these languages, such subjecthood tests as the control of PRO in infinitival complements do not hold. Note, however, that the former properties are not necessarily exclusive of subjects in these languages and may have other motivations. In total, one finds considerable correlations as to the syntactic behavior of the DAT argument across these languages in that they are endowed with only some few and not unambiguous subject properties.

To sum up, the 'ache'-verbs in Lithuanian, Latvian, Estonian, and Russian exhibit the same set of morphological and syntactic correspondences: They all show traces of denominal origin and they all exhibit the same degree of subjecthood of the DAT argument – a fact that can hardly be accidental. Meanwhile, none of these verbs are etymological cognates. Even the two closely related Baltic languages (Lithuanian and Latvian) exhibit two etymologically different verbs here. The etymological unrelatedness, on the one hand, and a number of striking correspondences in morphology and syntax, on the other, can only be accounted for by assuming a contact-induced convergence between the languages in this domain.

4.2 Predicatives

There is a large number of predicatives used with a copula 'to be' in Russian, Lithuanian, Latvian, Estonian, and Finnish, which have a dative-like marked experiencer.[10]

(6) Latvian
| Man | (ir) | žēl | +GEN/ACC |
| Man | (yra) | gaila | +GEN |

Russian
| Mne | ∅ | žal' | +GEN/ACC |
| I:DAT | (be:PRS.3) | sorry:ADV | |

Estonian
| Mul | on | kahju | +PART |
| I:ADESS | be:PRS.3SG | sorry | |

Finnish
| Minun | on | sääli | +PART |
| I:GEN | be:PRS.3SG | sorry | |

Finnish
| Minulla | on | sääli | +PART |
| I:ADESS | be:PRS.3SG | sorry | |

'I am sorry about (someone).'

Again, as in the case of verbs of pain discussed above, Latvian, Lithuanian, Russian, Estonian, and Finnish exhibit structurally the same pattern: DAT-(copula)-adv, which can optionally be extended with a genitive/partitive or (as a later innovation in Latvian and Russian) accusative case-marked object (see Holvoet, this volume, on Latvian). In all languages, the experiencer is

---

10 In present indicative clauses, the copula is optional in Baltic and Finnic and is impossible in Russian. It is otherwise obligatory in order for the clause to be marked for other tenses and moods.

case-marked with the case that correlates with the dative domain in that language. While Finnish preserves the older genitive alongside the more productive, adessive case marking, Estonian allows only for the adessive case marking on the experiencer in this construction. Both the genitive case in Finnish and the adessive case in Finnish and Estonian correlate with the dative case in Baltic and Russian in other constructions too. Recall that neither Finnish nor Estonian has dative case proper.

4.2.1 Morphological correlations

What is striking in this example is the fact that alongside the structural similarity of the patterns in different languages, there is no direct genetic inheritance in the morphology of the predicates even in such closely related languages as Finnish and Estonian or Latvian and Lithuanian. Thus, Latvian *žēl* is a very old borrowing from Old Russian *žāli,[11] exactly as is the Finnish *sääli*, which preserves the old ending *-i* and the original length of the root vowel. Thus, there has been a large degree of interaction between these languages on the lexical level from ancient times. The fact that there was a significant interference on the lexical level may suggest that the syntactic level was not untouched by language contact either, since a predicate can neither exist detached from its case frame, nor can it be uttered in isolation like, for instance, lexemes that denote artifacts. This means that the borrower always faces an utterance of a given predicate with its syntactic structure in the source language, and hence, (s)he is likely to copy the whole pattern.

4.2.2 Syntactic correlations

As in the case of verbs of pain, the DAT argument of the predicatives shows only a low degree of subjecthood: It can control reflexivization and tends to occupy the first position in the unmarked word order, but it fails to control the reference of the subjects of coordinated clauses (cf. 7). Latvian and Lithuanian are slightly different from the other languages in that sentences as in (7) are not entirely impossible here. Crucially, however, the subject left unexpressed in the conjoined clause is not controlled by the DAT argument in these languages as well. Thus, (7) is only grammatical

---

[11] The borrowing of Old Russian *žal'* into Latvian *žēl* shows such features as long vowel retention and the change from Old Russian *ā* to *ē* in Latvian, which are typical for borrowings dating back to no later than the twelfth century, cf. Seržant (2006) for details.

in Latvian or Lithuanian if the referent of the subject left unexpressed is otherwise retrievable from the context than just from the presence of the DAT argument:

(7) Finnish
*Pekan oli kylmä ja Ø haki huovan.[12]

Russian
*Pekke bylo xolodno i Ø prines odejalo

Latvian
?Pekam bija auksti un Ø atnesa segu.

Lithuanian
?Pekkui buvo šalta ir Ø atnešė antklodę.
Pekka:DAT COP:PST.3 cold:ADV and bring:PST.3 blanket
Intended meaning: 'Pekka was cold and fetched a blanket'

Subject control of PRO in infinitival complements results in ungrammaticality, cf. (8), which is ungrammatical in all languages under discussion:

(8) Lithuanian
*Ne-noriu būti šalta
NEG-want:PRS.1SG be:INF cold:ADV

Latvian
*Ne-gribu būt auksti
NEG-want:PRS.1SG be:INF cold:ADV

Russian
*Ne xoču byt' xolodno
NEG want:PRS.1SG be:INF cold:ADV

Estonian
*Ei taha olla külm
NEG want be:INF cold:ADV
Intended meaning: 'I don't want to be cold'

5 Both patterns outside the languages of concern

There are several criteria that make the patterns discussed typologically standing out with respect to the surrounding languages: (i) it is the morphological makeup

---

12 From Sands and Campbell (2001: 289).

of the verbs in Section 4.1 and of the predicatives in Section 4.2 that provides for the individuation on the typological background; (ii) it is their syntactic makeup that shows striking correlation on the background of the surrounding languages.

i. The recurrent morphological makeup of the respective verbs discussed in Section 4.1.1 at length is specific to the languages under investigation. Thus, one finds a different construction in, e.g., Czech *mam bolesti hlavy* (lit. 'I **have** a headache'). The alternative construction in this language *hlava mě bolí* (head:NOM I:ACC aches) matches morphologically to the pattern described in Section 4.1.1.

As regards the predicatives discussed in 4.2, Czech has analogical pattern *je mi líto* (is me:DAT pity) 'I am sorry'. However, as I have shown in Section 4.2.1, the predicative 'pity' is a borrowing from the oldest stage of Old Russian into Finnish and Latvian, which, again, suggests a somewhat closer relationship between the Eastern Circum-Baltic languages as opposed to the wider European background.

ii. When it comes to the case frame of the *ache*-verbs, one finds accusative case marking of the experiencer in Czech in contrast to the pattern under investigation. Furthermore, as Seržant and Bjarnadóttir (2014) show, the argument marking of the Russian verb *bolet'* has undergone a series of changes in the history of Russian, finally yielding structurally similar pattern to the one in Baltic and Finnic and quite different from the one that it had in Old Russian. Without going into details here, I just state that at some stage of development (approximately Late Old Russian), the experiencer marking of the corresponding Old Russian/Old Church Slavonic verb *boléti* was accusative (standard), dative or, later, the adessive PP (Danylenko 2003: 105–106, Krys'ko 2006: 117–119, Seržant & Bjarnadóttir 2014). Thus, Ukrainian dialects still preserve all three options,[13] while West Slavic languages opt for the accusative case marking as does Czech. Crucially, while West Slavic languages have generalized the accusative case marking, which has been the most frequent option in Old Russian too, Modern Russian has generalized the adessive PP and lost the accusative option altogether. Even more, it has also lost the option to encode the experiencer with the dative case in favor of the adessive PP that is the closest Russian counterpart of the Finnic adessive case. Baltic languages simply did not have this choice because the adessive case has been lost here. I take the rise and generalization of the adessive-like PP in Russian as a strong evidence in favor of the areal influence from Finnic.

---

13 Cf. also German that allows for both accusative and dative case marking of the experiencer with *schmerzen* 'to ache'.

As regards syntactic correlations found with the predicates under investigation, I concede, these do not define the Eastern Circum-Baltic area on their own in terms of discriminating it from the neighboring languages as do the more idiosyncratic morphological properties or common developments in the case marking. Thus, similar syntactic behavior is found in SAE languages (see Haspelmath 2001: 67–75). Nevertheless, the syntactic correlations additionally strengthen the claim that the pattern is syntactically uniform in the area – a fact that by no means is typologically motivated. As I have mentioned in Section 3, the syntactic behavior of the experiencer datives varies cross-linguistically considerably from Icelandic with all syntactic subject properties to English with none. The dative experiencers in Hindi, Marathi, and Nepali pass such subjecthood tests as *raising, equi-NP deletion (control), control over the reflexive, conjunction reduction* (Gupta & Tuladhar 1980), which makes them syntactically quite distinct from the Circum-Baltic dative experiencers (cf. also Masica 1976: 164 on the lack of parallels for the dative subjects of the South-Asian sprachbund). At the same time, the same tests have been shown positive for the other languages of the area not genetically related to Indo-Aryan, namely, the Dravidian languages. Thus, Kannada, a Dravidian language shows the same test values as Hindi or Nepali with regard to dative subjects (cf. the tests in Sridhar 1979). Analogically, the dative experiencer arguments of the East Caucasian (Nakh-Daghestanian) languages, e.g., in Agul, pattern syntactically rather with subjects of Western European languages, e.g., by allowing and controlling the co-referential omission (Ganenkov, Maisak, & Merdanova 2008), in contrast to the pattern discussed here. Finally, the cross-linguistic study of oblique subjects of Bhaskararao and Subbarao (2004) treating a number of dative or dative-like non-canonical subjects reveals that even those dative arguments that can be analyzed as non-canonical subjects vary as to how much behavioral subject properties they are endowed with.

Furthermore, as has been repeatedly claimed in the literature, a particular set of (behavioral and coding) subject properties is characteristic not only of a particular language, but rather of a particular construction and varies both intra- and cross-linguistically (cf. Croft 2001). Thus, Moore and Perlmutter (2000), while discussing the Russian dative first arguments, state that only those dative first arguments can be treated as a kind of subjects that trigger gender and number agreement while the others cannot.

To conclude, the syntactic tests provide an important, typologically rather idiosyncratic characteristic of the pattern. They support the claim of uniformity of the pattern in the languages under investigation, but at the same time, they establish a link to the Eastern part of the SAE (as described by Haspelmath 2001: 62). The latter does not come as a surprise, since one would not expect to find an abrupt boundary between the east of the CBA and the east of SAE, where the analogical construction would have a completely different syntactic makeup.

6 Conclusions

In this chapter, I have tried to make a case on how typologically recurrent features may also be shown to be driven by the areal diffusion processes. The main idea consists in "zooming-in" on the feature of concern establishing the typologically individual profile of the feature based on a set of its semantic and formal properties.

In Section 3, I have introduced my framework based on the RIC and RCI, which allow for individualizing particular features on the basis of their typological background and exclude inheritance as a potential reason for the correlation of their individual profiles.

In Section 4, I have discussed two subclasses of experiencer predicates in West Finnic, Baltic, and Russian. These predicates show striking structural parallelisms in lexical, morphological, and syntactic levels across the languages of the Eastern Circum-Baltic Area. At the same time, none of the discussed predicates are etymological cognates with any of its translational equivalents, even in such closely related languages as Lithuanian and Latvian (one exception may be the dialectal Lithuanian *sopėti* and Standard Latvian *sāpēt* 'to ache'). To provide sufficient evidence for the claim about the contact-induced nature of the phenomenon in question, I have formulated three characteristics (Section 3), at least one of which has to be met to make an areal account plausible and to exclude an independent parallel development. The innovative character and the lack of etymological counterparts in the ancestor language exclude inheritance as a factor in convergence. I have argued that all three characteristics are met in the case of verbs of pain and predicatives. As already mentioned, if one or more characteristics are met, then the chance of independent parallel development can be safely excluded as improbable.

The syntactic, morphological, and lexical coherence of the experiencer constructions across the languages of the Eastern Baltic area suggests that this pattern is areally induced. This claim does not exclude the fact that some of the constructions may be inherited and are possibly not acquired via language contact as such. This claim only implies that they must have been remodelled at some later stage of the language history in accordance with, and adjusting to, the prevalent areal pattern along their properties. I admit, thereby, that certain properties of the dative experiencer have been different in the respective languages before they entered the contact zone. In other words, my minimal claim is that the dative experiencer constructions discussed here must have been at least considerably adjusted to the areal pattern (thus commonly created) but not necessarily borrowed completely from one of the languages into another. Indeed, ancient Indo-European languages restrictedly do attest dative experiencers. Nevertheless, there are considerable differences between the ancient Indo-European languages such as Sanskrit, on the one hand, and Baltic and Russian, on the other hand, as regards the morphological makeup of the respective predicates, the degree of integration of dative experiencers into the case frame of the respective verbs and other properties.

Another case of adjustment and not of a complete borrowing is found with the independent partitive case (Seržant 2015). The reason for the changes found in the syntactic behavior and function is due to a certain degree of "assimilation" of the Baltic and Slavic independent "partitive" genitive case with the Finnic independent partitive case that results in the creation of a common, Finno-Baltic-Slavic *partitive-case* pattern. Both the independent partitive case of Finnic and the "partitive" function of the independent genitive case of Baltic and Russian are inherited from the respective proto-languages; nevertheless, they exhibit considerable permutations that cannot be explained but by mutual influence. The creation of a common core pattern consists of a number of rather small micro-processes that affect particular properties of a category, and for each of these micro-processes, the target and the source languages must be determined independently.

Although I have examined only a small group of predicates, the areal analysis can be readily extended to a broader class of verbs. Hakulinen (1955: 240–241, 243) cites a large number of Finnish verbs with non-canonically marked highest ranked arguments (traditionally referred to as impersonal verbs) alongside their Russian counterparts and shows that in both languages exactly the same case frame is used. The structural parallelism in the encoding of experiencer events in Finnic and Slavic is not confined to just dative-like case-marked experiencers. One also finds an overwhelming correlation in accusative or object-like case-marked experiencers across these languages. Thus, a number of experiencer predicates in Finnish (cited in Hakulinen 1955) and Estonian (Erelt & Metslang 2006: 262, Lindström 2013) encode the experiencer as a direct object (i.e., with the partitive case), which corresponds to the semantically equivalent predicates with accusative case-marked experiencers in Russian, Latvian, and Lithuanian.[14] Moreover, the DAT experiencers are frequently grammaticalized into obligees of modal verbs (cf., inter alia, Holvoet 2003, 2004 suggesting the possessive origin of

---

14 Note that the partitive case is a canonical option to encode direct objects in Finnic. The alternation between the accusative (traditionally referred to as genitive) object marking and the partitive object marking is conditioned by a variety of factors not related to the present discussion (actionality interpretation of the VP, NP-related properties, etc.), cf. Kiparsky (1998), Huumo (2010), and Seržant (forthcoming).

the DAT argument; Kettunen 1938: lxviii for Livonian) and non-canonical subjects of "ergative-like" perfects in this area (Seržant 2012).

Furthermore, the correspondence in the encoding of experiencer events can be extended to precursors of Swedish and Norwegian as well, since the ancestors of these languages had quite similar patterns. Thus, accusative and dative case-marked experiencers with some syntactic subject-like properties are well known from Old Norse, which preserves the original stage of development (Faarlund 2001; Eythórsson & Barðdal 2005). However, in Old Swedish, a number of experiencer predicates are also attested with a dative or accusative experiencers exhibiting quite delimited subset of the syntactic properties of nominative subjects, not sufficient to claim subjecthood (Falk 1997, Faarlund 2001). Parallel to Old Scandinavian is (Low) German, which has played an important role in the area of concern. This language equally has a number of experiencer predicates whose main argument is coded by the dative case and is not syntactically a subject in this language (Bayer 2004, pace Barðdal 2006).

I conclude that dative-like marked experiencers can be regarded as a feature that originally pertained to the entire Circum-Baltic Area and that represents one of its most important syntactic isoglosses in the Eastern part of the Circum-Baltic Area.

Acknowledgments

I am indebted to (alphabetically) Cori Andersen (Princeton), Peter Arkadiev (Moscow), Valgerður Bjarnadóttir (Stockhom), Chiara Fedriani (Pavia), Petar Kehayov (Tartu), Tuomas Huumo (Turku), and Björn Wiemer (Mainz) for their invaluable comments. All disclaimers apply.

Abbreviations

ACC	accusative	INF	infinitive
ADESS	adessive	NOM	nominative
ADJ	adjective	PART	partitive
ADV	adverb	PRS	present
ALLAT	allative	PST	past
COP	copula	REFL	reflexive
DAT	dative	SG	singular
GEN	genitive		

References

Ariste, Paul. 1968. *A Grammar of the Votic Language*. Indiana University Publications, Uralic and Altaic Series, 68. Bloomington: Indiana University Press.
Barðdal, Jóhanna. 2006. Construction-specific properties of syntactic subjects in Icelandic and German. *Cognitive Linguistics* 17(1): 39–106.
Bayer, Joseph. 2004. Non-nominative subjects in comparison. In Peri Bhaskararao & Karumuri Venkata Subbarao (eds.) *Non-nominative subjects*. Vol. 1, 49–76. Amsterdam, Philadelphia: John Benjamins.
Bhaskararao, Peri & Karumuri Venkata Subbarao (eds.). 2004. *Non-nominative subjects*. Vols. 1–2. Amsterdam, Philadelphia: John Benjamins.
Bickel, Balthasar. 2004. The syntax of experiencers in the Himalayas. In Peri Bhaskararao & Karumuri Venkata Subbarao (eds.) *Non-nominative subjects*. Vol. 1, 77–111. Amsterdam, Philadelphia: John Benjamins.
Bossong, Georg. 1998. Le marquage de l'experient dans les langues de l'Europe. In Jack Feuillet (éd.) *Actance et valence dans les langues de l'Europe*, 259–294. Berlin, New York: Mouton de Gruyter.
Croft, Wiliam. 2001. *Radical construction grammar. Syntactic theory in typological perspective*. Oxford: Oxford University Press.
Danylenko, A. 2003. *Predykaty, Vidminky i Diatezy v Ukraïns'kij Movi: Istoryčnyj i Typolohičnyj Aspekty*. (Predicates, cases and diatheses in Ukrainian: historical and typological aspects). Xarkiv: Oko.
Erelt, Matti & Helle Metslang. 2006. Estonian clause patterns – from Finno-Ugric to Standard Average European. *Linguistica Uralica* 42(4): 254–266.
Eythórsson, Thórhallur & Jóhanna Barðdal. 2005. Oblique subjects: A common Germanic inheritance. *Language* 81(4): 824–881.
Faarlund, Jan Terje. 2001. The notion of oblique subject and its status in the history of Icelandic. In Jan Terje Faarlund (ed.) *Grammatical relations in change*, 99–137. Amsterdam, Philadelphia: John Benjamins.
Falk, Cecilia. 1997. *Fornsvenska upplevarverb*. Lund: Lund University Press.
Ganenkov, Dmitry, Timur Maisak & Solmaz R. Merdanova. 2008. Involuntary agent as non-canonical subject in Agul. In Helen de Hoop & Peter de Swart (eds.) *Differential subject marking*, 173–198. Dordrecht: Springer.
Gupta, Sagar Mal & Jyoti Tuladhar. 1980. Dative subject constructions in Hindi, Nepali and Marathi and Relational Grammar. *Contributions to Nepalese Studies* 7(1–2): 119–153.
Hakulinen, Lauri. 1955. *Razvitie i struktura finskogo jazyka. II. Leksikologija i sintaksis.* [*The development and structure of Finnish II. Lexicology and Syntax.*] Moscow: Izdatel'stvo inostrannoj literatury.
Haspelmath, Martin. 2001. Non-canonical marking of core arguments in European languages. In Alexandra Y. Aikhenvald, R. M. W. Dixon & Masayuki Onishi (eds.) *Non-canonical marking of subjects and objects*, 53–83. Amsterdam, Philadelphia: John Benjamins.
Heine, Bernd. 2009. Identifying instances of contact-induced grammatical replication. In Samuel Gyasi Obeng (ed.) *Topics in descriptive and African linguistics. Essays in honor of distinguished professor Paul Newman*, 29–56. München, Newcastle: LINCOM Europa.
Holvoet, Axel. 2003. Modal constructions with 'be' and the infinitive in Slavonic and Baltic. *Zeitschrift für Slawistik* 48(4): 465–480.

Holvoet, Axel. 2004. Eine modale Konstruktion ostseefinnischer Herkunft im Lettischen. In Irma Hyvärinen, Petri Kallio & Jarmo Korhonen (eds.) *Etymologie, Entlehnungen und Entwicklungen. Fs. für J. Koivulehto zum 70. Geburtstag*, 117–127. Helsinki.

Huumo, Tuomas. 2010. Nominal aspect, quantity, and time: The case of the Finnish object. *Journal of Linguistics* 46(1): 83–125.

Keenan, Edward L. 1976. Towards a universal definition of "subject". In Charles N. Li (ed.) *Subject and topic*, 303–333. New York: Academic Press.

Kettunen, Lauri. 1938. *Livisches Wörterbuch mit grammatischer Einleitung*. Lexica Societatis Fenno-Ugricae V. Helsinki.

Kiparsky, Paul. 1998. Partitive case and aspect. In Miriam Butt & William Geuder (eds.) *The projection of arguments. Lexical and compositional factors*, 265–307. Stanford: CSLI Publications.

König, Ekkehard & Martin Haspelmath. 1998. Les constructions à possesseur externe dans les langues de l'Europe. In Jack Feuillet (ed.) *Actance et valence dans les langues de l'Europe*, 525–606. Berlin, New York: Mouton de Gruyter.

Klaiman, Miriam H. 1980. Bengali dative subjects. *Lingua* 51: 275–295.

Koptjevskaja-Tamm, Maria & Bernhard Wälchli. 2001. The Circum-Baltic languages: An areal-typological approach. In Östen Dahl & Maria Koptjevskaja-Tamm (eds.) *Circum-Baltic languages. Typology and contact*. Vol. 2, 615–750. Amsterdam, Philadelphia: John Benjamins.

Krys'ko, Vadim B. 2006. *Istoričeskij sintaksis russkogo jazyka: Ob"ekt i perexodnost'*. (Historical Syntax of Russian. The object and Transitivity) 2-nd ed. Moscow: Azbukovnik.

Lindström, Liina. 2013. Between Finnic and Indo-European: Variation and change in the Estonian experiencer-object construction. In Ilja A. Seržant & Leonid Kulikov (eds.) *The diachronic typology of non-canonical subjects*, 139–162. Amsterdam, Philadelphia: John Benjamins.

LIV[2]. 2001. *Lexikon der indogermanischen Verben. Die Wurzeln und ihre Primärstammbildun*. Zweite, erweiterte und verbesserte Auflage, bearbeitet von Martin Kümmel und Helmut Rix. Wiesbaden: Reichert.

Matras, Yaron & Sakel, Jeanette. 2007. Investigating the mechanisms of pattern replication in language convergence. *Studies in Language* 31(4): 829–865.

Masica, Colin P. 1976. *Defining a linguistic area: South Asia*. Chicago: University of Chicago Press.

Metuzāle-Kangare, Baiba & Kersti Boiko. 2001. Case systems and syntax in Latvian and Estonian. In Östen Dahl & Maria Koptjevskaja-Tamm (eds.) *Circum-Baltic languages. Typology and contact*. Vol. 2, 481–497. Amsterdam, Philadelphia: John Benjamins.

Moore, John & David M. Perlmutter. 2000. What does it take to be a dative subject? *Natural Language and Linguistic Theory* 18: 373–416.

Næss, Åshild. 2007. *Prototypical transitivity*. Amsterdam, Philadelphia: John Benjamins.

Onishi, Masayuki. 2001. Non-canonically marked subjects and objects: Parameters and properties. In Alexandra Yu. Aikhenvald, R. M. W. Dixon, & Masayuki Onishi (eds.) *Non-canonical marking of subjects and objects*, 1–52. Amsterdam, Philadelphia: John Benjamins.

Ostrowski, Norbert. 2006. *Studia z historii czasownika litewskiego. Iteratiwa. Denominatiwa*. Poznań: Wydawnictwo Naukowe UAM.

Sakel, Jeanette. 2007. Types of loan: Matter and pattern. In Yaron Matras & Jeanette Sakel (eds.) *Grammatical borrowing in cross-linguistic perspective*, 15–29. Berlin, New York: Mouton de Gruyter.

Sands Kristina & Lyle Campbell. 2001. Non-canonical subjects and objects in Finnish. In Alexandra Yu. Aikhenvald, R. M. W. Dixon, & Masayuki Onishi (eds.) *Non-canonical marking of subjects and objects*, 251–305. Amsterdam, Philadelphia: John Benjamins.
Seržant, Ilja A. 2004a. K voprosy ob obrazovanii adessiva (On the development of the adessive case). *Acta Linguistica Lithuanica* 51: 49–57.
Seržant, Ilja A. 2004b. Zur Vorgeschichte des Inessivs im Urostbaltischen. *Acta Linguistica Lithuanica 51: 59–67.*
Seržant, Ilja A. 2006. Vermittlungsrolle des Hochlettischen bei den Altrussischen und litauischen Entlehnungen im Lettischen. *Acta Linguistica Lithuanica* 55: 89–105.
Seržant, Ilja A. 2010. Phonologische Isoglossen des Hochlettischen, Nord-Ost-Litauischen, Nord-West-Russischen und Weißrussischen. *Baltic Linguistics* 1: 193–214.
Seržant, Ilja A. 2011. Die Entstehung der Kategorie Inagentiv im Tocharischen. In Thomas Krisch & Thomas Lindner unter redaktioneller Mitwirkung von Michael Crombach & Stefan Niederreiter, *Indogermanistik und Linguistik im Dialog. Akten der XIII. Fachtung der Indogermanischen Gesellschaft vom 21. bis 27. September 2008 in Salzburg*, 527–537. Wiesbaden: Reichert.
Seržant, Ilja A. 2012. The so-called possessive perfect in North Russian and the Circum-Baltic area. A diachronic and areal approach. *Lingua* 122: 356–385.
Seržant, Ilja A. 2013. Rise of canonical objecthood with the Lithuanian verbs of pain. *Baltic Linguistics* 4: 187–211.
Seržant, Ilja A. 2015. Independent partitive as a Circum-Baltic isogloss, *Journal Language Contact* 8: 341–418.
Seržant, Ilja A. & Valgerður Bjarnadóttir. 2014. Verbalization and non-canonical case marking of some irregular verbs in *-ē- in Baltic and Russian. In Artūras Judžentis, Tatyana Civjan & Maria Zavyalova (eds.) *Baltai ir Slavai: Dvasinių kulūtors sankritos. Balty I Slavjane: peresečenie duxovnyx kul'tur. Skiriama akademikui Vladimirui Toporovui atminti*, 218–242. Vilnius: Versmė.
Sjörgren, Joh. Andreas. 1861. *Livische Grammatik nebst Sprachproben.* Gesammelte Schriften. Band II. Theil I. St. Petersburg. Reprinted in: Unveränderter fotomechanischer Nachdruck der Originalausgabe. Leipzig: Zentralantiquariat der DDR. 1969.
Sridhar, S. N. 1979. Dative subjects and the notion of subject. *Lingua* 49: 99–125.
Stolz, Thomas. 1991. *Sprachbund im Baltikum? Estnisch und Lettisch im Zentrum einer sprachlichen Konvergenzlandschaft.* Bochum: Brockmeyer.
Thomason, Sarah G. 2007. *Language contact (an introduction).* 2nd Edition. Edinburgh. Edinburgh University Press.
Veenker, Wolfgang. 1967. *Die Frage des finnougrischen Substrats in der russischen Sprache.* Bloomington, IN: Indiana University.
Verhoeven, Elisabeth. 2010. Agentivity and stativity in experiencer verbs: Implications for a typology of verb classes. *Linguistic Typology* 14: 213–251.
Wälchli, Bernhard. 2012. Grammaticalization clines in space: Zooming in on synchronic traces of diffusion processes. In Björn Wiemer, Bernhard Wälchli & Björn Hansen (eds.) *Grammatical replication and borrowability in language contact*, 233–274. Berlin, New York: Mouton de Gruyter.

Nijolė Maskaliūnienė
9 Morphological, syntactic, and semantic types of converse verbs in Lithuanian

1 Introduction

As a type of paradigmatic relations in the lexicon, converseness came to the attention of linguists after the pioneering publications by Lyons (1963, 1968, 1977) in the United Kingdom and Apresjan (1967, [1974] 1995) in the Soviet Union.[1] However, although Lyons and Apresjan did spark some interest in the subject, lexical converses (LCs) remain one of the most under-investigated areas of lexical semantics, with most books on semantics offering a very limited discussion of converseness that rarely goes beyond one page in scope.

One reason for this neglect is that the number of lexemes that may enter into converse relations is very limited. Depending on the criteria adopted for identifying pairs of LCs (see Section 2), their number in a given language may range from about 100 to 300 lexemes. For instance, my corpus of Lithuanian LCs contains about 300 pairs of verbs collected from the *Dictionary of Modern Lithuanian* (DLKŽ 1972).[2] However, this hundred or so lexemes forms a very representative set, as most of these lexemes are at the very core of the vocabulary of every language. The periphery of this set (about 40 lexemes in Lithuanian) represents different kinds of marked vocabulary (see Section 6.2). As will be suggested in Section 4, the number of LCs in a given language also depends on its morphosyntactic characteristics: Certain types of LCs are only possible in some languages and are naturally absent in others. For instance, reflexive converses make a very distinct group in Lithuanian, but are not found in English where the same shift in perspective is expressed by a grammatical means, i.e., the passive voice, cf.:

(1) a. *Ežer-as*   ***at-spind-i***   *dang-ų.*
       lake-NOM.SG   PRF-shine-PRS.3   sky-ACC.SG
       'The lake reflects the sky.'

---

[1] As suggested by Apresjan ([1974] 1995: 256), this does not mean that this type of relation between words was entirely unknown before: some early references to such oppositions as *precede-follow* can be traced back to the works of Bally (1921) and Jespersen (1924); however, the first systematic treatments of converseness-related issues did not appear until about four decades later.
[2] For instance, in her unpublished doctoral thesis, Zueva (1980: 195–198) gives a list of 97 full and 77 partial ("pseudo-converse") verbal LCs in English, all of which are suppletives.

b. *Dang-us*　　　***at-si-spind-i***　　　*ežer-e.*
　　sky-NOM.SG　　PRF-REFL-shine-PRS.3　　lake-LOC.SG
　　'The sky is reflected in the lake.'

Naturally, the list of English LCs will be shorter than that of Lithuanian.

Among the most typical examples of LCs in English are pairs of verbs such as *precede-follow, buy-sell, bequeath-inherit, win-lose*, etc. As these pairs represent binary oppositions, each member of the pair is understood as the opposite of its counterpart. As a result, many semanticists treat LCs as antonyms (Jones 2002: 2, Ermanytė 2008: 27, Jakaitienė 2010: 134), even though taxonomies of antonymy involve, primarily, contrariety and complementarity (Murphy 2003: 196), converseness clearly being a category of a different nature. Leech (1974: 110–114), Palmer (1981: 97–100), and Cruse (1986: 231–233) draw a distinction between LCs and other types of lexical opposites, emphasizing the relational character of LCs, which is not characteristic of genuine antonyms, cf. LCs *A preceded B – B followed A* and antonyms *A entered the room; A left the room*.

This semantic approach to LCs has proved limited because the converse properties of words manifest themselves primarily at the level of syntax. For instance, Haspelmath (2002: 210) observes that verbs *like* and *please* and *rob* and *steal* are roughly synonymous, so that their different syntactic behavior cannot be predicted from their meaning; being synonymous paradigmatically, they produce conversely related sentences, cf.:

(2) a. *I **like** this song.*
　　b. *This song **pleases** me.*
(3) a. *Baba **stole** my bike from me.*
　　b. *Baba **robbed** me of my bike.*

(Haspelmath 2002: 210)

What this means is that the criteria used to define purely semantic categories as synonyms or antonyms are inadequate in dealing with LCs, the study of which goes hand in hand with problems of syntactic analysis, and in particular problems of the syntax-semantics interface, semantic and syntactic valencies, as well as changes in the rank of the arguments.[3]

The promotion of one of the arguments into the most prominent position in an utterance and its theme-rheme structure – usually associated with word

---

3 These aspects of the analysis of LCs were first discussed by Geniušienė (1987: 118–124) in her seminal work on the typology of reflexives; they formed the basis for the analysis of Lithuanian LCs in my (unpublished) doctoral dissertation (Maskaliūnienė 1989). More recently, Lithuanian reflexive LCs were discussed by Wiemer (2006: 291–297) in his study of actor-demoting devices in Lithuanian.

order – are also of importance as they constitute the communicative role of LCs.[4] These problems stretch far beyond the scope of a single article, the present study being limited to an empirical corpus-based classification of Lithuanian converse verbs, with a focus on their morphological (formal) properties, a description of the syntactic types of LCs based on their valency patterns and changes occurring in converse transformations, and finally the semantic types of Lithuanian LCs. As one might expect, all the characteristics are interrelated.

2 Defining converses and converse relations

Although the defining criteria for categorizing words as LCs are a matter of debate, there does exist some consensus in this regard. Thus, LCs can be defined as pairs of words – typically verbs – that take at least two arguments (i.e., are at least bivalent) and are capable of being used in two correlative constructions by virtue of having identical denotation and hence defining the same situation from the point of view of the situation's different participants, or referents. In other words, it is a relationship that holds between the following pairs of sentences:

(4) a. *John **preceded** Ann.*
    b. *Ann **followed** John.*
(5) a. *John **sold** the book to Ann.*
    b. *Ann **bought** the book from John.*

Another feature that most investigators point out as being characteristic of LCs is mutual inference. For example, *buying* always infers *selling*, *following* is impossible without *preceding*, and vice versa. Besides, the use of one or the other member in a converse construction is always associated with a change in the syntactic functions of the arguments denoting the same referents of the situation.

This article adopts a broader definition of LCs, where LCs may denote not only situations happening at the same time, but also those that may be separated in time and space, e.g., pairs of verbs like *siųsti* 'to send' – *gauti* 'to receive'; *klausti* 'to ask' – *atsakyti* 'to answer'. Their inference is also one-sided: e.g., *siųsti* 'send' does not imply *gauti* 'get', but *gauti* 'get' presupposes *siųsti* 'send'.

---

[4] The pragmatic role of LCs in distributing prominence between the focus (the most prominent component of sentence structure) and the non-focus is actually the same one that governs the choice between the active and passive forms of the verb (see Apresjan [1974] 1995: 257, Kastovsky 1981: 123, Huddleston 2002: 230, Maskaliūnienė 2003: 71; see also Kazenin 2001: 907–908, Geniušienė 2006: 31, 40, on the communicative purposes of the passive).

Moreover, the list of LCs includes verbs, mainly autoconverses, which allow a correlation not only between the first and second arguments, but between other arguments as well (cf. Apresjan [1974] 1995: 258). Usually, they denote partially coinciding situations, as in (6) and (7), known after Fillmore (1977) as "spray-paint cases":

(6) a. We **smeared**$_1$ the wall with paint.
    b. We **smeared**$_2$ paint on the wall.
(7) a. John **loaded**$_1$ the cart with apples.
    b. John **loaded**$_2$ apples onto the cart.

(Fillmore 1977: 79)

The definition of LCs then is broadened to include all verbs capable of producing conversely related sentences at the syntactic level on condition that no demotion of semantic arguments occurs as a result of the transformation. The latter restriction is important, as the demotion of arguments always involves a change in the meaning of the lexeme, while in the case of LCs, no such changes take place.[5]

It is evident that the criteria applied to LCs are also relevant to the constructions in (8) and (9): They refer to the same situation from the perspective of its different participants and they can be viewed as mutually inferable, with the syntactic functions of the arguments in the opposing sentences changing in the same manner as in (4) and (5), cf.:

(8) a. John **kissed** Ann.
    b. Ann **was kissed** by John.
(9) a. John **gave** the book to Ann.
    b. Ann **was given** the book [by John].

The only difference is that these syntactic changes are due to different factors: In LCs, the transformation is possible due to the lexical meaning of the verbs comprising a pair, while in (8) and (9), the syntactic functions of the arguments are changed by means of a grammatical operation (a change of the active form of the verb into the passive). It is therefore unsurprising that LCs have been treated as a voice phenomenon (Apresjan [1974] 1995: 264) or, conversely, that voice can be analyzed in terms of converseness. In the words of Wiemer, "in general, the

---

5 Argument demotion often occurs with anticausatives as in *They sell books – Books sell well* (Haspelmath 2002: 212) or reflexives of the type *Mother washes the child – The child washes himself*. In my opinion, verbs forming such oppositions should not be treated as LCs, but there also exists a view to the contrary (see Zueva 1980: 162).

passive may be understood as a converse relationship, too. But it differs in the regularity and range of verbs involved: Lexical converses are severely restricted because they require a very specific semantic relation between their two arguments" (2006: 292).

To sum up, the definition of LCs need not have the requirement of entirely identical denotations if a pair of verbs meets the condition of syntactic converseness – that is, if identical semantic arguments perform different syntactic functions at the syntactic level of representation. LCs that meet all the criteria discussed above may be regarded as full LCs, and those that denote partially matching situations may be viewed as partial LCs. These can involve differences in the way the situations are presented, and in particular differences of quantification (part vs. whole), stylistic and emotional coloring, and the like. Some additional parameters pertaining to the semantics of LCs are discussed below.

3 Converse relations in the verb system

In Lithuanian, as well as in other languages, converse relations can be observed within different lexical classes (e.g., prepositions, adjectives in the comparative degree, some nouns). However, they are particularly common in the verb domain (see Lyons 1977: 280, Apresjan [1974] 1995: 263).

The verb system of Lithuanian contains a variety of different realizations of the converse relation, including various lexicalized oppositions (phraseological units). The present discussion, however, will confine itself to converse oppositions of two different verbs and converse oppositions between two meanings of the same verb (converse polysemy, or autoconverses). Example (10) illustrates the converse opposition of two different verbs (suppletive converses):

(10) a. *Priežiūr-a* **lemi-a** *derl-ių.*
 upkeep-NOM.SG determine-PRS.3 yield-ACC.SG
 'Upkeep (of crops) determines yield.'

 b. *Derl-ius* **priklaus-o** *nuo priežiūr-os.*
 yield-NOM.PL depend-PRS.3 from upkeep-GEN.SG
 'The yield (of crops) depends on the upkeep.'

In addition to suppletives, this group also includes verbs of different derivational types (for details see Section 4), e.g., reflexives of the type *atspindėti* 'to reflect' – *at-si-spindėti* 'to be reflected' as in (1).

Converse polysemy is represented by oppositions of bivalent (11) or trivalent verbs (12). The latter are characterized by a converse relation between the second and third arguments, cf.:

(11) a. *Žol-ė*   **užžėl-ė₁**   *tak-ą.*
  grass-NOM.SG   overgrow-PST.3   path-ACC.SG
  'The grass has overgrown the path.'

  b. *Tak-as*   **užžėl-ė₂**   *žol-e.*
  path-NOM.SG   overgrow-PST.3   grass-INS.SG
  'The path has been overgrown with grass.'

(12) a. *J-is*   **šeri-a₁**   *karv-ę*   *šien-u.*
  he-NOM   feed-PRS.3   cow-ACC.SG   hay-INS.SG
  'He is feeding the cow hay.'

  b. *J-is*   **šeri-a₂**   *šien-ą*   *karv-ei.*
  he-NOM   feed-PRS.3   hay-ACC.SG   cow-DAT.SG
  'He is feeding hay to the cow.'

Although the converseness of a lexical item is evident only at the level of syntax, what underlies it is lexical material. As a result, LCs may be analyzed on at least three levels of representation: (i) the formal (morphological) level, with a focus on the derivational relations that hold between the verbs within a converse pair; (ii) the syntactic level, with a focus on the syntactic functions of the same arguments within pairs of syntactically converse sentences, and (iii) the level of the meaning of the verbs that make up a converse pair, which involves event structure, argument structure (semantic roles) and referent structure (RefS).

In this article, the correlation of the semantic and syntactic characteristics of Lithuanian LCs will be demonstrated through their diatheses in accordance with the theory developed by Geniušienė (1987) for reflexive verbs.[6] Diathesis accounts for the link between the RefS expressed in terms of the semantic classes of the referents of the denotational situation, the RolS of the semantic arguments and the SynS, or grammatical relations. This three-level diathesis is a convenient model that shows the range of the possible changes in the structure of verbal meaning that occur in the derivation of verbs (Geniušienė 1987: 54). It also reflects the interaction of changes at different levels of representation even if the verbs that form an opposition are not related derivationally.

---

[6] The only difference is that the term "semantic component structure" as used by Geniušienė (1987: 33–37) for the analysis of Lithuanian reflexives has here been replaced by the term "event structure" (cf. Levin 1993, Levin & Rappaport 2005).

4 Morphological types of Lithuanian lexical converses

As LCs constitute pairs of verbs, they can be classified on the basis of the type of derivation that defines its members. This principle of analysis is relevant because it supplements the semantic and syntactic classification of LCs by exposing the formal (morphological) types of the verbs, which allow converse transpositions between their arguments.

The present classification is based on the model proposed by Nedjalkov and Sil'nickij (1973) in their study of causativity, where they list the logical possibilities of morphological (formal) oppositions in causative verbs (see also Haspelmath 1993). Although Lithuanian LCs are not all causatives, the types of oppositions discussed in the above work present a good model for the description of Lithuanian LCs, namely,

1. Directional (or derivational) oppositions. In these oppositions, one member is formally derived from the other, the derived member being marked by an additional derivational morpheme (Nedjalkov & Sil'nickij 1973: 2). LCs of this type fall into two groups in accordance with the type of derivation:

(a) Pairs of converses in which one member is a reflexive derivative of the other, for example:

(13) a. *Snieg-as* **deng-ė** *žem-ę.*
snow-NOM.SG cover-PST.3 earth-ACC.SG
'Snow was covering the earth.'

b. *Žem-ė* **deng-ė-si** *snieg-u.*
earth-NOM.SG cover-PST.3-REFL snow-INS.SG
'The earth was getting covered with snow.'

The following verb pairs best exemplify this opposition: *atspindėti* 'to reflect' – *at-si-spindėti* 'to be reflected' (see 1), *apkloti* 'to shroud' – *ap-si-kloti* 'to shroud itself/oneself, to be shrouded', *absorbuoti* 'to absorb' – *absorbuoti-s* 'to absorb itself, to be absorbed', *remti* 'to support' – *remti-s* 'to be supported', *girdėti* 'to hear' – *girdėti-s* 'to be heard', *matyti* 'to see' – *matyti-s* 'to be seen, to be visible', *apnešti* 'to cover (with dirt)' – *ap-si-nešti* 'to become covered (with dirt)', etc.

(b) Pairs of converses in which one member is a prefixed derivative of the other. The prefixes involved are *ap-, api-, nu-, pra-, pri-*, all of which have the meaning of '(all) over, completely'. Consider the following:

(14) a. *Plauk-ai* **drib-o** *ant* *ak-ių.*
hair-NOM.PL fall-PST.3 on eye-GEN.PL
'Hair fell on the eyes.'

b. Ak-ys   **ap-drib-o**   plauk-ais.
    eye-NOM.PL   PRF-fall-PST.3   hair-INS.PL
    'The eyes got covered with hair.'

This type of directional (derivational) opposition is unlike the one with the reflexive marker because LCs of this type not only differ in terms of their argument hierarchies, but also undergo denotational shifts, as the use of a prefix in Lithuanian creates a "holistic" effect, leading to semantic perfectivization, an effect that is inherent in "spray-paint cases".

2. Non-directional oppositions. Nedjalkov and Sil'nickij (1973: 2) point out that in this type of opposition the distinction between its base and derived members is obscure, as both verbs have the same stem. They subdivide non-directional oppositions into correlative and converse. In correlative oppositions, the stems of both members intersect. That is, in addition to the part that coincides, they contain elements that differentiate them. The correlative type is further subdivided into correlative-radical and correlative-affixal. The members of a correlative radical (or root) opposition are distinguished by the partial non-coincidence of their root morphemes (e.g., Lith. *lūž-ti* 'break, become broken' and *lauž-ti* 'break'), while those of the correlative-affixal opposition have different alternating affixes (e.g., Lith. *iš-lie-ti* 'spill' and *ap-lie-ti* 'spill over' as in 15).

Converse oppositions fall into paradigmatic, where the members of the opposition differ in their morphological paradigms, and syntagmatic, where the different meanings of the members in the opposition are determined solely by their environment (cf. 16 and 17) Nedjalkov and Sil'nickij (1973: 2–3). My Lithuanian material indicates that of the four possibilities, only two types of non-directional oppositions exist among Lithuanian verbal converses, namely, correlative-affixal and syntagmatic.

(a) The members of correlative-affixal oppositions have different alternating affixes, for example:

(15) a. Mokin-ys   **iš-lie-jo**   rašal-ą   ant   sąsiuvin-io.
         student-NOM.SG   PRF-spill-PST.3   ink-ACC.SG   on   notebook-GEN.SG
         'The student spilt (all) ink on the notebook.'

     b. Mokin-ys   **ap-lie-jo**   sąsiuvin-į   rašal-u.
         student-NOM.SG   PRF-spill-PST.3   notebook-ACC.SG   ink-INS.SG
         'The student spilt (some) ink all over the notebook.'

Here also belong pairs such as *į-kloti* 'to put/lay (sth. in)' – *iš-kloti* 'to line (sth. with)', *iš-draikyti* 'to cover a place with sth.'– *pri-draikyti* 'to spread/scatter sth. over a place', and the like. LCs that form correlative-affixal oppositions differ in denotation: In (15a), the verb *išlieti* 'spill' suggests that all of the ink was spilt on the notebook (it does not necessarily mean that the entire notebook was covered with ink), while the verb *aplieti* in (15b), on the contrary, means that the entire notebook was covered with ink, without suggesting that all of the ink was spilt. Most such converses differ in terms of the semantics of part vs. whole.

(b) Syntagmatic oppositions are oppositions of two different meanings of the same verb (autoconverses) – in other words, oppositions of two lexemes whose conversibility is determined solely on the basis of their immediate context. Syntagmatic oppositions of LCs may involve either the two arguments of bivalent verbs as in (16) (cf. also 11) or the second and third arguments of trivalent verbs as in (17) (cf. also 6, 7, and 12):

(16) a. *Pel-ės*   ***knibžd-a$_1$***   *šiaud-uose.*
         mouse-NOM.PL   teem-PRS.3   hay-LOC.PL
         'Mice are teeming in the hay.'

    b. *Šiaud-ai*   ***knibžd-a$_2$***   *pel-ių.*
         hay-NOM.PL   teem-PRS.3   mouse-GEN.PL
         'The hay is teeming with mice.'

(17) a. *J-is*   ***apvynio-jo$_1$***   *kakl-ą*   *šalik-u.*
         he-NOM   wrap-PST.3   neck-ACC.SG   scarf-INS.SG
         'He has wrapped the neck with a scarf.'

    b. *J-is*   ***apvynio-jo$_2$***   *šalik-ą*   *ant*   *kakl-o.*
         he-NOM   wrap-PST.3   scarf-ACC.SG   on   neck-GEN.SG
         'He has wrapped a scarf around the neck.'

This type of opposition is actually characterized by semantic, rather than formal, derivation, the derived meaning of the verb being related to its base as a syntactic converse (for more detail concerning the determination of the base and the derived construction, see Section 5.2). It is noteworthy that in Lithuanian verbs whose different meanings are determined by their environment alone are fairly numerous. They form the largest group among Lithuanian LCs as well.[7]

---

[7] In English, non-directional (syntagmatic) oppositions are also fairly common. For instance, in his often-cited article, Salkoff (1983) presents a list of English verbs capable of producing alternations of the type *Bees are swarming in the garden – The garden is swarming with bees*; Fillmore (1977, 2000) discusses examples of the type *to load the truck with hay* and *to load hay onto the truck*; etc. English verb alternations are discussed in detail in Levin (1993); for a discussion of Lithuanian alternations, see Lenartaitė (2011, 2014). This type of converseness is also found in French and other Romance languages, but it is not typical of modern German (Dowty 2000: 127).

3. **Suppletive oppositions.** These oppositions are defined in terms of a "complete discrepancy between the root morphemes" of their members (Nedjalkov & Sil'nickij 1973: 2–3). Consider the following:

(18) a. Jon-as **parduod-a** man knyg-ą už 3 lit-us.
Jonas-NOM.SG sell-PRS.3 1SG.DAT book-ACC.SG for 3 litas-ACC.PL
'Jonas is selling me a book for 3 litas.'

b. Aš **perk-u** iš Jon-o knyg-ą
1SG.NOM buy-PRS.1SG from Jonas-GEN.SG book-ACC.SG
už 3 lit-us.
for 3 litas-ACC.PL
'I am buying a book from Jonas for 3 litas.'

Suppletive LCs are not exclusive to Lithuanian and are common at least to all Indo-European languages. Among the most typical examples are pairs such as *duoti* 'to give'– *imti* 'to take',[8] *turėti* 'to own' – *priklausyti* 'to belong', *dovanoti* 'to give (a present)' – *gauti* 'to receive, get', *palikti (palikimą, turtą)* 'to bequeath' – *paveldėti* 'to inherit', *vesti* 'to marry (of a man), to take as a wife' – *ištekėti* 'to marry (of a woman), to take as a husband',[9] *siųsti* 'to send' – *gauti* 'to receive', etc.

4. **Mixed types.** Different types of morphological oppositions can combine. For example, pairs such as *džiaugtis* 'to enjoy, to rejoice' – *džiuginti* 'to be a delight, to gladden' and *domėtis* 'to take an interest, to be interested' – *dominti* 'to interest' combine both derivational elements (the reflexive marker *-si-* as well as prefixes) and means of correlation (root alternation). Consider the following:

(19) a. Vaik-ų sėkm-ė mane **džiugin-a**.
child-GEN.PL success-NOM.SG 1SG.ACC delight-PRS.3
'The children's success gives me joy.'

---

8 Although *give* and *take* are considered prototypical LCs, it must be emphasized that the two verbs become LCs only under very specific conditions, namely, when we have both actions taking place at the same time, i.e., when an exchange actually occurs between the two referents. Being polysemous verbs, both of them are found in many different patterns of usage, when each can act independently of the other (e.g., *I took a book from the shelf*; *He gave some food to the dog*, etc.).
9 In Lithuanian, the pair *vesti* 'to marry (of a man), to take as a wife' – *ištekėti* 'to marry (of a woman), to take as a husband)' is a pair of LCs, but in other languages, verbs such as English '*marry*', German '*heiraten*', French '*épouser*', or Spanish '*casarse*' are a type of autoconverses, sometimes called symmetrical predicates (Lyons 1977) or treated as reciprocals (Nedjalkov 2007). In Russian, the opposition is between a verb and a verbal idiom, cf. '*ženit'sa – vyjti zamuž*'. It is evident that all these verb forms are interrelated in the sense that they can all express the same relationship no matter how different their morphology may be.

b. *Aš*   ***džiaug-iuo-si***   vaik-ų   sėkm-e.
   1SG.NOM   enjoy-PRS.1SG-REFL   child-GEN.PL   success-INS.SG
   'I am delighted with the children's success.'

LCs of this type, although relatively infrequent, form a clear group of about a dozen pairs of lexemes: *baisinti* 'to terrify' – *baisėtis* 'to be terrified/horrified', *bauginti* 'to scare' – *bijoti* 'to be afraid', *bauginti* 'to scare' – *būgštauti* 'to fear', *įbauginti* 'to intimidate' – *įbūgti* 'to get frightened', *dominti* 'to take interest' – *domėtis* 'to be interested', *sudominti* 'to cause interest' – *susidomėti* 'to get interested', *džiuginti* 'to make happy' – *džiaugtis* 'to rejoice, be happy', *gąsdinti* 'to intimidate, frighten' – *gąsčioti* 'to be frightened', *gąsdinti* 'to frighten, scare' – *gąstauti* 'to be afraid', *išgąsdinti* 'to startle' – *išsigąsti* 'to get startled', *pergąsdinti* 'to horrify' – *persigąsti* 'to get terrified/ horrified', *stebinti* 'to amaze' – *stebėtis* 'to be amazed'. In such pairs, one verb is a causative, while the other one derives from the root of which the first one forms a causative (with *in*-suffix)+RM. This can (cf. *dominti* 'to take interest' – *domėtis* 'to be interested'), but need not (cf. *džiuginti* 'to make happy' – *džiaugtis* 'to rejoice, be happy') go hand in hand with a change of conjugation.

5 Syntactic types of Lithuanian LCs

The classification of LCs according to their syntactic characteristics draws upon two criteria: (a) semantic valency, or to be more precise, the number of semantic arguments of the verbs comprising a converse pair that can be realized at the syntactic level and (b) the syntactic patterns of converse transformations as defined by the syntactic functions of the arguments that take part in the transformation.

5.1 Valency patterns of LCs

My material shows that semantically Lithuanian LCs are mostly bivalent and trivalent, but there are some four-valent and even five-valent LCs. The sum of these valencies determines the lexical meaning of the verb, and thus, they are semantically obligatory, although not necessarily realized at the syntactic level. For example, deletion of the fourth valency 'money' semantically reduces the pair of the verbs *buy* and *sell* to the meaning of *give* and *take*. By the same token, the meaning of the verbs *let*, *rent*, *hire* is determined by the existence of the fifth valency – a period of time for which something is *let*, *rented*, or *hired* (Apresjan [1974] 1995: 120).

Moreover, it is evident that there exists a correlation between the morphological types of LCs and their semantic valency. For instance, bivalent converses include the following morphological types of LCs:

All reflexive LCs (with the exception of the pairs *skolinti* 'to lend' – *skolinti-s* 'to borrow', which are four-valent (20) and *nuomoti* 'to let' – *nuomoti-s* 'to rent', with five valencies (21), as well as some prefixal verbs and part of syntagmatic LCs, such as *aplašėti$_1$* 'to drip, cover with drops' – *aplašėti$_2$* 'to become covered with drops' and a few suppletive LCs.

The greater part of Lithuanian LCs are semantically trivalent. They include most LCs of the correlative-affixal type, most suppletive LCs, and the major part of LCs that form syntagmatic oppositions, as well as some prefixal converses that form directional (derivational) morphological oppositions.

Four- and five-valent LCs are very few in number. Four-valent converses can be exemplified by pairs such as *pirkti* 'to buy' – *parduoti* 'to sell', *skolinti* 'to lend' – *skolinti-s* 'to borrow', and their synonyms. The pair *nuomoti* 'to let' – *nuomoti-s* 'to rent' represents a five-valent converse, cf.:

(20) a. *J-is   man   **paskolin-o**   knyg-ą   3 dien-oms.*
        he-NOM 1SG.DAT   lend-PST.3   book-ACC.SG   3 day-DAT.PL
        'He lent me the book for three days'

   b. *Aš   **pasiskolin-au**   iš   j-o   knyg-ą   3 dien-oms.*
       1SG.NOM   borrowed-PST.1SG   from   he-GEN   book-ACC.SG   3 day-DAT.PL
       'I have borrowed the book from him for 3 days'

(21) a. *J-is   **išnuomav-o**   man   but-ą   met-ams   už
        he-NOM   let-PST.3   1SG.DAT   flat-ACC.SG   year-DAT.SG   for
        1000 lit-ų.*
        1000 litas-GEN.PL
        'He has let me a flat for a year for a thousand litas'

   b. *Aš   **išsinuomo-jau** iš   j-o   but-ą   met-ams
       1SG.NOM   rent-PRS.1SG   from   he-GEN   flat-ACC.SG   year-DAT.SG
       už   1000 lit-ų.*
       for   1000 litas-GEN.PL
       'I have rented a flat from him for a year for a thousand litas'.

As is known, a verb's semantic arguments assume a syntactic realization, each verb being defined in terms of a specific valency pattern.[10] Only the valencies

---

[10] Lithuanian valency patterns are discussed in detail by Ambrazas (1986, 1997) and Sližienė (1986, 1994).

that must be realized at all times are considered syntactically obligatory, as the omission of the others does not affect the grammaticality of the sentence. A valency pattern, however, shows all the arguments, irrespective of their syntactic obligatoriness.

5.2 Types of syntactic transformations

LCs differ not only in terms of the number of arguments, but also in terms of which arguments participate in converse transformations. For the sake of convenience of description, each realization of a semantic argument in converse pairs will be assigned a number. In an unmarked (neutral) word order environment, the number of a given valency realization is determined on the basis of the syntactic obligatoriness of the respective argument and its relative positioning within the construction (cf. Apresjan [1974] 1995: 137–138). Thus, the argument acting as the subject (in the nominative case) is labeled as 1, the argument(s) acting as the direct object (in the accusative) is labeled as 2, the indirect object (in the dative or instrumental) or the oblique object (different case forms used with prepositions and the locative case) is labeled as 3. Oblique objects may be labeled as 4 and even 5 if the verb is four- or five-valent. Being optional and rather peripheral, however, they do not participate in converse transformations, which are discussed below.

For the purposes of the present research, the numbering of arguments refers to the base construction, as what we are interested in are the changes in the syntactic organization of the construction that occur as a result of converse transformations. The base construction in oppositions containing derived verbs is one with a non-derived or, in other words, formally simpler LC, cf.:

(22) a. *Kolon-os*   ***remi-a***   *skliaut-ą.*
          column-NOM.PL   support-PRS.3   arch-ACC.SG
          'The columns support the arch.'

      b. *Skliaut-as*   ***remi-a-si***   *į*   *kolon-as.*
          arch-NOM.SG   support-PRS.3-REFL   in   columns-ACC.PL
          'The arch is supported by columns.'

Typically, constructions with a formally simpler verb acting as the predicate illustrate a nominative-accusative argument arrangement as in (22a). As such, they are in agreement with the principle of case hierarchy (see Keenan & Comrie 1977), which is based on the "weight"[11] of the cases used to mark different syntactic functions and also the principle of syntactic hierarchy attributable to those syntactic functions:

subject (S) > direct object (DO) > indirect object (IO) > oblique object (OblO) (cf. Geniušienė 1987: 49).

In dealing with suppletive oppositions, there is no simpler verb form – both are equally "simple" (see Section 4). Therefore, the only applicable principle is that of syntactic hierarchy, with the base member of the opposition being defined in terms of a set of hierarchically higher syntactic functions. The numbers given to arguments can either be in agreement with the syntactic hierarchy or there may be no match between them, as LCs can involve discrepancies between the semantic argument structure of the verb and the realization of the arguments in syntax.

For example, in (23a), the nominative subject *Jonas* is labeled as 1, the accusative direct object *knygą* 'book' is 2, and the dative indirect object *man* '(to) me' is 3. In the second member of the opposition (23b), the realization of arguments 1 and 2 matches that of (23a); however, argument 3 is realized as a prepositional genitive *iš Jono* 'from Jonas'. This fact suggests treating sentence 23a as the base construction in relation to (23b), which is its converse, cf.:

(23) a.
	1		3	2
	Jon-as	***duod-a***	*man*	*knyg-ą.*
	Jonas-NOM.SG	give-PRS.3	1SG.DAT	book-ACC.SG

'Jonas is giving me a book.'

b.
	3			1	2
	Aš	***im-u***	*iš*	*Jon-o*	*knyg-ą.*
	1SG.NOM	take-PRS.3	from	Jonas-GEN.SG	book-ACC.SG

'I am taking a book from Jonas.'

---

[11] As is well known, the argument acting as the subject (in the nominative case) is always at the top of the hierarchy, the argument acting as the direct object (in the accusative) is in the second position, any indirect object arguments (either in the dative or prepositional case forms) come third, and arguments acting as adverbial modifiers (in the locative or prepositional case forms) are ranked lowest. This hierarchy is relevant only in the event of obligatory syntactic valencies, i.e., if any of the semantic arguments are realized by oblique cases or prepositional noun groups, they should be treated as syntactic arguments proper rather than as adjuncts, as is common in most Western traditions. For instance, the sentence *Medžiai atsispindi *(ežere)* 'The trees are reflected [in the lake]' would be grammatically incomplete if the semantic role of the locative were not realized at the syntactic level.

In other cases, and particularly where the converse opposition is based upon two meanings of the same verb, determining the base construction is a matter of interpretation. Consider the following:

(24) a.
    1   2   3
    Jon-as   **barst-o₁**   *smėl-į*   *ant*   *tak-o.*
    Jonas-NOM.SG   sprinkle-PRS.3   sand-ACC.SG   on   path-GEN.SG
    'Jonas is sprinkling sand on the path.'

  b.
    1   3   2
    Jon-as   **barst-o₂**   *tak-ą*   *smėl-iu.*
    Jonas-NOM.SG   sprinkle-PRS.3   path-ACC.SG   sand-INS.SG
    'Jonas is sprinkling the path with sand.'

Of the two, the former construction may be regarded as the base because the verb *barstyti₁* is conventionally defined as 'to sprinkle fine objects on the surface' (*pelenus* 'ashes', *druską* 'salt', *grūdus* 'grain', *smėlį* 'sand', *žvyrą* 'gravel', *monetas* 'coins', etc.), while *barstyti₂* means 'to cover by sprinkling' (DLKŽ). Besides, only (24a) survives the test of argument demotion. Thus, eliminating the prepositional phrase *ant tako* 'on the path' leaves the grammaticality of *barstyti smėlį* 'to sprinkle sand' unaffected, whereas eliminating either argument in (24b) would render the structure incomplete. Hence, the verb *barstyti₁* 'to sprinkle fine/grainy material' is to be regarded as primary to *barstyti₂* 'to cover by sprinkling'.

Bivalent converses are capable of only one type of transformation – namely, the transposition of arguments 1 and 2 (1, 2 → 2, 1). Consider the following examples:

(25) a.
    1   2
    Zuik-is   **iš-gąsdin-o**   *av-is.*
    hare-NOM.SG   PRF-startle-PST.3   sheep-ACC.PL
    'A hare startled the sheep.'

  b.
    2   1
    Av-ys   **iš-si-gand-o**   *zuik-io.*
    sheep-NOM.PL   PRF-REFL-startle-PST.3   hare-GEN.SG
    'The sheep got startled by a hare.'

(26) a.
    1   2
    Jon-as   **tur-i**   *šun-į.*
    Jonas-NOM.SG   have-PRS.3   dog-ACC.SG
    'Jonas has a dog.'

b.

	2		1
	Šuo	**priklaus-o**	Jon-ui.
	dog:NOM.SG	belong-PRS.3	Jonas-DAT.sg

'The dog belongs to Jonas.'

The principal difference between the derived sentences is that they have different surface realizations of the second argument. This argument can appear in the genitive (25b), dative (26b), instrumental (11b), locative (1b), or different prepositional case forms.

Adopting a symbolic notation for the different components of a converse construction makes it possible to present the structure of converse transformations as formulae. Thus, if the verb is labeled as V and the noun as N, with an indication of argument number and case index ($N1_{nom}$, $N2_{acc}$, and the like), the converse relations that define members within an opposition of bivalent LCs can be illustrated as follows:

$$N1_{nom} \; V \; N2_{acc} \rightarrow N2_{nom} \; V_{(prep)} N1_{gen/dat/ins/loc}$$

As expected, in a great majority of cases, the base construction of bivalent LCs has the nominative-accusative arrangement (as illustrated by the above examples). However, base constructions with bivalent LCs of the syntagmatic type include also instances of the nominative-locative arrangement, and the base structure is defined in terms of being stylistically neutral as opposed to its stylistically marked converse. Consider the following:

(27) a. Mišk-e   **aid-i₁**   šūv-iai.
         wood-LOC.SG   echo-PRS.3   gunshot-NOM.PL
         'Gunshots are echoing in the wood.'

   b. Mišk-as   **aid-i₂**   šūv-iais / nuo šūv-ių.
       wood-NOM.SG   echo-PRS.3   gunshots-INS.PL / from gunshots-GEN.PL
       'The wood is echoing with gunshots.'

(28) a. Kaim-e   **skamb-a₁**   dain-os.
         village-LOC.SG   ring-PRS.3   song-NOM.PL
         'Songs are ringing in the village.'

   b. Kaim-as   **skamb-a₂**   dainom-is /   nuo   dain-ų.
       village-NOM.SG   ring-PRS.3   song-INS.PL/   from   song-GEN.PL
       'The village is ringing with songs.'

The structural model of the above examples can be represented as follows:

$$N1_{nom} \; V \; N2_{loc} \rightarrow N2_{nom} \; V \; N1_{ins}/_{(prep)}N1_{gen}$$

Trivalent verbs allow a greater number of converse transpositions, as all three arguments can switch places. In theory, the transposition can have as many as five variants (Apresjan [1974] 1995: 267):

  (a) 1, 2, 3 → 2, 1, 3 (transposition of arguments 1 and 2)
  (b) 1, 2, 3 → 1, 3, 2 (transposition of arguments 2 and 3)
  (c) 1, 2, 3 → 3, 2, 1 (transposition of arguments 1 and 3)
  (d) 1, 2, 3 → 3, 1, 2 (transposition of all arguments)
  (e) 1, 2, 3 → 2, 3, 1 (transposition of all arguments)

However, it transpires from the data that not all of the variants are realized in practice. A converse transposition of arguments 2 and 3 is particularly common among Lithuanian trivalent LCs, as this syntactic model is principally characteristic of trivalent LCs that form non-directional morphological oppositions (syntagmatic and correlative-affixal) (cf. 12, 17, and 24). The syntactic model of these constructions can be represented as follows:

$$N1_{nom} \; V \; N3_{acc \; (prep)} \; N2_{gen/acc} \rightarrow N1_{nom} \; V \; N2_{acc} \; N3_{ins}$$

Another possibility of argument transposition in Lithuanian LCs is between arguments 1 and 3. Consider the following:

		1	2	3		
(29)	a.	*Tet-a*	***palik-o***	*nam-ą*	*sūnėn-ui.*	
		aunt-NOM.SG	bequeath-PST.3	house-ACC.SG	nephew-DAT.SG	

'The aunt bequeathed the house to her nephew.'

		3		2		1
	b.	*Sūnėn-as*	***paveldė-jo***	*nam-ą*	*iš*	*tet-os.*
		nephew-NOM.SG	inherit-PST.3	house-ACC.SG	from	aunt-GEN.SG

'The nephew inherited the house from his aunt.'

The following representation summarizes the syntactic model of the above constructions:

$$N1_{nom} \; V \; N2_{acc \; (prep)} N3_{dat/acc/ins} \rightarrow N3_{nom} \; V \; N2_{acc \; (prep)} N1_{gen}$$

A transposition of all arguments (1, 2, 3 → 2, 3, 1) is the least common type of restructuring in converse transformations. My material contains only one example of this type:

		1	2	3
(30)	a.	*Vad-as*	***apdovano-jo*** *kar-į*	*laikrodž-iu.*
		chief-NOM.SG	reward-PST.3 soldier-ACC.SG	watch-INS.SG

'The chief rewarded the soldier with a watch.'

	2		3		1
b.	*Kar-ys*	**gav-o**	*laikrod-į*	*iš*	*vad-o.*
	soldier-NOM.SG	receive-PST.3	watch-ACC.SG	from	chief-GEN.sg

'The soldier received a watch from the chief.'

The structural model of these constructions can be presented as follows:

$$N1_{nom} \; V \; N2_{acc} \; N3_{ins} \rightarrow N2_{nom} \; V \; N3_{acc} \; _{(prep)}N1_{gen}$$

In theory, two more types of converse transformation can be posited that involve the transposition of all arguments: 1, 2, 3 → 3, 1, 2 and 1, 2, 3 → 2, 3, 1. However, no evidence of those types has been found in the Lithuanian material. Apresjan ([1974] 1995: 268) provides the following example to illustrate the latter type in Russian, although it is evident that he numbers the arguments according to their position in the sentence (linear word order), without following the principle of syntactic hierarchy, cf.:

Russian

		1			2		3	
(31)	a.	*Ja*	**raskvita-ju-s'**		*s*	*toboj*	*za*	*èto.*
		1SG.NOM	get.even-FUT.1SG-REFL		with	2SG.INS	for	this.ACC.SG.N

'I will get even with you for this.'

		2		3		1	
	b.	*Ty*	*za*	*èto*	*mne*	**zaplat-iš.**
		2SG.NOM	for	this.ACC.SG.N	1SG.DAT	pay-FUT.2SG

'You will pay (me) for this.'

However, a different word order of the converse sentence is also possible:

		2	1		3	
	c.	*Ty*	*mne*	*za*	*èto*	**zaplat-iš.**
		2SG.NOM	1SG.DAT	for	this.ACC.SG.N	pay-FUT.2SG

'You will pay (me) for this.'

It seems that with a change of word order the transposition can be seen to affect arguments 1 and 2, more so that the argument *za èto* 'for this' may be omitted, without affecting grammaticality of the sentence. The same sentence is found in Lithuanian, cf.:

		1		2		3	
(32)	a.	*Aš*	*su*	*tavim*	*už*	*tai*	**atsiskaity-si-u.**
		1SG.NOM	with	2SG.INS	for	this	get.even-FUT-1SG

'I will get even with you for this.'

	2	1		3	
b.	*Tu*	*man*	*už*	*tai*	***sumokė-s-i.***
	2SG.NOM	1SG.DAT	for	this	pay-FUT-2SG

'You will pay (me) for this.'

The principle of syntactic hierarchy seems more reliable for determining the order of arguments in a transposition because in this case, their numbering does not depend on word order.

6 Semantic classification of LCs

6.1 Principles of the semantic classification of LCs

The first step in the semantic classification of verbal LCs is to analyze their event structure, followed by their grouping in accordance with the semantic type of the underlying verb: stative, actional, inchoative, or causative. These verb classes are traditionally considered primary (or basic) and as such constitute the first stage in any classification of verbs.[12]

The material under analysis suggests grouping Lithuanian LCs into two major classes in accordance with their event structure, namely, causative (e.g., *pirkti* 'to buy' – *parduoti* 'to sell', *duoti* 'to give' – *imti* 'to take') and stative (e.g., *remti* 'to support' – *remtis* 'refl. to be supported', *mėgti* 'to like' – *patikti* 'to like, appeal'). However, there are pairs that represent oppositions between a causative and an inchoative verb (e.g., *siųsti* 'to send' – *gauti* 'to receive', *palikti* 'to bequeath' – *paveldėti* 'to inherit'), or a causative and a stative (e.g., *bauginti* 'to scare' – *bijoti* 'to fear, be afraid'), etc. Usually, full LCs belong to the same semantic class, while partial LCs fall to different semantic classes.

LCs can be further classified into smaller lexical-semantic groups (LSGs) on the basis of the similarity of their individual lexical meanings. It is assumed that verbs of the same LSG share a number of semantic properties including not only their event structure and semantic role structure (RolS), but also some semantic features of a narrower scope, e.g., the semantic types of referents (cf. Geniušienė 1987: 37). However, as we have accepted a broad definition of LCs that subsumes all verbs capable of producing conversely related sentences without demoting their semantic arguments, it is necessary to broaden the definition of a LSG to remove the restriction of identical event structure and semantic RolS for verbs of

---

[12] In the last 30 years, the number of these primary verb classes and their labeling have changed, but their essence remains the same (for instance, the primary classes in Role and Reference Grammar, see Van Valin 2001).

the same LSG. For the purposes of this study, LCs are attributed to the same LSG if most of the event structure coincides, irrespective of whether they are full or partial LCs and whether or not their RolS is identical.

The event structure and the argument RolS are closely related, as each verb is associated with a particular event structure and with a relevant list of semantic roles that are meant to bring out similarities and differences in verb meaning that are reflected in argument expression (cf. Levin & Rappaport Hovav 2005: 35–36).[13]

The RefS is defined in terms of the number and semantic properties of the participants, or referents, in a given situation (Apresjan [1974] 1995: 99–100, Geniušienė 1987: 44–47). In line with the methodology proposed by Geniušienė (1987: 44–45), it is useful to separate the referent level from other levels of semantic analysis because the semantic properties of referents such as "human", "animate", "inanimate", "abstract", and the like may impose restrictions on a converse transformation. Consider the following:

(33) a. *His uncle **died** from/of pneumonia.*
b. *Pneumonia **killed** his uncle.*
(34) a. *Brutus **killed** Caesar.*
b. **Caesar **died** from/of Brutus.*

(Levin & Rappaport Hovav 2005: 40)

In (33) and (34), the pair of verbs *kill* and *die* may enter into a converse relationship and may thus be treated as a lexical converse pair if their RefS includes one human and one inanimate referent naming the cause of someone's death. If both referents are human, such a transformation would be semantically unacceptable.

6.2 Semantic types of LCs and their diatheses

The following principal LSGs underlie the lexical semantic classification of Lithuanian LCs:
i. Possessive relations. This LSG includes LCs, which in fact denote transfer of possession and may thus be further subdivided into nine smaller

---

[13] The discussion of the RolS of the verb in semantics, syntax, and elsewhere is so extensive that it is impossible to deal with the many different approaches here. In brief, different sets of semantic roles have been proposed, ranging from very general sets (in Role and Reference Grammar, there are only two: the actor and the undergoer, see Van Valin 2001: 206) to systems comprising as many as 20 or more individual roles identified through the analysis of the denotational situation (Fillmore 1977: 62, Huddleston 2002: 230–235; cf. also Apresjan [1974] 1995). In her dictionary of Lithuanian verb valency patterns, Sližienė (1994: 19–25) presents a list of as many as 24 semantic roles; in the Lithuanian Grammar (Ambrazas 1997: 603–604), meanwhile, there are only 14.

subgroups in accordance with the type of the transfer: giving-taking (*duoti* 'to give' – *imti* 'to take'), donating/awarding-receiving (*dovanoti* 'to donate' – *gauti* 'to receive'), buying-selling (*parduoti* 'to sell' – *pirkti* 'to buy'), borrowing-lending (*skolinti* 'to lend' – *skolintis* 'to borrow'), bequeathing-inheriting (*palikti* 'to bequeath' – *paveldėti* 'to inherit'), letting-renting (*nuomoti* 'to let' – *nuomotis* 'to rent'), supplying-receiving (*teikti* 'to supply' – *gauti* 'to get'), sending-receiving (via an intermediary) (*siųsti* 'to send' – *gauti* 'to receive'), and stable possessive relations (*turėti* 'to have' – *priklausyti* 'to belong').

ii. Spatial relations. This LSG subsumes three subgroups: LCs of support (*laikyti* 'to hold, support' – *laikytis* 'to be supported'), LCs of reflection (*atspindėti* 'to reflect' – *atsispindėti* 'to be reflected'), and LCs meaning permeability (*susiurbti* 'to absorb' – *susisiurbti* 'to be absorbed').

iii. Emotional relations. This LSG may be divided into three subgroups too. They include LCs of positive emotions (*žavėti* 'to fascinate' – *žavėtis* 'to admire, to be fascinated by'), LCs of negative emotions (*baugint* 'to scare' – *bijoti* 'to be afraid'), and LCs of passive perception (*sapnuoti* 'to be dreaming' – *sapnuotis* 'to be seeing something in a dream').

iv. Covering. This LSG subsumes six smaller subgroups, including those of covering a surface (*tiesti₁ staltiesę ant stalo* 'to lay a tablecloth on the table' – *tiesti₂ stalą staltiese* 'to lay a table with a tablecloth'), covering with fine objects (*barstyti₁ smėlį ant tako* 'to sprinkle sand on the path' – *barstyti₂ taką smėliu* 'to sprinkle the path with sand'), covering with vegetation (*Krūmai apaugo₁ tvenkinį* 'The shrubs have overgrown the pond' – *Tvenkinys apaugo₂ krūmais* 'The pond has been overgrown with shrubs'), covering by spreading (*tepti₁ sviestą ant duonos* 'to smear butter on the bread' – *tepti₂ duoną sviestu* 'to smear the bread with butter'), covering by sticking (*Purvas aplipo batus* 'Mud has stuck to the shoes' – *Batai aplipo purvu* 'The shoes have been caked with mud'), and that of uncontrolled covering (*Sniegas dengia laukus* 'Snow is covering the fields' – *Laukai dengiasi sniegu* 'The fields are being covered (lit. are covering themselves) with snow').[14]

v. Placement of object/obstruction (*užristi₁ akmenį ant tako* 'to roll a boulder over the path' – *užristi₂ taką akmeniu* 'to block the path with a boulder (i.e., to block the path by rolling a boulder over it').

vi. Cause and effect relations (*sąlygoti* 'to cause' – *priklausyti* 'to depend on').

vii. Victory and loss (*laimėti* 'to win' – *pralaimėti* 'to lose').

viii. Feeding (*šerti₁ karvę šienu* 'to feed a cow hay' – *šerti₂ šieną karvei* 'to feed hay to a cow').

---

14 Wiemer (2006: 293) refers to these verb pairs as LCs of physical contact.

ix. Flow of liquid (*Kraujas plūdo₁ iš žaizdos* 'Blood surged from the wound' – *Žaizda plūdo₂ krauju* 'The wound overflowed with blood').
x. Expressive/Color properties (*Pievoje marguoja₁ gėlės* 'Flowers are shimmering with color in the meadow' – *Pieva marguoja₂ gėlėmis / nuo gėlių* 'The meadow is shimmering with motley flowers'). LCs within the LSG of flow of liquid and expressive/color properties are on the periphery of converseness. Unlike most other LCs, commonly found in spoken Lithuanian, these are mainly found in fiction as they are a tool of imagery building.

A few LCs happen to be outside lexical-semantic grouping, representing individual instances, e.g.:

(35) a. *Iš t-os medžiag-os* **išein-a** *kostium-as.*
from that-GEN.SG.F fabric-GEN.SG come.out-PRS.3 suit-NOM.SG
'A suit can be made from that piece of fabric.'

b. *T-os medžiag-os* **užtenk-a** *kostium-ui.*
that-GEN.SG.F fabric-GEN.SG suffice-PRS.3 suit-DAT.SG
'That piece of fabric is enough for a suit.'

(36) a. *Nauj-i žodži-ai* **papild-o** *kalb-ą.*
new-NOM.PL.M word-NOM.PL supplement-PRS.3 language-ACC.SG
'New words supplement the language.'

b. *Kalb-a* **pasipild-o** *nauj-ais žodž-iais.*
language-NOM.SG supplement:REFL-PRS.3 new-INS.PL.M word-INS.PL
'The language supplements itself with new words.'

Analysis of the data indicates that there is a correlation between the formal properties of LCs and their semantics. For instance, most suppletives belong to the LSG of possessive relations; LCs of directional morphological derivation fall into LSGs of spatial relations, including such subgroups as support, reflection, and permeability. All LCs of the mixed type of derivation signify emotional relations, while LCs of non-directional (syntagmatic) derivation mainly represent LSGs of different types of covering, placement of object/obstruction, feeding, flow of liquid, expressive/color properties. Only in very few cases is an overlapping of several types of derivation observed within one and the same LSG (for example, reflexive derivatives *skolinti* 'to lend' – *skolinti-s* 'to borrow', *nuomoti* 'to let' – *nuomoti-s* 'to rent', and the like are in the LSG of possessive relations, which is mainly represented by suppletive oppositions).

It is noteworthy that the LSGs of converses exhibit several properties that distinguish them from other kinds of semantic groups of lexemes. First, LCs constitute two paradigms within an LSG: Two verbs form a pair by virtue of a converse relation that defines them – as such, they constitute a "horizontal" converse paradigm; on a vertical dimension, different converse verbs within an LSG engage in synonymic and/or hyponymic relations.

Second, based on their lexical meanings, the members of a converse pair belong to different vertical paradigms. For example, the LCs *išvežti, eksportuoti* 'to export' and *įsivežti, importuoti* 'to import' are related horizontally in terms of syntactic converseness, as illustrated below:

(37) a. Rusij-a **eksportuo-ja** medien-ą į Japonij-ą.
Russia-NOM.SG export-PRS.3 wood-ACC.SG to Japan-ACC.SG
'Russia exports wood to Japan.'

b. Japonij-a **importuo-ja** medien-ą iš Rusij-os.
Japan-NOM.SG import-PRS.3 wood-ACC.SG from Russia-GEN.SG
'Japan imports wood from Russia.'

At the same time, the verb *eksportuoti* 'to export' belongs to the vertical paradigm of verbs of "transfer", while *importuoti* 'to import' belongs to the paradigm of "receiving". Taken together, the two verbs are in a more generic LSG of "possessive relations".

Third, LCs are not mutually exclusive: The two vertical paradigms are asymmetrical, as one lexeme can form converse relations with two, or even more, lexemes. For example, the verb *gauti* 'to receive' can be in a converse relation with the verbs *duoti* 'to give', *dovanoti* 'to present, to give as a present', *tiekti* 'to supply', *apdovanoti* 'to reward', *išduoti* 'to produce, to give, to issue smb. with smth.', etc. Compare the way (38a) correlates with (38b–f):

(38) a. Aš **gav-au** iš j-o knyg-ą.
1SG.NOM receive-PST.1SG from he-GEN book-ACC.SG
'I got/received a book from him.'

b. J-is **dav-ė** man knyg-ą.
he-NOM give-PST.3 1SG.DAT book-ACC.SG
'He gave me a book.'

c. J-is **padovano-jo** man knyg-ą.
he-NOM present-PST.3 1SG.DAT book-ACC.SG
'He gave me a present of a book.'

d. *J-is* **tiek-ė** *man* *knyg-as.*
he-NOM supply-PST.3 1SG.DAT book-ACC.PL
'He supplied books to me.'

e. *J-is* **apdovano-jo** *mane* *knyg-a.*
he-NOM reward-PST.3 1SG.ACC book-INS.SG
'He rewarded me with a book.'

f. *J-is* **išdav-ė** *man* *knyg-ą.*
he-NOM issue-PST.3 1SG.DAT book-ACC.SG
'He issued a book to me.'

Graphically, this LSG may be represented as follows[15]:

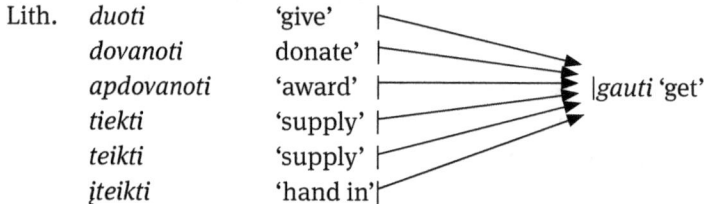

Lith. *duoti*   'give'
       dovanoti   'donate'
       apdovanoti 'award'
       tiekti   'supply'
       teikti   'supply'
       įteikti   'hand in'

|gauti 'get'

The LSG of possessive relations is the largest group in the corpus, with over 50 pairs of LCs. Formally, almost all of them are suppletives (except for six pairs of reflexive derivatives, e.g., *skolinti* 'to lend' – *skolinti-s* 'to borrow'). The majority of the subgroups contain LCs that are mainly trivalent. Most often their RefS contains two human referents and one inanimate referent – typically a thing (an object of the transfer, borrowing, inheriting, etc.) or, occasionally, an animal. The appearance of a fourth and fifth valency slot in the meaning of LCs signals a fourth and fifth referent in the RefS of the verb: Money, in the case of LCs of buying-selling, and money and a period of time in the case of letting-renting. LCs in the subgroup of possessive relations are bivalent. Although their referents may belong to different classes, the one that occurs in the function of the subject is usually human.

The RolS of trivalent LCs within this LSG correlates with the event structure of their meaning. For example, as all verbs in the base construction of the paradigm of 'giving' are causatives, the RolS of their meaning consists of an agent, a patient, and a beneficiary. At the same time, most of the verbs in the paradigm of 'receiving', which are inchoatives, are characterized by a RolS that involves

---

[15] The assymetry of the paradigm of LCs is also observable in other languages, and any of the vertical paradigms in opposition can be richer in synonyms or hyponyms. For instance, in English, contrary to Lithuanian, the LSG of property relations has a richer paradigm of verbs that refer to "receiving": for example, *confer* enters into a converse relationship with *take*, *get*, *receive*, *obtain* (Zueva 1980: 103).

a beneficiary, a source, and a patient. The RolS of the LCs differs because they describe the same denotational situation differently: The person receiving an object is understood as a beneficiary rather than an agent – a typical role for an inchoative verb of receiving – while the person transferring an object to the beneficiary, again, is not the agent, but the source of the transfer taking place.

As has been mentioned above (see Section 3), the correlation of the semantic and syntactic characteristics of Lithuanian LCs may be demonstrated through their diatheses, which show the link between the RefS and the RolS of the semantic arguments and the SynS, or grammatical relations. It has been established that syntactic rearrangements within pairs of converse constructions bring about two types of diathetical change:

  i. A change in the correlation pattern between elements on three levels – referential, role, and syntactic – with no impact on RolS.

(39) a. *Jon-as*   **ved-a**   *On-ą.*
Jonas-NOM.SG   take.as.a.wife-PRS.3   Ona-ACC.SG
AGENT   COMITATIVE
'Jonas is getting married to Ona.'

b. *On-a*   **ištek-a**   *už*   *Jon-o.*
Ona-NOM.SG   take.as.a.husband-PRS.3   for   Jonas-GEN.SG
AGENT   COMITATIVE
'Ona is getting married to Jonas.'

In these examples, the otherwise identical arguments are defined in terms of different syntactic functions, but the RolS of the verbs remains the same.

  ii. A change in the correlation pattern between elements at all levels, including RolS.

(40) a. *Jon-as*   **pardav-ė**   *knyg-ą*   *On-ai.*
Jonas-NOM.SG   sell-PST.3   book-ACC.SG   Ona-DAT.SG
AGENT=SUBJECT   BENEFICIARY=OBJECT
'Jonas sold a book to Ona.'

b. *On-a*   **pirk-o**   *knyg-ą*   *iš*   *Jon-o.*
Ona-NOM.SG   buy-PST.3   book-ACC.SG   from   Jonas-GEN.SG
AGENT=SUBJECT   SOURCE=OBJECT
'Ona bought a book from Jonas.'

Analysis of the data has highlighted 16 types of derived diatheses, 8 of which have the properties illustrated in (i) and the other 8 in (ii). The possibility of change in the RolS of verb meaning within a converse opposition depends upon the interpretation of the roles of the arguments in the two conversely related sentences: They may either coincide or be different. Examples of the 16 diatheses of converse constructions in Lithuanian are provided in the appendix.

7 Conclusions

1. Lithuanian LCs form three types of morphological (formal) opposition: (i) directional (derivational) oppositions, in which one member of the opposition is derived from the other; (ii) non-directional oppositions, in which both members of the opposition share the same stem, without being derived from each other; (iii) suppletive oppositions, in which the members of the opposition are not cognate lexemes. Of these, non-directional morphological oppositions represent the most sizeable group.

LCs cannot be defined in terms of a dedicated formal realization, as the above morphological (formal) types of opposition are not exclusive to LCs: The same types of opposition are also observable in other subsystems of the verb.

2. Based on the number of semantic arguments at their disposal (i.e., on their valency), LCs are bivalent, trivalent, and rarely four- and five-valent. The number of semantic valency slots determines the structural model of constructions headed by LCs. Bivalent converses allow only one type of converse transformation, which involves a transposition of arguments 1 and 2. Logically, trivalent LCs generate five types of converse transformation, of which only three types find support in the data: (i) transposition of arguments 1 and 2; (ii) transposition of arguments 2 and 3; (iii) transposition of arguments 1 and 3. Four- and five-valent LCs follow the same model of converse transformation as trivalent LCs.

3. The following correlations are observed between the logically independent properties of "morphological type" and "syntactic type":

　　i. Bivalent LCs typically involve verbs that form directional (derivational) morphological oppositions, as well as several verbs of the non-directional type and some suppletives. In this case, conversion affects arguments 1 and 2. The base constructions with such converses usually display a nominative-accusative or, less commonly, nominative-locative realization of the arguments. The converse counterparts of these constructions have a more varied argument realization, from nominative-genitive to nominative-prepositional.

　　ii. Trivalent LCs involve the majority of verbs that form non-directional (syntagmatic and correlative-affixal) morphological oppositions as well as most suppletives. Trivalent converses defined in terms of syntagmatic and correlative-affixal morphological oppositions are capable of only one type of converse transposition: that involving arguments 2 and 3.

Suppletive converses, on the other hand, illustrate all types of converse transposition.

iii. Four- and five-valent LCs involve either verbs that form directional morphological oppositions (reflexives) or suppletive verbs. In this case, the converse transposition affects arguments 1 and 3.

4. The semantic classification of LCs is based on the analysis of their event structure, RolS and RefS, which enables the classification of LCs into semantic classes and lexical-semantic groups. Full LCs belong to the same semantic classes and are either causative or stative, while two verbs that form a pair of partial LCs usually belong to different semantic classes, i.e., they form oppositions between a causative and an inchoative verb or a causative and a stative verb. LCs in Lithuanian fall into ten LSGs of different size.

Acknowledgments

I wish to express my most sincere gratitude to Emma Geniušienė for being my lifelong mentor and a model of dedication to linguistic study. I owe my everlasting interest in oppositions and syntactic transformations to her. I am also grateful to the editors of this volume, Peter Arkadiev, Axel Holvoet, and Björn Wiemer, for inviting me to this volume and for their valuable editorial comments and expert advice. I also thank Elżbieta Muskat-Tabakowska, who read the article and let me look at it from a different perspective, leading to a number of clarifications and, naturally, improvements of the text. A special word of thanks goes to my colleague Artūras Ratkus for his enthusiasm for this article and most selfless help while preparing the manuscript for publication.

Abbreviations

Glosses

ACC	accusative	NEG	negation
DAT	dative	NOM	nominative
FUT	future	PL	plural
GEN	genitive	PRF	(verbal) prefix
INS	instrumental	PRS	present tense
LOC	locative	PST	past tense
M	masculine	REFL	reflexive
N	neuter	SG	singular

Diatheses: Semantic roles

Ag	agent	Med	means
Ben	beneficiary	Pt	patient
Com	comitative	Pos	possessor
Exp	experiencer	Qag	quasi-agent
Ad	goal	O	source
Loc	locative	Stim	stimulus

Diatheses: Syntactic functions of cases attributed to the particular referents

S_{Nom} — subject in the nominative case
DO_{Acc} — direct object in the accusative
IO_{Gen} — indirect object in the genitive
IO_{Inst} — indirect object in the instrumental
$OblO_{Loc}$ — oblique object in the locative
$OblO_{(prep)Gen/(prep)Acc}$ — oblique objects with prepositions

Type of referents in the RefS

Pers person
NonP non-person

References

Ambrazas, Vytautas. 1986. Lietuvių kalbos sakinio sintaksinės ir semantinės struktūros vienetai [Units of the syntactic and semantic structure of the Lithuanian sentence]. In Vytautas Ambrazas (ed.) *Lietuvių kalbos sintaksės tyrinėjimai* [Studies in Lithuanian syntax], 4–44. Vilnius: Mokslas.

Ambrazas, Vytautas (ed.). 1997. *Lithuanian grammar*. Vilnius: Baltos lankos.

Apresjan, Jurij D. 1967. *Eksperimental'noje isledovanie semantiki russkogo glagola* [An experimental investigation of the semantics of the Russian verb]. Moskva: Nauka.

Apresjan, Jurij D. [1974] 1995. Leksičeskaja semantika [Lexical semantics]. 2nd edition. In Jurij D. Apresjan *Izbrannyje trudy* [Selected writings]. Tom I. Moskva: Jazyki russkoj kul'tury. (1st edition. Moscow: Nauka, 1974).

Bally, Charles. 1921. *Traîté de stylistique française*. 2nd edition. Paris.

Cruse, Alan D. 1986. *Lexical semantics*. Cambridge: Cambridge University Press.

DLKŽ – Kruopas, Jonas (ed.) *Dabartinės lietuvių kalbos žodynas* [Dictionary of Modern Lithuanian]. Vilnius: Mintis, 1972.

Dowty, David. 2000. 'The garden swarms with bees' and the fallacy of 'argument alternation'. In Yael Ravin & Claudia Leacock (eds.) *Polysemy: Theoretical and computational approaches*, 111–129. New York: Oxford University Press.

Ermanytė, Irena. 2008. *Antonimija ir antonimai* [Antonymy and antonyms]. Vilnius: Lietuvių kalbos instituto leidykla.

Fillmore, Charles J. 1977. The case for case reopened. In Peter Cole & Jerrold M. Sadock (eds.) *Syntax and semantics. Vol. 8: Grammatical relations*, 59–81. New York: Academic Press.

Fillmore, Charles J. & B. T. S. Atkins. 2000. Describing polysemy: The case of 'crawl'. In Yael Ravin & Claudia Leacock (eds.) *Polysemy: Theoretical and computational approaches*, 91–110. New York: Oxford University Press.

Geniušienė, Emma. 1987. *The typology of reflexives*. Berlin: Mouton de Gruyter.

Geniušienė, Emma. 2006. Passives in Lithuanian (in comparison with Russian). In Werner Abraham & Larisa Leisiö (eds.) *Passivization and typology. Form and function*, 29–61. Amsterdam, Philadelphia: John Benjamins.

Haspelmath, Martin. 1993. More on the typology of inchoative / causative verb alternations. In Bernard Comrie & Maria Polinsky (eds.) *Causatives and transitivity*, 86–120. Amsterdam, Philadelphia: John Benjamins.

Haspelmath, Martin. 2002. *Understanding morphology*. London: Arnold (Oxford University Press).

Huddleston, Rodney. 2002. The clause: Complements. In Rodney Huddleston & Geoffrey K. Pullum (eds.) *The Cambridge grammar of the English language*, 2013–2323. Cambridge: Cambridge University Press.

Jakaitienė, Evalda. 2010. *Leksikologija* [Lexicology]. Vilnius: Vilniaus universiteto leidykla.

Jespersen, Otto. 1924. *The philosophy of grammar*. New York: W. W. Norton and Company.

Jones, Steven. 2002. *Antonymy. A corpus-based perspective*. London, New York: Routledge.

Kastovsky, Dieter. 1981. Interaction of lexicon and syntax: Lexical converses. In Jürgen Esser & Axel Hübler (eds.) *Forms and functions. Papers in general, English and applied linguistics presented to Vilém Fried on the occasion of his 65th birthday*, 123–136. Tübingen: Narr.

Kazenin, Konstantin I. 2001. The passive voice. In Martin Haspelmath, Ekkehard Konig, Wulf Oesterreicher, & Wolfgang Raible (eds.) *Language typology and language universals. An international handbook of contemporary research.* Vol. 2, 899–916. Berlin: Walter de Gruyter.

Keenan, Edward L. & Bernard Comrie. 1977. Noun phrase accessibility and universal grammar. *Linguistic Inquiry* 8(1): 63–99.

Leech, Geoffrey N. 1974. *Semantics*. Harmondsworth: Penguin.

Lenartaitė, Kristina. 2011. *Argumentų raiškos alternavimas lietuvių kalboje* [Alternations of argument expression in Lithuanian]. Vilnius University PhD dissertation.

Lenartaitė-Gotaučienė, Kristina. 2014. Alternations in argument realization and problematic cases of subjecthood in Lithuanian. In Axel Holvoet & Nicole Nau (eds.) *Grammatical relations and their non-canonical encoding in Baltic*, 137–180. Amsterdam, Philadelphia: John Benjamins.

Levin, Beth. 1993. *English verb classes and alternations: A preliminary investigation*. Chicago: University of Chicago Press.

Levin, Beth & Malka Rappaport Hovav. 2005. *Argument realization*. New York: Cambridge University Press.

Lyons, John. 1963. *Structural semantics: An analysis of part of the vocabulary of Plato*. Oxford: Blackwell.

Lyons, John. 1968. *Introduction to theoretical linguistics*. Cambridge: Cambridge University Press.

Lyons, John. 1977. *Semantics*. Vol. 1. Cambridge: Cambridge University Press.
Maskaliūnienė, Nijolė. 1989. *Leksičeskie konversivy v litovskom jazyke* [Lexical converses in Lithuanian]. Vilnius University unpublished PhD dissertation.
Maskaliūnienė, Nijolė. 2003. Focus and perspective in the selection of lexical converses. *Kalbotyra* 53(3): 71–77.
Murphy, M. Lynne. 2003. *Semantic relations and the lexicon: Antonymy, synonymy and other paradigms*. Cambridge: Cambridge University Press.
Nedjalkov, Vladimir P. (ed.). 2007. *Reciprocal constructions*. Vols. 1–5. Amsterdam, Philadelphia: John Benjamins.
Nedjalkov, Vladimir P. & Silnitsky [Sil'nickij], Georgij G. 1973. The typology of morphological and lexical causatives. In Ferenc Kiefer (ed.) *Trends in Soviet theoretical linguistics*, 1–32. Dordrecht, Boston: Reidel. (Originally published in: Aleksandr A. Xolodovič (ed.) *Tipologija kauzativnyx konstrukcij: morfologičeskij kauzativ* [Typology of causative constructions: the morphological causative]. 20–50. Leningrad: Nauka, 1969.)
Palmer, Francis Roger. 1981. *Semantics*. 2nd edition. Cambridge: Cambridge University Press.
Salkoff, Maurice. 1983. 'Bees are swarming in the garden': A systematic synchronic study of productivity. *Language* 59(2): 288–346.
Sližienė, Nijolė. 1986. Lietuvių kalbos veiksmažodžių valentingumas ir sintaksinė klasifikacija (Valency and the syntactic classification of Lithuanian verbs). In Vytautas Ambrazas (ed.) *Lietuvių kalbos sintaksės tyrinėjimai* [Studies in Lithuanian syntax], 45–96. Vilnius: Mokslas.
Sližienė, Nijolė. 1994. *Lietuvių kalbos veiksmažodžių junglumo žodynas* [Dictionary of the Lithuanian verb co-occurrence]. I–II tomas. Vilnius: Mokslo ir enciklopedijų leidykla.
Van Valin, Robert D. Jr. 2001. *An introduction to syntax*. Cambridge: Cambridge University Press.
Wiemer, Björn. 2006. Relations between actor-demoting devices in Lithuanian. In Werner Abraham & Larisa Leisiö (eds.) *Passivization and typology. Form and function*, 274–309. Amsterdam, Philadelphia: John Benjamins.
Zueva, Elizaveta V. 1980. *Konversnyje otnošenija v leksike sovremennovo anglijskogo jazyka* [Converse relations in the lexicon of modern English]. Leningrad unpublished PhD dissertation.

Appendix

Diatheses of Lithuanian LCs

Jon-as   turi   nam-ą.
Jonas-NOM   has   house-ACC
'Jonas has a house.'

Δ_0 $\rightarrow$

Pers	NonP
Pos	Pt
S_{Nom}	DO_{Acc}

Nam-as   priklauso   Jon-ui.
house-NOM   belongs   Jonas-DAT
'The house belongs to Jonas.'

Δ_1

Pers	NonP
Pos	Pt
IO_{Dat}	S_{Nom}

Darb-as   lemia   sėkm-ę.
work-NOM assures   success-ACC
'Work assures success.'

Δ_0

NonP$_1$	NonP$_2$
Qag	Pt
S$_{Nom}$	DO$_{Acc}$

→

Sėkm-ė   priklauso nuo darb-o.
success-NOM depends on work-GEN
'Success depends on work.'

Δ_2

NonP$_1$	NonP$_2$
Qag	Pt
OblO$_{Gen}$	S$_{Nom}$

Jon-as   laimėjo   prieš   Petr-ą.
Jonas-NOM won   against Petras-ACC
'Jonas won against Petras.'

Δ_0

Pers$_1$	Pers$_2$
Ben	Com
S$_{Nom}$	DO$_{Acc}$

→

Petr-as   pralaimėjo Jon-ui.
Petras-NOM lost   Jonas-DAT
'Petras lost to Jonas.'

Δ_3

Pers$_1$	Pers$_2$
Com	Ben
IO$_{Dat}$	S$_{Nom}$

Jon-as   vedė   On-ą.
Jonas-NOM married Ona-ACC
'Jonas married Ona'

Δ_0

Pers$_1$	Pers$_2$
Ag	Com
S$_{Nom}$	DO$_{Acc}$

→

On-a   ištekėjo už   Jon-o.
Ona-NOM married for Jonas-GEN
'Ona married Jonas.'

Δ_4

Pers$_1$	Pers$_2$
Com	Ag
OblO$_{Gen}$	S$_{Nom}$

Kolon-os   laiko   stog-ą.
column-NOM.PL   support roof-ACC
'Columns support the roof.'

Δ_0

NonP$_1$	NonP$_2$
Qag	Pt
S$_{Nom}$	DO$_{Acc}$

→

Stog-as   laiko-si   ant kolon-ų.
roof-NOM   hold-REFL   on column-GEN.PL
'The roof is supported by columns.'

Δ_5

NonP$_1$	NonP$_2$
Qag	Pt
OblO$_{Gen}$	S$_{Nom}$

J-os   skon-is   mane   žavi.
she-GEN taste-NOM   1SG.ACC appeals
'Her taste appeals to me.'

Δ_0

Pers$_1$/NonP	Pers$_2$
Stim	Exp
S$_{Nom}$	DO$_{Acc}$

→

Aš   žaviuosi j-os   skoni-u.
1SG.NOM admire   she-GEN   taste-INS
'I admire her taste.'

Δ_6

Pers$_1$/NonP	Pers$_2$
Stim	Exp
IO$_{Ins}$	S$_{Nom}$

J-is sapnuoja kaln-us.
he-NOM dreams mountain-ACC.PL
'He sees mountains in his dream.'

J-am sapnuoja-si kaln-ai.
he-DAT dreams-REFL mountain-NOM.PL
'He is dreaming of mountains.'

Δ_0 → Δ_7

Pers$_1$	Pers$_2$/NonP
Exp	Stim
S$_{Nom}$	DO$_{Acc}$

Pers$_1$	Pers$_2$/NonP
Exp	Stim
IO$_{Dat}$	S$_{Nom}$

Snieg-as dengė žem-ę.
snow-NOM covered earth-ACC
'Snow was covering the earth.'

Žem-ė dengė-si snieg-u.
earth-NOM covered-REFL snow-INS
'The earth was getting covered with snow.'

Δ_0 → Δ_8

NonP$_1$	NonP$_2$
Med	Pt
S$_{Nom}$	DO$_{Acc}$

NonP$_1$	NonP$_2$
Med	Pt
IO$_{Ins}$	S$_{Nom}$

Ežer-as at-spindi dang-ų.
lake-NOM PREF-shines sky-ACC
'The lake reflects the sky.'

Dang-us at-si-spindi ežer-e.
sky-NOM PREF-REFL-shines lake-LOC
'The sky is reflected in the lake.'

Δ_0 → Δ_9

NonP$_1$	NonP$_2$
Qag	Pt
S$_{Nom}$	DO$_{Acc}$

NonP$_1$	NonP$_2$
Loc	Qag
OblO$_{Loc}$	S$_{Nom}$

Žem-ė sugėrė vanden-į.
soil-NOM drank water-ACC
'The soil absorbed the water.'

Vand-uo su-si-gėrė į žem-ę.
water-NOM PREF-REFL-drank to soil-ACC
'The water was absorbed into the soil.'

Δ_0 → Δ_{10}

NonP$_1$	NonP$_2$
Qag	Pt/Med
S$_{Nom}$	DO$_{Acc}$

NonP$_1$	NonP$_2$
Ad(Loc)	Qag/Med
OblO$_{(prep)Acc/Loc}$	S$_{Nom}$

Aš bijau šun-s.
1SG.NOM fear dog-GEN
'I am afraid of the dog.'

Šuo baugina mane.
dog:NOM scares 1SG.ACC
'The dog scares me.'

Δ_0 → $_S\Delta_{11}$

Pers$_1$	Pers$_2$/NonP
Exp	Stim
S$_{Nom}$	OblO$_{Gen/Ins}$

Pers$_1$	Pers$_2$/NonP
Exp	Ag/Qag
DO$_{Acc}$	S$_{Nom}$

Žol-ė   apaugo   tak-ą.
grass-NOM   overgrew   path-ACC
'Grass has overgrown the path.'

Δ_0

NonP$_1$	NonP$_2$
Qag	Pt
S$_{Nom}$	DO$_{Acc}$

→

Tak-as   apaugo   žol-e.
path-NOM   overgrew   grass-INS
'The path has been overgrown with grass.'

Δ_{12}

NonP$_1$	NonP$_2$
Med	Pt
OblO$_{Ins}$	S$_{Nom}$

Mam-a   užtiesė   stalties-ę
mother-NOM laid   tablecloth-ACC
ant stal-o.
on table-GEN
'Mother has laid a tablecloth on the table.'

Δ_0

Pers$_1$	NonP	Pers$_2$
Ag	Pt	Loc
S$_{Nom}$	DO$_{Acc}$	OblO$_{Gen}$

→

Mam-a   užtiesė   stal-ą
mother-NOM laid   table-ACC
stalties-e.
tablecloth-INS
'Mother has laid the table with a tablecloth.'

Δ_{13}

Pers$_1$	NonP	Pers$_2$
Ag	Med	Pt
S$_{Nom}$	OblO$_{Ins}$	DO$_{Acc}$

J-is   šeria karv-ę   šien-u.
he-NOM   feeds cow-ACC   hay-INS
'He is feeding a cow hay.'

Δ_0

Pers	Anim	NonP
Ag	Pt	Med
S$_{Nom}$	DO$_{Acc}$	OblO$_{Ins}$

→

J-is   šeria šien-ą   karv-ei.
he-NOM   feeds hay-ACC   cow-DAT
'He is feeding hay to a cow.'

Δ_{14}

Pers	Anim	NonP
Ag	Ben	Pt
S$_{Nom}$	OblO$_{Dat}$	DO$_{Acc}$

Tet-a   paliko   nam-ą
aunt-NOM   bequeathed   house-ACC
sūnėn-ui.
nephew-DAT
'The aunt bequeathed the house to her nephew.'

Δ_0

Pers$_1$	NonP	Pers$_2$
Ag	Pt	Ben
S$_{Nom}$	DO$_{Acc}$	IO$_{Dat}$

→

Sūnėn-as   paveldėjo nam-ą
nephew-NOM inherited house-ACC
iš tet-os.
from aunt-GEN
'The nephew inherited the house from his aunt.'

Δ_{15}

Pers$_1$	NonP	Pers$_2$
O	Pt	Ben
OblO$_{Gen}$	DO$_{Acc}$	S$_{Nom}$

Jon-as   duoda   man   knyg-ą.   *Aš   imu   knyg-ą   iš*
Jonas-NOM   gives   1SG.DAT   book-ACC   1SG.NOM   take   book-ACC   from
                                                    Jon-o.
                                                    Jonas-GEN

'Jonas is giving me a book.'   'I am taking a book from Jonas.'

Δ_0 → Δ_{16}

Pers$_1$	NonP	Pers$_2$
Ag	Pt	Ben
S$_{Nom}$	DO$_{Acc}$	IO$_{Dat}$

Pers$_1$	NonP	Pers$_2$
O	Pt	Ag
OblO$_{Gen}$	DO$_{Acc}$	S$_{Nom}$

Eiko Sakurai
10 Past habitual tense in Lithuanian

1 Introduction

This chapter presents detailed observations regarding aspectual characteristics of the past habitual tense with the suffix -*dav*- in Lithuanian. By referring to contrastive analysis with Russian, I will try to go beyond the already existing interpretations and to give a more comprehensive explanation of the functions of the past habitual tense. Moreover, this study will offer an analysis, based on the results of a questionnaire that I carried out in Lithuania in 2008–2009, of the divisions in the usage domain of the two past tenses of Lithuanian, i.e., the unmarked past tense and the past habitual tense, from the perspective of correlation with aspectual properties of verbs.

In normative "academic" grammars (LKG, GLJa, DLKG, and LG) or in related studies that follow this tradition, the past form with the suffix -*dav*- is defined as "past frequentative tense" (Lith. *būtasis dažninis laikas*; Russ. *prošedšee mnogokratnoe vremja*), which expresses a repeated action in the past, while the unmarked past tense is called "past single-time tense" (Lith. *būtasis kartinis laikas*; Russ. *prošedšee odnokratnoe vremja*). Along with the term "frequentative", "iterative" (Dambriūnas 1959, 1960, Genjušene 1989) and a most misleading term "imperfect" or "imperfectum consuetudinis" (Senn 1949, Safarewicz 1967) are also used. These definitions are not explicit enough to convey the properties of the two past forms in Lithuanian because the unmarked past form can denote not only a single-time situation, but also a repeated or frequent situation. Moreover, the past tense form with the suffix -*dav*- can quite naturally denote a non-frequentative iterative (defined as "discontinuative" by Xrakovskij 1997) or non-iterative (continuous or durative) situation as well.

While most scholars recognize that the past habitual form primarily denotes a situation that was repeated in the past, they also agree that it may denote or at least imply habitual meaning. For example, as Geniušienė (1997: 230) suggests, this tense form "serves to express situations repeated an indeterminate number of times in the past, with an implication of habituality and a remote past". However, I continue to hold the opinion given in my previous studies (Matsuya [=Sakurai] 1995, Sakurai 1997, 1999a,b) that the essence of this past tense lies in its habitual nature, and to define it as "past habitual tense", while calling the unmarked past tense as "simple past tense"[1] (see 1).[2]

(1) a. J-is   {kartais / dažnai / paprastai} **dirb-dav-o**   namie.
        he-NOM   sometimes   often   usually   work-HAB-PST.3   at.home
        'He {sometimes/often/usually} used to work at home.'

    b. J-is   {kartais / dažnai / paprastai} **dirb-o**   namie.
        he-NOM   sometimes   often   usually   work-PST.3   at.home
        'He {sometimes/often/usually} worked at home.'

In this regard, Comrie (1976) also assumes the Lithuanian past tense with the suffix *-dav-* to be a habitual form. Furthermore, Roszko and Roszko (2000, 2006) have made important contributions toward understanding the aspectual feature of this tense including its habitual nature.

I will now briefly explain the terms that are used in this chapter. The semantic definition of "habitual", adopted from Comrie (1976: 27–28), refers to "a situation which is characteristic of an extended period of time" and is distinguished from "iterativity", which means "the repetition or successive occurrence of several instances of the given situation". Also, "habitual" is distinguished from "frequentative", which is defined as a special type of "iterative", i.e., "iterative with small intervals between the repeated situations" and which is expressed mainly by adverbials like '*often*' (Xrakovskij 1997: 57–58).[3] Moreover, by following the approach of Comrie (1976) and Lindstedt (1984), I introduce the idea that habituals have a complex aspectual structure (which Lindstedt names the "nested aspect"). As I have already discussed in detail (1999b), I consider <habitual> as a complex tense-aspect category representing the relationship between the temporal-aspectual features at the macro-level of a situation and the features at the micro-level, i.e., internal structure of the individual micro-situations (e.g., in a sentence like *when Rimas was a student, he often used to meet her in the library*

---

[1] The main tense forms in Lithuanian are synthetic forms of present, simple past (non-habitual), past habitual, and future. Besides that, there exists what is traditionally called "compound forms" of each tense, i.e., analytic forms consisting of appropriate tense form of the verb *būti* 'be' and participles. The analytic forms with past participles (both active and passive participles) denote <perfect> (Geniušienė & Nedjalkov 1988, Genjušene 1990, Sakurai 1997, 2010) (the angle brackets < > are used in this chapter to indicate a semantic feature).

[2] Basically, the example sentences originated from the native consultants and the author of this chapter, which where then checked by native informants.

[3] Xrakovskij (1997: 52–58) notes that specialized frequentative tense forms have not been found in his data and considers the past tense forms with suffix *-dav-* in Lithuanian as specialized iterative tense forms.

and come home together [with her], past habitual functions to describe a macro-situation that is habitual, and each of whose micro-situation as well, i.e., *he met her in the library and came home together*).⁴ In this chapter, <habitual> and <habituality> pertain to semantic domains, whereas the term "past habitual" denotes the grammatical past habitual tense.

Furthermore, I hold on to the most general definition of "perfective" as a reference to a situation without regard to internal temporal structure, viewing a situation in its entirety as a single whole, and "imperfective" – as a reference to the internal temporal structure of a situation, to a situation without any internal structure, or to the repeated situations (cf. Comrie 1976, who explains subclasses of <imperfective> as in Table 1; see also Smith 1991).

In this chapter, the terms <perfective> and <imperfective> are used as semantic properties, whereas the terms "verbal aspect", "perfective verb", and "imperfective verb" (abbreviated as PFV and IPFV) – as grammatical-morphological category. As is well known, most simple verbs in Russian are defined as "imperfective verbs" (e.g., *pisat'* 'write'), prefixed derivatives of simple verbs – "perfective verbs" (e.g., *na-pisat'* 'write', *pere-pisat'* 'rewrite'), and suffixed derivatives of "perfective verbs" – "imperfective verbs" (e.g., *pere-pis-yva-t'* 'rewrite').

Tab. 1: Classification of aspectual oppositions (Comrie 1976: 25)

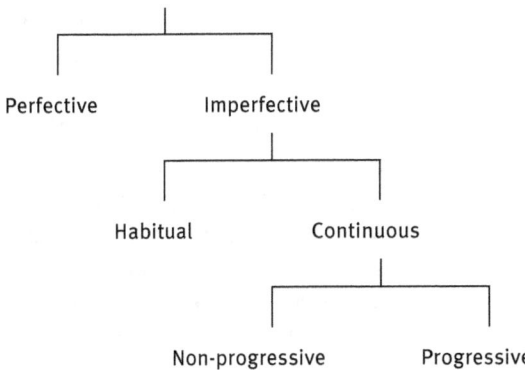

---

4 This issue is discussed by Dickey (2000) in terms of aspectual choice in the Slavic languages. The general properties of <habitual> from a typological point of view are reviewed in detail by Dahl (1985) and Bybee, Perkins, and Pagliuca (1994). Also, the broader discussions on <iterative> as the semantic type of the "plurality of situations" are provided by Xrakovskij (1989, 1997) and Šluinskij (2006).

Tab. 2: Time stability and types of situations (Lehmann 1994: 3298)

Static ←					→ Dynamic
Atelic			Telic		
Atemporal		Durative	Terminative	Ingressive	Punctual
Class membership	Property	State	Process	Event	

To describe the aspectual peculiarities of Lithuanian verbs, I use the terms "telic/atelic (bounded/non-bounded)". According to the traditional definition, a "telic (bounded) verb" is a verb conveying in its inherent lexical meaning the notion of boundaries and revealing a situation as moving toward those boundaries, while "atelic (non-bounded) verb" is a verb not conveying such a notion and revealing a situation as not having any boundaries (see Maslov 1948, 1962a,b, Garey 1957). However, in this chapter, the terms "telic/atelic", adopted from Lehmann (1994), are used in a wider sense: A telic verb (phrase) or predicate denotes a situation that is bounded at the start (ingressive), at the end (terminative), or both at the start and at the end (deliminative or punctual), while an atelic verb (phrase) or predicate denotes a situation that is open at both sides (durative or atemporal). Lehmann (1994) defines subclasses of telic/atelic meanings as in Table 2 (see also, for instance, Krifka 1998).

In addition, in this chapter, I use the general definition of "taxis", i.e., temporal order (or perspective), to denote an external temporal relation of one situation to another situation. The term "taxis" was introduced by Jakobson (1957: 4) as follows: "Taxis characterizes the narrated event in relation to another narrated event and without reference to the speech event." Later, Maslov (1978, 1984) and others suggested that the concepts of <simultaneity>, <anteriority>, and <posteriority> regularly appear as a result of interaction among aspectual forms (see also Bondarko 1987, 1996, Xrakovskij 2009; on taxis in Lithuanian, particularly Wiemer 2009). Speaking of the aspectual opposition of <perfective/imperfective>, typically <perfectivity> is related to taxis through the concept of <sequence>, while <imperfectivity> is related through <simultaneity>. The taxis relation is regarded as one of the most important functions of aspect.

This chapter is organized as follows. Section 2 reviews previous studies on the Lithuanian past habitual. Section 3 briefly discusses the essential differences of aspectual properties of verbs in Lithuanian and Russian by referring to their relationship with tense and taxis. Section 4 discusses in detail the concepts of <habituality> and <iterativity> already outlined in this section. The core of this chapter is constituted by Sections 5 to 8, in which the functions of the past habitual tense in Lithuanian are thoroughly explained. Section 5 presents the empirical study (questionnaire) I carried out. Section 6 examines the possibility of co-occurrence of the past habitual with adverbials as regards to <iterativity> and <habituality>. Section 7 analyzes the distribution of simple past forms and past habitual forms in Lithuanian by referring to contrastive analysis with Russian. Section 8 makes further observations on multiple functions of the past habitual tense in Lithuanian. Finally, Section 9 offers some conclusions based on my analysis.

2 Problems in previous studies on past habitual tense with suffix -dav-

In "academic" grammars, the past habitual tense with the suffix -dav- (as noted previously, traditionally called "the past frequentative tense") is defined as past tense that indicates a repeated action in the past. Consequently, no statements have been found that would define whether the meaning of this form pertains to <perfective> or <imperfective>.[5]

As yet, no consensus has been reached among scholars of Lithuanian who regard aspect to be a semantic category and who employ the concept of <perfective/imperfective> to analyze aspectual tense forms. To bring to light the problems involved in the previous studies, here I would like to provide an overview of representative interpretations of the form with the suffix -dav- (according to the terminology "imperfect" or "past iterative tense") offered by Senn (1949), who has given a very general explanation, and by Dambriūnas (1959), who has placed more emphasis on the analysis of aspect that is inherent in the tense form.

> Lithuanian has the same general types of verbal aspect as Russian. However, in contrast to Polish and Russian, Lithuanian has both aspects in all basic tenses, including the present tense [...] In addition, there is a so-called imperfectum consuetudinis, a past tense expressing habitual or iterative action. This tense, usually called imperfect has only imperfective aspect, irrespective of the form of the verb. Any verb, whether it be perfective or imperfective in the preterit, present, and future, becomes iterative, i.e. a special type of imperfective, in this tense (Senn 1949: 406).

---

5 In traditional studies, including the normative "academic" grammars, the idea that in Lithuanian "aspect" is a derivational category and is constituted by the binary opposition of "perfective/imperfective" in the "aspectual pairs" of verbs mainly formed with the help of prefixes and suffixes was accepted. Furthermore, it was not customary to regard tense forms as aspect forms as well (cf. Sližienė 1995).

> The Lithuanian verbal aspect can be determined only by explaining aspect of different verbal forms. [...] Forms of the past iterative tense (imperfectum consuetudinis) can also be manifold – imperfective, perfective, or neutral. [...] the past iterative form itself does not serve for expressing a certain aspect; it means past iterative or a habitual action. [...] Ordinarily, however, the aspect is as recognizable in these forms as in the other forms (Dambriūnas 1960: 151–157).

Senn assumes the past habitual form with the suffix *-dav-* to be completely imperfective. Yet, Dambriūnas is critical toward such a view and claims that the past habitual form can be neutral, imperfective, or perfective without being an aspectual form. Similar to Dambriūnas, Safarewicz (1967) does not recognize this tense as an aspectual form, but he offers an essentially different interpretation from that of Dambriūnas. See the following citation (4), translated from Polish by the author of this chapter.

> Thus, we come to the conclusion that imperfect itself in Lithuanian does not serve for expressing a certain aspect; rather, it should be recognized that verbs used in the form of imperfect in this case do not reveal whether they are perfective or imperfective (Safarewicz 1967: 350).

The prevailing interpretations of aspect of the form with the suffix *-dav-* can be summarized as follows:

i. "[The form] has only imperfective aspect, irrespective of the form of the verb" (Senn 1949: 406).
ii. "[The form] itself does not serve for expressing a certain aspect", but "can be imperfective, perfective, or neutral" (Dambriūnas 1960: 157–160).
iii. "[The form] itself does not serve for expressing a certain aspect" and "does not reveal whether they are perfective or imperfective" (Safarewicz 1967: 350).

I believe that the apparent lack of agreement among the available interpretations is the result of the presence of three unsolved problems:

1. The definitions of aspect itself and of aspectual properties of Lithuanian verbs differ among linguists.
2. There is no uniformity in the aspectual interpretation of <iterative> and <habitual>.
3. Investigations on how the usage of the past habitual tense differs from that of the simple past tense are not sufficient.

Regarding the first problem, as Wiemer (2001), Kardelis and Wiemer (2003), Pakerys and Wiemer (2007), and Arkadiev (2008, 2009, 2011, 2012) discussed in detail from a typological point of view, it should be admitted that interpreting "verbal aspect" in Russian and Lithuanian from the same perspective is rather dubious. It is important that, as I have also argued in the previous studies (Matsuya [=Sakurai] 1995, Sakurai 1997, 1999a,b, 2002, 2010), there is no basis for believing that verbs form "aspectual pairs" of "perfective/imperfective" in Lithuanian and for classifying them into so-called perfective, imperfective, or dual aspect (or biaspectual) verbs as is the case with verbal aspect in Russian. In fact, traditionally called "aspectual pairs" in Lithuanian considerably differs from Russian in both meaning and function. In my view, an important point is that in Russian where the verbal aspect is highly grammatical, the imperfective verb acts as an unmarked member in opposition to the marked perfective verb, and this pair of verbs forms the basis for the grammatical category of aspect. However, the situation in Lithuanian differs since the opposition of <perfective/imperfective> is realized only through the correlation between tense form and telic/atelic verbs. It should be said about the traditional definition of "verbal aspect" in Lithuanian that due to the biased focus on the formal peculiarities (or similarities to Russian) the underlying function of aspectual opposition is inappropriately perceived (Section 3 reviews this problem).

Regarding the second problem, I assign <imperfective> a broader meaning and, following Comrie (1976: 24–26), interpret <habitual> as a subclass of <imperfective>. Thus, I believe that this past habitual tense primarily should be dealt with as <imperfective>. It is important to recognize that from the functional perspective, the subclasses, including <habitual>, <continuous> (or <durative>) and <atemporal>, link together to form a single integrated concept of <imperfectivity> as a whole and to create a binary opposition with <perfective>, since the opposition <perfective/imperfective> is basically related to their functions in discourse. Meanwhile, <iterative>, which means a repeated situation, can be either <perfective> or <imperfective>. If a situation is repeated definite number of times, it can be viewed as <perfective> (e.g., *he pushed the button three times*), whereas, if a situation repeated indefinite number of times, it can be viewed as <imperfective> (e.g., *he was pushing the button many times*). <Habitual> meaning, however, can be either <iterative> or not, but is always primarily <imperfective>. (Section 4 discusses this problem in more detail.)

The major purpose of this chapter is to clarify the third problem, which is closely related to the first two, by differentiating the usage of the past habitual forms from the simple past tense forms. Regarding this, Mustejkis (1972), Genjušene (1989), Geniušienė (1997), and others note that when a "perfective verb" is unpaired with the corresponding "imperfective verb" or when a verb is a "dual aspect verb", the simple past form generally has <perfective> meaning and the past habitual form serves as a means of "imperfectivizing" (see 2).[6]

(2) a. *Visaip* **atsitik-dav-o** (**atsitik-o*) *mūsų kaim-e.*
 in.every.way happen-HAB-PST.3 (*happen-PST.3) our village-LOC.SG
 'lit. All kinds of things used to happen in our village.'

 b. *Rim-as dažnai* **atvažiuo-dav-o** (**atvažiav-o*)
 Rimas-NOM.SG often arrive-HAB-PST.3 (*come-PST.3)
 namo.
 home
 'Rimas often used to come home.'

The above idea seems to be widely accepted. However, it seems to focus partially on the function of the past habitual tense and does not explain the differences in usage between these two past forms. First, the past habitual tense does not denote simple (non-habitual) <durative> meaning. Second, in many cases, either the past habitual form or the simple past form of the same verb can be used[7] (see 3).

(3) *Rim-as dažnai* **{*dirb-o*/*dirb-dav-o*}** *namie.*
 Rimas-NOM.SG often work-PST.3/work-HAB-PST.3 at.home
 'Rimas often used to work at home.'

In my opinion, as defined in Section 1, by treating aspect of the past tense with the suffix *-dav-* as <habitual> with a complex semantic structure, it is possible to solve the problems remaining in the interpretations offered so far. To illustrate this point, I will distinguish two levels of aspect, that is, a level of the <habitual> macro-situation in interpretation (I) and a level of micro-situation (or sub-situation) enclosed within the macro-situation in interpretation (II). If the aspect of the past habitual tense is recognized from both perspectives as a complex

---

[6] Examples (2), (3), (9), and (11d) are taken from Genjušene (1989) and Geniušienė (1997) and are slightly modified by the author of this chapter.

[7] Note that in some dialects in Lithuanian, "habitual" is not a grammatical category like in the standard language and the past habitual forms are either used only rarely or do not exist at all. In those dialects, derivational iterative verbs with suffixes such as *-inė-* are in wider usage, and even in cases where the past habitual tense would be used in the standard language, it is usually replaced by the simple past tense (dialects of central Aukštaitija and western Dzūkija). Besides that, there are dialects where analytic forms combining an auxiliary with the infinitive are used instead of the suffix *-dav-* (Žemaitian dialect) (see LKG (2): 112; there are more up-to-date references in Arkadiev 2012: 83–84). In Latvian, which is very close to Lithuanian, this kind of past tense is not recognized.

semantic structure, these two interpretations would not contradict each other as in interpretation (III) (see 4).[8]

(4) a. *Visaip*   **atsitik-dav-o**   *Kaukaz-o*   *kaln-uose:*
       in.every.way happen-HAB-PST.3   Caucasus-GEN.SG mountains-LOC.PL
       kariau-dav-o   *kaimynin-ės*   *taut-os,*
       fight-HAB-PST.3   neighboring-NOM.PL   nation-NOM.PL
       susipeš-dav-o   *gimin-ės,*   **susipyk-dav-o**
       quarrel-HAB-PST.3   family-NOM.PL   fall.out.with.each.other-HAB-PST.3
       kunak-ai [...]
       allies-NOM.PL
       'lit. All kinds of things used to happen in Caucasian mountains: neighboring nations would fight, related families would quarrel, allies would fall out with each other [...]'

   b. *Kai*   *Rim-as*   *buv-o*   *student-as,*
      when   Rimas-NOM.SG   be-PST.3   student-NOM.SG
      j-is   *dažnai*   **dirb-dav-o**   *bibliotek-oje,*
      he-NOM   often   work-HAB-PST.3   library-LOC.SG
      kartais   *ten*   **sutik-dav-o**   *j-ą*
      sometimes   there   meet-HAB-PST.3   she-ACC
      ir   *kartu*   **atvažiuo-dav-o**   *namo.*
      and   together   arrive-HAB-PST.3   home
      'When Rimas was a student, he would often work in the library, would sometimes meet her there and come home together [with her].'

I propose that aspect of the past habitual tense at the level of the macro-situation is <habitual>, i.e., <imperfective>, while aspect at the level of the micro-situation (or sub-situation) can be either <perfective> or <imperfective>. For example, in example (4b), at the level of the micro-situation, individual micro-occurrences *'he worked in the library'* (<imperfective>), *'met her there'* (<perfective>), and *'came home together'* (<perfective>), which are referred to by past habitual forms, go together to construct the characteristic <habitual> macro-situation. In Lithuanian, this type of usage is characteristic of the past habitual tense; meanwhile, the simple past tense rarely denotes <habitual> meaning compared to the past habitual tense and typically does not refer to this kind of complex semantic

---

[8] Example (4a), which has been used as a typical example of the past habitual tense in the "academic" grammars, is originally cited from A. Vienuolis's novel *Kruvinojo keršto uola* [Rock of the Bloody Revenge].

structure of aspect. I would conclude that this is the essential functional difference between the two past tenses in Lithuanian (Sections 5 to 8 investigate this problem in detail).

3 Aspectual properties of Lithuanian verbs

Before making further observations, I will briefly touch upon the aspectual properties of Lithuanian verbs according to my previous studies (Matsuya [=Sakurai] 1995, Sakurai 1997, 1999a,b, 2002, 2008). It was assumed by Mustejkis (1972) and others that the system of "verbal aspect" that employs prefixes and suffixes to serve as markers of aspect has developed in Lithuanian in a same way as in Russian. This can be summarized as in Table 3.[9]

However, despite the similarities in the forms of verbs, there are remarkable differences between Lithuanian and Russian.[10] To begin with, in Russian, there is a dichotomy between perfective/imperfective pairs that are formed by the perfective

Tab. 3: Traditional interpretation of formation of "aspectual verbal pairs" in Lithuanian and in Russian

	Lithuanian	Russian
Simple verb (IPFV) 'write'	rašyti	pisat'
1. Prefixed verb (PFV) 'write'	rašyti→pa-rašyti	pisat'→na-pisat'
2. Prefixed verb (PFV) 'rewrite'	rašyti→per-rašyti	pisat'→pere-pisat'
3. Suffixed verb (IPFV) 'rewrite'	per-rašyti→per-raš-inė-ti	pere-pisat'→pere-pis-yva-t'

---

[9] For detailed observations on aspectual properties of Lithuanian verbs, see Dambriūnas (1959, 1960), Galnaitytė (1963, 1966), Safarewicz (1967), Mustejkis (1972), Paulauskienė (1979, 1994), Ambrazas (1984), Genjušene (1989, 1990), Geniušienė (1997), Wiemer (2001), Kardelis and Wiemer (2003), Holvoet and Čižik (2004), Pakerys and Wiemer (2007), and Arkadiev (2008, 2009, 2011, 2012).
[10] On the essential differences between aspectual systems in Lithuanian and in Russian, see in particular Wiemer (2001). Arkadiev (2008) also discusses this issue in detail and asserts that there is no need to postulate verbal aspect as a grammatical category in Lithuanian, while in Russian it can be regarded as grammatical, because there are morphosyntactic properties regularly associated with verbs of each of the aspects and regular grammatically conditioned interrelations between verbs of different aspects (partly captured by the notion of "aspectual pairs"). On the general problems of the notion of "aspectual pairs", see Plungian (2011: 409–410). On the issue of aspect and aspectuality, or actionality, see also Thelin (1978) and Bertinetto and Delfitto (2000).

verb being a prefixed derivative of the imperfective verb as 1 and 2 and the imperfective, which is a suffixed derivative of the perfective verb as 3. In contrast, in Lithuanian, prefixation does not necessarily render the simple verb <perfective>, as it does in Russian, nor does the suffixation render the prefixed verb <imperfective>.

In Lithuanian, the opposition 3 in Table 3 is not as productive as the Russian imperfectivizing suffixes, although in Lithuanian suffixation to the simple verb such as *raš-inė-ti* 'scribble' is even more productive than in Russian (Mustejkis 1972). Furthermore, the inherently telic verb, i.e., unprefixed simple telic verb such as *mirti* 'die', often does not build up an opposition like the Russian *umeret'* (PFV) – *umirat'* (IPFV) 'die'. The opposition between simple telic and atelic verbs cannot be clearly defined, that is, it presents a continuum/scale based on the degree of telicity. Thus, even though the relationship that starts the formation of a grammatical opposition similar to <perfective/imperfective> in Russian as in 1 can be observed, most oppositions among aspectually related Lithuanian verbs are more of a lexical nature as in 2. Thus, in Lithuanian aspect as a verbal category can be viewed as still in the process of grammaticalization.

As I have already discussed in my previous studies, in many cases, in Lithuanian, so-called aspectual pairs, which are traditionally interpreted as pairs of "perfective/imperfective verbs", should instead be defined as pairs of telic/atelic (or bounded/non-bounded) verbs (see also Section 1 and 2).[11] I consider many unprefixed Lithuanian verbs such as *skaityti* 'read', *rašyti* 'write', *eiti* 'go', or *dirbti* 'work', traditionally called "imperfective" verbs, to be inherently atelic verbs, which typically denote a <durative> or <atemporal> meaning.[12] Whereas prefixed Lithuanian verbs such as *per-skaityti* 'read through, finish reading' and *pa-rašyti* 'write, write up', traditionally called "perfective" verbs, are formally marked telic, i.e., highly telic verbs that typically denote an event.

It is important to note that the degrees of telicity among the group of unprefixed simple verbs, i.e., traditional "imperfective", in fact vary from relatively more (highly) telic verbs to less telic verbs. The unprefixed verbs that can denote a terminative process or an event without being bounded by any direct object or adverbials (e.g., *keltis* 'get up', *sėstis* 'sit down') are relatively more telic than the unprefixed verbs that denote a typically durative process (e.g., *eiti* 'go', *dirbti* 'work', *klausyti* 'listen') or state (*turėti* 'have', *žinoti* 'know', *būti* 'be') and thus

---

11 In this regard, there are more up-to-date and comprehensive references in the works of Arkadiev (previously cited) (footnote 9).

12 Note that atelic verbs can denote a terminative process or an event, mostly when they are bounded by direct objects (in accusative case) and/or by certain types of adverbials (see Dahl 1981).

are closer to the atelic side of the continuum. If the unprefixed verb is more telic, its traditional "perfective" counterpart, i.e., a prefixed verb (e.g., *at-si-kelti* 'get up', *at-si-sėsti* 'sit down') can be defined as formally marked or intensified telic verb (although, in fact, *at-si-kelti* and *keltis* have often been cited as "perfective/imperfective" pair in the previous studies).

Furthermore, I am of the opinion that the traditional "dual aspect (biaspectual) verbs", which express both <perfective> and <imperfective> meanings mainly depending on different tense forms, should be regarded simply as telic verbs. Among these, prefixed verbs (e.g., *at-eiti* 'come', *iš-važiuoti* 'leave (by transport)', *už-mesti* 'throw over') are formally marked as telic by prefixes, while simple verbs (e.g., *baigti* 'finish', *rasti* 'find', *gauti* 'get', *mirti* 'die') are unmarked, that is, they are inherently telic verbs. Note that these simple telic verbs can also be prefixed (e.g., *pa-baigti* 'finish', *su-rasti* 'find', and *nu-mirti* 'die'). In such cases, the prefixes function merely to intensify the telic meaning of verbs, and not to form telic verbs from atelic.

In addition, I consider the so-called iterative verbs with the suffix *-inė-* to be formally marked atelic verbs. The suffix *-inė-*, which adds iterative meaning both to unprefixed verbs (e.g., *šok-inė-ti* 'jump about, around, repeatedly', *važ-inė-ti* 'drive around, repeatedly') and to prefixed verbs (*per-raš-inė-ti* 'rewrite repeatedly', *at-im-inė-ti* 'take from repeatedly'), is commonly regarded as the most important "imperfectivizing" suffix, although it often also involves attenuative meaning.

Consequently, the grammatical <perfective/imperfective> meanings and functions obviously exist only in the tense-aspect system in Lithuanian, where the tense forms have a larger functional load compared to Russian. This is the point many scholars have agreed on (see, for instance, Dambriūnas 1959, 1960, Galnaitytė 1963, Musteikis 1972), although, at the same time, it has long been thought that, in Lithuanian, verbs are also classified as so-called perfective, imperfective, and dual aspect verbs analogously to Russian. In addition, one of the most important differences between Lithuanian and Russian has been considered that Lithuanian possesses very few "purely aspectual pairs" of verbs, many "dual aspect verbs", and many unpaired "perfective" and "imperfective" verbs (see Galnaitytė 1963).

In my opinion, although Lithuanian telic/atelic verbs are superficially similar to Russian perfective/imperfective verbs, they are essentially different in relations to tense and taxis. Most importantly, all Lithuanian verbs have both present and future tense forms and the prefixation to the present form of unprefixed verbs such as *skaityti* 'read' does not render the resultant form future tense, i.e., the prefixed verbs such as *per-skaityti* 'read through, finish reading' have present tense unlike Russian perfective verb such as *pro-čitat'* 'read through, finish reading', which have future tense, but not present tense. In relation to this, perfective/

imperfective verbs in Russian typically relates to the taxis relation <sequence/simultaneity> independently of tense, whereas telic/atelic verbs in Lithuanian are not directly related to the taxis.

In other words, the most important thing is that, unlike in Russian, the semantic distinction of <perfective/imperfective> in Lithuanian usually becomes evident through the combination of telic/atelic meanings of verbs and these tense forms. That is, in the case of telic verbs, the simple past and future tense forms basically denote <perfective> meaning (e.g., simple past – *jis per-skait-ė* 'he read through, finished reading', *at-ėj-o* 'came', *mir-ė* 'died'; future – *jis per-skaity-s* 'he will read through, will finish reading', *at-ei-s* 'will come', *mir-s* 'will die'), while in the case of atelic verbs the simple past and future tense forms basically denote <imperfective> (e.g., simple past – *jis skait-ė* 'he read, was reading', *ėj-o* 'went, was going'; future – *jis skaity-s* 'he will read, will be reading', *ei-s* 'will go, will be going'). Meanwhile, the present and past habitual tense forms of most verbs, whether telic or atelic, primarily denote <imperfective> meaning (e.g., present – *jis per-skait-o* 'he (repeatedly) reads through, is reading through, is finishing reading', *at-ein-a* '(repeatedly) comes, is coming', *miršt-a* '(repeatedly) die, is dying', *skait-o* 'reads, is reading', *ein-a* 'goes, is going'; past habitual – *jis per-skaity-dav-o* 'he used to read through', *at-ei-dav-o* 'used to come', *mir-dav-o* 'used to die', *skaity-dav-o* 'used to read', *ei-dav-o* 'used to go'), although telic verbs can denote <perfective> meaning at the level of the micro-situation, as I discuss in the next section.

4 Characteristics of <iterativity> and <habituality>

4.1 Differences between <iterativity> and <habituality>

In order to offer a clear definition of "habitual", I should start with an explanation of how it differs from "iterative", since the two meanings are frequently confused. I will use the term "iterative" for the simple repetition of situations (Comrie 1976), that is, for the repeated occurrences of an action on one particular occasion (Dahl 1994). The borderline between <iterativity> and <habituality> is not clear-cut; however, these meanings can be distinguished mainly by co-occurrence with adverbials.

Non-habitual <iterative> meaning co-occurs with aspectual adverbials denoting definite or indefinite number of times, while <habitual> meaning co-occurs with adverbials denoting frequency or habitual continuity. In this chapter, aspectual adverbials related to <iterative> and <habitual> meanings are classified below in (5) (cf. Xrakovskij 1987, 1989, 1997, Genjušene 1989, Sližienė 1995, Geniušienė 1997). The continuum of a to d shows how an iterative situation changes into a habitual one.

(5) Aspectual adverbials related to <iterative> and <habitual>
   a. Number of times (or counts)
      Definite number of times: *du kartus* 'two times', *dukart* 'twice'
      Indefinite number of times: *keletą kartų* 'several times', *daug kartų* 'many times'
   b. Cyclicity: *du kartus per savaitę* 'two times a week', *kasdien* 'every day', *kiekvieną vasarą* 'every summer'
   c. Frequency (interval or indefinite repetition): *retai* 'seldom', *kartais* 'from time to time, sometimes', *dažnai* 'often, frequently'
   d. Habitual continuity: *visada* 'always, all the time', *visuomet* 'always', *nuolat* 'permanently'

Moreover, adverbials concerning temporal localization are also important in highlighting the meanings of <iterativity> and <habituality>. In this chapter, adverbials related to <iterative> and <habitual> are defined in terms of (1) temporal definiteness, i.e., definite or indefinite time, (2) temporal localization, i.e., limited (short) or extended (long) period of time, and (3) temporal remoteness, i.e., regarding the past tense, close (recent), or remote (distant) past. The adverbials expressing (1) definite time, like *aštuntą valandą* 'at eight o'clock', (2) limited (short) period of time, like *tą dieną* 'that day', and (3) a close past, like *vakar* 'yesterday', are more naturally related to non-habitual <iterativity>. Meanwhile, the following types of adverbials related to temporal localization are regarded as more naturally related to <habituality>: adverbials expressing (1) indefinite time, like *tuo metu* 'that time', *anksčiau* 'previously', (2) extended period of time, like *vaikystėje* 'in childhood', and (3) remote past, like *senovėje* 'in the ancient past'.

4.2 Subclasses of <iterativity> and <habituality>

I propose to divide <iterativity> into two subclasses – <perfective iterativity> and <imperfective iterativity>. I define <perfective iterativity> as a reference to a repeated situation without regard to internal temporal structure, i.e., viewing a repeated situation in its entirety as a single whole. The meaning of <perfective iterativity> is typically expressed by adverbials referring to a definite number of times (e.g., *he pushed the button three times*). Meanwhile, the definition of <imperfective iterativity> points to the internal temporal structure of a repeated situation, viewing a successive situation as a linear continuity. The meaning of <imperfective iterativity> is typically expressed by

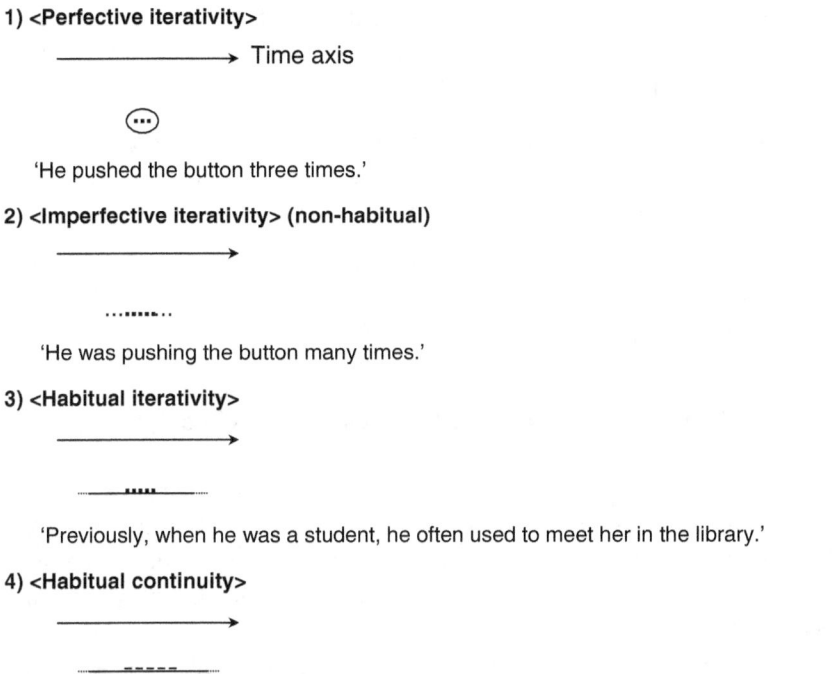

Fig. 1: Schematic illustrations of <iterative> and <habitual>.

adverbials meaning large indefinite number of times, non-habitual cyclicity, or frequency (e.g., *he was pushing the button many times/every minute*).

Furthermore, I propose to divide <habituality> into two subclasses as well – <habitual iterativity> and <habitual continuity>. <Habitual iterativity> is defined as a reference to a repeated situation characteristic of an extended period of time. The meaning of <habitual iterativity> is expressed by adverbials of habitual cyclicity or frequency (e.g., *he often used to meet her in the library*). Meanwhile, <habitual continuity> can be defined as a reference to a continuous situation characteristic of an extended period of time. The meaning of <habitual continuity> is typically expressed by adverbials of habitual continuity (e.g., *he always used to work in the library*).

The schematic illustrations of the aspectual meanings defined above are shown in the diagrams in Figure 1.

Note that the adverbials classified previously (Section 4.1) may be polysemous (see Padučeva 1996, Xrakovskij 1997); for example, adverbials such as *visada* 'always, all the time' or *nuolat* 'permanently' are related to <habitual continuity>

as well as to <iterativity>, depending on the meanings of the verbs and contexts (see 6). In example (6a), *visada* 'always' functions as adverbial of habitual continuity, while in example (6b), it refers to frequency.

(6) a. *Dur-ys*   *visada*   **bū-dav-o**   *atvir-os.*
door-NOM.PL   always   be-HAB-PST.3   open-NOM.PL
'lit. The doors always used to be open.'

b. *J-is*   *visada*   **atidary-dav-o**   *dur-is.*
he-NOM   always   open-HAB-PST.3   door-ACC.PL
'lit. He always used to open the doors.'

4.3 Taxis relations and complex semantic structure of <habituality>

Speaking of taxis relations, as defined above (Section 1), <perfectivity> is generally related to taxis through the concept of <sequence>, while <imperfectivity> is related through <simultaneity>. With regard to the taxis relations, the most important functional differences between <iterativity> and <habituality> are summarized as follows:

i. <perfective iterativity> typically refers to <sequence>, while (non-habitual) <imperfective iterativity> refers to <simultaneity>. For example, a situation such as **he pushed the button three times** and *the light went out* renders the meaning of <perfective iterativity> and the taxis of <sequence>, while a situation such as **he was pushing the button many times**, *but the light was still on* renders the meaning of <imperfective iterativity> and the taxis of <simultaneity>.

ii. The meaning of <habituality> is primarily related to taxis of <simultaneity> at the macro-level. For example, a habitual situation such as *when he lived alone,* **he always used to get up at eight o'clock** or **he used to read fairy tales for us**... *everyone loved him* renders the taxis of <simultaneity> at the macro-level.

iii. The meaning of both <habitual iterativity> and <habitual continuity> is typically related to taxis of <simultaneity> at the macro-level. Yet, at the micro-level, <habitual iterativity> renders <perfective> meaning, which is related to <sequence>, while <habitual continuity> renders <imperfective>, which is related to <simultaneity>. For example, a habitual situation such as *when he lived alone,* **he always used to get up at eight o'clock, come to our place and drink up two glasses of milk before breakfast** has the meaning of <habitual iterativity> in the macro-situation, as well as <perfective> meaning in each micro-situation. Here, taxis of the micro-situation is <sequence>, that is, the sub-events occur sequentially like *he got up→came to our place→drunk up two glasses of milk*. At the same time, this <habitual> macro-situation is complex <imperfective> as a whole and is related by <simultaneity> with the simple <imperfective> situation such as *he lived alone*. In contrast, a <habitual> situation such as **when he used to read (would be reading) fairy tales, usually we would be sitting and listening...** *everyone loved him* has the meaning of <habitual continuity> in the macro-situation and also entails the meaning of <imperfective> in each micro-situation. Here, taxis of the micro-situation is <simultaneity>, that is, the situations *he was reading fairy tales/ we were sitting/were listening* occur simultaneously. At the same time, this <habitual> macro-situation, as a whole, is related through complex <simultaneity> with the simple <imperfective> situation such as *everyone loved him*.

Consequently, in the cases where <habituality> involves <iterativity>, it may be possible to clearly render the aspectual opposition of each micro-situation, which together makes up a characteristic macro-situation. I believe that it is the most important functional difference between non-habitual <iterativity> and <habituality>. The complex semantic structure of <habituality> can be illustrated as in Figure 2.

1) Complex semantic structure of <habitual iterativity>

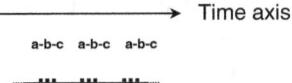 Time axis

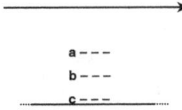

'When he lived alone, he always (a) used to get up at eight o'clock, (b) come to our place and (c) drink up two glasses of milk before breakfast.'

2) Complex semantic structure of <habitual continuity>

———————→

a - - -
b - - -
c - - -

'When he (a) used to read (would be reading) fairy tales, usually we (b) would be sitting and (c) listening. Everyone loved him.'

Fig. 2: Schematic illustrations of the complex semantic structure of <habituality>.

5 Data: The questionnaire

As remarked above, in Lithuanian, the meaning of <habituality> is expressed not only by past habitual forms, but also by simple past (non-habitual) forms. In what case and in what degree of appropriateness, although, are simple past forms or past habitual forms used in the expressions of <iterative> and <habitual>? In addition, how are telic/atelic meanings of verbs related to this problem? It should be said that previous studies on Lithuanian do not sufficiently discuss these issues. Therefore, I have made an attempt to analyze the distribution of simple past forms and past habitual forms based on the results of a questionnaire research that I conducted in Lithuania from 2008 to 2009.

The basic details concerning the questionnaire are as follows:
a. Informants (respondents): 282 Lithuanians (53 informants aged 10 to 20 years; 35 informants aged 20 to 30 years; 31 informants aged 30 to 40 years; 48 informants aged 40 to 50 years; 34 informants aged 50 to 60 years; 38 informants aged 60 to 70 years; 32 informants aged 70 to 80 years; 11 informants aged 80 to 90 years; 127 male informants; 155 female informants).
b. Personal details of informants requested: name, year of birth, age, place of birth, main place of residence, present place of residence, main place of residence of parents, present occupation, and, foreign language proficiency.
c. Structure of the questionnaire: questions on the appropriate (natural) usages of (i) past habitual forms and non-habitual simple past forms, (ii) analytic perfect forms and simple tense forms, (iii) present forms and future forms from the perspective of combination with telic/atelic verbs, and (iv) other questions.
d. Directions for completing the questionnaire: Informants were asked to evaluate some sentences by entering symbols representing the degree of appropriateness, using the symbol (++) to mean "very natural", (+) to mean "natural", (?) to mean "unnatural", (??) to mean "very unnatural", and (*) to mean "grammatically incorrect". The criterion for assessment was the question "Is the expression usually used in everyday life?".

The questionnaire was distributed to informants whose parents are native Lithuanian speakers. Those mostly from Vilnius (capital of Lithuania), Kaunas (located 103 km west of Vilnius), and Panevėžys (145 km north of Vilnius) participated in this research. All of these cities are located in the Highland Lithuanian region where Standard Lithuanian is spoken. Significant differences between dialects have not been identified as far as the results of this research are concerned.

In addition, Friedman's test is adopted in order to detect significant differences of acceptance levels. In this chapter, the term "statistical significance" is used in the sense of p-value and a fixed number p = 0.05 (5%) is regarded as a significance level. Thus, the differences of acceptance levels are referred to as statistically "significant" at the p < 0.05 level. According to Friedman's test, all tables in Sections 6 to 8, which present the results of questionnaire, are statistically significant (p < 0.001). Also, in this chapter, Scheffé's method is used for single-step multiple comparison procedure, which applies to the set of estimates of all possible contrasts among the factor level means. The results of tests by Scheffé's method are appended to the bottom of the tables.

6 Possibility of co-occurrence with adverbials concerning <iterativity> and <habituality> of two past tenses in Lithuanian

In this section, I will take a look at the co-occurrence of the two past tenses with adverbials concerning <iterativity> and <habituality>. Geniušienė (1997: 231) has already analyzed this subject as follows (words in parentheses [ ] here and below belong to the author of this chapter): "The past frequentative typically combines with adverbials of indefinite repetition [*dažnai* 'often' type]. Count adverbials are possible if only an adverbial of cyclicity [*du kartus per savaitę* 'two times a week' type] is present, [in such case,] where the difference between the imperfective and perfective is neutralised".

On this point, based on the results of questionnaire, I suggest that the possibility of co-occurrence with adverbials of definite number of times (or "definite counts") of the past habitual tense is in fact considerably low, yet it becomes higher with adverbials of indefinite number of times, especially if the number is large like *daug kartų* 'many times'. Meanwhile, the past habitual tense more naturally collocates with adverbials of cyclicity or frequency (see 7a and Tab. 4).

(7) a. *Aš*   *{du kartus / keletą kartų / daug kartų / kasdien / dažnai}*
I.NOM   two times   several times   many times   every day   often
sutik-dav-au   *j-ą*   *bibliotek-oje.*
meet-HAB-PST.1SG   she-ACC   library-LOC.SG
'I {two times/several times/many times/every day/often} used to meet her in the library.'

In contrast, the simple past tense of telic verbs naturally collocates with adverbials of definite number of times, less naturally with adverbials of large indefinite number of times like *daug kartų* 'many times' and does not at all collocate with adverbials of cyclicity or frequency (see 7b and Tab. 5).

(7) b. Aš   {du kartus / keletą kartų / daug kartų / kasdien / dažnai}
       I.NOM two times several times many times every day often
       sutik-au   j-ą   bibliotek-oje.
       meet-PST.1SG   she-ACC   library-LOC.SG
       'I {two times/several times/many times/every day/often} met (have met) her in the library.'

In my view, the possibility of co-occurrence with adverbials concerning temporal localization is also important in understanding the distinction between the two Lithuanian past tenses. According to the results of my questionnaire, the past habitual tense naturally collocates with adverbials expressing an indefinite time or a relatively remote (distant) past within an extended (long) period of time, like *vaikystėje* 'in childhood', *anksčiau* 'previously', or *senovėje* 'in the ancient past'. Meanwhile, adverbials expressing a definite time or a close (recent) past within a limited (short) period of time, like *vakar*

Tab. 4: The acceptance level of example (7a)

(7a)	++	+	?	??	*	Total (100%)	++	+	?	??	*
1. *du kartus* 'two times'	6	5	45	43	180	279	2%	2%	16%	15%	65%
2. *keletą kartų* 'several times'	7	48	81	46	97	279	3%	17%	29%	16%	35%
3. *daug kartų* 'many times'	65	107	66	14	27	279	23%	38%	24%	5%	10%
4. *kasdien* 'every day'	178	73	16	4	8	279	64%	26%	6%	1%	3%
5. *dažnai* 'often'	208	62	5	2	2	279	75%	22%	2%	1%	1%

Statistical significance: The differences of 1:2 ($\chi^2 = 20.500$), 2:3 ($\chi^2 = 92.327$), and 3:4 ($\chi^2 = 38.645$) are significant ($p < 0.001$), while the difference of 4:5 ($\chi^2 = 5.563$, $p = 0.2343$) is not significant.

Tab. 5: The acceptance level of example (7b)

(7b)	++	+	?	??	*	Total (100%)	++	+	?	??	*
1. *du kartus* 'two times'	179	95	4	1	0	279	64%	34%	1%	0%	0%
2. *keletą kartų* 'several times'	179	92	5	2	0	278	64%	33%	2%	1%	0%
3. *daug kartų* 'many times'	101	121	41	2	13	278	36%	44%	15%	1%	5%
4. *kasdien* 'every day'	1	16	38	35	188	278	0%	6%	14%	13%	68%
5. *dažnai* 'often'	5	12	65	47	149	278	2%	4%	23%	17%	54%

Statistical significance: The differences of 2:3 ($\chi^2 = 24.90163$) and 3:4 ($\chi^2 = 270.35515$) are significant ($p < 0.001$), while the differences of 1:2 ($\chi^2 = 0.03662$, $p = 0.9998$) and 4:5 ($\chi^2 = 2.52741$, $p = 0.6397$) are not significant.

Tab. 6: The acceptance level of example (8a)

(8a)	++	+	?	??	*	Total (100%)	++	+	?	??	*
1. *vakar* 'yesterday'	14	18	47	38	160	277	5%	6%	17%	14%	58%
2. *šią savaitę* 'this week'	25	70	77	35	70	277	9%	25%	28%	13%	25%
3. *šį mėnesį* 'this month'	62	118	62	15	20	277	22%	43%	22%	5%	7%
4. *vaikystėje* 'in childhood'	168	82	18	4	5	277	61%	30%	6%	1%	2%
5. *anksčiau* 'previously'	205	63	7	1	1	277	74%	23%	3%	0%	0%

Statistical significance: The differences of 1:2 ($\chi^2 = 36.041$), 2:3 ($\chi^2 = 52.249$), and 3:4 ($\chi^2 = 40.531$) are significant (p < 0.001), while the difference of 4:5 ($\chi^2 = 7.083$, p = 0.1315) is not significant.

'yesterday' or *tą dieną* 'that day', are seldom found with the past habitual tense (see 8a and Tab. 6).

(8) a. *{Vakar / šią savaitę / šį mėnesį / vaikystėje / anksčiau} aš*
 yesterday this week this month in childhood previously I.NOM
 sutik-dav-au *j-ą biblitek-oje.*
 meet-HAB-PST.1SG she-ACC library-LOC.SG
 '{Yesterday/this week/this month/in childhood/previously} I used to meet her in the library.'

In contrast, the simple past tense naturally collocates with adverbials expressing a definite time or a close past within a limited period of time, and if the verb is telic, it does not typically collocate with adverbials pointing to an indefinite time or a relatively remote past within an extended period of time (see 8b and Tab. 7).

(8) b. *{Vakar / šią savaitę / šį mėnesį / vaikystėje / anksčiau}*
 yesterday this week this month in childhood previously
 aš ***sutik-au*** *j-ą biblitek-oje.*
 I.NOM meet-PST.1SG she-ACC library-LOC.SG
 '{Yesterday/this week/this month/in childhood/previously} I used to meet her in the library.'

Meanwhile, it seems that the problem of the correlation between aspectual properties of verbs and the two past tenses is more complex than previously interpreted. Geniušienė (1997: 229–230) has given the following explanation concerning their co-occurrence with adverbials:

1. Unless the simple past tense form refers to an actual situation, imperfective verbs (e.g., *keltis* 'get up, rise'), except state verbs, combine with both types of adverbials (both *dažnai* 'often' type and *du kartus* 'two times' type).

Tab. 7: The acceptance level of example (8b)

(8b)	++	+	?	??	*	Total (100%)	++	+	?	??	*
1. *vakar* 'yesterday'	191	80	3	1	2	277	69%	29%	1%	0%	1%
2. *šią savaitę* 'this week'	177	95	4	0	1	277	64%	34%	1%	0%	0%
3. *šį mėnesį* 'this month'	119	140	15	0	3	277	43%	51%	5%	0%	1%
4. *vaikystėje* 'in childhood'	20	48	53	29	127	277	7%	17%	19%	10%	46%
5. *anksčiau* 'previously'	25	55	65	35	97	277	9%	20%	23%	13%	35%

Statistical significance: The difference of 2:3 ($\chi^2 = 10.5694$, p = 0.03185) and 3:4 ($\chi^2 = 258.6204$, p<0.001) is significant. Yet, the differences of 1:2 ($\chi^2 = 0.7263$, p = 0.9480) and 4:5 ($\chi^2 = 4.3397$, p = 0.3620) are not significant.

2. The simple past tense form of perfective verbs (e.g., *at-si-kelti* 'have gotten up, risen') typically combines with count adverbials (*du kartus* 'two times' type), to express iterativity.
3. In texts, the past frequentative of perfective verbs particularly often occurs with adverbials of indefinite repetition (*dažnai* 'often' type), to emphasize iterativity.

With the above in mind, I will try to give several examples of verbs that have been traditionally mentioned as typical examples of the so-called aspectual pair – *keltis* as "imperfective" and *at-si-kelti* as "perfective" – and reconsider the issue.

As shown by the results of my questionnaire, in the case of adverbials of definite number of times *du kartus* 'two times', and the adverbials of definite time or close past within a limited period of time *šią savaitę* 'this week', the simple past forms of both *keltis* and *at-si-kelti* 'get up' are almost equally accepted by the majority of the informants as "(very) natural". In contrast, the past habitual forms of these verbs are almost equally regarded as "(very) unnatural" or "grammatically incorrect" (see 9a and Tab. 8).

(9) a. *Šią savaitę j-is du kartus {kėl-ė-si/at-si-kėl-ė*
    this week he-NOM two times get.up-PST.3-REFL/PRF-REFL-get up-PST.3
    /kel-dav-o-si/at-si-kel-dav-o} anksti.
    /get.up-HAB-PST.3-REFL/PRF-REFL-get.up-HAB-PST.3 early
    'This week, he got up early two times.'

In the case of the adverbials of large indefinite numbers of times *daug kartų* 'many times' with the adverbials of temporal localization *šį mėnesį* 'this month' (the latter denotes a more extended (longer) time than *šią savaitę* 'this week'), the simple past form of *keltis* is the most acceptable. In this case, the acceptance level of the past habitual tense forms of both *keltis* and *at-si-kelti* is close to the same as the simple past form of *at-si-kelti* (see 9b and Tab. 9).

Tab. 8: The acceptance level of example (9a)

(9a)	++	+	?	??	*	Total (100%)	++	+	?	??	*
1. *kėl-ė-si* (get.up-PST.3-REFL)	161	107	11	3	0	282	57%	38%	4%	1%	0%
2. *at-si-kėl-ė* (PRF-REFL-get.up-PST.3)	152	116	8	3	3	282	54%	41%	3%	1%	1%
3. *kel-dav-o-si* (get.up-HAB-PST.3-REFL)	9	29	99	45	100	282	3%	10%	35%	16%	35%
4. *at-si-kel-dav-o* (PRF-REFL-get.up-HAB-PST.3)	8	23	79	45	127	282	3%	8%	28%	16%	45%

Statistical significance: The differences of 1:3 ($\chi^2 = 414.05261$), 1:4 ($\chi^2 = 474.25630$), 2:3 ($\chi^2 = 400.32048$), and 2:4 ($\chi^2 = 459.55157$) are significant ($p < 0.001$), while the differences of 1:2 ($\chi^2 = 0.11579$, $p = 1.000$) and 3:4 ($\chi^2 = 2.04245$, $p = 1.000$) are not significant.

Tab. 9: The acceptance level of example (9b)

(9b)	++	+	?	??	*	Total (100%)	++	+	?	??	*
1. *kėl-ė-si* (get.up-PST.3-REFL)	158	94	24	3	2	281	56%	33%	9%	1%	1%
2. *at-si-kėl-ė* (PRF-REFL-get.up-PAST.3)	58	132	68	5	18	281	21%	47%	24%	2%	6%
3. *kel-dav-o-si* (get.up-HAB-PST.3-REFL)	98	111	42	15	14	280	35%	40%	15%	5%	5%
4. *at-si-kel-dav-o* (PRF-REFL-get.up-HAB-PST.3)	69	103	58	17	33	280	25%	37%	21%	6%	12%

Statistical significance: The differences of 1:2 ($\chi^2 = 66.85118$, $p < 0.001$), 1:3 ($\chi^2 = 26.45017$, $p = 0.03355$), 1:4 ($\chi^2 = 77.58423$, $p < 0.001$) are significant, while the differences of 2:3 ($\chi^2 = 9.20081$, $p = 0.8668$), 2:4 ($\chi^2 = 0.39934$, $p = 1.000$), and 3:4 ($\chi^2 = 13.43383$, $p = 0.5688$) are not significant.

(9) b. Šį mėnesį   j-is   daug kartų
       this month   he-NOM   many times
       {kėl-ė-si/at-si-kėl-ė
       get.up-PST.3-REFL/PRF-REFL-get.up-PST.3
       /kel-dav-o-si/at-si-kel-dav-o}   anksti.
       /get.up-HAB-PST.3-REFL/PRF-REFL-get up-HAB-PST.3   early
       'This month, he got (was getting) up early many times.'

In the case of the adverbials of frequency *dažnai* 'often' and *šį mėnesį* 'this month', the acceptance level of the simple past and the past habitual is reversed.

Tab. 10: The acceptance level of example (9c)

(9c)	++	+	?	??	*	Total (100%)	++	+	?	??	*
1. kėl-ė-si (get.up-PST.3-REFL)	103	128	40	4	6	281	37%	46%	14%	1%	2%
2. at-si-kėl-ė (PRF-REFL-get.up-PST.3)	8	44	112	43	74	281	3%	16%	40%	15%	26%
3. kel-dav-o-si (get.up-HAB-PST.3-REFL)	182	82	9	3	5	281	65%	29%	3%	1%	2%
4. at-si-kel-dav-o (PRF-REFL-get.up-HAB-PST.3)	110	122	29	9	11	281	39%	43%	10%	3%	4%

Statistical significance: The differences of 1:2 ($\chi^2 = 214.08689$, $p < 0.001$), 1:3 ($\chi^2 = 28.90462$, $p = 0.01655$), 2:3 ($\chi^2 = 400.32048$, $p < 0.001$), 2:4 ($\chi^2 = 218.51936$, $p < 0.001$), 3:4 ($\chi^2 = 27.30700$, $p = 0.02633$) are significant, while the difference of 1:4 ($\chi^2 = 0.02271$, $p = 1.000$) is not significant.

In this case, the acceptance level of the simple past form of *at-si-kelti* is the lowest and the past habitual tense form of *keltis* is the most acceptable (see 9c and Tab. 10).

(9) c. Šį mėnesį   jis   dažnai   {kėl-ė-si/at-si-kėl-ė
       this month he-NOM   often   get.up-PST.3-REFL/PRF-REFL-get.up-PST.3
       /kel-dav-o-si/at-si-kel-dav-o}   anksti.
       /get.up-HAB-PST.3-REFL/PRF-REFL-get up-HAB-PST.3   early
       'This month, he often got (was getting) up early.'

Moreover, in the case of the adverbials of habitual continuity *visada* 'always' and the adverbials of relatively remote past within an extended period of time *kai jis gyveno vienas* 'when he lived alone', the past habitual form is more acceptable than the simple past tense of *keltis*. The past habitual tense form of *keltis* is the most acceptable, while the simple past tense form of *at-si-kelti* does not at all collocate with these types of adverbials (see 9d and Tab. 11).

(9) d. Kai   j-is   gyven-o   vien-as,   visada
       when   he-NOM   live-PST.3   one-NOM.SG   always
       {kėl-ė-si/at-si-kėl-ė
       get.up-PST.3-REFL/PRF-REFL-get.up-PST.3
       /kel-dav-o-si/at-si-kel-dav-o}   anksti.
       get.up-HAB-PST.3-REFL/PRF-REFL-get.up-HAB-PST.3   early
       'When he lived alone, he always used to get up early.'

The data examined in this section show that the explanations of Geniušienė (1997) can be expanded by the following:
1. The simple past forms of both unprefixed telic verbs like *keltis* 'get up' (traditionally called "imperfective") and of their prefixed counterparts like

Tab. 11: The acceptance level of example (9d)

(9d)	++	+	?	??	*	Total (100%)	++	+	?	??	*
1. *kėl-ė-si* (get.up-PST.3-REFL)	86	145	34	6	10	281	31%	52%	12%	2%	4%
2. *at-si-kėl-ė* (PRF-REFL-get.up-PST.3)	0	14	94	42	131	281	0%	5%	33%	15%	47%
3. *kel-dav-o-si* (get.up-HAB-PST.3-REFL)	209	67	4	0	1	281	74%	24%	1%	0%	0%
4. *at-si-kel-dav-o* (PRF-REFL-get.up-HAB-PST.3)	125	126	20	4	6	281	44%	45%	7%	1%	2%

Statistical significance: The differences of 1:2 ($\chi^2 = 299.13619$, p < 0.001), 1:3 ($\chi^2 = 70.06859$, p < 0.001), 2:3 ($\chi^2 = 658.75651$, p < 0.001), 2:4 ($\chi^2 = 412.66898$, p < 0.001), and 3:4 ($\chi^2 = 28.64387$, p = 0.01787) are significant, while the difference of 1:4 ($\chi^2 = 9.11256$, p = 0.8716) is not significant.

at-si-kelti ("perfective") most naturally collocate with the non-habitual iterative adverbials, i.e., the adverbials of definite number of times and the adverbials of definite close past within a limited period of time.

2. The simple past forms of verbs like *keltis* more naturally collocate with adverbials of large indefinite number of times than other forms, although the simple past forms of verbs like *at-si-kelti* and the past habitual forms of both *keltis* and *at-si-kelti* naturally collocate with such adverbials to a certain degree.
3. The past habitual forms of both verbs like *keltis* and *at-si-kelti* more naturally collocate with the adverbials of frequency than the simple past forms of verbs like *keltis*, whereas the simple past forms of verbs like *at-si-kelti* do not naturally collocate with such adverbials.
4. The past habitual forms of verbs like *keltis* and *at-si-kelti* quite naturally collocate with the habitual adverbials, i.e., the adverbials of habitual continuity and the adverbials of relatively remote past within an extended period of time.
5. In general, verbs like *keltis* more naturally collocate with adverbials denoting <iterativity> and <habituality> than verbs like *at-si-kelti*.

The results of the questionnaire demonstrate that the Lithuanian past tense with suffix *-dav-* is a grammatical habitual form that denotes <habituality> in the past without any lexical support, for example, adverbials. Along with this, it has become clear that the traditional interpretations of the correlation between aspectual properties of verbs and the two past tenses in Lithuanian need to be reconsidered (Section 7 will discuss this issue in more detail).

7 Expressions of ‹iterativity› and ‹habituality› in past tenses: A contrastive analysis with Russian

Based on the premises stated above, in this section, I will discuss the issue of the correlation between aspectual properties of verbs and the two past tenses in Lithuanian with respect to telicity of verbs. Referring to the differences between Lithuanian and Russian, I will consider the expression of ‹iterativity› and ‹habituality› in past tenses in Lithuanian, using the results of my questionnaire.

Russian fundamentally differs from Lithuanian in that it lacks any special habitual tense form. Since in Russian the aspectual opposition of ‹perfective/imperfective› is realized by means of pairs of perfective/imperfective verbs, only ‹perfective iterativity› is expressed by perfective verbs, while all other meanings, that is, the continuum of meanings ‹imperfective iterativity› – ‹habitual iterativity› – ‹habitual continuity› is expressed by the same past forms of imperfective verbs. Unlike in Russian, in Lithuanian, this continuum of three meanings is expressed by two past tense forms, that is, by the simple past forms and by the past habitual forms, in combination with telic/atelic (bounded/non-bounded) verbs.

7.1 Expressions of ‹iterativity›

In Russian, the meaning of ‹perfective iterativity› is expressed by perfective verbs with co-occurring adverbials of definite number of times. In addition, the verb form denoting ‹perfective iterativity› can naturally collocate with adverbials of punctual time, such as *v vosem' časov* 'at eight o'clock'. In Lithuanian, the meaning of ‹perfective iterativity› is not expressed by the past habitual forms, but solely by the simple past forms (see 10).

(10) Russ.
    On   *tri raza*   **na-davi-l**   *knopk-u*   *v vosem'*
    he.NOM   three times   PRF-push-PST(M.SG)   button-ACC.SG   in eight
    čas-ov.
    hour-GEN.PL

    Lith.
    J-is   *tris kartus*   **pa-spaud-ė**   *mygtuk-ą*   *aštunt-ą*
    he-NOM   three times   PRF-push-PST.3   button-ACC.SG   eighth-ACC.SG
    valand-ą.
    hour-ACC.SG
    'He pushed the button three times at eight o'clock.'

It is noteworthy that in Lithuanian the simple past forms of telic verbs typically render <perfective iterativity>; however, atelic verbs also can have this meaning, although they less naturally collocate with adverbials of definite number of times (see 11 and Tab. 12–13). Simple past tense forms of atelic verbs (with direct objects), like *klausyti (įrašą)* 'listen (to the record)' in example (11a) and *kartoti (tą žodį)* 'repeat (that word)' in example (11b), are regarded as "(very) natural" by most informants, although the acceptance level of prefixed counterparts of these verbs, *per-klausyti* 'listen, listen through to the end' in example (11a) and *pa-kartoti* 'repeat' in example (11b), are higher.

(11) a. J-is   du kartus   {klaus-ė/per-klaus-ė
       he-NOM   two times   listen-PST.3/PRF-listen-PST.3
       /klausy-dav-o/per-klausy-dav-o}
       /listen-HAB-PST.3/PRF-listen-HAB-PST.3   įraš-ą,
                                                 record-ACC.SG
       bet   ne   visk-ą   suprat-o.
       but   not   all-ACC   understand-PST.3
       'He listened to the record two times, but did not understand all.'

    b. J-is   du kartus   {kartoj-o/pa-kartoj-o
       he-NOM   two times   repeat-PST.3/PRF-repeat-PST.3
       /karto-dav-o/pa-karto-dav-o}   t-ą   žod-į,
       /repeat-HAB-PST.3/PRF-repeat-HAB-PST.3   that-ACC.SG word-ACC.SG
       bet   j-i   ne-suprat-o.
       but   she-NOM   NEG-understand-PST.3
       'He repeated that word two times, but she did not understand.'

The same goes for the case in which the suffix *-inė-* derives iterative verbs from the telic verbs. The simple past forms of unsuffixed telic verbs more

Tab. 12: The acceptance level of example (11a)

(11a)	++	+	?	??	*	Total (100%)	++	+	?	??	*
1. *klaus-ė* (listen-PST.3)	89	156	30	0	4	279	32%	56%	11%	0%	1%
2. *per-klaus-ė* (PRF-listen-PST.3)	201	65	6	2	5	279	72%	23%	2%	1%	2%
3. *klausy-dav-o* (listen-HAB-PST.3)	4	12	64	52	146	278	1%	4%	23%	19%	53%
4. *per-klausy-dav-o* (PRF-listen-HAB-PST.3)	6	12	48	51	161	278	2%	4%	17%	18%	58%

Statistical significance: The differences of 1:2 ($\chi^2 = 38.4562$), 1:3 ($\chi^2 = 298.9415$), 1:4 ($\chi^2 = 318.2018$), 2:3 ($\chi^2 = 551.8380$), and 2:4 ($\chi^2 = 577.8985$) are significant ($p < 0.001$), while the difference of 3:4 ($\chi^2 = 0.3006$, $p = 0.9999$) is not significant.

Tab. 13: The acceptance level of example (11b)

(11b)	++	+	?	??	*	Total (100%)	++	+	?	??	*
1. *kartoj-o* (repeat-PST.3)	45	164	54	8	9	280	16%	59%	19%	3%	3%
2. *pa-kartoj-o* (PRF-repeat-PST.3)	235	41	1	1	2	280	84%	15%	0%	0%	1%
3. *karto-dav-o* (repeat-HAB-PST.3)	3	25	84	54	114	280	1%	9%	30%	19%	41%
4. *pa-karto-dav-o* (PRF-repeat-HAB-PST.3)	12	22	76	55	114	279	4%	8%	27%	20%	41%

Statistical significance: The differences of 1:2 ($\chi^2 = 142.1862$), 1:3 ($\chi^2 = 177.4163$), 1:4 ($\chi^2 = 156.5702$), 2:3 ($\chi^2 = 637.2575$), and 2:4 ($\chi^2 = 597.1664$) are significant ($p < 0.001$), while the difference of 3:4 ($\chi^2 = 0.6512$, $p = 0.9987$) is not significant.

Tab. 14: The acceptance level of example (11c)

(11c)	++	+	?	??	*	Total (100%)	++	+	?	??	*
1. *perraš-inėj-o* (rewrite-ITER-PST.3)	68	127	61	11	14	281	24%	45%	22%	4%	5%
2. *perraš-ė* (rewrite-PST.3)	211	70	1	0	0	282	75%	25%	0%	0%	0%
3. *perraš-inė-dav-o* (rewrite-ITER-HAB-PST.3)	22	57	86	37	79	281	8%	20%	31%	13%	28%
4. *perrašy-dav-o* (rewrite-HAB-PST.3)	30	80	95	30	47	282	11%	28%	34%	11%	17%

Statistical significance: The differences of 1:2 ($\chi^2 = 137.9878$), 1:3 ($\chi^2 = 119.2280$), 1:4 ($\chi^2 = 52.9902$), 2:3 ($\chi^2 = 513.7466$), and 2:4 ($\chi^2 = 361.9985$) are significant ($p < 0.001$), while the difference of 3:4 ($\chi^2 = 13.2476$, $p = 0.06630$) is not significant.

naturally collocate with the adverbials of definite number of times than that of the derived iterative verbs with the suffix *-inė-* (see 11c and Tab. 14).

(11) c. *J-is   du kartus   {perraš-inėj-o/perraš-ė*
        he-NOM   two times   rewrite-ITER-PST.3/rewrite-PST.3
        /perraš-inė-dav-o/perrašy-dav-o}   laišk-ą.
        rewrite-ITER-HAB-PST.3/rewrite-HAB-PST.3   letter-ACC.SG
        'He rewrote the letter two times.'

If the telic verbs have no atelic counterpart, such as *pa-mesti* 'lose' (<*mesti* 'throw'), as a rule, only simple past forms of telic verbs are used to denote the meaning of <perfective iterativity> (see 11d and Tab. 15).

Tab. 15: The acceptance level of example (11d)

(11d)	++	+	?	??	*	Total (100%)	++	+	?	??	*
1. *pamet-ė* (lose-PST.3)	219	58	2	1	1	281	78%	21%	1%	0%	0%
2. *pames-dav-o* (lose-HAB-PST.3)	3	7	64	32	175	281	1%	2%	23%	11%	62%

Statistical significance: The difference of 1:2 ($\chi^2 = 393.265$) is significant ($p < 0.001$).

(11) d. Šį   mėnesį   j-is   du kartus   {*pamet-ė*/*pames-dav-o*}
       this   month   he-NOM   two times   lose-PST.3/lose-HAB-PST.3
       rakt-ą.
       key-ACC.SG
       'This month, he lost the key two times.'

In Russian, non-habitual <imperfective iterativity> is typically expressed only by imperfective verbs with co-occurring adverbials of large indefinite number of times. In addition, the verb form denoting <imperfective iterativity> can naturally collocate with adverbials of duration, such as *(načinaja) s vos'mi časov* 'from eight o'clock'. Meanwhile, in Lithuanian, this type of adverbials more naturally collocates with the simple past forms, although the past habitual forms also may collocate with them (see 12a).

(12) a. Russ.
       On   mnogo   raz   **davi-l**   knopk-u
       he.NOM   many   time(GEN.PL)   push-PST(M.SG)   button-ACC.SG
       s   vos'm-i   čas-ov.
       from   eight-GEN hour-GEN.PL

       Lith
       J-is   daug   kart-ų   {*spaud-ė*/*spaus-dav-o*}
       he-NOM   many   time-GEN.PL   push-PST.3/push-HAB-PST.3
       mygtuk-ą   nuo   aštuoni-ų   valand-ų.
       button-ACC.SG from   eight-GEN.PL   hour-GEN.PL
       'He was pushing the button many times from eight o'clock.'

In Lithuanian, the acceptance level of the simple past forms of atelic verbs, e.g., *klausyti* 'listen' in example (12b; Tab. 16), and *kartoti* 'repeat' in example (12c; Tab. 17), is almost equal to their prefixed counterparts, *per-klausyti* 'listen' and *pa-kartoti* 'repeat', respectively.

Tab. 16: The acceptance level of example (12b)

(12b)	++	+	?	??	*	Total (100%)	++	+	?	??	*
1. *klaus-ė* (listen-PST.3)	101	124	38	7	10	280	36%	44%	14%	3%	4%
2. *per-klaus-ė* (PRF-listen-PST.3)	131	105	30	5	9	280	47%	38%	11%	2%	3%
3. *klausy-dav-o* (listen-HAB-PST.3)	80	107	53	12	26	278	29%	38%	19%	4%	9%
4. *per-klausy-dav-o* (PRF-listen-HAB-PST.3)	75	105	52	21	26	279	27%	38%	19%	8%	9%

Statistical significance: The differences of 2:3 ($\chi^2 = 20.0778$, p = 0.005404) and 2:4 ($\chi^2 = 26.8361$, p < 0.001) are significant, while the differences of 1:2 ($\chi^2 = 3.6464$, p = 0.8195), 1:3 ($\chi^2 = 6.6114$, p = 0.4704), 1:4 ($\chi^2 = 10.6982$, p = 0.1523), and 3:4 ($\chi^2 = 0.4894$, p = 0.9995) are not significant.

(12) b. *J-is   daug kart-ų   {klaus-ė/per-klaus-ė*
 he-NOM   many time-GEN.PL   listen-PST.3/PRF-listen-PST.3
 /*klausy-dav-o/per-klausy-dav-o}   įraš-ą,   kad   gerai*
 /listen-HAB-PST.3/PRF-listen-HAB-PST.3   record-ACC.SG   that   well
 išmok-tų.
 learn-SBJV.3
 'He listened (was listening) to the record many times in order to learn well.'

 c. *J-is   daug kart-ų   {kartoj-o/pa-kartoj-o*
 he-NOM   many time-GEN.PL   repeat-PST.3/PRF-repeat-PST.3
 /*karto-dav-o/pa-karto-dav-o}   t-ą   žod-į,*
 /repeat-HAB-PST.3/PRF-repeat-HAB-PST.3   that-ACC.SG   word-ACC.SG
 kad   j-i   supras-tų.
 that   she-NOM   understand-SBJV.3
 'He repeated (was repeating) that word many times, so that she may understand.'

The same goes for the case of iterative verbs with the suffix *-inė-*. The acceptance level of the simple past forms of the iterative verbs like *perraš-inė-ti* 'rewrite (repeatedly)' in example (12d; Tab. 18), is almost equal to the unsuffixed telic verbs like *perrašyti* 'rewrite'.

(12) d. *J-is   daug kart-ų   {perraš-inėj-o/perraš-ė*
 he-NOM   many time-GEN.PL   rewrite-ITER-PST.3/rewrite-PST.3
 /*perraš-inė-dav-o/perrašy-dav-o}   laišk-ą.*
 rewrite-ITER-HAB-PST.3/rewrite-HAB-PST.3   letter-ACC.SG
 'He rewrote (was rewriting) the letter many times.'

Tab. 17: The acceptance level of example (12c)

(12c)	++	+	?	??	*	Total (100%)	++	+	?	??	*
1. *kartoj-o* (repeat-PST.3)	135	125	16	2	2	280	48%	45%	6%	1%	1%
2. *pa-kartoj-o* (PRF-repeat-PST.3)	155	98	18	2	7	280	55%	35%	6%	1%	3%
3. *karto-dav-o* (repeat-HAB-PST.3)	92	107	47	14	20	280	33%	38%	17%	5%	7%
4. *pa-karto-dav-o* (PRF-repeat-HAB-PST.3)	78	103	56	15	27	279	28%	37%	20%	5%	10%

Statistical significance: The differences of 1:3 ($\chi^2 = 20.3360$, p = 0.004888), 1:4 ($\chi^2 = 38.1980$), 2:3 ($\chi^2 = 26.4775$), and 2:4 ($\chi^2 = 46.4651$) are significant (p < 0.001), while the differences of 1:2 ($\chi^2 = 0.4046$, p = 0.9997) and 3:4 ($\chi^2 = 2.7919$, p = 0.9036) are not significant.

Tab. 18: The acceptance level of example (12d)

(12d)	++	+	?	??	*	Total (100%)	++	+	?	??	*
1. *perraš-inėj-o* (rewrite-ITER-PST.3)	130	117	22	7	4	280	46%	42%	8%	3%	1%
2. *perraš-ė* (rewrite-PST.3)	145	101	17	4	14	281	52%	36%	6%	1%	5%
3. *perraš-inė-dav-o* (rewrite-ITER-HAB-PST.3)	70	95	68	22	25	280	25%	34%	24%	8%	9%
4. *perrašy-dav-o* (rewrite-HAB-PST.3)	78	105	69	13	16	281	28%	37%	25%	5%	6%

Statistical significance: The differences of 1:3 ($\chi^2 = 56.5318$), 1:4 ($\chi^2 = 32.9910$), 2:3 ($\chi^2 = 66.6988$), and 2:4 ($\chi^2 = 40.8570$) are significant (p < 0.001), while the differences of 1:2 ($\chi^2 = 0.4201$, p = 0.9997) and 3:4 ($\chi^2 = 3.1506$, p = 0.8707) are not significant.

In the case of telic verbs that have no atelic counterpart, such as *pa-mesti* 'lose', simple past forms more naturally collocate with the adverbials of large indefinite number of times (see 12e and Tab. 19).

(12) e. Šį mėnesį j-is daug kart-ų {pamet-ė/pames-dav-o}
 this month he-NOM many time.GEN.PL lose-PST.3/lose-HAB-PST.3
 rakt-ą.
 key-ACC.SG
 'This month, he lost (was losing) the key many times.'

Meanwhile, in Russian only imperfective verbs can collocate with adverbials expressing a non-habitual cyclicity or frequency, whereas in Lithuanian the past habitual forms more naturally collocate with this type of adverbials than the simple past forms (see 13a).

Tab. 19: The acceptance level of example (12e)

(12e)	++	+	?	??	*	Total (100%)	++	+	?	??	*
1. *pamet-ė* (lose-PST.3)	139	106	21	4	11	281	49%	38%	7%	1%	4%
2. *pames-dav-o* (lose-HAB-PST.3)	74	54	68	29	56	281	26%	19%	24%	10%	20%

Statistical significance: The difference of 1:2 ($\chi^2 = 393.265$) is significant (p < 0.001).

(13) a. Russ.
    *Včera   noč'-ju   on   často   **davi-l***
    yesterday night-INS.SG he.NOM often push-PST(M.SG)
    knopk-u.
    button-ACC.SG

    Lith.
    *Vakar   nakt-į   j-is   dažnai **{spaud-ė/spaus-dav-o}***
    yesterday night-ACC.SG he-NOM often push-PST.3/push-HAB-PST.3
    mygtuk-ą.
    button-ACC.SG
    'Last night, he was often pushing the button.'

In Lithuanian, the simple past forms of prefixed telic verbs do not naturally collocate with the adverbials of non-habitual cyclicity or frequency. In the case of telic verbs without an atelic counterpart, as a rule, only past habitual forms are used with the adverbials of frequency, since the simple past forms of telic verbs generally render <perfective> meaning (see 13b and Tab. 20).

(13) b. *T-ą   dien-ą   j-ie   dažnai **{pamet-ė/pames-dav-o}***
    that-ACC.SG day-ACC.SG they-NOM often lose-PST.3/lose-HAB-PST.3
    rakt-ą.
    key-ACC.SG
    'That day, they were often losing the key.'

Tab. 20: The acceptance level of example (13b)

(13b)	++	+	?	??	*	Total (100%)	++	+	?	??	*
1. *pamet-ė* (lose-PST.3)	8	35	113	36	90	282	3%	12%	40%	13%	32%
2. *pames-dav-o* (lose-HAB-PST.3)	143	97	20	11	11	282	51%	34%	7%	4%	4%

Statistical significance: The difference of 1:2 ($\chi^2 = 393.265$) is significant (p < 0.001).

7.2 Expressions of <habituality>

In Russian, <habitual iterativity> is generally rendered by imperfective verbs with co-occurring adverbials expressing frequency or habitual continuity. In addition, verb forms denoting <habitual iterativity> can collocate with adverbials of punctual time, such as *v vosem' časov* 'at eight o'clock'. In Lithuanian, the meaning of <habitual iterativity> is more naturally expressed by the past habitual forms, although the simple past forms can also express this meaning (see 14a).

(14) a. Russ.
    Ran'še   *on*   *každ-yj*   *den'*   ***davi-l***
    previously   he.NOM   every-ACC.SG.M   day(ACC.SG)   push-PST(M.SG)
    knopk-u   *v vosem'*   *čas-ov.*
    button-ACC.SG   at eight   hour-GEN.PL

    Lith.
    Anksčiau   *j-is*   *kasdien*   **{*spaud-ė/spaus-dav-o*}**
    previously   he-NOM   every.day   push-PST.3/push-HAB-PST.3
    mygtuk-ą   *aštunt-ą*   *valand-ą.*
    button-ACC.SG   eighth-ACC.SG   hour-ACC.SG
    'Previously, he used to push the button at eight o'clock every day.'

In Lithuanian, <habitual iterativity> is most naturally expressed by the past habitual tense forms of telic verbs (see 14b and Tab. 21).

(14) b. *Kiekvien-ą*   *ryt-ą*   *j-is*   **{*gėr-ė/iš-gėr-ė***
    every-ACC.SG   morning-ACC.SG   he-NOM   drink-PST.3/PRF-drink-PST.3
    /*ger-dav-o/iš-ger-dav-o*}   *dvi*   *stiklin-es*
    drink-HAB-PST.3/PRF-drink-HAB-PST.3   two   glasses-ACC.PL
    pien-o.
    milk-GEN.SG
    'He used to drink two glasses of milk every morning.'

Tab. 21: The acceptance level of example (14b)

(14b)	++	+	?	??	*	Total (100%)	++	+	?	??	*
1. *gėr-ė* (drink-PST.3)	34	106	82	24	35	281	12%	38%	29%	9%	12%
2. *iš-gėr-ė* (PRF-drink-PST.3)	5	13	88	40	135	281	2%	5%	31%	14%	48%
3. *ger-dav-o* (drink-HAB-PST.3)	91	150	36	2	2	281	32%	53%	13%	1%	1%
4. *iš-ger-dav-o* (PRF-drink-HAB-PST.3)	236	38	4	1	1	280	84%	14%	1%	0%	0%

Statistical significance: The differences of 1:2 ($\chi^2 = 80.59$), 1:3 ($\chi^2 = 65.31$), 1:4 ($\chi^2 = 213.14$), 2:3 ($\chi^2 = 291.00$), 2:4 ($\chi^2 = 555.85$), and 3:4 ($\chi^2 = 42.48$) are significant ($p < 0.001$).

Tab. 22: The acceptance level of example (14c)

(14c)	++	+	?	??	*	Total (100%)	++	+	?	??	*
1. *perraš-inėj-o* (rewrite-ITER-PST.3)	81	132	49	12	8	282	29%	47%	17%	4%	3%
2. *perraš-ė* (rewrite-PST.3)	11	49	116	34	72	282	4%	17%	41%	12%	26%
3. *perraš-inė-dav-o* (rewrite-ITER-HAB-PST.3)	137	105	26	7	7	282	49%	37%	9%	2%	2%
4. *perrašy-dav-o* (rewrite-HAB-PST.3)	149	112	16	4	1	282	53%	40%	6%	1%	0%

Statistical significance: The differences of 1:2 ($\chi^2 = 164.893$), 1:3 ($\chi^2 = 14.884$), 1:4 ($\chi^2 = 31.125$), 2:3 ($\chi^2 = 278.859$), and 2:4 ($\chi^2 = 339.298$) are significant ($p < 0.001$), while the difference of 3:4 ($\chi^2 = 2.962$, $p = 0.3976$) is not significant.

The acceptance level of the past habitual forms of telic verbs is slightly higher than that of the derived iterative verbs with suffix *-inė-* (see 14c and Tab. 22).

(14) c. *J-is   dažnai   {perraš-inėj-o/perraš-ė*
       he-NOM   often   rewrite-ITER-PST.3/rewrite-PST.3
       /perraš-inė-dav-o/perrašy-dav-o}   laišk-us.
       rewrite-ITER-HAB-PST.3/rewrite-HAB-PST.3   letter-ACC.PL
       'He often used to rewrite the letters.'

Yet, when the telic verbs have no atelic counterpart, only past habitual forms can denote <habitual iterativity>. Regarding this, Geniušienė (1997) has noted: "The simple past tense form of dual aspect verbs like *duoti* 'give, have given', like most imperfective verbs, combine with both types of adverbials [both *dažnai* 'often' type and *du kartus* 'two times' type], though their past tense form usually has a perfective reading" (see also Genjušene 1989). As far as the results of my questionnaire are concerned, however, the simple past forms of this type of telic verbs (traditionally called "dual aspect") do not naturally collocate with the adverbials of frequency like *dažnai* 'often' (see 15 and Tab. 23–25).

(15) a. *J-is   dažnai   {baig-ė/baig-dav-o}   darb-ą*
       he-NOM   often   finish-PST.3/finish-HAB-PST.3   work-ACC.SG
       šešt-ą   valand-ą.
       sixth-ACC.SG hour-ACC.SG
       'He often used to finish work at six o'clock.'

   b. *J-is   dažnai   {gav-o/gau-dav-o}   laišk-us*
       he-NOM   often   receive-PST.3/receive-HAB-PST.3 letter-ACC.PL
       iš   nam-ų.
       from   home-GEN.PL
       'He often used to receive letters from home.'

Tab. 23: The acceptance level of example (15a)

(15a)	++	+	?	??	*	Total (100%)	++	+	?	??	*
1. *baig-ė* (finish-PST.3)	3	31	89	38	119	280	1%	11%	32%	14%	43%
2. *baig-dav-o* (finish-HAB-PST.3)	237	42	0	0	1	280	85%	15%	0%	0%	0%

Statistical significance: The difference of 1:2 ($\chi^2 = 541.70140$) is significant ($p < 0.001$).

Tab. 24: The acceptance level of example (15b)

(15b)	++	+	?	??	*	Total (100%)	++	+	?	??	*
1. *gav-o* (receive-PST.3)	3	48	87	36	107	281	1%	17%	31%	13%	38%
2. *gau-dav-o* (receive-HAB-PST.3)	239	40	0	0	2	281	85%	14%	0%	0%	1%

Statistical significance: The difference of 1:2 ($\chi^2 = 500.66879$) is significant ($p < 0.001$).

Tab. 25: The acceptance level of example (15c)

(15c)		++	+	?	??	*	Total (100%)	++	+	?	??	*
(1)	1. *mir-ė* (die-PST.3)	173	94	11	0	4	282	61%	33%	4%	0%	1%
	2. *nu-mir-ė* (PRF-die-PST.3)	111	122	40	3	6	282	39%	43%	14%	7%	2%
(2)	3. *mir-ė* (die-PST.3)	13	99	95	19	56	282	5%	35%	34%	1%	20%
	4. *mir-dav-o* (die-HAB-PST.3)	244	33	1	1	3	282	87%	12%	0%	0%	1%

Statistical significance: The differences of 1:2 ($\chi^2 = 15.44552$, $p = 0.03069$), 1:3 ($\chi^2 = 200.01159$, $p < 0.001$), and 3:4 ($\chi^2 = 339.53319$, $p < 0.001$) are significant.

(15) c. *J-is*   *{mir-ė/nu-mir-ė}*[(1)]   *nuo grip-o.*
       he-NOM   die-PST.3/PRF-die-PST.3   from influenza-GEN.SG
       Tuo   *met-u*   *žmon-ės*   *dažnai*
       that.INS.SG   time-INS.SG   people-NOM.PL   often
       {mir-ė/mir-dav-o}[(2)]   *nuo*   *grip-o.*
       die-PST.3/die-HAB-PST.3   from   influenza-GEN.SG
       'He died from influenza. At that time people often used to die from influenza.'

In Russian, the meaning of <habitual continuity> is expressed only by imperfective verbs, typically with co-occurring adverbials expressing habitual continuity like *vsegda* 'always'. In addition, <habitual continuity> can collocate with the adverbials of duration, such as *s vos'mi časov* 'from eight o'clock'. In Lithuanian, the meaning of <habitual continuity> is more naturally expressed by the past habitual forms, although it is also expressed by the simple past forms.

The important difference from <habitual iterativity> is that <habitual continuity> can only be expressed by atelic verbs in both languages (see 16a).

(16) a. Russ.
Ran'še   on   vsegda   rabota-l
previously   he.NOM   always   work-PST(M.SG)
s   vos'm-i   čas-ov.
from   eight-GEN hour-GEN.PL

Lith.
Anksčiau   j-is   visada   {dirb-o/dirb-dav-o}
previously   he-NOM   always   work-PST.3/work-HAB-PST.3
nuo   aštuoni-ų valand-ų
from   eight-GEN.PL hour-GEN.PL
'Previously, he always used to work from eight o'clock.'

As noted above, in Lithuanian, the meaning of <habitual continuity> is expressed by both the simple past forms and the past habitual forms of atelic verbs; however, the acceptance level of the simple past forms is obviously lower than that of the past habitual forms even in the case of verbs denoting state (see 16b,c and Tab. 26–27).

(16) b. *J-is   visada   {dirb-o/dirb-dav-o}   namie.*
         he-NOM   always   work-PST.3/work-HAB-PST.3   at home
         'He always used to work at home.'

     c. *Pas seneli-us   visada   {buv-o/bū-dav-o}   smagu.*
         at grandparent-ACC.PL   always   be-PST.3/be-HAB-PST.3   pleasant
         'It always used to be pleasant in grandparents' home.'

Tab. 26: The acceptance level of example (16b)

(16b)	++	+	?	??	*	Total (100%)	++	+	?	??	*
1. *dirb-o* (work-PST.3)	88	160	23	4	6	281	31%	57%	8%	1%	2%
2. *dirb-dav-o* (work-HAB-PST.3)	219	55	6	2	0	282	78%	20%	2%	1%	0%

Statistical significance: The differences of 1:2 ($\chi^2 = 118.667$) is significant ($p < 0.001$).

Tab. 27: The acceptance level of example (16c)

(16c)	++	+	?	??	*	Total (100%)	++	+	?	??	*
1. *buv-o* (be-PST.3)	54	173	35	10	10	282	19%	61%	12%	4%	4%
2. *bū-dav-o* (be-HAB-PST.3)	243	37	1	0	0	281	86%	13%	0%	0%	0%

Statistical significance: The differences of 1:2 ($\chi^2 = 287.380$) is significant ($p < 0.001$).

The acceptance level of the past habitual forms is higher than that of the simple past forms especially when the taxis relation between micro-situations making up a habitual macro-situation is expressed (see 17 and Tab. 28).

(17) Vaikyst-ėje,   kai   močiut-ė   {skait-ė/skaity-dav-o}⁽¹⁾
     childhood-LOC.SG when   grandma-NOM.SG   read-PST.3/read-HAB-PST.3
     pasak-as,   j-is   paprastai   {sėdėj-o/sėdė-dav-o}⁽²⁾
     fairy.tale-ACC.PL he-NOM usually   sit-PST.3/sit-HAB-PST.3
     prie   j-os   ir   {klaus-ė-si/klausy-dav-o-si}⁽³⁾.
     by   she-GEN and   listen-PST.3-REFL/listen-HAB-PST.3-REFL
     O   senel-is   visada   {dirb-o/dirb-dav-o}⁽⁴⁾
     and   grandpa-NOM.SG   always   work-PST.3/work-HAB-PST.3
     savo   kambar-yje.
     own   room-LOC.SG

'lit. In childhood, when grandma would read fairy tales, he usually would sit by her and listen. Grandpa always would work in his own room.'

As observed above, in Lithuanian, <habituality> is expressed more dominantly by the past habitual forms than by the simple past forms, especially when it is emphasized by the habitual adverbials. In the case of telic verbs, which are

Tab. 28: The acceptance level of example (17)

(17)		++	+	?	??	*	Total (100%)	++	+	?	??	*
(1)	1. skait-ė (read-PST.3)	24	158	67	14	19	282	9%	56%	24%	5%	7%
	2. skaity-dav-o (read-HAB-PST.3)	248	32	0	2	0	282	88%	11%	0%	1%	0%
(2)	3. sėdėj-o (sit-PST.3)	25	145	73	14	25	282	9%	51%	26%	5%	9%
	4. sėdė-dav-o (sit-HAB-PST.3)	250	30	0	2	0	282	89%	11%	0%	1%	0%
(3)	5. klaus-ė-si (listen-PST.3-REFL)	27	154	66	12	23	282	10%	55%	23%	4%	8%
	6. klausy-dav-o-si (listen-HAB-PST.3-REFL)	249	30	2	1	0	282	88%	11%	1%	0%	0%
(4)	7. dirb-o (work-PST.3)	29	177	47	9	20	282	10%	63%	17%	3%	7%
	8. dirb-dav-o (work-HAB-PST.3)	248	31	2	1	0	282	88%	11%	1%	0%	0%

Statistical significance: The differences of 1:2 ($\chi^2 = 388.3$), 3:4 ($\chi^2 = 418.0$), 5:6 ($\chi^2 = 378.2$), and 7:8 ($\chi^2 = 324.4$) are significant ($p < 0.001$).

generally <perfective> in the simple past forms, <habituality> can be expressed only by the past habitual forms. While even in the case of atelic verbs, which are generally <imperfective> in the simple past forms, <habituality> is expressed more dominantly by the past habitual forms.

8 Multiple functions of the past habitual tense in Lithuanian

8.1 Difference between Lithuanian and Russian

In view of the fact that aspectual systems of verbs ("verbal aspect") in Lithuanian and Russian were traditionally interpreted from the same perspective, I believe that it is worth comparing the expressions of <habituality> in Lithuanian and Russian parallel texts and focusing on their differences in order to define the proper functions of the past habitual tense in Lithuanian. Consequently, I will show that this past tense has multiple functions as habituals in discourse and should not be regarded as a "iterative" tense functioning as a "imperfectivizing" means in Lithuanian aspectual system.

In Russian, where only the past forms of imperfective verbs are used in order to express <habituality>, the reference to taxis relation in each micro-situation depends mainly on the lexical telic/atelic meaning of the verbs.[13] Whereas, in Lithuanian, <habituality> can be expressed by both past tenses; however, as regards telic verbs that have atelic counterpart or atelic verbs including stative verbs, there are also cases when the past habitual forms not combined with the habitual adverbials are even more dominantly used. The major difference in the functions is that the simple past tense generally expresses <habituality> only at the level of the macro-situation, whereas the past habitual tense also serves to express the aspectual opposition in the micro-situations that build the inner structure of a macro-situation. In this sense, the past habitual tense has multiple aspectual functions that comprise both the characteristic features of a habitual macro-situation and the individual features of micro-situations that constitute the macro-situation.

---

13 In Russian, the present forms of perfective/imperfective verbs are also sometimes used in order to more clearly reveal the aspectual <perfective/imperfective> opposition in each micro-situation that constitutes a habitual macro-situation. However, note that for perfective verbs, this is a highly marked case, and it requires irregular repetition and predominantly occurs with chains of events (not for single events). As lexical marker *byvalo* 'used to be' or *byvaet* 'happens' are often used in this case.

In comparing the following Russian and Lithuanian parallel texts, examples (18) and (19), which are constructed by the native consultants and the author of this chapter, in Russian, in both cases the past forms of imperfective verbs are used in order to express <habituality>, the taxis relations in each micro-situation are referred to by the lexical telic meaning (18) or atelic meaning (19) of verbs. In Lithuanian, however, both telic verbs (18) and atelic verbs (19) in the past habitual forms are used to reveal how taxis relation is built in each micro-situation that constitutes a habitual macro-situation. In these cases, the past habitual forms generally are not replaced by the simple past forms. This might be the reason why the past habitual forms most often appear repeatedly like a chain in texts.

(18) Russ.
Ran'še,   *kogda*   *on*   **ži-l**   *odin,*
previously   when   he.NOM   live-PST(M.SG)   one(NOM.SG.M)
vstava-l   *rano,*   **prixodi-l**   *k nam,*
get.up-PST(M.SG)   early   come-PST(M.SG)   to we.DAT
vypiva-l   *dva*   *stakan-a*   *molok-a*
drink.up-PST(M.SG)   two   glass-GEN.SG   milk-GEN.SG
pered   *zavtrak-om.*
before   breakfast-INS.SG

Lith.
Anksčiau,   *kai*   *j-is*   **gyven-o**   *vien-as,*
previously   when   he-NOM   live-PST.3   one-NOM.SG.M
at-si-kel-dav-o   *anksti,*   **atei-dav-o**   *pas*   *mus,*
PRF-REFL-get.up-HAB-PST.3   early   come-HAB-PST.3   to   we.ACC
iš-ger-dav-o   *dvi stiklin-es*   *pien-o*
PRF-drink-HAB-PST.3   two glass-ACC.PL   milk-GEN.SG
prieš   *pusryči-us.*
before   breakfast-ACC.PL
'Previously, when he lived alone, he used to get up early, come to our place and drink up two glasses of milk before breakfast.'

(19) Russ.
Ran'še,   *kogda*   *on*   *čita-l*   *skazk-i,*
previously   when   he.NOM   read-PST(M.SG)   fairy.tale-ACC.PL
my   **side-l-i**   *i*   **sluša-l-i.**
we.NOM   sit-PST-PL   and   listen-PST-PL
Vs-e   *ego*   **ljubi-l-i.**
all-NOM.PL   he.ACC   love-PST-PL

Lith.
Anksčiau, kai j-is **skaity-dav-o** *pasak-as,*
previously when he-NOM read-HAB-PST.3 fairy.tales-ACC.PL
mes **sėdė-dav-ome** *ir* **klausy-dav-ome.**
we.NOM sit-HAB-PST.1PL and listen-HAB-PST.1PL
Vis-i j-į **mylėj-o.**
all-NOM.PL.M he-ACC love-PST.3
'When he used to read (would be reading) fairy tales, usually we would be sitting and be listening. Everyone loved him.'

From the fact that there are many examples of this type of usage of past habitual forms even in texts translated from other languages that have no such special type of past tense, one can suppose that it is an important function of past habitual tense in Lithuanian. In contrast, in Russian the general past forms are usually used to express the same content (see 20; Russian and Lithuanian texts from A. Saint-Exupéry's *The Little Prince* [Le Petit Prince] translated from French).

(20) Russ. *Kogda ja* **vstrečal** *vzroslogo, kotoryj* **kazalsja** *mne razumnej i ponjatlivej drugix, ja* **pokazyval** *emu svoj risunok №1 – ja ego soxranil i vsegda nosil s soboju. Ja* **xotel** *znat', vpravdu li ètot čelovek čto-to ponimaet. No vse oni* **otvečali** *mne: «Èto šljapa». I ja uže ne* **govoril** *s nimi [...] Ja* **primenjalsja** *k ix ponjatijam. Ja* **govoril** *s nimi ob igre v bridž [...] I vzroslye* **byli** *očen' dovol'ny, čto poznakomilis's takim zdravomysljaščim čelovekom.*

Lith. *Kai* **sutik-dav-au** *suaugusį žmogų, kuris man* **atrody-dav-o** *bent kiek aiškesnio proto,* **ištir-dav-au** *jį savo piešiniu Nr.1, kurį buvau pasilikęs iš vaikystės.* **Norė-dav-au** *pasižiūrėti, ar tas žmogus tikrai ką supranta. Bet jis man visada* **atsaky-dav-o***: „Čia skrybėlė". Tada su juo* **nešnekė-dav-au** *[...]* **Prisitaiky-dav-au** *prie jo.* **Kalbė-dav-au** *su juo apie bridžą [...] Ir tas suaugęs žmogus* **bū-dav-o** *labai patenkintas, kad susipažino su tokiu protingu asmeniu.*

'Whenever I **met** one of them who **seemed** to me at all clear-sighted, I **tried** the experiment of showing him my Drawing Number One, which I have always kept. I **would try** to find out, so, if this was a person of true understanding. But, however it was, he, or she, **would** always **say**: "That is a hat". Then I **would never talk** to that person [...] I **would bring** myself down to his level. I **would talk** to him about bridge [...] And the grown-up **would be** greatly pleased to have met such a sensible man.'

All verb forms indicated by boldface in example (20) have been translated from the imperfect in French by the general past forms of imperfective verbs in Russian, while they are translated by the past habitual forms in Lithuanian. There are many examples of this type of difference between Russian and Lithuanian in translated texts.

8.2 Reference to internal aspectual complexity of <habituality>

In this subsection, I shall provide more details about how the past habitual forms and telicity/atelicity of verbs refer to internal aspectual complexity of <habituality> in Lithuanian. As has been noted before, the past habitual forms can express either <habitual iterativity> or <habitual continuity> at the level of macro-situation, depending on whether they are formed from telic or atelic verbs, respectively. At the same time, in the case of telic verbs, the past habitual forms can entail the meaning of <perfective> referring to <sequence>, while in the case of atelic verbs, they can entail <imperfective> referring to <simultaneity> in each repeated micro-situation that constitutes the macro-situation[14] (see 21 and 22) (in the examples below, the references in the parentheses [ ] provide the aspect of micro-situations).[15]

(21) *Kai j-is **per-skaity-dav-o** (*skaity-dav-o) pasak-as,*
when he-NOM PRF-read-HAB-PST.3 read-HAB-PST.3 fairy.tales-ACC.PL
*tuoj vis-i **nu-ei-dav-ome** gul-ti.*
immediately all-NOM.PL.M PRF-go-HAB-PST.1PL lie.down-INF
'When he **would finish reading** (HAB-PST (telic) [PFV] (*atelic [IPFV])) fairytales, we all **would go to bed** (HAB-PST (telic) [PFV]) immediately.'

(22) *Kai j-is **skaity-dav-o** (*per-skaity-dav-o) pasak-as,*
when he-NOM read-HAB-PST.3 PRF-read-HAB-PST.3 fairy.tales-ACC.PL
*mes vis-i **sėdė-dav-ome** ir **klausy-dav-ome**.*
we.NOM all–NOM.PL.M sit-HAB-PST.1PL and listen-HAB-PST.1PL
'While he **used to be reading** (HAB-PST (atelic) [IPFV] (*telic [PFV])) fairytales, we all **would be sitting** (HAB-PST (atelic) [IPFV]) and **listening** (HAB-PST (atelic) [IPFV]).'

---

[14] There are similar observations made by Savicki (2010) as to the use of simple and prefixed verbs in narrative text in Lithuanian.
[15] Examples (21) and (22) are taken from Dambriūnas (1960), only they are slightly modified, and the glosses and translations are given by the author of this chapter.

Example (21) illustrates the sequential relation of events in a micro-situation. In the subordinate clause 'when (he) would finish reading' in example (21), the past habitual form of the telic verb *per-skaity-dav-o* 'would finish reading' refers to <sequence> of micro-situations. When this verb is replaced by the past habitual form of the corresponding atelic verb *skaity-dav-o* 'would be reading', which refers to <simultaneity> of micro-situations, the sentence sounds like 'while he used to be reading fairy tales, we would all immediately go to bed' and the time relation of the events changes. Meanwhile, example (22) illustrates <simultaneity> of micro-situations. In the subordinate clause 'While (he) would read' in example (22), the past habitual form of the atelic verb *skaity-dav-o* 'would be reading' is used to express <simultaneity> of the micro-situations. When this form is replaced by the past habitual form of the telic verb *per-skaity-dav-o* 'would finish reading', the meaning of the sentence changes to 'when he would finish reading us fairytales, we would sit and listen', which distorts the time relation of the events[16] (see also 23 and 24).[17]

(23) *Mano vaikystės draugė Melanija **gyven-o** dviejų pedagogių šeimoje. [...] Motina ir teta [...] **norėj-o** padaryti iš Melanijos rašytoją. [...] Atėjusi dažnai **ras-dav-au** Melaniją apsiverkusią. **Atei-dav-au**, kai ji **bū-dav-o** viena, **atneš-dav-au** kortas, **prašy-dav-au**, kad man duotų saldumynų [...]. Tada man **buv-o** trylika metų.*

---

16 As the borderline between the telic/atelic verbs is rather unclear as already discussed in Section 3, there are ambiguous cases when the aspect and taxis of the micro-situation denoted by the same past habitual forms from telic verbs can be interpreted ambiguously, not only as <perfective> – <sequence>, but also as <imperfective> – <simultaneity>. However, this ambiguity is seldom found in texts and is usually resolved by context. See the following examples: Example (a) is the example of reference to <perfective> – <sequence> of micro-situation, while example (b) is the example of <imperfective> – <simultaneity>.
a. Kai   j-is   **grįž-dav-o**,   per-skaity-dav-o   laikrašt-į.
    when   he-NOM   come.back-HAB-PST.3   PRF-read-HAB-PST.3   newspaper-ACC.SG
    'After coming back (when he would come back) (HAB-PST (telic) [PFV]), he would finish reading the newspaper (HAB-PST (telic) [PFV]).'
b. Kai   j-is   **grįž-dav-o**,   skaity-dav-o   laikrašt-į.
    when   he-NOM   come.back-HAB-PST.3   read-HAB-PST.3   newspaper-ACC.SG
    'While coming back (when he would be coming back) (HAB-PST (telic) [IPFV]), he would be reading (HAB-PST (atelic) [IPFV]) the newspaper.'

17 Examples (23) and (28) are cited from B. Vilimaitė's novel *Užpustytas traukinys* [The Snowbound Train], and example (24) – from B. Radzevičius' novel *Link Debesijos* [To the Cloudland]. Examples are slightly modified and abridged by the author of this chapter.

'My childhood friend, Melanija, **lived** (PST (atelic)) in the family of two educators. Her mother and her aunt **wanted** (PST (atelic)) Melanija to become a writer. When I used to visit her, I **would** often **find** (HAB-PST (telic) [PFV]) Melanija in tears. When she **would be** (HAB-PST (atelic) [IPFV]) alone, I **would drop by** (HAB-PST (telic) [PFV]), **bring** cards (HAB-PST (telic) [PFV]), and **would beg** (HAB-PST (telic) [IPFV]) for some sweets. At that time I **was** (PST (atelic)) thirteen years old.'

In example (23), verbs *gyven-o* '(Melanija) lived', *norėj-o* '(mother and aunt) wanted', and *buv-o trylika metų* '(I) was thirteen years old', which denote non-habitual, simple durative situations, are used in the simple past forms, while the other verbs, which denote habitual situations, are used in the past habitual forms. Among these, telic verbs (phrases) in the past habitual forms *ras-dav-au* '(I) would find', *atei-dav-au* '(I) would drop by', and *atneš-dav-au* '(I) would bring cards' and *prašy-dav-au* '(I) would beg' clearly denote <perfective> meaning of the micro-situations, while atelic verb in the past habitual form *bū-dav-o* '(she) was alone' denotes <imperfective>.

(24) *Vyras [...] **nežinoj-o**, kad yra radiola. Tik ji **klausy-dav-o-si**. Kai **megz-dav-o** ar **siuvinė-dav-o**. **Sėdė-dav-o**, palenkusi galvą, [...] **niūniuo-dav-o** tą melodiją. Jeigu kas **pasibels-dav-o** į duris, **pašok-dav-o** kaip sugauta, skubiai **paslėp-dav-o** tą plokštelę ir **uždė-dav-o** kitą [...]*
'Her husband **didn't know** (PST (atelic)), that there was a radio-gramophone at home. She **used to be listening** (HAB-PST (atelic) [IPFV]) to it alone when she **would be knitting** (HAB-PST (atelic) [IPFV]) or **embroidering** (HAB-PST (atelic) [IPFV]). She **would be sitting** (HAB-PST (atelic) [IPFV]) with her head bent aside and **would be humming** a tune (HAB-PST (atelic) [IPFV]). If someone **would knock** (HAB-PST (telic) [PFV]) on the door, she **would jump up** (HAB-PST (telic) [PFV]), quickly **hide** (HAB-PST (telic) [PFV]) the record and **replace** (HAB-PST (telic) [PFV]) it with another one.'

In example (24), the fact that the micro-situations expressed by the past habitual forms represent both <perfective> (in the case of telic verbs) and <imperfective> (atelic verbs) clearly reveals differences in the taxis relations of unfolding events. In the first case, each event appearing in the micro-situation is in sequential relation ('(someone) knocked'→'(she) jumped up'→'hid away the record'→'replaced it with another one') with another, while in the second case, events relate through the relation of simultaneity ('(she) was listening'/'was knitting'/'was embroidering'/'was sitting'/'was humming a tune'). In such cases, the past habitual forms of telic verbs generally are not replaced by the simple past forms of atelic verbs – and vice versa.[18]

The results of my questionnaire clearly show that the past habitual forms are more dominantly used than the simple past tense forms when referring to internal aspectual complexity of <habituality> in correlation with telicity/atelicity of verbs (see 25 and 26). These examples in dialogue show that in a single interrogative sentence, presenting topic at the start of a conversation, i.e., typically functioning as conversation starter, the acceptance level of the past habitual forms is considerably lower than that of the simple past forms. In contrast, in a sentence providing a detailed description of a <habitual> situation, i.e., presenting reference to its internal complex aspectual structure, the acceptance level of the past habitual forms is obviously higher than that of the simple past forms. Taxis relations of <sequence> and <simultaneity> of micro-situations constructing the <habitual> macro-situation are referred to by the past habitual forms of telic verbs (25; Tab. 29) and atelic verbs (26; Tab. 30), respectively.

(25) A: – *Laima, ką tu {dar-ei/dary-dav-ai}*[(1)] *šį mėnesį, kai mūsų nebuvo namie?*
B: – *Aš nieko ypatingo {nedar-iau/nedary-dav-au}*[(2)].
Nuo ryto iki vakaro {žiūrėj-au/žiūrė-dav-au}[(3)] *televizorių...*
Kartais {skambin-o/pa-skambin-o/skambin-dav-o/pa-skambin-dav-o}[(4)] *draugės, {susitik-ome/susitik-dav-ome}*[(5)] *senamiestyje,*
kartu {pietav-ome/pa-pietav-ome/pietau-dav-ome/pa-pietau-dav-ome}[(6)].
'A: – Laima, what **were you doing**[(1)] this month, when we were not at home?
B: – I **was not doing**[(2)] anything special.
I **was watching**[(3)] television from morning to evening.
Sometimes friends **would call**[(4)], we **would meet**[(5)] in old town, **would dine**[(6)] together.'

---

18 The same usage of the past habitual forms of telic/atelic verbs can also be observed even when they render the meaning of non-habitual <imperfective iterativity>. This fact seems to cause misunderstanding about the past habitual tense in Lithuanian. However, this usage (i.e., as reference to non-habitual <imperfective iterativity>) of the past habitual forms is seldom observed in discourse or dialogue style in the first or second person, but is rather found in narrative texts, for example, in novels written in the third person.
Example: *Vagone* **buv-o** *daug žmonių. Traukinys* **susto-dav-o** *kiekvienoje stotelėje, ir jei* **atsidary-dav-o** *durys ir* **įlip-dav-o** *žmonės, tai* **bū-dav-o** *labai šalta. Kai jis* **išėj-o** *į tambūrą, traukinys staiga* **sustoj-o***, ir* **atsidar-ė** *durys.*
'There **were** (PAST (atelic)) many people in the passenger car. The train **would stop** (HAB-PST (telic)) at every station, and if doors **would open** (HAB-PST (telic) [PFV]) and people **would get on** (HAB-PST (telic) [PFV]), it was (HAB-PST (atelic) [IPFV]) very cold. When he **went out** (PAST (telic) [PFV]) to the platform, the train suddenly **stopped** (PAST (telic) [PFV]), and then the door **opened** (PAST (telic) [PFV]).'

Tab. 29: The acceptance level of example (25)

(25)		++	+	?	??	*	Total (100%)	++	+	?	??	*
(1)	1. *dar-ei* (do-PST.2SG)	190	82	5	1	4	282	67%	29%	2%	0%	1%
	2. *dary-dav-ai* (do-HAB-PST.2SG)	79	94	65	15	29	282	28%	33%	23%	5%	10%
(2)	3. *nedar-iau* (not.do-PST.1SG)	166	109	4	0	3	282	59%	39%	1%	0%	1%
	4. *nedary-dav-au* (not.do-HAB-PST.1SG)	99	99	53	15	16	282	35%	35%	19%	5%	6%
(3)	5. *žiūrėj-au* (watch-PST.1SG)	129	128	18	3	4	282	46%	45%	6%	1%	1%
	6. *žiūrė-dav-au* (watch-HAB-PST.1SG)	150	89	30	7	6	282	53%	32%	11%	2%	2%
(4)	7. *skambin-o* (call-PST.3)	11	66	88	38	79	282	4%	23%	31%	13%	28%
	8. *pa-skambin-o* (PRF-call-PST.3)	5	16	82	45	134	282	2%	6%	29%	16%	48%
	9. *skambin-dav-o* (call-HAB-PST.3)	127	129	17	6	3	282	45%	46%	6%	2%	1%
	10. *pa-skambin-dav-o* (PRF-call-HAB-PST.3)	205	70	4	1	2	282	73%	25%	1%	0%	1%
(5)	11. *susitik-ome* (meet-PST.1PL)	5	23	96	37	121	282	2%	8%	34%	13%	43%
	12. *susitik-dav-ome* (meet-HAB-PST.1PL)	229	49	3	1	0	282	81%	17%	1%	0%	0%
(6)	13. *pietav-ome* (dine-PST.1PL)	11	60	89	30	92	282	4%	21%	32%	11%	33%
	14. *pa-pietav-ome* (PRF-dine-PST.1PL)	9	32	86	42	113	282	3%	11%	30%	15%	40%
	15. *pietau-dav-ome* (dine-HAB-PST.1PL)	172	102	6	1	1	282	61%	36%	2%	0%	0%
	16. *pa-pietau-dav-ome* (PRF-dine-HAB-PST.1PL)	169	90	18	3	2	282	60%	32%	6%	1%	1%

Statistical significance: The differences of 1:2 ($\chi^2 = 99.01503$), 3:4 ($\chi^2 = 41.94407$), 7:9 ($\chi^2 = 233.14191$), 8:10 ($\chi^2 = 553.25808$), 11:12 ($\chi^2 = 587.18258$), 13:15 ($\chi^2 = 343.32731$), and 14:16 ($\chi^2 = 381.09770$) are significant ($p < 0.001$), while 5:6 ($\chi^2 = 0.21820$, $p = 1.000$) is not significant.

(26) A: – *Petrai, ką jūs šią vasarą {veik-ėte/veik-dav-ote}*[(1)] *Druskininkuose?*
B: – *Mes su seneliais {dirb-ome/dirb-dav-ome}*[(2)] *sode ir darže.*
A: – *Tikrai? Kasdien {dirb-ote/dirb-dav-ote}* [(3)] *per atostogas?*
B: – *Taip, bet kartais {atėj-o/atei-dav-o}*[(4)] *draugai,*
   mes kartu {maud-ėmė-s/maudy-dav-omė-s}[(5)],
   {žvejoj-ome/žvejo-dav-ome}[(6)]...
'A: – Petras, what **were** you **doing**[(1)] this summer in Druskininkai?
B: – We **were working**[(2)] with grandparents in the garden and the kitchen garden.
A: – Really? **Were** you **working**[(3)] every day during vacation?
B: – Yes, but sometimes friends **would come**[(4)], we **would bathe**[(5)] together, **would fish**[(6)]...'

Tab. 30: The acceptance level of example (26).

(26)		++	+	?	??	*	Total (100%)	++	+	?	??	*
(1)	1. *veik-ėte* (do-PST.2PL)	218	62	1	1	0	282	77%	22%	0%	0%	0%
	2. *veik-dav-ote* (do-HAB-PST.2PL)	39	83	91	18	51	282	14%	29%	32%	6%	18%
(2)	3. *dirb-ome* (work-PST.1PL)	165	99	13	1	4	282	59%	35%	5%	0%	1%
	4. *dirb-dav-ome* (work-HAB-PST.1PL)	121	91	47	3	20	282	43%	32%	17%	1%	7%
(3)	5. *dirb-ote* (work-PST.2PL)	102	137	30	2	11	282	36%	49%	11%	1%	4%
	6. *dirb-dav-ote* (work-HAB-PST.2PL)	165	87	23	3	4	282	59%	31%	8%	1%	1%
(4)	7. *atėj-o* (come-PST.3)	5	5	76	30	166	282	2%	2%	27%	11%	59%
	8. *atei-dav-o* (come-HAB-PST.3)	234	43	1	2	2	282	83%	15%	0%	1%	1%
(5)	9. *maud-ėmė-s* (bathe-PST.1PL-REFL)	30	113	71	15	53	282	11%	40%	25%	5%	19%
	10. *maudy-dav-omė-s* (bathe-HAB-PST.1PL-REFL)	235	44	1	1	1	282	83%	16%	0%	0%	0%
(6)	11. *žvejoj-ome* (fish-PST.1PL)	30	124	66	14	48	282	11%	44%	23%	5%	17%
	12. *žvejo-dav-ome* (fish-HAB-PST.1PL)	232	46	1	2	1	282	82%	16%	0%	1%	0%

Statistical significance: The differences of 3:4 ($\chi^2 = 20.14$, $p = 0.04348$), 1:2 ($\chi^2 = 304.3$), 7:8 ($\chi^2 = 700.8$), 9:10 ($\chi^2 = 325.3$), and 11:12 ($\chi^2 = 297.4$) are significant ($p < 0.001$), while 5:6 ($\chi^2 = 17.21$, $p = 0.1019$) is not significant.

8.3 Reference to <anteriority> as remote past

As I already cited in Section 1, Geniušienė (1997: 231) has used the term "remote past" to define the meaning of the past habitual form (cf. another term that is also used is "distant past"; see Sližienė 1995: 224). It should also be mentioned that the past habitual forms sometimes refer to <anteriority> and perform the function of expressing a remote past prior to the past time expressed by the simple past forms. This function is more often observed with the past habitual forms of atelic verbs (see 27 and 28).[19]

(27) *Mano atminimu viskas **pasikeit-ė**. Dabar pasaulis visai ne tas kaip anais laikais, kada aš mažas **buv-au**. O senovėje, kaip pasakoja mūsų tėvai, dar geriau **bū-dav-o**, dar linksmiau **gyven-dav-o**.*
'I remember that everything **changed** (PST (telic)). Now the world is not at all the same as in that time, when I **was** a child (PST (atelic)). But, in the past, as our parents tell us, it **used to be better** (HAB-PST (atelic)), and (people) **used to live** (HAB-PST (atelic)) more happily.'

(28) *Paskui ji **atsidūr-ė** Gedimino aikštėje, ten ji **mėg-dav-o** ramybėje lesinti balandžius, bet dabar aikštė **buv-o pagyvėjusi**, **šurmuliav-o** žmonės.*
'Then she **found herself** (PST (telic)) in Gediminas square, there she **used to like** (HAB-PST (atelic)) feeding pigeons in solitude, but now the square **had turned into** (PST PERFECT (telic)) a busier place, people **were making noise** (PST (atelic)) everywhere.'

Notice that the past perfect forms also refer to <anteriority> and have the function of expressing past-before-past (pluperfect), as *buvo pagyvėjusi* '(the square) had turned into a busier place' in example (28). Yet, the past habitual forms refer to an extended (longer) period of time and contrast with the recent past. In this point, the past habitual tense appears to be essentially different from the perfect, which refers to <anteriority> (+ <simultaneity>) and expresses some result or effect of the preceding situation.

The obvious difference between perfect and past habitual tense in this regard is, as Comrie (1976: 28) has stated, that "a further element of the meaning of these [past habitual] forms is that the situation described no longer

---

[19] Example (27), which has been used in the "academic" grammars, is originally cited from V. Krėvė's *Perkūnas, Vaiva ir Straublys* [Perkūnas, Vaiva and Straublys].

holds".[20] Thus, it would be an 'implicature' of the sentence *senovėje dar geriau* **bū-dav-o** (HAB-PST), *dar linksmiau* **gyven-dav-o** (HAB-PST) 'in the past it used to be better, (people) used to live more happily' in example (27) that 'it was no longer so good, people no longer lived so happily'. In the same way, it would be an implicature of the sentence *ten ji* **mėg-dav-o** (HAB-PST) *ramybėje lesinti balandžius* 'there she used to like feeding pigeons in solitude' in example (28) that 'she no more liked feeding pigeons there'. Consequently, if there is no disclaimer to the contrary, these sentences have an implicature that a previous situation no longer exists.

In contrast, the perfect generally entails that a resultant state or certain effect was or is still remaining simultaneously to the occurrence of the following situation. That is, a sentence such as *aikštė* **buv-o pagyvėjusi** (PST PERFECT) 'the square had turned into a busier place' in example (28) means that such a situation (or state) was continuing during the following situation. Thus, in such cases, the perfect forms cannot be replaced with the past habitual forms. Likewise, the past habitual forms in the sentences like example (27) or (28) cannot be replaced with the perfect forms, although they both refer to <anteriority>.

9 Summary and conclusions

In this chapter, I draw upon the perspective of contrastive analysis between Lithuanian and Russian and the questionnaire to prove that:
i. The essence of the Lithuanian past habitual tense, traditionally called "imperfect", "past frequentative", or "iterative", lies in its habitual nature. In the expressions of meanings of the domain of <iterativity> – <habituality>, the two Lithuanian past tense forms, i.e., the simple past form and the past habitual form, are used in a largely complementary fashion.
ii. The past habitual tense has multiple functions and is used to express not only <habituality> referring to <simultaneity> in a macro-situation, but also the opposition of <perfective/imperfective> referring to <sequence/simultaneity> in each micro-situation in combination with telic/atelic verbs, respectively.

---

20 This meaning of past habitual has defined as "discontinuous past" by Plungian and van der Auwera (2006), where the authors pointed out: "It seems that discontinuous past marking is found most often for habituals".

iii. The past habitual forms (typically with atelic verbs) sometimes refer to <anteriority> and denote a remote past prior to the past time expressed by the simple past forms. This use of the past habitual differs from the past perfect (pluperfect) in that the past habitual forms generally have an implicature that the situation described no longer exists.

The observations in this chapter are summarized in Table 31.

Tab. 31: <Iterativity> and <habituality> in the past tenses in Lithuanian

	(1) <PFV iterativity>	(2) <IPFV iterativity> (non-habitual)	(3) <habitual iterativity> micro-situation: <PFV> – <IPFV>	(4) <habitual continuity>
Taxis:	<sequence>	<simultaneity>	macro: <simultaneity> micro: <sequence> – <simultaneity>	
				– <anteriority>
Co-occurring adverbials:				
(a) Aspectual	Definite number of times	Indefinite number of times	macro: frequency – habitual continuity micro: punctual time – duration	
	Punctual time	Duration		
(b) Temporal localization	Definite time/limited period/close past – Indefinite time/extended period/ remote past			

	Past forms			
Russ.	PFV verbs	IPFV verbs	→	

Telic verbs ←——→ Atelic verbs

Lith.	Simple past forms		→	
			Telic verbs ←——→ Atelic verbs	
		← ——————	Past habitual forms	

▭ : More basic meaning
———→ : Scope of more peripheral meaning

The interpretation of <habitual> as a subclass of <imperfective> aspect was introduced by Comrie (1976) and has been widely accepted. However, discussions concerning the temporal-aspectual properties of <habitual> have not as yet been sufficient, not to mention that, in any discussion of aspect, preference will be given to examples from languages where aspect exists as grammatical category. Lithuanian, as a language that has specialized grammatical habitual tense forms, provides the clearest examples for investigations of the semantic distinctions and functions of <habituality>. Thus, it is hoped that my investigation in this chapter will contribute to a better understanding of habituals and of the correlation between tense and aspect.

Acknowledgments

I wish to thank Peter Arkadiev (Moscow), Axel Holvoet (Vilnius), Jun-ichi Sakuma (Nagoya), Tasaku Tsunoda (Tokyo), Björn Wiemer (Mainz), and the anonymous reviewers for their detailed and valuable comments on earlier versions of this paper, based partly on the results of my research in Lithuania (2008–2009), which was supported by the Japan Society for the Promotion of Science (JSPS). I am grateful to all my Lithuanian consultants, especially Ramutė Bingelienė (Vilnius), Jurgis Pakerys (Vilnius), and Renata Petroškevičienė (deceased; Tokyo), my Russian consultant, Ganna Šatoxina (Tokyo), my English consultant, Alice Lee (Tokyo), and my statistics consultant, Yoshihiko Asao (Buffalo), for their help, comments, and suggestions. Also, I would like to sincerely thank Aldona Paulauskienė (Vilnius) and Elena Urbanavičiūtė (Panevėžys) for their unconditional help with my research in Lithuania. All errors and shortcomings are of course my own.

Abbreviations

ACC	accusative	NOM	nominative
DAT	dative	PFV	perfective
GEN	genitive	PL	plural
HAB	habitual	PRF	(verbal) prefix
INS	instrumental	PST	past
IPFV	imperfective	REFL	reflexive
ITER	iterative	SBJV	subjunctive
LOC	locative	SG	singular
M	masculine		

References

Ambrazas, Vytautas. 1984. Dėl lietuvių kalbos veiksmažodžio morfologinių kategorijų [On the morphological categories of Lithuanian verbs]. *Baltistica* 20(2): 100–110.

Arkadiev, Peter M. [Arkad'jev, Petr]. 2008. Uroki litovskogo jazyka dlja slavjanskoj aspektologii [Lessons of Lithuanian for Slavic aspectology]. *Slavjanskoe jazykoznanie. XIV meždunarodnyj s"ezd slavistov. Oxrid, 10–16 sentjabrja 2008 g. Doklady rossijskoj delegacii* [Russian contributions to the 14th International Congress of Slavists, Oxrid, September 2008], 28–43. Moscow: Indrik.

Arkadiev, Peter M. [Arkad'jev, Petr]. 2009. Teorija akcional'nosti i litovskij glagol [Theory of actionality and Lithuanian verb]. *Balto-slavjanskie issledovanija* 18, 72–94. Moscow: Jazyki slavjanskix kul'tur.

Arkadiev, Peter M. 2011. Aspect and actionality in Lithuanian on a typological background. In Daniel Petit, Claire Le Feuvre & Henri Menantaud (eds.) *Langues baltiques, langues slaves*, pp. 57–86. Paris: Éditions CNRS.

Arkadiev, Peter M. [Arkad'jev, Petr]. 2012. Aspektual'naja sistema litovskogo jazyka (s privlečeniem areal'nyx dannyx). [The aspectual system of Lithuanian with references to areal data]. In Vladimir A. Plungjan (ed.) *Issledovanija po teorii grammatiki. Vypusk 6: Tipologija aspektual'nyx sistem i kategorij* [Studies in grammatical theory. Vol. 6. Typology of aspectual systems and categories]. *Acta Linguistica Petropolitana* 8 (2), 45–121. St. Petersburg: Nauka.

Bertinetto Pier Marco & Denis Delfitto. 2000. Aspect vs. actionality: Why they should be kept apart. In Östen Dahl (ed.) *Tense and aspect in the languages of Europe*, 189–226. Berlin, New York: Mouton de Gruyter.

Bondarko, Aleksandr V. 1987. *Teorija funkcional'noj grammatiki. Vvedenie. Aspektual'nost'. Vremennaja lokalizovannost'. Taksis*. [Theory of functional grammar. Introduction. Aspectuality. Temporal localization. Taxis]. Leningrad: Nauka.

Bondarko, Aleksandr V. 1996. *Problemy grammatičeskoj semantiki i russkoj aspektologii* [Problems of grammatical semantics and Russian aspectology]. St. Petersburg: Izdatel'stvo Sankt-Peterburgskogo universiteta.

Bybee, Joan L., Revere D. Perkins & William Pagliuca. 1994. *The evolution of grammar: Tense, aspect, and modality in the languages of the world*. Chicago: University of Chicago Press.

Comrie, Bernard. 1976. *Aspect*. Cambridge: Cambridge University Press.

Dahl, Östen. 1981. On the definition of the telic-atelic (bounded-nonbounded) distinction. In Philip J. Tedeschi & Annie Zaenen (eds.) *Syntax and Semantics, Vol. 14: Tense and aspect*, 79–90. New York: Academic Press.

Dahl, Östen. 1985. *Tense and aspect systems*. Oxfor, New York: Blackwell.

Dahl, Östen. 1994. Aspect. In Roland E. Asher (ed.) *The encyclopedia of language and linguistics*, vol. 1, 240–247. Oxford: Pergamon.

Dambriūnas, Leonardas. 1959. Verbal aspects in Lithuanian. *Lingua Posnaniensis* 7: 253–262.

Dambriūnas, Leonardas. 1960. *Lietuvių kalbos veiksmažodžių aspektai* [Verbal aspects in Lithuanian]. Boston: Lietuvių enciklopedijos leidykla.

Dickey, Stephen M. 2000. *Parameters of Slavic aspect. A cognitive approach*. Stanford, CA: CSLI Publications.

DLKG – Vytautas Ambrazas (ed.) 1994. *Dabartinės lietuvių kalbos gramatika* [Grammar of the modern Lithuanian]. Vilnius: Mokslo ir enciklopedijų leidykla.

Galnaitytė, Elzė. 1963. Osobennosti kategorii vida glagolov v litovskom jazyke (v sopostavlenii s russkim jazykom) [Peculiarities of the category of verbal aspect in Lithuanian in comparision with Russian]. *Kalbotyra* 7: 123–143.

Galnaitytė, Elzė. 1966. K voprosu ob imperfektivacii glagolov v litovskom jazyke [On the problem of imperfectivization of verbs in Lithuanian]. *Baltistica* 2: 147–158.

Garey, Howard B. 1957. Verbal aspect in French. *Language* 33: 91–10.

Genjušene [= Geniušienė], Emma Š. 1989. Mul'tiplikativ i iterativ v litovckom jazyke [Multiplicative and iterative in Lithuanian]. In Viktor S. Xrakovskij (ed.) *Tipologija iterativnyx konstrukcij* [Typology of iterative constructions], 122–132. Leningrad: Nauka.

Genjušene [= Geniušienė], Emma Š. 1990. Perfekt i vid v litovskom jazyke [Perfect and aspect in Lithuanian]. In Viktor S. Xrakovskij (ed.) *Tipologija i grammatika* [Typology and grammar], 135–140. Moscow: Nauka.

Geniušienė, E. 1997. The multiplicative and the iterative in Lithuanian. In Viktor S. Xrakovskij (ed.) *Typology of iterative constructions*, 220–240. München, Newcastle: LINCOM Europa.

Geniušienė, Emma Š. & Vladimir P. Nedjalkov. 1988. Resultative, passive, and perfect in Lithuanian. In Vladimir P. Nedjalkov (ed.) *Typology of resultative constructions*, 369–386. Amsterdam, Philadelphia: John Benjamins.

GLJa – Vytautas Ambrazas (ed.) 1985. *Grammatika litovskogo jazyka* [Grammar of the Lithuanian language]. Vilnius: Mokslas.

Holvoet, Axel & Veslava Čižik. 2004. Veikslo priešpriešos tipai [Types of aspectual opposition]. In Axel Holvoet & Loreta Semėnienė (eds.) *Gramatinių kategorijų tyrimai* [Studies on grammatical categories], 141–162. Vilnius: Lietuvių kalbos institutas.

Jakobson, Roman. 1957. Shifters, verbal categories, and the Russian verb. In Roman Jakobson, *Selected writings*, Vol. 2, 130–147. The Hague, Paris: Mouton.

Kardelis, Vytautas & Björn Wiemer. 2003. Kritische Bemerkungen zur Praxis der Erstellung litauischer Wörter-bücher, insbesondere von Mundarten – am Beispiel des slavischen Lehnguts und des 'veikslas'. In Norbert Ostrowski & Ona Vaičiulytė-Romančuk (red.), *Prace bałtystyczne. Język, literatura, kultura*, 45–72. Warszawa: Wydział Polonistyki UW.

Krifka, Manfred. 1998. The origins of telicity. In Susan Rothstein (ed.) *Events and grammar*, 197–236. Dordrecht: Kluwer.

LG – Vytautas Ambrazas (ed.). 1997. *Lithuanian grammar*. Vilnius: Baltos lankos.

LKG – Kazys Ulvydas (ed.). 1971. *Lietuvių kalbos gramatika* [Grammar of the Lithuanian language]. Vol. 2. Vilnius: Mintis.

Lehmann, Christian. 1994. Predicates: aspectual types. In Roland E. Asher (ed.) *The Encyclopedia of language and linguistics*, Vol. 6, 3297–3302. Oxford: Pergamon Press.

Lindstedt, Jouko. 1984. Nested aspects. In Casper de Groot & Hannu Tommola (eds.) *Aspect bound: A voyage into the realm of Germanic, Slavonic and Finno-Ugrian aspectology*, 177–192. Dordrecht: Foris.

Maslov, Jurij S. 1948 Vid i leksičeskoe značenie glagola v sovremennom russkom literaturnom jazyke [Aspect and the lexical meaning of the verb in the contemporary Russian literary language]. In Ju. S. Maslov, 1984, *Očerki po aspektologii* [Studies in aspectology], 48–65. Leningrad: Izdatel'stvo Leningradskogo universiteta.

Maslov, Jurij S. 1962a. Voprosy glagol'nogo vida v sovremennom zarubežnom jazykoznanii [Problems of the verbal aspect in modern non-Soviet linguistics]. In Jurij S. Maslov (ed.) *Voprosy glagol'nogo vida* [Problems of verbal aspect], 7–32. Moscow: Izdatel'stvo inostrannoj literatury.

Maslov, Jurij S. (ed.). 1962b. *Voprosy glagol'nogo vida* [Problems of verbal aspect]. Moscow: Izdatel'stvo inostrannoj literatury.
Maslov, Jurij S. 1978. K osnovanijam sopostavitel'noj aspektologii [Prolegomena to comparative aspectology]. In Jurij S. Maslov (ed.) *Voprosy sopostavitel'noj aspektologii* [Problems of comparative aspectology], 4–44. Leningrad: Nauka.
Maslov, Jurij S. 1984. *Očerki po aspektologii* [Essays in aspectology]. Leningrad: Izdatel'stvo Leningradskogo universiteta.
Matsuya [= Sakurai], Eiko. 1995. Aspect and compound tense in Lithuanian [In Japanese]. *Nagoya Working papers in Linguistics* 11: 1–50.
Mustejkis [= Musteikis], Kazimieras. 1972. *Sopostavitel'naja morfologija russkogo i litovskogo jazykov* [Contrastive morphology of Russian and Lithuanian]. Vilnius: Mintis.
Padučeva, Elena V. 1996. *Semantičeskie issledovanija (Semantika vremeni i vida v russkom jazyke; Semantika narrativa)* [Semantic studies (Semantics of tense and aspect in Russian; Semantics of narrative)]. Moscow: Jazyki russkoj kul'tury.
Pakerys, Jurgis & Björn Wiemer. 2007. Building a partial aspect system in East Aukštaitian Vilnius dialects of Lithuanian (Correlations between telic and activity verbs). *Acta Linguistica Lithuanica* 57: 45–97.
Paulauskienė, Aldona. 1979. *Gramatinės lietuvių kalbos veiksmažodžio kategorijos* [Grammatical categories of the Lithuanian verb]. Vilnius: Mokslas.
Paulauskienė, Aldona. 1994. *Lietuvių kalbos morfologija* [Lithuanian morphology]. Vilnius: Mokslo ir enciklopedijų leidykla.
Plungian, Vladimir A. & Johan van der Auwera. 2006. Towards a typology of discontinuous past marking. *Sprachtypologie und Universalienforschung* 59(4): 317–349.
Plungian, Vladimir A. 2011. *Vvedenie v grammatičeskuju semantiku: grammatičeskie značenija i grammatičeskie sistemy jazykov mira* [Introduction to grammatical semantics: Grammatical meanings and grammatical systems of the languages of the world]. Moscow: RGGU.
Roszko, Danuta & Roman Roszko. 2000. Litovskie glagol'nye formy s suffiksom *-dav-* [Lithuanian verbal forms with the suffix *-dav-*]. *Acta Baltico-Slavica* 25: 37–49.
Roszko, Danuta & Roman Roszko. 2006. Lithuanian frequentativum. *Études cognitives* 7: 163–172.
Safarewicz, Jan. 1967. Stan badań nad aspektem czasownikowym w języku litewskim [Situation of studies on verbal aspect in Lithuanian]. In *Studia językoznawcze*, 339–361. Warszawa: Państwowe Wydawnictwo Naukowe.
Sakurai, Eiko. 1997. Verbal aspect and meanings-functions of compound tenses in Lithuanian [In Japanese]. *Gengo Kenkyū: Journal of the Linguistic Society of Japan* 112: 98–131.
Sakurai, Eiko. 1999a. A contrastive analysis of the aspect systems of Russian and Lithuanian [In Japanese]. *Bulletin of Japan Association for the Study of Russian Language and Literature* 31: 82–97.
Sakurai, Eiko. 1999b. Verbal aspect and past habitual tense (with suffix *-dav-*) in Lithuanian [In Japanese]. *Nagoya Working Papers in Linguistics* 15: 137–170.
Sakurai, Eiko. 2002. Tense, aspect and temporal expressions in Baltic: An analysis by comparison with Slavic [in Japanese]. *Jinbun* 1: 55–72.
Sakurai, Eiko. 2008. Combination of past participles functioning as adverbials with main verbs in Lithuanian: Aspect and transitivity. *Acta Linguistica Lithuanica* 59: 81–108.

Sakurai, Eiko. 2010. Aspect and perfect in Lithuanian. Based on the contrastive aspectology with Russian [In Japanese]. *Jornal of the Institute of Language research* 15: 105–130.
Savicki, Lea. 2010. Preverbation and narrativity in Lithuanian: The distribution of finite simplex and compound verbs in narrative main clauses. *Baltic Linguistics* 1: 167–192.
Senn, Alfred E. 1949. Verbal aspects in Germanic, Slavic, and Baltic. *Language* 25(4): 402–409.
Sližienė, Nijolė. 1995. The tense system of Lithuanian. In Rolf Thieroff & Joachim Ballweg (eds.) *Tense systems in European languages*, vol. 2, 215–232. Tübingen: Niemeyer.
Smith, Carlota S. 1991. *The parameter of aspect*. Dordrecht: Kluwer.
Šluinskij, Andrej B. 2006. K tipologii predikatnoj množestvennosti: organizacija semantičeskoj zony [Toward a typology of predicative plurality: The structure of the semantic domain]. *Voprosy jazykoznanija* 1: 46–75.
Thelin, Nils B. 1978. *Toward a theory of aspect, tense and actionality in Slavic*. Stockholm: Almqvist and Wiksell.
Wiemer, Björn. 2001. Aspektual'nye paradigmy i leksičeskoe značenie russkix i litovskix glagolov (Opyt sopostavlenija s točki zrenija leksikalizacii i gramatikalizacii) [Aspectual paradigms and lexical meaning of Russian and Lithuanian verbs: Comparison from the perspective of lexicalization and grammaticalization]. *Voprosy jazykoznanija*. 2: 26–58.
Wiemer, Björn. 2009. Taksis v litovskom jazyke [Taxis in Lithuanian]. In Viktor S. Xrakovskij (ed.) *Tipologija taksisnyx konstrukcij* [Typology of taxis constructions], 161–216. Moscow: Znak.
Xrakovskij, Viktor S. 1987. Kratnost' [Situation plurality]. In Aleksandr V. Bondarko (ed.) *Teorija funkcional'noj grammatiki, t. 1: Vvedenie. Aspektual'nost'. Vremennaja lokalizovannost'. Taksis* [Theory of functional grammar. Introduction. Aspectuality. Temporal localization. Taxis], 124–152. Leningrad: Nauka.
Xrakovskij, Viktor S. 1989. Semantičeskie tipy množestva situacij i ix estestvennaja klassifikacija [Semantic types of the plurality of situations and their natural classification]. In Viktor S. Xrakovskij (ed.) *Tipologija iterativnyx konstrukcij*, 5–53. Leningrad: Nauka.
Xrakovskij, Viktor S. 1997. Semantic types of the plurality of situations and their natural classification. In Viktor S. Xrakovskij (ed.) *Typology of iterative constructions*, 3–64. München, Newcastle: LINCOM Europa.
Xrakovskij, Viktor S. (ed.). 2009. *Tipologija taksisnyx konstrukcij* [Typology of taxis constructions]. Moscow: Znak.

Aurelija Usonienė
11 Non-morphological realizations of evidentiality: The case of parenthetical elements in Lithuanian

1 Introduction

As has been already established in the linguistic literature on evidentiality, languages can have an obligatory grammatical category of evidentiality (e.g., Turkish) as opposed to those that do so optionally and can express evidential qualifications using the lexical inventory available in a language. In her seminal study on evidentiality, Aikhenvald (2004: 11) refers to the latter coding of evidential meanings as "evidential strategies". Although considering evidentiality exclusively as a grammatical category, this scholar does not discard the chances for lexical expressions to "provide historical sources for evidential systems" or that they "may reinforce grammatical evidentials" (Aikhenvald 2004: 10). In the present chapter, the coding of evidentiality that is not expressed by means of a set of verbal morphological markers is regarded as non-morphological.

One of the main objectives of the present study is to offer more evidence to support the point of view that in modern written Lithuanian lexical realizations dominate in the area of epistemicity (for this notion, cf. Boye 2012). Lately, there have been a number of studies published that demonstrate a preferred choice of the adverb(ial) strategy when expressing epistemic modality in Lithuanian (Usonienė & Šolienė 2010, Šolienė 2012). The given analysis concerns a few of the most common lexical markers of evidentiality, which are synchronically traceable back to complement taking predicate (CTP) clauses functioning as parenthetical elements in the sentence. These markers belong to the semantic-functional class of stance adverbials (Biber et al. 1999) in Lithuanian (Smetona & Usonienė 2012). The issue of the evidentiality of these parenthetical elements will be dealt with in the light of the process of adverbialization (Rissanen 1999, Traugott & Dasher 2002) and grammaticalization (Traugott 2010). The chapter begins with a very short overview of the morphological realizations of evidentiality in Lithuanian, which will be followed by a short description of the language data and methods of analysis in Section 2. Section 3 is devoted to an overview of quantitative findings that show frequency distributions of the expressions under analysis alongside the three basic patterns of use. Discussion of the types of evidential meaning expressed by the non-morphological realizations of evidentiality in Lithuanian is presented in Section 4. The last section contains a short summary and concluding remarks on the meaning and functions of the evidentials dealt with in the light of adverbialization and grammaticalization processes in language.

Lithuanian belongs to the group of languages that possesses a means of morphological marking of evidentiality, which is regarded as "evidential extensions of non-evidential categories" (Aikhenvald 2007: 209). The grammatical realizations of the linguistic category of evidentiality in Lithuanian have been extensively investigated by Ambrazas (1977a,b, 2006), Gronemeyer (1997), Holvoet (2001, 2004, 2007), Lavine (2006), Wiemer (2006, 2007a), and Kehayov (2008). The Lithuanian grammatical marking of evidentially, according to Wiemer (2006: 47) should be "characterized as being somehow intermediate between the system of Latvian (the language closest to Lithuanian in both genetic and areal terms) and the system of Bulgarian (and some other Balkan languages)". There are said to be two basic types of participles (an agreeing active participle, and a non-agreeing (so-called passive) participle -*ma/-ta*) that are used to express evidential meanings. The so-called construction 1 with an agreeing participle encodes reported evidentiality, while construction 2 with non-agreeing participles as a rule has an inferential reading, although "an occasional hearsay-function" has been observed with -*ta*- participles as well (Wiemer 2006: 43). The findings of the present analysis show that reportive reading is also common with non-agreeing passive and active participle forms of the verb *būti* 'be', namely *esama* 'be.PP.PRS.NAGR, *(ne)būsią* '(NEG)be.AP.FUT.NAGR, *(n)esą* '(NEG)be.AP.PRS.NAGR. Compare the following examples with agreeing participles in (1) and non-agreeing participles in (2) and (3), where both passive and active non-agreeing participles are used to mark second-hand information:

(1) Seseriai   sakė,   jog   jiems   viskas   žinoma,
    sister:DAT.SG say:PST.3 COMP   they:DAT all   know:PP.PRS.NAGR
    nes   aš   jau   **prisipažinęs**,   o   man
    because   I:NOM   already confess:AP.PST.NOM.SG.M   and   me:DAT
    melavo,   kad   sesuo   viską   **išpasakojusi**.
    lie:PST.3   COMP   sister:NOM.SG everything:ACC.SG   tell:AP.PST.NOM.SG.F
    'He said to the sister that everything was known to them because I had already confessed and they lied to me that the sister had told (them) everything.' (CCLL)

(2) Pensininkų   **esama**   apie   milijoną.
    retired:GEN.PL   be:PP.PRS.NAGR   about   million:ACC.SG
    'There is said to be about a million of retired people.' (CCLL)

(3) ... *vienas   kolega ...   paaiškino,   jog*
     one:NOM.SG.M   colleague:NOM.SG   explain:PST.3   COMP
     prof. Serbenta   sergąs,   o   be   jo
     prof. Serbenta   be.ill:AP.PRS.NOM.SG.M   and   without   he:GEN
     nesą   *kam   gudiškai   pirmininkauti.*
     NEG.be:AP.PRS.NAGR   who:DAT   in.Belarusian   chair:INF
     'a colleague explained that Prof. Serbenta is said to be ill and without him (as he says) there is nobody who can chair in Belarusian.' (CCLL)

The element of meaning that both types of participles seem to share is indirect evidence, which can easily be regarded as an unreliable source of information; therefore, it can trigger (by implicature) a reading of uncertainty, which is an epistemic qualification. Thus, the information conveyed is evidential often implying a slight shade of doubt toward the situation described. It should be noted that the first type of participles, i.e., agreeing participle forms, is very common in the complementation of communication and cognition verbs like *sakyti* 'say', *jausti* 'feel', *atrodyti* 'seem', and others (Gronemeyer & Usonienė 2001, Arkadiev 2012), e.g.,

(4) *Kol visi šie pakitimai nesutrikdo organizmo gyvybinės veiklos,*
     'Till all these changes do not affect the functioning of the organism,'
     *jis   **atrodo   esąs***   *sveikas.*
     it:NOM.M   seem:PRS.3   be:AP.PRS.NOM.SG.M   healthy:NOM.SG.M
     'it seems to be healthy.' (CorALit)

The analysis of the concordance of the progressive (PROG) present participle forms of the verb *būti* 'be', namely *besą* 'PROG.be.AP.PRS.NOM.PL.M' in the CCLL (Corpus of the Contemporary Lithuanian Language) has shown that about 90% of its use is in the complementation of the verb of appearance *pasirodyti* 'appear' (for more details, see Usonienė 2002).

(5) ... *mano   plaučiai   **pasirodė   besą***
         my   lung:NOM.PL   appear:PST.3   be:AP.PRS.NOM.PL.M
     švarūs ...
     clean:NOM.PL.M
     'My lungs appeared to be clean.' (CCLL)

However, the existing grammatical potential for coding evidential meanings is not very common in present-day Lithuanian. The so-called morphologically marked 'evidential' participle forms of the verb *būti* 'be' (*esama, būta, nesą, besą*, etc.)

are still used in written Lithuanian (fiction, news, academic register), but their frequency is not very high. However, in spoken Lithuanian, they are nearly extinct. There are only a few occurrences of *esama* 'be.PP.PRS.NAGR' and *būta* 'be.PP.PST.NAGR' and no cases of use of *nesą* 'NEG.be.AP.PRS.NAGR' in the sub-corpus of spoken Lithuanian in the CCLL, and only a few occurrences of *nesą* in the Corpus of Academic Lithuanian (CorALit).

Present-day language users prefer other means of expression, namely lexical or non-morphological marking of the source of information the author has for his/her assertion to be made. Among the most common lexical evidential markers in Lithuanian, mention can be made of a great number of so-called particles, parentheticals, and modals words, for instance, *matyt* 'evidently', *atrodo* 'apparently', *regis* 'seemingly', *girdi* 'reportedly' (<'you hear'), and many others as used in the following example:

(6) Niaukiasi, **matyt/ atrodo/ regis**, lis.
    get.cloudy:PRS.3 evidently/ apparently/ seemingly rain:FUT.3
    '(It's) getting cloudy, evidently/apparently/seemingly, (it) will rain.'

The three expressions used are circumstantial inferential evidentials. Overcast sky is a sign of rain, which serves as an evidence for the speaker's inference. However, in the description of situations when the source of information available is hearsay, the only acceptable alternatives are *atrodo* 'apparently' and *regis* 'seemingly', which means that they can also function as reportive evidentials. On the contrary, the use of inferential *matyt* 'evidently' is blocked in (6) because its meaning is incompatible with hearsay, e.g.,

(7) Pranešama,   kad   įvyko   avarija,
    report:PP.PRS.NAGR COMP   happen:PST.3   accident:NOM.SG
    atrodo/   regis/   *matyt,   yra   aukų.
    apparently/ seemingly/   evidently   be:PRS.3   victim:GEN.PL
    '(It is) reported that there was an accident, apparently/seemingly/evidently there are victims.'

In so-called condition→result cases, when the situation contains a direct indication to certain conditions (an *if*-clause) upon which the speaker's prediction is utterly dependent upon, only non-perceptual inferentials (like *matyt* 'evidently') seem to be preferable, while the use of circumstantial inferentials is blocked, as can be seen in (7):

(8) Jeigu neatsakė   į   klausimą,   **matyt/*atrodo/**
    if   NEG.answer:PST.3   in   question:ACC.SG   evidently/apparently/

***regis**   nežino.
seemingly   NEG.know:PRS.3
'If (s/he) hasn't answered the question, evidently/apparently/seemingly s/he doesn't know.'

Another dimension that might have effect upon the meaning of the given evidentials could be a degree of epistemic commitment, which is observed by many linguists (Mortelmans 2000, Plungian 2001, Aikhenvald 2004, Cornillie 2007, Wiemer 2010). Actually, the three expressions are regarded as epistemic modals of uncertainty in the Lithuanian grammar (Valeckienė 1998: 76) and one cannot deny the fact that they do imply a shade of uncertainty. In other words, they are non-factual and the reliability of knowledge/source of information is questioned.

Despite all the polemic regarding the content and realizations of evidentiality, the core interpretation of this linguistic category remains the same. It is the linguistic coding of the speaker's source of information that is available for the assertion made. Evidential markers are used by the speakers to indicate how the knowledge about the situation/proposition described has come to their awareness. In recent studies on lexical and grammatical evidentiality (Dendale & Van Bogaert 2007, Pietrandrea 2007, Wiemer 2007a,b, 2010, Squartini 2008, Boye & Harder 2009, Cornillie 2009, Pusch 2009, Whitt 2009, Diewald & Smirnova 2010, Boye 2012), much attention has been devoted to the issues of the category of evidentiality and its relation to the category of epistemic modality. A cross-linguistic category of epistemicity encompassing epistemic expressions of evidentiality and epistemic modality has been proposed by Boye (2012).

The subject of the present chapter is non-morphological realizations of evidentiality, which have so far received very little attention in Lithuanian linguistics (see, however, Usonienė 2002, 2003, Wiemer 2007b, Ruskan 2012). The area that needs in-depth research is a vast group of so-called parentheticals that comprises a great variety of linguistics expressions (particles, modal words, adverbs, parenthetical comment clauses) in Lithuanian. They can express a wide range of epistemic/evidential/evaluative qualifications (Thompson 2002: 146). The chapter will focus on parenthetical elements that can function as evidentials, namely *žinoma* 'is known, certainly', *manoma* '(is) believed/thought', *aišku* 'clearly, obviously', *matyt* 'evidently', *atrodo* 'apparently, seemingly', *tiesa* 'really, actually' (literally 'it is truth'), *žinia* 'be known' (literally '(it is the) message'). These evidential expressions will be claimed to be directly related to the corresponding CTPs (cf. Noonan 1985, Boye & Harder 2007, Van Bogaert 2009), namely verb-based CTPs *matyti* 'see', *atrodyti* 'seem', *žinoti* 'know', *manyti* 'think-that', adjective-based CTP *aišku* 'clear' and noun-based CTPs *tiesa* 'truth', *žinia* 'message, knowledge, news'. The purpose of the chapter is to see what evidential meanings are expressed by the Lithuanian parentheticals under analysis and which epistemic qualification (if any) is possible. The findings of the research can be also seen as offering support that the semantic-functional class of stance adverbials in Lithuanian should incorporate a great variety of linguistic realizations, parenthetical CTPs, and adverbial CTP clauses among them.

2 Data and method

The data have been collected from two monolingual corpora of written Lithuanian. The first one is the Corpus of Academic Lithuanian (CorALit; http://www.coralit.lt/), which is a specialized synchronic corpus of written Lithuanian. Its size is about 9 million words (8,670,613), and it represents five basic fields of science: biomedical sciences (B), humanities (H), physical sciences (P), social sciences (S), and technological sciences (T). The basic texts types included are monographs, textbooks, manuals, research articles, review articles, book reviews, and abstracts published in the period 1999–2009. The second source of the data is the sub-corpus of fiction in the Corpus of the Contemporary Lithuanian Language (CCLL; http://tekstynas.vdu.lt/), which contained about 7 million words (6,728,513) when the search was carried out (namely in the period of 2009–2010). As the size of the two corpora is different, when it is necessary to compare the number of occurrences of the elements contrasted, raw frequency numbers have been normalized per 1,000 words to make the comparison statistically valid.

This corpus-based study makes use of both quantitative and qualitative methods of analysis. I keep to the point of view of those linguists (Noël 2002: 16, Leech 2003: 228–231, Paradis 2003, Simon-Vandenbergen & Aijmer 2007: 6, Van Bogaert 2009: 130–132, Hasselgård 2010: 7), who regard frequency of linguistic expressions as a very important parameter in making conclusions about the linguistic system. Language use and frequency of occurrence are among most important factors in the development of various grammatical phenomena (constructions, forms, etc.). The given observation is directly related to the language data under analysis. For instance, the Lithuanian noun *tiesa* 'truth' is no longer a typical representative of this word class because its use is basically parenthetical and it has a broad range of functions characteristic of discourse markers; a marker for encoding evidentiality is one of them.

The two corpora used are not linguistically annotated; therefore, the search of linguistic forms was automatic, but the data analysis was basically manual.

As the subject of analysis concerns only certain forms of verbs, adjectives, and nouns that can function as CTPs and as parentheticals, the concordances of the matches collected had to undergo a detailed formal analysis. Thus, a purely formal analysis carried out follows a very simple pattern, which is based on a ternary opposition of (a) cases of use with default syntactic function of the word class the form belongs to vs. (b) cases of CTP use vs. (c) cases of parenthetical use. A detailed description of the main distinctions made for nouns, verbs, and adjectives is given in (9)–(11):

(9) Nouns
   a. subject/object/predicative;
   b. CTP (+*kad-*/*jog-*'that'clause);
   c. Parenthetical (initial, medial, final).

(10) Verb
   a. Lexical V-transitive (+NP)/V-intransitive (+AdvP);
   b. CTP (+*kad-*/*jog-*'that'clause);
   c. Parenthetical (initial, medial, final).

(11) Neuter adjectives
   a. Predicative;
   b. CTP (+*kad-*/*jog-*'that'clause);
   c. Parenthetical (initial, medial, final).

Consider examples (12)–(18), which illustrate the above classification. First, a few cases of use in pattern (a) will be given where the analyzed expressions function as full lexical items; then a few examples to illustrate cases of finite complementation in pattern (b); finally, the parenthetical use of the expressions under study will be demonstrated in pattern (c):

Pattern (a)
(12) *Ne   su   gera   **žinia**   atėjome.*
     NEG   with   good:INS.SG.F   message:INS.SG.F   come:PST.1PL
     'We have come with a piece of bad news.' (CCLL)

(13) *Viskas   **aišku**   ir   paprasta: ji   išėjo*
     everything   clear:NAGR   and   simple:NAGR   she   leave:PST.3
     ir ... nebesugrįš.
     and not.any.more.return:FUT.3
     'Everything's clear and simple: she has left and won't come back (again).' (CCLL)

(14) Šių   simptomų   etiologija   nėra
      this:GEN.PL   symptom:GEN.PL   etiology:NOM.SG.F   NEG:be:PRS.3
      žinoma ...
      know:PP.PRS.NOM.SG.F
      'The etiology of these symptoms is not known.' (CoRALit)

Pattern (b)

(15) Melaginga   **tiesa,**   **kad**   meilė   ateina
      false:NOM.SG.F   truth:NOM.SG   COMP   love:NOM.SG   come:PRS.3
      pati.
      self:NOM.SG.F
      'It's a false truth that love comes by itself.' (CCLL)

(16) ... logiškai   mąstant   buvo   **aišku,**
          logically   think:GER.PRS   be:PRS.3   clear:NAGR
      kad   priešginiauti...   beprasmiška ...
      COMP   contradict:INF   senseless:NAGR
      'Logically thinking it was clear that it was senseless to contradict.' (CCLL)

(17) ... pažiūrėk   į ...   veidą!   **Matyt,**   kad   šypsena
          look:IMP   at   face:ACC.SG   see:INF   COMP   smile:NOM.SG
      dirbtinė, ...
      artificial:NOM.SG.F
      'Look at her face! It is obvious that (her) smile is unnatural.'

Pattern (c)

(18) Žmogaus   kūnas,   **žinia,**
      human:GEN.SG   body:NOM.SG   message:NOM.SG
      irgi   iš   vandens.
      also   of   water:GEN.SG
      'The human body is known to be (constituted) of water.' (CCLL)

(19) ... bažnyčia,   **manoma,**   buvo   pastatyta
          church:NOM.SG   think:PP.PRS.NAGR   was   build:PP.PST.NOM.SG.F
      iki 1504 m.
      till 1504
      'The church is believed to have been built before 1504.' (CoRALit)

Instances of parenthetical use have been further subdivided according to the position of the parenthetical element in the sentence. Position is regarded as an important indicator of parenthetical status (Kaltenböck 2007, Van Bogaert 2009).

It can be sentence-initial and sentence-non-initial. Non-initial (medial and final) position is typically parenthetical, while initial position raises a few questions regarding the initial element in the sentence and its syntactic status (Brinton 2008: 11–12). This problem concerns cases when the sentence-initial position of *I think*-type parentheticals can be considered to be identical to the position of a matrix clause with complementizer-omission (*I think-Ø-S*). As deletion of the complementizer is a common phenomenon both in spoken and written language, there is a considerable amount of research devoted to the discussion of the semantic and grammatical status of complementizerless matrix clauses (Aijmer 1997, Thompson 2002, Wierzbicka 2006, Fischer 2007, Brinton 2008). Moreover, position might be function-dependent. Simon-Vandenbergen and Aijmer (2002–2003: 19) observe that "occurrence in the pre-front field (i.e. in the position preceding the front field in the proposition proper)" is formally a most typical position for discourse markers. The present analysis does not aim to establish a link between the position and a preferred evidential or pragmatic reading of the elements under study. These issues are to be the subject of further research.

The present chapter will not deal with a distinction between matrix clauses with zero-complementizer and sentence-initial parentheticals because for this purpose, a prosodic analysis is essential, which is impossible when dealing with written language data (for more details,[1] see Usonienė 2012, 2013). Therefore, complementizerless cases of sentence-initial position of the expressions under analysis will be regarded as parenthetical use, e.g., *Aišku, ji teisi* 'Actually she is right', *Matyt bijojo* ... 'Evidently s/he was afraid'. According to the position of their occurrence, parenthetical expressions under analysis are classified into initial, medial, and final. Consider a few examples that illustrate the positional flexibility of parenthetical *aišku* 'clearly, actually, obviously':

(20) Initial
  Aišku, jis viską žinojo iš anksto.
  clearly he:NOM everything:ACC.SG know:PST.3 beforehand
  'Obviously he knew everything beforehand.' (CCLL)

---

[1] There has been considerable polemic in the latest studies dealing with the issues of morphosyntactic independence of the complement clause and the status of the matrix clause (Thompson 2002, Boye & Harder 2007, Newmeyer 2010, Verhagen 2005, 2010). The fact that one-word-form parenthetical CTPs do not produce main information but function as "framing devices" means that they undergo adverbialization because they are inherently non-addressable, secondary, and grammatical (Usonienė 2013).

(21) Medial
... išokome   į   vagoną.
 jump:PST.1PL   in   carriage:ACC.SG
*Važiavome,   **aišku**,   be   bilietų.*
drive:PST.1PL   clearly   without   tickets:GEN
'We got into the carriage. We travelled, naturally, without tickets.' (CCLL)

(22) Final
*... ji   išgirdo   durų   dunkstelėjimą. Kostas,   **aišku**!*
 she:NOM   hear:PST.3   door:GEN.PL   thud:ACC.SG   Kostas:NOM   certainly
'She heard the door thud. It was Kostas, certainly/obviously.' (CCLL)

All of the expressions under study are used in different positions in the three patterns described above; however, their distribution in these patterns might be different. A greater or lesser frequency of parenthetical use might be indicative of the change of their status as a word class. For instance, *matyt* 'evidently' could be said to have nearly lost its link with the meaning of its lexical verb of direct visual perception *matyti* 'see'. Its concordance in the CorALit is constituted basically of the parenthetical use (~90%). The percentage of its parenthetical use in CCLL-fiction is even higher and reaches 91.5%, and its use in medial-sentence position constitutes 67.1%. As has been shown in Usonienė (2002, 2003), the development of this perception verb into an evidential marker in Lithuanian proceeds in two stages. First, it shifts to a verb of cognition when it functions as a CTP, and second, it parentheticalizes when omission of the complementizer increases its positional flexibility and it comes to be used as a marker of indirect evidentiality undergoing a further shift of meaning, which becomes more abstract and more speaker-oriented.

Before proceeding to a more detailed analysis of the evidential meanings conveyed by the expressions under study, however, a short overview of the quantitative findings might cast light on the real situation regarding language usage in present-day Lithuanian. In other words, it is important to find out whether there is any plausible evidence to regard some of the evidential expressions under analysis as belonging to a separate word class of function words. At the present time, according to the *Modern Lithuanian Dictionary* (MLD; http://dz.lki.lt/), some of these expressions are considered to be parentheticals, for instance *matyt* 'evidently', *žinia* 'the message is', *tiesa* 'the truth is', while the *Dictionary of the Lithuanian Language* (DLL; www.lkz.lt) regards them as modal words. The interpretation of the modal meanings is given in a circular way by offering a list of so-called synonymous expressions, meaning that all of them seem to share the semantic feature of a high degree of certainty/probability, e.g.,

(23) *žinia* → *žinoma* → **tikrai** → 'really' (DLL)

(24) *tiesa* → *beje* → *tiesa*, **tikrai** → 'really' (DLL)

The shortened infinitive form of the verb *matyti* 'to see', namely *matyt*, is regarded as a parenthetical. The evidential epistemic stance adverbial *atrodo* 'apparently' is, however, treated as a modal third-person present tense form of the verb *atrodyti* 'to seem', and it is introduced under the entry of the verb *atrodyti* 'to seem'. *Žinia* 'message/knowledge' is considered to be a modal word, but *tiesa* 'truth' is a parenthetical, while *ištiės, iš tiesų* 'in truth/actually' are regarded as adverbs. Thus, it is not clear how and why parentheticals are opposed to modal words and to adverbs.

The chapter is intended neither to assess the categorial part-of-speech status of these expressions nor to get involved into the polemic on the subtle aspects of morphosyntactic distinctions made among particles, parentheticals, modal words, adverbs, and various borderline cases in Lithuanian linguistics. However, the results of the quantitative and qualitative analysis of the given authentic empirical data can cast light on the issues mentioned in the light of the present-day language-in-use situation. Although no diachronic analysis is possible, synchronic data can also be indicative of the ongoing processes of adverbialization (Nevalainen 2004: 25) and grammaticalization. According to Traugott (2010: 36), a synchronic cline of grammaticality is unidirectional, "granulary", and with different "degrees of fusion".

3 Quantitative findings

The quantitative analysis of the data collected was started by comparing raw frequencies of the expressions studied in the concordances extracted from CorALit. The results are shown in Table 1.

As the data show, the most frequent is *žinoma* '(is) known, of course, certainly' and the least frequent is *žinia* 'be known/heard to be'. In the following quantitative parameter, which can indicate whether the expression is more commonly used as a lexical item or as a parenthetical; the latter use is characteristic of sentence adverbials and functional words. The following data in Table 2 show the distribution of the expressions in the three patterns that make a distinction among use of lexical items, CTPs, and parentheticals.

Tab. 1: Raw frequency of the expressions analyzed in CorALit

CorALit	Total raw
žinoma '(is) known' 'of course, certainly'	1,624
tiesa 'truth' 'in truth', 'really, actually'	1,135
atrodo '(it) seems' 'apparently, seemingly'	853
manoma '(is) thought' 'be thought/believed to'	757
matyt 'evidently'	672
aišku '(is) clear' 'clearly, obviously'	521
žinia 'message/knowledge' 'be known/heard to be'	133

Tab. 2: Distribution of expressions studied across the three patterns of use in the CorALit

CorALit	Total	Lexical item	CTP	Parenthetical
(kaip) žinoma '(as is) known' 'of course, certainly'	1,624	477 (29.4%)	437 (27%)	710 (43.7%)
tiesa 'truth' 'in truth', 'really, actually'	1,135	241 (21.2%)	8 (0.7%)	886 (78.1%)
atrodo '(it) seems' 'apparently, seemingly'	853	473 (55.3%)	184 (21.5%)	196 (23.2%)
manoma '(is) thought' 'be thought/believed to'	757	4 (0.5%)	701 (92.4%)	52 (7%)
matyt 'evidently'	672	–	9 (1.3%)	663 (98.7%)
aišku '(is) clear' 'clearly, obviously'	521	56 (10%)	295 (57%)	170 (33%)
žinia 'message/knowledge' 'be known/heard to be'	133	55 (41%)	6 (4.5%)	72 (54%)

As can be seen in Table 2, nearly all the concordance of *matyt* 'evidently' is made up of parenthetical use and a greater part of use of a noun-based CTP *tiesa* 'really, actually' is also parenthetical. *Manoma* 'be thought/believed to' functions basically as a CTP (92.4%), which means that all these expressions are used solely to express the speaker's epistemic attitude toward the proposition asserted. The attitude expressed concerns the source of information, and it will be dealt with in more detail in Section 4.

As has been explained in the introduction, parenthetical expressions were classified into initial, medial, and final according to the position of their occurrence.

Tab. 3: Overall distribution of parenthetical use of expressions in relation to their position in the sentence (CoRALit)

CoRALit	Parenthetical	Initial	Medial	Final
tiesa 'really, actually'	886	796	90	–
matyt 'evidently'	663	234	429	–
žinoma 'of course, certainly'	610	424	186	
kaip žinoma 'as is known'	100	73	27	
atrodo 'apparently, seemingly'	196	61	131	4
aišku 'clearly, obviously'	170	88	82	–
kaip žinia 'as is known'	43	25	18	
žinia 'be known/heard to be'	29	23	6	
manoma 'be thought/believed to'	52	2	50	–

Frequencies of parenthetical use in sentence-initial/medial/final position as calculated in the concordances extracted from CoRALit are given in Table 3.

The figures in Table 3 show that sentence-initial position is clearly predominant in the parenthetical use of *tiesa* 'really, actually', *žinia* 'be known/heard to be', and *žinoma* '(is) known, of course, certainly', which might be an important sign indicating differences in meaning and function. This issue needs an in-depth analysis of a larger amount of various data. According to Simon-Vandenbergen and Aijmer (2002–2003: 24), "the unmarked medial position of the Dutch *natuurlijk* can make it more of an adverb and less of a discourse marker". The same explanation is applicable to the Lithuanian *manoma* 'be thought/believed to', which is most frequent as a medial-position parenthetical. It seems to be exclusively an expression of propositional attitude and its concordance in the CoRALit is made up only of its functioning as a CTP or a medial-position parenthetical. *Manoma* 'be thought/believed to' indicates the source of information that is based on the level of knowledge in science and of common sense knowledge of the world in general. The role of the position of an expression in a sentence is also regarded as a very important indicator of its functions and meaning by Downing (2006). In her study on the use of *surely* in English, she observes that the initial *surely* is different from the medial used to "make a fairly confident prediction regarding the future, a fairly confident assumption regarding the present, and a reinforced deontic statement, respectfully" (Downing 2006: 45). Similarly, Van Bogaert (2009: 366) claims that *you know* when used with local scope "assumes initial position most often" and it has a function of a marker of metalinguistic awareness.

The analysis of the concordances extracted from the sub-corpus of fiction in CCLL also fully supports the quantitative findings in CorALit. The percentage of the lexical adjective *aišku* 'clear'NAGR (as in *Dabar viskas **aišku*** 'everything [is] clear now') is very low and it makes up about 13% of the overall matches. Only 43% of the occurrences of *žinia* 'message/knowledge' have been found to be lexical items and that of *tiesa* 'truth' is about 40%. The concordance of *matyt* 'evidently' consists of 92% (67% in the medial position) of its parenthetical (non-lexical) use, while that of *atrodo* 'apparently' is 67%.

As can be seen from the survey of the quantitative data findings, all the expressions analyzed can function as parentheticals in present-day Lithuanian. Their parenthetical frequency is very high both in written academic Lithuanian and in fiction. Fiction can be said to combine both written and spoken aspects of language, and although spoken Lithuanian data have not been analyzed, preliminary observations allow predicting a similar behavior. The majority of expressions are more frequent as parentheticals than lexical items, with the function of a CTP as an intermediate phase, which can serve as an illustration of the range of synchronic variation.

4 Evidential meanings

As has been stated, the focus of the analysis is to identify parenthetical use and specify possible evidential meanings of the items under analysis. All of the expressions under study are multifunctional. Their lexical meaning shifts and undergoes semantic bleaching, which is accompanied by the acquisition of a broad range of new functions: from markers of evidentiality (proposition-level qualification) to markers of affirmation (cf. response particles) and truth attesters (speaker-oriented qualification/function), etc. In the following sections, an overview of the types of evidential meanings that the expressions under study can develop is presented.

The meaning extension of the Lithuanian neuter (non-agreeing) adjective *aišku* 'clear' is synchronically observable and follows a most probably universal path of semantic change: from concrete and purely visual or perceptually 'clear' (24) to mental (25) and (26), and to more abstract 'clarity' based on reasoning (inference), which can serve as evidence for the speaker's judgment, hence the indication of the source of information (27). The given transition is also observed by Simon-Vandenbergen and Aijmer (2007: 256–257) who note that "the step from 'it is easy to see' to 'we all know' is a small one". This three-step semantic shift of Lithuanian *aišku* 'clear' can be illustrated by the following examples in (25) to (28):

(25) ... *matomas* ... ***aiškių*** *ribų* *darinys* ...
see:PP.PRS.NOM.SG.M clear:GEN.PL borders:GEN.PL structure:NOM.SG.M
'a structure with clear borders (can be) seen.' (CorALit)

(26) *Jūs nematėt ir negirdėjot.*
you(PL):NOM NEG.see:PST.2PL and NEG.hear:PST.2PL
*Aišku? Tikriausiai visiems buvo **aišku**,*
clear:NAGR probably all:DAT be:PST.3 clear:NAGR
nes ... pasidarė tylu.
because become:PST.3 silent:NAGR
'You haven't seen and heard (anything). (Is it) clear? (It) must have been clear to everybody because silence fell.' (CCLL)

(27) *Šis tebetylėjo ... Dabar neabejotinai tapo*
this:NOM.SG.M keep.silence:PST.3 now undoubtedly become:PST.3
***aišku**, **kad** tas esąs*
clear:NAGR COMP that:NOM.SG.M be:AP.PRS.NOM.SG.M
absoliutus nebylys.
absolute:NOM.SG.M mute:NOM.SG.M
'The man kept silent ... Now, undoubtedly, it became obvious that he was absolutely mute.' (CCLL)

(28) ... *priešais namus vis sukinėjasi neaiškus tipas. Žvalgosi, nueina ir vėl sugrįžta.*
'There's always a stranger near the house. He comes and goes, and keeps looking around.
***Aišku**, seklys.*
clear:NAGR tracker:NOM.SG
'Obviously, a snoop.' (CCLL)

The evidential meaning expressed by a CTP *aišku* 'clear'NAGR in (27) and a parenthetical in (28) is circumstantial inferential (cf. Squartini 2008: 925). Both examples contain a detailed description of evidence[2] that is crucial for the judgment made by the speaker. This is not the only function of *aišku*. Its meaning

---

[2] A more detailed analysis of the types of evidence expressed by the evidential adjectives *aišku* 'clear'NAGR, *akivaizdu* 'evident/obvious', *panašu* 'likely' in Lithuanian is given by Ruskan (2012).

extension proceeds further, which leads to its functioning as an emphatic particle in (29), as an affirmation marker in (30), or as a contrast marker in (31), e.g.,

(29) Abu ... svarstė, ar panašus.
both wonder:PST.3 whether similar:NOM.SG.M
– Taip, **aišku,** panašus, – tvirtino Kostas...
yes clear:NAGR similar:NOM.SG.M affirm:PST.3 Kostas
'Both were wondering whether he was similar. – Yes, of course, he is similar, – Kostas said.' (CCLL)

(30) ... jie plaukioja kartu su banginiais. Aišku?
they:NOM swim:PRS.3 together with whale:INS.PL clear:NAGR
– **Aišku, aišku,** mokslinčiau.
clear:NAGR clear:NAGR brainbox:VOC
'... they swim together with whales. Is it clear? – Yeah, sure, brainbox.' (CCLL)

(31) Šią dūdelę padariau pats.
this:ACC.SG.F fife:ACC.SG make:PST.1SG self:NOM.SG.M
Aišku, ne fleita, tačiau groti galima...
clear:NAGR NEG flute:NOM.SG but play:INF possible:NAGR
'I have made this fife myself. Actually, it is not a flute but one can play (it).' (CCLL)

In (31), *aišku* 'clearly, actually' is also used to make the speaker's statement more tentative before introducing a counterclaim, the function that is characteristic of the English *actually* as shown by Aijmer (2003: 30). This is the function characteristic of hedging devices. I cannot utterly agree with the remark made by one of the reviewers that the evidential reading seems to persist in (29) to (31). If we start measuring a degree of 'evidential content', it might be still discernible in (29), where *aišku* 'actually' is used to stress the reliability of evidence, which is interpreted as 'unquestionable', hence the emphasis on a high degree of certainty/truthfulness. With regard to the mode of the development of the range of functions discussed, no attempt is made to claim that it is a result of a linear step-by-step development through time. The coexistence of these alternatives in time might be as well seen as a radial splitting of the core meaning. However, a universal tendency of the development has been proved by many diachronic studies to be unidirectional and gradual (Rissanen 1999, Traugott 2007, 2010).

The function of a marker of affirmation is also common for *žinoma* 'is known', the meaning and function of which can be said to be identical to *aišku* 'of course' in the following example:

(32) Ar   galėsi   ateiti   padėti   sutvarkyti? – **Aišku/žinoma.**
      Q   can:FUT.2SG   come:INF   help:INF   tidy.up:INF   of course/sure
      'Will you be able to come and help tidy up? – Sure/of course'

Actually, the shift in meaning of *žinoma* '(is) known' proceeds along the same path as that of *aišku* '(is) clear', i.e., from denoting mere "possession" of knowledge to indicating previous knowledge as the speaker's source of information, hence inference with a high degree of commitment on the part of the speaker.

(33) **Žinoma**   apie 100   pneumokokų   serotipų.
      know:PP.PRS.NAGR   about 100   pneumococs:GEN.PL   serotypes:GEN.PL
      'About 100 pneumococcal serotypes are known.' (CorALit)

(34) Gerai **žinoma,**   kad   lengviau   ligos   išvengti, ...
      well   know:PP.PRS.NAGR   COMP   easier   illness:GEN.SG   avoid:INF
      'It is well known that it is easier to avoid an illness.' (CorALit)

(35) Aukštesnieji   organizmai,   **žinoma,**
      higher:NOM.PL.M.DEF   organism:NOM.PL   know:PP.PRS.NAGR
      yra   ... sudėtingesni.
      be:PRS.3   more.complex:NOM.PL.M
      'Higher organisms, naturally, are more complex.' (CorALit)

The function of *žinoma* 'naturally/certainly' in (35) is to inform the addressee that the information in the proposition expressed is not new and should be expected as it is general knowledge. This meaning is truth-conditional and the speaker expresses his/her strong confidence in the factuality of the situation described, which can be regarded as an epistemic extension of the given evidential meaning. As the author's judgment relies upon previous knowledge and well-known facts, the function of using *žinoma* 'naturally/certainly' is also to point out that it is shared knowledge. Thus the inferential *žinoma* 'naturally/certainly' belongs to the sub-domain of indirect evidentiality, the meaning of which seems to be in parallel to the English *surely* (cf. Downing 2006: 41) or *of course* (cf. Simon-Vandenbergen & Aijmer 2002–2003: 31), the expressions that belong to the semantic domain of certainty.

Similarly, *žinia* 'be known to' and *kaip žinia* 'as is known' are also inferential evidentials; however, they do not seem to be unmarked in terms of the speaker's confidence. The basic function of the two is to refer to the existence of 'objective' knowledge, which is the evidence whereupon the speaker bases his/her judgment. Pragmatically *žinia* 'be known to' and *kaip žinia* 'as is known' are more addressee-oriented, because they are used to remind the addressee that what is said is not new information – by contrast, it is shared knowledge. In this sense, the meaning conveyed can be regarded as intersubjective because it concerns the position of the addressee. Consider the following examples from academic Lithuanian:

(36) *Nepriklausomybės   deklaracija,   žinia,...*
independence:GEN.SG declaration:INS.SG news:NOM.SG
nedisponuojame,   ji ...   nusimetė, ...
NEG.possess:PRS.1PL it:NOM   get.lost:PST.3
'We do not have, as is known, the declaration of independence, it has been lost.' (CorALit)

(37) *... paveldimomis   ligomis,   kaip   žinia, ...*
inherited:INS.PL.F disease:INS.PL as   message:NOM.SG
dažniau   serga   grynaveisliai   šunys.
more.often   be.ill:PRS.3   pedigree:NOM.PL.M   dog:NOM.PL
'... inherited diseases are known to be more common in pedigree dogs' (CorALit)

The evidential meaning expressed by knowledge-based *žinia* parentheticals in academic Lithuanian can be seen as corresponding to the evidential meaning of the "passive matrices of infinitival complements" (Noël 2001: 270), which denote "a subjective intrusion by the speaker/writer" and "signal that the speaker/writer of the sentence is not the (sole) judge by calling in an unspecified source, from whose implied existence the relative factuality of the statement can be inferred". The content of the two linguistic expressions is nearly identical; however, their realization is very different and language structure-dependent. English prefers passive matrices that are on the path to auxiliarihood (Noël 2001), while Lithuanian makes use of reduced[3] parenthetical CTP clauses. In spoken Lithuanian, both markers (*žinia/kaip žinia* '(as) is known') are used to signal shared and common sense knowledge, which occasionally can be based on hearsay; hence, in some cases, these expressions can

---

3 Reduction in the Lithuanian parenthetical CTP clause means the omission of the grammatical subject, copular verb, and the complementizer. Compare the two following expressions with a full CTP clause (a) and a 'bare' CTP clause (b):

a. *Yra   žinoma,   kad* S
   be:PRS.3   know:PP.PRS.NAGR   COMP S
   'It is known that S'
b. Ø *žinoma* Ø S

have the reading characteristic of reportive evidentials as well. Compare the two sets of examples from the sub-corpus of fiction in (38–39) and (40):

(38) **Shared knowledge → generic inference**
*Bet šventė, **kaip žinia,***
but celebration:NOM.SG as knowledge:NOM.SG
nesitęsia amžinai.
NEG.continue:PRS.3 eternally
'But celebration, as we know, does not last forever.' (CCLL)

(39) *Patarinėti, **žinia**, visuomet nesunku ir*
advise:INF knowledge:NOM.SG always NEG.hard:NAGR and
malonu.
pleasant:NAGR
'To give advice, we know, is always easy and pleasant.' (CCLL)

(40) **Hearsay → reportive**
Kapitono veidas turi latviškų bruožų, o latviai,
'The captain's face has got Latvian features, and Latvians
***žinia**, visada buvo geri karininkai ....*
message:NOM.SG always be:PST.3 good:NOM.PL.M officer:NOM.PL
are known to have always been good officers...' (CCLL)

The given reportive reading in (40), as opposed to generic inferential *žinia* 'be known to' in (38) and (39), is not based on generic inference. The evidence about Latvians being good officers in this case is based on hearsay or inferred from it.

The opinion-based evidential *manoma* 'think-that'PP.PRS.NAGR can be also regarded as corresponding to the English passive matrices *be thought/believed to, be supposed to*, which are markers of evidentiality (Noël 2001). In academic Lithuanian, *manoma* 'be thought to' functions basically as an evidential CTP. When it parentheticalizes, it prefers the medial position in the sentence (as discussed in Section 3) and retains its evidential meaning, e.g.,

(41) *Kultūrinė salota, **manoma**, kilo*
cultured:NOM.SG.F lettuce:NOM.SG think:PP.PRS.NAGR develop:PST.3
iš Vakarų Europoje ... augančios ... rūšies.
from Western Europe:LOC.SG growing:GEN.SG.F species:GEN.SG
'Cultured lettuce is believed to have come from the species growing in Western Europe.' (CorALit)

The meaning conveyed is intersubjective, i.e., based on shared knowledge. When used parenthetically, it is non-addressable like the other parentheticals under study. It is always the content of the 'host' clause that is addressed by tag questions *tikrai?* 'really', *ar ne?* lit. 'whether not'. This fact also supports the claim made that these expressions are undergoing grammaticalization.

The truth-based parenthetical *tiesa* 'actually, really' is also a marker of evidentiality and expresses a circumstantial inferential meaning as in the following example:

(42) *Lankytojų,   **tiesa**,   be   mūsų   daugiau   nėra.*
    customer:GEN.PL actually   without   us:GEN   more   NEG:be:PRS.3
    'Actually/in fact, there are no more customers without us.' (CCLL)

Tiesa 'actually, really' can combine both features of actuality and subjectivity, which can lead to the meaning of assessment of truth with a high degree of confidence on the part of the speaker as in (36):

(43) *Bolševikai,   **tiesa**,   dabar   valdo,*
    Bolshevik:NOM.PL   truth:NOM.SG   now   rule:PRS.3
    bet   ar   ta   jų   valdžia   ilgam?
    but   Q   this   their   power:NOM.SG   long:DAT.SG.M
    'Bolsheviks are really in power now but is their rule for long?' (CCLL)

The initial *tiesa* 'actually, really' is predominantly used as the truth attester *really* in English (cf. Paradis 2003: 198), e.g.,

(44) ***Tiesa**,   vėjo ...   malūnai   žinomi*
    truth:NOM.SG   wind:GEN.SG   mill:NOM.PL   known:NOM.PL.M
    nuo   neatmenamų   laikų.
    from   immemorial:GEN.PL   time:GEN.PL
    'Really/in truth, windmills have been known from time immemorial.'
    (CorALit)

As a discourse marker, *tiesa* 'actually, really' can also perform a number of other functions (like emphasizing, clarifying, changing the subject, etc.); however, they will not be dealt with in this chapter.

As was discussed and illustrated in the introductory section, the perception-based parentheticals *matyt* 'evidently' and *atrodo* 'apparently' are evidentials proper. As the source of information is always inference, they belong to the type of indirect evidentials. Alongside the distinction made between their evidential meanings in terms of non-perceptual inference (*matyt* 'evidently') and circumstantial (*atrodo* 'apparently') inference, mention can be also made of the difference in the degree of non-factuality they seem to be able to indicate. *Atrodo* 'apparently' tends to express a lesser degree of probability regarding the situation or event assessed by the speaker, while *matyt* 'evidently' looks to denote a somewhat lesser degree of non-factuality, which at the same time can imply a higher confidence of the speaker. Compare examples (45) and (46), where the use of *matyt* 'evidently' in (46) is blocked because of the speaker's common-sense knowledge and conjectural inference is incompatible with the counterfactual content 'that a splitting headache can blow up':

(45) Galva   plyšta   iš   skausmo,   kad
     head:NOM.SG   split:PRS.3   from   ache:GEN.SG COMP
     atrodo   sprogs.
     apparently   explode:FUT.3
     'I've got a splitting headache. It seems that my head will explode.'

(46) Galva   plyšta   iš   skausmo,   kad
     head:NOM.SG   split:PRS.3   from   ache:GEN.SG COMP
     ****matyt** sprogs.
     evidently   explode:FUT.3
     'I've got a splitting headache. Evidently my head will explode'

Moreover, the evidential meaning expressed by *matyt* 'evidently' correlates with factuality from the point of view of the author, while *atrodo* 'apparently' is more epistemic. These two multifunctional stance adverbials can also function as hedging devices in academic Lithuanian (for more details, see Šinkūnienė 2011, 2012).

In summary, all the parenthetical elements discussed are evidential. The speaker's judgment can be based on inference or hearsay; hence, they are inferential or reportive evidentials, i.e., markers of indirect evidentiality. They can also develop other epistemic qualifications, and depending on the context, these evidentials can be used to express the speaker's confidence in the validity of the proposition.

5 Concluding remarks

The basic questions dealt with above have concerned the shift of meaning and function of some parenthetical CTPs, which are regarded as non-morphological realizations of evidentiality in Lithuanian. As frequency of occurrence has been regarded as a very important indicator/factor of possible meaning change, quantitative parameters have been taken into consideration. An attempt has been also made to offer evidence in support of the hypothesis that the paths of semantic change and syntactic behavior of the CTPs under study share some features in common. All of these expressions might be said to be prototypically lexical items, which can be used as CTPs and due to the complementizer omission they can easily parentheticalize and acquire a variety of functions: from adverbial to discourse markers. Thus, it is not only diachronic development but also synchronic relations that can offer information on the relationship between grammatical and non-morphological (lexical) evidentiality.

All the expressions analyzed when used as parentheticals are markers of indirect evidentiality. These expressions can be traced back to the lexical items they are related to and undergo shifts in meaning that can lead to semantic bleaching. As has been observed in many works, it is not only the purely metaphorical extension of meaning, which seems to be at work in the process of adverbialization. The role of the construction an expression occurs in most frequently is an important factor and a driving force influencing the meaning shifts and functioning of these lexical items. In the given case, a parenthetical use is directly related to the ability of a lexical expression to function as a CTP, meaning that it can have scope over a proposition. Therefore, the acquisition of proposition-wide scope via being used as a CTP clause seems to be one of the positive conditions that can trigger further movement toward its flexibility, especially with the omission of the complementizer.

When used parenthetically, all the expressions develop the meaning and functions that are characteristic of sentence adverbials: no propositional meaning, non-addressability, high syntactic flexibility (increase in syntactic distributional properties), paradigmatic reduction, semantic shift. The parenthetical expressions analyzed can be regarded as evidential adverbials that cannot be said to have utterly lost their link with their 'source', a lexical item the connection with which is still obvious and transparent, although some of them, like *matyt* 'evidently' or *žinoma* 'of course, certainly', *tiesa* 'really/actually', can be said to have advanced further on the path toward grammaticalization. Their patterns of use contain a very low percentage of their use as full lexical items. The only expression that persists to function as a CTP clause is *manoma* 'be thought/believed to' because its parenthetical use in the medial position is fairly low in academic Lithuanian (7% in its CorALit concordance). Grammaticalization of the evidential realizations under study can also be supported by the feature of inherent non-addressability (Boye & Harder 2007: 586), which is characteristic of their meaning.

All of these items undergo adverbialization, however differently from the cline described by Traugott and Dasher (2002). These evidential adverbials do not start as predication adverbials. By contrast, they come from CTP clauses that acquire freedom by reductions occurring in their construction and start functioning as sentence adverbials. Their positional flexibility is triggered by the omission of the complementizer. Then these evidential adverbials can proceed further by acquiring the function of discourse markers by way of conveying subjective and inter-subjective meanings that demonstrate various aspects of author's involvement. Thus, they are multifunctional and the range of their semantic-functional variation is synchronically observable in the use of present-day Lithuanian.

Acknowledgments

The research is in progress, and this pilot study has been partially carried out within the framework of project no. LIT-2-34 (*Author Stance in the Lithuanian Academic Discourse*) funded by the Research Council of Lithuania, and the kind assistance of my doctoral student Erika Jasionytė is very much appreciated. I am also pleased to acknowledge partial sponsorship of an MA student Inga Pranckevičiūtė's research practice at the Corpus Lab of the Faculty of Philology carried out within the framework of the project "Promotion of Students' Scientific Activities", which is implemented by the Research Council of Lithuania and is a part of "The Researchers Career Programme (2007–2013)" initiated by the Ministry of Education and Science. Special thanks are due to the reviewers and editors for their constructive criticism and advice, which has been very beneficial when working on the revision of the chapter. And last but not least, I wish to express my gratitude to Mark Fearon for his editing of the text.

Abbreviations

Data sources

CCLL   Corpus of Contemporary Lithuanian Language (http://tekstynas.vdu.lt/)
CorALit Corpus of Academic Lithuanian (http://coralit.lt)
DLL   Dictionary of the Lithuanian Language (www.lkz.lt).

Glosses

1	first person	CTP	complement taking predicate
2	second person	DAT	dative
3	third person	DEF	definite
ACC	accusative	F	feminine
AP	active participle	FUT	future
COMP	complementizer	GEN	genitive

GER	gerund	PL	plural
IMP	imperative	PP	passive participle
INF	infinitive	PRS	present
INS	instrumental	PROG	progressive
LOC	locative	PST	past
M	masculine	Q	question particle/marker
NAGR	non-agreeing	SG	singular
NEG	negation, negative	VOC	vocative
NOM	nominative		

References

Aijmer, Karin. 1997. *I think* – an English modal particle. In Toril Swan & Olaf J. Westwik (eds.) *Modality in Germanic languages*, 1–47. Berlin, New York: Mouton de Gruyter.

Aijmer, Karin. 2003. Discourse particles in contrast: The case of *in fact* and *actually*. In Andrew Wilson, Paul Rayson & Tony McEnery (eds.) *Corpus linguistics by the Lune. A Festschrift for Geoffrey Leech*, 23–35. Frankfurt am Main: Peter Lang.

Aikhenvald, Alexandra Yu. 2004. *Evidentiality*. Oxford: Oxford University Press.

Aikhenvald, Alexandra Yu. 2007. Information source and evidentiality: What can we conclude? *Rivista di Linguistica* 19(1): 207–227.

Ambrazas, Vytautas. 1977a. Netiesioginės nuosakos *(modus relativus)* paplitimas ir kilmės problema [Oblique mood and the problem of its origin]. *Lietuvių kalbotyros klausimai* 17: 7–54.

Ambrazas, Vytautas (ed.). 1997b. *Lithuanian grammar*. Vilnius: Baltos Lankos.

Ambrazas, Vytautas. 2006. *Lietuvių kalbos istorinė sintaksė* [Historical syntax of the Lithuanian language]. Vilnius: Lietuvių kalbos instituto leidykla.

Arkadiev, Peter. 2012. Participial complementation in Lithuanian. In Volker Gast & Holger Diessel (eds.) *Clause linkage in cross-linguistic perspective: Data-driven approaches to cross-clausal syntax,* 285–334. Berlin, New York: Mouton de Gruyter.

Biber, Douglas, Stig Johansson, Geoffrey Leech, Susan Conrad & Edward Finegan. 1999. *Longman grammar of spoken and written English*. London: Longman.

Boye, Kasper. 2012. *Epistemic meaning (A crosslinguistic and functional-cognitive study)*. Berlin, New York: Mouton de Gruyter.

Boye, Kasper & Peter Harder. 2007. Complement-taking predicates. Usage and linguistic structure. *Studies in Language* 31(3): 569–606.

Boye, Kasper & Peter Harder. 2009. Evidentiality. Linguistic categories and grammaticalization. *Functions of Language* 16(1): 9–43.

Brinton, Laurel J. 2008. *The comment clause in English*. Cambridge: Cambridge University Press.

Cornillie, Bert. 2007. *Evidentiality and Epistemic Modality in Spanish (Semi-) Auxiliaries: A Cognitive-Functional Approach*. (Applications of Cognitive Linguistics 5.) Berlin/New York: Mouton de Gruyter.

Cornillie, Bert. 2009. Evidentiality and epistemic modality. *Functions of Language* 16(1): 44–62.

Dendale, Patrik & Julie Van Bogaert. 2007. A semantic description of French lexical evidential markers and the classification of evidentials. *Rivista di Linguistica* 19(1): 65–98.
Diewald, Gabriele & Elena Smirnova. 2010. Evidentiality in European languages: The lexical grammatical distinction. In Gabriele Diewald & Elena Smirnova (eds.) *Linguistic realization of evidentiality in European languages,* 1–14. Berlin, New York: Mouton De Gruyter.
Downing, Angela. 2006. The English pragmatic marker *surely* and its functional counterparts in Spanish. In Karin Aijmer & Anne-Marie Simon-Vandenbergen (eds.) *Pragmatic markers in contrast,* 39–58. Amsterdam: Elsevier.
Fischer, Olga. 2007. The development of English parentheticals: A case of grammaticalization? In Ute Smit, Stefan Dollinger, Julia Hüttner, Gunther Kaltenböck & Ursula Lutzky (eds.) *Tracing English through time. Explorations in language variation,* 99–114. Wenen: Braumüller.
Gronemeyer, Claire. 1997. *Evidentiality in Lithuanian.* Working papers, 46: 93–112. Lund University.
Gronemeyer, Claire & Aurelia Usonienė. 2001. Complementation in Lithuanian. In Claire Gronemeyer, *Lying the boundaries of syntax: Studies in the interfaces between syntax, semantics and lexicon,* 105–135. Lund University.
Hasselgård, Hilde. 2010. *Adjunct adverbials in English.* Cambridge: Cambridge University Press.
Holvoet, Axel. 2001. On the paradigm of the oblique mood in Lithuanian and Latvian. *Linguistica Baltica* 9: 69–86.
Holvoet, Axel. 2004. Evidencialumo kategorija [The category of evidentiality]. In Axel Holvoet & Loreta Semėnienė (eds.) *Gramatinių kategorijų tyrimai,* 105–120. Vilnius: Lietuvių kalbos institutas.
Holvoet, Axel. 2007. *Mood and modality in Baltic.* Kraków: Wydawnictwo Uniwersytetu Jagiellońskiego.
Kaltenböck, Gunther. 2007. Position, prosody, and scope: The case of English comment clauses. *Vienna English Working Papers* 16(1): 3–38.
Kehayov, Petar. 2008. *An areal-typological perspective to evidentiality: The cases of the Balkan and Baltic linguistic areas.* Tartu: Tartu University Press PhD dissertation.
Lavine, E. James. 2006. Is there a passive evidential strategy in Lithuanian? In Jacqueline Bunting et al. (eds.) *Papers from the 42nd regional meeting of the Chicago Linguistic Society,* 41–55. Chicago: Chicago Linguistics Society.
Leech, Geoffrey. 2003. Modality on the move: The English modal auxiliaries 1961–1992. In Roberta Facchinetti, Manfred Krug & Frank Palmer (eds.) *Modality in Contemporary English,* 191–240. Berlin/New York: Mouton De Gruyter.
Mortelmans, Tanja. 2000. On the 'evidential' nature of 'epistemic' use of the German modals *müssen* and *sollen. Belgian Journal of Linguistics* 14: 131–148.
Nevalainen, Terttu. 2004. Three perspectives on grammaticalization: Lexico-grammar, corpora and historical sociolinguistics. In Hans Lindqvist & Christian Mair (eds.) *Corpus approaches to grammaticalization in English,* 1–31. Amsterdam, Philadelphia: John Benjamins.
Noël, Dirk. 2001. The passive matrices of English infinitival complement clauses. Evidentials on the road to auxiliarihood? *Studies in Language* 25(2): 255–296.
Noël, Dirk. 2002. Believe-type matrix verbs and their complements. Corpus-based investigations of their functions in discourse. Universiteit Gent PhD dissertation.
Newmeyer, Frederick J. 2010. A critique of Thompson's analysis of object complements. In Kasper Boye & Elisabeth Engberg-Pedersen (eds.) *Language usage and language structure,* 3–44. Berlin, New York: Walter de Gruyter.

Noonan, Michael. 1985. Complementation. In Timothy Shopen (ed.) *Language typology and syntactic description*, Vol. 2, 42–140. Cambridge: Cambridge University Press.
Paradis, Carita. 2003. Between epistemic modality and degree: The case of *really*. In Roberta Facchinetti, Manfgred Krug & Frank Palmer (eds.) *Modality in contemporary English*, 191–217. Berlin, New York: Mouton de Gruyter.
Pietrandrea, Paola. 2007. The grammatical nature of some epistemic-evidential adverbs in spoken Italian. *Rivista di Linguistica* 19(1): 39–63.
Plungian, Vladimir. 2001. The place of evidentiality within the universal grammatical space. *Journal of Pragmatics* 33: 349–357.
Pusch, Claus D. 2009. Noun-based complement-taking constructions as modal markers: Distributional and discourse-functional aspects in a Romance and cross-linguistic perspective. In *Societas Linguistica Europaea 42nd Annual Meeting. Book of Abstracts. Workshop on "Modality at Work"*, 68–69. Lisbon: Universidade de Lisboa.
Rissanen, Matti. 1999. On the adverbialization of RATHER: Surfing for historical data. In Hilde Hasselgård & Signe Oksefjell (eds.) *Out of corpora: Studies in honour of Stig Johansson*, 49–59. Amsterdam, Atlanta, GA: Rodopi.
Ruskan, Anna. 2012. Evidential adjectives in Lithuanian academic discourse. *Kalbotyra* 64(3): 103–123.
Simon-Vandenbergen, Anne-Marie & Karin Aijmer. 2002–2003. The expectation marker *of course* in a cross-linguistic perspective. *Languages in Contrast* 4(1): 13–43.
Simon-Vandenbergen, Anne-Marie & Karin Aijmer. 2007. *The semantic field of modal certainty. A corpus-based study of English adverbs*. Berlin, New York: Mouton de Gruyter.
Šinkūnienė, Jolanta. 2011. *Autoriaus pozicijos švelninimas rašytiniame moksliniame diskurse: gretinamasis tyrimas*. [Hedging in written academic discourse: A cross-linguistic and cross-disciplinary study]. Vilnius University PhD dissertation.
Šinkūnienė, Jolanta. 2012. Adverbials as hedging devices in Lithuanian academic discourse: A cross-disciplinary study. In Aurelija Usonienė, Nicole Nau & Ineta Dabašinskienė (eds.) *Multiple perspectives in linguistic research on Baltic languages*, 137–167. Newcastle upon Tyne: Cambridge Scholars Publishing.
Smetona, Antanas & Aurelija Usonienė. 2012. Autoriaus pozicijos adverbialai ir adverbializacija lietuvių mokslo kalboje. [Stance adverbials and adverbialization in academic Lithuanian]. *Kalbotyra* 2012(3): 124–139.
Šolienė, Audronė. 2012. Epistemic necessity in a parallel corpus: Lithuanian vs. English. In Aurelija Usonienė, Nicole Nau & Ineta Dabašinskienė (eds.) *Multiple perspectives in linguistic research on Baltic languages*, 10–42. Newcastle upon Tyne: Cambridge Scholars Publishing.
Squartini, Mario. 2008. Lexical vs. grammatical evidentiality in French and Italian. *Linguistics* 46(5): 917–947.
Thompson, Sandra. 2002. "Object complements" and conversation: Towards a realistic account. *Studies in Language* 26: 125–164.
Traugott, Elizabeth Closs. 2007. Discourse markers, modal particles, and contrastive analysis, synchronic and diachronic. *Catalan Journal of Linguistics* 6: 139–157.
Traugott, Elizabeth Closs. 2010. (Inter)ubjectivity and (inter)subjectification: A reassessment. In Kristin Davidse, Lieven Vandelanotte & Hubert Cuykens (eds.) *Subjectification, intersubjectification and grammaticalization*, 29–74. Walter de Gruyter.
Traugott, Elisabeth Closs & Richard B. Dasher. 2002. *Irregularity in syntax*. Cambridge: Cambridge University Press.

Usonienė, Aurelia. 2002. *On syntax-semantics interface: Verbs of perception in English and Lithuanian*. Vilnius University Dr. habil. dissertation.
Usonienė, Aurelia. 2003. Extension of meaning: Verbs of perception in English and Lithuanian. In Katarzyna M. Jaszczolt & Ken Turner (eds.) *Meaning through language contrast: The Cambridge papers*, Vol. 1, 193–220. Amsterdam, Philadelphia: John Benjamins.
Usonienė, Aurelia & Audrone Šoliene. 2010. Choice of strategies in realizations of epistemic possibility in English and Lithuanian. A corpus-based study. *International Journal of Corpus Linguistics* 15(2): 291–316.
Usonienė, Aurelija. 2012. Komplementiniai predikatai ir jų multifunkcionalumas. Lietuvių kalbos tekstynais paremtas tyrimas. [Complement taking predicates and their multifunctionality. A Lithuanian corpora-based study]. *Darbai ir dienos* 58: 223–233.
Usonienė, Aurelija. 2013. On the morphosyntactic status of complement-taking predicate clauses in Lithuanian. *Acta Linguistica Hafniensia* 45(1): 73–99
Valeckienė, Adelė. 1998. *Funkcinė lietuvių kalbos gramatika* [Functional grammar of Lithuanian]. Vilnius: Mokslo ir enciklopedijų leidybos institutas.
Van Bogaert, Julie. 2009. *The Grammar of complement-taking mental predicate constructions in present-day spoken British English. A corpus-based study of their syntactic, semantic and pragmatic behaviour as members of a constructional taxonomy*. University of Gent, Faculty of Arts and Philosophy PhD dissertation.
Verhagen, Arie. 2005. *Constructions of intersubjectivity: Discourse, syntax, and cognition*. Oxford: Oxford University Press.
Verhagen, Arie. 2010. Usage, structure, scientific explanation, and the role of abstraction by linguists and by language users. In Kasper Boye & Elisabeth Engberg-Pedersen (eds.) *Language usage and language structure*, 45–72. Berlin, New York: Walter de Gruyter.
Whitt, Richard. J. 2009. Auditory evidentiality in English and German: The case of perception verbs. *Lingua* 119: 1083–1095.
Wiemer, Björn. 2006. Grammatical evidentiality in Lithianian (A typological assessment). *Baltistica* 36: 33–49.
Wiemer, Björn. 2007a. Kosvennaja zasvidetel'stvovannost' v litovskom jazyke. [Marking of indirectness in Lithuanian]. In Viktor S. Xrakovskij (ed.) *Ėvidencial'nost' v jazykax Evropy i Azii*. [Evidentiality in the languages of Europe and Asia], 197–240. Saint Petersburg: Nauka.
Wiemer, Björn. 2007b. Lexical markers of evidentiality in Lithuanian. *Rivista di Linguistica* 19(1): 173–208.
Wiemer, Björn. 2010. Hearsay in European languages: Toward an integrative account of grammatical and lexical marking. In Gabriele Diewald & Elena Smirnova (eds.) *Linguistic realization of evidentiality in European languages*, 56–130. Berlin, New York: Mouton De Gruyter.
Wierzbicka, Anna. 2006. *English: Meaning and culture*. Oxford: Oxford University Press.

Kirill Kozhanov
12 Lithuanian indefinite pronouns in contact

1 Introduction

The "era" of Lithuanian contact studies truly began in the 1960s and 1970s of the last century. There was more attention paid to the problem of language contact after investigating the Lithuanian dialects spoken outside of Lithuania and thus surrounded and dominated by other languages. Before that, the issue of borrowing in Lithuanian dialects was considered with regard to Slavic influence in old Lithuanian texts (Skardžius 1931) and some Eastern Aukštaitian dialects (e.g., Otrębski 1932). Dialectal studies were continued in the 1950s when dialects were systematically investigated for the atlas of the Lithuanian language database (Morkūnas 1977–1991). In the 1960s and 1970s, a number of articles (e.g., Vidugiris 1960, Grinaveckienė 1969, etc.) and monographs (e.g., Smoczyński 1972) on the Aukštaitian dialects surrounded by other languages appeared. This study evolved into a more general investigation of Slavic-Lithuanian contacts in the domain of phonetics and phonology, conducted by Tamara Sudnik (1975), as well as several collections of articles (e.g., Toporov 1972), which initiated the still-ongoing series *Balto-slav'anskie issledovanija* [Balto-Slavic studies] published in Moscow. However, attention was mostly paid to the description of the dialects and their phonetics and lexical borrowings. The issues of grammatical borrowing were discussed only sporadically: Apart from the aforementioned article by Grinavickienė (1969), only a few more works fully devoted to grammatical borrowing can be named (e.g., Grinaveckienė 1974, Ambrazas 1985); for a recent overview, see Wiemer (2009: 357–366). One exception, however, is an interesting attempt to describe the Circum-Baltic language area as a Sprachbund, made by Dahl and Koptjevskaja-Tamm (2001). Works by Wiemer (e.g., 2003, 2004, 2009) and Wiemer, Vladyko, and Kardelis (2004) have also significantly contributed to the investigation of Lithuanian language contacts and the linguistic description of the area.

Over the last 30 years, significant developments in contact linguistics have been achieved (see, for example, Matras 2009: 1–2), including cross-linguistic studies of grammatical borrowings (see e.g., Matras & Sakel 2007). In this chapter, I address the issue of grammatical borrowing in Lithuanian and aim to show how complex, and unfortunately, under-investigated, this field of study is using as the example indefinite pronouns.

In the fundamental cross-linguistic work on indefinites supplied by Haspelmath (1997: 184–186), two primary means of borrowing indefiniteness markers are singled out: direct borrowing and calquing. In a more recent work, Matras (2009: 198–199) adds more examples of direct borrowing not only of indefiniteness markers, but of whole indefinite pronouns. In this article, I will use the terminology of borrowings as identified by Sakel (2007): matter loans (MAT), in which both function and phonological form are replicated in the recipient language, and pattern borrowing (PAT), in which only the functional pattern of the source language is replicated. The following variants of borrowed patterns are listed: "organization, distribution, and mapping of grammatical and semantic meaning" (Sakel 2007: 15). The notion of MAT- and PAT-loans is well described in the literature: For example, earlier the terms "importation" and "substitution" (Haugen 1950), "borrowing" and "transfer" (Treffers-Daller & Mougeon 2005: 95), or "global" and "selective copying" (Johanson 2008: 64) and many others were proposed to MAT- and PAT-borrowings, respectively.

Since the situations most favorable for borrowing are those of "unidirectional bilingualism with weak normative support of the recipient language" (Matras 2009: 198), I will mostly use the data from Lithuanian dialects under strong influence of Slavic languages, i.e., eastern and southern Aukštaitian dialects. Nevertheless, the data from the Corpus of the Modern Lithuanian Language (Dabartinės lietuvių kalbos tekstynas, LKT, http://tekstynas.vdu.lt/), the Dictionary of the Lithuanian Language (Lietuvių kalbos žodynas, LKŽ, http://www.lkz.lt/), and the Internet will also be taken into account, as they contain many examples of dialectal and colloquial forms. To illustrate Polish data, the examples were taken from the Corpus of the Polish Language (Korpus języka polskiego IPI PAN, KJP, http://korpus.pl/), and the National Corpus of Polish (Narodowy korpus języka polskiego, NKJP, http://nkjp.pl/). In Section 2, I will discuss the system of Lithuanian indefinite pronouns, its structure and functions in standard language, and analyze the differences that can be found in the dialects with a special focus on the Lithuanian dialect of Ramaškonys (Belarusian *Romaškancy*) spoken in northwestern Belarus. Then I will discuss the indefiniteness markers[1] that were borrowed directly (MAT-borrowing) in Section 3 and calqued (PAT-borrowing) in Section 4. In Section 5, I will summarize the results of the article. Although I will analyze the following markers as borrowed, Haspelmath's caveat that sometimes "it is hard to prove that language contact played a role in the creation of a particular type of indefiniteness marker because it might as well have arisen independently" (1997: 186) will be kept in mind.

---

[1] It should be noted that the languages under analysis do not possess grammaticalized indefinite articles that is why indefinite articles will not be discussed.

2 Lithuanian indefinite pronouns

2.1 The system of Standard Lithuanian

According to the criteria proposed by Haspelmath (1997: 10–12), indefinite pronouns consist of an element that refers to an ontological category (thing, person, place, etc.), which is expressed in Lithuanian by interrogatives, and an indefiniteness marker. Thus, in Lithuanian, it is possible to single out the following basic series of indefinite pronouns with the markers *kaž-*, *nors-*, *bet-*, *kai-*, and *nie-*. There is also an unmarked series of indefinites, formally identical to interrogatives: *kas*, *koks*, *kuris*, etc. In the language of fiction, *X-ne-X* series (e.g., *kas ne kas* 'someone') can be used. There is also an indefinite determiner *joks* used with negation.

Almost all of the above-mentioned indefinite pronouns contain units referring to the following ontological categories: thing, person, property, place, time, manner, amount, and determiner. The *kaž-*series also includes a "why"-based pronoun *kažkodėl* 'for some reason.'[2] On the other hand, only four elements of the *X-ne-X* series (*kas ne kas* 'someone', *kur ne kur* 'somewhere', *kuris ne kuris* 'some', and *kada ne kada* 'from time to time') are normally used.

Haspelmath (1997: 31–52) postulates nine main functions that can be expressed by indefinites: (1) specific known, (2) specific unknown, (3) irrealis non-specific, (4) conditional, (5) question, (6) comparative, (7) free choice, (8) indirect negation, and (9) direct negation (see 1–9).

(1) Turi-u   **kai k-ą**   tiktai   tau   vien-ai
    have-PRS.1SG   INDF what-ACC.SG   only   you(SG):DAT.   one-DAT.SG.F
    pasaky-ti.[3]
    say-INF
    'I've got something to say that's for your ears alone.'

(2) **Kažk-as**   atėj-o.
    who:INDF-NOM.SG   COME-PST.3
    'Somebody came (I don't know who).'

(3) Aplanky-k-ite   mane   **kada nors**.
    VISIT-IMP-2PL   I:ACC   when INDF
    'Visit me sometime.'

---

2 As an anonymous reviewer pointed out, a 'why'-indefinite exists neither in Polish nor in Latvian and can be probably considered a result of East Slavic influence. However, the form *czemuś* 'for some reason' does exist in Polish, so the fact of influence is not so obvious.
3 Unmarked examples (1)–(3), (5), and (7) are taken from Haspelmath (1997).

(4) Jeigu **k-as** skund-ė, tai melav-o.
    if who:INDF-NOM complain-PST.3 then lie-PST.3
    'If someone complained, he lied.' (LKT)

(5) Tu skait-ei **k-ą nors** apie maj-ų
    you-NOM.SG read-PST.2SG what-ACC INDF about MAYA-GEN.PL
    kultūr-ą?
    culture-ACC.SG
    'Have you read anything about the culture of the Mayas?'

(6) Man buv-o daug malon-iau š-ie šlap-i
    I:DAT be-PST.3 much pleasant-COMP this-NOM.PL wet-NOM.PL
    fejerverk-ai
    firework-NOM.PL
    negu **kok-ia** praktišk-a dovan-a.
    than what:INDEF-NOM.SG.F practical-NOM.SG.F present-NOM.SG
    'These wet fireworks made me feel much better than any practical gift
    [I might have gotten].' (LKT)

(7) Nupirk man k-ą nors paskaity-ti – O k-ą? –
    buy:IMP(2SG) I:DAT what-ACC INDF read-INF and what-ACC
    Bet k-ą.
    INDF what-ACC
    'Buy me something to read. – What? – Whatever.'

(8) J-ie sudauž-ė kab-ant-į žibint-ą,
    they-NOM break-PST.3 hang-PRS.PA-ACC.SG.M torch-ACC.SG
    be **joki-o** šūvi-o.
    without any-GEN.SG.M shot-GEN.SG
    'They broke a hanging lamp without any shot.' (LKT)

(9) Bet aš **niek-o** ne-suprasi-u, aš toki-a
    but I:NOM nothing-GEN NEG-understand:FUT-1SG I:NOM such-NOM.SG.F
    kvail-a.
    stupid-NOM.SG.F
    'But I will understand nothing, I am so stupid.' (LKT)

A semantic map, showing which functions can be expressed by which Lithuanian indefinites, is also provided in the appendix of the book (Haspelmath 1997: 275). The distribution of the functions of Lithuanian indefinites has been studied in more detail and revised by Kozhanov (2011). The modified distributional map of Lithuanian indefinites taken from the latter work is provided in Figure 1. Ø stands for a lack of any marker as in (4) and (6).

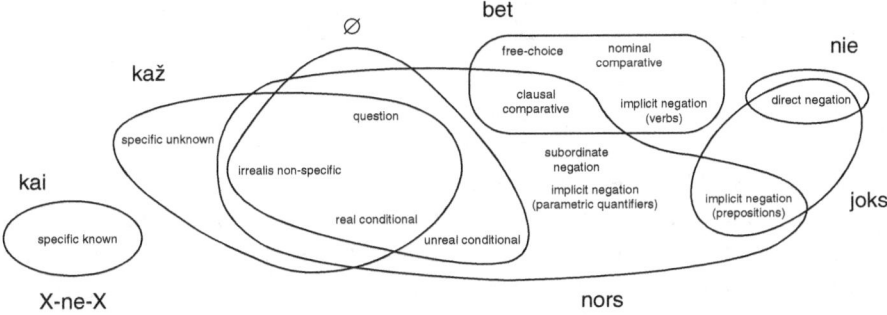

Fig. 1: Functions of Lithuanian indefinite pronouns.

2.2 Lithuanian dialectal indefinites: The system of the Ramaškonys dialect

Indefinites in Lithuanian have never been discussed from the perspective of language contact. Short comments and description of indefinites that differ from the ones found in the standard language can be sometimes found in grammatical descriptions of dialects (e.g., Jašinskaitė 1959: 193, Vidugiris 1960: 123, Aleksandravičius 1964: 128). In these cases, however, the description of the semantics of indefinites is usually limited to their translation into the standard language. Probably, the most comprehensive information on the dialectal variety of indefinites is provided by Zinkevičius (1966: 436–440) in his fundamental work on Lithuanian dialectology. The Slavic origin of some of the dialectal indefiniteness markers (*bile-*, *ne-*) is indicated in this work; however, Zinkevičius does not discuss the issues of their semantics or use, nor does he match them with their counterparts in the source language. More examples of borrowed or calqued indefiniteness markers can be found on the website of the State Commission of the Lithuanian Language (*Valstybinė lietuvių kalbos komisija*, VLKK, http://www.vlkk.lt/). This commission aims at addressing issues related to the Lithuanian language policy. One component of the site is a list of non-standard forms that speakers of Lithuanian should avoid in their speech. The *-tai* and *ne-* markers of indefinites are part of this list (see Sections 4.1 and 4.2). In the answers of the consultancy bank, provided by VLKK, the *bile* marker is also mentioned (see Section 3.2).

A major difference between Lithuanian dialects and the standard language with respect to indefinite pronouns is the clear tendency to use bare interrogative-indefinites instead of series with overt markers in the dialects. Such a trend, mostly for the irrealis non-specific function, undoubtedly exists in colloquial speech as well. However, in dialects, bare interrogative-indefinites usually replace both the *nors-* and *kaž-*series, i.e., the distinction of specific/non-specific indefinites is weak and likely to disappear. The free-choice function (the *bet-*series in Standard Lithuanian) is often expressed by constructions like *kur nori* 'where you want; wherever you want', *kiek nori* 'how much you want; as much as you want', etc. In other words, within a dialect, fewer indefiniteness markers are used, and indefiniteness is often expressed by non-grammaticalized constructions.

As an example, I will discuss the results of an analysis of approximately 200 pages of texts from the dialect of Ramaškonys, the southernmost South Aukštaitian dialect of Lithuanian (Tuomienė 2008). Ramaškonys is now a village in the Hrodna region of Belarus where for many years Lithuanian existed in a situation of bilingualism and multilingualism. As a result, the dialect has experienced significant influence from Slavic languages. All indefinite pronouns found in these texts have been analyzed with respect to their functions. First, I compared the series with standard indefiniteness markers found in the texts (the number of examples is shown in Table 1) to the functions expressed by these series in the standard language. In most cases, the low incidence of the examples demonstrates that this series is not usually used in the dialect.

Among 288 examples of indefinite pronouns I have found in the texts from Ramaškonys, only negative pronouns seem to be identical to the ones in the standard language. However, even among the negative indefinites, there are examples of MAT-borrowings from Polish, e.g., *nigdy* 'never' in example (10).

(10) Nog   t-o,   sak-o,   čės-o   **nigdy**   nėj-au
     from   that-GEN.SG.M   say-PRS.3   time-GEN.SG   never   NEG:go-PST.1SG
     švent-ą   dien-ą   aš   palavo-t.[4]
     saint-ACC.SG   day-ACC.SG   I:NOM   hunt-INF
     'After that time, he says, I never went hunting on a Saint Day.' (Tuomienė 2008: 116)

Tab. 1: Standard indefinites in the texts of the dialect of Ramaškonys

kaž-	nors	kai	bet	nie-	joks	X ne X	Ø
3	2	1	1	61	17	–	76

---

4 Since I analyze morphology and do not need phonetic dialectal features, I use transposed spelling of the examples proposed by Bacevičiūtė et al. (2004: 21).

The non-specific functions are usually expressed by bare interrogative-indefinites. The two examples of the use of the *nors-* indefiniteness marker found in the sample are probably influenced by the standard language. In one of these examples, the pronoun is used "incorrectly", i.e., the indefinite pronoun, which in the standard language appears only in the non-specific function, is used in the specific context known to the speaker of the dialect:

(11) *Aš   sėdži-u   ir   mezg-u   **k-ą nors**.*[5]
     I:NOM   sit-PRS.1SG   and   knit-PRS.1SG   what-ACC INDF
     'I am sitting and knitting something.' (Tuomienė 2008: 172).

The specific unknown series of indefinites usually has the indefiniteness marker *tai* (seen in a total of 126 examples!). Only three examples with the standard marker *kaž-* were found in the texts, and they should be considered as influenced by the standard language. (Cf. the texts of the Northeast Aukštaitian dialect, spoken around the town of Mielagėnai, eastern Lithuania, in the Ignalina region (Kardelis 2006), where all examples with the *kaž*-marker are indicated as influenced by the standard language (see Kardelis 2006: 60, 110 etc.)). The free-choice function in Ramaškonys is usually expressed by special constructions, as already mentioned above, e.g., *k-nori* (cf. 3). The status of *nori* in such sentences as (12) can probably be viewed as a non-grammaticalized indefiniteness marker, inasmuch as these constructions have the free-choice meaning. Haspelmath (1997: 134–135) considers such constructions to be a source for free-choice indefinites in many languages.

(12) *Materijol-ą   pirk   ir   staty-k   k-ą*
     material-ACC.SG   buy:IMP(2SG)   and   build-IMP(2SG)   what-ACC
     ***nor-i**.*
     want-PRS.2SG
     'Buy material and build whatever you want.' (Tuomienė 2008: 243)

The only example of the use of the *kai-*series seems to calque the construction from the standard language, shown in (13). In such constructions, the *kai-*series is not employed in the specific known function it usually expresses but indicates an indefinite number, cf. Russian *nekotorye* 'some.'

(13) ***Kai kur-ie***   *i   rusišk-ai   maža   kalb-a.*
     INDF what-NOM.PL.M   and   Russian-ADV   little   speak-PRS.3
     'Some (young people) also speak Russian a little.' (Tuomienė 2008: 206)

---

[5] The examples is not from an iterative context, so *nors-*series should not be possible.

I found only two examples in the texts where indefinites are used in the free-choice function. However, one of them, where the marker *bet* (identical to the standard free-choice marker) is used, represents the secondary meaning of free-choice indefinites that can be roughly described as 'something of bad quality, poorly, etc.' (cf. 14).

(14) An-is   ne   **bet kap**   verki-a,   nu   taip   kaip   reiki-a,
     they-NOM.PL   NEG   INDF how   cry-PRS.3   well that   how   need-PRS.3
     verki-a.
     cry-PRS.3
     'They don't *just* cry, they cry like they're supposed to (i.e., weep loudly).'
     (Tuomienė 2008: 206)

This meaning is derived from the free-choice meaning: 'any'>'anything of any quality'>'something of bad quality.' Since no other examples of *bet*-indefinites can be found in the sample, the analyzed example can be considered a borrowing from the standard language.

Another example of the use of indefinites in the free-choice function is calqued from the neighboring Slavic languages: *nors kur* 'anywhere' from Belarusian *xoc' dz'e*, Russian *xot' gd'e* 'anywhere', as in (15). There are more calqued forms in this sentence, cf. *nudavė* 'passed', vs. Standard Lithuanian *išlaikė* 'id.', Russian *sdal* 'passed'; *pastot* 'to enter (university)' vs. Standard Lithuanian *įstoti* 'id.', Russian *postupit'* 'id.'.

(15) Nudav-ė   egzamin-ų,   tai   t-as   tada   jau   galėj-o
     give-PST.3   exam-GEN.PL   so   that-NOM.SG.M   then   already   can-PST.3
     nors kur   pasto-t.
     INDF where   enter-INF
     'He passed the exams, and then he could enter any place (university).'
     (Tuomienė 2008: 123)

There are more examples of indefiniteness markers and even whole indefinite pronouns in this dialect that are directly borrowed or copied. A few words should be said with respect to the marker of the specific indefinite series *-tai*, which is considered to be copied from Slavic *-to*. This marker will be discussed in more detail below. In the dialect of Ramaškonys, instead of the standard demonstrative pronouns *šitas, šita, tai*, the pronouns *itas, ita, itai* are used. However, when used as an indefiniteness marker instead of the dialectal *itai*, the form *tai* occurs, as in (16). Such a form might be explained by the influence of the Slavic *-to* with no initial vowel.

(16) Visa   **kada tai**   itai   brang-iai   kainoj-o,   labai   brang-iai.
     everything   when INDF   this   expensive-ADV   cost-PST.3 very   expensive-ADV
     'Once all this was expensive, very expensive.' (Tuomienė 2008: 243)

There are also examples in which the indefiniteness marker is declined along with the interrogative, cf. (17).

(17) Tadu   pon-as   susimislij-o,   tinai   savo   jau   tinai
     then   lord-NOM.SG   think-PST.3   there   own   already   there
     koki-am t-am   tarn-ui   sak-o.
     what-DAT.SG.M INDF-DAT.SG.M   servant-DAT.SG   say-PRS.3
     'Then the landlord thought it over and told one of his servants.'
                                                              (Tuomienė 2008: 210)

It can be concluded from the investigation of the texts of Ramaškonys that the dialectal system of indefinite pronouns, including their usage, can differ in important respects from that of the standard language, and that language contact can play a role in this divergence. Some indefinites can be entirely replaced by a borrowed counterpart (-*tai* instead of *kaž*-), while others can display variable behavior and be expressed by the markers used in the standard language, as well as by borrowed ones. At the same time, it should be said that the notion of "being replaced" is given from the perspective of the standard language, and the exact time when the non-standard form of indefinite pronoun came into use can hardly be established. In other words, we usually cannot tell with full certainty whether the marker in question was borrowed and has replaced the marker identical to that of the standard language, or it developed independently before the grammaticalization of its counterpart in the standard language. However, the results of this analysis show the main tendencies of the "borrowability" of indefinite pronouns in Lithuanian. A more detailed investigation will be carried out in Section 3.

3 MAT-borrowing of indefinites

Indefinite pronouns are borrowed quite often, as they belong to "the explicit presupposition-processing apparatus" (Matras 2009: 198), i.e., they present new information and at the same time refer to background knowledge and play a large role in the speaker-hearer relationship in communication. As was mentioned above, indefinites are usually borrowed "in situations of unidirectional bilingualism with weak normative support of the recipient language" (Matras 2009: 198). The Lithuanian dialects surrounded by other languages (especially Slavic) represent such a case. However, borrowed indefinites can be found in the speech of the urban population as well.

Both (MAT- and PAT-) types of borrowing indefinites are attested in Lithuanian dialects. Some markers can be directly borrowed from the surrounding languages, e.g., *bile* from Polish, or *abi* from Belarusian. Sometimes borrowed markers are phonetically adapted, cf. the variants of the marker *abi/aby*: the Belarusian sound [ɨ] is kept intact ([abɨ]) or adapted to Lithuanian phonetic system ([ab'i]). Examples of PAT-borrowing can also be found: Instead of the standard specific indefiniteness marker *kaž-*, the form *-tai*, which is calqued from Slavic *to*, is used. In Lithuanian, MAT-borrowing appears in separate dialects (maybe even only in a limited number of cases), e.g., *abi* marker (in the variant of *aby*) borrowed from Belarusian in the Eastern Aukštaitian dialect of Gervėčiai (Belarusian *Herv'aty*), the Hrodna region (Kardelytė 1975: 70), as well as within larger territories, e.g., the *bile*-marker of free-choice indefinites from Polish can be found in many Lithuanian dialects in various regions. Some borrowings occur only in dialectal speech, while others can be found in literary written speech as well. In many cases, the exact source of the borrowing can hardly be firmly established, as the pattern exists in a few languages; *bile* exists not only in Polish but is also used in Belarusian dialects. Some indefiniteness markers are used in all three Slavic languages that surround Lithuanian, e.g., *ne-* in Polish, Belarusian, and Russian. In such cases, the source is marked as "Slavic."

The cases of MAT-borrowings in the domain of indefinite pronouns in Lithuanian are represented by a few examples of the use of the originally Slavic indefiniteness markers.

3.1 Borrowing of *abi*

In the southern Lithuanian dialects, the free-choice marker *abi*, borrowed from Belarusian, can regularly be found. It is represented in both adapted and non-adapted versions *abi* and *aby*, but only the adapted version was included in LKŽ (cf. 18 and 19).

(18) Belarusian
U vixur-y žycc'-a dumk-i čalavek-a l'otaj-uc'
in whirlgig-LOC.SG life-GEN.SG thought-NOM.PL man-GEN.SG fly-PRS.3PL
aby-dze, tol'ki ne l'a svaj-oj duš-y.
indf-where only NEG near own-GEN.SG.F soul-GEN.SG
'In the whirligig of life a person's thoughts fly anywhere except near his soul.'[6]

(19) Lithuanian
Man **abi k-as** ger-ai.
me:DAT INDF what-NOM good-ADV
'Anything is good for me.' (LKŽ)

---

[6] http://tululu.ru/read67906/37/.

It seems quite regular in Lithuanian dialects that not only the indefiniteness marker is borrowed, but also other function words that were a source for the marker (cf., 20).

(20) Kiaul-es   gan-ė,   **abi**   gyv-os   bū-tų.
      pig-ACC.PL   shepherd-PST.3 so   alive-NOM.PL.F   be-SBJV.3
      'They would graze pigs just to stay alive.'

3.2 Borrowing of *bile*

One of the most widespread borrowed indefiniteness markers in Lithuanian dialects is *bile* [b'il'e], which has phonetically non-adapted variants *byle*, *by* [bil'e, bi], *and* the variant *bele(n)* [b'el'en].[7] However, it can also be easily found in urban speech. In LKŽ, almost the full series of *bile* and *by* are represented. Many examples are attested in the Corpus of Lithuanian (cf. 21).

(21) Pas   mus   **bile k-am**   galima   užei-ti...
      at   we.ACC   INDF who-DAT   possible   come-INF
      'Anyone is allowed to drop by our house.' (LKT)

Fraenkel (1962: 42) states that this indefiniteness marker originated from Polish *byle*. It is interesting that the same marker is found in some Latvian dialects,[8] which can be explained either as the direct influence of Polish or by contact with Lithuanian (Fraenkel 1962: 42). A prepositional indefiniteness marker of the same origin and the same meaning *byl'a-* is used in the western dialects of Belarusian as well (Steškovič 1979: 36). The main function of the *bile*-series is expression of the free-choice function (cf. 22).

(22) **Bile katr-a**   merg-a   ai-tų   su   tavim,   kad   tik
      INDF what-NOM.SG.F   girl-NOM.SG   go-SBJV.3   with   you.sg:INS   what   only
      ves-tai!
      marry-SBJV.2SG
      'Any girl would go with you, if only you marry her!' (LKT)

---

[7] Zinkevičius (1966: 436) explains the sound [e] in the last form by the influence of the literary marker *bet*. However, the forms with final *-n*, broadly used in colloquial speech, cannot be easily explained.

[8] It is also used in the Romani variety of Lithuania, cf. *bili kon* 'anyone', *bili so* 'anything' (Beinortienė 2011: 36). It should also be said that no indefiniteness markers of Lithuanian origin are attested in Lithuanian Romani, which can probably be explained by the sociolinguistic situation in the country, as well as by historical circumstances of language development: the Roma people came to Lithuania from the Polish-speaking territories.

In the Lithuanian dialects neighboring with Polish, this marker seems to be the only variant of the free-choice series (see Niewulis 2001: 66).

However, the use of *bile* as an indefiniteness marker seems to be secondary with respect to the function of a particle or conjunction with the meanings 'as soon as, only, only if', since there are dialects where *bile* occurs only as a particle or conjunction (e.g., 23).

(23) **Bile** tik gav-o pinig-ų i išleid-o.
just only get-PST.3 money-GEN.PL and spend-PST.3
'As soon as they got some money, they spent it.' (LKŽ)

The particle function of *bile* is identical to the use of Polish *byle*, which can be a particle or conjunction, cf. the use of the second *byle* in (24), and an indefiniteness marker (although, Polish *byle*-series has marginal status and is only one of the ways to express the free-choice function; Haspelmath 1997: 271).

(24) Polish
Na oślep, tam i z powrot-em, bez wyjść-ia,
blindly there and with return-INS.SG without way.out-GEN.SG
*bez cel-u, **byle** gdzie, **byle** dal-ej.*
without purpose-GEN.SG INDF where only far-COMP
'Blindly, back and forth, with no way-out, with no purpose, anywhere, just to move ahead.' (KJP)

Polish *byle* can also be used in the free-choice function without a pronoun.

(25) Polish
*Sprzedadz-ą nas przy **byle** okazj-i.*
sell:FUT-3PL we:ACC at any occasion-GEN.SG
'They will sell us at any opportunity.' (KJP)

In Polish, the *byle*-series can also have a secondary, negative meaning of bad quality (as discussed above for Lithuanian), like in (26).

(26) Polish
*Odżywia-ł-a się **byle jak**, przez cał-y dzień dodaj-ąc*
nourish-PST-3SG.F REFL INDF how through entire-ACC day:ACC.SG add-NV
sobie energi-i mocn-ą herbat-ą.
yourself:DAT energy-GEN.SG strong-INS.SG.F tea-INS.SG
'She didn't eat well, all day long sustaining her energy with strong tea.' (KJP)

Compared to the Polish examples, *byle* in Lithuanian dialects seems to be more regular in expressing the free-choice function. Additionally, despite the meaning of examples like (26), recently, in Lithuanian youth slang, probably via conventionalization of irony, it has acquired a new meaning 'very good' (cf. 27).

(27) | Kreid-a | man | atrod-o | yra | **belen kok-s**
chalk-NOM.SG | I:DAT | seem-PRS.3 | be:PRS.3 | INDF what-NOM.SG.M
Kalci-o | *šaltin-is –* | *kreid-ą* | *valgy-ti* | *sveika.*
calcium-GEN.SG | source-NOM.SG | chalk-ACC.SG | eat-INF | healthy

'Chalk, I think, is a very good source of Calcium – it is healthy to eat chalk.'[9]

To express this "new" meaning the variant of the indefinite *bele(n) koks* is usually used. A similar highly expressive meaning is seen with the indefinite *belen kaip* 'strongly, big time', cf. examples like *belen kaip įspūdingai* 'really amazing'.[10] Other members of the *bele(n)*-series do not express such a meaning, or at least I have not found such examples. These meanings, which have developed in the last decade, are still probably being formed. In general, this is a very good example of how a borrowed element can acquire meanings and functions that are completely different from those of the source language.

The development of the free-choice meaning of the *bile*-series in Lithuanian may be in some way supported by the variant borrowed from Belarusian *abi* whose main function is free-choice as well. There are examples when these two markers are even contaminated in the forms like *abile* (cf. 28), Zinkevičius also mentions the form *abet* (1966: 436).

(28) | *Miel-i,* | *nori-u* | *paskelb-ti* | *e-adresiuk-ą* | *ir*
dear-NOM.PL.M | want-PRS.1SG | publish-INF | e-mail_adress-ACC.SG | and
bendrau-ti | *apie* | *"abile" k-ą.* | |
communicate-INF | about | INDF what-ACC | |

'Dear friends, I want to publish my e-mail address and talk about "whatever".' (LKT)

3.2 Borrowing of *koc*

There are more variants of the borrowing of the free-choice marker: *koc'/xoc*. The indefiniteness markers *xoc'/koc'* are attested neither in LKT, nor in LKŽ. The only function ascribed to these elements (in the variant *koc*) in the dictionary is one of the particle 'at least'. However, a few examples, when *koc* is used as an indefiniteness marker, are found in dialectal texts. This indefiniteness marker is usually used in the dialects that have come into contact with Belarusian, which

---

[9] http://www.games.lt/g/forum.forum_zinutes/74257.4?sev=page.
[10] http://wn.com/Ispudingai.

also explains why some variants have *c'* in the end, cf. Belarusian *xoc'* 'at least'. For instance:

(29) Im-k   an   save   **xot' k-o.**
     take-IMP.2SG   in   self:ACC   INDF what-GEN.SG
     'Take whatever you want.' (Vidugiris 2004: 224)

3.3 Borrowing of *nebūt*

Another borrowed Slavic indefiniteness marker is *nebūt*, which can mostly be found in the southern dialects of Lithuanian, in contact with Belarusian. It seems to be calqued from Belarusian *nebudz'*. Its main function in Slavic languages, viz. irrealis non-specific, seems to be retained in Lithuanian:

(30) Operacij-a,   ten   **k-ą nebūt**   prapjau-t   do   iščisti-t.
     operation-NOM.SG   there   what-ACC INDF   cut-INF   and   clean-INF
     'Surgery: [you know,] to cut something or other, then clean it out.'
     (Vidugiris 1998: 276)

There are examples when this marker means 'in any old way, barely, poorly':

(31) Nu   vaik-ai   **kap nebut**   gyven-a,   o   an-as   jau
     well   child-NOM.Pl   how INDF   live-PRS.3   but   he-NOM   already
     ne-rak   susiem.
     NEG-see:PRS.3   at all
     'The children live somehow, but he already doesn't see at all.' (Petrauskas & Vidugiris 1987: 58)

3.4 Borrowing of *kalvek*

Another borrowed indefiniteness marker found in Lithuanian dialects is *kalvek* (*kalvėk*). It comes from Western Slavic, cf. Polish *kolwiek*, Slovak *kol'vek*. Lithuanian dialects have probably borrowed it from Polish, but its existence in some Belarusian varieties should also be taken in mind. According to Haspelmath (1997: 271), its Polish counterpart's main functions include question, conditional, indirect negation, comparative, and free-choice (cf. 32), where the indefinite is used in the free-choice function:

(32) Polish
     Cokolwiek   teraz   powie-m,   obró-ci się   przeciwko   mnie
     what:INDF   now   say-PRS.1SG   turn-INF REFL   against   I:ACC
     'Whatever I'll say now will turn against me.' (NKJP)

The examples found in Lithuanian dialects show that its functions are very close to the ones found in Polish, cf. question 33, but also irrealis non-specific function 34:

(33) *Maž*   *pristig-ai*   **k-o kalvėk?**
maybe   lack-PST.2SG   what-GEN INDF
'Maybe you need something?' (LKŽ)

(34) *Aš*   *tau*   **k-ą kalvek**   *nupirk-si-u*
I:NOM   you_sg:DAT   what-ACC INDF   buy-FUT-1SG
'I will buy you something' (LKŽ)

It seems to exist only in dialects, as no examples are given by LKT as well all the speakers living in Vilnius I asked about the form have never heard it in everyday speech. Probably, its use in the dialects is limited to some point, cf. the remark in the dictionary of Dievėniškės saying that the marker is used only with *kas* ir *kaip* interrogatives (Mikulėnienė, Morkūnas, & Vidugiris 2005: 238). As in a few other cases with borrowed from Polish markers, the marker *kol'v'ek* is also found in the Old Belarusian texts as well as in some Belarusian dialects (Steškovič 1979: 34–35).

3.5 Borrowing of negative pronouns

Haspelmath (1997: 184) writes that he knows of no case when an entire indefinite pronoun has been borrowed. His observations hold with regard to Lithuanian as well: Mostly, only indefiniteness markers are borrowed, while the pronominal components are kept. However, I have found several examples of the entire negative pronoun *nigdi* (or *nigdy*) 'never' being borrowed from Polish. It might seem peculiar in the light of the fact that the system of negative pronouns seems to be the most stable one. This puzzle can be explained by the exceptional nature of this pronoun, which is not derived in accordance to the general pattern, cf. pl. *kto* 'who'>*nikt* 'nobody', *kiedy* 'when'>**nikiedy*, but *nigdy* 'never'. This form differs from the other members of the series, which makes it more likely to be borrowed than substituted by the counterpart in the recipient language.

(35) *Tadu bus*   *muzik-a,*   *kadu nor-i,*   **nigdi**   *ku tai*
then be:FUT.3   music-NOM.SG   when want-PRS.2SG   never   where INDF
išvažo.
go:PRS.2SG
'There will be music whenever you want, you never go anywhere.'
(Kardelis 2006: 95)

3.6 Borrowing of *žėdnas*

Another borrowed indefinite negative pronoun is *žėdnas* 'none, any' borrowed from Polish *żaden* 'id.'. Old Belarusian also borrowed this pronoun from Polish, and its variants *žadenъ*, *žadny* were regularly used in the ducal chancery style (cf. Steškovič 1979: 30–31). It has an interesting history: According to LKŽ, its only meaning is 'every', which contradicts Zinkevičius's (1966: 321) statement that it retains the meaning of the Polish source 'none'. In fact, examples of both meanings can be found in the dialects (and only in the dialects; there were no examples of this pronoun found in LKT):

(36) **Žėdn-am** gryb-e yra kirmėli-ų.
every-LOC.SG.M mushroom-LOC.SG be:PRS.3 worm-GEN.PL
'There are worms in every mushroom.' (LKŽ)

The negative meaning of this pronoun is found only in the contexts with direct negation:

(37) Gyven-k-it kaip mes, paukšteli-ai, ne-bus tarp
live-IMP-2PL how we-NOM.SG bird-NOM.PL NEG-be:FUT.3 between
jums **žėdn-ų** zdrod-ų, prapul-s vis-i
you(PL):DAT any-GEN.PL betrayal-GEN.PL dissapear-FUT.3 all-NOM.PL.M
neprieteli-ai.
enemy-NOM.PL
'Live like us, birds, there will be no betrayals between you, all enemies will disappear' (LKŽ)

In Lithuanian dialects, *žėdnas* is often used in the constructions *žėdnas bevienas*, *žėdnas vienas*, or *kožnas žėdnas* with the meaning 'every' (cf. 38).

(38) **Žėdn-as** bevien-as nor-i geriau.
every-NOM.SG.M one-NOM.SG.M want-PRS.3 better
'Every one and single [person] wants it to be better.' (LKŽ)

Contemporary Polish *żaden* does not have this meaning, but the data from other languages show that the meaning 'every' has probably emerged in Polish and was borrowed together with the pronoun, cf. the meanings of the pronoun in old Ukrainian and old Belarusian (Mel'nyčuk 1985: 204).[11] The development of this meaning can be probably reconstructed this way: 'no one'>'anyone' in negative contexts>'anyone, every' in positive contexts.

---

[11] Although the meaning 'every' is singled out for old Ukrainian and old Belarusian by Mel'nyčuk (1985: 204), I did not find any good examples of *żaden* with the meaning 'every' in non-negated contexts for old Belarusian by Žurauski (1989: 242–243).

To conclude this discussion of MAT-borrowing, it should be said that borrowing mostly affects the series used in the free-choice function. This fact can probably be interpreted as an argument for the relatively late development of a special series of indefinite pronouns expressing this function in Lithuanian. The borrowed markers usually can be used in other functions as well (mostly as discourse particles). In some cases, the borrowed series can develop new meanings, as in the case with *bele(n) k-*. Sporadic loans tend to keep the meaning they express in the source language (*koc'*), while old and widely used loans (*bile*) are likely to develop new functions. All borrowed indefiniteness markers (*abi, bile, koc'*) with the free-choice meaning have other functions, as particles or conjunctions. As stated by Matras (2009: 193), discourse markers are "at the very top of the borrowability hierarchy", which can also be taken to mean that the function of the discourse marker is more easily borrowed than that of the indefiniteness marker. The function of indefiniteness markers might have not be directly borrowed and could have developed later by analogy with the source language. This brings us to the discussion of another type of borrowing – PAT-loans.

4 PAT-borrowing of indefiniteness marker

4.1 Borrowing of *tai*

Commonly accepted as a calque from Russian, the indefiniteness marker *-tai* is found both in dialects and in the speech of urban population. This marker is used so widely that the Lithuanian language commission listed it as a "grave language mistake" (see paragraph 1.3.12 of the list, http://www.vlkk.lt/lit/lt/klaidos/zodyno3).

Indeed, Russian and Lithuanian examples of the use of *-to* and *-tai* show high similarity (cf. 39).

(39) Lithuanian
    a. *knyg-a*   *apie*   *kok-į **tai***   *šlykšt-ų*
         book-SG.NOM about   what-ACC.SG.M INDF despicable-ACC.SG.M
         sen-į   *Anglij-oje*
         old.man-ACC.SG   England-LOC.SG

    Russian
    b. *knig-a*   *o*   *kak-om-**to***   *protivn-om*
         book-SG.NOM about   what-LOC.SG.M INDF despicable-LOC.SG.M
         starik-e   *v*   *Angli-i*
         old.man-LOC.SG   in   England-LOC.SG
         'a book about some despicable old man in England'

Another function of the Russian element *to* is that of the neuter demonstrative pronoun. The Lithuanian counterpart of this element is *tai* (see Valeckienė 1974), whose use might be revised under the influence of Russian. The *-to* marker is also widespread in the northeastern dialects of Belarusian (Steškovič 1979: 35). An indirect argument for the "calquing origin" of this indefiniteness marker in Lithuanian is another calqued expression, *būk tai*, Russian *budto* 'as if, allegedly'. This example is fascinating, as it reflects the etymology of the Russian word containing the imperative of the verb *byt'* 'be' and the demonstrative *to* (cf. Vasmer 1986: 231): One would argue that this etymology is realized by the speakers even until now.

However, the origin of *tai* as an indefiniteness marker remains vague: It is very difficult to say whether this marker was calqued or developed independently. In forms like *kažkas tai* 'someone', *kažkoks tai* 'some' containing, in fact, two indefiniteness markers, viz. *kaž-* and *tai*, the question as to which element was added later can hardly be answered with precision. Such forms can be a result of either hypercorrection by adding the standard marker *kaž-* to forms like *kas tai* or reinforcement of the standard specific unknown series by adding the calqued indefiniteness marker.

Traditionally, two main functions of Lithuanian *tai* are singled out: (1) a demonstrative pronoun of the so-called neuter gender and (2) a particle or conjunction. In both Valeckienė's articles (1974, 1977), where these functions are described in detail, there is no mention of the use of *tai* as indefiniteness marker (even though dialectal material is analyzed).

The examples of the use of *tai* as a series marker show that in most cases, the functions of the pronouns of the *tai*-series are identical to their Russian counterparts, as well as to the standard *kaž*-series. The main function of this series is specific unknown:

(40) Aš   ne-pamen-u   tiksliai,   bet   žin-au,   kad
     I:NOM   NEG-remember-PRS.1SG   exact-ADV   but   know-PRS.1SG   that
     kaž-k-as tai   įvyk-o,   kad   aš   ten   pradėj-au
     what:INDF-NOM.SG INDF   happen-PST.3 that I:NOM there start-PST.1SG
     įsči-ose   aug-ti.
     womb-LOC.PL   grow-INF
     'I do not remember exactly, but I know that something happened and I started to grow in the womb.' (LKT)

The "correct" variants proposed by the Lithuanian language commission as alternatives to the "wrong" *tai*-series sometimes differ in meaning from the original sentences (cf. 41).

(41) Stat-ant   užtvank-ą   gal-i   atsiras-ti   ir
     build-CNV   embankment-ACC.SG   can-PRS.3   appear-INF   and
     (kaž)koki-ų tai (= tam tikrų) gamt-os   apsaug-os
     what:INDF-GEN.PL INDF   nature-GEN.SG protection-GEN.SG
     pažeidim-ų.
     violation-GEN.PL
     'When building an embankment, certain violations in the preservation of the environment may take place.' (VLKK)

Here the proposed correction *tam tikras* 'certain' refers not to a non-specific object, but rather to a specific one, cf. *kai*-series vs. *kaž*-series.

4.2 Borrowing of *ne-*

Another series with calqued indefiniteness marker is the specific unknown *ne*-series, which seems to be widespread both in colloquial speech and in the dialects (e.g., 42).

(42) *Brol-is*   *tavo*   *tur-i*   **nek-ą**   *prieš*   *tave.*
     brother-NOM.SG   your   have-PRS.3   what:INDF-ACC   against   you.sg:ACC
     'Your brother has something against you.' (LKŽ)

In contrast to other cases where I could find only some examples of the use of borrowed indefiniteness marker, the full *ne*-series can be reconstructed on the grounds of LKŽ, LKT, or dialectal texts. The dictionaries mark it as calqued from the Slavic *ne*-series, for instance, LKŽ, whose main function is also specific unknown (cf. 43).

(43) Russian
     Nekto   zašel   v   komnat-u.
     who:INDF.NOM   come.in:PST.SG.M   in   room-ACC.SG
     'Someone came into the room.'

The State Commission of the Lithuanian Language names the use of *nekuris*, *nekurie* 'some' a grave mistake (see paragraph 1.3.6. of the list, http://www.vlkk.lt/lit/lt/klaidos/zodyno3) and proposed correction in (44). However, the borrowed or calqued nature of this marker can hardly be proven. The development of non-negative indefinite pronouns from the negative ones is typologically widespread (see Haspelmath 1997: 230). The *ne*-series exists in all Slavic languages neighboring with Lithuanian – in Polish, Russian, and Belarusian. In all these languages, its main function is specific unknown.

(44) **Nekur-ie**   *ligoni-ai (= Kai kurie; Kurie ne kurie ligoniai; Vienas kitas ligonis)*
some:INDF-NOM.PL.M patient-NOM.PL
nuo   sunki-ų   komplikacij-ų   miršt-a.
from   difficult-GEN.PL   complication-GEN.PL   die-PRS.3
'Some patients die because of serious complications.' (VLKK)

Haspelmath argues for the explanation of the origin of this series that was proposed in the works of Brugmann and Delbrück. These linguists treated the *ne*-series of indefinite pronouns in Lithuanian and other Indo-European languages as the result of "reanalysis of a negative indefinite co-occurring with verbal negation as a non-negative indefinite" (Haspelmath 1997: 230). There seems to be some kind of mistake in Haspelmath's data, because the *ne*-series is probably calqued from Slavic, since the Lithuanian indefinite of this origin is *nėkas*, cf. the negation *nė* (Fraenkel 1962: 492). It can be used in negative contexts as well as in specific unknown ones (cf. 45 and 46).

(45) **Nėk-o**   ne-saky-k!
nothing-GEN   NEG-say-IMP.2SG
'Do not say anything!' (LKŽ)

(46) Tur-iu   tau   **nėk-ą**   pasaky-tie
have-PRS.1SG   you:DAT   INDF:what-ACC   say-INF
'I have something to tell you.' (LKŽ)

Haspelmath has some problems dealing with Lithuanian indefinite pronouns of the *ne-* type, as they are usually used as a part of "the reduplicative combinations *kas nekas, kada nekada*" (Haspelmath 1997: 232). If this suggestion is correct, and the indefinites of the *X ne X* type contain the *ne-* indefinites, it could probably be an argument in favor of the borrowed origin of this series.

4.3 The *X ne X* case

The case of the *X ne X* series is a little bit mysterious. Haspelmath calls it "marginal", meaning that it does not contain all members of the general paradigm. In addition, it is marginal in the sense of its use. Usually the pronouns of this series appear only in literary texts and already seem to be very old-fashioned. They are never used in colloquial speech, and I could not find any examples of this series in the dialectal texts. The origin of this series is not clear. The problems Haspelmath dealt with in discussing these forms can be explained if its borrowed nature is assumed. Haspelmath (1997: 232) admits that he does not know "the function of the negation *ne-* in such combinations". The Polish origin could explain the restriction of this series to the literary style in Lithuanian. However, this series is also used in Belarusian, cf., *xto-nixto, što-ništo, jaki-nijaki*, but it might have emerged also as a result of contacts with Polish. One of the arguments in favor of the Polish calque hypothesis is that this series is used in the same specific known function:

(47) Polish
*Jest   on   dosyć   woln-y,   a   nawet   **gdzieniegdzie***
be:PRS.3SG   he:NOM   quite   free-NOM.SG and   even   where:INDF
odbieg-a   od   łaciński-ego   oryginał-u.
diverge-PRS.3SG   from   Latin-GEN.SG.M   original-GEN.SG
'It [the translation] is quite free, and sometimes even diverges from the Latin original.' (KJP).

(48) Lithuanian
*Lėk-ėme   lygi-ais   lauk-ais,   **kur ne kur**   išdyg-dav-o*
fly-PST.1PL   plain-INS.PL   field-INS.PL   where:INDF   drift-HAB-PST.3
stači-os   raudon-os   uol-os.
straight-NOM.PL.F   red-NOM.PL.F   rock-NOM.PL
'We were flying through plain fields, in some places straight red rocks appeared.' (LKT)

On the other hand, the *X ne X* series is not very widespread in Polish and can be found in Latvian as well (Haspelmath 1997, 277).[12] The best way out is certainly a detailed investigation of this form in Polish dialects. Along with the aforementioned *bile* forms, this could be also an interesting contribution to the influence of Polish on the Baltic languages.

4.4 PAT-borrowing of negative pronouns

A few more words should be said about the negative pronouns. It has already been stated that this category of indefinites seems to be more stable than others (apart from the MAT-borrowed *nigdy* 'never'). However, one more example can be interpreted as testifying to Slavic influence: In the dialects, the negative determiner *niekoks* is found, cf. Russian *nikakoj* 'none'.

---

[12] An interesting fact is that the existence of forms like *so-na-so* in Latvian Romani is explained by the influence of Lithuanian (Manuš-Belugin 1973: 138).

(49) Ne-buv-o čia **niekoki-os** jau spatičk-os su
 NEG-be-PST.3 here any-GEN.SG.F already meeting-GEN.SG with
 partizan-ais.
 guerrilla-INS.PL
 'There was no fight whatsoever with guerrilla warriors.' (Petrauskas & Vidugiris 1987: 18)

(50) Russian
 Nikak-ogo somnenij-a zdes' i by-t' ne mož-et.
 any-GEN.SG doubt-GEN.SG.N here and be-INF NEG can-PRS.3SG
 'There cannot be any doubt here.'

Obviously, this form can be explained by the dialect-internal process of paradigm levelling, i.e., the form *nie-koks* was constructed on the model of other negative pronouns like *nie-kas*, *nie-kur*, etc. Still, this process could be influenced or supported by the surrounding languages.

In general, it is more difficult to prove that calquing took place, since very often the "suspicious" elements can also be explained as an independent development. The use of this form of negative indefinites is supported by the fact that the calqued series discussed above (*ne-*, *-tai*) are more regular both structurally (usually all members of the series are used) and geographically.

5 Conclusions

Functional words, and indefinite pronouns as a subtype thereof, are easily borrowed. In the Lithuanian dialects that are dominated by other languages (as the one of Ramaškonys), more loans can be found. There are both MAT-loans, i.e., the form is directly borrowed, and PAT-loans, with a calqued functional pattern. In the dialects of the areas where Lithuanian is the dominant language, the number of loans is much lower. In these cases, the borrowings are usually PAT-loans of older periods when Lithuanian played a subordinate role in the sociolinguistic hierarchy of the area (i.e., when Polish, Belarusian, and Russian were more prestigious for various reasons). In general, PAT-loans are also likely to be typical for the whole linguistic area, i.e., such patterns can be found in several surrounding languages (see Sakel 2007: 21–25).

All cases of borrowed indefinites, together with the cases when the borrowed nature is impossible to prove, are listed in Table 2. The acquisition of a secondary meaning in Lithuanian is marked by (+), while (–) means that the use of the borrowed element is identical to the one of the source language. The existence of the element exclusively in the dialect or in the speech of the city population is

Tab. 2: Borrowed indefinites in Lithuanian and its dialects

Specific known	Specific unknown	Free choice	Negative
X ne X? (–)OL	*tai*-series (–)DC	*bile*-series (+)DC	*nigdi* (–)OD
	ne-series (–)DC	*koc'*-series (–)OD	*žėdnas* (–?)OD
	nebūt-series (–)OD	*abi*-series (–)OD	
	kalvek-series (–)OD		

marked by OD (only dialectal), OL (only literary), and DC (dialects and colloquial speech). The interrogation mark is put when there are doubts of the borrowed origin of a marker or a meaning.

Table 2 shows that the free-choice function is more likely to be replaced by loans and that usually the meanings of the borrowed indefiniteness markers are kept identical to the source language model. The interrogation mark with the pronoun *žėdnas* is meant to show that there are no data that the meaning 'everyone' did not develop independently. The interrogation mark with the *X ne X* series shows there is doubt on the borrowed nature of the marker.

In general, the investigation of Lithuanian indefinite pronouns demonstrates that the complex system of Lithuanian emerges as even richer when the borrowed elements used in the dialects and colloquial speech are taken into consideration. Further study of contact for Lithuanian grammatical forms and patterns might help to describe the linguistic situation in the area, as well as to understand the trends in the development of the borrowed elements.

Acknowledgments

I thank the editors of the volume, Mikhail Oslon, and two anonymous reviewers, for many useful comments on the earlier versions of this paper, and Cori Anderson, for improving my English. All errors remain my own.

Abbreviations

Glosses

ACC	accusative	COMP	comparative
ACT	active	DAT	dative
ADV	adverb	F	feminine
CNV	converb	FUT	future

GEN	genitive		NEG	negation
HAB	habitual		NOM	nominative
IMP	imperative		PA	active participle
INDF	indefinite		PL	plural
INF	infinitive		PST	past
INS	instrumental		PRS	present
LOC	locative		REFL	reflexive
M	masculine		SBJV	subjunctive
N	neuter		SG	singular

Sources

KJP   Korpus języka polskiego IPI PAN [The Corpus of the Polish Language] http://korpus.pl

LKT   Dabartinės lietuvių kalbos tekstynas [The Corpus of the Modern Lithuanian Language] http://tekstynas.vdu.lt

LKŽ   Lietuvių kalbos žodynas [The Dictionary of the Lithuanian language] http://lkz.lt

NKJP   Narodowy korpus języka polskiego [The National Corpus of Polish] http://nkjp.pl

VLKK   Valstybinė lietuvių kalbos komisija [The State Commission of the Lithuanian language] http://www.vlkk.lt

References

Aleksandravičius, Juozas. 1964. Kretingos tarmės įvardis [Pronouns in the dialect of Kretinga]. *Kalbotyra* 10: 121–128.

Ambrazas, Vytautas. 1985. Nekotorye sledy balto-finnskix kontaktov v sintaksise baltijskix jazykov [Some traces of Balto-Finnic contacts in syntax of the Baltic languages.] In Regina Volkaitė-Kulikauskienė (ed.) *Problemy etnogeneza i etničeskoj istorii baltov* [Problems of ethnogenesis and ethnic history of the Balts], 188–196. Vilnius: Mokslas.

Bacevičiūtė, Rima, Audra Ivanauskienė, Asta Leskauskaitė, & Edmundas Trumpa (eds.). 2004. *Lietuvių kalbos tarmių chrestomatija* [Lithuanian dialects reader]. Vilnius: Lietuvių kalbos instituto leidykla.

Beinortienė, Vida. 2011. *Romų kalba* [The Romani language]. Panevėžys: Panevėžio vaikų dienos užimtumo centras.

Dahl, Östen & Maria Koptjevskaja-Tamm (eds.). 2001. *The Circum-Baltic languages: Typology and contact.* Vols. 1–2. Amsterdam, Philadelphia: John Benjamins.

Fraenkel, Ernst. 1962. *Litauisches etymologisches Wörterbuch*, Bd. I. Heidelberg: Winter; Göttingen: Vandenhoeck & Ruprecht.

Grinaveckienė, Elena. 1969. Lietuvių ir slavų gramatinio kontaktavimo reiškiniai pietryčių Lietuvoje [Cases of Lithuanian and Slavic grammatical contact in south-eastern Lithuania]. *Lietuvių kalbotyros klausimai* 11: 219–229.
Grinaveckienė, Elena. 1974. Vlijanie belorusskoj grammatičeskoj sistemy na lazunskij govor litovskogo jazyka [Influence of Belarusian grammar system on the Lithuanian dialect in Lazūnai]. In Marija Sivickienė, *Dialektologičeskij sbornik. Materialy IV dialektologičeskoj konferencii po izučeniju govorov i jazykovyx kontaktov v Pribaltike* [Dialectological collection. Materials of the IV dialectological conference on dialects and language contacts in the Baltic region], 46–56. Vilnius.
Haspelmath, Martin. 1997. *Indefinite pronouns*. Oxford: Clarendon Press.
Haugen, Einar. 1950. The analysis of linguistic borrowing. *Language* 26(2): 210–231.
Jašinskaitė, Irena. 1959. Biržų tarmės įvardis [Pronouns in the dialect of Biržai]. *Lietuvių kalbotyros klausimai* 2: 187–193.
Johanson, Lars. 2008. Remodelling grammar. Copying, conventionalization, grammaticalization. In Pieter Siemund & Noemi Kintana (eds.) *Language contact and contact languages*, 61–79. Amsterdam, Philadelphia: John Benjamins.
Kardelis, Vytautas (comp.). 2006. *Mielagėnų apylinkių tekstai* [Texts from in the localities of Mielagėnai]. Vilnius: Lietuvių kalbos institutas.
Kardelytė, Jadvyga. 1975. *Gervėčių tarmė* [The dialect of Gervėčiai]. Vilnius: Mintis.
Kozhanov, Kirill. 2011. Notes on the use of Lithuanian indefinite pronouns. *Baltic Linguistics* 2: 79–110.
Manuš-Belugin, Leksa. 1973. O vlijanii baltijskix jazykov na dialekt latyšskix cygan [On the influence of the Baltic languages on the dialect of Latvian Roma]. *Latvijas PSR Zinātņu Akedēmijas vēstis* 4(309): 124–139.
Matras, Yaron. 2009. *Language contact*. New York: Cambridge University Press.
Matras, Yaron & Jeanette Sakel (eds.). 2007. *Grammatical borrowing in cross-linguistic perspective*. Berlin, New York: Mouton de Gruyter.
Mel'nyčuk, Oleksandr Savyč (ed.). 1985. *Etimolohičnyj slovnyk ukrajins'koji movy.* [Etymological dictionary of Ukrainian]. T.2. Kyjiv: Institut movoznavstva imeni O.O. Potebni.
Mikulėnienė, Danguolė, Kazys Morkūnas, & Aloyzas Vidugiris (eds). 2005. *Dieveniškių šnektos žodynas* [Dictionary of the Dieveniškės dialect]. T. 1: A.-M. Vilnius: Lietuvių kalbos institutas.
Morkūnas, Kazys (ed.). 1977–1991. *Lietuvių kalbos atlasas* [Atlas of the Lithuanian language]. T.1: Leksika [Lexics]. T.2: Fonetika [Phonetics]. T.3: Morfologija [Morphology]. Vilnius: Mokslas.
Niewulis, Jowita. 2001. Punsko tarmės įvardžių savitumas [Features of pronouns in the dialect of Punsk]. In Józef Marcinkiewicz & Norbert Ostrowski (eds.) *Munera lingvistica et philologica Michaeli Hasiuk dedicata*, 63–67. Poznań: Katedra Skandynawistyki i Baltologii UAM w Poznaniu.
Otrębski, Jan. 1932. *Wschodniolitewskie narzecze twereckie* [Eastern Lithuanian dialects of Tverečius]. Część III. Zapożyczenia słowiańskie [Slavic borrowings]. Kraków.
Petrauskas, Jonas & Aloyzas Vidugiris. 1987. *Lazūnų tarmės tekstai* [Text samples of the Lazūnai dialect]. Vilnius: Mokslas.
Sakel, Jeanette. 2007. Types of loan: Matter and pattern. In Yaron Matras & Jeanette Sakel (eds.) *Grammatical borrowing in cross-linguistic perspective*, 15–30. Berlin, New York: Mouton de Gruyter.
Skardžius, Pranas. 1931. *Die slavischen Lehnwörter im Altlitauischen*. Kaunas: Spindulys.

Smoczyński, Wojciech. 1972. *Teksty gwarowe z Białostocczyny z komentarzem językowym* [Dialectal text samples from the region of Białostok with linguistic comments]. Warszawa.

Steškovič, Tatjana. 1979. Mestoimenija v belorusskom jazyke [Pronouns in Belarusian]. Habilitation thesis summary. Minsk.

Sudnik, Tamara. 1975. *Dialekty litovsko-slavjanskogo pograničʼja. Očerki fonologičeskix sistem* [Dialects of Lithuanian-Slavic border. Essays on phonological systems.]. Moscow: Nauka.

Toporov, Vladimir N. (ed.). 1972. *Balto-slavjanskij sbornik* [Balto-Slavic miscellany]. Moscow: Nauka.

Treffers-Daller, Jeanine & Raymond Mougeon. 2005. The role of transfer in language variation and change: Evidence from contact varieties of French. *Bilingualism: Language and Cognition* 8: 93–98.

Tuomienė, Nijolė. 2008. *Ramaškonių šnektos tekstai* [Text samples of Ramaškonys dialect]. Vilnius: Lietuvių kalbos institutas.

Valeckienė, Adelė. 1974. Bevardės giminės forma *tai* ir jos santykis su kitomis įvardžių formomis [The neuter gender form *tai* and its relations with other forms of the pronoun]. *Lietuvių kalbotyros klausimai* 15: 35–75.

Valeckienė, Adelė. 1977. Forma *tai* ir jos variantai lietuvių kalbos tarmėse [The form *tai* and its variants in Lithuanian dialects]. *Lietuvių kalbotyros klausimai* 17: 55–75.

Vasmer, Max. 1986. *Etimologičeskij slovarʼ russkogo jazyka* [Etymological dictionary of the Russian language]. Vol 1. Moscow: Progress.

Vidugiris, Aloyzas. 1960. Zietelos tarmės įvardis [Pronouns in the dialect of Zietela]. *Lietuvių kalbotyros klausimai* 3: 113–131.

Vidugiris, Aloyzas. 1998. *Zietelos šnektos žodynas* [The dictionary of the dialect of Zietela]. Vilnius: Mokslo ir enciklopedijų leidybos institutas.

Vidugiris, Aloyzas. 2004. *Zietelos lietuvių šnekta* [Lithuanian dialect of Zietela]. Vilnius: Presvika.

Wiemer, Björn. 2003. Dialect and language contacts on the territory of the Grand Duchy of Lithuania from the 15th century until 1939. In Kurt Braunmüller & Gisella Ferraresi (eds.) *Aspects of multilingualism in European language history*, 105–143. Amsterdam, Philadelphia: John Benjamins.

Wiemer, Björn. 2004. Population linguistics on a micro-scale. Lessons to be learnt from Baltic and Slavic dialects in contact. In Bernd Kortmann (ed.) *Dialectology meets typology. Dialect grammar from a cross-linguistic perspective*, 497–526. Berlin, New York: Mouton de Gruyter.

Wiemer, Björn. 2009. Zu entlehnten Verbpräfixen und anderen morphosintaktischen Slavismen in litauischen Insel- und Grenzmundarten. In Lenka Scholze & Björn Wiemer (eds.) *Von Zuständen, Dynamik und Veränderung bei Pygmäen und Giganten*, 347–391. Bochum: Brockmeyer.

Wiemer, Björn, Irina Vladyko, & Vytautas Kardelis. 2004. *Močʼ* i *umetʼ* – funkcionalʼnye peresečenija dvuch modalʼnyx glagolov v govorax litovsko-slavjanskogo pograničʼja [*Močʼ* 'be able to' i *umetʼ* 'to know to': Functional overlapping of the two modal verbs in the dialects of Lithuanian and Slavic border]. *Balto-slavjanskie issledovanija* 16: 142–167. Moscow: Indrik.

Zinkevičius, Zigmas. 1966. *Lietuvių dialektologija* [Lithuanian dialectology]. Vilnius: Mintis.

Žurauski, Arkadzʼ Iosifavič. (ed.). 1989. *Histaryčny slounik belaruskaj movy* [Historical dictionary of Belarusian]. T. 9. Minsk: Navuka i texnika.

Bernhard Wälchli

13 *Ištiktukai* "eventives" – The Baltic precursors of ideophones and why they remain unknown in typology

1 Why Lithuanian of all European languages? The Neogrammarians and a Samogitian bishop

According to the classical definition by Doke (1935: 118) for Zulu ideophones are "[a] vivid representation of an idea in sound. A word, often onomatopoeic, which describes a predicate, qualificative or adverb in respect to manner, colour, sound, smell, action, state or intensity". The typological treatment of ideophones in the modern literature is typically limited to the languages of Africa, Australia, South America, and South East Asia. Indo-European languages are hardly mentioned in the standard volume on ideophones by Voeltz and Kilian-Hatz (2001). Creissels (2001: 75) goes as far as to claim that ideophones do "not correspond to any of the categories traditionally recognized in descriptions of European languages".[1] However, there is at least one European language, where ideophones have long been recognized to be a part of speech: Lithuanian. They have a different name, however: *ištiktukai* "particles for what happens; 'happenlings' or – a less awkward translation – 'eventives'". "Eventive" is also the term used by Andersen (2009).

This chapter discusses Lithuanian ideophones both from the point of view of their very specific history in Lithuanian grammar writing (Section 2) and from the point of view of their typological properties (Section 3). In many languages, ideophones index spoken modality, rural environment, and communal society. However, in Lithuanian ideophones are particularly prominent in a sample of written language, a novel by the Samogitian[2] Bishop Motiejus Valančius published in 1863, which has been particularly important for the history of their grammatical description. In Section 2, I argue that this is no contradiction since the novel uses ideophones as a stylistic device to establish rural identity in a time when Lithuanian was heavily suppressed. Section 3 then continues with discussing the particular properties of Lithuanian ideophones from a cross-linguistic

---

1 For a recent and comprehensive survey, see Dingemanse (2012).
2 Samogitia or Žemaitija is "Lower" Lithuania, the northwestern part of Lithuania in contrast to High Lithuania (Aukštaitija).

point of view. I argue that Lithuanian ideophones have several properties typical of a word class marking events, notably event number (Section 3.2) and valency. Unlike ideophones in many other languages they do not associate with bleached light verbs (Section 3.5). In these respects, they resemble the so-called verboids in Russian, such as *gljad'* 'look' and *xvat'* 'grab' (Nikitina 2012).

The term *ištiktukai* 'eventive'[3] has been coined by the most influential normative grammarian of Lithuanian Jonas Jablonskis (also publishing under the name Rygiškių Jonas). He writes – thirteen years before Doke's classical definition: "Iš jaustukų tarpo išskiriami yra dažnai būtųjų ištikimų vaizdelaičiai, vadinamieji ištiktukai: *burbt, čiūzt, barkšt...*" ["Among interjections one has to distinguish a group of markers for past events, so-called eventives *burbt, čiūzt, barkšt...*"] (Jablonskis 1922 sections 282–283 [1957: 353]).[4] Jablonskis' name for ideophones *ištiktukas* 'eventive' is an excellent characterization of the part of speech. One of the most characteristic functions of ideophones in many languages is to express salient events. As Noss (2001: 268) writes, for instance, about Gbaya and Sotho: "In Gbaya expression, ideophones 'show' what the speaker has seen or experienced. They enable the audience to participate 'in a happening' as Daniel Kunene has written about Southern Sotho ideophones."

Jablonskis (1922) was the first grammarian to give the phenomenon a name, but he was not the first one to describe it. Prior to Jablonskis work, Lithuanian ideophones had already been treated extensively by the German Neogrammarian August Leskien (1902/1903: 165), who clearly distinguishes them from interjections proper, but fails to give the category a name:

> Ich beschränke aber die Aufgabe auf solche Ausdrücke, mit denen man Bewegungs-, Licht-, und Schallerscheinungen nachahmend, ausmalend oder verdeutlichend begleitet, schliesse also aus die eigentlichen Interjektionen, ebenso Nachahmungen von Tierschreien, Lockrufen u. dgl., da hierin das Litauische nichts besonders Bemerkenswerthes bietet.[5]

---

[3] Danylenko (this volume) calls them "onomatopoeic particles".
[4] Jašinskaitė (1975: 4) argues that it was Žiugžda (1961: 221) who first considered *ištiktukai* to be a part of speech. It is true that Jablonskis (1922) does not strictly call them a part of speech, but he clearly sets them apart from interjections.
[5] Similarly, Paul (1909: 180) subsumes what we know as ideophones under interjections, but they are clearly a distinct group within interjections: "Sie sind Reaktionen gegen plötzliche Erregungen des Gehörs-oder Gesichtssinnes ... Sie werden dann auch bei der Erinnerung und Erzählung der solche plötzliche Erregung wirkenden Vorgänge gebraucht. Ich meine Wörter wie nhd. *paff, patsch, bardautz, perdauz, bauz, blaff, buff, puff, bums, futsch, hurre, husch, hussa, klacks, klaps, kladderadatsch, knacks, plump, plumps, ratsch, rutsch, schrumm, schwapp, wupp* etc."

Note that this was at a time when many of the best linguists of the days went to Lithuania to do fieldwork on Lithuanian dialects because Lithuanian was considered to be one of the most important languages for Indo-European studies and was believed to be heavily endangered. Leskien's work again is difficult to imagine without its major source: a little novel, *Palangos Juzė*, full with ideophones published by the Samogitian Bishop Motiejus Valančius in 1863 at a time when publishing Lithuanian books was very difficult. After the Polish-Lithuanian insurrection of 1863, there was a ban on writings in Polish and Lithuanian in Latin script (1866 to 1904) in the Tsarist Empire, and Bishop Valančius was one of the major organizers of book smuggling from Prussia. Despite the prohibition, Lithuanian books were secretly available in most Lithuanian villages. It was one thing to make books available, another one to write books that would be of interest for the Lithuanian peasants and which could strengthen their national self-esteem. Valančius' booklet serves this purpose in an excellent manner, as we will see shortly, and ideophones are one of several stylistic devices marking rural identity. *Palangos Juzė* also inspired other linguists such as Alfred Senn (1924, 1966) to work about Lithuanian ideophones,[6] and it is also a major source for this article. Another important source is the monograph on ideophones by Jašinskaitė (1971) assembling many examples from Lithuanian literature and from dialects.

Let us now consider an example from Valančius: two sentences with eight ideophones (or six if we disregard the elements associated to cries of animals as suggested by Leskien). Note that full reduplication plays an important role, it expresses event number (multiple events), as will be discussed in Section 3.2. In the example, all ideophones are marked in boldface, and at the end of the examples, a list with all ideophones is given with a few lexical remarks about each of them. The example is about a "wolf", and we will see shortly that the characterization of animals or of persons compared to animals is a characteristic context of use for ideophones in Lithuanian.

---

[6] Senn (1966) uses the German term *Verbalinterjektionen* 'verbal interjections' to translate *ištiktukai*.

(1) Ideophones in nineteenth-century Lithuanian literature (Valančius [1863] 1996: 41)[7]

Ant	gal-o	vis-i	su-šok-o		ant	vilk-o,
on	end-GEN.SG	all-NOM.PL.M	PV-jump-PST.3		on	wolf-GEN.SG

čiupt	ger-ai	nu-tvėr-ė,	**brūkš**	pa-trauk-ė,	**benc**
IDEO	good-ADV	PV-seize-PST.3	IDEO	PV-draw-PST.3	IDEO

iš-vert-ė		ir	**takš**	**takš**	muš-ti	pradėj-o.
out-turn-PST.3		and	IDEO	IDEO	beat-INF	begin-PST.3

Vilk-as,	girdi,	pirma	**cypt**	**cypt**	cyp-ė,
wolf-NOM.SG	HEARSAY	first	IDEO	IDEO	squeak-PST.3

paskiaus	**vau**	**vau**	kauk-ė,	ant	gal-o	**strapt**
then	IDEO	IDEO	howl-PST.3	on	end-GEN.SG	IDEO

stoj-o-s		ir	**tabalai**	**tabalai**	pa-bėgo,	nė
stand.up-PST.3-REFL		and	IDEO	IDEO	PV-flee-PST.3	not

uodeg-os	ne-be-palik-ęs.
tail-GEN.SG	not-more-leave-CNV:SS:ANT:SG:M

'In the end all jumped on the wolf, **čiupt** grasped it well, **brūkš** pulled it, **benc** knocked it down, and began to beat it **takš takš**. The wolf first **cypt cypt** squeaked, then **vau vau** howled and in the end got up **strapt** and escaped **tabalai tabalai**, without leaving a tail.'[8]

čiupt	'quick seizing', related verb *čiupti* 'grasp, seize'
brūkš(t)	= *briaukš(t)* 'quick pulling away, cutting off'
benc	'intensive falling on the ground', no related verb
takš(t)	'heavy beating', related to *taškyti* 'splash', iterative of *tėkšti* (pres. *teškiu*) 'hit, splash'
cypt	'squeaking', related verb *cypti* 'squeak'
strapt	'sudden end or beginning of a movement', no related verb
tabalai	'staggering', no related verb.

In (1), the "wolf" is not really a true wolf. The example describes a game young people play in the evening after work. In the narrative, a long dispute

---

[7] This and all other examples from Valančius are given in modern Lithuanian standard orthography after the 1996 edition of Valančius. Example (1) reads as follows in the original orthography: *Ant gała wisi suszoka ąnt wiłka, cziupt gieraj nutwiere, bruksz patraukie, bęnc iszwerte ir taksz taksz muszti pradieje. Wiłkas girdi pirmu cipt cipt cipe, paskiaus wau wau kaukie, ąnt gała strapt stojes ir tabałai tabałai pabiega, nie uodigos nebipalikies.*
[8] I adopt the strategy of the English translator of Wilhelm Busch's *Max und Moritz* not to translate ideophones: *Knacks! – Da bricht der Stuhl entzwei*; 'Knacks! The chair breaks! down they go', *Schwapp! – Da liegen sie im Brei.* 'Schwapp! – into a trough of dough!'

between the "shepherd" and the "wolf" precedes the scene described in (1). The game starts as follows:

> "Still gasping [from the previous game] I said: – Well, now, Peliksas, you are the wolf, and Izidorius shall 'tend the sheep'. Immediately they pushed Peliksas, as the wolf, into a corner and encircled him with chairs as if fencing with a fence. Isidorius took a long crutch, gathered together some ten boys and girls and said: – I am tending the sheep; I will scare the wolf with the crutch and chase it with the dogs." (translation BW here and elsewhere in this chapter)

Similarly in (2), the "fox" is not a fox, but a girl:

(2) Ideophones in early Lithuanian literature (Valančius 1996: 42)

Lap-ė	**šmurkš**	po	lov-ą.	Vis-i		su-šuk-o:
fox-NOM.SG	IDEO	under	bed-ACC.SG	all-NOM.PL.M		PV-cry-PST.3
"Še,	še	mes	regėj-om,	lįs-ki-t		po
here	here	we:NOM	see-PST.1PL	creep-IMP-2PL		under
įtiestuv-ę!"	Pa-lind-usi-am			**čakš**	į-kand-o.	
bed-ACC.SG	PV-creep-PTC:PST:A-DAT:SG:M			IDEO	in-bite-PST.3	
T-as	**ai**	**ai**	su-šuk-o	ir	sak-ė:	"Ei,
that-NOM.SG.M	IDEO	IDEO	PV-cry-PST.3	and	say-PST.3	INTERJ,
štis	tu		laukan!"	Kit-am	lend-ant	**sprakt**
INTERJ	you[SG].NOM		out	other-DAT.SG.M	creep-CNV:DS:SIM	IDEO
į-spyr-ė	į	galv-ą;	t-as	**capt**	su-grob-ė	
PV-kick-PST.3	in	head-ACC.SG	that-NOM.SG.M	IDEO	PV-grasp-PST.3	
lap-ei	už	uodeg-ą,	bet	t-a		
fox-DAT.SG	behind	tail-ACC.SG	but	that-NOM.SG.F		
iš-trauk-usi		**blykš**	pa-si-rod-ė		po	
PV-draw-CNV:SS:ANT:SG:F		IDEO	PV-REFL-show-PST.3		under	
stal-u.	Ap-nik-ta			**purst**	**purst**	
table-INS.SG	PV-disappear-PTC:PST:PASS:SG:F			IDEO	IDEO	
braiž-ė	it	kat-ė,	su-gau-t-a			
scratch-PST.3	as	cat-NOM.SG	PV-catch-PTC:PST:PASS-NOM:SG:F			
klapst	**klapst**	su	dant-imis	brazdin-o,	smeig-ė-s	
IDEO	IDEO	with	tooth-PL:INS	rustle-PST.3	try-PST.3-REFL	
kąs-ti	ir	tarsi	ap-mir-ė.	Vis-i	**ki**	**ki**	**ki**
bite-INF	and	as.if	PV-die-PST.3	all-NOM.PL.M	IDEO	IDEO	IDEO
juok-ė-s.	Bet	lap-ė,	staiga	atgij-usi,		
laugh-PST.3-REFL	but	fox-NOM.SG	quickly	recover-CNV:SS:ANT:SG:F		
strup	stoj-o-s	ir	**pataukš**	pro		
IDEO	stand.up-PST.3-REFL	and	IDEO	trough		
dur-is	iš-spruk-o.					
door-ACC:PL	PV-slip-PST.3					

'[Standing up we caught 'the fox', who was a girl. Standing on the floor of the hut, I said: "Do you know what, neighbors, unfortunately a fox has intruded into our place, she slew a goose and a chicken, we should catch her." Mykolas asked: "What kind of fox is it?" I answered: "The fox is not tall, has a narrow beak, broad eyes, upright ears, teeth like an organ...bent claws and a long tail like a broom. She dresses the same sometimes like a girl." Mykolas replied: "I have seen such a one scurrying in the corner of the hut behind the table. So then, let us catch her."] The fox **šmurkš** away under the bed. All cried: "Here, here, we have seen her, creep under the bed." The one who tried was bitten **čakš**. He cried **ai ai** and said: "Hush you out!" The next got his head kicked **sprakt**; he **capt** caught the fox by her tail, but after she was drawn out **blykš** disappeared under the table. Pounced on, she scratched **purst purst** like a cat, when caught crunched **klapst klapst** with her teeth, tried to bite and seemingly calmed down. Everybody **ki ki ki** laughed. But the fox, quickly recovering, **strup** rose up and **pataukš** slipped away by the door.'

šmurkš	'quick entering into something', derived verb *šmurkšterėti* 'quick entering'
sprakt	related to *spragėti* 'decrepitate', *sprakseti* 'hail hits the window'
capt	'quick grasping'
blykš	'sudden lightning'
purst	'flapping (wings)'
klapst	'rattling, clattering'
strup(t)	'sudden end or beginning of a movement'
pataukš	'sound of hitting something firm with a firm object, running'.

Valančius wrote mainly in Polish. He kept a detailed record of his life and also of many different aspects of his time. For instance, he documented both the daily running battle with Tsarist authorities in the era of Russification and which days he was ill (*Diariusz zdrowia mego* 'Diary of my health', Valančius 2003: 544–549). In the same spirit, *Palangos Juzė* is intended to document not only his own life but also the Lithuanian way of life during a time when that way of life was heavily endangered. This is stated explicitly in the preface to *Palangos Juzė*:

> People's customs change like everything else in the world changes eternally. Observing this, I started to write down not only the customs, but also the games and plays of people of our time. Also because future generations should know what happened to the Samogitians and Lithuanians at the end of our nineteenth century. Knowing that the Lithuanians especially like the things of God, I inserted here and there some new spiritual songs.

Those learning to read should read this booklet if they like it, and if you do not like it, throw it into the stove. And if everybody will do as he likes, there will remain at least one booklet somewhere that future generations will read laughing. The names of places and roads and farmsteads mentioned in this booklet as well as the first and last names of people are not invented by the writer, but real.

The plot of *Palangos Juzė* goes as follows: The peasant Jonas Viskantas from Palanga brings his son Jūzupas (Juzė) to Klaipėda to a German tailor (*kaip ožaitį į turgų **ve ve** bliaunantį* "like a young **ve ve** crying billy goat to the market"), and he shall learn a trade. At the time, Klaipėda (Memel) is the major city in "Small Lithuania", which was a part of Prussia and mainly Protestant, but Juzė is, of course, a good Catholic. After three years, the son comes home; he has run away because the tailor always beats him (*šmiaukš šmiaukš su bizūnu per nugarą* "**šmiaukš šmiaukš** with the whip over the back"). As a migrant tailor, eighteen-year-old Juzė now travels across the whole of Lithuania and learns much about the various customs of the Lithuanian people. Special reference is made to the games and dances of young people, and the youth teaches each other all the songs they know. After four years, Juzė turns home, he has made it, he has three brown horses, a wife, and a child. In thirteen evenings, he tells what he has gone through. Only in passing did the Catholic attitude of the author comes through, and only marginally the resistance against Russification is alluded to.

2 *Palangos Juzė* and the oral, rural, and narrative character of ideophones

We have seen above that Lithuanian *ištiktukai* are a special feature of a particular work in Lithuanian literature, that is, of a certain kind of written language. How can this be reconciled with the general finding that ideophones are characteristic of spoken language summarized in the following statement: "Ideophones are part of an informal language register" (Kilian-Hatz 2001: 156)?

Spoken informal language is a very large domain. Let us first consider in more detail what kind of spoken language is particularly favorable for ideophones. Three factors are frequently mentioned in the literature: communal society, rural environment, and narrative function, as illustrated with quotations in the following paragraphs:

Communal society: Ideophones are characteristic for communal society, for oral and visual society "in which people form themselves into conversational clusters, or take advantage of any situations that throw them together in their daily existence such as a bus shelter, a bus, a train, the village pump, and any situation where people find themselves so to say 'trapped' for a significant amount of time" (Kunene 2001: 190). According to Childs (2001), ideophones are quintessentially social and mark local identity and solidarity.

Rural environment: "Urbanized speakers of a language have a poorer inventory of ideophones than their more traditional co-ethnics and use ideophones less competently" (Samarin 2001: 323). "Ideophones mark one as being rural, non-urban, as something of a country hick" (Childs 2001: 66). According to Childs (2001), Zulu is losing its ideophones due to urbanization. "Concerning the use of ideophones in Wolaitta we observe that existing written materials (school text books and Bible translations) have few ideophones. It seems that people in the towns use ideophones less frequently than those in the countryside" (Amha 2001: 49).

Narrative function: Ideophones in Gbaya "are particularly prevalent in the folktale" (Noss 2001: 260). The function of ideophones "is to dramatize a narration" (Kilian-Hatz 2001: 156). The performative function of level shift evokes in the hearer the illusion of a direct participation (Kilian-Hatz 2001: 157).

It is important to note that narrative here means a particular oral kind of narration. Narrative in a wider sense also includes historical novels and large parts of the Bible. What is meant here is a performed (dramatized) narrativity, making ample use of mimesis (Güldemann 2008). As far as folklore is concerned, the frequency of ideophones in Lithuanian folktales is well known at least since Leskien (1902/1903). Now, there is no reason why oral folktales could not be written down. Actually, it was a favored activity of the Neogrammarians and their predecessors to collect and write down Lithuanian folktales. In transferring speaking to writing, its characteristic oral properties – as far as they are not restricted to the spoken modality a priori, such as intonation – can be reduced or kept; they can even be reinforced. This is what happens in *Palangos Juzė*. The ideophones are stereotypically reinforced as a stylistic device to evoke orality and thereby local identity. The text is designed to be attractive for young people on the countryside. In a time where the distribution of Lithuanian books is strongly obstructed by the authorities, it is meant to reach the most remote Lithuanian villages, and even if written, it is intended to be performed. A large part of the booklet consists of songs (both traditional style and spiritual) that are there for singing, not for reading only. *Ištiktukai* in *Palangos Juzė* are definitely a device to mark Lithuanian local identity and solidarity. This comes with a certain portion of chauvinism. People who are not Lithuanians and Catholics are negatively characterized and treated badly, in the same way as the "wolves" and "foxes" in young people's games discussed above.

(3) Valančius (1996: 37–38)

Aš	pa-jut-au	kaži	k-ą	čiupno-jant	mano
I:NOM	PV-feel-PST.1SG	INDEF	who-ACC	grasp-CNV:DS:SIM	my
kišen-ę,	**čapt** už	rank-ą		nu-tvėr-iau,	veiz-iu
bag-ACC.SG	IDEO behind	hand-ACC.SG		PV-catch-PST.1SG	see-PRS.1SG
k-ame	ne-buv-ęs			žyd-as;	niek-o
who-LOC	NEG-be-PTC:PST:ACT:M:SG			Jew-NOM.SG	nothing-GEN
ne-lauk-dam-as,		**pliaukš**	j-am	per	aus-į,
NEG-wait-CNV:SS:SIM-SG:M		IDEO	he-DAT	through	ear-ACC.SG
takš	per	antr-ą,	**tvinkt**	treči-ą	kart-ą,
IDEO	through	second-ACC.SG	IDEO	third-ACC.SG	time-ACC.SG
žyd-as		**benc**	pa-virt-o.	Kit-i	vaikiuk-ai
Jew-NOM.SG		IDEO	PV-turn-PST.3	other-NOM.PL.M	guy-NOM.PL
bakš	**bakš**	su-dav-ė	j-am	su bat-ų	kuln-imis,
IDEO	IDEO	PV-give-PST.3	he-DAT	with shoe-GEN.PL	heel-INS.PL
žyd-as	tačiaus	tylė-jo		it nebyl-ys,	o
Jew-NOM.SG	however	keep.still-PST.3		as.if mute-NOM.SG	but
iš-spruk-ęs		iš	mūsų	rank-ų,	pa-bėg-o. //
PV-slip-CNV:SS:ANT:SG:M		out.of	our	hand-GEN.PL	PV-flee-PST.3
Pradė-jo	varp-us	**dzen**	**dzen**	skamb-in-ti;	
begin-PST.3	bell-ACC.PL	IDEO	IDEO	ring-CAUS-INF	
iš-gird-ę		**šmukš**	su-lind-om	vis-i	
PV-hear-CNV:SS:ANT:PL:M		IDEO	PV-creep-PST.3	all-NOM.PL.M	
į	bažnyči-ą.				
into	church-ACC.SG				

'I felt somebody grabbing at my bag, **čapt** caught him by the arm, looked around watched – where was it not a Jew – promptly **pliaukš** slapped him in the ear, and **takš** in the other one, and **tvinkt** a third time, the Jew **benc** stumbled down. The other guys **bakš bakš** kicked him with boot heels, but the Jew remained silent as if dumb and slipping out of our hands, escaped. The bells started ringing **dzen dzen**; hearing this, we all **šmukš** entered the church.'

The marking of a certain type of written language as oral with the function of dramatizing narration is paralleled in a completely different modern register, Internet chat, where ideophones have a similar function as smileys and quotation marks, which are all devices to mimic spoken language. Consider example (4), where we encounter the context type "narrating own mishaps", which is characteristic of ideophone use and also occurs in *Palangos Juzė*.

(4) Example from chat: Use type "narrating own mishaps"

Užėj-au	kartą	pas	mam-ą,	šnek-amės,	kav-ą
go-PST.1SG	once	to	mother-ACC.SG	speak-PRS.1PL.REFL,	coffee-ACC.SG

dar-omės.	Na,	**gurkš**	"kav-ut-ės"	ir	žiūr-im
make-PRS.1PL.REFL	INTERJ	**IDEO**	coffee-DIM-GEN.SG	and	look-PRS.1PL

vien-a	į	kit-ą	**blink.gif**
one-NOM.SG.F	in	other-ACC.SG	

pa-si-rod-o	kav-ą	ne-virt-u	vanden-iu
PV-REFL-show-PRS.3	coffee-ACC.SG	NEG-cooked-INS.SG.M	water-INS.SG

už-pyl-ėm	**LOTULIUKAS.GIF**
PV-pour-PST.1PL	

'Once I went to see my mother, we talked, made coffee. Well, **gurkš** "coffee" and we looked at each other SMILEY apparently we had poured unboiled water over the coffee SMILEY [and this with two cooks in the kitchen SMILEY]'.
supermama.lt/forumas/index.php?showtopic=238862&mode=threaded&pid= 14373525 (2008 01 21, 13:13)

Apart from the factors communal society, rural environment, and narrative function, there is another important factor: the element of play. Ideophones are characteristic of playful language and frequently occur in child-directed speech, as is expressed vividly in the following passage from a handbook article on field methods:

> Serendipitous events can produce spontaneous types of language that are hard to elicit and that may never appear in texts. I had studied the Muskogean language Chickasaw for eight years and hundreds of hours before I began bringing my new baby Alex to visit my Chickasaw teacher, Catherine Willmond. One day, she took him on her lap and patted with his hand on the table in front of them, telling him,
>
> (1) Pas pas pas aachi
>   pas pas pas say
>
> I had never heard this type of sentence before, but discovered that it was a type of 'expressive' construction used to describe noises that speakers feel is particularly appropriate for illustration presented to children. (Catherine's remark could be translated either 'He's going *pas pas pas* (making a slapping noise),' or as a command addressed to him, 'Go *pas pas pas* (make a slapping noise)!'" (Munro 2001: 132–133)

Playful language does not mean only using language for fun, but has again a performative element. Both in Catherine Willmond's Chickasaw game played with Alex and in Valančius' "wolf" and "fox" games, ideophones serve to emphasize the performative character of speech.

Child-directed speech has also something to do with rurality if considered from the point of view of politeness. In rural settings, people are more likely to talk more often to people they know than in urban settings. In speaking to adult non-familiar persons, preservation of face is a more serious issue than in speaking to personal friends, relatives, and children. This makes urban speech more formal on average than rural speech.

The narrative and performative functions of ideophones have been associated with their incompatibility with negation in many languages. According to Kilian-Hatz (2001: 157), "[t]he incompatibility of ideophones and negation can be explained by their dramaturgic function". In *Palangos Juzė*, there is only a single example of ideophones used under the scope of negation. This example is very instructive in that it shows that ideophones are incompatible with irreality rather than with negation. *Ištiktukai* occur with events that have happened; that is to say with realized events, not with unrealized, future, or possible or impossible events, hence Jablonskis' statement that ideophones are associated with past events. In (5), there is a counterfactual construction with a negation in the apodosis. A counterfactual combined with a negation results in assertion. Actually, here, it is an emphatic kind of assertion, which is a favorable context for the use of an ideophone despite the formal negation marker on the verb. What matters is that the event has occurred, not whether or not it is formally marked for negation:

(5) Ideophone with a formally negated verb, expressing a realis event (Valančius 1996)

Rasi   bū-čiau   ir   smerči-op   už-si-muš-ęs...
perhaps   be-SBJV.1SG   and dead-ALL   PV-REFL-hit-PTC:PST:A:M:SG
*kad   rietė-dam-as   bū-čiau   **capt***
when   roll-CNV:SS:SIM-SG:M   be-SBJV.1SG   IDEO
ne-nu-si-tvėr-ęs   auganč-io   alksn-io.
NEG-PV-REFL-catch-PTC:PST:A:M:SG growing-GEN.SG.M   alder-GEN.SG
'Perhaps I would even have perished to death...if I had not **capt** grabbed a growing aldertree.'

We can summarize the results of this section as follows: If ideophones mark rurality – as is frequently stated in the literature on ideophones – they can also be used as a stylistic device to establish rural identity. This happens in Valančius' *Palangos Juzė*: One of its major aims is to foster the Lithuanian rural self-esteem in times of repression of Lithuanian culture in the Tsarist Empire. Furthermore, ideophones have a playful element. It is not surprising that they occur exactly in descriptions of games in *Palangos Juzė*. The games serve the same purpose as the many songs in *Palangos Juzė*: They are suggestions for performance in leisure time for young Lithuanian peasants, and this is one of the aspects that make the booklet particularly appealing for them. Hence, Lithuanian ideophones show that ideophones are not only oral and visual, but that they can also be used in written language as a means to evoke orality stereotypically. The same holds for the modern use of ideophones in Internet chats.

3 Particular features of Lithuanian *ištiktukai* and universals of ideophones

3.1 Introduction

In Sections 1 and 2, I argued that Lithuanian ideophones have an interesting history because of the way they have been used in written texts and the way they have been treated by linguists. In this section, I will now discuss structural properties of Lithuanian ideophones. This issue is important both for their description in Lithuanian and from a cross-linguistic perspective. As will be demonstrated, Lithuanian ideophones exhibit several language-specific properties. Identifying those as such helps us gain insight into the typology of ideophones by being able to tell apart those properties that are recurrent in most known languages and those that are rescricted to single languages or areas.

Let us begin here with some very general features that are not particularly striking. It is well known that ideophones in all kinds of languages exhibit peculiar traits in phonology and skewed phonotactic distributions (see e.g., Childs 1994: 181, Dingemanse 2012: 656, Danylenko, this volume, for details on Lithuanian and East Slavic). Lithuanian is no exception in this respect. Ideophones frequently contain phonemes or phonemes in particular positions that are not generally characteristic of other parts of speech. For instance, most words beginning with *č* are ideophones or associated with ideophones, while *č* is generally common word-internally. A quote from the etymological dictionary is as follows: "Die meisten Wörter unter *č* sind Fremdwörter oder onomatopoetische Bildungen; um nicht jedes onomat. Wort einzeln zu behandeln, werden sie nach semasiologischen Gesichtspunkten zusammengefasst" (Fraenkel 1962/5: 71). Even more specific is the phoneme /c/: "c ist überhaupt kein im Litauischen möglicher Laut ausser in Schallnachahmungen und Fremdwörtern..." (Leskien 1902/3: 180). For a very thorough treatment of the phonology of sound verbs (related to ideophones) in the related language Latvian, see Urdze (2010, discussed extensively in Wälchli 2010).

Another general point is that ideophones have to be considered to be an integral part of the grammar and lexicon. As claimed by Ameka (2001: 25), progress in ideophone research "has been hampered by emphasizing the peripheral and the irregular nature of ideophones".[9] It is interesting to note that there is a very similar point made by Leskien (1902/1903: 165): "Interjektionen und Schallnachahmungen erfahren in den Grammatiken selten liebevolle Behandlung, weil sie meist als nicht so recht zur Sprache gehörig angesehen werden". In this context, it is important to note that "[i]deophones are collectable" (Samarin 2001: 321) like items of any other part of speech and that "[i]deophones belong to the lexicon of a language" (Samarin 2001: 326). This was self-evident for Leskien (1902/1903). His article ends with a comprehensive glossary of Lithuanian ideophones. Hence, I do not agree with Andersen (2009) that *ištiktukai* are a "para-lexical part of speech", but rather take sides with the Lithuanian grammar tradition that they are a part of speech of Lithuanian *tout court*.

In the following sections, five particular aspects of Lithuanian ideophones will be discussed that are both language-specific and fit into the general typology of ideophones at the same time. In Section 3.2, the tendency of Lithuanian to express event number by full reduplication is discussed (reduplication is known to be pervasive in ideophones in general). In Section 3.3, lengthening of vowels is discussed as an instance of the general tendency of ideophones for iconic sound symbolism. Lithuanian, with its length distinction and tone opposition on long syllable cores, is particularly suitable to mark such distinctions. Ideophones are often argued to be morphologically simple in contrast to verbs. In Lithuanian, however, the majority of ideophones have formal characteristics, some of which are even related to grammatical categories (notably the infinitive, see also Danylenko, this volume). In Section 3.4, I discuss to what extent Lithuanian ideophones are morphologically complex. In Section 3.5, I present the syntactic constructions of ideophones that are largely conforming to those discussed in the literature, except that the cross-linguistically widespread construction with semantically bleached verbs for "say", "go", or "do" are virtually absent and that it is characteristic for Lithuanian ideophones to be used with arguments (as if they were verbs with the valency of verbs). Finally, in Section 3.6, I show data that demonstrate that there are many ideophones derived from verbs that do not follow the cross-linguistically well-known grammaticalization path of ideophone+light verb

---

9 This is generally the case for the phenomena summarized under the term "mimesis" in Güldemann (2008): iconic representational gestures, non-lingusitic sound imitations, ideophones, and direct reported discourse.

condensation (which is not available in Lithuanian due to lack of bleached light verbs with ideophones).

3.2 Reduplication and event number

Event number is typically marked on verbs and hence "may reasonably be taken as a type of verbal aspect" (Corbett 2000: 247). But there is no reason why it could not be marked on a word class other than verbs expressing events, such as ideophones. Unlike participant number, event number does not specify the number of subjects or objects or other noun phrases, but the number of events, most commonly the opposition between single event and multiple events (Corbett 2000: 246, Mithun 1988: 217, cf. also Newman's notion of pluractionality 2006).

In Lithuanian, full reduplication (iteration) of ideophones expresses event number, and its absence, the lack of pluractionality at least in *Palangos Juzė* and probably also in other varieties of Lithuanian (see the many examples in Jašinskaitė 1975 conforming to the distinction). This has been observed already by Senn (1966), who expresses it succinctly but somewhat cryptically as follows: "Durch wiederholte oder andauernde Handlung erzeugter wiederholter oder andauernder Naturlaut wird durch Wiederholung des Schallwortes nachgeahmt" [Repeated or persisting natural sound, produced by repeated or persisting events, is imitated by a repetition of the sound word.] (Senn 1966: 308). Senn's statement implicitly contains a diachronic explanation – the development starts with repeated sound being expressed by repeated ideophones – and a synchronic motivation for the opposition: iconicity. Reduplication in *ištiktukai* is also extensively discussed by Andersen (2009: 130), who distinguishes different degrees of iconicity: "the single iteration is not to be understood as representing a single repetition, but as a common metaphor for multiple events or event parts".[10]

The opposition is illustrated in examples (6) and (7) from the Ninth Evening in *Palangos Juzė*, where the story becomes highly ethnographical, describing the process of courtship and the subsequent wedding. Courtship follows strict rules. The suitor does not speak himself, his companion speaks for him, and as soon as the request is made to the father of the bride, the daughter immediately disap-

---

[10] Andersen (2009) argues that the reduplication in *ištiktukai* in Lithuanian is one of several areas in Baltic morphology where reduplication is renewed after Baltic and Slavic have lost the productive devices of reduplication of Indo-European. This is an interesting approach, but I find it too difficult to reconstruct the use of ideophones in Indo-European to be sure whether there is really an innovation in Lithuanian.

pears, which is stated in (6). Her act of slipping out is momentary, which is why it is expressed in (6) with a non-reduplicated ideophone.

(6) Single event>simplex (Valančius 1996: 69)

...dukt-ė	**šmurkš**	spruk-o	oran	ir	kaip
daughter-NOM.SG	IDEO	slip-PST.3	out	and	like
pel-el-ė	po	šluot-a	pa-si-slėp-ė		
mouse-DIM-NOM.SG	under	broom-INS.SG	PV-REFL-hide-PST.3		

'[Having heard those words] the daughter **šmurkš** slipped out and hid like a mouse under the broom.'

The beating of the heart, however, when the daughter reappears consists of multiple events, which is why it is expressed by a reduplicated ideophone in (7).

(7) Multiple event>full reduplication (Valančius 1996: 69)

At-rad-us	į-ėj-o	raudon-a,	kaip	vėž-ys
PV-find-CNV:DS:ANT	PV-go-PST.3	red-NOM.SG,F	like	crab-NOM.SG
iš-vir-t-as,		širdi-is	j-os	**timpt** **timpt**
PV-cook-PTC:PST:PASS-NOM:SG:M		heart-NOM.SG	she-GEN	IDEO IDEO
greit-ai	muš-ė	kaip	gaid-ys	sparn-us,
quick-ADV	beat-PST.3	like	rooster-NOM.SG	wing-ACC:PL
giedo-ti	norė-dam-as			
sing-INF	want-CNV:SS:SIM-SG:M			

'After they found her she entered with a face red like a cooked crab, her heart beat quickly **timpt timpt** like a rooster "beats" with his wings when it wants to sing.'

Note again the comparison with animals in (6) and (7) – mouse, crab, and rooster. It is important to point out that the aspectual distinction in ideophones is rather different from the well-known perfective-imperfective aspect opposition in Slavic languages.

Example (8a,b) is used to illustrate the close relationship between aspect and number, with predicates meaning 'sit down'. If several persons sit down, they do so at various places and usually not exactly simultaneously (8b, multiple event); with a single subject, however, sitting down is a single event (8a):

(8) Single and multiple event (Valančius 1996: 80, 51)

a.
motyn-a	**plekš**	at-si-sėd-o	ant	vien-a
woman-NOM.SG	IDEO	PV-REFL-sit-PST.3	on	one-INS.SG.F
skryni-a				
box-INS.sg				

'the woman **plekš** sat down on a box'

b. | *vis-i* | ***plekš*** | ***plekš*** | *su-sėd-o* | *ant* | *pamat-u*
   | all-NOM.PL.M | **IDEO** | **IDEO** | PV-sit-PST.3 | on | ground-INS.SG

'all **plekš plekš** sat down on the ground'

It is well known that repeated ideophones tend to express plurality. Kilian-Hatz (2001: 158) notes for Kxoe: "Reduplication always denotes, when used with ideophones, a kind of plurality, i.e. an increase of intensity concerning states or e.g. colors". In *Palangos Juzė*, full reduplication of ideophones is arguably fully grammaticalized as an expression of event number. Reduplicated ideophones are slightly more frequent (54.2%, 115 tokens) than their non-reduplicated counterparts (45.8%, 97 tokens). It is therefore not clear whether reduplicated ideophones should be considered the marked or the unmarked member of the opposition. Lithuanian verbs also have derivational means to express iterativity lexically, but these are more idiosyncratic than with ideophones. Interestingly, iterativity is more grammaticalized in ideophones than in verbs.

It is not difficult to find other examples beyond *Palangos Juzė*, where Lithuanian ideophones express event number. Example (9) is from a modern newspaper interview with an expert on pollution who explains that pollution is not caused only by big multinational companies, but also by ordinary people who are negligent and simply do not care. The example given is a stereotypical neighbor who throws garbage on the street. It starts with the already familiar comparison with an animal: The woman has the double chin of a mouse. (It is as unusual in Lithuanian as in English to imagine double chins of mice. For our purposes, it suffices to note that there is a comparison with an animal, not so much what is means exactly.) The first ideophone *dirst* – which is repeated – stands for repeated side glancing. Then *čiupt* 'grasping' and *šliūkšt* 'pouring' are momentary events. Note that the ideophones are used here without concomitant verbs; they take the valency of verbs they "replace": *šliūkšt* 'pouring' takes a direct object in the accusative case and a goal complement, *dirst* 'glancing' comes with several dependent directional adverbs.

(9) From a newspaper interview with an expert about pollution

štai	*ji,*	*guv-i*	*moterišk-ė,*		
voilà	she:NOM	swift-NOM.SG.F	woman-NOM.SG		
pel-yt-ės		*pasmakr-ė,*	*žvitri-u*		*žvilgsni-u*
mouse-DIM-GEN.SG		under.chin-INS.SG	brisk-INS.SG.M		glance-INS.SG
tik	***dirst-dirst***	*kairėn*	*dešinėn,*	*viršun*	*apačion*	*aha,*
only	**IDEO-IDEO**	to.left	to.right	up	down	aha
niekas	*ne-mat-o,*	*tai*	*staiga*	***čiupt***	*ir*	***šliūkšt***
nobody	NEG-see-PRS.3	so	quickly	**IDEO**	and	**IDEO**
piln-ą	*kibir-iok-ą*		*šiukšli-ų*		*į*	
full-ACC.SG	bucket-AUGM-ACC.SG		sweeping-GEN.PL		in	

gatv-ę,	ant	šaligatvi-o,	vos	ne
street-ACC.SG	on	sidewalk-GEN.SG	hardly	not
praeivi-ams	ant	galv-ų…		
passersby-DAT.PL	on	head-GEN.PL		

'[From details not worth of any attention, pecadillo, the most common non-educatedness, for example, when even from the opposite house of my neighbor:] Voilà she, the swift woman, with the double-chin of a mouse, with a brisk glance only **dirst dirst** (side-glancing) to the left to the right, down, up, aha, nobody sees it, then quickly **čiupt** (grasping) and **šliūkšt** (pouring) a full bucketone sweepings on the street, on the sidewalk, almost on the heads of passers-by. [The motive for justification of all dirtmakers and litterers is the same, from oil and coal barons until untidy builders – oh, it is a pecadillo, nothing happens, I am not the only one who litters.]'

It is not always clear what reduplication in ideophones means, which is illustrated in the anecdote in (10) given here in full length without glossing. The anecdote plays with the fact that it is difficult to point to the exact meaning of the reduplication, but the addressee's response can be taken as evidence that reduplication usually means something, especially when used contrastively.[11] The addressee is suspicious that the difference means something and must be reassured that it does not.

(10) Anekdotas
Sėdi Chaimas su geriausiu draugu kalėjimo kameroje ir garsiai svajoja:
– Kai mus išleis iš kalėjimo, kaip mums bus gera. Nueisim į mano krautuvę, tu nupirksi didelį batoną ir butelį limonado. Paskui nueisim į parką, atsisėsim ant suoliuko ir taip skaniai valgysim. Tu **krimst**, aš **krimst, krimst**. Tu **gurkšt**, aš **gurkšt, gurkšt**.
– Palauk-palauk, o kodėl tu du kartus **krimst-krimst** ir **gurkšt-gurkšt**?
– Taigi mes su tavim geriausi draugai!
'Chaimas sits with his best friend in a prison cell and dreams aloud:
– If they'll let us out of the prison, we will live so well. We'll go to my shop, you will buy a big loaf of bread and a bottle of soda. Then we'll go to the park, sit on a bank and eat. You **krimst**, I **krimst krimst**. You **gurkšt**, I **gurkšt gurkšt**.
– Wait a moment, and why you twice **krimst-krimst** and **gurkšt-gurkšt**?
– How can you doubt that we are the very best of friends?'

---

[11] I am grateful to Mark Dingemanse for this remark.

Based on the material in Jašinskaitė (1971), Andersen (2009) argues that there is only a weak correlation between eventive (=ideophone) iteration and aspect: Iterated eventives represent either an activity or a process (imperfective equivalent) or a composite event (perfective equivalent). Partial reduplication (e.g., *buburgt*), however, tends to go together with perfectivity as well as infixed stem extensions, apophony, or prefixation. I agree with Andersen (2009: 132) that "[e]ventives with the prefix *pa-* are perfective; but also without the prefix, simple eventives are mostly equivalent to a perfective verb" while there is no strict (im)perfectivity opposition in ideophones. However, it seems to me that Senn's approach in its modern interpretation of event number captures a more general principle at least for *Palangos Juzė*. The material of Jašinskaitė (1971) is more difficult to interpret because it comes from most different sources. It cannot be taken for granted that full reduplication has the same function in all varieties of Lithuanian. A further analysis of the function of reduplication in Lithuanian is a promising task for Lithuanian corpus linguistics.

3.3 Lengthening of vowels

It is well known that ideophones tend to make extensive use of iconic sound symbolism. For Lithuanian, it is particularly important to note the possibility to use vowel length. In long syllable cores (long vowels, long diphthongs, and vowels with tautosyllabic nasal or liquid), there is, furthermore, a tonal distinction between so-called acute and circumflex intonation (see, for instance, Daugaviete, this volume). This yields three different variants for many ideophones (Table 1).

Tab. 1: Three variants of ideophones with differing in vowel length and tone[12]

Short	*trùkt* 'a slight twitching drawing'
Long acute	*trūkt* 'same, but with a stronger grasp'
Long circumflex	*trũkt* 'same, with stronger grasp, but with more slowly performed action'

With some ideophones, it is possible to mark phonologically a three-way slowness distinction: *pùrst* 'flapping with wings', *pūrst* 'slower', *pũrst* 'still slower' (Niedermann et al. 1951–1986: III, 459).[13]

---

[12] However, there are many dialects where the distinction between *trūkt* (acute) and *trũkt* (circumflex) etc. is neutralized.
[13] A long vowel before a tautosyllabic sonorant is a fairly uncommon phenomenon in Lithuanian and testifies to the specific phonology of ideophones.

As pointed out above, exploiting length distinctions in ideophones is not unusual. For instance, Childs points out for Gbaya: "A common type of universal iconicity is that associated with expressive lengthening or (unlimited) reduplication common with ideophones. In each case the prolongation represents a lengthy or repeated action or state, in some cases standing in contrast with a non-prolonged form." For instance, Gbaya *fɛɛ* 'a breath of air', *fɛɛɛ* 'a long breath of air'; *dirr* 'a rumble like thunder', *dirrr* 'a long rolling rumble like thunder or like an earthquake' (Noss 1985: 242 quoted in Childs 1994: 193).

What makes Lithuanian special is that its phonology is particularly well suited to mark such iconic distinctions in ideophones phonologically (as far as vowels are concerned) (see also Jašinskaitė 1975: 45).

3.4 Simplex form or complex morphology

In modern literature, we typically find statements to the effect that ideophones do not have any morphological affixes and do not express any major grammatical categories. For instance, according to Killian-Hatz (2001: 156), "[i]deophones are simplexes, i.e. they are not marked for person, tense and mood like verbs, and they are not marked for case, gender and number like nouns". We have seen in Section 3.2, that there is an exception, as far as the category of event number or iterative aspect is concerned. This section, however, deals with suffixes (or rather pseudo-suffixes) of Lithuanian ideophones.

Many Lithuanian ideophones end in -*t*; this is reminiscent of the infinitive ending -*ti* (-*t* in many Žemaitian dialects). According to Leskien, -*t* actually derives from the infinitive, but let us consider first how -*t* in ideophones is distributed in a corpus. In *Palangos Juzė*, there is free variation in the following four ideophones only without any difference in meaning *brink(t)* 'throw, spread (money)', *cyp(t)* 'squeak', *šmukš(t)* 'move away, in, to another place', *strup(t)* 'stand up'. Put differently, for most ideophones, -*t* (where it occurs) is clearly part of the lexical entry and cannot therefore express a grammatical category. Consequently, the extension -*t* cannot be described as a morpheme proper: It does not bear any meaning. Jašinskaitė (1975: 20) calls it a "formant". This formant -*t* is highly characteristic for the phonotactics of Lithuanian ideophones. Of 212 ideophone tokens in *Palangos Juzė*, 72 (34%) end in -*t*, but we must hasten to add that in 71 of 72 cases, -*t* is preceded by at least one consonant. The characteristic structure is thus -*(C)Ct* rather than -*t*.

Now why should ideophones be associated with the infinitive? The Lithuanian infinitive derives diachronically from a dative case of a verbal noun and is thus beyond any suspicion not of onomatopoeic origin. If there is a diachronic connection, ideophones – or rather only some of them – derive from infinitives, not the other way round (see also Danylenko, this volume). Leskien (1902/1903) provides the following reasons for such a scenario:

i. There is a second infinitive in Lithuanian -*tè* marking emphasis and always combined with a finite verb form of the same stem (*figura etymologica*): *degtè dėga* 'burn.INFII burn.PRS3 'it burns intensively'. It should further be taken into account that -*tè* can be shortened to -*t* in Žemaitian. Ideophones sometimes look as if they have the same stem as the accompanying verb. Thus, they share with the second infinitive the function of intensification and a predilection for *figura etymologica*. However, -*te* can certainly not be the source of -*t* in ideophones, given that ideophones in the East Aukštaitian dialect of Tverečius have -*ć* originating from -*ti* (Norbert Ostrowski, p.c.).

ii. Like the imperative in Russian, the Lithuanian infinitive can express a suddenly occurring event in a narrative (Leskien 1902/1903: 182, Senn 1966: 470).

(11) Infinitive used to express a sudden event (Senn 1966: 470)
 šuo, *pa-mat-ęs* *lap-ę*
 dog:NOM.SG PV-see-CNV:SS:ANT:SG:M fox-ACC.SG
 nu-bėg-ant, *j-ą* **gin-ti-s**
 PV-run-CNV:DS:SIM 3-ACC:SG:F **chase-INF-REFL**
 'When the dog saw the fox running away, it chased after it immediately.'

However, such uses of the infinitive are not frequent, at least in modern Lithuanian.

If the -*t* originates from *figura etymologica* constructions, we might expect that it still collocates with this function. This is not the case in *Palangos Juzė*. Of 212 ideophone tokens, 22 (or 10.4%) occur in *figura etymologica* constructions, nine of which have -*t*. A χ^2 test does not reveal any correlation of -*t* with *figura etymologica* within ideophones (p=0.62). In sum, a clear connection between infinitive and -*t* in ideophones cannot be established either synchronically or diachronically.

More important than the association of -*(C)Ct* with the infinitive is the fact that many Lithuanian ideophones generally have characteristic formants, -*t* only being one of them (see Jašinskaitė 1975: 20–31 for an extensive discussion). The sequence -*kš* is even more common (89 tokens, or 42%). The two most characteristic endings have a complementary distribution in *Palangos Juzė*: Only 4 tokens have -*kšt* and only 56 have neither -*kš* nor -*(C)Ct* (χ^2, p=8.5e–14). These sequences are of crucial importance for ideophones as has already been observed by Leskien. He argues that Lithuanian ideophones have a fixed "grammatical form" ending on -š or -t and derived from a root that must end on a consonant. Ideophones can be derived from verb stems unless these end on a vowel.[14] Similarly, Metuzāle-Kangere (1991) and Urdze (2010) argue for Latvian, that Latvian sound verbs have characteristic sequences k+šķ and k+st.

Now, the lack of a synchronic collocation of -t with *figura etymologica* does not invalidate the connection of ideophones with the infinitive. Some ideophones look like infinitives or are fake infinitives, which means that they would have the form of an infinitive. Lithuanian verb derivation makes extensive use of ablaut (see Stang 1942). Consider the following two examples with the ideophone *žvilgt* 'glancing', cognate with the verb *žvelgti* 'look, glance', and its iterative (and reflexive) derivation *žvalgytis* 'look around': *žvilgt žvilgt ap-si-žvalgė* 'IDEO IDEO around-REFL-look:ITER-PST.3>looked around' (Valančius 1996: 50) and *žvilgt pa-žvelg-iau* 'IDEO PV-look-PST.1SG>I glanced' (Valančius 1996: 37). The verb *žvilgti* exists as a variant of *žvelgti* with a different ablaut grade.

We can conclude that (some) Lithuanian ideophones share with the infinitive some formal and functional peculiarities without there being any clear general correlations. However, most Lithuanian ideophones are not simplex, but have a -(C)t or -(k)š enlargement, which has no morphological function, but rather marks the forms phonologically as ideophones (see also Andersen 2009: 125–132 for the discussion of other morphological processes in *ištiktukai*).

3.5 Ideophones used with the valency of verbs and the lack of bleached light verbs

The discussion of ideophones cannot be separated from the constructions where they appear. In the literature, the following three construction types are probably most frequently referred to: (i) the use of ideophones in isolation, (ii) the combination with verbs that express the same or a similar meaning that is often partly redundant, as argued by Derbyshire (1977: 178) for Hixkaryána (e.g., *nomokyatxkonà, àhpo* 'they_used_to_come, action_of_arriving'), and (iii) the combination with

---

14 "Die von den Grammatikern unerörtert gelassene Eigentümlichkeit ist, dass die Schallworte im Litauischen eine feste grammatische Form haben. Sie enden auf *t, st, szt* und müssen von (sic!) dem *t* konsonantischen Anlaut des zu Grunde liegenden verbalen oder nicht verbalen Elementes haben, das ich im folgenden der Kürze wegen als Wurzel bezeichnen werde, so dass man, so weit ich habe beobachten können, von Verben vokalisch auslautender Wurzel, z.B. *ló-ti* bellen, solche Rufe nicht bildet" (Leskien 1902/1903: 168).

bleached light verbs, most characteristically 'go', 'do/make', and/or 'say', as in English *Ding-dong went the door bell*.

A characteristic feature of Lithuanian ideophones is that type (iii) – used with bleached light verbs – is almost completely lacking. In *Palangos Juzė*, it is not attested and also in Jašinskaitė (1975), there are hardly any examples. This does not mean that ideophones cannot be combined with 'go' and 'say', but if they are, they are rather of type (ii): The verbs are used in their literal meaning as in (12):

(12) Ideophone with motion event (Valančius 1996: 13)
 bet nugis **styri** **styri** *ei-kim gul-ti*
 but now **IDEO** **IDEO** go-IMP.1PL sleep-INF
 'but let us now **styri styri** go to bed'

In (12), *eiti* 'go' is used in its literal sense of motion; *styrì* specifies the manner of motion 'slow going with stiff legs (from cold or long sitting)'. Actually, the use of ideophones to express motion events (notably manner of motion) is very common in Lithuanian. The first two semantic groups of Jašinskaitė (1975: 57–70) in her semantic subclassification are horizontal and vertical motion.

However, it might be argued that the use of type (iii) with light verbs is a secondary development, due to grammaticalization – or more specifically, semantic bleaching. Lithuanian could then be taken as an example to show that there are languages where stage (ii) is attested, but (iii) is lacking. A problem with this argument is that type (iii) is not the exception, but rather the rule in the languages of the world. For most languages where ideophones have been described, there are also examples with 'go', 'say' (or other non-verbal quotative markers), or 'make' beyond their literal motion, speech, or production domain uses. This holds even for most European languages; consider (13) from Italian:

(13) Italian (Sicilian) (Camilleri 1998)
 ciaf, **ciaf**, *fac-ev-a distint-amente la sabbia vagnàt-a*
 IDEO **IDEO** make-IPV:PST-3SG distinctive-ADV ART:F sand wet-F
 'ciaf, ciaf, made the wet sand distinctively' [from the steps of the mafia-hired killer approaching]

This means that what would have to be explained is why Lithuanian lacks type (iii), rather than why English, German, Italian, Mordvin (Wälchli 2005: 164), and all the other languages have it.

A compensation for the lacking type (iii) is another construction type that is not frequently discussed in the literature on ideophones: the use of ideophones instead of verbs and with the valency of the verbs they can be claimed to replace (see also Andersen 2009: 126).[15] In example (14) from a newspaper article, the ideophone *triaukš* 'eating' has an accusative object in the same way as the verb *valgyti* 'eat' would have in this context and the verb phrase headed by the ideophone is coordinated with another verb phrase headed by the verb form *užsigers* 'will drink until filled'. The verb form is marked for future tense, which is used here in a habitual sense. Despite the conditional construction, the ideophone is not at all out of place here because the contextual interpretation is factual. This is what parents and elder children do, and following their example, so do babies.

(14) Ideophone with the valency of a verb and coordinated with a verb
Kūdikiai   mok-o-si   turė-dam-i
baby-NOM.PL   learn-PRS3-REFL have-CNV:SS:SIM-NOM:PL:M
prieš   ak-is
before   eye-ACC.PL
pavyzd-į –   jus.
example-ACC.SG   you[2PL:ACC]
Taigi   jei   mam-a,   tėt-is,   vyresn-ieji
thus   if   mummy-NOM.SG   daddy-NOM.SG   elder-DEF.NOM.PL.M
*broli-ai   ir   ses-ės   kasdien   **triaukš***
brother-NOM.PL   and   sister-NOM.PL   every.day   **IDEO**
saldaini-us,   traškuči-us,   pusfabrikači-us   bei
sweet-ACC.PL   snack-ACC.PL   half.fabricate-ACC.PL   and
už-si-ger-s   gazuot-ais   gėrim-ais
PV-REFL-drink-FUT.3   carbonated-INS.PL   drink-INS.PL
ūgtelė-jęs   mažyl-is   dary-s
grow.quickly.a.bit-PTC.PST.ACT.NOM.SG.M   little.one-NOM.SG   do-FUT.3
lygi-ai   t-ą   pat-į.
exactly   that-ACC.SG   self-ACC.SG

'Babies learn by keeping in front of their eyes an example – you. So if mother, father, elder brothers and sisters every day **triaukš** sweets, snacks, convenience food and tank up with carbonated drinks, the quickly a little growing little one will do the same.'

---

15 Tom Güldemann points out to me that the same is possible in Shona:
*imbwá   héyo   **pikú**   nyáma   mu-mbá   washu   toro*
9.dog   PRES:9.DEM   **IDEO:snatch**   meat   INE-house   IDEO:run   IDEO:disappear
'There is the dog **taking** the meat from the house, running off and disappearing' (Fortune 1971: 250).

To put it differently, it looks as if Lithuanian ideophones can behave syntactically as if they were verbs and exhibit a high degree of syntactic integration in this use.[16] For further examples of this use, see examples (4) and (9). There is no research on exactly how frequent this construction type is, but it is perhaps not equally common for all varieties of Lithuanian. According to Zinkevičius (1981: 201), *ištiktukai* replacing verbs are characteristic of those parts of Lithuania where they are more widespread: Žemaitian (Low Lithuanian) and in Eastern Aukštaitian (Eastern High Lithuanian) rather than in Central Lithuanian where they are more restricted. However, *Palangos Juzė* is an obvious counterexample. Even though ideophones are frequent in that text, there are only seven occurrences (3.3%) without an accompanying verb (in some of them, there is a prepositional complement or a dative object, but there is no example with a direct object). The types of syntactic constructions ideophones can occur in various varieties of Lithuanian and their correlation with the overall frequency of ideophones is a topic for further research. We can conclude, however, that Lithuanian ideophones are cross-linguistically unusual in that they show no tendency to be used with semantically bleached verbs; furthermore, in some varieties of Lithuanian, they can be used instead of full verbs and "take over" their valency.

3.6 Ideophones from verbs by derivation rather than condensation

The construction of ideophones with light verb collocations is important not only because it is cross-linguistically frequent, but also because it represents a well-investigated diachronic path from ideophones to verbs, especially in northern Australian languages. McGregor (2001: 2005) argues that "ideophones represent an important historical source for [Uninflected Verbs] in northern Australian languages", and according to Schultze-Bernd (2001), uninflected predicates (co-verbs) in Jaminjung and other northern Australian languages have ideophone-like characteristics. Even though McGregor does not argue that the scenario for Australia is universal, it is profitable to consider it here to show in what way Lithuanian is different.

The univerbation of ideophone plus light verb is no option in Lithuanian for the development of new verbs, although there are many verbs in Lithuanian

---

[16] See Dingemanse (in press) for a discussion of the typological relevance of the notion of syntactic integration of ideophones.

containing elements reminiscent of ideophones. This means that there must be at least two ways to travel from ideophones to verbs:
i. Condensation of ideophone+light verb collocations (compound verb construction, McGregor 2001)
ii. Verbal derivation from ideophones (in languages where the derivation of verbs from most different parts of speech is very common)[17]

Let us first summarize McGregor's (2001: 214) scenario for the development of compound verb constructions (co-verb+light verb) in northern Australia:
1. The class of ideophones is expanded.
2. Simultaneously, ideophones are frequently used with 'say' (instead of 'he swam' 'splash he said').
3. This means of expression catches on.
4. Other light verbs ('go', 'hit', 'sit', 'put', 'catch', 'give', 'fall') are used analogically.
5. The original simple verbal expressions are outdated.
6. The light verbs can become meaningless conjugation class markers and the compound verb constructions are condensed to a new productive class of verbs. As soon as this stage is reached, the cycle can start anew.

According to McGregor (2001: 218), there is reason to believe that this sequence of processes has occurred more than once in the history of Australian languages.

While this scenario may be appropriate for the explanation of developments in northern Australian languages, it is doubtful whether it is compatible with all languages with ideophones. In Lithuanian, there is no evidence for a stage 2. Lithuanian is thus a counterargument against a scenario where the construction with 'say/do' is a universal precondition for the expansion of a class of ideophones. Note also that some of the "other verbs" in McGregor's scenario are characteristic for ideophone-verb constructions in Lithuanian, notably 'hit', 'catch', and 'fall'. It is thus not necessarily the case that 'say/do' is historically prior to 'hit', 'catch', and 'fall'; 'say' and 'do' simply have more potential to become more general light verbs and hence to be the major motor of such a grammaticalization, but this does not mean that 'say/do' is the only point where an expansion can start.

---

[17] For a similar argument concerning delocutive verbs – which are often derived from ideophones – see Plank (2005: 481): "Wherever delocutive expression is genuinely morphological rather than syntactic, the re-analysis of existing non-delocutive morphology, or rather its re-use for yet another purpose, with the earlier functions continuing to be catered for, is a diachronic scenario far commoner than univerbation…"

In Lithuanian, there is no evidence of ideophone+verb combinations resulting in lexical verbs. However, verbs can be derived from ideophones (verb derivation is overall very productive). On the one hand, general verbal suffixes are used, such as the causative *-in-*; on the other hand, there are specific suffixes to derive verbs from ideophones. Delocutive verbs provide an important link to causative verbs (see Plank 2005 for a typological survey). In (15), the causative derivation in *į̃-krūpšt-in-ti* 'into-IDEO-CAUS-INF' seems to be motivated by delocutive origin (making the sound *krūpšt*, which characterizes the manner of motion, and is then turned into a motion verb with the prefix *į̃-* 'into' in the context of a motion event clause).

(15) Causative derivation from ideophones (Valančius 1996: 14)
*T-uo   tarpu   **krūpšt   krūpšt**   į̃   trob-ą*
that-INS.SG.M   between   **IDEO   IDEO**   in   hut-ACC.SG
*į̃-**krūpšt**-in-o   bobel-ė̃*
PV-[IDEO-CAUS>]drag-PST.3   old.woman-NOM.SG
'An old woman dragged herself **krūpšt krūpšt** into the hut.'

In Lithuanian, there are entire types of verbs preferably derived from ideophones. Senn calls them interjectional verbs (1966: 297) or momentive verbs (1929: 112). The suffix *-telėti*, (variant *-terėti*) expresses events occurring only a single time and enduring only for a moment. Already Leskien notes that these verbs mostly derive from ideophones: "Dass eine ziemliche Anzahl der Verba auf *-terėti* (*-telėti*) unmittelbar von Rufen herkommt, ist sicher. Der Ausruf *bumbt*...ist Grundlage zum Verbum *bùmbtelėti* bums! hinfallen, *cínkt* klirr! zu *cínktelėti*...klirren, *cvánkt* bei plötzlichem Schlag, zu *cvánktelėti*..." (Leskien 1902/1903: 180). Momentive verbs share with ideophones their propensity to distinguish duration formally (see Section 3.2). Aside from *-telėti*, there is another shorter affix *-telti* (variant *-terti*) expressing an especially short duration (distinction made only in infinitive stem, not in the present or the past). The two affixes can be combined with different degrees in the root marking iconic length distinctions as well (see Section 3.3): *dèptelėti* 'throw a sharp short glance at sth.', *dė̃ptelėti* 'throw a slightly longer sharp short glance at sth.', *dèptelti* 'throw a very short sharp glance at sth.', *dė̃ptelti* 'throw a slightly longer very short sharp glance at sth' (Senn 1929: 112).

It is often hard to decide whether a verb is derived from an ideophone or the other way round. But there are many verbs that are associated with related ideophones, e.g., *styrì* 'slow going with stiff legs (from cold or after long sitting)' in (12). The verb *styrinėti* 'go around with one's legs apart bashfully, nakedly, go on tiptoes' could be derived from *styrì*, but *styrì* is probably derived in turn from *stirti* 'become rigid', related to German *starr* 'rigid', Classical Greek *stereós* 'rigid'.

The connection between ideophones and verbs is not restricted to Lithuanian. Baltic, Slavic, and Germanic languages have a large range of verbal derivations from ideophones especially for inchoatives, as has been stated, for instance, for Slavic by Meillet: "Le slave s'est servi de ce procédé [suffixe i.-e. -ske-] pour former des verbes expressifs en -skati, -štati indiquant en particulier des bruits, verbes qui de par leur sens ne comportent guère d'étymologie précise: ainsi trěskati « faire du fracas »..." (Meillet 1934: 215). Stang (1942: 135) associates the characteristic st-suffix in Baltic inchoative present stem formation with Germanic sound verbs in -s-to such as Gothic kriustan 'crunch', Middle High German krīsten 'groan', Old Norse gnesta 'crack' (see also Brugmann 1916: 371). We may conclude with Leskien that the derivational relation between verbs and ideophones is not unidirectional. Ideophones can be derived from verbs and vice versa: "In der That ist die Beziehung von Ausrufen und Verben nach beiden Seiten hin: Rufe aus Verben, Verba aus Rufen, im Litauischen sehr ausgedehnt" (Leskien 1902/1903: 166).

In the literature on ideophones, deriving verbs from ideophones is sometimes seen as an aspect of "deideophonization" (Childs 2001: 66). Deideophonization is the process by which ideophones are lost or become less frequent, for instance, in urban varieties of African languages. However, deriving verbs from ideophones does not necessarily entail that the ideophones themselves disappear. I do not know to what extent we can speak of deideophonization in Lithuanian. Indeed, there are many texts and entire registers of Lithuanian where ideophones are extremely rare or completely lacking. It is possible, but difficult to prove that things have been different five centuries ago when Lithuanian was only a spoken language. However, if Brugmann, Stang, and Meillet are right, it is likely that ideophones have played a considerable role in the makeup of verbal derivation in at least some Indo-European languages, which is only conceivable if ideophones have been salient in language use at that time (this issue is further treated in Danylenko, this volume).

4 Conclusions

Contrary to opposite claims in the modern literature on ideophones, ideophones are a traditionally recognized part of speech in at least one European language, Lithuanian. Their name *ištiktukai* 'eventives' (Jablonskis 1922) is a very good characterization of the phenomenon. Lithuanian ideophones are well described due to the work of Neogrammarians (in particular August Leskien and Alfred Senn). At the end of the nineteenth century, many of the best linguists of their time did fieldwork in Lithuanian in the same vein as typologists today do fieldwork on languages in Amazonia and New Guinea. Leskien and Senn developed an interest in ideophones largely because of their abundance in one single book *Palangos Juzė*, itself a sole specimen of nineteenth-century Lithuanian literature. Its author, Bishop Motiejus Valančius, used several stylistic devices to strengthen the identity and solidarity among the rural population. This is well in line with the characterization of ideophones as rural, quintessentially social, and marking local identity in the modern literature.

The Neogrammarian work on ideophones is not known by many typologists because of an obvious rupture of tradition. Neogrammarians are associated primarily with sound laws and not with fieldwork or the description of morphosyntactic categories. This is related to a more or less tacit assumption among many typologists that Indo-European languages are not interesting. They are simply not "exotic" enough. Indo-European tends to be identified implicitly with written Standard Average European and the diversity of the family is ignored. However, unusual categories in exotic languages are passed on most easily if described in a most non-exotic meta-language, preferably English. As a meta-language, Lithuanian is much too exotic to be taken note of. Furthermore, for traditional Lithuanian linguists, the idea that their language boasts a part of speech that is known predominantly from African and Australian languages is not particularly appealing.

Most properties of Lithuanian *ištiktukai* are well in line with the characterization of ideophones in the modern literature (and many of them have long been described by Leskien, Senn, and others). The interaction with tone is of particular interest (Section 3.3) and likewise a tendency to grammaticalize reduplication as event number (Section 3.2). There are, however, some rather specific characteristics, notably the pseudo-morphological "formants" (Section 3.4) and the lack of (bleached) combinations with 'say' and 'do' light verbs. The complete lack of compound verb constructions with 'do' and 'say' makes Lithuanian ideophones important for the study of the relationship of ideophones and verbs. There is no evidence in Lithuanian for a cyclic development of verbs from compound verb constructions. Rather verbs can be derived directly from ideophones by productive processes of word formation. Comparative evidence suggests that derivations from ideophones have contributed considerably to the inventory of verbs in Baltic, Slavic, and Germanic, even though reconstruction is particularly difficult in this domain due to the dynamic nature of ideophones.

Acknowledgments

I would like to thank Tom Güldemann, Christiane Schiller, Mark Dingemanse, the editors, and four anonymous reviewers for many useful comments, and I am highly indebted to Ljuba Veselinova for her many excellent suggestions for reformulation, which have considerably improved the paper.

Abbreviations

1	1st person	INE	inessive
2	2nd person	INF	infinitive
3	3rd person	INS	instrumental
9	Bantu noun class 9	INTERJ	interjection
ACC	accusative	IPV	imperfective
A(CT)	active	ITER	iterative
ADV	adverb	LOC	locative
ALL	allative	M	masculine
AUGM	augmentative	NEG	negation
CAUS	causative	NOM	nominative
CNV	converb	PASS	passive
DAT	dative	PL	plural
DEF	definite form of adjectives	PRES	presentative
DEM	demonstrative	PRS	present
DIM	diminutive	PST	past
DS	different subject	PTC	participle
F	feminine	PV	preverb
FUT	future	REFL	reflexive/middle
GEN	genitive	SBJV	subjunctive
IDEO	ideophone/*ištiktukas*	SG	singular
IMP	imperative	SIM	simultaneous
INDEF	indefinite	SS	same subject

Participles in adverbial function are glossed as converbs according to typological practice.

References

Ameka, Felix. 2001. Ideophones and the nature of the adjective word class in Ewe. In Erhard F. K. Voeltz & Christa Kilian-Hatz (eds.) *Ideophones*, 25–48. Amsterdam, Philadelphia: John Benjamins.

Amha, Azeb. 2001. Ideophones and compound verbs in Wolaitta. In Erhard F. K. Voeltz & Christa Kilian-Hatz (eds.) *Ideophones*, 49–62. Amsterdam, Philadelphia: John Benjamins.

Andersen, Henning. 2009. Reduplication in Slavic and Baltic: Loss and renewal. *Morphology* 19: 113–134.
Brugmann, Karl. 1916. *Grundriss der vergleichenden Grammatik der indogermanischen Sprachen. Vergleichende Laut-, Stammbildungs- und Flexionslehre*. Zweiter Band, dritter Teil. Strassburg: Trübner.
Camilleri, Andrea. 1998. *Il cane di terracotta*. Palermo: Sellerio.
Childs, G. Tucker. 1994. African ideophones. In Leanne Hinton, Johanna Nichols & John J. Ohala (eds.) *Sound symbolism*, 178–204. Cambridge: Cambridge University Press.
Childs, G. Tucker. 2001. Research on ideophone, whither hence? In Erhard F. K. Voeltz & Christa Kilian-Hatz (eds.) *Ideophones*, 63–73. Amsterdam, Philadelphia: John Benjamins.
Corbett, Greville G. 2000. *Number*. Cambridge: Cambridge University Press.
Creissels, Denis. 2001. Setswana ideophones as uninflected predicative lexemes. In Erhard F. K. Voeltz & Christa Kilian-Hatz (eds.) *Ideophones*, 75–85. Amsterdam, Philadelphia: John Benjamins.
Derbyshire, Desmond C. 1977. Discourse redundancy in Hixkaryana. *International Journal of American Linguistics* 43.3: 176–188.
Dingemanse, Mark. 2012. Advances in the cross-linguistic study of ideophones. *Language and Linguistics Compass* 6(10): 654–672.
Dingemanse, Mark (in press). Expressiveness and system integration. On the typology of ideophones, with special reference to Siwu. To appear in *Sprachtypologie und Universalienforschung*.
Doke, Clement Martin. 1935. *Bantu linguistic terminology*. London: Longmans.
Fortune, George. 1971. Some notes on ideophones and ideophonic constructions in Shona. *African Studies* 30(3/4): 237–257.
Fraenkel, Ernst. 1962/1965. *Litauisches etymologisches Wörterbuch*. Bd. I–II. Heidelberg: Winter.
Güldemann, Tom. 2008. *Quotative indexes in African languages: a synchronic and diachronic survey*. Berlin, New York: Mouton de Gruyter.
Jablonskis, Jonas. 1922. *Rygiškių Jono Lietuvių kalbos gramatika* [A Lithuanian grammar by Rugiškių Jonas]. 2nd ed. Kaunas, Vilnius "Švyturio" bendrovės leidinys. In Jablonskis, Jonas. 1957. *Rinktiniai raštai* [Collected writings] T. I: 183–433. Vilnius: Valstybinė politinės ir mokslinės literatūros leidykla.
Jašinskaitė, Irena. 1971. Ištiktukai [Ideophones]. In Kazys Ulvydas (ed.) *Lietuvių kalbos gramatika* [The grammar of the Lithuanian language]. Vol. 2: *Morfologija* [Morphology], 734–746. Vilnius: Mintis.
Jašinskaitė, Irena. 1975. *Lietuvių kalbos ištiktukai* [Lithuanian ideophones]. Vilnius: Mintis.
Kilian-Hatz, Christa. 2001. Universality and diversity. Ideophones from Baka and Kxoe. In Erhard F. K. Voeltz & Christa Kilian-Hatz (eds.) *Ideophones*, 155–163. Amsterdam, Philadelphia: John Benjamins.
Kunene, Daniel P. 2001. Speaking the act. The ideophone as a linguistic rebel. In Erhard F. K. Voeltz & Christa Kilian-Hatz (eds.) *Ideophones*, 183–191. Amsterdam, Philadelphia: John Benjamins.
Leskien, August. 1902/1903. Schallnachahmungen und Schallverba im Litauischen. *Indogermanische Forschungen* 13: 165–212.
McGregor, William. 2001. Ideophones as a source of verbs in Northern Australian languages. In Erhard F. K. Voeltz & Christa Kilian-Hatz (eds.) *Ideophones*, 205–221. Amsterdam, Philadelphia: John Benjamins.
Meillet, Antoine. 1934. *Le slave commun*. Paris: Champion.

Metuzāle-Kangere, Baiba. 1991. Verba strepentia and morphological development in Latvian and Lithuanian. In Norbert Boretzky, Werner Enninger, Benedikt Jessing & Thomas Stolz (eds.) *Sprachwandel und seine Prinzipien. Beiträge zum 8. Bochum-Essener Kolloquium über "Sprachwandel und seine Prinzipien" vom 19.10. – 21.10.1990 an der Ruhruniversität Bochum*, 194–205. Bochum: Brockmeyer.

Mithun, Marianne. 1988. Lexical categories and the evolution of number marking. In Michael Hammond & Michael Noonan (eds.) *Theoretical morphology: Approaches in modern linguistics*, 211–234. San Diego: Academic Press.

Munro, Pamela. 2001. Field linguistics. In Mark Aronoff & Janie Rees-Miller (eds.) *The handbook of linguistics*, 130–149. Oxford: Blackwell.

Newman, Paul. 2006. Pluractionals (distributives). In Keith Brown (ed.) *Encyclopedia of language and linguistics*. 2nd edition, 640–641. Oxford: Elsevier.

Niedermann, Max, Alfred Senn, & Anton Salys. 1951–1968. *Wörterbuch der litauischen Sprache*. Heidelberg: Winter.

Nikitina, Tatiana. 2012. Russian verboids: A case study in expressive vocabulary. *Linguistics* 50(2), 165–189.

Noss, Philipp A. 1985. The ideophone in Gbaya syntax. In Gerrit J. Dimmendahl (ed.) *Current Approaches to African Linguistics*, Vol. 3, 241–255. Dordrecht: Foris.

Noss, Philipp A. 2001. Ideas, phones and Gbaya verbal art. In Erhard F. K. Voeltz & Christa Kilian-Hatz (eds.) *Ideophones*, 259–270. Amsterdam, Philadelphia: John Benjamins.

Paul, Hermann. 1909. *Prinzipien der Sprachgeschichte*. 4th edition. Halle: Niemeier.

Plank, Frans. 2005. Delocutive verbs, cross-linguistically. *Linguistic Typology* 9(3): 459–491.

Samarin, William J. 2001. Testing hypotheses about African ideophones. In Erhard F. K. Voeltz & Christa Kilian-Hatz (eds.) *Ideophones*, 321–337. Amsterdam, Philadelphia: John Benjamins.

Schultze-Bernd, Eva. 2001. Ideophone-like characteristics of uninflected predicates in Jaminjung (Australia). In Erhard F. K. Voeltz & Christa Kilian-Hatz (eds.) *Ideophones*, 355–373. Amsterdam, Philadelphia: John Benjamins.

Senn, Alfred. 1924. Lautnachahmende Bildungen in den Schriften von Motiejus Wolonczauski. *Tauta ir žodis* 2: 456–462.

Senn, Alfred. 1929. *Kleine Litauische Sprachlehre*. Heidelberg: Groos.

Senn, Alfred. 1966. *Handbuch der litauischen Sprache. Bd. 1: Grammatik*. Heidelberg: Winter.

Stang, Christian S. 1942. *Das slavische und baltische Verbum*. Oslo: Dybwad.

Urdze, Aina Marite. 2010. *Ideophone in Europa. Die Grammatik der lettischen Geräuschverben*. Bochum: Brockmeyer.

Valančius, Motiejus. [1863] 1996. *Palangos Juzė*. Vilnius: Baltos Lankos.

Valančius, Motiejus. 2003. *Namų užrašai*. Sudarė Aldona Prašmanaitė. Vilnius: Baltos Lankos.

Voeltz, Erhard F. K. & Christa Kilian-Hatz (eds.). 2001. *Ideophones*. Amsterdam, Philadelphia: John Benjamins.

Wälchli, Bernhard. 2005. *Co-compounds and natural coordination*. Oxford: Oxford University Press.

Wälchli, Bernhard. 2010. Baltische Geräuschverben und Ideophone. Eine Herausforderung für die Sprachtypologie. Rez. von Aina Marite Urdze: Ideophone in Europa. Die Grammatik der lettischen Geräuschverben. *Baltic Linguistics* 1: 167–179.

Zinkevičius, Zigmas. 1981. *Lietuvių kalbos istorinė gramatika* [A historical grammar of Lithuanian] Vol. 2. Vilnius: Mokslas.

Žiugžda, Juozas. 1961. *Lietuvių kalbos gramatika* [A grammar of Lithuanian]. Kaunas: Valstybinė pedagoginės literatūros leidykla.

Andrii Danylenko
14 The chicken or the egg? Onomatopoeic particles and verbs in Baltic and Slavic
To William R. Schmalstieg

1 Introduction

There is no disguising the fact that one of the problems for ascertaining the status of the onomatopoeic particles in Baltic and of the analogous formations in Slavic is their reconstruction. Thus, to adequately describe forms like Lith. *čiùpt*, Ukr. *xap*, Rus. *xvat'*, Bel. *xvac'* representing the act of grabbing, Bulg. and USorb. *buch* referring to thumping, and the like (Danylenko 2003: 204–205), it is necessary to determine their derivational relation to the corresponding verbs. In other words, one should answer a chicken-and-egg question vexing specialists in Baltic since Leskien (1902/1903: 166) and in Slavic ever since Lomonosov (1755: 167) – which came first, the onomatopoeic particle or the corresponding verb?

With this puzzle in mind, I will first review semantic, formal (syntactic), and morphophonemic properties of the onomatopoeic particles in Lithuanian and East Slavic, which will be proxies for the Baltic and Slavic languages, respectively, in this chapter (Sections 2.1–2.3). Most of these properties are discussed in descriptive grammars and can serve as a backdrop for a palliative theory premised on the analysis of the corresponding lexicalizing (expressive) devices applied to the formation of onomatopoeic particles. Among those devices, for example, are expression (phonetic) reduction and root apophony, which are employed to form iconic representations of auditorily and non-auditorily based experiential dimensions of states, activities, and actions (Section 4.1). Following Potebnja (1941: 187–191), I will expand on my previous explanation of onomatopoeic formations in East Slavic and Lithuanian (Danylenko 2003: 204–223; see Sections 3.1–3.2.1). My ultimate objective will be to argue, first, that prototypical onomatopoeic particles are "extracted" from the corresponding onomatopoeic verbs and, second, that the subsequent lexicalization of such particles in Lithuanian and East Slavic depends on different procedurals (*Aktionsarten*) as encoded in the base onomatopoeic verbs (see Sections 4.1–4.3). Unlike aspects, which are obligatory grammatical categories, the procedurals are optional, derivational categories that modify the meaning of a lexical verb (Andersen 2009a: 125; cf. Maslov 1948), including the onomatopoeic verb, and ultimately the semantics of a particle "extracted" from such a verb.

Onomatopoeic particles warrant here some terminological disambiguation. Thus, for East Slavic, I will deal with verb-related onomatopoeic formations, called "deverbal" (Karskij [1911] 2006: 58) or "verbal" interjections (Šaxmatov 1941: 472), predicative or verbal particles (Potebnja 1941: 189).[1] For Lithuanian, I will primarily focus on verb-related onomatopoeic *ištiktùkai* 'exclamatory interjections' that, sharing the root with the respective onomatopoeic verbs, refer primarily to actions associated often with acoustic and visual effects or impressions (Ambrazas 1997: 440); cf. *šlèpt* alongside *šlep(s)nóti* 'to walk, plod' (Ulvydas 1971: 257). Andersen (2009a) has recently employed the term "eventive" as a Lithuanian part of speech that represents events, a characteristic captured by the native term Lith. *ištiktùkai* (cf. *ištìkti* 'to occur').[2] Unlike interjections (cf. Senn 1966: 308) or particles, 'eventives' describe or represent situations, which, according to Andersen (2009a: 113, 125), is really a defining feature of "eventives" as a para-lexical part of speech (see Wälchli, this volume). However, the postulated description or representation of situations by "eventives" is not relevant for present purposes. I will concentrate instead on the lexicalization of such formations, which may ultimately delineate the derivational vector between the particles and verbs.

2 Profiling onomatopoeic particles

The Lithuanian and East Slavic onomatopoeic particles demonstrate similar semantic (Section 2.1) and syntactic features (Section 2.2), although varying morphophonemic properties (Section 2.3).

2.1 Semantic features

Due to a parallelism (or association) between different domains of experience – which will allow onomatopoeia to represent visual and other phenomena – some of the onomatopoeic particles are associated with non-auditorily based impressions

---

[1] For a synopsis of terms used in East Slavic linguistics and their discussion, see Mustejkis [Musteikis] (1972: 196).
[2] Unlike the term "happenlings" viewed by Wälchli as "precursors [?–A.D.] of ideophones" in this volume, the term "eventive" looks more appropriate in this case. In fact, derivationally, the latter form is more in line with regular English-language linguistic terms of the type *stative*, *inchoative*, *iterative*, *nominative*, *adjective*, and so forth, all ending in the suffix *-ive*. The term "verboid" coined by Nikitina (2012) is hardly acceptable either since it inadvertently obscures the categorical interrelation between the onomatopoeic particles and the corresponding verbs.

of light, time, and so forth. This is why particles usually refer to "dynamic" actions like walking, falling, beating, cutting, and so forth (cf. Ambrazas 1997: 440, 447; Potebnja 1941: 189). Apart from the sounds of insects, birds, or animals, as well as the sound, sight, and/or sensation of physical phenomena in the environment and human-made devices, the onomatopoeic particles represent the sound, sight, and/or sensation of

1. locomotion (e.g., walking, running, jumping, tumbling) or movement (e.g., striking, cutting, breaking, grabbing, stabbing) or
2. physiological activities and events (e.g., speaking, eating, swallowing, weeping, coughing, snoring, glancing, side-stitch, heartbeat, expiring) (Andersen 2009a: 125–126)

Sound-imitating words not related to verbs, including Lithuanian *jaustùkai* 'interjections' like *diñ diñ* (cf. Senn 1966: 304–305) and respective interjections in East Slavic like Ukr. *dzen'-dzen'* 'ding dong' are not analyzed in this chapter. Sometimes, however, it is difficult to tell the difference between verb-related and verb-unrelated (imitative) onomatopoeic particles in East Slavic like Ukr. *šubovst'*, referring to one's violent plunge into water next to a secondary formation, *šubovstnuty* 'to cast oneself into water' (Potebnja 1941: 188–189), and especially in Lithuanian where sound and light are allegedly always intimately associated with locomotion or movement, be they real or imaginary (Leskien 1902/1903: 165); cf. *trinkt* 'a bang, hit, knock', or *blýkst*, referring to a flash of light and so forth (Ambrazas 1997: 440–441). Interestingly, by contrast, in Latvian both sound and visual impressions seem to be divorced in the onomatopoeic verbs and corresponding onomatopoeic particles. Urdze (2010: 95) argues that verb forms with the thematic vowel -*ē*- are, by and large, related to the "sound", while verbs with the thematic vowel -*ī*- cover, in the main, visual impressions; cf. Latv. *gārkstēt* 'to breathe stertorously' and *bakstīt* 'to poke'.

2.2 Syntactic features

Syntactically, particles are used in both languages as predicates, being able to take over and replace not only any tense, mood, number, person, but also the argument structure of the corresponding verbal predicate. Although uninflected, onomatopoeic particles may be conjoined with finite verbs or function as finite verbs. In the latter case, they represent an activity or action and may be intransitive or transitive (see 1a,b); in the former case, the onomatopoeic particle marks a prominent feature of the situation represented by the verb (Potebnja 1941: 190–191, Andersen 2009a: 125) (see 2a,b).

(1) a. Lith. jìs   trèpt   į   žẽm-ę
             he.NOM   stamp.PART   in   ground-ACC.SG
             'He stamped the ground.'

    b. Rus. on   xvat'   molodc-a   za   nog-i
             he   grab.PART   fellow-ACC.SG   at   legs-ACC.PL
             'He grabbed the fellow by his feet.'

(2) a. Ukr. Zyrk!   j   vzdri-v   Marusj-u
             glance.PART   and   see-PST(M.SG)   Marusja-ACC.SG
             'He glanced, and saw Marusja.'

    b. Lith. liūt-as,   tìk   čiùpt,   t-ą   ženklẽl-į
             lion-NOM.SG   only   grab.PART   this-ACC.SG   sign-ACC.SG
             skait-ė
             read-PST3
             'The lion only grab! and read the letter' (cf. Schleicher 1856: 339)

2.3 Morphophonemic differences

What distinguishes the Lithuanian onomatopoeic particles from the parallel formations in East Slavic is a set of its own lexicalizing devices, including total and partial reduplication, which are used to form more or less expressive onomatopoeic particles.

(3) Lith.   dur-ìs   tràkš!   tràkš!   añt   rãkt-o
             door-ACC.PL   click.PART   click.PART   on   key-GEN.SG
             'He locked the door with two turns of the key'

                                                           (Andersen 2009a: 126)

However, reduplication patterns whether inherited or renewed in Lithuanian, are of little importance for our discussion of the relationship between the onomatopoeic particles and verbs. It is worth, instead, of homing in on morphophonemic differences in the *Auslaut* of the Lithuanian and East Slavic particles, which are likely to reflect differences in the process of their lexicalization (Section 4.1) and categorialization (Section 4.2).

To begin with, the Lithuanian particles under consideration demonstrate root vowel apophony, which is not found (any longer to that extent) in East Slavic. From this point of view, the onomatopoeic particles and corresponding verbs in Lithuanian are prone to demonstrate a kind of mirror-image relationship. Thus, Senn (1966: 309) argued that the verb *tráukti* 'to pull' could have given rise to *trùkt* denoting "a slight pull", *trūkt* (with the full vocalism and the acute intonation) denoting a more energetic pull and, finally, *trũkt* (with the circumflected root) referring to the strongest pull (cf. Ulvydas 1971: 741). The above-mentioned derivational chain does not look persuasive since the long vowel accents in these particles can be secondary and the grave accent type can be easily associated with the verb *trùktelėti* 'to give a (small) pull'; cf. *trùkteli* in Eastern High Lithuanian (Ulvydas 1971: 260).

(4) Lith. *tráukti* ~
    trùkt 'a small pull'
    trūkt 'a strong pull'
    trũkt 'a very strong pull'

Meanwhile, one onomatopoeic particle can be juxtaposed with more than one verb with the same root, although a different root vowel:

(5) Lith. *žiòps* ~
    žiópčioti, žiopsė́ti 'to gape around'
    žiõplinėti, žiõplinti 'to walk around gaping at things'
    žiópterėti, žiópteleti 'to walk around gaping at things'
    (Schmalstieg 2000: 197; cf. Nesselmann 1851: 550)

In East Slavic, the situation is different. Here onomatopoeic particles tend to be associated with semelfactive verbs in *-nu-*, hence Ukr. *xap~xapnuty* 'to take a grab' rather than the iterative *xapaty* 'to grab', similarly *bax~baxnuty* not *baxaty* 'to bang', *bux~buxnuty* not *buxaty* 'to thump', *hup~hupnuty* not *hupaty* 'to stamp', *stuk~stuknuty* not *stukaty* 'to knock', *tris'~trisnuty* not *triskatys'* 'to crack', and so forth (Vyxovanec' & Horodens'ka 2004: 388); cf. Rus. *bax, bux, top, stuk, tres'*.

The above-mentioned unequivocal relationship can be tentatively explained by the prehistoric loss of tone and vowel alternation in East Slavic, although the so-called expressive lengthening of the root vowel was a common Balto-Slavic phenomenon (Endzelīns 1971: 227). The proportion for the expressive lengthening in the Balto-Slavic period might have been the following: the long root vowel in Baltic as in *brýd-o-ti* 'to stand in water into which one has forded' next to the Slavic verb forms with the suffix *-ā-* like *bĭr-a-ti* 'to take' (Schmalstieg 1993: 409). It is not therefore incidental that Stepanov (1989: 196) compared the short and long vowel contrast in Lithuanian particles like *grìbš* and *grýbš* 'grab' with the Slavic formations of a "new imperfective aspect", e.g., *umъrěti/umirati* 'to die'. Since the original zero-grade root with the *-ā-* suffix verb had durative value, which passed to stative in Balto-Slavic and from stative it began to serve as the preterit to *-e*-grade (cf. Stang 1966: 376–379), it is no surprise that onomatopoeic particles with original zero-grade verb roots with durative (or multiplicative) semantics cannot be found in East Slavic. Logically, such a particle might be linked primarily with a semelfactive verb.

In this respect, particles like Ukr. (and Rus. dial.) *zyrk* where *-y-* is a deviation from the regular reflex of the vowel in the *CьSC* group (Shevelov 1979: 292) can be paired with the verb *zyr(k)-nu-ty* 'to take a glance' referring to a single momentary action, rather than *zyrk-a-ty* 'to take glances, to stare' with the reflex *-y-* motivated by affectivity in the two verbs; cf. Rus. dial. *zyrit'* 'to ogle', *zorit'* 'to watch' (Vasmer 1953, 1: 461, 465), OCS *zьrěti*, and Ukr. *zrity* 'to stare'. However, the deviation with *y* may easily be, at least in part, archaic and preserve petrified pre-*jer* stage vowel in the corresponding verb (Shevelov 1979: 292).

Tentatively, one can state that iconicity in the case of deviation with *y* could first have encompassed the verb involved rather than the corresponding particle *zyrk* (with a secondary *-k-*). The latter replicated on the categorialization of the semelfactive verb *zyr(k)nuty*; cf. a parallel formation *zyr* with the same expressive lengthening of the root vowel.

3 Unpacking the derivational gridlocks

3.1 The case of Lithuanian

Scholarly tradition has taken for granted that onomatopoeic verbs in Lithuanian and Latvian were derived from the onomatopoeic particles (Ulvydas 1971: 242, 734, Ambrazas 1997: 442, Schmalstieg 2000: 125, 194, 200; cf. Bergmane et al. 1959: 331). Premised on Metuzāle-Kangere (1991), Urdze (2010: 81–82), however, posited a more intricate derivational process that could have taken place in both directions, i.e., from the particle to the verb and the other way around. Remarkably, a similar two vector-valued solution to this puzzle was first outlined by Leskien (1902/1903: 166), who tried to reconcile the opposite views propounded by Schleicher (1856: 338–339) and Kurschat (1876: 74, 125–126), respectively. What Urdze (2010: 179) innovated on is the postulation of some onomatopoeic roots as bases for both onomatopoeic particles and corresponding verbs as illustrated in (6).

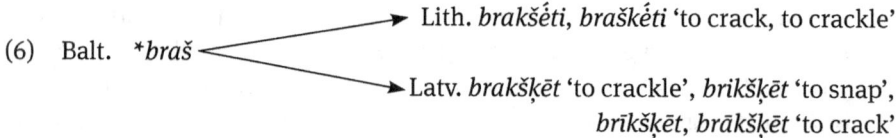

(6) Balt. **braš* → Lith. *brakšė́ti, braškė́ti* 'to crack, to crackle'
→ Latv. *brakšķēt* 'to crackle', *brikšķēt* 'to snap', *brīkšķēt, brākšķēt* 'to crack'

Unlike Latvian, however, whose onomatopoeic verbs demonstrate characteristic sound sequences of *k* or *p* with the sibilant *s* in combination with a plosive, consonant sequences in the *Auslaut* of Lithuanian particles are more variegated, looking even chaotic and less prototypical (Urdze 2010: 91–92). To take the most regular formant -*t*-, it is commonly preceded by the voiceless consonants *k*, *p*, *s*, *š*, and clusters *kš* and *ks* (Ulvydas 1971: 736, Ambrazas 1997: 442); conspicuously, clusters *kšt* (or *kšč*) and eventually *kš* and *šk* are attested in non-auditorily based verbs, likewise; cf. *šmakštelėti* 'to pick, to poke a little' (Urdze 2010: 90–91).

Some onomatopoeic particles in -*t*- occur also without this formant, e.g., *bràkšt~bràkš* 'crack', which allows some authors to treat particles like *lìnkt* or *drìkst*, *drýkst* as derivatives from verbs of the type *liñkti* 'to bend, slope', *drìksti*, *drė̃ksti* 'to tear' (Ambrazas 1997: 442). Strangely enough, verbs denoting momentary or "diminutive-multiplicative" actions like *drìkstelėti*, *drìkstelti*, *drìksterėti*, *drìksterti* (Stepanov 1989: 185), which all have the same formant -*t*- as part of the suffixes -*tel(ė)ti*, -*ter(ė)ti*, are not routinely taken into consideration in such cases (cf. Ulvydas 1971: 260). In order to resolve this misconstruction, Urdze (2010: 87–88, 90) came up with a twofold explanation. To substantiate parallel formations *táukšt~táukš* 'knock, tap', the author treated -*t*- as part of the infinitive marker -*ti* as in *taũkšti* 'to chatter, rattle'. At the same time, Urdze (2010: 87–88) admitted that the formant -*t*- might be part of a different suffix in the verbs *taũkščioti* (where -*č*-<*-*t*'-), *taúkštelėti*, and *taúkšterėti* 'to knock, tap, rap', which all allegedly were derived from the particle *táukšt*. Thus, unlike *taũkš-t-i*, in the above-mentioned three forms -*t*- could belong to the derivational base of the onomatopoeic particle, being part of the cluster *kšt* (cf. Ulvydas 1971: 253, 258).

At first blush, the above argumentation corroborates the historical tendency to insert a *k* before sibilants in Baltic (Stang 1966: 108). Yet the usual metathesis *sk>ks/zg>gz* in Baltic, and especially in Lithuanian (Machek 1957: 68), brings to mind verb formations with the suffix -*sk*- in Slavic and Baltic with or without parallels in other Indo-European languages (Meillet 1912: 197–198). Denoting the intensity of an action or a kind of pejorative attenuation (or both simultaneously) (Machek 1957: 77), verbs with the suffix -*sk*- reveal derivational patterns, which seem to be at variance with Urdze's theory. Just to cite a few examples, I will mention Sl. *bliskati/blъščati*, Ukr. *blyščaty* 'to shine' as compared with the particles Bel. *blis'*, Rus. *bles'*, Ukr. *blys'* 'shine, flash'. The palatalized final *s'* in the latter formations is a result of the phonetic reduction of the cluster *sk>s>s'* as postulated for the onomatopoeic semelfactive verbs Ukr. *blysnuty*, Bel. *blisnuc'*, Rus. *blesnut'* (<*blъs(k)nuti*) (Danylenko 2003: 219). The parallel Lithuanian *blizgéti* 'to shine, flash' can be expanded with *blìgsti*, *blìgznóti*, and *blìgstelėti*, *blìkšterėti*, *blìksterėti* 'to flash a little bit' next to *blìkst* with the diminutive, and a kind of the multiplicative meaning (cf. Leskien 1902/1903: 187); cf. *blýkstereti* 'to flash quite a bit' (Ulvydas 1971: 260).

All in all, based exclusively on morphophonemic features, especially consonant clusters in the *Auslaut*, it is difficult, if at all possible, to determine which came first in Lithuanian, the onomatopoeic particle or the corresponding verb.[3]

3.2 The case of East Slavic

For East Slavic, it has also been maintained that the onomatopoeic verbs are derivative of the corresponding particles (Voznyj 1963: 113), which are reminiscent of the erstwhile aorist of asigmatic or partly sigmatic stem, the most productive mode of formation in late Indo-European. Šaxmatov (1941: 206, 472), for instance, hypothesized that Rus. *dvig* 'move' could have arisen from the asigmatic aorist form *dvigъ* and Rus. *bac* 'smack, bang' from a sigmatic aorist form of the type 1SG *basъ* 'I bunted'; cf. the infinitive Sl. *bosti* 'to pierce, to bunt'.

3.2.1 The Slavic injunctive

Stepanov (1981) tried to harmonize the development of the formant -*s*-, frequently encountered in the *Auslaut* of Slavic onomatopoeic particles, with the existence of the Baltic *s*-future like *duo-s-iu* give-FUT-1SG 'I shall give' and so forth (Stang 1966: 397), identical in form to the sigmatic aorist in Slavic of the type 1SG *něsъ* 'I carried' (Stepanov 1989: 169–201). Stepanov's argumentation was premised on the following tenets. First, Balto-Slavic inherited an Indo-European formation with the thematic suffix -*syo*-, which, having eventually disappeared in Slavic, was substituted for by a periphrastic future formation in Slavic and partly in Baltic (Stepanov 1981: 114). The solitary participle *byšęšt*-, regarded as evidence for the erstwhile existence of the *s*-future in Slavic, corresponds ultimately with the future participle in Lithuanian *būsiant*-. As Stepanov (1989: 114, footnote 3)

---

[3] According to Andersen (2009a: 127), Lithuanian non-imitative ("deverbal") eventives (onomatopoeic particles) might have derived from a lexical verb root, optionally modified with vowel apophony and/or with a consonant or vowel suffix, e.g., *traũk-ti→trùk-t* 'pull'. Yet it is not clear in this case, if there is any categorical connection between the base verb root and its derivative eventive. Otherwise, it is hard to explain why the eventive *trùk-t* was formed from *traũk-ti* and not from *trùk-teleti* 'to give a (small) pull' or dial. *trùk-teli* (see Section 2.3), especially since the eventives are commonly used in colloquial discourse or peripheral northwestern (lowland) and eastern (upland) dialects (Andersen 2009a: 127).

admitted, that participle must be left out of account, since it is a fairly late innovation formed from the aorist *byšę*, thus having originally not only a future but also a past (anterior) meaning ("having become") (Szemerényi 1999: 286). Second, in Baltic and Slavic, a new future formation emerged, which was an uncharacterized present-aorist form reminiscent of Rus. *pryg* 'jump' and Lith. *klùp* 'stumble', identified today as onomatopoeic particles (Stepanov 1989: 194–195). Despite its morphological ambivalence, such formations in certain semantic and syntactic environments could function as a 3SG form of the putative Indo-European injunctive (Stepanov 1981: 114–115).[4]

Revealing the perfective semantics, Russian "injunctives" never take prefixes and, when representing predicates, may render a momentary action perceived as past, present, or future. All the "injunctives" are paired with respective onomatopoeic verbs. According to Stepanov (1981: 119–120), the latter should have derived from the "injunctives" following the historical restructuring of preterit stems since it is impossible to extract particles from the verbs with the help of modern morphological rules.

The author should be given credit for bringing together the historical and comparative dimensions of the problem. However, the reconstruction of derivational technique applied to the formation of "injunctives" can hardly determine the vector of derivation and answer the question as to which comes first – the onomatopoeic particle or the corresponding onomatopoeic verb?

4 A palliative approach

A palliative approach was first offered by Potebnja (1941: 189–191), who, based on the analysis of lexicalizing devices (Section 4.1), treated onomatopoeic particles as derivative of the corresponding verbs (Section 4.2).

4.1 Lexicalizing devices

According to Potebnja (1941: 189–190), the loss of *k, t* after *s*, or *z(g)* in the *Auslaut* was evidence that the corresponding particles were derivative of the verbs

---

[4] It is customary to use this term for the unaugmented imperfect or aorist indicative of Old Indic or Aryan when they have a modal function (Szemerényi 1999: 263; cf. Kuryłowicz 1964: 111). Stepanov (1981: 115), however, treated the postulated Slavic-Baltic injunctive as an "unaugmented representative of the augmented forms", in general.

denoting a single momentary action (*odnokratnye glagoly* 'semelfactive verbs') in East Slavic. Otherwise, it would be difficult to explain the existence of Ukr. *ljas'* 'smack', *xljas'* 'slam', *brjaz'* 'jingle', *trjas'* 'smack', all with a palatalized sibilant in word final position, rather than *ljask, *xljast, *brjazg, *trjask in comparison with the nouns *ljask, brjazk, tresk* retaining the final obstruent (cf. Shevelov 1979: 731–732).

By the argument outlined in the preceding paragraph, it follows that the phonetic reduction in the *Auslaut* of onomatopoeic particles might have happened after their "extraction" from the verbs; hence, a somewhat impressionistic, although close to reality, identification of the particles as "truncated verbs" in the work of Mustejkis [Musteikis] (1972: 198). The phonetic reduction was accompanied by what I called elsewhere (Danylenko 2003: 218–222) "semantic palatalization" marking a "diminutive" representation of the semelfactive action. This "semantic palatalization" is of iconic nature, whence its use in both auditorily (cf. Ukr. *brjaz'* 'jingle') and non-auditorily based (cf. Ukr. *trjas'* 'smack') particles; cf. also Bel. *hljadz'* next to Rus. *gljad'* 'glance', Ukr. *skok* 'jump', and *skic'* 'jump (a bit)' (with the palatalized consonant *c'* (<*t'*) and the *i*-reflex of the etymological *o*) next to the more regular *skik* without any palatalization but with ikavism; also Rus. dial. *kid'* and *kid* from *kinut'* 'to throw' (Danylenko 2003: 219).

In addition to the "semantic" palatalization, the East Slavic particles can take substantivizing suffixes as found, for instance, in the particle Ukr. *smyk-ec'* from *smyknut'* 'to pull, tear', which is close to Lith. *trùkt*, referring to a slight pull, rather than to *trūkt* or even *trūkt* referring to the strongest pull; cf. *nomina agentis* Ukr. *mr-ec'* 'deceased', *žn-ec'* 'reaper'. Of particular interest also are substantivizing suffixes in such particles as Rus. dial. *kid-yx* (from *kid-nu-ti* 'to throw'?) referring to a more energetic single momentary action in comparison with a lower degree of intensity in the particles Bel. dial. *kid-el', kidz-el', kidz-en'* 'throw', where -*d* (-*dz'*) is part of the stem (Danylenko 2003: 219–221).

As shown, the intensity of a notion is rendered in East Slavic not through the lengthening of the root vowel as in Lithuanian, but through the simplification (phonetic reduction) of the word final cluster and a change in the articulation (palatalization) of the final sibilant as well as the use of substantivizing suffixes.

Meanwhile, the occurrence of the formant -*t*- in the Lithuanian *ištiktùkai* after, in particular, sibilants and the metathetic clusters *ks/kš* might be sufficient evidence of the derivative nature of onomatopoeic particles in Lithuanian (Potebnja 1941: 191). It is worth citing again *tráks-t~tárks-t~tréks-t* 'crackle, bang' (ESl. *trjasъ*<*tręsk-nu-t'* 'to smack') next to *treškėti, traškėti, tarškėti* 'to crackle', and especially *tárkštereti* 'to jungle, crackle a little bit'. The appearance of -*t*- after a sibilant in final position can be explained in a twofold manner.

First, one needs to bear in mind that the use of a sibilant in this position meets a tendency not only in Slavic, but also in other Indo-European languages (cf. Urdze 2010: 4–5), in particular in German (Leskien 1902/1903: 181); the metathesis of *ks/kš* from *-sk-* (Shevelov 1965: 141) could be provoked, in fact, by its word-final position with the sibilant rendering residually the intensity of a notion as observed in East Slavic onomatopoeic particles. Second, since *-t* seems to be optional in parallel formations like *bràkš~bràkšt* '[small] crack', we can postulate the relationship between, on the one hand, *bràkš* and *bràkšt* and, on the other hand, *bràkštelėti/bràkšterėti* 'to crack a little bit'; cf. 'oft und leise zittern' in Nesselmann (1851: 343; cf. Ulvydas 1971: 22, 259). In short, since the word-final sibilant refers to the intensity of action and the optional formant *-t* denotes the multiplicative character of such an action, one can then construe the following correspondence with [often] dependable on the use of the *t*-formant:

(7) *bràkš* '[small + [often]] crack'

bràkšt '[small + often] crack'

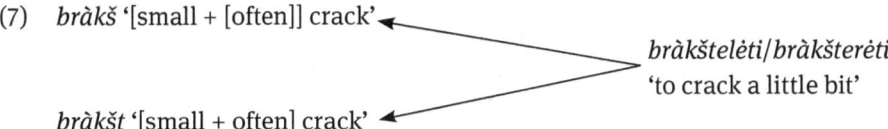

bràkštelėti/bràkšterėti 'to crack a little bit'

What is left to ascertain is the vector of derivation, which Potebnja (1941: 191; cf. Schleicher 1856: 338–339) directed from the verb toward a particle. There are some persuasive arguments corroborating his hypothesis (see Section 4.2).

4.2 The procedural meaning

In Lithuanian, the categorialization of onomatopoeic particles can be exemplified with the help of verbs in *-tel(ė)ti* and *ter(ė)ti*, where the formant *-t-* is comparable with the Slavic "multiplicative" suffix **-ot/-et* or **-ъt-/-ьt-* (Vondrák 1906: 450–451, Shevelov 1979: 102, footnote 12) as found, for instance, in Rus. dial. *stuk-ot-et'*, Ukr. *hrjuk-ot-ity*, Bel. *hrjuk-ot-ac'* 'to bang, to knock quite a bit' and Rus. dial. *tup-ot-et'*, Ukr. *tup-ot-ity*, Bel. *tup-ot-ac'* 'to tramp a little bit', respectively; cf. Lith. *tàpšterėti* 'to tap slightly a little bit' (Voznyj 1963: 117, Danylenko 2003: 212). Unlike East Slavic, where the categorialized meaning of the onomatopoeic particles is conceived of in terms of a single momentary action as illustrated by the base verb in *-nu-*, the Lithuanian onomatopoeic particles tend to denote a "multiplicative-diminutive" action as exemplified in the base verbs in *-tel(ė)ti* and *-ter(ė)ti* (cf. Keydana 1998: 133). Mustejkis [Musteikis] (1972: 197) also juxtaposed most representative onomatopoeic particles in Lithuanian with the same derivational class of verbs ending in *-tel(ė)ti* and *-ter(ė)ti*. He argued, however, that the particles denote a "momentary action" without any diminutive nuance in their meaning, although on another page (Mustejkis [Musteikis], 1972: 130), he admitted a diminutive connotation in these verbs.

Note that the postulated multiplicativity is based on the notion of a particular "quantum" of action viewed potentially as a series of discrete small actions (cf. Dolinina 1999: 189); intensity can acquire the diminutive or, in the case of the root vowel lengthening, the intensive or intensive-durative value. As a result, the corresponding value of the intensity can be ideally retained in the short and long vowel contrast in both onomatopoeic particles and verbs (see 8a,b), while discrepancies in (4) and (5) (see Section 2.3) may be a corollary to independent derivational transformations in the particles and verbs.

(8) a. *žvìlgt ~ žvìlgterėti* 'to look around'
         žvýlgt ~ žvýlgterėti 'to look around more intensely'

   b. *dèpt ~ dèptel(ė)ti, dèpter(ė)ti* 'to cast a glance'
         dė̃pt ~ dė̃ptel(ė)ti, dė̃pter(ė)ti 'to cast a longer glance'
                                                              (Endzelīns 1971: 224–225, Balčikonis 2002, 20: 1117–1118).

The verbs in *-tel(ė)ti* and *-ter(ė)ti* are thus typologically representative, although not unique, for the understanding of the categorialization of onomatopoeic particles in Lithuanian. Along with the base onomatopoeic verbs, they denote the multiplicativity and intensity of an action, acquiring variegated attenuations dependent on root vowel apophony and stem formation, including predesinential stem suffixes like *-n-o-ti*, *-sn-o-ti/-šn-o-ti*, *-n-y-ti*, and so forth (Ulvydas 1971: 247–268) and in some cases the prefix *pa-* (see Section 4.3).

Prototypically, the derivation of a particle begins with the expression (phonetic) reduction ("truncation") of a verb in *-tel(ė)ti* and *-ter(ė)ti*, referring to a multiplicative action conceived of as a series of short constituent "individualized actions" (cf. "individualized singularity" in Dolinina 1999: 189). This type of expression reduction does not involve either lexical or syntactic change in the "extracted" particle, thus being, conceivably, of paradigmatic nature. All this allowed (Mustejkis [Musteikis], 1972: 195, 200) to treat the resulting particles ("truncated verbs") as a separate verbal category, although Andersen (2009a: 113) recently called them "a para-lexical part of speech" (see also Wälchli, this volume). Eventually, a new onomatopoeic particle can become associated with another verb, sharing the same root and tending, in general, to harmonize its procedural value with that of the particle. In other words, the onomatopoeic particle "extracted" from a verb with an obvious quantifying procedural like a multiplicative and diminutive meaning can be eventually associated with another verb with a different predesinential stem suffix but a similar procedural value.

In (9), several random examples are cited from Ulvydas (1971: 247–268), Schmalstieg (2000: 118–200), and Urdze (2010: 92–94) in order to illustrate the procedural similarity of the onomatopoeic verbs and the respective particles. Since the procedural meaning is influenced by different predesinential suffixes, including the common Indo-European suffix *-sk-* with the meaning of intensity of an action for Balto-Slavic and the suffix *-ina-/*-ena-* (Stang 1966: 371–372), the categorialization may look in some cases rather vague. Not surprisingly, a series of short (diminutive) constituent actions may get blurred into the multiplicative meaning and the other way around.

(9)

Suffix	Onomatopoeic verb	Ištiktùkas	Procedural meaning of the particle
-ė-ti	treškė́ti 'to crackle'	trèkšt	multiplicative-[diminutive]
-kš/šk-ė-ti	brakšė́ti/braškė́ti 'to crackle'	bràkš, bràkšt	multiplicative-[diminutive]
-in-ti	bárškinti 'to knock'	bárkšt	multiplicative-[diminutive]
-en-ti	stukénti 'to knock'	stùkt	multiplicative-diminutive
-s-en-ti	čepsénti 'to smack one's lips'	čèpt	multiplicative-diminutive
-š-en-ti	brukšénti 'to crackle'	brùkšt	multiplicative-intensive
-(š)č-io-ti	mìrkčioti 'to blink'	mìrkt	multiplicative-diminutive
-n-o-ti	vepnóti 'to chatter'	vèpt	multiplicative-diminutive
-sn-o-ti	bak(s)nóti 'to poke'	bàkt, bàkst	multiplicative-diminutive
-šn-o-ti	pakšnóti 'to drip'	pàkšt	multiplicative-diminutive
-s-y-ti	kiáksyti 'to yap'	kiáukt	multiplicative-durative
-š-y-ti	bàkšyti 'to urge'	bàkšt	multiplicative-diminutive

Thus, the main difference between the categorialization of the East Slavic and Lithuanian onomatopoeic particles lies in their procedural characteristics "borrowed" from the base verbs. The procedural meaning of the East Slavic particles is shaped by the notion of semelfactive action, which today is obligatorily coupled with the aspectual meaning of perfective base verbs in *-nu-* like Rus. *tresnut'* 'to crack; to smack', *prygnut'* 'to jump' (cf. Musteijkis [Musteikis] 1972: 131). In Lithuanian, the meaning of the onomatopoeic particles is conceived of as multiplicative with a certain degree of intensity of the respective action, divorced, however, from any grammatical (aspectual) interpretation of action in its completion (Danylenko 2003: 216, 335–337).

4.3 The prefixed onomatopoeic particles

The occurrence of prefixed onomatopoeic particles, especially those ending in *-t* like *pabràkšt* 'crack', *pastrìkt* 'hop', and the like is different from an analogous perfectivization, based on aspect-driving prefixes, in East Slavic. Synchronically, there is a great number of perfective-imperfective-looking pairs of prefixed vs. unprefixed verbs in Lithuanian, in particular with the semantically bleached prefix *pa-*; cf. *darýti:padarýti* 'to make' (Keydana 1998: 131). However, different prefixes always modify only the lexical meaning of the verb and are not a grammatical feature in Lithuanian (cf. Hewson & Bubenik 1997: 146, 148; Mustejkis [Musteikis] 1972: 126). According to Arkadiev (2011, 82), a prefix, when added in order to express the transition point between previous state and the one denoted by the verb or between the process and the resulting state, changes the actional property of the verb, which, for our case, may acquire a multiplicative meaning. A result of such a procedural modification is observed, for instance, in the prefixed verb with the lengthened zero-grade *-ū-* root vowel *pa-lūk-ėti* 'to wait a little bit'. This multiplicative pattern with the prefix *pa-*, the lengthened grade of the root, and present conjugation in *-i* (with a diminutive attenuation) has been extended to other verbs, whence the quantifying (multiplicative) procedural meaning in the following formations:

(10) *pa-bėg-ėti* 'to run a little bit'
pa-ėj-ėti 'to walk a little bit'
pa-kyl-ėti 'to rise a little bit'
pa-nėš-ėti 'to carry a little bit'

(Schmalstieg 2000: 117).

The difference between the prefixed derivatives and their unprefixed counterparts in Lithuanian is not in the Slavic sense aspectual, but lexical, which looks to be in accord with Dolinina's (1999) argumentation that distributivity does not belong to the domain of aspect, but to that of quantification. Sawicki (2000: 141) reports a similar opinion, according to which no compound (prefixed) verb should be considered a perfective member of an aspectual opposition in Lithuanian. We can add that the prefixes in verbal derivatives play in Lithuanian an important role in conveying various fine procedural distinctions (*Aktionsarten*) only (cf. Arkadiev 2011: 82–83).

It would not be therefore overdoing it to say that the prefix *pa-* has no perfectivizing function in Lithuanian (cf. Andersen 2009a: 132), thus differing from the prefix *po-* in East Slavic, where the procedural meaning of a single momentary action is always coupled with the perfective value. This is why neither *po-* nor any other prefix is ever attested in the eastern Slavic onomatopoeic particles, whereas onomatopoeic verbs in *-nu-* can take various prefixes without changing its procedural (semelfactive) meaning (see 11a). By contrast, Lithuanian verbs in *-tel(ė)ti* and *-ter(ė)ti* are not used with the prefix *pa-*, whereas particles can take this prefix, thus adding "the meaning of the onset of action or sound" (Ambrazas 1997: 444; see 11b) or, in fact, strengthening the multiplicativity of a particular (singularized) "quantum" of action.

(11) a. Rus. *pryg* ~ **pod-pryg*
   prygnut' ~ *pod-prygnut'* 'to jump up'
 b. Lith. *blìnk* ~ *pa-blìnk*
   blìnkteléti ~ **pa-blìnkteléti* 'to throw, to bang quite a bit'

In Belarusian, Ukrainian, and, to a lesser extent, Russian dialects, one encounters derivatives with the doubled prefix *po-po-* (Lith. *pa-*) (Zjalinskaja 1975: 23, Karskij [1911] 2006: 391): Ukr. *po-po-xodyty*, Bel. *pa-pa-xadzic'*, Rus. *po-po-xodit'* 'to walk around a little bit' (Lith. *pa-ėj-ėti*), Ukr. *po-po-nosyty*, Bel. *pa-pa-nasic'*, Rus. *po-po-nosit'* 'to carry around a little bit' (Lith. *pa-nėš-ėti*). Such double-prefixed derivatives in Ukrainian and Belarusian can render contextually various degrees of the intensity of multiplicative action, e.g., Ukr. *po-po-jisty* 'to eat a little bit (picking many small pieces of food)' as opposed to Bel. (dial.) *pa-pa-jëdac'* 'to eat much (picking many pieces of food)' (Danylenko 2011: 167–168). Interestingly, one comes across Lithuanian dialectal forms tending sporadically, arguably under the Belarusian influence, to take the doubled prefix *pa-pa-* with an iconic (expressive) element in their meaning, e.g., *pa-pa-riñkti* (=*suránkioti*) 'to choose, pick [one by one]' and *pa-pa-mìršti* (=*užmìršti*) 'to forget' (Grinaveckienė 1969: 221).

Thus, the pattern with the (doubled) prefix *pa-pa-* and the lengthened (iconic) grade in Lithuanian conveys a twofold quantifying procedural of a particular action that may be conceived as multiplicative with a certain degree of intensity but not "completed", as has been mentioned, in the Slavic aspect sense (Danylenko 2003: 216, 335–337).

5 Conclusions

The onomatopoeic particles in East Slavic and Lithuanian share most of their semantic (Section 2.1) and syntactic features (Section 2.2), but stand apart morphophonemically (Section 2.3) as a result of different expression (phonetic) reduction (Section 4.1) and procedural categorialization (Section 4.2).

Used as uncharacterized predicates in both languages, the onomatopoeic particles represent activities or actions through their auditorily and non-auditorily-based experiential dimensions. Morphophonemically, however, they are different.

First, Lithuanian onomatopoeic particles are characterized by root vowel apophony, which practically died out in East Slavic. Second, they also vary in word-final consonant clusters, which, in fact, are genetically related to the respective clusters in East Slavic. Most telling in this respect is a connection between ESl. *sk* and metathetic Lith. *kš/ks~šk/sk*, which, as Machek argued, refer to the intensity of an action sometimes coupled with a pejorative connotation. In Lithuanian, such clusters are regularly expanded with the help of the formant -*t*-. Typologically representative of the Lithuanian onomatopoeic particles, this formant seems to be the main marker of multiplicativity as rendered by both onomatopoeic particles and respective verbs in this language; cf. *bràkš~bràkšt* 'crackle' next to *bràkštelėti/bràkšterėti* 'to crackle a little bit'.

In East Slavic, the onomatopoeic particles reveal different consonant clusters in the *Auslaut* as a result of a more advanced reduction in phonetic substance (the loss of the final *k/g* and *t* in clusters *sk/zg* and *st*) and application of more advanced lexicalizing devices of the "semantic palatalization" of the final consonants like Ukr. *ljas'* 'smack' from **ljask-(nu-ti)* and the use of substantivizing suffixes like Ukr. -*ec'*, Rus. -*yx*, Bel. -*el'*, and -*en'* (see Section 4.1).

The foregoing analysis allows us to argue that, in both Lithuanian and East Slavic, the prototypical onomatopoeic particles (with the exception of sound-imitating forms) are derivative of the onomatopoeic verbs. The categorialization of the onomatopoeic particles, accompanied by expression reduction and the use of lexicalizing devices, depends on procedural characteristics of the base verb. The Lithuanian base verbs tend to denote multiplicative actions conceived of, as a rule, through the lower (diminutive) degree of their intensity. In East Slavic, however, the base verbs in -*nu*- denote single momentary actions viewed in their completion without any attenuation in terms of a lower or higher degree of the intensity of action. In other words, Lithuanian *ištiktùkai* are lexically specified only for quantifying procedurals (and their possible combinations like a multiplicative-diminutive meaning), but not for the aspectual distinction, while onomatopoeic particles in East Slavic are characterized by the lexical procedural of a single momentary action. The association of Eastern Slavic particles with the perfective aspect became historically possible after the reanalysis of procedural categories (Andersen 2009b: 125).

At this point, one may well wonder how long onomatopoeic particles have been in existence in Lithuanian and East Slavic. Based on a qualitative difference between base vowel and reduplicant vowel in pairs like *bokšt→ba-bokšt* 'poke, jab', Andersen (2009a: 133) suggested that particles could have emerged prior to the vowel shift in much of the Lithuanian language area before 1550. Leskien (1902/1903: 166) drew attention to a number of Lithuanian particles that had precise correspondences in Latvian and concluded that the category was ancient. In East Slavic, the onomatopoeic particles could become "extracted" from verbs before the opposition of perfective vs. imperfective became obligatory for all verbs, that is, tentatively, before (or at) the 1300s when a steep rise in the development of patterns of aspectual derivation became first attested (cf. Silina 1982). Thus, whatever their age, the extraction of particles and their categorialization in Lithuanian and East Slavic should be linked with the historical formation of procedural categories in the verbal systems of the two languages (Potebnja 1941: 46–62).

Acknowledgments

I would like to thank William R. Schmalstieg and Robert Orr as well as the reviewers and the editors of the volume for valuable comments on the earlier version of this paper. I alone am responsible for any shortcomings.

Abbreviations

1	first person	Lith.	Lithuanian
3	third person	M	masculine
ACC	accusative	PART	particle
AOR	aorist	PST	past
Bel.	Belarusian	Rus.	Russian
Bulg.	Bulgarian	SG	singular
dial.	dialectal	Sl.	Slavic
ESl.	East Slavic	Ukr.	Ukrainian
F	feminine	USorb.	Upper Sorbian
Latv.	Latvian		

References

Ambrazas, Vytautas (ed.). 1997. *Lithuanian grammar*. Vilnius: Baltos lankos.
Andersen, Henning. 2009a. Reduplication in Slavic and Baltic: Loss and renewal. *Morphology* 19: 113–134.

Andersen, Henning. 2009b. On the origin of the Slavic aspects. In Vit Bubenik, John Hewson & Sarah Rose (eds.) *Grammatical change in Indo-European languages*, 123–140. Amsterdam, Philadelphia: John Benjamins.

Arkadiev, Peter M. 2011. Aspect and actionality in Lithuanian on a typological background. In Daniel Petit, Claire Le Feuvre & Henri Menantaud (eds.) *Langues baltiques, langues slaves*, 57–86. Paris: CNRS Editions.

Balčikonis, Juozas et. al. 1941–2002. *Lietuvių kalbos žodynas* [Dictionary of the Lithuanian Language], vol. 1–20. Vilnius: Valstybinė politinės ir mokslinės literatūros leidykla.

Bergmane, Anna., Rūdolf Grabis, M. Lepika & Evalds Sokols (eds.). 1959. *Mūsdienu latviešu literārās valodas gramatika: fonētika un morfoloģija* [Grammar of the modern Latvian literary language: Phonetics and morphology]. Rīga: Latvijas PSR Zinātņu Akadēmijas izdevniecība.

Danylenko, Andrii. 2003. *Predykaty, vidminky i diatezy v ukrajins'kij movi: istoryčnyj i typolohičnyj aspekty* [Predicates, cases, and diatheses in the Ukrainian language: Historical and typological aspects]. Xarkiv: Oko.

Danylenko, Andrii. 2011. Linguistic and cultural border crossings in the Grand Duchy of Lithuania or, can the Grand Duchy of Lithuania be defined as a *Sprachareal*?' In Daniel Petit, Claire Le Feuvre & Henri Menantaud (eds.) *Langues baltiques, langues slaves*, 141–183. Paris: CNRS Editions.

Dolinina, Inga. 1999. Distributivity: More than aspect. In Werner Abraham & Leonid Kulikov (eds.) *Tense-aspect, transitivity, and causativity: Essays in honor of Vladimir Nedjalkov*, 185–205. Amsterdam, Philadelphia: John Benjamins.

Endzelīns, Jānis. 1971. *Comparative phonology and morphology of the Baltic languages*. The Hague, Paris: Mouton.

Grinaveckienė, Elena. 1969. Lietuvių ir slavų kalbų gramatinio kontaktavimo reiškiniai pietryčių Lietuvoje [Some contact phenomena in the grammar of Lithuanian and Slavic in South-Eastern Lithuania]. *Lietuvių kalbotyros klausimai* 11: 219–229.

Hewson, John & Vit Bubenik. 1997. *Tense and aspect in Indo-European languages. Theory, typology, diachrony*. Amsterdam, Philadelphia: John Benjamins.

Karskij, Efimij Fëdorovič. [1911] 2006. *Belorusy. Vol. 2: Jazyk belorusskogo naroda*. Minsk: Belaruskaja Ėncyklapedyja.

Keydana, Götz. 1998. Aspekt im älteren Litauischen. *Linguistica Baltica* 7: 119–145.

Kurschat, Friedrich. 1876. *Grammatik der littauischen Sprache*. Halle: Verlag der Buchhandlung des Weisenhauses.

Kuryłowicz, Jerzy. 1964. *The inflectional categories of Indo-European*. Heidelberg: Carl Winter.

Leskien, August. 1902/1903. Schallnachahmungen und Schallverba im Litauischen. *Indogermanische Forschungen* 13: 165–212.

Lomonosov, Mixajlo. 1755. *Rossijskaja grammatika* [The Russian grammar]. Sanktpeterburg: Imperatorskaja Akademija Nauk.

Machek, Václav. 1957. Slavische Verba mit Suffixalem *sk*. *Slavistična revija* 10: 67–80.

Maslov, Jurij Sergeevič. 1948. Vid i leksičeskoe značenie glagola v russkom jazyke [Aspect and lexical meaning of the verb in the Russian language]. *Izvestija Akademii Nauk SSSR. Serija literatury i jazyka* 7(4): 303–316.

Meillet, Antoine. 1912. *Introduction à l'étude comparative des langues indo-européennes*. Paris: Librairie Hachette.

Metuzāle-Kangere, Baiba. 1991. Verba strepentia and morphological developments in Latvian and Lithuanian. In Norbert Boretzky, Werner Enninger & Benedikt Jeßing (eds.)

Sprachwandel und seine Prinzipien. Beiträger zum 8. Bochum-Essener Kolloquium über "Sprachwandel und seine Prinzipien" vom 19.10 – 21.10.1990 an der Ruhruniversität Bochum, 194–205. Bochum: Brockmeyer.

Mustejkis [Musteikis], Kazimieras. 1972. *Sopostavitel'naja morfologija russkogo i litovskogo jazykov* [Comparative morphology of Russian and Lithuanian]. Vilnius: Mintis.

Nesselmann, George Heinrich Ferdinand. 1851. *Wörterbuch der litauischen Sprache*. Königsberg: Verlag der Gebrüder Vornträger.

Nikitina, Tatiana. 2012. Russian verboids: A case study in expressive vocabulary. *Linguistics* 50(2): 1–30.

Potebnja, Aleksandr Afanas'evič 1941. *Iz zapisok po russkoj grammatike* [From the notes on the Russian grammar]. Vol. 4. Moscow, Leningrad: Izdatel'stvo Akademii nauk SSSR.

Sawicki, Lea. 2000. Remarks on the category of aspect in Lithuanian. *Linguistica Baltica* 8: 133–142.

Schleicher, August. 1856. *Handbuch der litauischen Sprache. Vol. 1: Litauische Grammatik*. Prag: J. G. Galve'sche Buchverlag.

Schmalstieg, William R. 1993. Lengthened grade iteratives in the Baltic and Slavic languages. In Robert A. Maguire & Alan Timberlake (eds.) *American contributions to the Eleventh International Congress of Slavists, Bratislava, August-September 1993: Literature, linguistics, poetics*, 408–413. Columbus, OH: Slavica.

Schmalstieg, William R. 2000. *The historical morphology of the Baltic verb*. Washington, DC: Institute for the Study of Man.

Senn, Alfred. 1966. *Handbuch der litauischen Sprache. Vol. 1: Grammatik*. Heidelberg: Carl Winter.

Shevelov, George Y. 1965. *A prehistory of Slavic*. New York: Columbia University Press.

Shevelov, George Y. 1979. *A historical phonology of the Ukrainian language*. Heidelberg: Carl Winter.

Silina, Vera Borisovna 1982. Istorija kategorii glagol'nogo vida. In Ruben Ivanovič Avanesov and Valerij Vasil'evič Ivanov (eds.) *Istoričeskaja grammatika russkogo jazyka. Morfologija. Glagol* [Russian historical grammar. Morphology. The verb], 158–279. Moscow: Nauka.

Stang, Christian S. 1966. *Vergleichende Grammatik der baltischen Sprachen*. Oslo, Bergen, Tromsö: Universitetsforlaget.

Stepanov, Jurij S. 1981. Balto-slavjanskij in"junktiv i sigmatičeskie formy [The Balto-Slavic injunctive and sigmatic forms]. *Baltistica* 18(2): 112–125.

Stepanov, Jurij S. 1989. *Indoevropejskoe predloženie* [The Indo-European sentence]. Moscow: Nauka.

Szemerényi, Oswald J. L. 1999. *Introduction to Indo-European linguistics*. Oxford: Oxford University Press.

Šaxmatov, Aleksej Aleksandrovič 1941. *Sintaksis russkogo jazyka* [*The syntax of Russian*]. Leningrad: Učpedgiz.

Ulvydas, Kazys (ed.). 1971. *Lietuvių kalbos gramatika* [The Grammar of the Lithuanian Language]. Vol. 2: *Morfologija* [Morphology]. Vilnius: Mintis.

Urdze, Aina Mārīte. 2010. *Ideophone in Europa. Die Grammatik der lettischen Geräuschverben*. Bochum: Brockmeyer.

Vasmer, Max. 1952–1958. *Russisches etymologisches Wörterbuch* 1–3. Heidelberg: Carl Winter.

Vondrák, Wenzel. 1906. *Vergleichende slavische Grammatik. Vol. 1: Lautlehre und Stammbildungslehre*. Göttingen: Vandenboeck und Ruprecht.

Voznyj, Teodozij Mykhajlovyč. 1963. Vidvyhukovi j zvukonasliduval'ni formy dijesliv na *-a-ty*, *-ka-ty* (*-at'*, *-ka-t'*, *-a-c'*, *-ka-c'*) [The onomatopoeic forms of verbs in *-a-ty*, *-ka-ty* (*-at'*, *-ka-t'*, *-a-c'*, *-ka-c'*)]. In Ivan Kos'tjantynovyč Bilodid (ed.) *Slavistyčnyj zbirnyk*, 112–141. Kyjiv: Vydavnyctvo Akademiji nauk Ukrajins'koji RSR.

Vyxovanec', Ivan & Kateryna Horodens'ka. 2004. *Teoretyčna morfolohija ukrajins'koji movy* [The theoretical morphology of the Ukrainian language]. Kyjiv: Pul'sary.

Zjalinskaja, H. D. 1975. Dzejasloŭnyja asnovy z prefiksam *pa-* (*po-*) va ŭsxodneslavjanskix movax [Verbal stems with the prefix *pa-*(*po-*) in East Slavic]. *Belaruskaja mova i movaznaŭstva* 3: 20–27.

Index of languages

Compiled by Auksė Razanovaitė

Apurinã 66
Aukštaitian 2, 3, 14, 60, 117, 119, 123, 127, 176–183, 186, 191–192, 194–196, 465
– North-East Aukštaitian 8, 471
– East Aukštaitian 3, 58, 176–178, 180, 187, 189, 190–192, 196, 465–466, 474, 510, 514
  – South Aukštaitian 3, 58, 111, 176–178, 185, 188, 190, 466, 470
  – West(ern) Aukštaitian 3, 23, 176–180, 182, 185, 188, 189, 190, 192, 195
– Prussian Aukštaitian 181, 182
– Ramaškonys dialect 466, 469, 470–473, 486
– Mielagėnai dialect 471
– Gervėčiai dialect 474
Australian languages 514–515, 518
Austrian German 203

Baltic 1–6, 8, 10, 12–14, 18, 20–24, 27–30, 32–35, 38–42, 44–45, 47–48, 50, 52, 56–73, 127, 142, 144, 149, 156–159, 182, 304, 325, 327–328, 332, 334–335, 337–339, 341–343, 465, 485, 504, 517–518, 523, 527, 529–531, 539
– East Baltic 1, 2, 3, 18, 58, 59, 132, 134, 330, 343
– West Baltic 3
Balto-Slavic 40, 61, 68–69, 128, 527, 530, 535
Belarusian 58–59, 325, 472–475, 477–480, 482–483, 485–486, 537
Bulgarian 64, 329, 438

Čakavian 114, 124
Celtic 128
Chickasaw 500
Common Baltic 10, 58, 61
Croatian 114–115, 124–125, 128, 132, 204
Curonian 2–3, 149, 152, 182–183
Curonian dialects 327–328

Dutch 204, 449
Dzukian see *South Aukštaitian*

English 5–6, 32, 267, 278, 309, 331, 342, 349–350, 452, 454–456, 506, 512
– Old English 309
Estonian 10, 44, 61, 163–167, 183, 191, 325–328, 333–340, 344

Faroese 310
Finnic 2–3, 10, 41, 43–44, 57, 59–62, 72, 111, 132, 134, 142, 144, 156, 325–327, 329, 335, 338, 341, 343–344
Finnish 44, 64, 204, 269, 271, 314, 325–328, 333, 335–341, 344
French 15, 62, 357, 358, 423

Gbaya 492, 498, 509
German 3, 44, 54, 59, 204, 225, 266, 304, 326, 345, 512, 516–517, 533
Germanic 30, 47, 517–518
Greek 124, 204
– Classical Greek 516

Hittite 124
Hixkaryána 511
Huichol 112–113
Hungarian 203–204, 329

Icelandic 266–267, 272, 304, 310, 332, 342
Indo-European 14, 21, 43, 50, 52, 62–63, 113–114, 124, 128, 129, 169, 331, 334, 343, 344, 358, 484, 491, 493, 504, 517–518, 529– 531, 533, 535
Indo-Aryan 342
– Middle Indo-Aryan 131
Italian 15, 62, 204, 512
– Sicilian 512
Italic 128

Jaminjung 514

Kayardild 66
Kxoe 506

Latgalian 1–6, 9, 11–13, 15, 18, 20–22,
    25–26, 28–29, 35–36, 38–40, 46, 51,
    53–58, 61, 65, 70, 149
Latvian 1–6, 8, 9–15, 18–22, 24, 25, 27–36,
    38–54, 56–72, 111, 116, 122, 131–134,
    140–153, 155–157, 159, 164, 166–168,
    179, 182–186, 189, 191, 193, 195,
    235–237, 240–246, 248, 254, 255,
    300–304, 306–314, 316, 318, 319,
    325, 327, 328, 331, 333–341, 343,
    344, 438, 455, 475, 485, 502, 511,
    525, 528, 539
– Low Latvian 2, 3, 57, 59, 149, 150
– High Latvian 2–4, 51, 57, 149–153, 182
– Central Latvian 3, 149–153, 155, 182
– Livonian dialects, Livonianized Latvian
    3, 149, 150, 152
– West Latvian 153, 183, 185, 195
– East Latvian 153, 155, 166, 182, 183, 185,
    186, 194
– Old Latvian 18, 27, 51, 66, 306, 307, 314
Lithuanian 1–18, 20–25, 28–31, 33–34,
    36–73, 111, 115–117, 119, 123, 129, 132,
    139–144, 157, 168–196, 203–205,
    207–229, 263–274, 279–281, 284–287,
    290–292, 294–295, 306, 310, 325,
    328, 331, 333–340, 343–344, 349–351,
    353, 355–361, 365–368, 370, 373–375,
    383–384, 386–395, 400–402, 407–409,
    411, 413, 414–415, 417–423, 430–432,
    437–442, 446–447, 449–451, 454–455,
    457–459, 465–470, 472–487, 491–498,
    501–504, 506, 508–512, 514–518,
    523–530, 532, 533–539
– Eastern Lithuanian 328
– East High Lithuanian 58, 514, 527
– High Lithuanian see *Aukštaitian*
– Low Lithuanian see *Žemaitian*
– Junkilai dialect 121
– Kelmė dialect 121
– Raseiniai dialect 120, 177
– Šaukėnai dialect 121
– Váiguva dialect 121
Livonian 3, 44, 61, 70, 140–143, 156–160,
    162–163, 165–167, 182, 183–186,
    191, 193, 194, 195, 326, 327, 328,
    333–335

Makua 112
Mediterranean languages 203
Mordvin 512

Nahuatl 115
Nehrungskurisch 67

Old Norse 345, 517
Old Prussian 2, 3, 6, 14, 18

Persian 114, 128
– Modern Persian 112, 113
Prussian Aukštaitian see *Aukštaitian*
Polish 5, 33, 58, 59, 61, 62, 64, 325, 387,
    388, 466, 470, 473, 474, 475, 476, 478,
    479, 480, 483, 485, 486, 493, 496
– *polszczyzna kresowa* 58
Portuguese 64

Romance 30, 32, 357
Romani
– Lithuanian Romani 475
– Latvian Romani 485
Russian 5, 9, 11, 13, 33, 35, 47, 54, 58–62,
    71–73, 203, 204–230, 235, 238,
    240–242, 245, 254, 255, 267–269,
    271, 272, 274, 276, 287, 288, 325–329,
    332–344, 358, 366, 383, 385–389,
    392–395, 408, 411, 413, 415, 417,
    420–423, 430, 471, 472, 474, 481–483,
    485, 186, 492, 510, 531, 537

Samogitian see *Žemaitian*
Sanskrit 131, 344
Selonian 2, 3, 149, 151
Semigalian 2, 3, 149
Serbian-Croatian 114–115, 124–125, 128, 132
Slavic 8, 13, 14, 32–35, 37–38, 43, 45, 47,
    50–51, 57, 59–62, 66, 70, 73, 128–129,
    203, 212, 241, 269, 325, 327, 329, 334,
    344, 385, 465–466, 469–470, 472–474,
    478, 483–485, 505, 517–518, 523, 527,
    529–531, 533, 536–537
– East Slavic 35, 43, 51, 57–58, 62, 326, 467,
    502, 523–527, 530, 532–533, 535–539
– West Slavic 30, 58, 341
Sorbian, Upper 523

Sotho 492
Spanish 115, 203, 204, 279, 358
Štokavian 114
Swedish 3, 64, 345

Tagalog 112
Tamian dialects 2
Turkish 204, 437

Ukrainian 341, 480, 537
Uralic 134

Vedic Sanskrit 112, 113, 128

Wolaitta 498, 519

Žemaitian 2, 3, 70, 111, 116, 119–120,
    122–125, 127–134, 176, 514
– North Žemaitian 131–134, 177–179, 195
– South Žemaitian 120, 125, 133, 177–178,
    180, 195
– West Žemaitian 176–178
Zulu 491, 498

Index of subjects

Compiled by Auksė Razanovaitė and Benita Riaubienė

ablaut 12, 37, 511
abstract noun (see *noun*)
accent 8–11, 51, 111–116, 121, 123–125, 128, 130, 132, 134, 139–140, 142, 159, 164–167, 169–176, 178–183, 185–167, 188, 191–195, 228, 527
– retraction 113–115, 124, 125
– secondary 116, 120–121
accentual paradigm (see *paradigm*)
accentuation 7–8, 130, 173, 175
accusative (see *case*)
action nominal 19
actor 60, 350, 368, 378
acute 115, 117–119, 121–127, 129–134, 139–142, 164, 169–174, 176, 178–181, 183–188, 190–195, 508, 527
– intonation 121, 123, 527
adessive (see *case*)
adjective 14–19, 41–42, 47, 50, 53, 55, 60, 117, 139, 206–209, 237, 240, 353, 443, 451
– (in)definite 16–18, 41, 65, 519
– diminutive 207, 229
– neuter 42, 60, 225, 443
adjunct 45–46, 263, 269, 277, 280, 284–285, 362
adposition 41, 52
adverb 33, 35, 44, 53, 206–208, 238, 240, 243–244, 246, 249, 253–255, 273, 326, 362, 437, 441, 447, 449, 491, 506
– diminutive 208
– relational 44
– stance 52
adverbial 28, 45–46, 73, 268, 273, 281, 293, 362, 384, 387, 393, 395–398, 401–411, 413–417, 419–420, 437, 442, 458
– sentence 447, 458
– stance 437, 442, 447, 457
adverbialization 437–438, 445, 447, 458
agglutination 16
agreement 14–15, 28–29, 43–44, 60, 162, 207, 216, 221, 225, 306, 311, 315–316, 319, 320, 342, 361–362, 388
– predicate nominal 42

Aktionsarten 32, 235, 240–243, 258, 523, 536
analogy 36, 60, 158, 175, 191, 293, 481
analytical habitual (see *tense*)
anaptyxis 129, 153, 155
animacy 14–15, 44, 61, 268, 277, 302–303, 308, 314
antecedent 54, 300
anterior(ity) 29–31, 60, 386, 429–431, 531
anticausative 35, 352
apocope 111, 117–121, 128, 131–132, 154, 164
aquamotion 48
areal 3, 6, 10, 14, 23, 30, 43–44, 56–57, 59–62, 64, 68, 70, 72, 74, 134, 140, 142, 181, 307, 329–331, 341, 343–344, 438
– clines 59, 61–62, 67
– convergence 57, 60, 72
– linguistics 2, 39, 68, 72, 330
argument
– demotion 36, 320, 352, 363
– expression 293, 368
– structure 35, 66, 72, 264, 287, 289, 291, 293–295, 313, 319, 354, 362, 525
aspect 23, 31–35, 38, 40, 44, 365, 240–241, 245, 253, 259, 271, 312, 385–394, 416, 420, 432, 504–505, 508–509, 523, 527, 536, 538
– derivational 66
– imperfective 33, 37, 245, 387–388, 432, 505, 527
– inflectional 35
– perfective 33, 538
aspectual pair 242, 253, 387, 289, 392–394, 404
atelic 32, 271, 386, 389, 393–395, 400, 408–411, 413–414, 416, 418, 420–421, 423–426, 430–431
attenuative 71, 235–236, 243–247, 254–258, 394
augmentative 208–209, 236, 240, 255–256, 259
Ausdruck (Bühler) (see *expressive function*)
autosegmental theory 8

Index of subjects — 547

auxiliary 24–25, 27, 29, 32, 43, 270, 307, 315, 318–319, 390
– modal 40, 53
avertive 24–25

biclausal 27
bilingualism 11, 466, 470, 473
borrowing 34, 50, 51, 73, 132, 143–144, 148, 168–171, 307, 331–332, 339, 341, 344, 369, 372, 465–466, 470, 472–475, 477–481, 483, 485–486

case assignment rule 46
case
– accusative 18, 27, 29, 39, 61, 71, 243, 247–248, 263–265, 267–275, 280–281, 284–294, 304, 306, 308–315, 320–321, 329, 333, 338, 341, 344–345, 361–362, 364, 374, 393, 506, 513
– adessive 60, 325–328, 339, 341
– dative 18, 27, 43–44, 46, 60–61, 64, 66, 71–72, 131, 263–265, 267–268, 270, 276, 279, 281–284, 291, 294, 299–300, 303, 305, 307, 310–313, 316, 318–319, 325–330, 332, 338–339, 341–345, 361–362, 364, 509, 514
– genitive 28, 31, 39, 41, 43, 46, 64, 71, 122, 225, 227, 263–265, 267, 268, 270, 272–276, 281–284, 294, 306–310, 321, 326–328, 338–339, 344, 362, 364, 374
– inherent 14, 32, 37, 56, 71, 155, 187, 263, 265–269, 279–280, 284, 294, 302, 327, 356, 386–387, 393–394, 445, 458
– instrumental 18, 42, 66, 71, 263–265, 269, 276, 278–281, 285–294, 361, 364
– nominative 15–16, 27–30, 39, 42–43, 59–60, 71, 139, 225, 227, 263, 267, 270, 272, 277–278, 289, 294, 299–301, 303–307, 310–315, 317–321, 325, 329, 334, 336, 345, 361–362, 364, 374, 524
– semantic 263, 265–266, 268–269, 279–281, 284–286, 293–294
– structural 263–269, 272–276, 279–280, 284, 286, 294
– vocative 15, 18, 44, 215, 217
case hierarchy 303, 311, 361
case theory 71, 263, 265–266, 269, 272, 279, 286, 293–294

categorialization 526, 528, 533–535, 537–539
causative 36, 38, 48, 244, 289, 334, 352, 355, 359, 367, 372, 375, 516
– construction 43
– suffix 36, 334
– verb (see *verb, causative*)
causativity 37, 355
Circum-Baltic Area (CBA) 30, 56, 325–326, 329–330, 334, 342–343, 345
circumflex 70, 116–120, 122–125, 127–128, 130–131, 133, 139–142, 169–174, 176, 178–188, 190–196, 508
– intonation 117, 127–128, 508
classificatory categories 48
clause 15, 27–30, 40–41, 43–46, 52, 55–56, 62, 64, 66, 113–114, 264–265, 267, 280–284, 286, 293–295, 299, 301–306, 308, 314, 319–320, 336, 338–339, 424, 437, 440–443, 445, 454, 456, 458, 516
– adverbial 46
– complement 29–30, 41, 45–46, 64, 113, 445
– embedded 55, 314
– existential 43
– independent 55
– infinitival 27, 46, 264, 282, 314
– main 30, 113, 264, 281, 283–284
– relative 27, 46, 314
– small 43
cognitive semantics 47–48, 52
communal society 491, 497, 500
comparative construction 41, 43
complementation 31, 45–46, 54, 304, 439, 443
– clausal 46, 54
complementizer 41, 44–46, 52–53, 66, 445–446, 454, 458
complement-taking predicate (CTP) 30, 73, 437, 441–443, 445–451, 454–455, 457–458
complex sentence 1, 28, 40, 44
compound 33, 50, 305, 315, 384, 515, 518, 536
conduit metaphor 47
conjugation 22, 359, 515, 536
conjunction 41, 44, 52, 53, 336, 342, 476, 481–482

connective 52
connotation 35, 203–204, 213, 215, 244,
　　253, 534, 538
consonant 7, 9–12, 15, 21–22, 63, 65, 131,
　　140, 142, 144, 157, 160, 162–164, 169,
　　192, 208, 212, 225–226, 511, 529–530,
　　532, 538
– alternation 21–22, 208
– cluster 12, 160, 163, 530, 538
– geminate 144, 157, 160–161, 163, 169
– palatalized 7, 11, 532
continuative 24–25, 65, 383
continuous 209, 383, 385, 389,
　　397, 430
converb 27–28, 519
converse 48, 72, 349–375
– autoconverse 352–353, 357–358
– lexical (LCs) 48, 349, 353, 355, 368
– reflexive 349
– syntactic 353, 357, 371,
coordination 30, 40, 247, 304–306, 311,
　　317, 319
corpus, corpora 2, 5–6, 49, 51, 53, 55,
　　67–69, 71, 73, 204, 208, 212, 229,
　　236, 286, 349, 351, 372, 439–440,
　　442, 450, 455, 459, 466, 475,
　　508–509
Courland (see *Kurzeme*)

dative (see *case*)
debitive 21, 27–28, 40, 43, 46, 61, 65,
　　299–300, 311–320
declension 14–20, 224, 225–227
definiteness 14, 16, 268, 396
deideophonization 517
delimitative 71, 235, 243–245, 248, 254
delocutive verb 515–516
derivative 49, 203–204, 206–207, 229,
　　238, 355, 370, 372, 385, 393, 529–532,
　　536–538
dialect
– continuum 2, 24, 57, 133–134
– geography 1, 57–58, 68
– peripheral 58
diathesis 354
– diathetical change 373
differential subject/object marking 39, 42,
　　61, 268

diminutive 37–38, 50, 53, 70–71, 203–215,
　　217–221, 223–229, 235–241, 243–247,
　　249–251, 253, 255–258, 529,
　　532–536, 538
– noun (see *noun, diminutive*)
diphthong 7, 9, 11, 65, 70–71, 115, 117–118,
　　128, 139–146, 154, 156–164, 166–172,
　　176, 179–181, 183–195, 508
diphthongal sequence 65, 139–148, 150–154,
　　156, 158–159, 161–162, 164, 166–169,
　　171–172, 176, 179–181, 183–195
discourse marker 52, 442, 445, 449, 456,
　　458, 481
Distributed Morphology 18–19
durative 32, 243, 383, 386, 389–390, 393,
　　425, 527, 534, 535

emotion(al) 203, 207–210, 213, 215, 219, 236,
　　238–240, 247, 353, 369–370
endearment 203, 205–207, 236–237
epistemicity 437, 441
etymology 13, 47, 50, 482
event 32, 34, 48, 74, 249, 269, 280, 292,
　　294, 312, 329, 332, 344–345, 354, 362,
　　386, 393, 399, 420, 424, 425, 456,
　　492–493, 500–501, 503–506, 508, 510,
　　512, 516, 524–525
– structure 265, 269, 287, 289, 293–295,
　　354, 367, 368, 372, 375
– number 492–493, 503–504, 506,
　　508–509, 518
eventives (see *ideophones*)
evidential(ity) 15, 21, 27–28, 30–31, 40, 42,
　　52–53, 55, 60, 66, 73, 272, 315,
　　437–442, 445–447, 450–458
– inferential 31, 440, 453
– marking 27, 31
– meaning 437–439, 442, 446, 450–451,
　　453–457
– non-agreeing 28, 30, 53, 440, 455, 457
– reportive 28, 53, 440, 455, 457
experiencer 60, 72, 302, 304, 307, 312–313,
　　318, 325–330, 332, 338, 341–345
experimental research 8, 10, 156
exponence 14, 19, 22, 65
– cumulative 14
expressive function 52, 240
expressivity 239–240, 255–257

Index of subjects — 549

folk etymology 47
folk song 39
function word 52, 446, 475
fusion 16, 447
future (see *tense*)

gender 14–16, 18, 28–32, 60, 208, 213, 216–217, 224–227, 229, 315, 342, 482, 509
– control(ler) 15, 31
– neuter 14–15, 482
– target 15, 60
genitive (see *case*)
glossematics 8
glottal stop 116, 123, 133, 146, 158, 178–180
glottalization 10
grammaticalization 27, 35, 41, 61, 64, 393, 437–438, 447, 456, 458, 473, 503, 512, 515
grave (intonation) 116–118, 123, 164, 170, 172, 363, 481, 483, 527

habitual 21, 23–24, 28, 32, 37, 65, 72–73, 383–391, 395–409, 411, 413, 414–426, 429–431, 513
have-perfect (see *tense, perfect*)
hearsay 53, 438, 440, 454–455, 457, 494
hedges 52, 56
heterosemy, heterosemic expressions 52–53
homonymy
– inflectional (see *syncretism*)
hortative (see *mood*)
hypocoristics 206–207, 211–213, 215, 217, 223

ictus 70, 111, 116–117, 119–134
ideophones 73, 491–495, 497–518, 523–539
illocution 52, 55–56, 209
imperative (see *mood*)
imperfective 23, 32–34, 37, 73, 235, 240–243, 245–246, 248, 253–254, 385–389, 391–408, 411, 415–417, 420–421, 423–426, 430, 432, 505, 508, 527, 536, 539
impersonal 31, 42–43, 60–61, 66, 279, 299, 344
inchoativity 37
inference 351, 440, 450, 453, 455–457
inferential (see *evidential*)

infinitive 21–27, 46, 53, 59, 208, 255, 281, 282–284, 291, 314, 390, 447, 503, 509–511, 516, 529–530
infixation(al) 21, 65
inflection 12–16, 18–22, 24–27, 29, 32–33, 35, 38, 46, 48, 57, 64–65, 119, 124, 156, 208, 212, 225–228, 299, 311–312
– double 18, 65
– pleonastic 16
instrumental (see *case*)
interjection 208, 241, 492–493, 516, 524–525
intonation 7, 9–11, 65, 112, 116–117, 119–124, 127–128, 131, 133–134, 173, 196, 209, 213, 498, 508, 527
– sentential 11
irrealis 27, 45, 467, 469, 478–479
ištiktukai (see *ideophones*)
iterative 235, 241, 383–385, 387–390, 394–397, 400, 407, 409–410, 412, 416, 420, 430, 471, 494, 509, 511, 524, 527
iterativity 37, 241, 384, 386–387, 395–399, 401, 404, 407–411, 415–416, 418, 423, 426, 430–431, 506

Kurzeme 3, 142, 149–150, 152–154, 185

language
– acquisition 210, 236
– contact 57, 59, 73, 326, 330–331, 339, 343, 465–466, 469, 473
– shift 58–59
– spoken 204, 227, 497, 499, 517
lengthening 70–71, 139–143, 145, 147–156, 159–162, 165–168, 171–172, 174, 176, 178–196, 206, 503, 508–509, 527–528, 532, 534
Leskien's Law 123, 174
level pitch 10, 123, 171
lexicalization 523–524, 526
loanwords 51, 57, 68
logophoric constructions 30, 54

markedness 18, 240
marking
– head/dependent 44
metathesis 12, 529, 533

mimesis 498, 503
modifier 41, 52, 59, 362
mood 21, 33, 45, 65, 205, 250, 272, 311–312, 315, 509, 525
– hortative 21, 53
– imperative 2, 13, 21–22, 53, 66, 211, 213, 241, 253–254, 256, 482, 510
– indicative 45, 338, 446–447, 531
– optative 21
– permissive 21
– subjunctive 21–23, 25–26, 45
mora 70, 114, 117–118, 125, 128, 140, 142–144, 146, 154–156, 164, 166–167, 171–173, 176, 190, 193–195
morphologization 27
morphotactic (rule) 12–13
multiplicative 37, 527, 529, 530, 533–538
multiplicativity 37, 534, 537–538

narrative 53–54, 423, 426, 494, 497–498, 510
– back-/foreground 53
– function 497–498, 500–501
narrativity 498
nasal deletion 12
necessity 27, 29, 40, 46
negation 24, 66, 272–275, 467, 478, 480, 484–485, 501
Neogrammarians 4, 6, 37, 52, 67–68, 491–492, 498, 517–518
nominative (see *case*)
non-finite 21, 24, 40, 46, 59–60, 265, 282
noun phrase 41, 44, 263, 265–270, 275, 277–278, 280, 283–284, 290, 293, 301, 504
noun
– abstract 35, 205, 207
– collective 50
– diminutive 204, 206–207
– reflexive 37
– relational 44
numeral 18, 41, 50, 206, 226, 240

object
– nominative 39, 59, 314, 319
– non-canonical 42
obliqueness 72, 299, 301–302, 321
– adjustment 311, 321
– hierarchy 72, 300, 302–303, 311

– mismatch 311
obstruent 144, 154, 157–162, 164–165, 169
– voiceless 10, 144, 157, 159–160, 162, 188
operator 52
opposition
– binary 350, 387, 389
– converse 353, 356, 363, 373
– correlative-affixal 356, 374
– correlative 356
– correlative-radical (root) 356
– derivational 355–356, 360, 374
– directional 355–356, 360, 374
– non-directional 356–357, 365, 374
– paradigmatic 356
– suppletive 358, 362, 370, 374
– syntagmatic 357, 360, 374
optative (Indo-European) (see *mood*)

paradigm 13–14, 16–20, 53, 116, 121, 126, 129–130, 203, 228, 334, 356, 371, 486
– accentual 15–16
– defective 19
– nominal 20, 71
– verbal 27
parenthetical 55–56, 73, 440, 441–443, 445–451, 454–456, 458
participle 14–15, 19, 21, 27–31, 33, 40, 43, 45, 53, 59–61, 66, 270–271, 276, 280, 305, 315, 384, 438–439, 519, 530–531
– active 28, 30, 384, 438
– active anteriority (see *participles, past active*)
– declinable 27
– inflected 28, 30, 45, 53
– -*ma/-ta* (Lithuanian) 31, 60, 438
– neuter 53, 60–61
– passive 28, 43, 270, 277, 279–280, 294, 384, 438
– past active 29–30, 60
– present active 25, 53
– uninflected 28, 45
particle 24, 44, 52–53, 59, 208, 440–441, 447, 450, 452, 476–477, 481–482, 491, 523–535, 537–539
– onomatopoeic (see *ideophones*)
– turn-opening 53
– verb(al) 36, 44, 49, 59, 524

passive 28–31, 35, 40, 42–43, 61, 64, 66, 263, 265, 270–272, 276–280, 311–312, 318–319, 350–353, 369, 454–455
- backgrounding (see *passive, impersonal*)
- dynamic 43, 318
- foregrounding 61
- impersonal 42, 60, 66, 279
- non-agreeing 272
- resultative 43, 271, 318
passivization 71, 263, 265, 270, 272, 276–279, 294, 309, 319
past (see *tense*)
past habitual (see *tense*)
pejorative 205–206, 209, 226, 240–241, 252, 529, 538
perdurative 243
perfect (see *tense*)
permissive (see *mood*)
pivot-controller 304–306, 311, 317, 319–320
phonology 6, 8, 10–12, 65, 67, 70, 73, 117, 170, 196, 465, 502, 508–509
- autosegmental 11
- generative 12
phonotactics 10–11, 509
pitch reattachment 118
Polish Livonia 3
politeness 56, 209, 221, 223, 228, 501
polysemy 48, 353–354
possession 274, 368, 453
- external 43
- predicative 40, 43, 60
possessor 238, 329
- external 44, 61, 326–327
- predicative 327–338
possibility 29, 40, 61
postposition 18, 66
pragmatic function 53, 71, 203–204, 206–207, 209–210, 214, 218, 223–224, 228–229, 236
Prague School structuralism 12
prefix 12, 21, 24–25, 27, 33, 38, 44, 59, 71, 209, 235, 241–246, 250, 252, 255, 258, 291–292, 355–356, 358, 387, 392, 394, 508, 516, 531, 534, 536–537
- permissive 21
- restrictive 21

- spatial 33
- verbal 59, 174–175
prefixation 33, 36, 38, 71, 242, 245, 248, 250, 252, 393, 394, 508
preposition 43–44, 52, 267, 275, 294, 328, 353, 361
préverbe vide 242, 245
procedural 523, 534, 537–538
process 32, 34, 242, 386, 393, 508, 536
prominence contour (see *syllable, peak*)
pronoun 5, 14, 16–18, 20, 27, 35, 54–55, 63, 69, 174–175, 208, 313–314, 336, 467, 470–472, 476, 479–480, 482, 484–487
- anaphoric 55
- demonstrative 13–14, 54, 308, 472, 482
- indefinite 18, 35, 73, 465–467, 469–474, 479, 481, 483–484, 486–487
- interrogative 14, 66
- personal 13, 15, 240
- reflexive 27, 300, 313, 316, 335
proposition 52, 441, 445, 448, 450, 453, 457–458
prototype
- lexical 38
proximative reading 34
Prussian Lithuania 3
punctual 386, 408, 415, 431

quotation 53

realis/irrealis distinction 45
reanalysis 29, 126, 484, 538
reciprocal 358
- natural 48
reduplication 493, 503–509, 518, 526
referential conflict 54
reflexive 35, 48, 287, 291, 300, 332, 342, 350, 352–355, 360, 370, 372, 375, 511
- marker 35, 65, 291–292, 356, 358
- noun (see *noun*)
- pronoun (see *pronoun*)
- verb (see *verb*)
reflexivization 35, 300–301, 304–305, 316–317, 320, 335, 337, 339
relational noun (see *noun*)
relative clause (see *clause*)
reportive (see *evidential*)

resultative (see also *perfect*) 29–30, 43, 271, 280, 288–289, 294, 318
– *have*-resultative 62
– object-oriented 30
– subject-oriented 30
rural 58, 497–498, 501, 518
– identity 491, 493, 501
– environment 491, 497–498, 500
rurality 501

Saussure's Law 123–124, 131, 174
semantic
– component structure 354
– map 468
– palatalization 532, 538
semelfactive 37, 245, 527–529, 532, 535, 537
semi-diphthong (see *diphthongal sequences*)
sentence prosody 9, 66
sequence 46, 386, 395, 398–399, 423–424, 426, 430
simple past (see *tense*)
simultaneity 46, 242, 245, 386, 395, 398–399, 423–426, 429–430
situation 32, 37
Slavicism 50–51
smallness 203, 205–208, 220, 235–236, 241, 259
sociolinguistics 47, 57
sonorant 10, 115, 118, 139, 142, 144, 152, 154–155, 157–158, 160–162, 164, 169, 187–188, 191–192, 508
sonority contour (see *vowel, quality*)
sound symbolism 503, 508
speech 53, 56, 68–69, 73, 204, 206, 209–210, 216, 219–222, 224–225, 228, 237, 240–241, 254, 256, 386, 469, 473–475, 481, 483–484, 486–487, 501
– act 45, 49, 56, 203, 209, 211, 215, 217–219, 249
– adult-directed (ADS) 204, 214, 219, 223
– child-centered 203
– child-directed (CDS) 203–204, 206, 208–211, 214–216, 223, 241, 500–501
– pet-centered 203
– register 203
– reported 53, 55
– represented 53
– situation 204, 209–210, 214–216, 218–219, 223–224
spray-paint case 356
Standard Average European (SAE) 56, 329, 342, 518
standardization 2
standard language 3, 8, 12, 14, 49, 52, 117, 140, 147, 149, 176, 178, 182, 185–189, 196, 390, 466, 469–473
state 32, 244, 271, 386, 393, 403, 418, 430, 491, 509, 523, 536
stative 44, 49, 72, 332, 334, 367, 375, 420, 524, 527
stem 13, 15–16, 20–23, 28, 32–33, 35–38, 48–49, 53, 59, 116, 126, 175, 181, 205–208, 212, 224–225, 228, 248, 291, 356, 374, 508, 510–511, 530–532, 534–535
– alternation 14, 18, 21–22, 65, 225
– derivation 32–33, 48
– ictus 117, 121–122, 125–126, 130, 132–133
– infinitive 21–22, 516
– past (tense) 21, 28
– present (tense) 21, 28, 517
– unprefixed 37
stress 8, 10, 14–15, 116, 125, 132, 141–144, 146, 148, 169–170, 172–174, 176, 183, 188–196, 206, 227–228
– clash 116, 129–130
– fixed initial 10
– free mobile 8, 65, 173
– retraction 12, 70, 134, 188
subject 28, 30, 43, 53, 60–63, 71–72, 263, 265, 267, 270, 272–273, 276–277, 279–282, 294, 299–307, 309, 311, 313–315, 318–320, 332, 336–337, 339–340, 342, 345, 361–362, 372, 454, 504
– animate 43
– deletion 46
– intransitive 43–44, 301, 304, 311, 319–321
– non-canonical 42, 72, 301, 303–304, 342, 345
– oblique 43, 304, 342
– properties 304–306, 311, 319–320, 332, 336–337, 342
– quasi-subject 301–304, 306, 310, 319, 321
– quirky 304

Index of subjects — 553

subjecthood 42, 299–300, 302–306, 315, 319, 325, 332, 335, 337, 339, 342, 345
– criteria 42
– diffuse 304, 320
– recoverable 304, 317
subjunctive (see *mood*)
subordination 30
subordinator 46
substratum 111
– Finnic 3, 10, 44, 61, 132
suffix
– causative 36
– syllabic 22, 175
suffixation 21, 33, 36–37, 50, 205, 393
Suffixaufnahme 18
supine 46
suppletion 13, 312
Swedish Livonia (see *Vidzeme*)
switch reference 28
syllable 70, 111–112, 114–134, 141–142, 144–148, 150–151, 153–154, 156, 158–159, 162, 164–167, 169–175, 179–181, 185–188, 190–195, 206, 212, 225
– accent 10–11, 51
– heavy 142, 144, 154, 159–165, 167, 169–170, 172, 174, 185, 188, 191
– intonation 7, 65
– length 10, 189
– light syllable 144, 155, 159–160, 162, 164, 170, 172
– long 70, 116–117, 120, 122, 164, 174, 503, 508
– peaks 65
– short 70, 117, 120, 124–125, 163–164, 174, 192
– stressed 10–11, 116, 129–130, 140, 142, 144, 148, 159, 162, 168–169, 176, 189, 191, 193–194, 196
– structure 7, 9–10, 71, 119, 154, 156, 195
– unstressed 10–11, 146–148, 157, 164, 174, 188, 196
– weight 143–144, 157–158, 168, 184, 195
syncategorematic words (see *function words*)
syncretism 14, 32

syntactic
– hierarchy 362, 366–367
– integration 514
– tightening 30

TAM system 28
taxis 28, 45–46, 386, 394–395, 398–399, 419–421, 424–426
telic 32, 44, 248, 386, 393–395, 400–401, 403, 406, 408–410, 412–416, 419–421, 423–426, 429–430
temporal localization 396, 402, 404
tense 21, 23–24, 28–29, 32–33, 64, 271, 312–313, 338, 384, 386–389, 394–395, 400, 432, 509, 525
– analytical habitual 24
– compound 33, 315
– future 21, 30, 394–395, 513
– past 3, 21, 25, 30, 32, 270, 383–384, 387–388, 390, 392, 396, 401–403, 407–408, 420, 422, 430
  – habitual 72–73, 383–391, 395, 401–404, 406, 415, 416, 420, 422, 426, 429–430
  – simple 29, 384, 388–391, 395, 401, 403–404, 406, 409, 416, 420, 426
– perfect 29, 40
  – *have*-perfect (Lithuanian) 30, 66
  – periphrastic 21
– present 3, 21, 30, 387, 394–395, 447
theta (thematic) role 263, 265–269, 277, 279–280, 284, 293–294, 302
tonal 8, 10, 70, 111–112, 115, 139, 144–145, 147–148, 155–156, 164, 171, 184–185, 194–195, 508
tone 7, 10, 70, 115–116, 123–124, 126–129, 131–133, 139, 142, 145–156, 158–159, 164, 166, 169, 172, 182, 185–186, 194–195, 503, 518, 527
– broken 116, 122–124, 126–129, 131–134, 146–147, 149–151, 153, 158, 186
– falling 145–152, 154
– level 145–148, 151–152, 154, 164
– rising 149, 151, 153, 155, 158, 166, 182
– secondary displaced 122, 131, 133–134
topic 299, 302, 305–306, 318, 336
transitional zone 56, 328
transitivity 28, 37, 273, 276, 309, 311, 321, 332

utterance finality 112, 115

valency 35, 48, 312, 359, 374, 492, 503, 506, 511–514
– pattern 42–43, 311–313, 351, 360–361, 368
– realization/surface realization 361, 364
– semantic 359–360
– slot 372, 374
– syntactic 28
variationist framework 57, 69
verb
– auxiliary (see *auxiliary*)
– biaspectual 34, 389, 394
– causative 38, 289, 355
– denominal 48, 50, 334
– intransitive 21, 29, 244
– light 492, 504, 511–512, 515, 518
– mixed 22
– (of) motion 47, 49, 244, 264, 281, 516
– of pain 310, 338–339, 343
– one-place 28
– phasal 34
– primary 22, 48, 175, 367
– reflexive 286–287, 291, 354
– reflexive-benefactive 36, 62
– suffixal 22
– telic 248, 386, 389, 393–395, 400–401, 406, 408–410, 412–416, 419–421, 423–426, 430
– transitive 30, 309
verboid 492, 524

Vidzeme 3, 149–153
vocative (see *case*)
voice 28, 31, 33, 35, 40, 279, 311–312, 318, 352
– marked 40
– middle 35, 40
– orientation 28–29
vowel
– apophony 526, 530, 534, 538
– change 21, 150
– front 7
– high 147, 150, 152, 154, 170, 172, 177, 179, 182–183, 186–187, 189–190, 192
– length(ening) 70, 141, 150, 152, 154–155, 159, 188–189, 191, 194, 508, 534
– quality 10–11, 65, 153, 169
– quantity 10
– reduction 12
– short 10, 70, 111, 115–118, 130, 141, 144, 148, 154–155, 157–158, 160, 162, 164, 166, 169, 189, 192

word
– length 10, 207, 224, 226
– order 9, 42, 66, 129, 269, 274–275, 281, 302, 316, 318, 320, 335, 337, 339, 361, 366–367
  – NP-internal 40
word-final position 11, 70, 112, 115, 532–533
word-formation 236, 239, 245, 248, 255

zero marking 63

www.ingramcontent.com/pod-product-compliance
Lightning Source LLC
Chambersburg PA
CBHW070254240426
43661CB00057B/2555